ETHICAL ISSUE IN DEATH AND DYING

Second Edition

Edited By

Tom L. Beauchamp
Robert M. Veatch

Georgetown University

**Interdisciplinary Programs
in Health and Humanities
Michigan State University**

Prentice Hall
Upper Saddle River, New Jersey 07458

Library of Congress Cataloging-in-Publication Data

Ethical issues in death and dying / edited by Tom L. Beauchamp, Robert
    M. Veatch. —2nd ed.
        p.   cm.
    Includes bibliographical references.
    ISBN 0-13-282732-8
    1. Terminal care—Moral and ethical aspects.   2. Euthanasia—Moral
and ethical aspects.   3. Suicide—Moral and ethical aspects.
4. Right to die.   I. Beauchamp, Tom L.   II. Veatch, Robert M.
[DNLM: 1. Ethics, Medical.   2. Death.   3. Euthanasia.   4. Suicide.
5. Terminal Care.   W 50 E825 1996]
R726.E773   1996
179'.7—dc20
DNLM/DLC   95-9228
for Library of Congress   CIP

Acquisitions editors: *Ted Bolen/Charlyce Jones Owen*
Editorial assistant: *Meg McGuane*
Production editor: *Jean Lapidus*
Copy editor: *Maria Caruso*
Manufacturing buyer: *Lynn Pearlman*
Cover credit: Rushing stream, Olympic National Park
            Photographer: Grant V. Faint
            Photo courtesy of The Image Bank
Cover design: *Wendy Alling-Judy*

©1996 by Prentice-Hall, Inc.
Simon & Schuster/A Viacom Company
Upper Saddle River, New Jersey 07458

Printed in the United States of America
10 9 8 7 6 5 4 3 2 1

ISBN 0-13-282732-8

PRENTICE-HALL INTERNATIONAL (UK) LIMITED, *LONDON*
PRENTICE-HALL OF AUSTRALIA PTY. LIMITED, *SYDNEY*
PRENTICE-HALL CANADA INC., *TORONTO*
PRENTICE-HALL HISPANOAMERICANA, S.A., *MEXICO*
PRENTICE-HALL OF INDIA PRIVATE LIMITED, *NEW DELHI*
PRENTICE-HALL OF JAPAN, INC., *TOKYO*
SIMON & SCHUSTER ASIA PTE. LTD., *SINGAPORE*
EDITORA PRENTICE-HALL DO BRASIL, LTDA., *RIO DE JANEIRO*

For Dan Callahan and Seymour Perlin

Contents

Preface

This volume is an almost entirely recast version of the first edition, published in 1978, with Dr. Seymour Perlin as one of the co-editors. Dr. Perlin could not join us in this new edition, but was able to meet with us and make suggestions for its content. We are grateful for his support—now and in the past.

When the first edition went to press in late 1976, biomedical ethics in its modern form was a struggling and much underdeveloped field. The changes in the literature of this field between the first edition and this second edition were immense, and consequently the second edition has introduced changes so major that it is, in effect, a different book. However, the book retains some of the same chapter breakdowns and chapter headings.

Bibliographies have been placed at the end of each chapter and at the end of the volume. This material was compiled with the help of professional librarians at the National Reference Center for Bioethics Literature of the Kennedy Institute. We acknowledge with appreciation the assistance provided by the information retrieval project at the library, which kept us in touch with the most important literature and reduced the burdens of research. A talented research staff including William Stempsey, S. J., Marcia Uddoh, David Bekelman, and Catherine Marshall also assisted us in various stages of manuscript preparation. Miranda Kobritz and Kier Olsen provided invaluable service in checking the final manuscript, and Moheba Hanif saw the full manuscript through to completion. We also wish to thank Ted Bolen of Prentice Hall for helpful and supportive editorial advice.

Tom L. Beauchamp
Robert M. Veatch

ACKNOWLEDGMENTS

The authors thank the following reviewers for their helpful advice and criticism: Donald B. Marquis, *Univ. of Kansas*; Marta E. Flores-Muñoz, *Milwaukee Area Technical College*; Sarah Brabant, *Univ. of Southwestern Louisiana*; James F. Childress, *Univ. of Virginia*; Delpha J. Camp, *Univ. of Oregon*; and Barbara J. Paul, *Temple Univ.*

1

The Definition of Death

INTRODUCTION

Until recently, there was no controversy over what it means for a human to die. When the heart stopped beating for more than a few minutes, the heart could not be made to beat again. All the body's organ systems shut down in short order. It was apparent that death had occurred.

New medical technologies and new medical vision beginning in the middle of the twentieth century changed all that. The artificial respirator made it possible for a patient to breathe indefinitely. If oxygen was brought to the blood stream, other organs, especially the heart, could continue to function for an indefinite period as well. We discovered that even with a beating heart, sometimes other body functions were severely compromised. In cases of serious neurological trauma caused by a stroke or an accident, the major portions of brain tissue—potentially the entire brain—might be destroyed. The brain tissue is very vulnerable to periods of lack of oxygen.

The realization that patients could be maintained with beating hearts even though major brain functions had ceased, posed serious ethical and policy questions. One issue was whether some patients were so irreversibly damaged that it would be acceptable—morally and legally—to stop life-support and let the patient die. That question has turned out to be one of the most important and controversial of the contemporary period of medical ethics. It will be taken up in later chapters in this volume.

A second somewhat different question is raised by some of these cases: Precisely when should society begin to treat such injured patients as dead? Some severely impaired, brain-injured patients are clearly alive, but might be allowed to die because there is no intervention that is deemed worth pursuing. Others may actually be so irretrievably compromised that they can be said to have already died. Determining exactly when brain-injured patients die has been a major controversy since 1967. In that year South African surgeon Christiaan Barnard removed the heart from a severely

1

injured patient and transplanted it into a fellow human who was near death from heart failure. The evolution of the transplantation of human organs suddenly made it vitally important to know precisely when death occurred. Assuming that organs could only be removed from people after they were dead, calling a patient dead who is without brain function but still has a beating heart could make all the difference. There was suddenly an enormous importance to what had previously been only an academic question.

A committee was formed at Harvard Medical School to examine the definition of death. Its report had as its objective establishing criteria for measuring that the brain tissue was completely and irreversibly destroyed. Although at the time the questions were not precisely formulated, two separate issues had to be resolved. The first was a social policy question: when do we want to treat the human being as a deceased individual? Treating the individual as a dead person is a decision that he or she is no longer a member of the human moral and legal community. Does the individual lose this status when the heart irreversibly stops beating, or does that status cease when the brain function stops irreversibly? That is an ethical or policy question about which no amount of medical science can provide a definitive answer.

The second issue is more technical: If the irreversible loss of brain function is important for deciding an individual is dead, how can neurologists and other experts accurately measure the irreversible loss of the brain's functions? These questions have turned out to be deceptively complex. Part of the problem has been linguistic. Many people to this day speak of "brain death," but that term is ambiguous. The term could refer to the "death" of the brain, that is, its irreversible destruction, or it could refer to the death of the individual as a whole based on the destruction of the brain. If brain death means only that the individual has a dead brain, it is logically possible that the individual as a whole could still be considered alive. That, in fact, is the view held by those who continue to believe in a heart-oriented definition of death. They could consistently say that the individual is alive, but has a dead (or destroyed) brain.

On the other hand, if brain death refers to the death of the individual as a whole, then we are using the term to refer to something quite different. We are saying that society should treat the individual the way we treat dead people whenever the brain is irreversibly destroyed. Deciding that the individual as a whole is dead is a social or ethical decision to treat the individual the way dead people are treated. The pronouncement of death is a social statement that one is no longer part of the human community. Of course, even the dead deserve respect, but there is a significant change in the status of individuals when we decide they are dead. We would begin speaking of the individual in the past tense. A spouse assumes the role of widow or widower. Life insurance policies must be paid; health insurance policies cease. A grieving process begins in a way that is not appropriate for those who are said only to be dying. If the dead person happened to be President of the United States, the Vice President would automatically assume the office when death is pronounced (but not when the President is merely said to be dying).

By 1970 these issues had become so critical that a public resolution was necessary. That year, the state of Kansas became the first jurisdiction to adopt a brain-oriented definition of death. Now all jurisdictions within the U.S. and almost all other countries throughout the world have adopted a definition of death based on irreversible loss of brain function. The debate about when an individual should be considered dead was reviewed by the President's Commission for the Study of Ethical Problems in Medicine and Biomedical and Behavioral Research in 1981. That report, an excerpt of which is the first selection in this chapter, summarizes the issues and arguments.

If a policy decision is made to pronounce people dead when there is irreversible loss of all functions of the entire brain, then the technical question must be addressed. How would someone measure that the brain has irreversibly ceased? It is important to stress that the loss must be irreversible. It is a serious mistake to refer to patients who temporarily cease heart or brain function as dead. Death is an irreversible condition. Each individual dies only once. Thus, it is a mistake to say that people were "clinically dead, but recovered." They may have been clinically in cardiac arrest or even neurological arrest, but they never died if they recovered functioning. Thus, any measures of the destruction of the brain must support the claim that the loss is irreversible.

The Medical Consultants to the President's Commission formulated a set of criteria for measuring the death of the brain. For those who believe that an individual dies when there is irreversible loss of all the functions of the entire brain, the claim is made that these criteria measure what can be taken as the death of the individual. However, not everyone is convinced that society should treat the individual as dead precisely when there is irreversible loss of all functions of the entire brain. One group, represented by philosophers such as Hans Jonas, whose essay is included here, are not convinced that individuals who maintain considerable organic function outside the brain—including heart beat and respiration (albeit maintained mechanically)—should be considered dead. They recognize this choice as a moral, religious, or philosophical one, not one that can be made solely on the basis of scientific evidence. It appears that a small, but significant minority will continue to hold that an individual with a beating heart is still alive even if that heart is maintained mechanically and there is no brain function. These views are held by many Orthodox Jews, many people of Japanese heritage, many native Americans, and others.

While one group has dissented from the definition of death based on irreversible loss of all brain function by insisting that the heart or respiratory function remain the basis for pronouncing death, others have questioned this view from another direction. They agree that death should be pronounced based on irreversible loss of neurological function, but they reject the idea that literally every function of the entire brain must be lost before an individual is dead. They argue that human life involves both organic and mental functioning and that when mental function is irreversibly destroyed, then the individual should be treated as dead. Neurologically, this means that death could occur even though certain lower brain functions remain in tact.

Reflexes mediated through the brain stem control eye blink, pupil dilation, and cough. Technically, it is possible for these lower brain centers to be functional while the higher brain activities—those in the cerebrum—responsible for consciousness are irretrievably lost. Some holders of this view believe that it is acceptable to pronounce death when these higher functions are destroyed. This position is often referred to as a *higher-brain-oriented definition of death*. It is contrasted with the now–older view, that can be called the *whole-brain-oriented definition of death*.

While it might appear that there are three well-defined options—the cardiac, whole-brain, and higher-brain views—in fact there may be many more. Once one accepts that not all functions of the entire brain must be destroyed for death to occur, there is much room for debate over exactly which functions must be lost. Even among those who hold the whole-brain view, it is not always clear whether it is cellular function or functioning that involves groups of interacting cells that is critical. Some claim that the presence of measurable electrical function is sufficient to show the brain is not dead whereas others are willing to claim, somewhat confusedly, that a brain is dead when all clinical functions are lost even if electrical activity remains. Some even insist that it is not loss of function, but anatomical destruction of the tissues that must occur before death takes place. There turns out to be many different variations on the definition of death, no one of which is likely to command universal acceptance in the near future. For this reason, some have advocated a limited range of choice whereby one definition would be selected as a state's default definition, while individuals who strongly objected could execute an advance directive picking some alternative provided it was within reason and did not pose insurmountable social and health problems. The State of New Jersey has become the first state to adopt a limited conscience clause that permits religious objectors to the state's whole-brain-type statute to be considered alive until the heart irreversibly stops.

A final controversy is posed by the realization that some infants are born with a condition known as anencephaly. These infants have only rudimentary brain tissue, never enough cerebral tissue to permit consciousness. Holders of a higher-brain-oriented definition of death would logically hold that these infants are dead (they have never been alive) even though they are able to maintain heart beat and respiration for what is usually a brief period of time.

Realizing that these infants can never become conscious and will inevitably die fairly soon unless heroic efforts are used to maintain bodily functions, some have proposed using the anencephalic as a source of organs. The parents of Baby Theresa, whose case is described in the last selection in this chapter, wanted to donate their daughter's organs to help other children live. Some would recognize such proposals as an example of the higher-brain-oriented view. They would claim that anencephalic infants as well as the permanently vegetative adult who, by definition, can never become conscious again, should be pronounced dead. This does not mean that such individuals would immediately be buried; for aesthetic or other reasons we may want to wait until all body functions cease even though the individual is already dead. Just as we would never bury someone who was breathing on a ventilator who was pronounced dead by whole-brain criteria, we would not bury someone breathing spontaneously or whose heart was still beating. For aesthetic or other reasons we would wait until all major functions cease.

Others are claiming that instead of calling such anencephalic infants and permanently vegetative patients dead, we could create exceptions to the rule that life-prolonging organs can never be procured until the individual is dead. Defenders of this view have the complex problem of explaining why a living human being should in this case be used solely for the purpose of benefiting another. Normally we do not accept the notion that living individuals can be so used. A case can be made that the very decision that it is acceptable to procure organs is a sign that the proponents of taking the organs believe that death has occurred. According to this view society should treat the individual the way we treat dead people. Those who oppose procuring organs may be concerned about a slippery-slope problem; they may believe that, if we take organs from anencephalic infants, we would be inclined to take them from other severely impaired infants. If no principled difference can be found on which to draw a sharp line, then permitting taking of organs from anencephalics could lead to taking them from other infants in cases in which we are convinced doing so would be wrong.

These selections taken together present a sampling of the range of views on the definition of death.

THE EMERGENCE OF A BRAIN-ORIENTED DEFINITION

Defining Death: Medical, Legal, and Ethical Issues in the Definition of Death*

PRESIDENT'S COMMISSION FOR THE STUDY OF ETHICAL PROBLEMS IN MEDICINE AND BIOMEDICAL AND BEHAVIORAL RESEARCH

The President's Commission came into being in 1980 to examine at the national level critical ethical issues in the biomedical sciences. Made up of lay people and professionals in the relevant fields of medicine, nursing, law, and ethics, it generated consensus statements on some of the critical issues of the day. Its endorsement of the definition of death based on the irreversible loss of all functions of the entire brain established a public policy consensus that humans shall be pronounced dead when all brain functions are lost irreversibly, even if the heart and respiratory function continue. The Commission spoke only on the policy issue of a general standard for pronouncing death, leaving the question of how to measure and confirm the death of the brain to a group of consultants.

The enabling legislation for the President's Commission directs it to study "the ethical and legal implications of the matter of defining death, including the advisability of developing a uniform definition of death."[1] In performing its mandate, the Commission has reached conclusions on a series of questions which are the subject of this Report. In summary, the central conclusions are:

1. That recent developments in medical treatment necessitate a restatement of the standards traditionally recognized for determining that death has occurred.
2. That such a restatement ought preferably to be a matter of statutory law.
3. That such a statute ought to remain a matter for state law, with federal action at this time being limited to areas under current federal jurisdiction.
4. That the statutory law ought to be uniform among the several states.
5. That the "definition" contained in the statute ought to address general physiological standards rather than medical criteria and tests, which will change with advances in biomedical knowledge and refinements in technique.

*Source: President's Commission for the Study of Ethical Problems in Medicine and Biomedical and Behavioral Research, *Defining Death: Medical, Legal, and Ethical Issues in the Definition of Death.* Washington, DC: U.S. Government Printing Office, 1981, pp. 1–7, 15–20, 32–38.

6. That death is a unitary phenomenon which can be accurately demonstrated either on the traditional grounds of irreversible cessation of heart and lung functions or on the basis of irreversible loss of all functions of the entire brain.

7. That any statutory "definition" should be kept separate and distinct from provisions governing the donation of cadaver organs and from any legal rules on decisions to terminate life-sustaining treatment.

To embody these conclusions in statutory form the Commission worked with the three organizations which had proposed model legislation on the subject, the American Bar Association, the American Medical Association, and the National Conference of Commissioners on Uniform State Laws. These groups have now endorsed the following statute, in place of their previous proposals:

Uniform Determination of Death Act

An individual who has sustained either (1) irreversible cessation of circulatory and respiratory functions, or (2) irreversible cessation of all functions of the entire brain, including the brain stem, is dead. A determination of death must be made in accordance with accepted medical standards.

The Commission recommends the adoption of this statute in all jurisdictions in the United States. . . .

The accepted standard for determining death has been the permanent absence of respiration and circulation. A question arises about continued reliance on the traditional standard because advances in medical technique now permit physicians to generate breathing and heartbeat when the capacity to breathe spontaneously has been irretrievably lost. Prior to the advent of current technology, breathing ceased and death was obvious. Now, however, certain organic processes in these bodies can be maintained through artificial means, although they will never recover the capacity for spontaneous breathing or sustained integration of bodily functions, for consciousness, or for other human experiences.

Such artificially maintained bodies present a new category for the law (and for society), to which the application of traditional means for determining death is neither clear nor fully satisfactory. The Commission's mandate is to study and recommend ways in which the traditional legal standards can be updated in order to provide clear and principled guidance for determining whether such bodies are alive or dead.

Although it is in most respects straightforward, "the matter of defining death" seemed troublesome enough to be included in the Commission's statutory mandate for several reasons. Most important, consideration of the new approaches to the determination of death has resulted in attention being paid to underlying questions about the meaning of life and death. Concerns about diagnosing death by measuring the presence or absence of brain functions has occasioned a reexamination of the traditional techniques. Consequently, questions have been posed about the scientific and clinical bases for the traditional standard for death and about the understanding of human life upon which that standard rests.

Furthermore, other changes in medical abilities have contributed to the concern about the "definition" of death. For example, the importance customarily accorded to a person's beating heart in differentiating the living from the dead is challenged when a "dead" person's heart can beat in the chest of a "living" person whose own heart has not merely stopped but has been removed from his or her body.

Finally, confusion arises—which can only be dispelled by the application of accepted medical standards in each individual case—because the same technology not only keeps heart and lungs functioning in some who have irretrievably lost all brain functions but also sustains other, less severely injured patients. Inexact medical and legal descriptions of these two categories of cases have led to a blurring of the important distinction between patients who are *dead* and those who are or may be *dying*. . . .

Traditionally, the cessation of heartbeat and of breathing were regarded by the lay and medical communities alike as the definitive signs of death. The law, through the judgments of courts in deciding individual cases, articulated this general view. In the oft-quoted words of *Black's Law Dictionary,* the common law mirrored the physician's "definition" of death "as a total stoppage of the circulation of the blood, and a cessation of the animal and vital functions consequent thereon, such as respiration, pulsation, etc."[2]

Developments in medical technology and practice . . . have prompted an examination of the adequacy of the traditional view of the proper way to determine whether death has occurred. Since respiration is controlled by brain centers, the loss of function in those centers used to mean that breathing (and consequently heartbeat) would never return. Mechanical respirators and related therapy now enable physicians to reverse the failure of respiration and circulation in many victims of conditions such as cardiac arrest or trauma. If blood flow to the brain is restored quickly enough (usually this must be within several minutes), these victims may eventually recover unassisted breathing. But the brain cannot regenerate neural cells to replace ones that have permanently stopped metabolizing. Hence, longer periods without blood flow (ischemia) or oxygen (anoxia) may cause complete and irreversible loss of all brain functions. When the entire brain has been so severely damaged, spontaneous respiration can never return even though breathing may be maintained by artificial means for some time (typically, several days).

Although physicians find themselves unable to rely on respiration and circulation as a means of diagnosing death in artificially maintained, comatose patients, they have developed means of detecting the existence or nonexistence of brain functions and the potential for reversibility in such patients. These tests are intended to measure the organic functioning of the brain, not the mere existence of cellular activity which may continue in some brain cells—as in cells of other organs, such as the heart and lungs—for varying lengths of time after the organ has lost the ability to fulfill any of its functions in an organized manner. From the evidence presented at the Commission's July 11, 1980 meeting and in the biomedical literature, the Commission concludes that proof of an irreversible absence of functions in the entire brain, including the brainstem, provides a highly reliable means of declaring death for respirator-maintained bodies. . . .

If death were entirely a medical matter, the process of "redefinition" might have been left in the hands of the health professions. . . . But, as the Congress and the President signified in referring this task to an interdisciplinary, broadly based public body for study, the standards by which death is determined have significance and consequences that are not limited to medical ones. Accordingly, the standards by which death is to be recognized should be arrived at publicly, although it will remain for physicians to continue to develop criteria and tests and to apply them in reaching individual diagnoses. . . .

THE INTERRELATIONSHIPS OF BRAIN, HEART, AND LUNG FUNCTIONS

The brain has three general anatomic divisions: the cerebrum, with its outer shell called the *cortex;* the cerebellum; and the brainstem, composed of the midbrain, the pons, and the medulla oblongata. Traditionally, the cerebrum has been referred to as the "higher brain" because it has primary control of consciousness, thought, memory and feeling. The brainstem has been called the "lower brain," since it controls spontaneous, vegetative functions such as swallowing, yawning, and sleep-wake cycles. It is important to note that these generalizations are not entirely accurate. Neuroscientists generally agree that such higher brain functions as cognition or consciousness probably are not mediated strictly by the cerebral cortex; rather, they probably result from complex interrelations between brainstem and cortex.

Respiration is controlled in the brainstem, particularly the medulla. Neural impulses originating in the respiratory centers of the medulla stimulate the diaphragm and intercostal muscles, which cause the lungs to fill with air. Ordinarily, these respiratory centers adjust the rate of breathing to maintain the correct levels of carbon dioxide and oxygen. In certain circumstances such as heavy exercise, sighing, coughing, or sneezing, other areas of the brain modulate the activities of the respiratory centers or even briefly take direct control of respiration.

Destruction of the brain's respiratory center stops respiration, which in turn deprives the heart of needed oxygen, causing it too to cease functioning. The traditional signs of life—respiration and heartbeat—disappear: the person is dead. The "vital signs" traditionally used in diagnosing death thus reflect the direct interdependence of respiration, circulation and the brain.

The artificial respirator and concomitant life-support systems have changed this simple picture. Normally, respiration ceases when the functions of the diaphragm and intercostal muscles are impaired. This results from direct injury to the muscles or (more commonly) because the neural impulses between the brain and these muscles are interrupted. However, an artificial respirator (also called a ventilator) can be used to compensate for the inability of the thoracic muscles to fill the lungs with air. Some of these machines use negative pressure to expand the chest wall (in which case they are called "iron lungs"); others use positive pressure to push air into the lungs. The respirators are equipped with devices to regulate the rate and depth of "breathing," which are normally controlled by the respiratory centers in the medulla. The machines cannot compensate entirely for the defective neural connections since they cannot regulate blood gas levels precisely. But, provided that the lungs themselves have not been extensively damaged, gas exchange can continue and appropriate levels of oxygen and carbon dioxide can be maintained in the circulating blood.

Unlike the respiratory system, which depends on the neural impulses from the brain, the heart can pump blood without external control. Impulses from brain centers modulate the inherent rate and force of the heartbeat but are not required for the heart to contract at a level of function that is ordinarily adequate. Thus, when artificial respiration provides adequate oxygenation and associated medical treatments regulate essential plasma components and blood pressure, an intact heart will continue to beat, despite loss of brain functions. At present, however, no machine can take over the functions of the heart except for a very limited time and in limited circumstances (e.g., a heart-lung machine used during surgery). Therefore, when a severe injury to the heart or major blood vessels prevents the circulation of the crucial blood supply to the brain, the loss of brain functioning is inevitable because no oxygen reaches the brain.

CONCLUSION: THE NEED FOR RELIABLE POLICY

Medical interventions can often provide great benefit in avoiding *irreversible* harm to a patient's injured heart, lungs, or brain by carrying a patient through a period of acute need. These techniques have, however, thrown new light on the interrelationship of these crucial organ systems. This has created complex issues for public policy as well.

For medical and legal purposes, partial brain impairment must be distinguished from complete and irreversible loss of brain functions or "whole brain death." The President's Commission regards the cessation of the vital functions of the entire brain—and not merely portions thereof, such as those responsible for cognitive functions—as the only proper neurologic basis for declaring death. This conclusion accords with the overwhelming consensus of medical and legal experts and the public.

Present attention to the definition of death is part of a process of development in social attitudes and legal rules stimulated by the unfolding of biomedical knowledge. In the nineteenth century increasing knowledge and practical skill made the public confident that death could be diagnosed reliably using cardiopulmonary criteria. The question now is whether, when medical intervention may be responsible for a patient's respiration and circulation, there are other equally reliable ways to diagnose death.

The Commission recognizes that it is often difficult to determine the severity of a patient's injuries, especially in the first few days of intensive care following a cardiac arrest, head trauma, or other similar event. Responsible public policy in this area requires that physicians be able to distinguish reliably those patients who have died from those whose injuries are less severe or are reversible. . . .

THE "WHOLE BRAIN" FORMULATIONS

One characteristic of living things which is absent in the dead is the body's capacity to organize and regulate itself. In animals, the neural apparatus is the dominant locus of these functions. In higher animals and man, regulation of both maintenance of the internal environment (homeostasis) and interaction with the external environment occurs primarily within the cranium.

External threats such as heat or infection, or internal ones such as liver failure or endogenous lung disease, can stress the body enough to overwhelm its ability to maintain organization and regulation. If the stress passes a certain level, the organism as a whole is defeated and death occurs.

This process and its denouement are understood in two major ways. Although they are sometimes stated as alternative formulations of a "whole brain definition" of death, they are actually mirror images of each other. The Commission has found them to be complementary; together they enrich one's understanding of the definition. The first focuses on the integrated functioning of the body's major organ systems, while recognizing the centrality of the whole brain, since it is neither revivable nor replaceable. The other identifies the functioning of the whole brain as the hallmark of life because the brain is the regulator of the body's integration. The two conceptions are subject to similar criticisms and have similar implications for policy.

The Concepts

The functioning of many organs—such as the liver, kidneys, and skin—and their integration are vital to individual health in the sense that if any one ceases and that function is not restored or artificially replaced, the organism as a whole cannot long survive. All elements in the system are mutually interdependent, so that the loss of any part leads to the breakdown of the whole and, eventually, to the cessation of functions in every part.[3]

Three organs—the heart, lungs, and brain—assume special significance, however, because their interrelationship is very close and the irreversible cessation of any one very quickly stops the other two and consequently halts the integrated functioning of the organism as a whole. Because they were easily measured, circulation and respiration were traditionally the basic "vital signs." But breathing and heartbeat are not life itself. They are simply used as signs—as one window for viewing a deeper and more complex reality: a triangle of interrelated systems with the brain at its apex. As the biomedical scientists who appeared before the Commission made clear, the traditional means of diagnosing death actually detected an irreversible cessation of integrated functioning among the interdependent bodily systems. When artificial means of support mask this loss of integration as measured by the old methods, brain-oriented criteria and tests provide a new window on the same phenomenon.

On this view, death is that moment at which the body's physiological system ceases to constitute an integrated whole. Even if life continues in individual cells or organs, life of the organism as a whole requires complex integration, and without the latter, a person cannot properly be regarded as alive.

This distinction between systemic, integrated functioning and physiological activity in cells or individual organs is important for two reasons. First, a person is considered dead under this concept even if oxygenation and metabolism persist in some cells or organs. There would be no need to wait until all metabolism had ceased in every body part before recognizing that death has occurred.

More important, this concept would reduce the significance of continued respiration and heartbeat for the definition of death. This view holds that continued breathing and circulation are not in themselves tantamount to life. Since life is a matter of integrating the functioning of major organ systems, breathing and circulation are necessary but not sufficient to establish that an individual is alive. When an individual's breathing and circulation lack neurologic integration, he or she is dead.

The alternative "whole brain" explanation of death differs from the one just described primarily in the vigor of its insistence that the traditional "vital signs" of heartbeat and respiration were merely surrogate signs with no significance in themselves. On this view, the heart and lungs are not important as basic prerequisites to continued life but rather because the irreversible cessation of their functions shows that the brain had ceased functioning. Other signs customarily employed by physicians in diagnosing death, such as unresponsiveness and absence of pupillary light response, are also indicative of loss of the functions of the whole brain.

This view gives the brain primacy not merely as the sponsor of consciousness (since even unconscious persons may be alive), but also as the complex organizer and regulator of bodily functions. (Indeed, the "regulatory" role of the brain in the organism can be understood in terms of thermodynamics and information theory.[4]) Only the brain can direct the entire organism. Artificial support for the heart and lungs, which is required only when the brain can no longer control them, cannot maintain the usual synchronized integration of the body. Now that other traditional indicators of cessation of brain functions (i.e., absence of breathing) can be obscured by medical interventions, one needs, according to this view, new standards for determining death, that is, more reliable tests for the complete cessation of brain functions.

Critique

Both of these "whole brain" formulations—the "integrated functions" and the "primary organ" views—are subject to several criticisms. Since both of these conceptions of death give an important place to the integrating or regulating capacity of the whole brain, it can be asked whether that characteristic is as distinctive as they would suggest. Other organ systems are also required for life to continue, for example, the skin to conserve fluid, the liver to detoxify the blood.

The view that the brain's functions are more central to "life" than those of the skin, the liver, and so on, is admittedly arbitrary in the sense of representing a choice. The view is not, however, arbitrary in the sense of lacking reasons. As discussed previously, the centrality accorded the brain reflects both its overarching role as "regulator" or "integrator" of other bodily systems and the immediate and devastating consequences of its loss for the organism as a whole. Furthermore, the Commission believes that this choice overwhelmingly reflects the views of experts and the lay public alike.

A more significant criticism shares the view that life consists of the coordinated functioning of the various bodily systems, in which process the whole brain plays a crucial role. At the same time, it notes that in some adult patients lacking all brain functions it is possible through intensive support to achieve constant temperature, metabolism, waste disposal, blood pressure, and other conditions typical of living organisms and not found in dead ones. Even with extraordinary medical care, these functions cannot be sustained indefinitely—typically, no longer than several days—

but it is argued that this shows only that patients with nonfunctional brains are dying, not that they are dead. In this view, the respirator, drugs, and other resources of the modern intensive-care unit collectively substitutes for the lower brain, just as a pump used in cardiac surgery takes over the heart's function.

This criticism rests, however, on a premise about the role of artificial support vis-á-vis the brainstem which the Commission believes is mistaken or at best incomplete. While the respirator and its associated medical techniques do substitute for the functions of the intercostal muscles and the diaphragm, which without neuronal stimulation from the brain cannot function spontaneously, they cannot replace the myriad functions of the brainstem or of the rest of the brain. The startling contrast between bodies lacking all brain functions and patients with intact brainstems (despite severe neocortical damage) manifests this. The former lie with fixed pupils, motionless except for the chest movements produced by their respirators. The latter can not only breathe, metabolize, maintain temperature and blood pressure, and so forth, on their own but also sigh, yawn, track light with their eyes, and react to pain or reflex stimulation.

It is not easy to discern precisely what it is about patients in this latter group that makes them alive while those in the other category are not. It is in part that in the case of the first category (i.e., absence of all brain functions) when the mask created by the artificial medical support is stripped away what remains is not an integrated organism but "merely a group of artificially maintained subsystems."[5] Sometimes, of course, an artificial substitute can forge the link that restores the organism as a whole to unified functioning. Heart or kidney transplants, kidney dialysis, or an iron lung used to replace physically impaired breathing ability in a polio victim, for example, restore the integrated functioning of the organism as they replace the failed function of a part. Contrast such situations, however, with the hypothetical of a decapitated body treated so as to prevent the outpouring of blood and to generate respiration: continuation of bodily functions in that case would not have restored the requisites of human life.

The living differ from the dead in many ways. The dead do not think, interact, autoregulate or maintain organic identity through time, for example. Not all the living can always do all of these activities, however; nor is there one single characteristic (e.g., breathing, yawning, etc.) the loss of which signifies death. Rather, what is missing in the dead is a cluster of attributes, all of which form part of an organism's responsiveness to its internal and external environment.

While it is valuable to test public policies against basic conceptions of death, philosophical refinement beyond a certain point may not be necessary. The task undertaken in this Report, as stated at the outset, is to provide and defend a statutory standard for determining that a human being has died. In setting forth the standards recommended in this Report, the Commission has used "whole brain" terms to clarify the understanding of death that enjoys near universal acceptance in our society. The Commission finds that the "whole brain" formulations give resonance and depth to the biomedical and epidemiological data. Further effort to search for a conceptual "definition" of death is not required for the purpose of public policy because, separately or together, the "whole brain" formulations provide a theory that is sufficiently precise, concise and widely acceptable.

Policy Consequences

Those holding to the "whole brain" view—and this view seems at least implicit in most of the testimony and writing reviewed by the Commission—believe that when respirators are in use, respiration and circulation lose significance for the diagnosis of death. In a body without a functioning brain these two functions, it is argued, become mere artifacts of the mechanical life supports. The lungs breathe and the heart circulates blood only because the respirator (and attendant medical interventions) cause them to do so, not because of any comprehensive integrated functioning. This is "breathing" and "circulation" only in an analogous sense: the function and its results are similar, but the source, cause, and purpose are different between those individuals with and those without functioning brains.

For patients who are not artificially maintained, breathing and heartbeat were, and are, reliable signs either of systemic integration and/or of continued brain functioning (depending on which approach one takes to the "whole brain" concept). To regard breathing and respiration as having diagnostic significance when the brain of a respirator-supported patient has ceased functioning, however, is to forget the basic reasoning behind their use in individuals who are not artificially maintained.

Although similar in most respects, the two approaches to "whole brain death" could have slightly different policy consequences. The "primary organ" view would be satisfied with a statute that contained only a single standard—the irreversible cessation of all functions of the entire brain. Nevertheless, as a practical matter, the view is also compatible with a statute establishing irreversible cessation of respiration and circulation as an alternative standard, since it is inherent in this view that the loss of spontaneous breathing and heartbeat are surrogates for the loss of brain functions.

The "integrated functions" view would lead one to a "definition" of death recognizing that collapse of the organism as a whole can be diagnosed through the loss of brain functions as well as through loss of cardiopulmonary functions. The latter functions would remain an explicit part of the policy statement because their irreversible loss will continue to provide an independent and wholly reliable basis for determining that death has occurred when respirators and related means of support are not employed.

The two "whole brain" formulations thus differ only modestly. And even conceptual disagreements have a context; the context of the present one is the need to clarify and update the "definition" of death in order to allow principled decisions to be made about the status of comatose respirator-supported patients. The explicit recognition of both standards—cardiopulmonary and whole brain—solves that problem fully. In addition, since it requires only a modest reformulation of the generally accepted view, it accounts for the importance traditionally accorded to heartbeat and respiration, the "vital signs" which will continue to be the grounds for determining death in the overwhelming majority of cases for the foreseeable future. Hence, the Commission, drawing on the aspects that the two formulations share and on the ways in which they each add to an understanding of the "meaning" of death, concludes that public policy should recognize both cardiopulmonary and brain-based standards for declaring death.

NOTES

1. 42 U.S.C. §1802 (1978).
2. *Black's Law Dictionary,* (4th ed.). St. Paul, MN: West Publishing Co., (1968) at 488:

> DEATH. The cessation of life; the ceasing to exist; defined by physicians as a total stoppage of the circulation of the blood, and a cessation of the animal and vital functions consequent thereon, such as respiration, pulsation, etc.

But see *Black's Law Dictionary* (5th ed.) West Publishing Co., St. Paul, Minn. (1979) at 170, which now includes an entry under the heading "brain death," citing recent statutes and court cases.

3. Germain Grisez and Joseph M. Boyle, Jr. *Life and Death with Liberty and Justice: A Contribution to the Euthanasia Debate.* Notre Dame, IN: University of Notre Dame Press, (1979) at 59–61.

> If death is understood in theoretical terms as the permanent termination of the integrated functioning characteristic of a living body as a whole, then one can see why death of higher animals is usually grasped in factual terms by the cessation of the vital functions of respiration and circulation which correlates so well with bodily decomposition. Breathing is the minimum in "social interaction." However, considering the role of the brain in the maintenance of the dynamic equilibrium of any system which includes a brain, there is a compelling reason for defining death in factual terms as that state of affairs in which there is complete and irreversible loss of the functioning of the entire brain. To accept this definition is not to make a choice based on one's evaluation of various human characteristics, but is to assent to a theory which fits the facts.

Id. at 77.

4. Julius Korein. "The Problem of Brain Death: Development and History," *Annals of the New York Academy of Science* 315 (1978), 19.
5. James L. Bernat, Charles M. Culver, and Bernard Gert. "On the Definition and Criterion of Death," *Annals of Internal Medicine* 94 (1981), 389, 391.

> . . . When the respirator maintains the organism, it is questionable whether there is complete and irreversible loss of the functioning of the entire brain. But this is a question to be settled by empirical inquiry, not by philosophy. Philosophically, we answer the objection by saying that if the functioning of the brain is the factor which principally integrates any organism which has a brain, then if that function is lost, what is left is no longer as a whole an organic unity. If the dynamic equilibrium of the remaining parts of the system is maintained, it nevertheless as a whole is a mechanical, not an organic system.

Grisez & Boyle, *op. cit.* at 77.

Guidelines for the Determination of Death*

Report of the Medical Consultants on the Diagnosis
of Death to the President's Commission for the Study
of Ethical Problems in Medicine and Biomedical
and Behavioral Research

As the President's Commission developed a consensus in favor of a whole-brain-oriented definition of death, it turned to a distinguished group of neurological experts to address the question of how clinicians could measure and confirm that the brain had irreversibly ceased functioning. A group of 55 experts in the medical sciences developed what has become the standard set of criteria (at least in the United States) for measuring the irreversible loss of the functions of the entire brain.

More than half of the states now recognize, through statutes or judicial decisions, that death may be determined on the basis of irreversible cessation of all functions of the brain. Law in the remaining states has not yet departed from the older, common law view that death has not occurred until "all vital functions" (whether or not artificially maintained) have ceased. The language of the statutes has not been uniform from state to state, and the diversity of proposed and enacted laws has created substantial confusion. Consequently, the American Bar Association, the American Medical Association, the National Conference of Commissioners on Uniform State Laws, and the President's Commission for the Study of Ethical Problems in Medicine and Biomedical and Behavioral Research have proposed the following model statute, intended for adoption in every jurisdiction.

Uniform Determination of Death Act

An individual who has sustained either (1) irreversible cessation of circulatory and respiratory functions, or (2) irreversible cessation of all functions of the entire brain, including the brain stem, is dead. A determination of death must be made in accordance with accepted medical standards. . . .

THE CRITERIA FOR DETERMINATION OF DEATH

An individual presenting the findings in either section A (cardiopulmonary) or section B (neurologic) is dead. In either section, a diagnosis of death requires that

*Source: President's Commission for the Study of Ethical Problems in Medicine and Biomedical and Behavioral Research, *Defining Death: Medical, Legal, and Ethical Issues in the Definition of Death.* Washington, D.C.: U.S. Government Printing Office, 1981, pp. 159–166.

16

both cessation of functions, as set forth in subsection 1, and irreversibility, as set forth in subsection 2, be demonstrated.

A. AN INDIVIDUAL WITH IRREVERSIBLE CESSATION OF CIRCULATORY AND RESPIRATORY FUNCTIONS IS DEAD.

    1. *CESSATION* IS RECOGNIZED BY AN APPROPRIATE CLINICAL EXAMINATION.

        Clinical examination will disclose at least the absence of responsiveness, heartbeat, and respiratory effort. Medical circumstances may require the use of confirmatory tests such as an ECG.

    2. *IRREVERSIBILITY* IS RECOGNIZED BY PERSISTENT CESSATION OF FUNCTIONS DURING AN APPROPRIATE PERIOD OF OBSERVATION AND/OR TRIAL OF THERAPY.

        In clinical situations where death is expected, where the course has been gradual, and where irregular agonal respiration or heartbeat finally ceases, the period of observation following the cessation may be only the few minutes required to complete the examination. Similarly, if resuscitation is not undertaken and ventricular fibrillation and standstill develop in a monitored patient, the required period of observation thereafter may be as short as a few minutes. When a possible death is unobserved, unexpected, or sudden, the examination may need to be more detailed and repeated over a longer period, while appropriate resuscitative effort is maintained as a test of cardiovascular responsiveness. Diagnosis in individuals who are first observed with rigor mortis or putrefaction may require only the observation period necessary to establish that fact.

B. AN INDIVIDUAL WITH IRREVERSIBLE CESSATION OF ALL FUNCTIONS OF THE ENTIRE BRAIN, INCLUDING THE BRAINSTEM, IS DEAD.

        The "functions of the entire brain" that are relevant to the diagnosis are those that are clinically ascertainable. Where indicated, the clinical diagnosis is subject to confirmation by laboratory tests as described in the following. Consultation with a physician experienced in this diagnosis is advisable.

    1. *CESSATION* IS RECOGNIZED WHEN EVALUATION DISCLOSES FINDINGS OF a AND b:

        a. CEREBRAL FUNCTIONS ARE ABSENT, AND . . .

        There must be deep coma, that is, cerebral unreceptivity and unresponsivity. Medical circumstances may require the use of confirmatory studies such as EEG or blood flow study.

        b. BRAINSTEM FUNCTIONS ARE ABSENT.

        Reliable testing of brainstem reflexes requires a perceptive and experienced physician using adequate stimuli. Pupillary light, corneal, oculocephalic, oculovestibular, oropharyngeal, and respiratory (apnea) reflexes should be tested. When these reflexes cannot be adequately assessed, confirmatory tests are recommended. . . .

        Peripheral nervous system activity and spinal cord reflexes may persist after death. True decerebrate or decorticate posturing or seizures are inconsistent with the diagnosis of death.

    2. *IRREVERSIBILITY* IS RECOGNIZED WHEN EVALUATION DISCLOSES FINDINGS OF a AND b AND c:

        a. THE CAUSE OF COMA IS ESTABLISHED AND IS SUFFICIENT TO ACCOUNT FOR THE LOSS OF BRAIN FUNCTIONS, AND . . .

Most difficulties with the determination of death on the basis of neurologic criteria have resulted from inadequate attention to this basic diagnostic prerequisite. In addition to a careful clinical examination and investigation of history, relevant knowledge of causation may be acquired by computed tomographic scan, measurement of core temperature, drug screening, EEG, angiography, or other procedures.

b. THE POSSIBILITY OF RECOVERY OF ANY BRAIN FUNCTIONS IS EX-CLUDED, AND . . .

The most important reversible conditions are sedation, hypothermia, neuromuscular blockade, and shock. In the unusual circumstance where a sufficient cause cannot be established, irreversibility can be reliably inferred only after extensive evaluation for drug intoxication, extended observation, and other testing. A determination that blood flow to the brain is absent can be used to demonstrate a sufficient and irreversible condition.

c. THE CESSATION OF ALL BRAIN FUNCTIONS PERSISTS FOR AN APPRO-PRIATE PERIOD OF OBSERVATION AND/OR TRIAL OF THERAPY.

Even when coma is known to have started at an earlier time, the absence of all brain functions must be established by an experienced physician at the initiation of the observation period. The duration of observation periods is a matter of clinical judgment, and some physicians recommend shorter or longer periods than those given here.

Except for patients with drug intoxication, hypothermia, young age, or shock, medical centers with substantial experience in diagnosing death neurologically report no cases of brain functions returning following a 6-hour cessation, documented by clinical examination and confirmatory EEG. In the absence of confirmatory tests, a period of observation of at least 12 hours is recommended when an irreversible condition is well established. For anoxic brain damage where the extent of damage is more difficult to ascertain, observation for 24 hours is generally desirable. In anoxic injury, the observation period may be reduced if a test shows cessation of cerebral blood flow or if an EEG shows electrocerebral silence in an adult patient without drug intoxication, hypothermia, or shock.

Confirmation of clinical findings by EEG is desirable when objective documentation is needed to substantiate the clinical findings. Electrocerebral silence verifies irreversible loss of cortical functions, except in patients with drug intoxication or hypothermia. . . .

Complete cessation of circulation to the normothermic adult brain for more than 10 minutes is incompatible with survival of brain tissue. Documentation of this circulatory failure is therefore evidence of death of the entire brain. . . . Without complicating conditions, absent cerebral blood flow . . . in conjunction with the clinical determination of cessation of all brain functions for at least 6 hours, is diagnostic of death.

COMPLICATING CONDITIONS

A. Drug and Metabolic Intoxication

Drug intoxication is the most serious problem in the determination of death, especially when multiple drugs are used. Cessation of brain functions caused by the sedative and anesthetic drugs such as barbituates, benzodiazepines, meprobamate, methaqualone, and trichloroethylene, may be completely reversible even though they produce clinical cessation of brain functions and electrocerebral silence. In cases where there is any likelihood of sedative presence, toxicology screening for all likely drugs is required. If exogenous intoxication is found, death may not be declared until the intoxicant is metabolized or intracranial circulation is tested and found to have ceased.

Total paralysis may cause unresponsiveness, areflexia, and apnea that closely simulates death. Exposure to drugs such as neuromuscular blocking agents or aminoglycoside antibiotics, and diseases like myasthenia gravis are usually apparent by careful review of the history. Prolonged paralysis after use of succinylcholine chloride and related drugs requires evaluation for pseudo-cholinesterase deficiency. If there is any question, low-dose atropine stimulation, electromyogram, peripheral nerve stimulation, EEG, tests of intracranial circulation, or extended observation, as indicated, will make the diagnosis clear. . . .

Some severe illnesses (e.g., hepatic encephalopathy, hyperosmolar coma, and preterminal uremia) can cause deep coma. Before irreversible cessation of brain functions can be determined, metabolic abnormalities should be considered and, if possible, corrected. Confirmatory tests of circulation or EEG may be necessary.

B.   Hypothermia

Criteria for reliable recognition of death are not available in the presence of hypothermia (below 32.2°C core temperature). The variables of cerebral circulation in hypothermic patients are not sufficiently well studied to know whether tests of absent or diminished circulation are confirmatory. Hypothermia can mimic brain death by ordinary clinical criteria and can protect against neurologic damage due to hypoxia. Further complications arise since hypothermia also usually precedes and follows death. If these complicating factors make it unclear whether an individual is alive, the only available measure to resolve the issue is to restore normothermia. Hypothermia is not a common cause of difficulty in the determination of death.

C.   Children

The brains of infants and young children have increased resistance to damage and may recover substantial functions even after exhibiting unresponsiveness on neurological examination for longer periods than do adults. Physicians should be particularly cautious in applying neurologic criteria to determine death in children younger than 5 years.

D.   Shock

Physicians should also be particularly cautious in applying neurologic criteria to determine death in patients in shock because the reduction in cerebral circulation can render clinical examination and laboratory tests unreliable.

Non-Brain Formulations
The Alternative to the
Brain-Based Definitions*

President's Commission for the Study
of Ethical Problems in Medicine and Biomedical
and Behavioral Research

As it developed its report expressing a consensus in favor of a whole-brain-oriented definition of death, The President's Commission also examined the arguments surrounding what it called the *non-brain formulations*. At first these might appear to be based on the loss of the individual's heart beat or respiration, but the commissioners realized that bodily fluids might continue to flow mechanically with an artificial heart or even a heart-lung machine. In the excerpt presented, the Commission reviews the concepts and policy implications of continuing the traditional policy of pronouncing persons dead when they irreversibly lose functions related to the flow of bodily fluids.

THE NON-BRAIN FORMULATIONS

The Concepts.   The various physiological concepts of death so far discussed rely in some fashion on brain functioning. By contrast, a literal reading of the traditional cardiopulmonary criteria would require cessation of the flow of bodily "fluids," including air and blood, for death to be declared. This standard is meant to apply whether or not these flows coincide with any other bodily processes, neurological or otherwise. Its support derives from interpretations of religious literature and cultural practices of certain religious and ethnic groups, including some Orthodox Jews[1] and Native Americans.[2]

Another theological formulation of death is, by contrast, not necessarily related to any physiologic phenomenon. The view is traditional in many faiths that death occurs the moment the soul leaves the body.[3] Whether this happens when the patient loses psychological capacities, loses all brain functions, or at some other point, varies according to the teachings of each faith and according to particular interpretations of the scriptures recognized as authoritative.

Critique.   The conclusions of the "bodily fluids" view lack a physiologic basis in modern biomedicine. While this view accords with the traditional criteria of death, as noted above, it does not necessarily carry over to the new conditions of the intensive care unit—which are what prompts the reexamination of the definition of death. The flow of bodily fluids could conceivably be maintained by machines in the

*Source: President's Commission for the Study of Ethical Problems in Medicine and Biomedical and Behavioral Research, *Defining Death: Medical, Legal, and Ethical Issues in the Definition of Death.* Washington, D.C.: U.S. Government Printing Office, 1981, pp. 41–43.

absence of almost all other life processes; the result would be viewed by most as a perfused corpse, totally unresponsive to its environment.

Although the argument concerning the soul could be interpreted as providing a standard for secular action, those who adhere to the concept today apparently acknowledge the need for a more public and verifiable standard of death. Indeed, a statute incorporating a brain-based standard is accepted by theologians of all backgrounds.4

Policy Consequences.   The Commission does not regard itself as a competent or appropriate forum for theological interpretation. Nevertheless, it has sought to propose policies consistent with as many as possible of the diverse religious tenets and practices in our society.

The statute does not appear to conflict with the view that the soul leaves the body at death. It provides standards by which death can be determined to have occurred, but it does not prevent a person from believing on religious grounds that the soul leaves the body at a point other than that established as marking death for legal and medical purposes.

The concept of death based upon the flow of bodily fluids cannot be completely reconciled with the proposed statute. The statute is partially consistent with the "fluids" formulation in that both would regard as dead a body with no respiration and circulation. As noted previously, the overwhelming majority of patients, now and for the foreseeable future, will be diagnosed on such basis. Under the statute, however, physicians would declare dead those bodies in which respiration and circulation continued solely as a result of artificial maintenance, in the absence of all brain functions. Nonetheless, people who believe that the continued flow of fluids in such patients means they are alive would not be forced by the statute to abandon those beliefs nor to change their religious conduct. While the recommended statute may cause changes in medical and legal behavior, the Commission urges those acting under the statute to apply it with sensitivity to the emotional and religious needs of those for whom the new standards mark a departure from traditional practice. Determinations of death must be made in a consistent and evenhanded fashion, but the statute does not preclude flexibility in responding to individual circumstances after determination has been made.

NOTES

1. J. David Bleich. "Neurological Criteria of Death and Time of Death Statutes," in Fred Rosner and J. David Bleich (eds.). *Jewish Bioethics.* New York: Hebrew Publishing Co., (1979) at 303–316.
2. Telephone conversation with Richard E. Grant, Assistant Professor of Nursing, Arizona State University, July 17, 1981.
3. Milton McC. Gatch. "Death: Post-Biblical Christian Thought" in Warren T. Reich (ed.). *Encyclopedia of Bioethics* (v.1). New York: Macmillan Publishing Co., (1976) at 249, 250; Saint Augustine, *The City of God,* Vernon H. Bourke (ed). Garden City, NY: Image Books, (1958) at 269, 277; J. David Bleich, "Establishing Criteria of

Death," in Fred Rosner and J. David Bleich (eds.). *Jewish Bioethics,* New York: Hebrew Publishing Co., (1979) at 285.

4. Bernard Haring. *Medical Ethics,* Notre Dame, IN: Fides Publishers, Inc., (1973) at 136; Charles J. McFadden, "The Dignity of Life: Moral Values in a Changing Society," Huntington, IN: Our Sunday Visitor, Inc., (1976) at 202; Paul Ramsey, op. cit. at 59–112; Seymour Siegel, "Updating the Criteria of Death," 30 *Conservative Judaism* 23 (1976); Moses D. Tendler, "Cessation of Brain Function: Ethical Implications In Terminal Care and Organ Transplant," *Annals of the New York Academy of Science* 315 (1978), 394. *See also* pp. 13–14 supra and accompanying notes for a summary of the religious views presented to the Commission.

Against the Stream
Comments on the Definition and Redefinition of Death*

HANS JONAS

The movement to a brain-oriented definition of death was stimulated by the Report of the Harvard Ad Hoc Committee to Examine the Definition of Brain Death. In 1968 it proposed treating the death of the brain as the death of the individual.

One of the earliest critics of the move to a new brain-oriented definition of death was Hans Jonas. Jonas expressed concern that human life will be devalued if those with seriously compromised neurological function are treated as if they were dead. He urges caution in accepting the newer formulations.

Jonas believes that the criteria the Harvard Committee proposes may be appropriate criteria for permitting death to take place unopposed, but should not be seen as criteria for death itself. Jonas sees no sharp borderline (medical or otherwise) between life and death, doubts that the requirement of spontaneous functioning is useful, and sees much of the "definition" debate as covertly asking what should be done with the patient rather than whether the patient is dead.

Also, Jonas does not see reference either to central nervous system function or brain functions as directly relevant to the problem of a *definition* of death. He sees in modern technology only new capacities for sustaining life, not new ways of determining death. Indeed, Jonas thinks such capacities might easily lead to premature declarations of death, especially where there is need for transplant organs. Consequently, he tends toward acceptance of the conservative or traditional list of medical criteria for the determination that death has occurred. He even concludes that "no definition of death is needed." Rather, more careful moral reasoning about what to do with such patients is needed—not a new definition.

The by now famous "Report of the Ad Hoc Committee of the Harvard Medical School to Examine the Definition of Brain Death" advocates the adoption of "irreversible coma as a new definition of death." The report leaves no doubt of the practical reasons "why there is need for a definition," naming these two: relief of patient, kin, and medical resources from the burdens of indefinitely prolonged coma; and removal of controversy on obtaining organs for transplantation. On both counts, the new definition is designed to give the physician the right to terminate the treatment of a condition which not only cannot be improved by such treatment, but whose mere prolongation by it is utterly meaningless to the patient himself. The last consideration, of course, is ultimately the only valid rationale for termination (and for termination only!) and must support all the others. It does so with regard to the reasons mentioned under the first head, for the relief of the patient means automatically also that of his family, doctor, nurses, apparatus, hospital space, and so on. But the other reason—freedom for organ use—has possible implications that are not equally covered by the primary rationale, which is the patient himself. For with this primary rationale (the senselessness of mere vegetative function) the Report has strictly speaking defined not death, the ultimate state, itself, but a criterion for permitting it to take place unopposed—for example, by turning off the respirator. . . . But if "the patient is declared dead on the basis of these criteria," that is, if the comatose individual is not a patient at all but a corpse, then the road to other uses of the definition, urged by the second reason, has been opened in principle and will be taken in practice, unless it is blocked in good time by a special barrier. What follows is meant to reinforce what I called "my feeble attempt" to help erect such a barrier on theoretical grounds. . . .

I contend that, pure as this interest, viz., to save other lives, is in itself, its intrusion into the *theoretical* attempt to define death makes the attempt impure; and the Harvard Committee should never have allowed itself to adulterate the purity of its scientific case by baiting it with the prospect of this *extraneous*—though extremely appealing—gain. But purity of theory is not my concern here. My concern is with certain practical consequences which under the urgings of that extraneous interest can be drawn from the definition and would enjoy its full sanction, once it has been officially accepted. . . .

The difference between "organism as a whole" and "whole organism" . . . is perhaps brought out more clearly if for "whole organism" we write "every and all parts of the organism." If this is the meaning, then I have been speaking throughout of "death of the organism as a whole," not of "death of the whole organism"; and any ambiguity in my formulations can be easily removed. Local subsystems—single cells or tissues—may well continue to function locally, that is, to display biochemical activity for themselves (e.g., growth of hair and nails) for some time after death, without this affecting the definition of death by the larger criteria of the whole. But respiration and circulation do not fall into this class, since the effect of their functioning, though performed by subsystems, extends through the total system and insures the functional preservation of its other parts. Why else prolong them artificially in prospective "cadaveric" organ donors (e.g., "maintain renal circulation of cadaver kidneys in situ") except to keep those other parts "in good shape"—viz., alive—for eventual transplantation? The comprehensive system thus sustained is even capable of continued overall metabolism when intravenously fed, and then, presumably, of diverse other (e.g., glandular) functions as well—in fact, I suppose, of pretty much everything not involving neural control. There are stories of comatose patients lingering on for months with those aids; the metaphor of the "human vegetable" recurring in the debate (strangely enough, sometimes in support of redefining death—as if "vegetable" were not an instance of life!) says as much. In short, what is here kept going by various artifices must—with the caution due in this twilight zone—be equated with "the organism as a whole" named in the classical definition of death—much more so, at least, than with any mere, separable part of it.

Nor, to my knowledge, does that older definition specify that the functioning whose "irreversible cessation" constitutes death must be spontaneous and does not count for life when artificially induced and sustained (the implications for therapy would be devastating). Indeed, "irreversible" cessation can have a twofold reference: to the function itself or only to the spontaneity of it. A cessation can be irreversible with respect to spontaneity but still reversible with respect to the activity as such—in which case the reversing external agency must continuously substitute for the lost spontaneity. This is the case of the respiratory movements and heart contractions in the comatose. The distinction is not irrelevant, because if we could do for the disabled brain—let's say, the lower nerve centers only—what we can do for the heart and lungs, viz., *make* it work by the continuous input of some external agency (electrical, chemical, or whatever), we would surely do so and not be finicky about the resulting function's lacking spontaneity: the functioning as such would matter. Respirator and stimulator could then be turned off, because the nerve center presiding over heart contractions (etc.) has again taken over and returned *them* to being "spontaneous"—just as systems presided over by circulation had enjoyed spontaneity of function when the circulation was only nonspontaneously active. The case is wholly hypothetical, but I doubt that a doctor would feel at liberty to pronounce the patient dead on the ground of the nonspontaneity at the cerebral source, when it can be *made* to function by an auxiliary device.

The purpose of the foregoing thought-experiment was to cast some doubt (a layman's, to be sure) on the seeming simplicity of the spontaneity criterion. With the stratification and interlocking of functions, it seems to me, organic spontaneity is distributed over many levels and loci—any superordinated level enabling its subordinates to be naturally spontaneous, be its own action natural or artificial.

The point with irreversible coma as defined by the Harvard group, of course, is precisely that it is a condition which precludes reactivation of any part of the brain in *every* sense. We then have an "organism as a whole" minus the brain, maintained in some partial state of life so long as the respirator and other artifices are at work. And here the question is not: has the patient died? but: how should he—still a patient—be dealt with? Now *this* question must be settled, surely not by a definition of death, but by a definition of man and of what life is human. That is to say, the question cannot be answered by decreeing that death has already occurred and the body is therefore in the domain of things; rather it is answered by holding, for example, that it is humanly not justified—let alone, demanded—to artificially prolong the life of a brainless body. This is the answer I myself would advocate. On that philosophical ground, which few will contest, the physician can, indeed should, turn off the respirator and let the "definition of death" take care of itself by what then inevitably happens. (The later utilization of the corpse is a different matter I am not dealing with here, though it too resists the comfortable patness of merely utilitarian answers.) The decision to be made, I repeat, is an axiological one and not already made by clinical fact. It begins when the diagnosis of the condition has spoken: it is not diagnostic itself. Thus, as I have pointed out before, no redefinition of death is needed; only, perhaps, a redefinition of the physician's presumed duty to prolong life under all circumstances.

But, it might be asked, is not a definition of death made into law the simpler and more precise way than a definition of medical ethics (which is difficult to legislate) for sanctioning the same practical conclusion, while avoiding the twilight of value judgment and possible legal ambiguity? It would be, if it really sanctioned the same conclusion, and no more. But it sanctions indefinitely more: it opens the gate to a whole range of other possible conclusions, the extent of which cannot even be foreseen, but some of which are disquietingly close at hand. The point is, if the comatose patient is by definition dead, he is a patient no more but a corpse, with which can be done whatever law or custom or the deceased's will or next of kin permit and sundry interests urge doing with a corpse. This includes—why not?—the protracting of the in-between state, for which we must find a new name ("simulated life"?), since that of "life" has been preempted by the new definition of death, and extracting from it all the profit we can. There are many. So far the "redefiners" speak of no more than keeping the respirator going until the transplant organ is to be removed, then turning it off,[1] then beginning to cut into the "cadaver," this being the end of it—which sounds innocent enough. But why must it be the end? Why turn the respirator off? Once we are assured that we are dealing with a cadaver, there are no logical reasons against (and strong pragmatic reasons for) going on with the artificial "animation" and keeping the "deceased's" body on call, as a bank for life-fresh organs, possibly also as a plant for manufacturing hormones or other biochemical compounds in demand. I have no doubts that methods exist or can be perfected which allow the natural powers for the healing of surgical wounds by new tissue growth to stay "alive" in such a body. Tempting also is the idea of a self-replenishing blood bank. And that is not all. Let us not forget research. Why shouldn't the most wonderful surgical and grafting experiments be conducted on the complaisant subject-nonsubject, with no limits set to daring? Why not immunological explorations, infection with diseases old and new, trying out of drugs? We have the active cooperation of a functional organism declared to be dead: we have, that is, the advantages of the living donor without the disadvantages imposed by his rights and interests (for a corpse has none). What a boon for medical instruction, for anatomical and physiological demonstration and practicing on so much better material than the inert cadavers otherwise serving in the dissection room! What a chance for the apprentice to learn in vivo, as it were, how to amputate a leg, without his mistakes mattering! And so on, into the wide open field. After all, what is advocated is "the full utilization of modern means to maximize the value of cadaver organs." Well, this is it. . . .

Now my point is a very simple one. It is this. We do not know with certainty the borderline between life and death, and a definition cannot substitute for knowledge. Moreover, we have sufficient grounds for suspecting that the artificially supported condition of the comatose patient may still be one of life, however reduced—that is, for doubting that, even with the brain function gone, he is completely dead. In this state of marginal ignorance and doubt the only course to take is to lean over backward toward the side of possible life. It follows that interventions as I described should be regarded on a par with vivisection and on no account be performed on a human body in that equivocal or threshold condition. And the definition that allows them, by stamping as unequivocal what at best is equivocal, must be rejected. But mere rejection in discourse is not enough. Given the pressure of the—very real and very worthy—medical interests, it can be predicted that the permission it implies in theory will be irresistible in practice, once the definition is installed in official authority. Its becoming so installed must therefore be resisted at all cost. It is the only thing that still can be resisted; by the time the practical conclusions beckon, it will be too late. It is a clear case of *principiis obsta.*

The foregoing argumentation was strictly on the plane of common sense and ordinary logic. Let me add, somewhat conjecturally, two philosophical observations.

I see lurking behind the proposed definition of death, apart from its obvious pragmatic motivation, a curious revenant of the old soul-body dualism. Its new apparition is the dualism of brain and body. In a certain analogy to the former it holds that the true human person rests in (or is represented by) the brain, of which the rest of the body is a mere subservient tool. Thus, when the brain dies, it is as when the soul departed: what is left are "mortal remains." Now nobody will deny that the cerebral aspect is decisive for the human quality of the life of the organism that is man's. The position I advanced acknowledges just this by recommending that with the irrecoverable total loss of brain function one should not hold up the naturally ensuing death of the rest of the organism. But it is no less an exaggeration of the cerebral aspect as it was of the conscious soul, to deny the extracerebral body its essential share in the identity of the person. The body is as uniquely the body of this brain and no other, as the brain is uniquely the brain of this body and no other. . . .

My second observation concerns the morality of our time, to which our "redefiners" pay homage with the best of intentions, which have their own subtle sophistry. I mean the prevailing attitude toward death, whose faintheartedness they indulge in a curious blend with the toughmindedness of the scientist. The Catholic Church had the guts to say: under these circumstances let the patient die—speaking of the patient alone and not of outside interests (society's, medicine's, etc.). The cowardice of modern secular society which shrinks from death as an unmitigated evil needs the assurance (or fiction) that he is already dead when the decision is to be made. The responsibility of a value-laden decision replaced by the mechanics of a value-free routine. Insofar as the redefiners of death—by saying "he is already dead"—seek to allay the scruples about turning the respirator off, they cater to this modern cowardice which has forgotten that death has its own fitness and dignity, and that a man has a right to be let die. . . .

NOTE

1. This has turned out to be too charitable an assumption.

Establishing Criteria of Death*

J. DAVID BLEICH

In addition to the philosophical objections to the brain-oriented definition of death, certain religious groups have opposed such a move. Native American objections and some of those from Japan reflect traditions that are religious in character, as are some objections from certain right-to-life groups. The clearest religious objection to a brain-based definition of death, however, has come from the Orthodox Jewish community. That group has long associated life with breath or the capacity to breathe. They support a more traditional view of the definition of death that links death to irreversible loss of cardiac and respiratory function. They have not insisted that the respiration be spontaneous and therefore have not insisted that the brain function be intact for an individual to be alive. J. David Bleich, a rabbinical scholar at Yeshiva University in New York, represents this perspective.

The task of defining death is not a trivial exercise to be relegated to the purview of the lexicographer. It is perhaps the most pressing concern in the field of bioethics. The formulation of such a definition involves an attempt to arrive at an understanding of the very essence of human life and an endeavor to identify the nature of the ephemeral substance which is lost at the time of death.

The loss of that elusive component which transforms the human organism into a living being effects a change in the moral and legal status of the individual. The traditional view is that death occurs upon the separation of the soul from the body. Of course, the occurrence of this phenomenon does not lend itself to direct empirical observation. Accordingly, traditional definitions of death have focussed upon cessation of circulatory and respiratory functions as criteria of the ebbing of life. *Black's Law Dictionary* (rev. 4th ed. 1968), in recording the accepted legal definition, describes death as " . . . total stoppage of the circulation of the blood, and a cessation of the animal and vital functions consequent thereupon, such as respiration, pulsation, etc."

Contemporary medical science has developed highly sophisticated techniques for determining the presence or absence of vital bodily functions. Moreover, improvements in resuscitatory and supportive measures now at times make it possible to restore life as judged by the traditional standards of persistent respiration and continuing heart beat. This can be the case even when there is little likelihood of an individual recovering consciousness following massive brain damage. These new medical realia have led to a reassessment of traditional definitions of death. Some

---

*Source: J. David Bleich, "Establishing Criteria of Death," *Tradition*, 13, 1973: 90–113. © The Rabbinical Council of America. Also reprinted from *Contemporary Halakhic Problems*, Vol. 1, J. David Bleich, ed. © 1977, pp. 372–393. Published KTAV Publishing House. Reprinted by permission.

members of the scientific community now advocate that previously accepted criteria of death be set aside and have formulated several proposals for a redefinition of the phenomenon of death.

Chief among these is the now popular concept frequently, though inaccurately, referred to as brain death. According to this view, death is equated with the complete loss of the body's integrating capacities as signified by the activity of the central nervous system and is determined by the absence of brain waves as recorded by an electroencephalogram over a period of time. It is most interesting to note that reports have appeared, both in the popular press and in scholarly publications, of a significant number of instances in which patients have made either partial or complete recoveries despite previous electroencephalogram readings which registered no brain activity over an extended period of time.[1]

Several years ago the Ad Hoc Committee of the Harvard Medical School to Examine the Definition of Brain Death was established. The published report of this committee[2] states that its primary purpose was to "define irreversible coma as a new criterion of death." In order to arrive at a clinical definition of irreversible coma, the Ad Hoc Committee recommends establishment of operational criteria for the determination of the characteristics of a permanently nonfunctioning brain. The three recommended criteria are: (1) lack of response to external stimuli or to internal need; (2) absence of movement or breathing as observed by physicians over a period of at least one hour; (3) absence of elicitable reflexes ("except in some cases through the spinal cord").[3] A fourth criterion, a flat, or isoelectric, electroencephalogram, is recommended as being "of great confirmatory value" but not of absolute necessity. Subsequently, Dr. Henry K. Beecher, the chairman of the Ad Hoc Committee, noted, "Almost everybody else has required the use of the electroencephalogram. We think it adds helpful confirmatory evidence, but we do not think that it is necessary by itself."[4] The procedure advocated by the Ad Hoc Committee calls for repetition of the relevant tests following a lapse of 24 hours. Repeated examinations over a period of 24 hours or longer are required in order to obtain evidence of the irreversible nature of the coma.

Most revealing is the quite candid statement of the committee chairman: "Only a very bold man, I think, would attempt to define death. . . . I was chairman of a recent *ad hoc* committee at Harvard composed of members of five faculties in the university who tried to define irreversible coma. We felt we could not define death. I suppose you will say that by implication we have defined it as brain death, but we do not make a point of that."[5]

More recently, the adequacy of even this notion of brain death has been challenged in some quarters. Proponents of a broader definition ask, "Why is it that one must identify the entire brain with death; is it not possible that we are really interested only in man's consciousness: in his ability to think, reason, feel, interact with others and control his body functions consciously?"[6] According to this latter view, death is to be equated with irreversible loss of consciousness. If this definition were to gain acceptance, the effect would be that in cases where the lower brain function is intact while the cortex, which controls consciousness, is destroyed, the patient would be pronounced dead.

Much of the debate concerning the definition of death misses the mark. A definition of death cannot be derived from medical facts or scientific investigation alone. The physician can only describe the physiological state which he observes; whether the patient meeting that description is alive or dead, whether the human organism in that physiological state is to be treated as a living person or as a corpse, is an ethical and legal question. The determination of the time of death, insofar as it is more than a mere exercise in semantics, is essentially a theological and moral problem, not a medical or scientific one. . . .

It must be emphasized that in all . . . questions involving the very heart of a physician's obligations with regard to the preservation of human life, halakhic Judaism demands of him that he govern himself by the norms of Jewish law whether or not these determinations coincide with the mores of contemporary society. Brain death and irreversible coma are not acceptable definitions of death insofar as Halakhah is concerned. The sole criterion of death accepted by Halakhah is total cessation of both cardiac and respiratory activity. Even when these indications are present, there is a definite obligation to resuscitate the patient, if at all feasible. Jewish law recognizes the malformed, the crippled, the terminally ill, and the mentally retarded as human beings in the full sense of the term. Hence, the physician's obligation with regard to medical treatment and resuscitation is in no way diminished by the fact that the resuscitated patient may be a victim of brain damage or other debilitating injury.

Of late, there has been increased discussion of a patient's right to "die with dignity" and a general urging that physicians not overly prolong the lives of comatose patients who are incurably ill. It is exceedingly difficult to argue against an individual's right to "die with dignity." This phrase, so pregnant with approbation, bespeaks a concept which is rapidly joining motherhood, the Fourth of July, and apple pie as one of the great American values.

Certainly one has a right to dignity both in life and in death. But is death, properly speaking, a *right?* Suicide is forbidden both by religious and temporal law. It is proscribed because Western culture has long recognized that man's life is not his own to dispose of at will. This fundamental concept is expressed most cogently by Plato in his *Phaedo.* Socrates, in a farewell conversation with his students prior to his execution, speaks of the afterlife with eager anticipation. Thereupon one of his disciples queries, if death is so much preferable to life, why did not Socrates long ago take his own life? In a very apt simile, Socrates responds that an ox does not have the right to take its own life because it thereby deprives its master of the enjoyment of his property.[7] Man is the chattel of the gods, says Socrates. Just as "bovicide" on the part of the ox is a violation of the proprietor-property relationship, so suicide on the part of man constitutes a violation of the Creator-creature relationship.

Man does not possess absolute title to his life or to his body. He is but the steward of the life which he has been privileged to receive. Man is charged with preserving, dignifying, and hallowing that life. He is obliged to seek food and sustenance in order to safeguard the life he has been granted; when falling victim to illness and disease he is obliged to seek a cure in order to sustain life. Never is he called upon to determine whether life is worth living—this is a question over which God remains sole arbiter.

Surely, even on the basis of humanistic assumptions, one must recognize that human life must remain inviolate. As long as life is indeed present, the decision to terminate such life is beyond the competence of man. In pragmatic terms, a decision not to prolong life means precluding the application of some new advance in therapeutics that would secure a remission or cure for that patient should a breakthrough occur. But, more fundamentally, man lacks the right to assess the quality of any human life and to determine that it is beneficial for that life to be terminated; all human life is of inestimable value. If the comatose may be caused to "die with dignity," what of the mentally deranged and the feeble-minded incapable of "meaningful" human activity? Withdrawal of treatment leads directly to overt acts of euthanasia; from there it may be but a short step to selective elimination of those whose life is deemed a burden upon society at large.

Undoubtedly, caring for a patient *in extremis* places a heavy burden upon the family, the medical practitioner and hospital facilities. It is natural for us, both individually and collectively, to harbor feelings of resentment because of the toll exacted from us. But we must recognize that preservation of any value demands sacrifices. Above all, we must be on guard against self-interest cloaked in altruism, against allowing self-serving motives to find expression in the language of idealism.

Attempts have been made in the past to make the right to life subservient to other values. The results have been tragic. Hannah Arendt and others have pointed out that in the scale of values accepted in Germany during the World War II era, obedience to law took priority over the sanctity of human life. Yet we have refused to accept this argument as a valid line of defense, because we believe it to be self-evident that the right to life is a right which has been endowed upon all men by their Creator. A person's right to life, as long as it does not conflict with another's right to life, is inviolate. And the right to life precludes the right to hasten death either overtly or covertly. The teachings of Judaism in this regard are nowhere expressed more eloquently than in the *Siddur:*

> My God, the soul which You have placed within me is pure. *You* have created it; *You* have fashioned it; *You* have breathed it into me and *You* preserve it within me; *and You will at some time take it from me* and return it to me in the time to come. As long as the soul is within me I will give thanks unto You . . .

NOTES

1. *Jerusalem Post,* November 14, 1968; *Hirntod* (Stuttgart, 1969), pp. 63, 66, 98, and 106. See Jacob Levy, *Mavet Mohi, Ha-Ma'ayan,* Nisan 5732, p. 25; J. B. Brierly, J. H. Adams, D. I. Graham, et al., "Neocortical Death after Cardiac Arrest," *Lancet* 2:560–565, 1971; Hadassah Gillon, "Defining Death Anew," *Science News* 95 (January 11, 1969), p. 50; Harold L. Hirsch, *Case and Comment,* September-October 1974; *Rochester Democrat and Chronicle,* March 19, 1975, p. 19. Cf. also Henry K. Beecher, "Definitions of 'Life' and 'Death' for Medical Science and Practice," *Annals of the New York Academy of Sciences,* vol. 169, art. 2 (January 21, 1971), pp. 471–472; E. Bental and U. Leibowitz, "Flat Electroencephalograms During 28 Days

in Case of 'Encephalitis,'" *Electroenceph. Clinical Neurophysiology,* XIII (1961), 457–460; R. G. Bickford, B. Dawson and H. Takeshita, "EEG Evidence of Neurologic Death," *Electroencephalography Clinical Neurophysiology,* XVIII (1965), 513–514; T. D. Bird and F. Plum, "Recovery from Barbituate Overdose Coma with Prolonged Isoelectric Electroencephalogram," *Neurology,* XVIII (1968), 456–460; R. L. Tentler et al., "Electroencephalographic Evidence of Cortical 'Death' Followed by Full Recovery: Protective Action of Hypothermia," *Journal of the American Medical Association,* CLXIV (1957), 1667–1670; P. Braunstein, J. Korein et al., "A Simple Bedside Evaluation of Cerebral Blood Flow in the Study of Cerebral Death." *The American Journal of Roentgeneology Radium Therapy and Nuclear Medecine,* CXVIII (1973), 758; and P. Braunstein, I. Kricheff, et al., "Cerebral Death: A Rapid and Reliable Diagnostic Adjunct Using Radiosotopes," *Journal of Nuclear Medecine,* XIV (1973), 122.

2. "A Definition of Irreversible Coma." *Journal of the American Medical Association,* vol. 205, no. 6 (August 5, 1968), pp. 337–340.

3. This modification appears in Beecher, *Annals,* p. 471.

4. *Loc. cit.*

5. *Loc. cit.*

6. Robert M. Veatch, "Brain Death: Welcome Definition or Dangerous Judgment?" *Hastings Center Report,* II, no. 5 (November 1972), p. 11.

7. In halakhic literature this concept is developed by Radbaz in his commentary on Rambam, *Hilkhot Sanhedrin* 18:6. It is a basic halakhic principle that, while a defendant's testimony is accorded absolute credibility with regard to establishing financial liability, a confession of guilt is never accepted as evidence of criminal culpability. Citing the verse "Behold, all souls are Mine" (Ezek. 18:4), Radbaz explains that while material goods belong to man and may be disposed of at will, the human body is the possession of God and may be punished only by Him. See also Rambam, *Hilkhot Roze'ah* 1:4 and *Shulhan Arukh ha-Rav,* VI, *Hilkhot Nizkei Guf* 4.

CONTROVERSIES SURROUNDING THE DEFINITION

The "Higher Brain" Formulations*

President's Commission for the Study of Ethical Problems in Medicine and Biomedical and Behavioral Research

While the defenders of a brain-oriented definition of death have gradually prevailed over those holding out for a heart-oriented formulation, a newer dispute has arisen within the brain-oriented camp. It appeared that the brain-based definitions would eventually carry the day and the controversy would disappear, but as the neurological basis for pronouncing death became more accepted, some began to ask for more precise information about whether literally all functions of the entire brain needed to be lost for someone to be pronounced dead. A so-called *higher-brain formulation* emerged that favored pronouncing death when only the "higher" functions were lost. This had generally been defined to refer to cerebral functions or to consciousness. (Since some cerebral functions have nothing to do with consciousness, it would be possible to have some isolated cerebral function and still no capacity for consciousness.)

In the section that follows, the Commission rejects these higher-brain formulations. In the process they present what they see as problems with such views.

THE "HIGHER BRAIN" FORMULATIONS

When all brain processes cease, the patient loses two important sets of functions. One set encompasses the integrating and coordinating functions, carried out principally but not exclusively by the cerebellum and brainstem. The other set includes the psychological functions which make consciousness, thought, and feeling possible. These latter functions are located primarily but not exclusively in the cerebrum, especially the neocortex. The two "higher brain" formulations of brain-oriented definitions of death discussed here are premised on the fact that loss of cerebral functions strips the patient of his psychological capacities and properties.

A patient whose brain has permanently stopped functioning will, by definition, have lost those brain functions which sponsor consciousness, feeling, and thought. Thus, the higher brain rationales support classifying as dead bodies which meet "whole brain" standards. . . . The converse is not true, however. If there are parts of the brain which have no role in sponsoring consciousness, the higher brain formulation would regard their continued functioning as compatible with death.

*Source: President's Commission for the Study of Ethical Problems in Medicine and Biological and Behavioral Research, *Defining Death: Medical, Legal, and Ethical Issues in the Definition of Death*. Washington, D.C.: U.S. Government Printing Office, 1981, pp. 38–41.

The Concepts.   Philosophers and theologians have attempted to describe the attributes a living being must have to be a person.[1] "Personhood" consists of the complex of activities (or of capacities to engage in them) such as thinking, reasoning, feeling, human intercourse which make the human different from, or superior to, animals or things. One higher brain formulation would define death as the loss of what is essential to a person. Those advocating the personhood definition often relate these characteristics to brain functioning. Without brain activity, people are incapable of these essential activities. A breathing body, the argument goes, is not in itself a person; and, without functioning brains, patients are merely breathing bodies. Hence personhood ends when the brain suffers irreversible loss of function.

For other philosophers, a certain concept of "personal identity" supports a brain-oriented definition of death.[2] According to this argument, a patient literally ceases to exist as an individual when his or her brain ceases functioning, even if the patient's body is biologically alive. Actual decapitation creates a similar situation: the body might continue to function for a short time, but it would no longer be the "same" person. The persistent identity of a person as an individual from one moment to the next is taken to be dependent on the continuation of certain mental processes which arise from brain functioning. When the brain processes cease (whether due to decapitation or to "brain death") the person's identity also lapses. The mere continuation of biological activity in the body is irrelevant to the determination of death, it is argued, because after the brain has ceased functioning the body is no longer identical with the person.

Critique.   Theoretical and practical objections to these arguments led the Commission to rely on them only as confirmatory of other views in formulating a definition of death. First, crucial to the personhood argument is acceptance of one particular concept of those things that are essential to being a person, while there is no general agreement on this very fundamental point among philosophers, much less physicians or the general public. Opinions about what is essential to personhood vary greatly from person to person in our society—to say nothing of intercultural variations.

The argument from personal identity does not rely on any particular conception of personhood, but it does require assent to a single solution to the philosophical problem of identity. Again, this problem has persisted for centuries despite the best attempts by philosophers to solve it. Regardless of the scholarly merits of the various philosophical solutions, their abstract technicality makes them less useful to public policy.

Further, applying either of these arguments in practice would give rise to additional important problems. Severely senile patients, for example, might not clearly be persons, let alone ones with continuing personal identities; the same might be true of the severely retarded. Any argument that classified these individuals as dead would not meet with public acceptance.

Equally problematic for the "higher brain" formulations, patients in whom only the neocortex or subcortical areas have been damaged may retain or regain spontaneous respiration and circulation. Karen Quinlan is a well-known example of a person who apparently suffered permanent damage to the higher centers of the brain but whose lower brain continues to function. Five years after being removed from the respirator that supported her breathing for nearly a year, she remains in a persistent vegetative state but with heart and lungs that function without mechanical assistance.[3] Yet the implication of the personhood and personal identity arguments is that Karen Quinlan, who retains brainstem function and breathes spontaneously, is just as dead as a corpse in the traditional sense. The Commission rejects this conclusion and the further implication that such patients could be buried or otherwise treated as dead persons.

Policy Consequences. In order to be incorporated in public policy, a conceptual formulation of death has to be amenable to clear articulation. At present, neither basic neurophysiology nor medical technique suffices to translate the "higher brain" formulation into policy. First, it is not known which portions of the brain are responsible for cognition and consciousness; what little is known points to substantial interconnections among the brainstem, subcortical structures and the neocortex. Thus, the "higher brain" may well exist only as a metaphorical concept, not in reality. Second, even when the sites of certain aspects of consciousness can be found, their cessation often cannot be assessed with the certainty that would be required in applying a statutory definition.

Even were these difficulties to be overcome, the adoption of a higher brain "definition" would depart radically from the traditional standards. As already observed, the new standard would assign no significance to spontaneous breathing and heartbeat. Indeed, it would imply that the existing cardiopulmonary definition had been in error all along, even before the advent of respirators and other life-sustaining technology.

In contrast, the position taken by the Commission is deliberately conservative. The statutory proposal offers legal recognition for new diagnostic measures of death, but does not ask for acceptance of a wholly new concept of death. On a matter so fundamental to a society's sense of itself—touching deeply held personal and religious beliefs—and so final for the individuals involved, one would desire much greater consensus than now exists before taking the major step of radically revising the concept of death.

Finally, patients declared dead pursuant to the statute recommended by the Commission would be also considered dead by those who believe that a body without higher brain functions is dead. Thus, all the arguments reviewed thus far are in agreement that irreversible cessation of *all* brain functioning is sufficient to determine death of the organism.

NOTES

1. H. Tristram Engelhardt, Jr. "Defining Death: A Philosophical Problem for Medicine and Law," 112 *Annual Review Respiratory Disease* 587 (1975); Robert M. Veatch, "The Whole-Brain Oriented Concept of Death: An Out-moded Philosophical Formulation," 3 *Journal of Thanatology* 13 (1975).

2. Michael B. Green and Daniel Wikler. "Brain Death and Personal Identity," 9 *Philosophical and Public Affairs* 105 (1980); Bernard Gert, "Personal Identity and the Body," *Dialogue* 458 (1971); Roland Puccetti, "The Conquest of Death" 59 *The Monist* 252 (1976); Azriel Rosenfeld, "The Heart, the Head and the Halakhah, *New York State Journal of Medicine* 2615 (1970).
3. "Karen Ann Quinlan: A Family's Fate," May 26, 1981, *Washington Post,* A at 1, col. 1.

The Impending Collapse of the Whole-Brain Definition of Death*

ROBERT M. VEATCH

In the years since the 1981 President's Commission report that rejected a higher-brain formulation, the controversy has grown. More and more people realize how implausible it is to insist that literally every last function of the entire brain must be dead before an individual can be pronounced dead based on brain criteria. From the early years of the debate it was recognized that isolated cells might survive and produce electrical activity indicating that there is remaining cellular function. There was a general agreement to ignore this form of cellular life. More recently it has been realized that small groups of cells might still survive even if all the tests of the Medical Consultants to the Commission were fulfilled. Recently, certain hormonal regulations by the brain have been shown to survive. One response might be to call for a revision of the tests to measure brain function to insist that literally all functions be lost. Another response, as is suggested in the following reading, is to press for a further modification of the definition of death so that death can be pronounced in the presence of these residual functions.

For many years there has been lingering doubt, at least among theorists, that the currently fashionable "whole-brain-oriented" definition of death has things exactly right. I myself have long resisted the term "brain death" and will use it only in quotation marks to indicate the still common, if ambiguous, usage. The term is ambiguous because it fails to distinguish between the biological claim that the brain is dead and the social/legal/moral claim that the individual as a whole is dead because the brain is dead. An even greater problem with the term arises from the lingering doubt that individuals with dead brains are really dead. Hence, even physicians are sometimes heard to say that the patient "suffered brain death" one day and "died" the following day. It is better to say that he "died" on the first day, the day the brain was determined to be dead, and that the cadaver's other bodily functions ceased the following day. For these reasons I insist on speaking of persons with dead brains as individuals who are dead, not merely persons who are "brain dead."

The presently accepted standard definition, the Uniform Determination of Death Act, specifies that an individual is dead who has sustained "irreversible cessation of all functions of the entire brain, including the brain stem."[1] It also provides an alternative definition specifying that an individual is also dead who has sustained "irreversible cessation of circulatory and respiratory functions." The President's Commission for the Study of Ethical Problems in Medicine and Biomedical and Behavioral Research made clear, however, that circulatory and respiratory function loss are important only as indirect indicators that the brain has been permanently destroyed (p. 74).

*Source: Robert M. Veatch, "The Impending Collapse of the Whole-Brain Definition of Death," *Hastings Center Report* 23, no. 4 (1993):18–24. Reproduced by permission. © The Hastings Center.

DOUBTS ABOUT THE WHOLE-BRAIN-ORIENTED DEFINITION

It is increasingly apparent, however, that this consensus is coming apart. As long ago as the early 1970s some of us doubted that literally the entire brain had to be dead for the individual as a whole to be dead.[2]

From the early years it was known, at least among neurologists and theorists who read the literature, that individual, isolated brain cells could be perfused and continue to live even though integrated supercellular brain function had been destroyed. When the uniform definition of death said *all functions of the entire brain* must be dead, there was a gentleman's agreement that cellular level functions did not count. The President's Commission recognized this, positing that "cellular activity alone is irrelevant" (p. 75). This willingness to write off cellular level functions is more controversial than it may appear. After all, the law does not grant a dispensation to ignore cellular level functions, no matter how plausible that may be. Keep in mind that critics of soon-to-be-developed higher brain definitions of death would need to emphasize that the model statute called for loss of *all* functions.

By 1977 an analogous problem arose regarding electrical activity. The report of a multicenter study funded by the National Institutes of Neurological Diseases and Stroke found that all of the functions it considered important could be lost irreversibly while very small (2 microvolt) electrical potentials could still be obtained on EEG. These were not artifact but real electrical activity from brain cells. Nevertheless, the committee concluded that there could be "electrocerebral silence" and therefore the brain could be considered "dead" even though these small electrical charges could be recorded.[3]

It is possible that the members of the committee believed that these were the result of nothing more than cellular level functions, so that the same reasoning that permitted the President's Commission to write off little functions as unimportant would apply. However, no evidence was presented that these electrical potentials were arising exclusively from cellular level functions. It could well be that the reasoning in this report expanded the existing view that cellular functions did not count to the view that some minor supercellular functions could be ignored as long as they were small.

More recently the neurologist James Bernat, a defender of the whole-brain-oriented definition of death, has acknowledged that:

> the bedside clinical examination is not sufficiently sensitive to exclude the possibility that small nests of brain cells may have survived . . . and that their continued functioning, although not contributing significantly to the functioning of the organism as a whole, can be measured by laboratory techniques. Because these isolated nests of neurons no longer contribute to the functioning of the organism as a whole, their continued functioning is now irrelevant to the dead organism.[4]

The idea that functions of "isolated nests of neurons" can remain when an individual is declared dead based on whole-brain-oriented criteria certainly stretches the plain words of the law that requires, without qualification, that *all functions of the entire brain* must be gone. That exceptions can be granted by individual private citizens based on their personal judgments about which functions are "contributing significantly" certainly challenges the integrity of the idea that the whole brain must be dead for the individual as a whole to be dead.

There is still another problem for those who favor what can now be called the "whole-brain definition of death." It is not altogether clear that the "death of the brain" is to be equated with the "irreversible loss of function." At least one paper appears to hold out not only for loss of function but also for destruction of anatomical structure.[5] Thus we are left with a severely nuanced and qualified whole-brain-oriented definition of death. For it to hold as applied in the 1990s, one must assume that function rather than structure is irreversibly destroyed and that not only can certain cellular-level functions and microvolt-level electrical functions be ignored as "insignificant," but also certain "nests of cells" and associated supercellular-level functions can as well.

By the time the whole-brain-oriented definition of death is so qualified, it can hardly be referring to the death of the whole brain any longer. What is particularly troublesome is that private citizens—neurologists, philosophers, theologians, and public commentators—seem to be determining just what brain functions are insignificant.

THE HIGHER-BRAIN-ORIENTED ALTERNATIVE

The problem is exacerbated when one reviews the early "brain death" literature. Writers trying to make the case for a brain-based definition of death over a heart-based one invariably pointed out that certain functions were irreversibly lost when the brain was gone. Then, implicitly or explicitly, they made the moral/philosophical/religious claim that individuals who have irreversibly lost these key functions should be treated as dead.

While this function-based defense of a brain-oriented definition of death served the day well, some of us realized that the critical functions cited were not randomly distributed throughout the brain. For instance, Henry Beecher, the chair of the Harvard Ad Hoc Committee, identified the following functions as critical: "the individual's personality, his conscious life, his uniqueness, his capacity for remembering, judging, reasoning, acting, enjoying, worrying, and so on."[6]

Of course, all these functions are known to require the cerebrum. If these are the important functions, the obvious question is why any lower brain functions would signal the presence of a living individual. This gave rise to what is now best called the *higher-brain-oriented definition of death:* that one is dead when there is irreversible loss of all "higher" brain functions. At first this was referred to as a cerebral or a cortical definition of death, but it seems clear that just as some brain stem functions may be deemed insignificant, likewise, some functions in the cerebrum may be as well. Moreover, it is not clear that the functions of the kind Beecher listed are always necessarily localized in the cerebrum or the cerebral cortex. At least in theory someday we may be able to build an artificial neurological organ that could replace some functions of the cerebrum. Someone who was thinking, feeling, reasoning, and carrying on a conversation through the use of an artificial brain would surely be recognized as alive even if the cerebrum that it had replaced was long since completely dead. I have preferred the purposely ambiguous term "higher brain function," as a way to make clear that the key philosophical issue is which of the many brain functions are really important. . . .

CRITICISMS OF THE HIGHER BRAIN FORMULATIONS

Several defenders of the whole-brain-oriented concept have claimed that defining death in terms of loss of certain significant brain functions involves a change in the concept of death. This, however, rests on the implausible claim of Alex Capron, the executive director of the President's Commission, that the move from a heart-oriented to a whole-brain-oriented definition of death is not a change in concept at all, but merely the recognition of new diagnostic measures for the traditional concept of death. . . .

Most understood this as a significant change in concept. In any case, even if there is a greater change in moving to a definition of death that identifies certain functions of the brain as significant, the mere fact that it is a conceptual change should not count against it. Surely, the critical question is which concept is right, not which concept squares with traditional views.

A second major charge against the higher-brain-oriented formulations has been that we are unable to measure precisely the irreversible loss of these higher functions based on current neurophysiological techniques. By contrast it has been assumed that the irreversible loss of all functions of the entire brain is measurable based on current techniques.

Although lay people generally do not realize it, the measurement of death based on any concept can never be 100 percent accurate. The greatest error rates have certainly been with the heart-oriented concepts of death. . . .

There is even newly found ambiguity in the notion of irreversibility.[7] We are moving rapidly toward the day when organs for transplant will be obtained from non-heart-beating cadavers who have been determined to be dead based on heart function loss. It will be important for death to be pronounced as quickly as possible after the heart function has been found irreversibly lost. It is not clear, however, whether death should be pronounced when the heart has permanently stopped (say, following a decision based on an advance directive to withdraw a ventilator), but could be started again. In the minutes when it could be started, but will not be because the patient has refused resuscitation, can we say that the individual is dead?

Likewise, it is increasingly clear that we must acknowledge some, admittedly very small, risk of error in measuring the irreversible loss of all functions of the entire brain.

None of this should imply that the death of the brain cannot be measured with great accuracy. But it is wrong to assume that similar or greater levels of accuracy cannot be obtained in measuring the irreversible loss of key higher functions, including consciousness. The literature on the persistent vegetative state repeatedly claims that we can know with great accuracy that consciousness is irreversibly lost.[8] . . .

Even if we could not presently measure accurately the loss of key higher functions such as consciousness, that would have a bearing only on the clinical implementation of the higher-brain-oriented definition, not the validity of the concept it-self. Defenders of the higher brain formulation might continue to use the now old-fashioned measures of loss of all function, but only because of the assurance that if all functions are lost, the higher functions certainly are. Such a conservative policy would leave open the question of whether we could some day measure the loss of higher functions accurately enough to use the measures clinically.

Still another criticism is the claim that any higher brain formulation would rely on a concept of personhood or personal identity that is philosophically controversial. Personhood theories are notoriously controversial. It is simply wrong, however, to claim that any higher-brain-oriented concept of death is based on either personhood or personal identity theories. I, for one, have acknowledged the possibility that there are living human beings who do not satisfy the various concepts of personhood. As long as the law is only discussing whether someone is a living individual, the debate over personhood is irrelevant.

Perhaps the most serious charge against the higher-brain-oriented formulations is that they are susceptible to the so-called slippery slope argument.[9] Once one yields on the insistence that all functions of the entire brain must be irreversibly gone be-fore an individual is considered dead, there seems to be no stopping the slide of elim-inating functions considered insignificant. The argument posits that once totally and permanently unconscious individuals who have some other brain functions (such as brain stem reflexes) remaining are considered dead, someone will propose that those with only marginal consciousness similarly lack significant function and soon all manner of functionally compromised humans will be defined as dead. Since being la-belled dead is normally an indicator that certain moral and legal rights cease, such a slide toward considering increasing numbers of marginally functional humans as dead would be morally horrific.

But is the slippery slope argument plausible? In its most significant form, such an argument involves a claim that the same principle underlying one appar-ently tolerable judgment also entails other, clearly unacceptable judgments. For example, imagine we were trying to determine whether the elderly could be ex-cluded from access to certain health care services based on the utilitarian prin-ciple of choosing the course that produced the maximum aggregate good for so-ciety. The slippery slope argument might be used to show that the same principle entails implications presumed clearly unacceptable, such as excluding health care from the socially unproductive. To the extent that one is certain that the empiri-cal assumptions are correct . . . and one is confident that such an outcome would be morally unacceptable, then one might attempt to use slippery slope argu-ments to challenge the proposal to withhold health care from the elderly. The same principle used to support one policy also entails other policies that are clearly unacceptable.

The slippery slope argument is valid insofar as it shows that the principle used to support one policy under consideration entails clearly unacceptable implications when applied to different situations. In principle, there is no difference between the small, potentially tolerable move and the more dramatic, unacceptable move. How-ever, as applied to the definition of death debate, the slippery slope argument can actually be used to show that the whole-brain-oriented definition of death is less defensible than the higher-brain-oriented one.

As we have seen, the whole-brain-oriented definition of death rests on the claim that irreversible loss of all functions of the entire brain is necessary and sufficient for an individual to be dead. That, in effect, means drawing a sharp line between the top of the spinal cord and the base of the brain (i.e., the bottom of the brain stem). But is there any principled reason why one would draw a line at that point?

In the early years of the definition of death debate, the claim was made that an individual was dead when the central nervous system no longer retained the capacity for integration. It was soon discovered, however, that this could be taken to imply that one was "alive" as long as some spinal cord function remained. That was counterintuitive (and also made it more difficult to obtain organs for transplant). Hence, very early on it was agreed that simple reflexes of the spinal cord did not count as an indicator of life. Presumably the principle was that reflex arcs that do not integrate significant bodily functions are to be ignored.

But why then do brain stem reflexes mediated through the base of the brain stem count? By the same principle, if spinal reflexes can be ignored, it would seem that some brain stem reflexes might be as well. An effort to show that brain stem reflexes are more integrative of bodily function is doomed to fail. At most there are gradual, imperceptible gradations in complexity between the reflexes of the first cervical vertebra and those of the base of the brain stem. Some spinal reflexes that trigger extension of the foot while the contralateral arm is withdrawn certainly cover larger distances.

Whatever principle could be used to exclude the spinal reflexes surely can exclude some brain stem reflexes as well. We have seen that the defenders of the whole-brain-oriented position admit as much when they start excluding cellular level functions and electrical functions. Certainly, those who exclude "nests of cells" in the brain as insignificant have abandoned the whole brain position and are already sliding along the slippery slope.

By contrast the defenders of the higher-brain-oriented definition of death can articulate a principle that avoids such slipperiness. Suppose, for example, they rely on classical Judeo-Christian notions that the human is essentially the integration of the mind and body and that the existence of one without the other is not sufficient to constitute a living human being. Such a principle provides a bright line that would clearly distinguish the total and irreversible loss of consciousness from serious but not total mental impairments.

Likewise, the integration of mind and body provides a firm basis for telling which functions of nests of brain cells count as significant. It avoids the hopeless task of trying to show why brain stem reflexes count more than spinal ones or trying to show exactly how many cells must be in a nest before it is significant. There is no subjective assessment of different bodily functions, no quibble about how much integration there must be for the organism to function as a whole. The principle is simple. It relies on qualitative considerations: when, and only when, there is the capacity for organic (bodily) and mental function present together in a single human entity is there a living human being. That, I would suggest, is the philosophical basis for the higher-brain-oriented definition of death. It avoids the slippery slope on which the defenders of the whole-brain-oriented position have found themselves; it, and only it, provides a principled reason for avoiding the slippery slope.

CONSCIENCE CLAUSES

There is one final development that signals the demise of the whole-brain-oriented definition of death as the single basis for declaring death. It should be clear by now that the definition of death debate is actually a debate over the moral status of human beings. . . .

In a pluralistic society, we are not likely to reach agreement on such moral questions, which is why no one definition of death has carried the day thus far. When one realizes that there are many variants on each of the three major definitions of death, each of which has some group of adherents, it seems unlikely that any one position is likely to gain even a majority any time soon. For example, defense of the higher-brain-oriented position stands or falls on the claim that the essence of the human being is the integration of a mind and a body, a position reflecting religious and philosophical assumptions that are not beyond dispute. . . . These are disputes not likely to be resolved soon.

As a society we have a method for dealing with fundamental disputes in religion and philosophy. We tolerate diversity and affirm the right of conscience to hold minority beliefs as long as actions based on those beliefs do not cause insurmountable problems for the rest of society. That is precisely what in 1976 I proposed doing in the dispute over the definition of death.[10] I proposed a definition of death with a conscience clause that would permit individuals to choose their own definition of death based on their religious and philosophical convictions. I did not say at the time, but should have, that the choices would have to be restricted to those that avoid violating the rights of others and avoid creating insurmountable social problems for the rest of society. . . . There are minimal public health considerations that would set limits on the choices available, but certainly the three major options would be tolerable: heart-, whole-brain-, and higher-brain-oriented definitions.

The state of New Jersey has gone part of the way recently by adopting a law with a conscience clause that would permit religious objectors to designate in advance that a heart-oriented definition should be used in pronouncing their deaths.[11] Since it is now widely accepted that anyone can write an advance directive mandating withdrawal of life support once one is permanently unconscious, any persons who favor a higher-brain-oriented definition of death already have the legal right to make choices that end up with them dead in anyone's sense of the term very shortly after they had lost higher brain functions. Permitting them to designate that they be called dead when they are permanently unconscious changes very little. . . .

CRAFTING NEW PUBLIC LAW

Changing current law to conform to these suggestions will be complex and should be done with deliberate speed, but it should be done. Two changes would be needed in the current definition of death: (1) incorporating the higher brain function notion and (2) incorporating some form of the conscience clause.

Present law makes persons dead when they have lost all functions of the entire brain. It is uniformly agreed that the law should incorporate only this basic concept of death, not the precise criteria or tests needed to determine that the whole brain is dead. That is left up to the consensus of neurological experts.

All that would be needed to shift to a higher brain formulation is a change in the wording of the law to replace "all functions of the entire brain" with some relevant, more limited alternative. There are at least three options: references to higher brain functions, cerebral functions, or consciousness. . . .

The language that seems best if integration of mind and body is what is critical is "irreversible cessation of the capacity for consciousness." That is, after all, what the defenders of the higher brain formulations really have in mind. (If someone were to claim that some other "higher" function is critical, that alternative could simply be plugged in.) As is the case now, the specifics of the criteria and tests for measuring irreversible loss of capacity for consciousness would be left up to the consensus of neurological expertise, even though measuring irreversible loss of capacity for a brain function such as consciousness involves fundamentally nonscientific value judgments. If the community of neurological expertise claims that irreversible loss of consciousness cannot be measured, so be it. We will at least have clarified the concept and set the stage for the day when it can be measured with sufficient accuracy. We have noted, however, that neurologists presently claim they can in fact measure irreversible loss of consciousness accurately.

A second significant change in the definition of death would be required to incorporate the conscience clause. It would permit individuals, while competent, to execute documents choosing alternative definitions of death that are, within reason, not threatening to significant interests of others. While the New Jersey law permits only the alternative of a heart-oriented definition, my proposal, assuming irreversible loss of consciousness were the default definition, would permit choosing either heart-oriented or whole-brain-oriented definitions as alternatives.

The New Jersey law presently permits only competent adults to execute such conscience clauses. This, of course, excludes the possibility of parents choosing alternative definitions for their children. I had long ago proposed that, just as legal surrogates have the right to make medical treatment decisions for their wards provided the decisions are within reason, so they should be permitted to choose alternative definitions of death provided the individual had never expressed a preference. This would, for example, permit Orthodox Jewish parents to require that the state continue to treat their child as alive even though he or she had suffered irreversible loss of consciousness or of total brain function. (Whether the state also requires insurers to continue paying for support of these individuals deemed living is a separate policy issue.) While the New Jersey law tolerates only variation with an explicitly religious basis, I would favor variation based on any conscientiously formulated position. . . . This leads to a proposal for a new definition of death, which would read as follows:

> An individual who has sustained irreversible loss of consciousness is dead. A determination of death must be made in accordance with accepted medical standards.
>
> However, no individual shall be considered dead based on irreversible loss of consciousness if he or she, while competent, has explicitly asked to be pronounced dead

based on irreversible cessation of all functions of the entire brain or based on irreversible cessation of circulatory and respiratory functions.

Unless an individual has, while competent, selected one of these definitions of death, the legal guardian or next of kin (in that order) may do so. The definition selected by the individual, legal guardian or next of kin shall serve as the definition of death for all legal purposes.

If one favored only the shift to consciousness as a definition of death without the conscience clause, only paragraph one would be necessary. One could also craft a similar definition using the whole-brain-oriented definition of death as the default definition. . . .

A PRINCIPLED REASON FOR DRAWING THE LINE

It has been puzzling why what at first seemed like a rather minor debate over when a human was dead should have persisted as long as it has. Many thought the definition of death debate was a technical argument that would be resolved in favor of the more fashionable, scientific, and progressive brain-oriented definition as soon as the old romantics attached to the heart died off. It is now clear that something much more complex and more fundamental is at stake. We have been fighting over the question of who has moral standing as a full member of the human moral community, a matter that forces on us some of the most basic questions of human existence: the relation of mind and body, the rights of religious and philosophical minorities, and the meaning of life itself. . . .

I am convinced that the now old-fashioned whole-brain-oriented definition of death is becoming less and less plausible as we realize that no one really believes that literally all functions of the entire brain must be irreversibly lost for an individual to be dead. Unless there is some public consensus expressed in state or federal law conveying agreement upon exactly which brain functions are insignificant, we will all be vulnerable to a slippery slope in which private practitioners choose for themselves exactly where from the top of the cerebrum to caudal end of the spinal cord to draw the line. There is no principled reason to draw it exactly between the base of the brain and the top of the spine. Better that we have a principled reason for drawing it. To me, the principle is that for human life to be present—that is, for the human to be treated as a member in full standing of the human moral community—there must be integrated functioning of mind and body. That means some version of a higher-brain-oriented formulation.

NOTES

1. President's Commission for the Study of Ethical Problems in Medicine and Biomedical and Behavioral Research, *Defining Death: Medical, Legal and Ethical Issues in the Definition of Death* (Washington, DC: U.S. Government Printing Office, 1981), p. 2. Page numbers for subsequent citations are in the text.

2. Robert M. Veatch. "The Whole-Brain-Oriented Concept of Death: An Outmoded Philosophical Formulation," *Journal of Thanatology* 3 (1975): 13–30.

3. Earl A. Walker et al. "An Appraisal of the Criteria of Cerebral Death: A Summary Statement," *JAMA* 237 (1977): 982–986, at 983.

4. James L. Bernat. "How Much of the Brain Must Die on Brain Death?" *The Journal of Clinical Ethics* 3, no. 1 (1992):21–26, at 25.

5. Paul A. Byrne, Sean O'Reilly, and Paul M. Quay. "Brain Death: An Opposing Viewpoint," *JAMA* 242 (1979): 1985–1990.

6. Cited in Robert M. Veatch, *Death, Dying, and the Biological Revolution* (New Haven: Yale University Press, 1976), p. 38.

7. David J. Cole. "The Reversibility of Death," *Journal of Medical Ethics* 18 (1992): 26–30.

8. Ronald B. Cranford and Harmon L. Smith. "Some Critical Distinctions between Brain Death and the Persistent Vegetative State," *Ethics in Science and Medicine* 6 (Winter 1979): 199–209; Phiroze L. Hansotia, "Persistent Vegetative State," *Archives of Neurology* 42 (1985): 1048–1052.

9. James L. Bernat. "How Much of the Brain Must Die on Brain Death?" pp. 21–26.

10. Robert M. Veatch. *Death, Dying, and the Biological Revolution,* pp. 72–76.

11. New Jersey Declaration of Death Act (1991), *New Jersey Statutes Annotated,* Title 26, 6A-1 to 6A-8.

In Re T.A.C.P. (Baby Theresa)

SUPREME COURT OF FLORIDA
609 SO. 2D 588 (FLA. 1992)

As organ transplantation became more successful and the need for organs increased, we realized that there is a serious shortage. People began looking for other sources of organs. One source was a group of infants born with a serious condition known as *anencephaly*. Literally meaning "without a brain," the term has been used to refer to a group of infants who, in fact, may have rudimentary brain tissue, especially at the level of the brain stem. Such infants lack the capacity for consciousness. They can never feel pain or any emotion. Yet with enough brain stem tissue present some such infants can be maintained, usually for short periods of time. Their heart and respiratory function may be sufficient to preserve organs that are viable for transplant. Such infants are not dead based on heart criteria. They are not even dead based on whole-brain criteria since significant brain functions remain. They would, of course, be dead based on higher-brain criteria, but no jurisdiction adopted such a definition of death. Baby Theresa was born to a Florida couple who recognized that their daughter could not survive. They wanted her organs to be used to bring life to another. They asked that the infant be declared dead so that organs could be procured. The Florida Supreme Court rejected this proposal, insisting that it would be up to the legislature to make any change in the definition of death.

BARKETT, C.J., and OVERTON, McDONALD, SHAW, GRIMES, KOGAN and HARDING, JJ., concur.

I. Facts

At or about the eighth month of pregnancy, the parents of the child T.A.C.P. were informed that she would be born with anencephaly. This is a birth defect invariably fatal,[1] in which the child typically is born with only a "brain stem" but otherwise lacks a human brain. In T.A.C.P.'s case, the back of the skull was entirely missing and the brain stem was exposed to the air, except for medical bandaging. The risk of infection to the brain stem was considered very high. Anencephalic infants sometimes can survive several days after birth because the brain stem has a limited capacity to maintain autonomic bodily functions such as breathing and heartbeat. This ability soon ceases, however, in the absence of regulation from the missing brain.

In this case, T.A.C.P. actually survived only a few days after birth. The medical evidence in the record shows that the child T.A.C.P. was incapable of developing any sort of cognitive process, may have been unable to feel pain or experience sensation due to the absence of the upper brain,[2] and at least for part of the time was placed on a mechanical ventilator to assist her breathing. At the time of the hearing below, however, the child was breathing unaided, although she died soon thereafter.

On the advice of physicians, the parents continued the pregnancy to term and agreed that the mother would undergo caesarean section during birth. The parents agreed to the caesarean procedure with the express hope that the infant's organs would be less damaged and could be used for transplant in other sick children. Although T.A.C.P. had no hope of life herself, the parents both testified in court that they wanted to use this opportunity to give life to others. However, when the parents requested that T.A.C.P. be declared legally dead for this purpose, her health care providers refused out of concern that they thereby might incur civil or criminal liability.

The parents then filed a petition in the circuit court asking for a judicial determination. After hearing testimony and argument, the trial court denied the request on grounds that . . . Florida Statute . . . would not permit a determination of legal death so long as the child's brain stem continued to function.

II. The Medical Nature of Anencephaly

A statement by the Medical Task Force on Anencephaly ("Task Force") printed in the New England Journal of Medicine[3] generally described "anencephaly" as "a congenital absence of major portions of the brain, skull, and scalp, with its genesis in the first month of gestation." [David A. Stumpf et al., *The Infant with Anencephaly,* 322 New Engl. J. Med. 669, 669 (1990)]. The large opening in the skull accompanied by the absence or severe congenital disruption of the cerebral hemispheres is the characteristic feature of the condition. (*Id.*)

The Task Force defined anencephaly as diagnosable only when all of the following four criteria are present:

(1) A large portion of the skull is absent. (2) The scalp, which extends to the margin of the bone, is absent over the skull defect. (3) Hemorrhagic, fibrotic tissue is exposed because of defects in the skull and scalp. (4) Recognizable cerebral hemispheres are absent. (*Id.* at 670)

Anencephaly is often, though not always, accompanied by defects in various other body organs and systems, some of which may render the child unsuitable for organ transplantation. (*Id.*) . . . We emphasize that the child T.A.C.P. clearly met the four criteria described above. . . .

The Task Force reported that the medical consequences of anencephaly can be established with some certainty. All anencephalics by definition are permanently unconscious because they lack the cerebral cortex necessary for conscious thought. Their condition thus is quite similar to that of persons in a persistent vegetative state. Where the brain stem is functioning, as it was here, spontaneous breathing and heartbeat can occur. In addition, such infants may show spontaneous movements of the extremities, "startle" reflexes, and pupils that respond to light. Some may show feeding reflexes, may cough, hiccup, or exhibit eye movements, and may produce facial expressions. (*Id.* at 671–72.) . . .

Anencephalic infants may reflexively avoid painful stimuli where the brain stem is functioning and thus is able to command an innate, unconscious withdrawal response; but the infants presumably lack the capacity to suffer. (*Id.* 672.) It is clear, however, that the incapacity to suffer has not been established beyond all doubt. (*See id.*) . . .

There appears to be general agreement that anencephalics usually have ceased to be suitable organ donors by the time they meet all the criteria for "whole brain death," i.e., the complete absence of brainstem function. [Stephen Ashwal et al., *Anencephaly: Clinical Determination of Brain Death and Neuropathologic Studies,* 6 Pediatric Neurology 233, 239 (1990)]. There also is no doubt that a need exists for infant organs for transplantation. Nationally, between thirty and fifty percent of children under two years of age who need transplants die while waiting for organs to become available. [Joyce L. Peabody et al., *Experience with Anencephalic Infants as Prospective Organ Donors,* 321 New Eng. J. Med. 344, 344 (1989)]. . . .

III. Legal Definitions of "Death" & "Life"

There are a few Florida authorities that have addressed the definitions of "life" and "death" in somewhat analogous though factually distinguishable contexts. Florida's Vital Statistics Act, for example, defines "live birth" as

> the complete expulsion or extraction of a product of human conception from its mother, irrespective of the duration of pregnancy, which, after such expulsion, breathes or shows any other evidence of life such as beating of the heart, pulsation of the umbilical cord, and definite movement of the voluntary muscles, whether or not the umbilical cord has been cut or the placenta is attached. (§ 382.002(10), Fla.Stat. (1991))

Conversely, "fetal death" is defined as:

> death prior to the complete expulsion or extraction of a product of human conception from its mother if the 20th week of gestation has been reached and the death is indicated by the fact that after such expulsion or extraction the fetus does not breathe or show any other evidence of life such as beating of the heart, pulsation of the umbilical cord, or definite movement of voluntary muscles. (§ 382.002(7), Fla.Stat. (1991))

From these definitions, it is clear that T.A.C.P. was a "live birth" and not a "fetal death," at least for purposes of the collection of vital statistics in Florida. These definitions obviously are inapplicable to the issues at hand today, but they do shed some light on the Florida legislature's thoughts regarding a definition of "life" and "death."

Similarly, an analogous (if distinguishable) problem has arisen in Florida tort law. In cases alleging wrongful death, our courts have held that fetuses are not "persons" and are not "born alive" until they acquire an existence separate and independent from the mother. [E.g., *Duncan v. Flynn,* 358 So.2d 178, 178–79 (Fla.1978)]. We believe the weight of the evidence supports the conclusion that T.A.C.P. was "alive" in this sense because she was separated from the womb, and was capable of breathing and maintaining a heartbeat independently of her mother's body for some duration of time thereafter. Once again, however, this conclusion arises from law that is only analogous and is not dispositive of the issue at hand. . . .

We thus are led to the conclusion that no legal authority binding upon this Court has decided whether an anencephalic child is alive for purposes of organ donation. In the absence of applicable legal authority, this Court must weigh and consider the public policy considerations at stake here. . . .

IV. Common Law & Policy

[4,5] The question remaining is whether there is good reason in public policy for this Court to create an additional common law standard applicable to anencephalics. . . .

Our review of the medical, ethical, and legal literature on anencephaly discloses absolutely no consensus that public necessity or fundamental rights will be better served by granting this request.

We are not persuaded that a public necessity exists to justify this action, in light of the other factors in this case—although we acknowledge much ambivalence about this particular question. We have been deeply touched by the altruism and unquestioned motives of the parents of T.A.C.P. The parents have shown great humanity, compassion, and concern for others. The problem we as a Court must face, however, is that the medical literature shows unresolved controversy over the extent to which anencephalic organs can or should be used in transplants. . . .

A presidential commission in 1981 urged strict adherence to the Uniform Determination of Death Act's definition, which would preclude equating anencephaly with death. [President's Commission for the Study of Ethical Problems in Medicine, Biomedical and Behavioral Research, *Defining Death Medical, Legal and Ethical Issues in the Determination of Death* 2 (1981)]. Several sections of the American Bar Association have reached much the same conclusion. [National Conference on Birth, Death, and Law, *Report on Conference,* 29 Jurimetrics J. 403, 421 (Lori B. Andrews et al. eds. 1989)].

Some legal commentators have argued that treating anencephalics as dead equates them with "nonpersons," presenting a "slippery slope" problem with regard to all other persons who lack cognition for whatever reason. [Debra H. Berger, *The Infant with Anencephaly: Moral and Legal Dilemmas,* 5 Issues in L. & Med. 67, 84–85 (1989)]. Others have quoted physicians involved in infant-organ transplants as stating, "[T]he slippery slope is real," because some physicians have proposed transplants from infants with defects less severe than anencephaly. [Beth Brandon, *Anencephalic Infants as Organ Donors: A Question of Life or Death,* 40 Case Western L.Rev. 781, 802 (1989–90)].

We express no opinion today about who is right and who is wrong on these issues—if any "right" or "wrong" can be found here. The salient point is that no consensus exists as to: (a) the utility of organ transplants of the type at issue here; (b) the ethical issues involved; or (c) the legal and constitutional problems implicated.

V. Conclusions

Accordingly, we find no basis to expand the common law to equate anencephaly with death. We acknowledge the possibility that some infants' lives might be saved by using organs from anencephalics who do not meet the traditional definition of "death" we reaffirm today. But weighed against this is the utter lack of consensus, and the questions about the overall utility of such organ donations. The scales clearly tip in favor of not extending the common law in this instance.

NOTES

1. We are mindful that some parties argue that anencephaly is not invariably fatal and that some anencephalics actually live for many years. We find that this argument arises from a misperception about the nature of anencephaly as it is defined by a consensus in the medical community. The living children described by the parties actually are not anencephalic, because they do not meet the definitive medical criteria. These medical criteria are discussed further.
2. There was some dispute about this point. Our resolution of the case, however, renders the dispute moot.
3. The statement also was approved by the American Academy of Pediatrics, the American Academy of Neurology, the American College of Obstetricians and Gynecologists, the American Neurological Association, and the Child Neurology Society. David A. Stumpf et al., *The Infant with Anencephaly,* 322 *New England Journal of Medicine* 669, 669 n.* (1990).

Brain Death, Religious Freedom, and Public Policy
New Jersey's Landmark Legislative Initiative*

ROBERT S. OLICK**

The persistence of the controversy over the definition of death and the realization that the choices required religious or philosophical decisions rather than just good medical science led many to treat the issue as a matter of public policy. In many policy choices a pluralistic society will try to accommodate diversity of opinion rather than forcing all members of the society to accept a single view, even if that view represents the majority opinion. People began approaching the definition of death in this manner. Such an approach could permit individuals, while competent, to choose an alternative definition to be used in determining their own deaths. Some proposals would extend that choice to the next of kin in cases in which the individual has not spoken on the subject while competent. To avoid confusion, a state would probably need to choose some default definition to be used when a choice has not been made for the individual.

The State of New Jersey, stimulated by dissent on the brain-oriented definition of death from Jewish and other groups, accepted a whole-brain definition of death that permitted religious objectors to execute a declaration requiring that a heart-based definition be used in pronouncing their deaths. The New Jersey law does not permit secular philosophical dissent and does not permit any objectors to opt for a higher-brain formulation.

ABSTRACT. "Whole brain death" (neurological death) is well-established as a legal standard of death across the country. Recently, New Jersey became the first state to enact a statute recognizing a personal religious exemption (a conscience clause) protecting the rights of those who object to neurological death. The Act also mandates adoption through the regulatory process of uniform and up-to-date clinical criteria for determining neurological death.

INTRODUCTION

In the decade since the President's Commission for the Study of Ethical Problems in Medicine and Biomedical and Behavioral Research (the President's

*The views expressed in this article are those of the author and not necessarily those of the New Jersey Commission on Legal and Ethical Problems in the Delivery of Health Care.
**Source: "Brain Death, Freedom, and Public Policy." *Kennedy Institute of Ethics Journal,* Vol. 1, No. 4, 275–288, © 1991 by The Johns Hopkins University Press.
The author wishes to express his appreciation to Paul W. Armstrong, Michael Vollen, and the members of the Bioethics Commission for the privilege of joining in the shared dialogue and labors of the New Jersey Bioethics Commission.

Commission) issued its influential report, *Defining Death* (1981), the irreversible cessation of all functions of the entire brain, including the brain stem (commonly known as "whole brain death"), has come to be widely accepted as death by the medical and legal communities and by the public across the United States. The President's Commission argued that the determination of death should be addressed at the state level, in the "laboratory of the states," but it also strongly urged that all states adopt a uniform statute on determining death (President's Commission 1981, p. 8). At least twenty-five state legislatures have enacted the Uniform Determination of Death Act (UDDA), or some variant of it, jointly drafted and approved by major professional groups and the President's Commission in 1980 and 1981 (UDDA 1990, prefatory note; President's Commission 1981, p. 119). Whole brain death is now uniformly recognized as a legal standard of death by statute or court decision in all fifty states and the District of Columbia.[1]

Ten years after the President's Commission report, and fifteen years after the New Jersey Supreme Court's seminal opinion in the case of Karen Ann Quinlan (*In re Quinlan*, 70 N.J. 10, 355 A.2d 647, *cert. denied sub nom. Garger v. New Jersey,* 429 U.S. 922 (1976)), New Jersey has again distinguished itself by putting its unique stamp on issues in death and dying. In its recent enactment of statutory law to govern the declaration of death, New Jersey joins its sister states in recognizing whole brain death as a legal standard of death.[2] In two important respects, however, New Jersey's statute goes beyond the law of other states, possibly signaling new directions in the policy debate regarding the declaration of death.

Of greatest import, the Act recognizes a religious exemption (a conscience clause) designed to respect the personal religious beliefs of those who do not accept neurological criteria for the determination of death, making New Jersey the first state to recognize a conscience clause in its statutory law. A second unique feature of the new law is its mandate that legally recognized uniform criteria for the determination of death on the basis of neurological criteria be adopted through the regulatory process, and that these criteria be updated with advances in medical science and technology. Signed into law in Spring 1991, the New Jersey Declaration of Death Act was originally drafted and recommended by the New Jersey Commission on Legal and Ethical Problems in the Delivery of Health Care (informally known as the New Jersey Bioethics Commission).[3]

Drawing on the deliberations of the Bioethics Commission and the vigorous legislative debate, this article discusses these two unique features of the New Jersey approach to public policy on the declaration of death, focusing primarily on the religious exemption. The analysis also touches upon several subsidiary questions raised and addressed by the new law.

THE RELIGIOUS EXEMPTION

What emerged early in the deliberations was the shared understanding that legal adoption of neurological death was objectionable to the traditional and religiously-based beliefs and practices of some of the state's diverse and pluralistic citizenry. Most significantly affected by this issue are those in the Orthodox Jewish community who adhere to the traditional belief identifying life with continued circulatory and respiratory activity, even if artificially maintained. For Orthodox Jews holding this theological position (there are differing views within the Orthodox community itself), "one whose heart still beats still lives; despite the irreversible cessation of brain function; and it would be an act of murder to disconnect such an individual from a respirator . . . " (Zweibel 1989, p. 49). Neurological death is also objectionable to some Japanese who adhere to religious and cultural understandings that such a death would be unnatural and premature, as it would hasten destruction of the unity of "human beings as completely integrated mind-body units" and disturb important dying rituals (Kimura 1991, p. 125). Modern neurological criteria may also violate the cultural and religious traditions of some Native Americans (President's Commission 1981, p. 41).

Thus, when death occurs is not solely a medical judgment about a biological fact, it is also a value judgment, which for some rests on personal religious beliefs or moral convictions. The social and policy choice is whether the state's general interests in uniform legal recognition of neurological death justify giving the law's permission to compel those with contrary personal religious beliefs to accept neurological criteria for declarations of their own deaths (New Jersey Commission 1990, pp. 19–20; Veatch 1989a, pp. 53–58).[4]

The widely accepted answer to this question is that societal interests in a uniform standard of death are so strong as to preclude statutory recognition of a conscience clause. This position, advanced by the President's Commission and more recently endorsed by the Hastings Center (Hastings Center 1987, p. 87), is embodied in state laws nationally. While the New York State Task Force (1986, p. 11) reached a similar conclusion with respect to the legislative role, laudably New York also has promulgated regulations calling for the "reasonable accommodation" of religious or moral objections to neurological death (New York Codes 1987).

The New Jersey law reaches a different conclusion and expresses a strong conviction that the societal need for uniformity should yield to and accommodate personal interests of a distinct minority of the population in the exercise of their religious beliefs. Meaningful protection demands empowerment of the individual through statutory recognition of a religious exemption. Thus, the Act provides that when the religious exemption applies (see the discussion of implementation that follows) death is to be declared, and the time of death fixed, only upon irreversible cessation of heartbeat and respiration. Artificial maintenance of the patient's circulatory and respiratory functions is not to be discontinued solely on the ground of the patient's neurological status. Physicians and other health care providers responsible for the patient's care should continue to provide cardio-respiratory support (such as a respirator) until it is determined that irreversible cessation of all heart and lung functions has occurred, and that death may be declared in accordance with this standard (New Jersey Commission 1991, p. 7). Generally in the adult patient this will occur within a matter of days, or in rare cases weeks, of the diagnosis of neurological death (Youngner et al. 1989, p. 2205). It is important to recognize that the Act does not allow individuals to choose any novel or idiosyncratic standard for the declaration of death; it only permits those with conscientious beliefs to reject neurological criteria for death and to choose that their time of death shall be determined upon irreversible cessation of circulatory and respiratory functions.[5]

Beyond the insistence of some medical and legal professionals that acceptance of neurological death admits of no value judgments and no exceptions, the most common arguments proffered against the religious exemption have been variations on the President's Commission's contention that "(w)ere a non-uniform standard permitted, unfortunate and mischievous results are easily imaginable" (President's Commission, 1981, p. 80). To the extent this view predicts confusion over the applicability of health or life insurance coverage, the New Jersey law anticipates and resolves this dilemma. When the religious exemption has been invoked, "death shall be declared, and the time of death fixed, solely upon the basis of cardio-respiratory criteria." Thus, as a legal matter, the patient has not died even though neurological death has been confirmed. Furthermore, the Act expressly provides that health payments are to continue and that no discrimination for the exercise of religious beliefs is permitted. Life insurance would be triggered only when death has been declared. A uniform legal standard for time of death when the exemption is applied should also obviate any true concerns regarding property transfers or the rights of beneficiaries under testamentary wills, as well as when criminal homicide prosecutions or wrongful death actions should be tried.[6]

Some members of the health care community have argued that a religious exemption would diminish the already scarce supply of transplantable organs. Yet, this contention ignores the fact that only the few with strong convictions are likely to make the necessary effort to invoke the exemption. Since those who reject neurological death on religious (or moral) grounds consider themselves alive until cardio-respiratory functions irretrievably cease, consent to removal of organs would likely be incompatible with their beliefs. Those who might make an exception by giving higher priority to saving the life of another will probably make this known as well. Further, as a practical matter, consent to organ retrieval is most unlikely after an assault on the dignity of the patient and grieving family members when told that their loved one has been, or is about to be, declared dead and that the hospital will not honor his or her religious beliefs to the contrary.

The most serious ethical and social challenge to the religious exemption is the patient in need of the scarce respirator or ICU bed supporting the neurologically dead patient. An early draft of the conscience clause considered by the Bioethics Commission sought to address this problem, stating that where scarce life-sustaining treatments or technologies such as a respirator must be allocated, the law should not preclude the granting of priority to the patient in imminent need for whom the treatment or technology in question might, in the exercise of reasonable medical judgment, be life-saving and offer greater probability of long-term survival or other medical benefit. (Hospitals should be able to move the neurologically dead patient out of the ICU.) Ultimately, this issue proved unworkable and inappropriate for statutory resolution, largely due to the difficulty of crafting legal guidelines for the exercise of "reasonable" judgment, and the related concern that to embody this principle in statute would give those who did not favor the exemption "an out," and would undermine the goal of respecting religious beliefs on this important question.

While the new law thus remains silent here, the prior draft sets forth the ethically appropriate response that should guide health care providers where a bona fide allocation question arises in emergency circumstances. Treatment and care should be provided to the patient who can reasonably benefit from it, particularly if the treatment may be life-saving. As a matter of both policy and practice, religious freedom in this area ought to yield to the competing interests of patients in dire need for whom the scarce treatment or technology offers reasonable medical benefit.

The Scope of a Religious Exemption

The New Jersey law extends express protection to "personal religious beliefs." In contrast, the original proposal emanating from the Bioethics Commission applied to "personal religious beliefs and moral convictions." The more limited language eventually enacted represents a political compromise accommodating those who in principle could not accept the idea of an exemption, but recognized both its symbolic and political importance. In theory and in practice, however, this should prove a distinction without a difference.

There is no compelling reason to distinguish among "truly" religious beliefs, nor to respect only religious and not moral values, in a matter so fundamental as when one's own death occurs. In a pluralistic society, protection for sincerely held claims of conscience ought not to hinge upon whether personal convictions are grounded in a particular religious tradition or ultimately rest on belief in a Supreme Being. This principle has also received legal recognition, where courts and legislatures have generally avoided defining "religion," or parsing out whether one set of beliefs should be characterized as "truly religious" but another not. In the analogous context of conscientious objection to participation in war, the U. S. Supreme Court has stated that *conscientious* objection extends to a strongly held belief "parallel to that filled by the Orthodox belief in God," and has iterated the time-honored principle that the sincerity, but not the "truth," of personal beliefs is a proper subject of inquiry (*United States v. Seeger*, 380 U.S. 163 (1965), pp. 166, 184–85; Goldberg 1988, p. 1256). This line of reasoning suggests that if subjected to judicial scrutiny, the religious exemption is likely to be construed to protect sincerely held beliefs even if out of keeping with mainstream thought in the patient's professed religious tradition, and to extend to moral convictions as well.

This approach should similarly govern implementation of the exemption in clinical practice. The New Jersey law imposes no duties on physicians or other health care professionals to become theological experts or to ascertain whether the patient's objection is truly religiously based. Indeed, what is asked of the physician is that if he or she has "reason to believe," based upon available and reliable information, that the patient's religious beliefs would be violated by a declaration of neurological death, then he or she should refrain from declaring death on this basis. This standard both contemplates and permits a limited inquiry into the sincerity and basis of the patient's beliefs. Absent unusual circumstances, such as emergency allocation of life-support to another patient, there should be little reason for physicians and hospitals to seek to distinguish the truly religious, the religious, and the moral in the forum of conscience.

This is not to say, however, that all objections to neurological death are entitled to respect regardless of their basis. Most importantly, the right of conscience belongs to the patient, not to the family. Loved ones are not authorized by the New Jersey law to substitute their own beliefs for the patient's. Nor should family denial of death in time of bereavement be taken as an expression of the patient's conscientious beliefs. Of course, as with all critical medical decisions sensitivity to loved ones is of paramount importance; clarifying misunderstandings about neurological death and some delay in declaring death and removing respirator may be appropriate in particular cases.[7]

Implementing a Religious Exemption

In the quest for consensus, framing the legal parameters for practical implementation of a conscience clause presented the greatest challenge to the Bioethics Commission, and ultimately became the key issue in securing the support of medical and legal groups for the final version of the legislation. The central concern here was how information about the patient's religious beliefs would become known, and the responsibilities of health care professionals to ascertain the patient's beliefs.

Under the new law, the exemption is triggered when the patient's religious beliefs have actually been communicated to the physician authorized to declare death, giving the physician "reason to believe" that the patient's religious beliefs would be violated by a declaration of death on the basis of neurological criteria. The act places initial responsibility with the patient, family, or others who may be knowledgeable about the patient's religious beliefs, such as a personal physician, religious leader, or close friend, to provide information about the patient's religious beliefs regarding the declaration of death. Oral statements about the patient's beliefs from knowledgeable family members, religious leaders, or others are sufficient to invoke the exemption.

Nonetheless, those who object to neurological death would be well-advised to document their wishes in advance, such as in an advance directive or similar written document. The advance directive forms developed by the Bioethics Commission and widely distributed throughout the state are designed to allow those with such religious objections to make this known along with other directions and instructions for their future care. The "halachic living will" developed by Agudath Israel of America allows individuals to document their commitment to Jewish law, and to direct that a Rabbi of the individual's choosing be consulted regarding "the method and timing of determination of death" before death is determined. Affected religious communities may also wish to maintain their own registries for consultation in time of need.

This approach to implementation represents the most significant amendment to the Bioethics Commission's proposal that prevailed in the legislative process. The Bioethics Commission had recommended that the physician authorized to declare neurological death, or another designated person, make reasonable and good faith efforts to ascertain the patient's personal religious beliefs (or moral convictions). This more active role for the health care professional, characterized by many as an obligation of "affirmative inquiry," met strong resistance in the broader health care community. Several professional organizations successfully urged shifting the responsibility for raising the issue of conscience to the patient and family and away from the health care professional. The enacted language should offer greater legal protection and comfort to health care providers. For those who are strongly motivated to make known (and hopefully document) their objections to neurological death it should make little difference to ensuring respect for their wishes.

Cognizant of the difficult and sensitive nature of conversations in such circumstances, a further concern was that the law afford a great deal of flexibility and discretion for those responsible for the patient's care to structure conversation in a manner appropriate to the sensibilities of the family. Responsibility for respecting the patient's objections ultimately rests with the responsible physician (and the institution), but it is contemplated that conversations with the family may also be carried out by other responsible health care providers, such as nurses, social workers, or others experienced in bereavement counseling. Family members and others should clearly understand that they are being asked about the beliefs of the patient; they are not being asked for their own consent to declaring the patient dead or to withdrawing life-sustaining treatment. Nor should families receive a detailed or legalistic explanation of the exemption provision. Initiation of more extensive discussion becomes appropriate when initial conversation with family members or others suggests that the patient may harbor conscientious objection to neurological criteria for declaring death. . . .

IMPLICATIONS FOR FUTURE POLICY

New Jersey's statutory enactment challenges widely accepted judgments of how to weigh society's interests in uniform standards for the determination of death against respect for personal conscientious beliefs held by a distinct minority of its citizens. The New Jersey Declaration of Death Act, together with New York's regulatory approach, signals a new direction for the development of public policy governing the declaration of death in pluralistic communities. Whether formal recognition of a conscience clause serves as a model for the evolution of policy in other states may well depend upon our willingness to look at the question of when death occurs as a moral and policy issue and not merely as a medical one. It will also depend upon the religious and cultural diversity of communities participating in the public policy process within the "laboratories" of the several states.

NOTES

1. For a list of the statutes and judicial opinions, see Charlotte Goldberg (1988, p. 1207, nn. 59–60). The most recent enactments are *Minn. Stat.* 1991 (West Supp.), sec. 145.135; *N.D. Cent. Code* 1989 (Michie Supp.), secs. 23-06.3-01 to .3-02; *S.D. Laws*

Ann. 1991 (Michie Supp.), sec. 34-25-18.1; and *Utah Code Ann.* 1991 (Michie Supp.), secs. 26-34-1 to 26-34-2.

2. The new law codifies prior New Jersey Supreme Court case law recognizing whole brain death (*Strachan v. John F. Kennedy Memorial Hospital,* 109 N.J. 523, 538 A.2d 346 (1988)).

3. The New Jersey Bioethics Commission was established in November 1985 as a permanent legislative study commission (P.L. 1985, Chapter 363). The Bioethics Commission is mandated to provide a comprehensive and scholarly examination of the impact of advancing technology on health care decisions, and is directed to make recommendations for health policy to the legislature, the governor, and the citizens of New Jersey. Comprised of a diverse and multidisciplinary body of twenty-seven appointed members, the Bioethics Commission brings to the public policy process a broad spectrum of expertise, opinions, and perspectives in medicine, nursing, law, ethics, and theology, and includes representatives of the executive and legislative branches of state government, and of New Jersey's professional and public communities. The Bioethics Commission's process and deliberations, which included more than twenty open meetings and six public hearings over the course of approximately two years of formal deliberations on issues in death and dying, are discussed at greater length in *Problems and Approaches in Health Care Decisionmaking: The New Jersey Experience,* the Bioethics Commission's first comprehensive report, issued in 1990.

   The proposed New Jersey Declaration of Death Act was formally approved by the Bioethics Commission on June 8, 1988, by a near unanimous vote of 20 in favor, 1 opposed, and 1 abstention. The proposal was first introduced in the legislature on June 16, 1988, and was signed into law by Governor James J. Florio on April 8, 1991 (see *Wall Street Journal,* 10 April 1991, p. B8). The Declaration of Death Act's religious exemption complements the institutional conscience provision for private religiously-affiliated facilities in the companion New Jersey Advance Directives for Health Care Act, enacted on July 11, 1991.

4. Of these (potentially) affected groups, the Jewish community was politically active in support of a conscience clause. Special mention should be made of the tireless efforts of one Orthodox Jewish organization, Agudath Israel of America, a New York–based grassroots movement with chapters in thirty states across the country, which was instrumental in translating the proposed legislation into political reality.

5. The New York regulation directs each hospital to develop its own written policy to govern neurological death, which is to include "a procedure for the reasonable accommodation of the individual's religious or moral objection to the determination as expressed by the individual, or by the next of kin or other person closest to the individual." The regulations are silent, however, on the meaning of "reasonable accommodation," leaving this to be determined at the local level by each hospital (New York Codes 1987, sec. 400.16(e)(3)).

6. The statute also establishes the legal standard for time of neurological death: "If death is to be declared upon the basis of neurological criteria, the time of death shall be upon the conclusion of definitive clinical examinations and any confirmation necessary to determine the irreversible cessation of all functions of the entire brain, including the brain stem" (New Jersey Declaration of Death Act 1991, sec. 4d.). Under the Act, when the religious exemption applies the neurologically dead patient is not legally dead and considers himself or herself to be alive. Consequently, the Act is careful to address itself to the time when death *shall be declared* and assiduously avoids speaking in terms of when the patient *is dead,* the formulation used in the UDDA and many state statutes.

7. The role of family consent raises further issues which cannot be addressed here. For example, in cases of neurological death in children, should parents be entitled to insist upon continued treatment on the basis of their own religious objections? (Veatch 1989b, p. 216).

REFERENCES

BELSH, JERRY. 1988. Testimony at Public Hearing held by the New Jersey Commission on Legal and Ethical Problems in the Delivery of Health Care, 13 April.

GOLDBERG, CHARLOTTE K. 1988. Choosing Life After Death: Respecting Religious Beliefs And Moral Convictions In Near Death Decisions. *Syracuse Law Review* 39: 1197–1260.

Hastings Center. 1987. *Guidelines on the Termination of Life-Sustaining Treatment and the Care of the Dying.* New York.

KIMURA, RIHITO. 1991. Japan's Dilemma With The Definition of Death. *Kennedy Institute of Ethics Journal* I: 123–131.

LYNN, JOANNE. 1989. The Definition of Death: Unresolved Controversies. In *Pediatric Brain Death And Organ/Tissue Retrieval: Medical, Ethical, and Legal Aspects,* ed. Howard H. Kaufman, pp. 65–72. New York: Plenum Medical Book Company.

Medical Consultants on the Diagnosis of Death to the President's Commission for the Study of Ethical Problems in Medicine and Biomedical and Behavioral Research. 1981. Guidelines for the Determination of Death. *Journal of the American Medical Association* 246: 2184–2186.

New Jersey Declaration of Death Act. 1991 (West). *New Jersey Statutes Annotated.* Title 26, secs. 6A-1 to 6A-8.

New Jersey Commission on Legal and Ethical Problems in the Delivery of Health Care. 1990. *Problems and Approaches in Health Care Decisionmaking: The New Jersey Experience.* New Jersey.

———. 1991. The New Jersey Declaration of Death Act: Statute and Commentary. *New York Codes, Rules and Regulations.* 1987. Title 10, sec. 400.16.

New York State Task Force on Life and The Law. 1986. *The Determination of Death.* New York.

President's Commission for the Study of Ethical Problems in Medicine and Biomedical and Behavioral Research, 1981. *Defining Death: Medical, Legal, and Ethical Issues in the Definition of Death.* Washington, DC: U.S. Government Printing Office.

Task Force on Brain Death in Children. 1987. *Pediatrics* 80 (2):298–300.

Uniform Determination of Death Act. 1990 (West Supp.). Uniform Laws Annotated. Title 12, pp. 320–323.

VEATCH, ROBERT M. 1989a. *Death, Dying, and the Biological Revolution: Our Last Quest for Responsibility.* New Haven and London: Yale University Press.

———. 1989b. The Definition of Death: Unresolved Controversies. In *Pediatric Brain Death And Organ/Tissue Retrieval: Medical, Ethical, and Legal Aspects,* ed. Howard H. Kaufman, pp. 207–218. New York: Plenum Medical Book Company.

YOUNGNER, STUART, et al. 1989. "Brain Death" and Organ Retrieval: A Cross-sectional Survey of Knowledge and Concepts Among Health Professionals. *Journal of the American Medical Association* 261: 2205–2210.

ZWEIBEL, DAVID. 1989. Accommodating Religious Objections to Brain Death: Legal Considerations. *Journal of Halacha and Contemporary Society* XVII: 49–68.

SUGGESTED READINGS FOR CHAPTER 1

A. EMERGENCE OF A BRAIN-ORIENTED DEFINITION

1. Summary of the Issues and Arguments

CAPRON, ALEXANDER M., and LEON R. KASS. "A Statutory Definition of the Standards for Determining Human Death: An Appraisal and a Proposal." *University of Pennsylvania Law Review* 121 (1972):87–118.

GERVAIS, KAREN GRANDSTAND, *Redefining Death*. New Haven: Yale University Press, 1986.

GREEN, MICHAEL B., and DANIEL WIKLER. "Brain Death and Personal Identity." *Philosophy and Public Affairs* Winter 1980; 9(2): 105–133.

KAUFMAN, HOWARD H. (ed.). *Pediatric Brain Death and Organ/Tissue Retrieval*. New York: Plenum Publishing Corporation, 1989.

KOREIN, JULIUS (ed.). *Brain Death: Interrelated Medical and Social Issues*. New York: The New York Academy of Sciences, 1978.

LAMB, DAVID. *Death, Brain Death and Ethics*. Albany: State University of New York Press, 1985.

Law Reform Commission of Canada. *Criteria for the Determination of Death*. Ottawa: Ministry of Supply and Services, 1979.

President's Commission for the Study of Ethical Problems in Medicine and Biomedical and Behavioral Research. *Defining Death: Medical, Legal and Ethical Issues in the Definition of Death*. Washington, DC: U.S. Government Printing Office, 1981.

VEATCH, ROBERT M. "Definitions of Life and Death: Should There Be Consistency." In Margery W. Shaw and A. Edward Doudera (eds.) *Defining Human Life*. Ann Arbor, MI: AUPHA Press, 1983, pp. 99–113.

WIKLER, DANIEL, and ALAN J. WEISBARD. "Appropriate Confusion Over 'Brain Death'." *Journal of the American Medical Association* April 21, 1989; 261(15):2246.

YOUNGNER, STUART J., SETH C. LANDFELD, CLAUDIA J. COULTON, et al. "'Brain Death' and Organ Retrieval." *Journal of the American Medical Association* April 21, 1989; 261(15):2205–2210.

2. Measurement of the Death of the Brain

ASHWAL, STEPHEN, and SANFORD SCHNEIDER, "Brain Death in Children, I, II." *Pediatric Neurology* 3 (1987):5–10, 69–78.

Harvard Medical School. "A Definition of Irreversible Coma. Report of the Ad Hoc Committee of the Harvard Medical School to Examine the Definition of Brain Death." *Journal of the American Medical Association* 205 (1968):337–340.

SHEWMON, D. ALAN. "Commentary on Guidelines for the Determination of Brain Death in Children." *Annals of Neurology* 24 (1988):789–791.

Task Force for the Determination of Brain Death in Children. "Guidelines for the Determination of Brain Death in Children." *Neurology* 37 (1987):1077–1078.

Task Force on Death and Dying, Institute of Society, Ethics and the Life Sciences. "Refinements in Criteria for the Determination of Death: An Appraisal." *Journal of the American Medical Association* 221 (1972):48–53.

WALKER, A. EARL. *Cerebral Death*, Baltimore-Munich: Urban & Schwarzenberg, 1981.

3. Critique of Brain-Oriented Definition

BYRNE, PAUL A., SEAN O'REILLY, and PAUL M. QUAY. "Brain Death—An Opposing Viewpoint." *Journal of the American Medical Association* 242 (1979):1985–1990.
ROSNER, FRED. "The Definition of Death in Jewish Law." *Tradition* 1969; 10(4):33–39.
TOMLINSON, TOM. "The Conservative Use of the Brain-Death Criterion—A Critique." *Journal of Medicine and Philosophy* 9 (1984):377–393.

B. CONTROVERSIES SURROUNDING THE DEFINITION

1. Summary of the Higher-Brain Definition Debate

BERNAT, JAMES L. "How Much of the Brain Must Die on Brain Death?" *The Journal of Clinical Ethics* Spring 3(1, 1992):21–26.
BRIERLEY, J.B., J.A.H. ADAM, D.I. GRAHAM, and J.A. SIMPSON. "Neocortical Death After Cardiac Arrest." *Lancet* 2 (September 11, 1971):560–565.
Council on Scientific Affairs and Council on Ethical and Judicial Affairs. "Persistent Vegetative State and the Decision to Withdraw or Withhold Life Support." *Journal of the American Medical Association* 263 (1990):426–430.
CRANFORD, RONALD B., and HARMON L. SMITH. "Some Critical Distinctions Between Brain Death and the Persistent Vegetative State." *Ethics in Science and Medicine* 6 (Winter 1979):199–209.
VEATCH, ROBERT M. "Brain Death and Slippery Slopes." *The Journal of Clinical Ethics* Fall 3(3, 1992):181–187.
VEATCH, ROBERT M. "The Whole-Brain-Oriented Concept of Death: An Outmoded Philosophical Formulation." *Journal of Thanatology* 3 (1975):13–30.

2. The Controversy Over Organ Procurement from Anencephalic Infants

ARRAS, JOHN, and SCHLOMO SHINNAR. "Anencephalic Newborns as Organ Donors: A Critique." *Journal of the American Medical Association* 259(15, 1988):2284–2285.
CAPLAN, A.L. "Ethical Issues in the Use of Anencephalic Infants as a Source of Organs and Tissues for Transplantation." *Transplantation Proceedings* 20(4, 1988):42–49.
CAPRON, ALEXANDER. "Anencephalic Donors: Separate the Dead from the Dying." *Hastings Center Report* 17 (February, 1987):5–9.
FLETCHER, JOHN, JOHN ROBERTSON, and MICHAEL HARRISON. "Primates and Anencephalics as Sources for Pediatric Organ Transplants." *Fetal Therapy* 1(2-3, 1986): 150–164.
FOST, NORMAN. "Organs from Anencephalic Infants: An Idea Whose Time Has Yet Come." *Hastings Center Report* 18 (October/November 1988):5–10.
ROSNER, FRED. "The Anencephalic Fetus and Newborn as Organ Donors." *New York State Journal of Medicine* 88 (July, 1988):360–366.
SHEWMON, D. ALAN, ALEXANDER M. CAPRON, WARNICK J. PEACOCK, et al. "The Use of Anencephalic Infants as Organ Source—A Critique." *Journal of the American Medical Association* March 24/31, 261(12, 1989):1773–1781.
WALTERS, JAMES, and STEPHEN ASHWAL. "Organ Prolongation in Anencephalic Infants: Ethical and Medical Issues." *Hastings Center Report* 18 (October/November 1988):19–27.

3. Debate Over Discretion in Choosing Among Definitions (including New Jersey law)

New Jersey Declaration of Death Act (1991). *New Jersey Statutes Annotated.* Title 26, 6A-1 to 6A-8.

BIBLIOGRAPHICAL SOURCES AND REFERENCE WORKS

MEINKE, SUE A. *Anencephalic Infants as Potential Organ Sources: Ethical and Legal Issues* Washington, D.C.: The Kennedy Institute of Ethics, 1989.
REICH, WARREN (ed.). *Encyclopedia of Bioethics.* New York: Macmillan, 1995, articles on:

Death: Anthropological Perspectives
Death: Eastern Thought
Death: Western Philosophical Thought
Death: Western Religious Thought
Death in the Western World
Death: Art of Dying
Death, Attitudes Toward
Death Education
Hospice and End of Life Care

2

Truth Telling with Dying Persons

INTRODUCTION

One of the key issues in the ethics of terminal care is the controversy over what the dying patient should be told about his or her diagnosis. In many cultures the standard pattern is for the clinician to refrain from telling the dying patient about the diagnosis. This approach has been used in Japan, Eastern Europe, and many Latin countries as well as in the Hippocratic tradition.

The Hippocratic Oath includes a pledge in which the physician swears to "share precepts and oral instruction and all the other learning to my sons and to the sons of him who has instructed me . . . , but to no one else."[1] This view of knowledge is common in ancient cultures. Knowledge is seen as powerful, potent, and dangerous. If it falls into the wrong hands, it can do great harm. In philosophical terms, Hippocratic physicians are committed to the principles of beneficence and nonmaleficence, of doing good and avoiding harm. They apply these principles in a special way, however. The only benefits and harms that count are those affecting the patient.

ATTITUDES ABOUT DISCLOSURE

This view is reflected in traditional Hippocratic attitudes about disclosure of diagnoses to terminally ill patients. It was widely believed by physicians from ancient times until the middle of the twentieth century that disclosure of diagnoses to patients could often cause serious problems. It was believed that the patient could be traumatized by the bad news, leading to depression, unwillingness to cooperate in medical treatment, and worse. Many medical students have been told stories of patients who committed suicide on being told of a terminal diagnosis. However, efforts to document these stories have generally been unsuccessful.

From surveys of physicians we know, that for American physicians, the pattern up until the 1960s was reluctance to disclose. In a study published in 1962, Donald Oken asked physicians what their usual policy was about disclosure of a terminal cancer diagnosis.[2] Only 12 percent usually told cancer patients of their diagnosis. The Oken study is described in the first reading in this chapter.

While physicians were reporting that their usual policy was not to disclose, patients, when they were surveyed, indicated by large percentages that they wanted this information. In a 1957 study by Samp and Curreri, 87 percent of patients and visitors in a waiting room of a tumor clinic said that they believed cancer patients should be told.[3] In a similar study by Branch, 88 percent of cancer-free patients said that they would want to be told.[4]

The first reading in this chapter reveals that a dramatic change took place in physician attitudes by the end of the 1970s. Dennis Novack and his colleagues asked the same question that had been asked by Oken. By this time, 98 percent of physicians reported that their usual policy was to tell cancer patients of their diagnoses.[5]

The key question, from the point of view of one interested in the ethics of terminal care, is what happened to produce this dramatic shift in an attitude that had apparently been more or less stable over many centuries. Why would attitudes shift from 88 percent having a usual policy of nondisclosure to 98 percent having a usual policy of telling?

PHILOSOPHICAL FOUNDATIONS OF TRUTH TELLING

Hippocratic Paternalism

Traditionally, physicians have been committed to the moral principle of doing good for their patients. The Hippocratic Oath, for example, requires the physician to strive to benefit the patient according to the physician's ability and judgment and to protect the patient from harm. Most traditional physicians, when asked why they refrained from making disclosures of terminal diagnoses, would say that they had a duty to protect the patient from harm. It is clear that they believed that such disclosures had a potential for harm. If they were committed to doing whatever was necessary to avoid harming the patient and they believed that disclosures were likely to be harmful, then they felt they had a moral duty not to disclose, perhaps even to lie to the patient. This approach, which can be called *Hippocratic paternalism,* is found in the reading by Bernard Meyer. He treats information as if it were medicine—dispensing it only when he believed it would be beneficial.

Social Utilitarianism

Sometimes Hippocratic physicians may sound like holders of another moral position. Classical utilitarians are committed to the view that an action is morally right if it will produce as much or more good than any alternative action. Classical utilitarians differ from Hippocratic paternalists in at least one important way. Utilitarians consider the consequences to all affected parties, not just the one most immediately affected. They take into account the benefits and harms for all persons throughout the society. Thus in medicine, utilitarians would consider the effects of a physician's action not only on the patient, but also on all other people who were affected. In allocating medical resources, this would require considering the effect on other parties who will not get scarce resources if the resources are used on the patient under consideration. It would also require considering the effects on the patient's family and friends. It would even require including the effects on the physician and the other members of the health care team.

It is apparent that is some cases doing what will most benefit the patient (the Hippocratic requirement) will simultaneously not be most beneficial for other parties. In fact, the net consequences, taking into account how every person is affected, might be worse if the physician does what will benefit the patient than if the physician follows some other course of action.

Henry Sidgwick is one of the classical utilitarians. In his most famous work, *Methods in Ethics,* he includes a section in which he justifies nondisclosure to patients on grounds of what he calls *expediency.* He is simply applying his general utilitarian method to the problem of disclosure of diagnoses. Although he does not discuss the issue, Sidgwick's approach could in today's world lead to a conclusion that a physician should disclose an HIV diagnosis against the wishes of the patient, if the overall effect on others, including those who could be exposed to the virus, was weighty enough to override the harm to the patient's interests.

This suggests that some classical utilitarians could reach a conclusion that it is sometimes morally necessary for the physician to disclose information to the patient or others on the grounds that the consequences will be better than if a nondisclosure policy were followed.

Some medical ethicists have assessed consequences in a way that has led them to conclude that disclosure of diagnoses is required. Hippocratic physicians would reach this conclusion on the grounds that the patient would benefit more from the disclosure than from nondisclosure, whereas utilitarians would reach this conclusion by considering the consequences for all parties. Richard C. Cabot is a physician who has argued for disclosure on the grounds that the consequences will usually be better if the disclosure is made.

In defending disclosure on consequentialist grounds, Hippocratic physicians will point to the anxiety that can arise if one suspects one has cancer or some other terminal illness, but does not know for sure. Others have pointed to better cooperation in treatment of patients who know their diagnosis. Still others have stressed other psychological benefits that accrue with knowing one's diagnosis. Classical utilitarians will add to these considerations the possible benefits to society that come from disclosure such as the societal benefit resulting from patients being able to plan for the care of loved ones, make more prudent decisions about use of society's resources for treatment, and other concerns that affect the welfare of third parties.

Arguments Grounded in Duty

Not everyone who debates the subject of what dying patients should be told will approach the problem by trying to calculate the consequences—either consequences for the patient or consequences for everyone in the society. Some people consider lying and truth telling simply a matter of duty. Some philosophers such as Immanuel Kant, whose essay on truth telling is included in this chapter, hold that it is simply wrong to lie. Honesty, they claim, is an inherent duty of morality that is not dependent on whether telling the lie does harm.

While many people hold that lying is intrinsically wrong, there is considerable dispute about cases in which a physician might claim not to be lying, but simply withholding the truth. Philosophically it is more complex to determine whether a moral duty not to lie also includes a duty to tell the truth. Surely, people are not morally obliged to say everything they know. It seems much easier to identify a dishonest statement than to figure out whether one must disclose something that is known.

Ordinary citizens clearly do not have to disclose everything they know about a friend or neighbor. We would probably destroy friendships if we did. Yet physicians taking care of dying patients seem to be in a special role. They may have special duties to disclose in certain circumstances even if people outside this special role need not disclose.

For example, in research medicine, it is almost universally believed that, if an investigator wants to use a human as a subject for research, he or she has duties to disclose, not simply duties to avoid lying. Likewise, many people believe clinicians providing therapeutic care for patients have duties to disclose truthfully that go beyond the duty to avoid lying. They may hold this view because physicians have a related moral duty to get informed consent for the therapies being offered or because there is some implied contractural relation between patient and physician. Some patients may believe that if they go to the physician to get a diagnosis, there is an implied contract that the physician will truthfully disclose the diagnosis if one is established. Thus, for Kantians and others who believe that disclosure is a moral duty independent of consequences, the duty may go beyond the obligation not to lie to include disclosure of certain information that the patient needs to consent to treatment or that the patient is expecting as part of the patient/physician relation. This sense of duty does not occur in Hippocratic medicine and may not occur in some forms of utilitarian ethics.

Sometimes this sense of duty gets expressed in terms of rights. The patient might claim that he or she simply has the right to the truth about the diagnosis. An approach based on rights is often seen as connected to the ethics of duty. In both cases, consequences are not enough to justify overriding the purported duty or right. Some hold that rights and duties are reciprocal: if one person has a duty, then someone else often has a rights claim against that person. Together they stand in contrast to approaches that make decisions and policies by appeal to consequences of actions.

Mixed or Balancing Approaches

Appeals to consequences and to duties and rights are both powerful. Many people see both approaches as valid. But if one accepts the principles of beneficence and nonmaleficence and also the principles of veracity or fidelity to contracts, then in some cases one must determine what should be done when these two kinds of appeals are in conflict.

Some people will try to rank-order the principles. Some in the Kantian tradition would say that the consequences never justify a lie, whereas utilitarians like Sidgwick might claim that only the consequences can justify behavior. Many people, however, see both kinds of appeals as important. They may try to include both kinds of principles balancing competing claims and giving priority to those that are "more weighty." The last group of readings in this chapter provide several different examples of writers who balance the competing claims to protect patients from harms of disclosure and the duty to fulfill contracts and avoid lying. As we shall see, some people may balance these competing claims by giving strong emphasis to the consequences to provide exceptions to the general duty to disclose, while others will permit the consequences to override this duty only in extreme or exceptional cases.

NOTES

1. Edelstein, Ludwig. "The Hippocratic Oath: Text, Translation and Interpretation." In Temkin, Owsei, and C. Lilian Temkin (eds.) *Ancient Medicine: Selected Papers of Ludwig Edelstein.* Baltimore, MD: The Johns Hopkins Press, 1967, p. 6.
2. Oken, Donald. "What to Tell Cancer Patients: A Study of Medical Attitudes," *Journal of the American Medical Association* 175 (April 1, 1961):1120–1128.
3. Samp, Robert J., and Anthony R. Curreri. "A Questionnaire Survey on Public Cancer Education Obtained from Cancer Patients and their Families," *Cancer* 10 (1957): 382–384.
4. Branch, C.H. "Psychiatric Aspects of Malignant Disease," *CA: Bulletin of Cancer Progress* 6 (1956):102–104.
5. Novack, Dennis H., Robin Plumer, Raymond L. Smith, Herbert Ochitill, Gary R. Morrow, and John M. Bennett. "Changes in Physicians' Attitudes Toward Telling the Cancer Patient," *Journal of the American Medical Association* 241 (March 2, 1979):897–900.

Changes in Physicians' Attitudes Toward Telling the Cancer Patient*

DENNIS H. NOVACK, MD; ROBIN PLUMER;
RAYMOND L. SMITH; HERBERT OCHITILL, MD;
GARY R. MORROW, PhD; JOHN M. BENNETT, MD**

Empirical data about physicians attitudes toward disclosing a terminal diagnosis have shaped the literature on the ethics of what to tell dying patients. In 1961 Donald Oken surveyed 219 American physicians and found that 88 percent followed a usual policy of not disclosing the diagnosis to the patient. In a study published in 1979, Dennis Novack and his colleagues repeated essentially the same study, but they found that at that time 98 percent of physicians followed a usual policy of disclosing. Their article summarizes the attitudes of physicians and patients, considers how they have changed over the years, and begins to address the reasons why this abrupt change took place.

In answer to a questionnaire administered in 1961, 90% of responding physicians indicated a preference for not telling a cancer patient his diagnosis. To assess attitudinal changes, the same questionnaire was submitted to 699 university-hospital medical staff. Of 264 respondents, 97% indicated a preference for telling a cancer patient his diagnosis—a complete reversal of attitude. As in 1961, clinical experience was the major policy determinant, but the 1977 population emphasized the influence of medical school and hospital training. Our respondents indicated less likelihood that they would change their present policy or be swayed by research. Clinical experience was the determining factor in shaping two opposite policies. Physicians are still basing their policies on emotion-laden personal conviction rather than the outcome of properly designed scientific studies. (*JAMA* 241:897–900, 1979)

*Source: "Changes in Physicians' Attitudes Toward Telling the Cancer Patient." *Journal of the American Medical Association,* v. 241 (March 2, 1979), pp. 897–900, copyright 1979, American Medical Association.
**From the University of Rochester Medical Center (Dr. Novack, Mr. Plumer, Mr. Smith, Dr. Ochitill, and Dr. Morrow), and the University of Rochester Cancer Center (Dr. Bennett), Rochester, NY. Dr. Novack is currently with the University of Virginia, Charlottesville, Va. Dr. Ochitill is currently with San Francisco General Hospital, San Francisco.
This study was supported in part by grants R18-CA-19861 and CA11198 from the US Department of Health, Education, and Welfare, and the Rochester Plan at the University of Rochester, Rochester, NY.
Donald Oken, MD, and George Engel, MD, provided valuable suggestions during preparation of the manuscript.
Copies of the questionnaire used can be obtained from Dennis H. Novack, MD, PO Box 432, University of Virginia Medical Center, Charlottesville, VA 22908.

A number of surveys since 1953 have investigated the physician's approach to the cancer patient regarding the issue of disclosing the diagnosis.

Of 442 physicians surveyed through the mail in 1953, 31% said they always or usually tell the patient, while 69% said they usually do not or never tell the patient. Of those who generally did not make the diagnosis known, exception occurred when the patient refused treatment or needed to plan. Of those inclined to share the diagnosis, reluctance arose when they were discouraged by the family or afraid of the patient's response.[1] In 1960, of 5,000 physicians, 16% said that they always told the patient, and 22% responded that they never told the patient. The rest sometimes told the patient. Their decisions were influenced by such factors as the stability of the patient, the insistence by the patient or family, the necessity for the patient to put affairs in order, and the unavailability of anyone else who could be told.[2]

In Oken's[3] survey of 219 physicians at Michael Reese Hospital, based on questionnaires and personal interviews, 90% generally did not inform the patient. Although more than three fourths of the group cited clinical experience as the major determinant of their policies, the data bore no relationship to length of experience or age. Many showed inconsistencies in attitudes, personal bias, and resistance to change and to further research, suggesting that emotion-laden a priori personal judgments were the real determinants of policy. Underlying were feelings of pessimism and futility about cancer.

By 1970 a questionnaire survey responded to by 178 physicians showed that 66% sometimes inform the patient, 25% always tell the patient, and only 9% never tell the patient.[4] This suggests a modification of previous practice. To assess whether this represents a genuine change, the present survey was undertaken.

METHODS

The survey population consisted of 699 physicians whose names appeared in the *Physician Staff Directory* of Strong Memorial Hospital. Only pathologists and psychiatrists were excluded.

All subjects received an 18-item structured questionnaire through the mail almost identical to Oken's questionnaire in 1961, which covered physicians' attitude and practice toward the cancer patient.

RESULTS

Two hundred seventy-eight, or 40% usable responses, were returned from a single mailing. Nine specialties were represented: internal medicine represented 35% of total returns; pediatrics, 7.5%; obstetrics and gynecology, 2.5%; surgery and neurosurgery 10%; oncology, 11.7%; family practice, 2.1%; radiology, 2.1%; subspecialty, 18.7%; others, 7.9%; and specialty not indicated, 2.5%. The sample appeared to represent a cross section of specialties within the hospital's physician population, with the exceptions that oncology was slightly overrepresented, and surgery and obstetrics and gynecology were slightly underrepresented.

In comparing the 1977 and 1961 populations, the present sample had a mean age of 37 years and was 91% men, while the 1961 sample had a mean age of 50 years

TABLE 1.   Physicians' Policies About Telling Cancer Patients

	Do not tell, no. (%)		Tell, no. (%)	
Exceptions	1977	1961	1977	1961
Never	1(0.4)	18(9)	17(7)	0(0)
Very rarely	2(0.8)	90(47)	152(61)	6(3)
Occasionally	1(0.4)	56(29)	71(28)	10(5)
Often	2(0.8)	5(3)	5(2)	8(4)
Usual policy	6(2)	169(88)	245(98)	24(12)

1961 data from Oken[3].

and was 97% men. Oken reported that the great bulk of physicians in the sample were in active private practice in addition to taking a regular part in the teaching program. Two thirds of our respondents were older than 31 years and were involved in the practice of their specialties. Many took an active role in the hospital's teaching program.

As shown in Table 1, 98% reported that their general policy is to tell the patient. Two thirds of this group say that they never or very rarely make exceptions to this rule. This stands in sharp contrast with Oken's 1961 data, which showed that 88% generally did not tell the patient, with 56% saying that they never or very rarely made exceptions to this rule.

No differences between specialties were found, with the exception that the pediatricians, while reporting that their usual policy is to tell the patient, make exception to this rule more frequently than other physicians. With minor exceptions this lack of specialty difference was a consistent finding for all questionnaire items.

The results seem to indicate that the many factors that went into the decision to tell the patient influenced not only whether a physician would tell the patient but also the manner in which he made the diagnosis known, perhaps influencing the timing or wording of the communication.

The four most frequent factors considered in the decision to tell the patient were age (56%), intelligence (44%), relative's wish about telling the patient (51%), and emotional stability (47%).

Four factors most frequently believed to be of special importance were the patient's expressed wish to be told (52%), emotional stability (21%), age (11%), and intelligence (10%).

Eighteen percent of the sample reported they were less likely to tell a child, while approximately 10% were inclined to tell a patient who was old or who had poor comprehension. Fourteen percent said that they would tell the patient less frequently or might delay telling if they thought the patient was prone to depression or suicide. Approximately 12% would tell the patient somewhat more frequently if personal affairs needed to be put in order.

The bases of policies in 1977 and 1961 are tabulated in Table 2.

The topic of communication with the cancer patient seems to be more frequently discussed now in medical schools and hospital training programs. Twenty-

TABLE 2.   Sources From Which Policies Were Acquired

Source	Every source, no. (%)		Major source, no. (%)	
	1977	1961	1977	1961
Medical school teaching	59(24)	14(7)	7(3)	0(0)
Hospital training	128(53)	72(35)	33(15)	10(5)
Clinical experience	222(92)	191(94)	153(70)	146(77)
Illness in friends or family	89(37)	61(30)	15(7)	15(8)
Other	22(9)	24(12)	10(5)	17(9)
Total	520*	362*	218(100)†	188(100)†

*More than one answer can be given by respondent.
†Figures rounded to nearest percent.

four percent of the 1977 sample vs. 7% in the 1961 sample mention medical school teaching, and 53% of our sample vs. 35% in 1961 mention hospital training as sources from which policies are acquired.

As before, clinical experience was given the major credit in both studies, with more than 90% citing it as a source and more than 70% citing it as a major source. As in Oken's data, analysis of the age of respondents citing clinical experience as a major policy determinant showed that younger physicians were just as likely to cite clinical experience as their seniors. Seventy-four percent of our group (and 86% of Oken's group) said that their policy had not changed in the past.

Thus, as in 1961, it appears that personal and emotional factors are of major importance in shaping policy, perhaps even more so in the present study. Subsequent to the general inquiry, "How did you acquire your policy?" it was specifically asked if personal issues were determinants. Seventy-one percent of the 1961 survey and 92% of the current survey reported that personal elements were involved. Again, as in 1961, these respondents were about equally divided as to whether these factors were most important. The physicians specializing in oncology (12% of total respondents) indicated that personal factors were less important in shaping their policies, suggesting that they believed there was some objective policy to be followed that was independent of personal considerations.

There is further evidence of the continuing importance of personal and emotional factors in shaping policy. Our sample evidences an even greater resistance to change and opposition to further research. Questioned about the likelihood of policy change in the future, our respondents show significantly less likelihood that they would change their policy in the future ($P < .01$). Five percent said that there was no possibility of change, 48% said that change was very unlikely, and 34% said that change was unlikely, although they were not sure. Only 9% said that change was probable, and 4% said that it was certain.

This resistance to change was also evident with 28% responding that their policy would not be swayed by research as opposed to 16% of Oken's sampling. Only 15% of our sample said that perhaps their policy would be changed; 29% responded this way in 1961. One of the comments seemed to sum up the general feeling: "I would not be swayed by research (but I think my opinion is correct)."

Responses to the last two survey questions are perhaps indicative of the conviction with which the present policies are held. One hundred percent (vs. 60% of the 1961 sample) indicated a preference for being told if they themselves had cancer. One hundred percent thought that the patient has the right to know.

COMMENT

There appears to have been a major change in physicians' attitudes concerning telling patients their diagnosis of cancer. Even if only those physicians who believed strongly about telling the patient responded to our survey, there has still been a significant change since Oken's study. Indeed, there is some evidence that our results may be representative of more widely held views. In a recent study in which 50 patients undergoing radiotherapy were interviewed, 94% used the word "cancer" or "malignant tumor" to describe the reason for being treated. All patients were told their diagnosis by the physician who referred them for therapy.[5] How might we account for this change in attitude? Our respondents' written replies and additional comments suggest several explanations.

Therapy for many forms of cancer has notably improved in recent years. Oken's data suggested that the great majority of physicians believed that cancer connoted certain death. As many patients shared this pessimism, this common belief was often an effective deterrent to free communication. Today advances in therapy have brought longer survival, improved quality of life, and, in many cases, permanent cure. Physicians believe they can offer their cancer patients more hope.

There has been an increase in public awareness of cancer at many levels. The media are constantly presenting evidence of the ubiquity of carcinogens. Public figures such as Betty Ford and Happy Rockefeller spoke openly about their malignant neoplasms. The American Cancer Society publicizes the "Seven Danger Signals of Cancer." Perhaps all of this has led to a lesser stigmatization of cancer, a greater ease in talking about its reality, and a greater awareness of its signs and symptoms.

Oken suggested that most physicians thought that the diagnosis of cancer, with its expectation of death, deprived the patient of hope, and hence they were reluctant to tell cancer patients the diagnosis. Our data suggest that this attitude has also changed. Even when death is expected from the disease, physicians are nevertheless telling their patients the diagnosis. Perhaps improved therapy allows physicians to be overly optimistic with their patients. Perhaps some physicians feel more comfortable in relating to dying patients. At least, many understand better the dying process. This is certainly due, in part, to the recent upsurge of interest in death and dying. Good empirical studies have been done, and many authors have made important contributions to our knowledge in this field.[6-12] This knowledge may have led to more effective communication with dying patients, a reduction in the fear that the dying process necessarily engenders loss of hope, and a greater understanding of the concerns and needs of dying patients. Our data show that these issues are more frequently discussed in medical schools and hospital training programs.

Perhaps more patients are being told because more need to know. Many university hospitals are major clinical research centers, and patients who agree to participate in research protocols must be told their diagnosis to satisfy the legal requirements of informed consent. At the University of Rochester, in 1975, 15% of patients with all newly diagnosed cancer participated in national protocols.

It is impossible to know to what extent the literature on telling the cancer patient has shaped attitudes. If it has had any effect, however, it would be in the direction of encouraging frankness. Koenig[13] systematically reviewed 51 articles appearing in the professional journals between 1946 and 1966 that discussed the treatment of fatally ill patients. He concluded that the tendency of authors appears to be strongly in favor of informing fatally ill patients of their conditions. This has been more recently reaffirmed by Cassem and Stewart,[14] who, in suggesting a general policy of frankness, cite two sets of empirical studies. The first set includes those studies in which patients were asked whether or not they should be told. These indicate overwhelming positive favor for telling. The second set looks at the effects of telling on patients and their families. These studies dispelled the myth of the harm that telling the patient might engender.

The comments of some of our respondents indicate that the reason for the present reversal in attitude is due, in part, to more sweeping social changes. The rise in the consumerism movement and increasing public scrutiny of the medical profession have altered the physician-patient relationship. In this era of "patients' rights," an attitude of frankness feels right and, indeed, given the current disputatious atmosphere of medical practice, may be the safest one to adopt.

Many questions remain. Do physicians tell patients they have "cancer," or are euphemisms such as "tumor" or "growth" still widely used, and if so what does that mean for the communication process? Are changing attitudes on telling the patient accompanied by the emotional support that a patient's knowledge of his diagnosis may demand of a physician? Saunders[15] wrote, "The real question is not 'What do you tell your patients?' but rather, 'What do you let your patients tell you?' " Now that we tell our patients more, are we also listening more? Unfortunately one survey cannot answer these questions.

Is the present policy of telling the patient the best policy? The majority of our respondents cite clinical experience as shaping their present policy, even though most of them have never had experience with another policy. The majority of Oken's respondents also cited clinical experience in shaping the exact opposite policy. While not discounting the value of clinical experience, its use as a determinant of policy must be called into question.

Our data suggest that, as in Oken's study, the present policy is supported by strong belief and emotional investment in its being right. One hundred percent of our respondents stated that patients have a right to know. Yet in asserting this in a blanket manner, are physicians sometimes abdicating a responsibility to make subtle judgments in individual cases? Do patients also have a right not to know?

Is it possible to determine who should be told what, when, and how? What are the criterions by which we judge if telling is right? Patient evaluation in future studies on telling might include assessments of compliance with the medical regimen, quality of communication with physician and family members, ratings of adjustment to illness, or psychological tests of depression and anxiety.

Our respondents' written comments seem to indicate that the current policy of telling the patient is accompanied by increased sensitivity to patients' emotional needs. There is some evidence that telling is the best policy.[16] Yet how rational is the process of deciding what to tell the patient with cancer? Even though the policies have reversed, many physicians are still basing their communication with cancer patients on emotion-laden personal convictions. They are relying on honesty, sensitivity, and patients' rights rather than focusing on the following relevant scientific psychological question: Does telling the diagnosis of cancer help or harm (which) patients and how? Only further systematic research can answer these questions.

NOTES

1. Fitts W.T. Jr., Ravdin I.S. What Philadelphia physicians tell patients with cancer. *JAMA* 153:901–904, 1953.
2. Rennick D. (ed). What should physicians tell cancer patients? *N Med Material* 2:51–53, 1960.
3. Oken D. What to tell cancer patients: A study of medical attitudes. *JAMA* 175:1120–1128, 1961.
4. Friedman H.S. Physician management of dying patients: An exploration. *Psychiatric Medicine* 1:295–305, 1970.
5. Mitchell G.W., Glicksman A.S. Cancer patients: Knowledge and attitudes. *Cancer* 40:61–66, 1977.
6. Feifel H. (ed). *The Meaning of Death.* New York: McGraw-Hill Book Co Inc, 1959.
7. Saunders C. Care of the dying. *Nursing Times* 55:960–961, 994–995, 1031–1032, 1067–1069, 1091–1092, 1129–1130, 1959.
8. Hinton J. M. *Dying.* Baltimore: Penguin Books Ltd, 1967.
9. Glaser B.G., Strauss A.C. *Awareness of Dying.* Chicago: Aldine Publishing, 1965.
10. Kübler-Ross E. *On Death and Dying.* New York, MacMillan, 1969.
11. Engel G.L. Psychological responses to major environmental stress, in *Psychological Development in Health and Disease.* Philadelphia, W. B. Saunders, 1962, pp. 272–305.
12. Greene W.A. The physician and his dying patient, in Troupe S.B., Greene W.C. (eds). *The Patient, Death and the Family.* New York: Charles Scribner's Sons, 1974, pp. 85–99.
13. Koenig R.R. Anticipating death from cancer—physician and patient attitudes. *Michigan Medicine* 68:899–905, 1969.
14. Cassem N.H., Stewart R.S. Management and care of the dying patient. *International Journal of Psychiatry in Medicine* 6:293–304, 1975.
15. Saunders C. The moment of truth: Care of the dying person, in Pearson L. (ed): *Death and Dying.* Cleveland: Case Western Reserve University Press, 1969, pp. 49–78.
16. Gerle B., Landen G., Sandblom P. The patient with inoperable cancer from the psychiatric and social standpoint. *Cancer* 13:1206–1217, 1960.

ARGUMENTS GROUNDED IN CONSEQUENCES

Truth and the Physician*

BERNARD C. MEYER

The traditional approach of physicians to the question of disclosure of terminal illness to patients was grounded in the Hippocratic dictum that the physician should always strive to benefit the patient and keep the patient from harm according to the physician's ability and judgment. In the following essay (dating from 1968), physician Bernard Meyer follows this approach. He argues that information should always be given when it will serve a medical purpose, but should be withheld when it might be harmful to the patient. It is the welfare of the patient that is the standard of reference.

TRUTH AS ABSTRACT PRINCIPLE

There are . . . pitfalls . . . that complicate the problem of telling patients the truth about their illness. There is the naïve notion, for example, that when the patient asserts that what he is seeking is the plain truth he means just that. But as more than one observer has noted, this is sometimes the last thing the patient really wants. Such assertions may be voiced with particular emphasis by patients who happen to be physicians and who strive to display a professional or scientifically objective attitude toward their own condition. Yet to accept such assertions at their face value may sometimes lead to tragic consequences, as in the following incident.

> A distinguished urological surgeon was hospitalized for a hypernephroma, which diagnosis had been withheld from him. One day he summoned the intern into his room, and after appealing to the latter on the basis of we're-both-doctors-and-grown-up-men, succeeded in getting the unwary younger man to divulge the facts. Not long afterward, while the nurse was momentarily absent from the room, the patient opened a window and leaped to his death. . . .

Discussion of Known Truth

Still another misconception is the belief that if it is certain that the truth is known it is all right to discuss it. How mistaken such an assumption may be was

*Source: In *Ethical Issues in Medicine: The Role of the Physician in Today's Society,* E. Fuller Torrey, ed. Copyright © 1968, pp. 166–177 (slightly edited). Published by Little, Brown and Company. Reprinted by permission of the author and Little, Brown and Company.

illustrated by the violent rage a recent widow continued to harbor toward a friend for having alluded to cancer in the presence of her late husband. Hearing her outburst one would have concluded that until the ominous word had been uttered, her husband had been ignorant of the nature of his condition. The facts, however, were different, as the unhappy woman knew, for it had been her husband who originally had told the friend what the diagnosis was.

DENIAL AND REPRESSION

The psychological devices that make such seeming inconsistencies of thought and knowledge possible are the mechanisms of repression and denial. It is indeed the remarkable capacity to bury or conceal more or less transparent truth that makes the problem of telling it so sticky and difficult a matter, and one that is so unsusceptible to simple rule-of-thumb formulas. For while in some instances the maintenance of denial may lead to severe emotional distress, in others it may serve as a merciful shield. For example,

> A physician with a reputation for considerable diagnostic acumen developed a painless jaundice. When, not surprisingly, a laparotomy revealed a carcinoma of the head of the pancreas, the surgeon relocated the biliary outflow so that postoperatively the jaundice subsided. This seeming improvement was consistent with the surgeon's explanation to the patient that the operation had revealed a hepatitis. Immensely relieved, the patient chided himself for not having anticipated the "correct" diagnosis. "What a fool I was!" he declared, obviously alluding to an earlier, albeit unspoken, fear of cancer.

Among less sophisticated persons the play of denial may assume a more primitive expression. Thus a woman who had ignored the growth of a breast cancer to the point where it had produced spinal metastases and paraplegia, attributed the latter to "arthritis" and asked whether the breast would grow back again. The same mental mechanism allowed another woman to ignore dangerous rectal bleeding by ascribing it to menstruation, although she was well beyond menopause.

In contrast to these examples is a case reported by Winkelstein and Blacher of a man who, awaiting the report of a cervical node biopsy, asserted that if it showed cancer he wouldn't want to live, and that if it didn't he wouldn't believe it.[1] Yet despite this seemingly unambiguous willingness to deal with raw reality, when the chips were down, . . . this man too was able to protect himself through the use of denial.

From the foregoing it should be self-evident that what is imparted to a patient about his illness should be planned with the same care and executed with the same skill that are demanded by any potentially therapeutic measure. Like the transfusion of blood, the dispensing of certain information must be distinctly indicated, the amount given consonant with the needs of the recipient, and the type chosen with the view of avoiding untoward reactions. This means that only in selected instances is there any justification for telling a patient the precise figures of his blood pressure, and that the question of revealing interesting but asymptomatic congenital anomalies should be considered in light of the possibility of evoking either hypochondriacal ruminations or narcissistic gratification.

Under graver circumstances the choices confronting the physician rest upon more crucial psychological issues. In principle, we should strive to make the patient sufficiently aware of the facts of his condition to facilitate his participation in the treatment without at the same time giving him cause to believe that such participation is futile. "The indispensable ingredient of this therapeutic approach," write Stehlin and Beach, "is free communication between [physician] and patient, in which the latter is sustained by hope within a framework of reality."[2] What this may mean in many instances is neither outright truth nor outright falsehood but a carefully modulated formulation that neither overtaxes human credulity nor invites despair. . . .

If what has been set down here should prove uncongenial to some strict moralists, one can only observe that there is a hierarchy of morality, and that ours is a profession which traditionally has been guided by a precept that transcends the virtue of uttering truth for truth's sake; that is, "So far as possible, do no harm." Where it concerns the communication between the physician and his patient, the attainment of this goal demands an ear that is sensitive to both what is said and what is not said, a mind that is capable of understanding what has been heard, and a heart that can respond to what has been understood.

NOTES

1. C. Winkelstein and R. Blacher, Personal communication, 1967.
2. J.S. Stehlin and K.A. Beach, "Psychological aspects of cancer therapy," *Journal of the American Medical Association* 197 (1966), 100.

The Classification of Duties—Veracity*

HENRY SIDGWICK

While Hippocratic physicians are oriented to benefit for the patient, classical utilitarians are committed to maximizing net benefit taking into account all possible individuals in the society who might be affected by an action. Henry Sidgwick was a classical utilitarian. In *Methods of Ethics,* he includes a section in which he explains the duty of veracity or truth telling. He also takes up the question of exceptions to this duty and cites medical communication of the physician to the patient as an example of a case in which more harm than good might arise from being honest. Criticizing the views of Immanuel Kant (see the reading later in this chapter), Sidgwick holds out "expediency" as the ultimate criterion of whether it is necessary to speak the truth. He defines expediency in terms of "weighing the gain of any particular deception against the imperilment of mutual confidence involved in all violation of truth." Thus, he has in mind not just the impact on the particular patient of an act of dishonesty, but also the impact the act will have on all future attempts to rely on truthful communication.

In the first place, it does not seem clearly agreed whether Veracity is an absolute and independent duty, or a special application of some higher principle. We find (*e.g.*) that Kant regards it as a duty owed to oneself to speak the truth, because "a lie is an abandonment or, as it were, annihilation of the dignity of man." And this seems to be the view in which lying is prohibited by the code of honour, except that it is not thought (by men of honour as such) that the dignity of man is impaired by *any* lying: but only that lying for selfish ends, especially under the influence of fear, is mean and base. In fact, there seems to be circumstances under which the code of honour prescribes lying. Here, however, it may be said to be plainly divergent from the morality of Common Sense. Still, the latter does not seem to decide clearly whether truth-speaking is absolutely a duty, needing no further justification: or whether it is merely a general right of each man to have truth spoken to him by his fellows, which right however may be forfeited or suspended under certain circumstances. Just as each man is thought to have a natural right to personal security generally, but not if he is himself attempting to injure others in life and property: so if we may even kill in defence of ourselves and others, it seems strange if we may not lie, if lying will defend us better against a palpable invasion of our rights: and Common Sense does not seem to prohibit this decisively. And again, just as the orderly and systematic slaughter which we call war is thought perfectly right under certain circumstances, though painful and revolting: so in the word-contests of the law-courts, the lawyer is commonly held to be justified in untruthfulness within strict rules and limits: for an

*Source: Henry Sidwick, "The Classification of Duties Veracity," *Methods of Ethics,* copyright © 1907, pp. 312–317.

advocate is thought to be over-scrupulous who refuses to say what he knows to be false, if he is instructed to say it.[1] Again, where deception is designed to benefit the per-son deceived, Common Sense seems to concede that it may sometimes be right: for example, most persons would not hesitate to speak falsely to an invalid, if this seemed the only way of concealing facts that might produce a dangerous shock: nor do I perceive that any one shrinks from telling fictions to children, on matters upon which it is thought well that they should not know the truth. But if the lawfulness of benevolent deception in any case be admitted, I do not see how we can decide when and how far it is admissible, except by considerations of expediency; that is, by weighing the gain of any particular deception against the imperilment of mutual confidence involved in all violation of truth.

The much argued question of religious deception ("pious fraud") naturally suggests itself here. It seems clear, however, that Common Sense now pronounces against the broad rule, that falsehoods may rightly be told in the interests of religion. But there is a subtler form in which the same principle is still maintained by moral persons. It is sometimes said that the most important truths of religion cannot be conveyed into the minds of ordinary men, except by being enclosed, as it were, in a shell of fiction; so that by relating such fictions as if they were facts, we are really performing an act of substantial veracity.[2] Reflecting upon this argument, we see that it is not after all so clear wherein veracity consists. For from the beliefs immediately communicated by any set of affirmations inferences are naturally drawn, and we may clearly forsee that they will be drawn. And though commonly we intend that both the beliefs immediately communicated and the inferences drawn from them should be true, and a person who always aims at this is praised as candid and sincere: still we find relaxation of the rule prescribing this intention claimed in two different ways by at least respectable sections of opinion. For first, as was just now observed, it is sometimes held that if a conclusion is true and important, and cannot be satisfactorily communicated otherwise, we may lead the mind of the hearer to it by means of fictitious premises. But the exact reverse of this is perhaps a commoner view: viz. that it is only an absolute duty to make our actual affirmations true: for it is said that though the ideal condition of human converse involves perfect sincerity and candour, and we ought to rejoice in exhibiting these virtues where we can, still in our actual world concealment is frequently necessary to the well-being of society, and may be legitimately effected by any means short of actual falsehood. Thus it is not uncommonly said that in defence of a secret we may not indeed *lie*,[3] *i.e.* produce directly beliefs contrary to fact; but we may "turn a question aside," *i.e.* produce indirectly, by natural inference from our answer, a negatively false belief; or "throw the inquirer on a wrong scent," *i.e.* produce similarly a positively false belief. These two methods of concealment are known respectively as *suppressio veri* and *suggestio falsi,* and many think them legitimate under certain circumstances: while others say that if deception is to be practised at all, it is mere formalism to object to any one mode of effecting it more than another.

On the whole, then, reflection seems to show that the rule of veracity, as commonly accepted, cannot be elevated into a definite moral axiom: for there is no real agreement as to how far we are bound to impart true beliefs to others: and while it is contrary to common sense to exact absolute candour under all circumstances, we yet find no self-evident secondary principle, clearly defining when it is not to be exacted.

NOTES

1. It can hardly be said that the advocate merely *reports* the false affirmations of others: since the whole force of his pleading depends upon his adopting them and working them up into a view of the case which, for the time at least, he appears to hold.
2. E.g. certain religious persons hold–or held in 1873–that it is right solemnly to affirm a belief that God created the world in 6 days and rested on the 7th, meaning that 1 : 6 is the divinely ordered proportion between rest and labour.
3. Cf. Whewell, *Elements of Morality,* Book ii. Chapter xv. § 299.

The Use of Truth and Falsehood in Medicine
An Experimental Study*

RICHARD C. CABOT

Those who focus on maximizing good consequences (whether consequences for the patient or consequences for all in the society) will often conclude that there are times when expediency justifies lying to the patient. However, that need not be one's conclusion. Some who determine moral right and wrong by the consequences of actions might conclude that the harms done by lying and failing to speak truthfully are greater than the expected gains. These judgments will, in part, be based on empirical evidence about the effects of lying, but they will also incorporate evaluative judgments about how bad certain consequences are. For example, when it is argued that the outcome of disclosure of a terminal diagnosis will be suicide, one must assess whether that claim is true as well as how bad an outcome suicide would be.

Richard C. Cabot, a famous physician in the early years of the twentieth century, admits to using reasoning from consequences to justify lying to patients early in his career, but in the following essay he reveals that his opinion about the consequences of lying changed as he practiced medicine. He concludes that often the outcome will be better if one truthfully reveals the diagnosis and prognosis to patients.

TRUTH AND FALSEHOOD IN PROGNOSIS

That it is a bad thing to lie about a prognosis we all admit, as a general rule, but there are cases when it is not easy to see what harm it does when the good that it does is very evident indeed.

A patient has gastric cancer. He is told that he has neuralgia of the stomach, and feels greatly relieved by the reassurance, for the effect of psychic influences is nowhere more striking than in gastric cancer (as the cases quoted in Osler's textbook show). Meantime the truth is told to the patient's wife, and she makes whatever preparations are necessary for the inevitable end. Now what harm can be done by such a lie as this? That sufferer is protected from those anticipations and forebodings which are often the worst portion of his misery, and yet his wife, knowing the truth and thoroughly approving of the deception, is able to see to it that her husband's financial affairs are straightened out and to prepare, as well as may be, for his death. Surely this seems a humane and sensible way to ease the patient's hard path, and who can be the worse off for it?

I answer, "Many may be worse off for it, and some must be." The patient himself is very possibly saved some suffering. But consider a minute. His wife has now

*Source: Richard C. Cabot. "The Use of Truth and Falsehood in Medicine: An Experimental Study," *American Medicine* 5 (1903): 344–49.

acquired, if she did not have it already, a knowledge of the circumstances under which doctors think it merciful and useful to lie. She will be sick herself some day, and when the doctors tell that she is not seriously ill, is she likely to believe them?

I was talking not long ago on this subject with a girl of 22. "Oh, of course, *I* never believe what doctors say," was her comment, "for I've helped 'em lie too often and helped fix up the letters that were written so that no one should suspect the truth."

In other words, we have added to the lot of one person, the sufferings which we spare another. We rob Peter to pay Paul.

But it is not likely that the mischief will be so closely limited. There are almost always other members of the family who are let into the secret, and intimate friends, either before or after the patient's death, find out what is going on. Then there are nurses and servants from whom it is rarely wise or possible to keep hidden the actual state of affairs. All told, I doubt if there are less than a dozen souls on the average who are enlightened by such a case in regard to the standards of the physician in charge and so of the profession he represents. I have heard such things talked over among "the laity," and, as a rule, not one, but several cases are adduced to exemplify the prevailing customs of medical men in such circumstances.

We think we can isolate a lie as we do a case of smallpox, and let its effect die with the occasion that brought it about. But is it not common experience that such customs are infectious and spread far beyond our intention and beyond our control? They beget, as a rule, not any acute indignation among those who get wind of them (for "how," they say, "could the doctor do otherwise"), but rather a quiet, chronic incredulity which is stubborn, just in proportion as it is vitally important in a given case to get at the real truth, as in the case of King Edward before mentioned.

You will notice that I am not now arguing that a lie is, in itself and apart from its consequences, a bad thing. I am not saying that we ought to tell the truth in order to save our own souls or keep ourselves untainted. I am saying that a lie saves present pain at the expense of greater future pain, and that if we saw as clearly the future harm as we see the present good, we could not help seeing that the balance is on the side of harm. It is intellectual short-sightedness.

I have told fully my share of lies, under the impression, shared I think, by many of the profession, that it is necessary in exceptional cases to do it for the good of the patient and his friends, but since I have been experimenting with the policy of telling the truth (at first cautiously, but lately with more confidence), I have become convinced that the necessity is a specious one, that the truth works better for all concerned, not only in the long run, but in relatively short spurts, and that its good results are not postponed to eternity, but are discernible within a short time. . . .

So in medicine, if a patient asks me a straight question I believe it works best to give him a straight answer, not a rough answer, but yet not a lie or a prevarication. I do not believe it pays to give an answer that would justify a patient in saying (in case he happened to find out the truth):—"that doctor tried to trick me." I have heard a patient say that, apropos of a lie told by one of the most high-minded and honorable physicians I know, and I do not believe it advisable for any of us to expose ourselves to the chance of rousing that sort of indignation in a patient.

A straight answer to a straight question is what I am recommending, not an unasked presentation of the facts of the patient's case. He may not care to know those facts any more than I care to know the interesting details of dental pathology in which my dentist might wish to instruct me; I leave all that to him. Just so my patient may very properly prefer to be told nothing about his disease, trusting that I shall do my best and let him know when there is anything for him to do in the matter.

But a straight answer does not mean for me what is often called the "blunt truth," the "naked truth," the dry cold facts. The truth that I mean is a true *impression,* a fully drawn and properly shaded account such as is, as I well know, very difficult to give. . . .

But better than either a misleading half truth or a pleasing lie, is an attempt so to answer the patient's question that he shall see not only what he can't do and can't hope for, but what he can do and what there is to *work* for hopefully. . . .

ARGUMENTS GROUNDED IN DUTY

On a Supposed Right to Tell Lies from Benevolent Motives*

IMMANUEL KANT

Meyer, Sidgwick, and Cabot reason differently about the question of disclosure of terminal diagnosis, but they all agree that consequences (either consequences to the patient or consequences to society) determine what is moral. Against this appeal to consequences, Immanuel Kant views ethics as a matter of duty. He believes that there may be actions, such as deceiving a dying patient, that could protect the patient from harm and still be morally wrong. For Kant, the wrongness of an action is in the very form of the act; not in its consequences. Hence, he addresses what he calls the "supposed" right to lie from benevolent motives.

It is to be remarked, first, that the expression "to have a right to the truth" is unmeaning. We should rather say, a man has a right to his own *truthfulness* (*veracitas*), that is, to subjective truth in his own person. For to have a right objectively to truth would mean that, as in *meum* and *tuum* generally, it depends on his *will* whether a given statement shall be true or false, which would produce a singular logic.

Now, the first question is whether a man—in cases where he cannot avoid answering Yes or No—has the *right* to be untruthful. The *second* question is whether, in order to prevent a misdeed that threatens him or someone else, he is not actually bound to be untruthful in a certain statement to which an unjust compulsion forces him.

Truth in utterances that cannot be avoided is the formal duty of a man to everyone, however great the disadvantage that may arise from it to him or any other; and although by making a false statement I do no wrong to him who unjustly compels me to speak, yet I do wrong to men in general in the most essential point of duty, so that it may be called a lie (though not in the jurist's sense), that is, so far as in me lies I cause that declarations in general find no credit, and hence that all rights founded on contract should lost their force; and this is a wrong which is done to mankind.

If, then, we define a lie merely as an intentionally false declaration towards another man, we need not add that it must injure another; as the jurists think proper to put in their definition (*mendacium est falsiioquium in praejudicium alterius*). For it always injures another; if not another individual, yet mankind generally, since it

*Source: Immanuel Kant. "On the Supposed Right to Tell Lies from Benevolent Motives," translated by Thomas Kingsmill Abbott and reprinted in Kant's *Critique of Practical Reason and Other Works on the Theory of Ethics*. London: Longmans, 1909 [1797], pp. 361–65.

vitiates the source of justice. This benevolent lie *may,* however, by *accident* (*casus*) become punishable even by civil laws; and that which escapes liability to punishment only by accident may be condemned as a wrong even by external laws. For instance, if you have by a lie hindered a man who is even now planning a murder, you are legally responsible for all the consequences. But if you have strictly adhered to the truth, public justice can find no fault with you, be the unforeseen consequence what it may. It is possible that whilst you have honestly answered Yes to the murderer's question, whether his intended victim is in the house, the latter may have gone out unobserved, and so not have come in the way of the murderer, and the deed therefore have not been done; whereas, if you lied and said he was not in the house, and he had really gone out (though unknown to you), so that the murderer met him as he went, and executed his purpose on him, then you might with justice be accused as the cause of his death. For, if you had spoken the truth as well as you knew it, perhaps the murderer while seeking for his enemy in the house might have been caught by neighbours coming up and the deed been prevented. Whoever then *tells a lie,* however good his intentions may be, must answer for the consequences of it, even before the civil tribunal, and must pay the penalty for them, however unforeseen they may have been; because truthfulness is a duty that must be regarded as the basis for all duties founded on contract, the laws of which would be rendered uncertain and useless if even the least exception to them were admitted.

To be *truthful* (honest) in all declarations is therefore a sacred unconditional command of reason, and not to be limited by any expediency. . . .

Truthfulness As a
Prima Facie Duty*

W. D. ROSS

The position of Kant, which totally excludes consequences from the justification of deception of dying patients, strikes many as too much of a rejection of the appeals to consequences that were seen in Meyer, Sidgwick, and Cabot. Some philosophers have addressed this problem by acknowledging that both consequences and the intrinsic characteristics of an action (such as whether it includes a lie or a deception) are relevant to the conclusion about what patients ought to be told. W. D. Ross, the early twentieth century British philosopher, proposes an approach in which both perspectives are incorporated. He tries to accommodate the view of Kant and also of Moore and Rashdall, who work in the tradition of Sidgwick.

It is necessary to say something by way of clearing up the relation between *prima facie* duties and the actual or absolute duty to one particular act in particular circumstances. If, as almost all moralists except Kant are agreed, and as most plain men think, it is sometimes right to tell a lie or to break a promise, it must be maintained that there is a difference between *prima facie* duty and actual or absolute duty. When we think ourselves justified in breaking, and indeed morally obliged to break, a promise in order to relieve some one's distress, we do not for a moment cease to recognize a *prima facie* duty to keep our promise, and this leads us to feel, not indeed shame or repentance, but certainly compunction, for behaving as we do; we recognize, further, that it is our duty to make up somehow to the promisee for the breaking of the promise. We have to distinguish from the characteristic of being our duty that of tending to be our duty. Any act that we do contains various elements in virtue of which it falls under various categories. In virtue of being the breaking of a promise, for instance, it tends to be wrong; in virtue of being an instance of relieving distress it tends to be right. Tendency to be one's duty may be called a parti-resultant attribute, i.e., one which belongs to an act in virtue of some one component in its nature. *Being* one's duty is a toti-resultant attribute, one which belongs to an act . . . in virtue of its whole nature and of nothing less than this.[1] . . . .

NOTE

1. But cf. the qualification in p. 33, n. 2.

*Source: W. D. Ross. *The Right and the Good.* p. 28. Oxford: Oxford University Press, 1930. By permission of Oxford University Press.

EXAMPLES OF MIXED OR BALANCING APPROACHES

Telling the Truth*

JENNIFER JACKSON

The readings in this chapter thus far have not generally distinguished carefully between outright lying to patients and mere deception. Jennifer Jackson, a philosopher at Leeds University in Great Britain, takes up this issue in the reading that follows. Working generally in the tradition of Ross, she examines both utilitarian and nonutilitarian dimensions of the distinction between lying and deception. She sees a more stringent *prima facie* duty to avoid lying, but is more accepting of deceptions unless they would involve a breach of trust. Those reading this essay will want to ask whether cases of terminal illness in which physicians are expected to get an adequately informed consent for treatment would require disclosures for which deception would involve breaches of trust.

It should . . . be noted that if you share . . . the view that doctors and nurses do not enjoy a general dispensation from the duty everyone else is under not to lie and if you also share [the] view that intentional deception is tantamount to lying, you must take a pretty dim view of the reputability of medical practice past and present. Has not benevolent deception always been part and parcel of accepted medical practice—"he who cannot dissimulate cannot cure"?[1]

If doctors did think they had a special duty not to deceive intentionally we should expect it to get a mention in their codes and declarations. But it does not: not until 1980[2] and then there is only the bland pronouncement that doctors should "deal honestly"—no guidance is provided as to whether that means "Tell no lies" or "Don't hide the truth" or "Tell all." Current practice suggests that doctors do not interpret it as prohibiting benevolent deception.

Admittedly, many doctors past and present are sceptical about the therapeutic value of benevolent deception though perhaps none deny that there are some occasions when it is plainly in a patient's interests to be deceived. What these situations are and how common are not questions we need pursue here. We are addressing a prior question: whether the benevolent deception of a patient by his doctor is, like lying, generally contrary to duty. If it is, then the question whether or not benevolent deception is therapeutic in certain circumstances, though perhaps fascinating from the point of view of cause and effect, ceases to have any bearing on the question of right and wrong.

*Source: Jennifer Jackson, "Telling the Truth," *Journal of Medical Ethics,* Vol. 17 (1991): 5–9. Published by BMJ Publishing Group.

Here I hope to establish the importance of differentiating lying from intentional deception and to point up some of the practical implications for good medical practice of the differences to which I draw attention. My discussion is divided into three parts. In Part I, I distinguish lying from intentional deception. In Part II, I enquire how far everyone is obliged (1) to tell the truth and (2) to refrain from deliberate deception. In Part III, I enquire whether doctors are obliged (1) to tell the truth and (2) to refrain from deliberate deception when others, in general, are not.

PART I—SOME DISTINCTIONS

Deception in General

A deceives B if and only if A causes B to be misled. My doctor's dour expression gives me the (false) impression that the symptoms which I am relating to him are sinister: I am misled.

Deceiving may be voluntary or involuntary. In the former case, my doctor maybe means to frighten me a little so that he can persuade me to adopt healthier habits. In the latter case, where his deception of me is involuntary, he is not putting on that expression for my benefit, still less to mislead me. He is perhaps simply following the advice of Securis that a doctor's "countenance must be lyke one that is given to studye and sadde"[3]—advice which Securis offers to counter the risk run by the doctor who is always laughing, who is in danger of being "taken for a lewde person."[4]

A sub-species of voluntary deception is: *intentional deception.* Voluntary deception is intentional if and only if A aims to mislead B: that is, if A acts as he does *in order* to mislead B. Perhaps my doctor's dour expression initially has nothing to do with me—it is directed not at me but at the clouds gathering outside the window. He is half-listening to me while fretting over whether it will be raining by the time surgery ends and whether he will have to postpone his game of golf yet again. If he notices my misapprehension, recognises its cause, and does nothing to correct it then his deception of me which was initially involuntary becomes voluntary. If he does nothing to correct it because he realises how it might help him to bring me to my senses, then his deception of me becomes intentional as well as voluntary.

Lying

A lies to B if and only if A, in order to mislead B, informs B that something is the case although A believes that it is not the case. Lying is not a sub-species of intentional deception, on the account given above, since B need not be "taken in" by A's lies. I ask my doctor, "Have you been talking to my husband?" and he replies "No" although he has and I already know it. I was just putting my doctor's honesty to the test. He lies to me but I am not deceived.

Whereas all liars intend to deceive not all who intentionally deceive tell lies. One way in which the discrepancy emerges is this—intentional deception like lying, does not require that A be communicating with B. Thus, for example if I, noticing that you are eavesdropping on my private conversation with someone else, say something false in order to mislead you, I am intentionally deceiving you but I am not lying to you. Intentional deception need not, of course, involve assertion of any kind. . . .

PART II—TELLING THE TRUTH AS A GENERAL OBLIGATION

Does Everyone Have a Duty Not to Tell Lies?

Do people have a duty, at least a *prima facie* duty, not to tell lies—and if so, what is its source? . . . Necessities, moral or otherwise, must have an explanation—there must always be a reason *why* we must. . . . But what kind of explanation we should be looking for in regard to "moral" necessities and what counts as sufficient explanation are questions we cannot hope to dispose of adequately in a few incidental remarks.

One kind of explanation of the wrongness of lying, though, that is, I think, manifestly inadequate locates its wrongness in the harm suffered by those to whom we lie: as if a person taken in by a lie is *ipso facto* harmed thereby. Suppose my doctor asks if I have taken my medicine and I lyingly reply that I have. The doctor wanted to know—but not for his own good: his remaining in ignorance does not damage him. Yet it is still the case that I have lied to him.

In seeking an explanation of the wrongness of lying we need rather to reflect on the necessity for any community to preserve trust and the crucial role upholding a rule against lying plays here. Just how strict a rule against lying it is necessary to uphold is not so easy to establish—although in view of the importance of preserving trust as the basis of fellowship and the extreme difficulty of restoring it in a community if once it is lost, it would seem that a pretty firm teaching is called for. . . .

If we are prepared to recognise any duties at all, we will surely include at least a *prima facie* duty not to tell lies.

Does Everyone Have a Duty Not Intentionally to Deceive?

In contrast to the case with lying the answer appears to be no. We all intentionally deceive one another daily without a second thought. Women wear make-up, men cover their incipient balding with strategic combings, we smile at each other's feeble witticisms even though we are not amused and we feign delight over gifts which fail to please. To be sure the fact that we all behave in a certain way without scruple is no proof that our behaviour is in fact innocent. But in this particular instance, I submit, there is no good reason to fault our behaviour. Are we not quite able to enjoy fellowship as a community despite a public tolerance of the many tricks of deceit we continually practise on one another, for example in casual conversation?

But when we enter a special relationship in which there is an understanding, explicit or implicit, between the parties the situation can change. The understanding may itself impose special duties and corresponding rights. Where such a special relationship exists, intentional deception in regard to certain matters may involve a betrayal of trust. Only then is it *prima facie* unjust. But B does not suffer such a betrayal unless (1) B has put trust in A and (2) B was entitled to do so.

PART III—TELLING THE TRUTH AS A SPECIAL OBLIGATION OF DOCTORS

When Is Lying to Patients Morally Defensible?

Even doctors who would defend lying as an acceptable feature of normal medical practice may agree with the rather feeble-sounding conclusion I have drawn in Part II, that everyone has at least a *prima facie* duty not to tell lies. They simply argue that often they are obliged to set aside this merely *prima facie* duty in order to fulfill their first duty as doctors—to care for their patients.

Two points deserve comment here. This defence of lying assumes (i) the patient's deception is often necessary (ii) where deception is justified, lying is justified.

(i) Is it true that doctors often have no alternative in fulfilling their caring duties—that deliberate deception is often therapeutically necessary? Perhaps doctors would want this question to be made more specific if it is to be sensibly discussed—is deception of child-patients or dying patients, or depressed patients often necessary? Be that as it may, the question does need to be made more specific in another way—in view of the inherent vagueness of the notion of necessity. A particular treatment, for example, may be said to be necessary in order to cure a patient—or to do so without enormous expense, or trouble, or distress to the patient. Thus, when it is said that lying is therapeutically necessary, we may need further clarification as to how, in what way, it is necessary.

There is, moreover, a lack of precision about a duty of care as opposed to say a duty not to commit adultery or a duty to pay one's debts. The duty of care is open-ended. There being virtually no end to what you can do in accordance with the duty of care it is far from clear what you must do in order to fulfill this duty. Legally, a doctor's duty of care is measured against the yardstick of normal practice. But morally?

In view of the vagueness about the notion of necessity and the imprecision about requirements imposed by a duty of care, we should not be surprised to find that doctors who agree that they have a duty not to lie and a duty of care may still disagree when presented with the same case history whether the one duty is overridden by the other.

Suppose, for example, that while doing a locum for a colleague away on holiday, you are called to attend a patient who is dying of cancer and whose relatives tell you that she does not know and must not be told: the truth, they insist, would kill her more swiftly than the disease. But what if when you meet her, she asks you point blank: "Have I got cancer?" Could you be justified in lying?

In anticipation of finding yourself in such a situation let us suppose that you consult with some colleagues—they do not agree in their advice. Dr. Noteller agrees with the relatives. He cites cases he has encountered in which patients upon being told the truth have died with unexpected suddenness as if, indeed, the news precipitated their demise. Why risk that for patients whose diseases might otherwise allow them weeks, even months, of tolerable existence? Thus, does Dr. Noteller counsel you to withhold the truth and, if necessary, lie rather than shatter the patient's hopes. Dr. Teller disagrees with the relatives. He dismisses the tales of patients dying because allegedly "they could not live with the truth." This happens only where the doctors concerned botch the telling, he insists, and do not follow it up with proper conselling. It is not necessary to lie or even to deceive in such a case. On the contrary, the patient and the relatives should be told the truth so that they can be freed from the isolating trap of deception that makes dying an unnecessarily lonely experience for both parties. But the patient and the relatives need help and support to come to terms with reality. Thus does Dr. Teller counsel you *not* to lie. Indeed he urges that the patient be told the truth.

(ii) Supposing that there is often (seen to be) a therapeutic justification for doctors deliberately deceiving their patients, it does not follow that lying to them is thereby justified. Even if, as in the above case, you are asked point blank, "Have I got cancer?" you are not forced either to lie or tell. Suppose you agree with Dr. Teller but think that it would be better for her to be told by her own doctor than by a relative stranger—you mean to persuade him to talk to her as soon as he returns. Meanwhile you can evade even a direct question without actually lying. You could say, perhaps: "I don't know your case fully . . . I have not talked about your case in depth with your specialist. You should talk to him."

Many people fall in with a utilitarian approach to ethics—for them, our questions as to when lying to patients is morally defensible turns on the overall harm/benefit of lying—whether it would be for the best to lie, bearing in mind all relevant interests (which would doubtless, include the interests of other people, for example, family, nursing staff). Once it is established as it surely would be, that in some cases deliberate deception *is* for the best, the further question of whether to accomplish it by a lie, or an equivocation, evasion or whatever becomes a mere technicality of no particular moral significance, to be decided again by applying the same procedure of weighing costs against benefits. Those who adopt this approach are understandably impatient with fine distinctions such as I have attempted—to them these are a practical irrelevance—certainly not to be inflicted on doctors addressing questions of medical ethics.

But this utilitarian approach to the ethics of lying seems to me to be radically misguided. The distinctions to which I drew attention in Part I were not proffered merely as an example of minute philosophising but as of *practical* relevance to the issues before us, for example, whether lying to patients is morally defensible.

As I argued in Part II the wrongness of lying is not to be located in the harm suffered by the person lied to—nor, I now would add, by the harm suffered generally, bearing in mind, for example, its effect on observers. It is to be explained rather in terms of the need a community (any community) has to maintain a firm rule against lying—a rule the function of which is to preclude lying as a practical option, as a possible method for achieving whatever aims we happen to have. And if as a community we need the rule we cannot allow ourselves the freedom to set aside the rule whenever an occasion presents where it appears that so doing would be for the best: that would be to abandon the rule—it would lose its essential function.

Yet the very question I have posed: "When is lying to patients morally defensible?" rather invites us to adopt a utilitarian approach—it invites us to review the plight of patients in various situations to see whether lying is never, sometimes, or often, justified. On my account of the wrongness of lying maybe we should not allow ourselves to be drawn into a discussion of what harm there is in setting this rule aside in regard to patient A or patient B.

Now some utilitarians would actually share my misgivings about what I have been calling the utilitarian approach and which they would call, rather, an act utilitarian approach. They too, as rule utilitarians, argue that there are certain rules which a community needs to uphold and which we should be learning to follow as a matter of course in our day-to-day activities without stopping to calculate consequences though meanwhile, they say, in our less active more reflective moments, we should be reviewing and revising our rules in the light of our day-to-day experience—seeking always to develop our rules so as to improve them.[5]

How does the position I am advocating in regard to lying differ from that of the rule utilitarians? If the rule against lying is, as I have allowed, *prima facie,* it may on occasion be morally defensible for doctors to lie to their patients. How else then are we to decide on what occasion except by considering, as rule utilitarians do, what departures from the rule would be for the best?

But I have not defended a rule against lying on the grounds that we need to live by this rule so that we may achieve what is for the best. Why suppose it is *necessary* to aim for the best? We may doubt anyway whether that aim is even intelligible. Rather, I have maintained that we need the rule just so as to get by—whatever particular further aims we happen to have in life. If the rule would still allow us to get by if certain departures were generally allowed, then the departures *can* be allowed. If the rule would only allow us to get by if certain departures were allowed, then the departures *must* be allowed.

When Is Intentional Deception of Patients Morally Defensible?

Suppose that many people think . . . that, morally speaking, deliberate deception and lying are on the same footing. In their view then the one practice poses just as much of a threat to trust as does the other. Such a supposition, if it comes to be widely shared is self-fulfilling.

But I do not think that this view *is* widely shared. It is not shared, at any rate, outside the medical context: as I have argued, we practise deliberate deception on one another in a variety of ways that we believe pose no significant threat to trust: for example, by putting someone off the scent so as to keep a planned treat a surprise: a stratagem, it may be noted, which we play on our friends with whom we care most to preserve trust.

Perhaps, though, it can be shown that doctors have a special duty not to deceive their patients, a duty which derives from another duty universally acknowledged by doctors, *viz* their duty of care. While some might protest that it is this very duty of care which makes benevolent deception on occasion not just permissible but obligatory, it might be argued that on the contrary from the duty of care may be derived a duty to maintain trust (without which a patient cannot be got to follow advice) and, from that duty derives another, to refrain from deception. . . .

This pronouncement has a certain force and simplicity about it. On examination it is not so clear, though, what is being asserted. Firstly, should we go along with the assertion that the absence of truth is a casualty? A casualty for whom? After all, truth can be withheld without recourse to deception—and without any injury to those shielded from it: there are many things that we are better off not knowing (the result of a match if we are about to watch the replay) or that we ought not to be told (a doctor has many confidences to keep). Secondly, non-deceptive withholding of truth aside, it remains unclear whether the truth which is being said to underpin trust is a matter of not telling lies (my view) or also a matter of not deliberately deceiving. . . . In other words, the saying could be cited in support of either view; it does not tell in favour of one against the other.

I conclude that while doctors generally speaking should have no truck with lying, deliberate deception need not in general pose a significant threat to trust.

NOTES

1. Hoffman F. *Medicus politicus,* part 3, ch 4, vol 5:24: "qui enim nescit simulare, nescit curare." The *Medicus politicus* (separately paginated) is in the "second part" of a two-volume *Operum omnium physico-medicorum supplementum,* Geneva, 1749. These two volumes are a supplement to Hoffman's *Opera omnia physico-medico* (6 vols). Geneva, 1748.
2. Higgs R. On telling patients the truth. In Lockwood M. (ed.) *Moral dilemmas in modern medicine.* Oxford: Oxford University Press, 1985, 190–191.
3. Securis J. *A detection and querimonie of the daily enormitites and abuses committed in physick.* London: 1566. SIG A iv recto. (This was the way pages were numbered at that time: by signature, by letter and number, and by right-hand [recto] or left-hand [verso] page.)
4. See reference 3: SIG a iv verso.
5. For recent discussion of rule utilitarian, or as some would now prefer, indirect utilitarian, ethics see the ongoing debate between R. M. Hare and his critics in: Seanor D., Fotion N., eds. *Hare and critics.* Oxford: Oxford University Press, 1988.

Truth in Our Intercourse with the Sick*

Worthington Hooker

While Jackson appears open to the possibility of deceiving the patient without violating trust, Worthington Hooker, a nineteenth century American physician, balances the competing claims in a different manner. First, he seems skeptical (as was Cabot some years later) that truthful disclosure to terminally ill patients will harm the patient. But, after looking at several reasons focused on consequences to the patient, he turns to the impact on the community of a rule that the truth may be sacrificed in urgent cases. He concludes that falsehoods are never permitted and sees deception as something that should not be practiced, but he holds open the possibility that in some cases not all information need be disclosed. The physician, he believes has a right to withhold certain truthful information for the good of the patient. This essay was written well before the era of the doctrine of informed consent, and it is important to ask whether a similar conclusion could be reached when it is the duty of the physician to obtain an adequately informed consent for treatment.

The question that presents itself is not, let it be understood, whether the truth shall in any case be *withheld,* but whether, in doing this, real falsehood is justifiable, in any form, whether direct or indirect, whether palpable or in the shape of equivocation.

And we may also remark, that the question is not, whether those who practice deception upon the sick are guilty of a criminal act. This depends altogether on the motive which prompts it, and it is certainly often done from the best and kindest motives. The question is stripped of all considerations of this nature, and comes before us as a simple practical question—whether there are any cases in which, for the sake of benefiting our fellow men, perhaps even to the saving of life, it is proper to make an exception to the great general law of truth.

The considerations which will bring us to a clear and undoubted decision of this question, are not all to be drawn from the preciousness of the principle of truth, as an unbroken, invariable, and ever-present principle, the soul of all order, and confidence, and happiness, in the wide universe. But the principle of expediency also furnishes us with some considerations that are valuable in confirming our decision, if not leading us to it. In truth, expediency and right always correspond, and would be seen to do so, if we could always see the end from the beginning.

I will remark upon each of the considerations as I present them.

*Source: Worthington Hooker. Physician and Patient: Or, a Practical View of the Mutual Duties, Relations and Interests of the Medical Profession and the Community. New York: Baker and Schribner, 1849, pp. 359–382.

First.   It is erroneously assumed by those who advocate deception, that the knowledge to be concealed from the patient would, if communicated, be essentially injurious to him. . . .

Secondly.   It is also erroneously assumed that concealment can always or generally be effectually carried out. There are so many ways by which the truth can be betrayed, even where concerted plans are laid, guarded at every point, that failure is much more common than success, so far as my observation has extended. Some unguarded expression or act, even on the part of those who are practising the concealment, or some information communicated by those who are not in the secret, perhaps by children, or some evidence casually seen, very often either reveals the truth or awakens suspicion and prompts inquiry which the most skillful equivocation may not be able to elude. The very air that is assumed in carrying on the deception often defeats the object. . . .

Thirdly.   If the deception be discovered or suspected, the effect upon the patient is much worse than a frank and full statement of the truth can produce. If disagreeable news, for example, be concealed from him, there is very great danger that it will in some way be revealed to him so abruptly and unexpectedly, as to give him a severe shock, which can for the most part be avoided when the communication is made voluntarily. And then, too, the very fact that the truth has been withheld, increases, for obvious reasons, this shock. . . .

Fourthly.   The destruction of confidence, resulting from discovered deception, is productive of injurious consequences to the persons deceived. The moment that you are detected in deceiving the sick, you at once impair or even destroy their confidence in your veracity and frankness. Everything you do afterward is suspected, and a full and unshrinking trust is not accorded to you even when you deserve it, though you may try to obtain it by the most positive and solemn assurances. If, for example, you wish to encourage a patient, and you tell him that though the bow of hope is dim to his eye, it is bright to your own: "Ah!" he will think if he does not say, "how do I know but that it is as dim to him as it looks to me—he has deceived me once, and perhaps he does now." . . .

Fifthly.   The *general* effect of deception aside from the individual which it is supposed it will benefit, is injurious. The considerations on which I have already remarked, have had regard entirely to the person that is deceived, and I think that I have shown most clearly, that even taking this narrow view of the influence of deception, it is in almost all cases a bad influence: and therefore as we cannot tell in what cases this influence will be good, it is impolitic, and should be entirely discarded. Let us now go farther, and looking beyond the individuals who are the subjects of the deception, we shall see its influence extending all around from these individuals, as so many radiating points of influence, leavening the whole mass of society with a most poisonous leaven. It is not an influence that can be shut up in the case of any individual, in that one breast, or within that one chamber of sickness.

That confidence, which should always exist in the intercourse of the sick with their physicians and friends, and which may be made the channel of great and essential benefits to them, is materially impaired, often even destroyed by such deception. And this effect is unfortunately not confined to those who practice it, but the imputation rests upon others. The distrust thus produced often exerts a depressing influence in those cases, where the cordial influence of hope is most urgently needed, and where it can be administered in consonance with the most scrupulous veracity. It is well if, under such circumstances, the physician can appeal to the patient's own experience of his frankness in all his previous intercourse with him. . . .

I need barely say in concluding my remarks on this consideration, that the momentary good which occasionally results to *individual* cases from deception, is not to be put in comparison, for one moment, with the vast and permanent evils of a *general* character, that almost uniformly proceed from a breach of the great law of truth. And there is no warrant to be found for shutting our eyes to these general and remote results, in our earnestness to secure a particular and present good, however precious that good may be—a plain principle, and yet how often it is disregarded.

Sixthly.   If it be adopted by the community as a common rule, that the truth may be sacrificed in urgent cases, the very object of the deception will be defeated. For why is it that deception succeeds in any case? It is because the patient supposes that all who have intercourse with him deal with him truthfully—that no such common rule has been adopted. There is even now, while the policy on this subject is unsettled and matter of dispute, enough distrust produced to occasion trouble. And if it should become a settled policy under an acknowledged common rule, the result would be *general* distrust, of course defeating deception at every point. And yet if it be proper to deceive, then most clearly is it proper to proclaim it as an adopted principle of action. Else we are driven to the absurd proposition, that while it is right to practice deception, it is wrong to say to the world that it is right.

It is in vain to say that the evil result which would attend this adoption of occasional deception, as the settled policy of the medical profession, would find a correction in the very terms of the rule which should be adopted, viz. that the case must be an urgent one to warrant deception, and there must be a fair prospect that it can be carried through without discovery. For every patient that was aware of the adoption of such a rule, might and often probably would suspect that his own case is considered as coming within the terms of the rule.

Seventhly.   Once open the door for deception, and you can prescribe for it no definite limits. Every one is to be left to judge for himself. And as present good is the object for which the truth is to be sacrificed, the amount of good, for which it is proper to do it, can not be fixed upon with any exactness. Each one is left to make his own estimate, and the limit is in each one's private judgment, in each one's individual case as it arises. And the limit, which is at first perhaps quite narrow, is apt to grow wider, till the deception may get to be of the very worst and most injurious character. . . .

I have now finished the examination of the various considerations which have been suggested to my mind in relation to this subject. And I think that they settle the question as to the expediency of deception beyond all doubt. I think it perfectly evident, that the good, which may be done by deception in a *few* cases, is almost as nothing, compared with the evil which it does in *many* cases, when the prospect of its doing good was just as promising as it was in those in which it succeeded. And when we add to this the evil which would result from a *general* adoption of a system of deception, the importance of a strict adherence to truth in our intercourse with the sick, even on the ground of expediency, becomes incalculably great. . . .

I wish not to be understood as saying that we should never take pains to withhold knowledge from the sick, which we fear might be injurious to them. There are cases in which this should be done. All that I claim is this—that in withholding the truth no deception should be practised, and that if sacrifice of the truth be the necessary price for obtaining the object, no such sacrifice should be made. . . . I do not agree with him, that in withholding the truth we have the right to *put absolute falsehood in its place.*

It is always a question of expediency simply, whether the truth ought to be withheld. And it is a question that depends, for its proper decision, upon a variety of considerations in each individual case.

It is by no means true that all direct questions on the part of the sick must be directly and fully answered. For example, suppose the patient asks the physician, "Do you think on the whole that I shall recover"—a question that is sometimes asked under very embarrassing circumstances. If the physician thinks that he will probably not recover, he has no right to say to him that he will, for this would be falsehood. But he has a right, and it is his duty if he thinks it for the good of the patient, to withhold his opinion from him, if he can do it without falsehood or equivocation. He may say to him something like this: "It is difficult to decide that question. Perhaps it is not proper for me at this stage of your case to attempt to do it. You are very sick, and the issue of your sickness is known only to God. I hope that remedies will do so and so (pointing out somewhat the effects ordinarily to be expected) but I cannot tell." Something of this kind, varied according to the nature of each case, especially in the amount of hope communicated, it is perfectly consistent with truth and good faith to say; and very often when more is said, even in very dangerous cases, the physician goes beyond the limits which infinite wisdom has thought best to set to his knowledge. It is very common, as the reader has already seen in the preceding chapter, for persons to recover, particularly in cases of acute disease, when the physician had supposed that they would die. This fact should make him somewhat cautious in giving definite opinions to the sick in relation to the probable final result of their sickness.

SUGGESTED READINGS FOR CHAPTER 2

A. EXCERPTS FROM SURVEY DATA

AITKEN-SWAN, JEAN, and E.C. EASSON. "Reactions of Cancer Patients on Being Told Their Diagnosis." *British Medical Journal* (March 21, 1959):779–783.

BLUMENFIELD, MICHAEL, NORMAN B. LEVY, and DIANE KAUFMAN. "Current Attitudes of Medical Students and House Staff Toward Terminal Illness." *General Hospital Psychiatry* 1(4, December 1979):306–310.

BRANCH, C.H. "Psychiatric Aspects of Malignant Disease." *CA: Bulletin of Cancer Progress* 6 (1956):102–104.

FITTS, WILLIAM T., JR., and I.S. RAVDIN. "What Philadelphia Physicians Tell Patients with Cancer." *Journal of the American Medical Association* 153 (1953):901–904.

KELLY, WILLIAM D., and STANLEY R. FRIESEN. "Do Cancer Patients Want to Be Told?" *Surgery* 27 (June 1950):822–826.

NOVACK, DENNIS H., BARBARA J. DETERING, ROBERT ARNOLD, et al. "Physician's Attitudes Toward Using Deception to Resolve Difficult Ethical Problems." *Journal of the American Medical Association* 261(20, May 26, 1989):2980–2985.

OKEN, DONALD. "What to Tell Cancer Patients: A Study of Medical Attitudes." *Journal of the American Medical Association* 175 (April 1, 1961):1120–1128.

REA, M. PRISCILLA, SHIRLEY GREENSPOON, and BERNARD SPILKA. "Physicians and the Terminal Patient: Some Selected Attitudes and Behavior." *Omega* 6(4, 1975): 291–302.

SAMP, ROBERT J., and ANTHONY R. CURRERI. "A Questionnaire Survey on Public Cancer Education Obtained from Cancer Patients and their Families." *Cancer* 10 (1957):382–384.

SIMINOFF, L.A., J.H. FETTING, and M.D. ABELOFF. "Doctor-Patient Communication about Breast Cancer Adjuvant Therapy." *Journal of Clinical Oncology* 7 (1989): 1192–1200.

TRAVIS, TERRY A., RUSSELL NOYES, JR., and DENNIS R. BRIGHTWELL. "The Attitudes of Physicians Toward Prolonging Life." *International Journal of Psychiatry in Medicine* 5 (No. 1, 1974):17–26.

VEATCH, ROBERT M., and ERNEST TAI. "Talking About Death: Patterns of Lay and Professional Change." *Annals of the American Academy of Political and Social Science* 447 (January 1980):29–45.

B. MORAL ARGUMENTS ABOUT TRUTH TELLING

BOK, SISSELA. *Lying: Moral Choice in Public and Private Life.* New York: Pantheon Books, 1978.

BRODY, HOWARD. *Placebos and the Philosophy of Medicine.* Chicago: University of Chicago Press, 1980.

BURNUM, JOHN F. "Secrets about Patients." *New England Journal of Medicine* 324 (April 18, 1991):1130–1133.

CABOT, RICHARD C. "The Use of Truth and Falsehood in Medicine," as edited by Jay Katz from the 1909 version. *Connecticut Medicine* 42 (1978):189–194.

HIGGS, ROGER. "On Telling Patients the Truth." In Beauchamp, Tom L., and Leroy Walters (eds.). *Contemporary Issues in Bioethics,* 4th ed. Belmont, CA: Wadsworth, 1994, pp. 137–142.

LUND, CHARLES C. "The Doctor, the Patient and the Truth." *Annals of Internal Medicine* 24 (1946):957–958.

PIATT, LOUIS M. "The Physician and the Cancer Patient." *Ohio State Medical Journal* 42 (1946):371–372.

QUILL, TIMOTHY E., and PENELOPE TOWNSEND, "Bad News: Delivery, Dialogue, and Dilemmas." In Beauchamp, Tom L., and LeRoy Walters (eds.). *Contemporary Issues in Bioethics,* 4th ed. Belmont, CA: Wadsworth, 1994, pp. 131–136.

SCHÖNE-SEIFERT, BETTINA, and CHILDRESS, JAMES F. "How Much Should the Patient Know and Decide?" *CA-A Cancer Journal for Clinicians* 36 (1986):85–94.

SIEGLER, MARK. "Pascal's Wager and the Hanging of Crepe." *New England Journal of Medicine* 293 (October 23, 1975):853–857.

VANDEVEER, DONALD. "The Contractual Argument for Withholding Medical Information." *Philosophy & Public Affairs* 9 (1980):198–205.

VEATCH, ROBERT M. "She'll be Happier if She Never Knows: The Patient's Right and Obligation to Have the Truth." *Death, Dying, and the Biological Revolution.* New Haven: Yale University Press, 1989, pp. 166–196.

VEATCH, ROBERT M. *Case Studies in Medical Ethics.* Cambridge, MA: Harvard University Press, 1977, Chapters 6 and 12.

WEIR, ROBERT. "Truthtelling in Medicine." *Perspectives in Biology and Medicine* 24 (Autumn 1980):95–112.

BIBLIOGRAPHICAL SOURCES AND REFERENCE WORKS

REICH, WARREN (ed.). *Encyclopedia of Bioethics.* New York: Macmillan, 1995, articles on:

Autonomy
Informed Consent
Mental Illness
Natural Law
Paternalism
Patients' Rights
Virtue and Character

3

Suicide

INTRODUCTION

Suicide is a major medical and social problem. It is the second-ranking cause of death among college students (after accidents) and the eighth-ranking cause of death in North America. The problem is worsening. The rate of suicide for adolescent and college-aged populations tripled between 1960 and 1995, and rates have increased dramatically for some types of seriously ill patients. For example, the suicide rate among AIDS patients is approximately 35 times the rate of the general population.[1]

The major objective of this chapter is to evaluate classical and contemporary assessments of the justifiability of both suicide and interventions to prevent suicide. Chapters 4 and 5 present moral and legal justifications of assisted suicide.

The Definition of Suicide

A person who aids, encourages, or counsels a suicide commits a felony in many legal jurisdictions. Whether a physician or a friend who helps a person die has helped a *suicide* is therefore a practical question of criminal behavior, not merely a distanced philosophical inquiry. But how do we know whether an act qualifies as suicide?

There are two primary reasons for conceptual uncertainty about the nature of suicide. First, social attitudes are commonly reflected in a culture's conception of suicide. If suicide is socially disapproved, the definition of "suicide" in that society may reflect this disapproval by eliminating the possibility that any permissible or praiseworthy action could count as a suicide. For example, if covering an exploding grenade with one's body in order to save others is regarded as praiseworthy, whereas suicide is disapproved, then a reason exists to believe that this sacrificial action is not suicidal. Nevertheless, if suicide is widely approved in a culture under some conditions, then actions that are risky and that may eventuate in death might be considered suicides. For example, a doctor who experimented on herself for the benefit of her patients knowing that the experiment could cause death, and who did die, might be classified a suicide.

A second reason for conceptual confusion arises from differing assessments of suicidal *motives*. Sacrificial acts and actions in response to serious illnesses are perhaps the most troublesome. For example, when a spy takes his life in order not to reveal secrets or when a patient terminates life-saving equipment attached to her body, we may be uncertain whether the acts constitute suicide, even if the acts clearly involve an *intentional* taking of life. In other cases of mixed motives we may be similarly perplexed. For example, when someone is playing Russian Roulette to win money and have a better life, but the gun fires and the person dies, is it a suicide or not?

Problems for many definitions of "suicide" are presented by refusal of treatment with the intent to die, sacrificial acts, martyrdom that could have been avoided, actions that risk near certain death or mutilation, addiction-induced overdoses, coercion to self-caused death, and the like. These conceptual problems are compounded by moral views and psychological theories about voluntariness and the rationality of suicide, as well as about the role of depression and delirium in causing the actions. Some definitions of "suicide" have tried to take account of these cases by not requiring suicidal intent, but only foreknowledge of death or the acceptance of a risk of death. These different definitions have led to disagreements over cases, for example, whether Socrates and Samson committed suicide. These problems, together with leading definitions of suicide, are discussed in the articles by Manuel Velasquez and Tom Beauchamp, who assess the leading standard definitions, offer alternatives of these definitions, and then criticize opponents' views.

Classical Problems in the Morality of Suicide

Next in this chapter we encounter two influential classical writers on suicide: the medieval philosophical theologian St. Thomas Aquinas (1224–1274) and the eighteenth-century Scottish philosopher David Hume (1711–1776). These two starkly different philosophies of suicide both use moral arguments about the permissibility and impermissibility of suicide that center on questions of whether suicide violates some fundamental obligation.

Attempts to answer these questions about moral permissibility usually appeal to one or more of three moral principles. The first is a principle of community responsibility: The suicide should consider not only his or her interests, but the interests of all affected. This principle does not demand that society's interests are always overriding. Rather it demands a weighing and balancing of considerations by the person contemplating suicide. The second is a principle of self-determination: The suicide is said to have the right to do whatever he wishes with his or her life, as long as the action does not seriously limit the rights of others. The third is a sanctity-of-life principle: The suicide is always wrong if he or she *intends* to take life, because the intentional taking of human life is always wrong. This third principle is sometimes also linked to obligations to God, who gives the gift of life.

Different reasons for invoking one or the other of these principles are found in the articles by Aquinas and Hume. Hume's arguments rely on premises about the right to self-determination and on an account of community obligations. He urges us to balance a variety of interests in assessing the morality of suicide. An autonomous suicide, from Hume's perspective, is permissible (and on occasion laudable) if, on balance, more value is produced for the individual or more value is produced for society than would be produced by not performing the act of taking one's life. Aquinas's arguments rely on premises about obligations to God and community and also call on related views about the sanctity of life. Hume's essay is not expressly organized as a point-by-point reply to Aquinas, but he does present arguments against each of the major Thomistic arguments. Hume's utilitarian and libertine arguments in defense of the moral acceptability of some acts of suicide have long been thought to provide important counterexamples to the claims Aquinas makes about duty to God and community and about the sanctity of life.

Prevention, Intervention, and Control of Suicide

Many potential suicides have been thwarted by strategies such as reporting suicide threats, suicide hotlines, getting persons into treatment, and the like. It is widely believed that obligations to prevent suicide override a person's right to commit suicide, a view reflected in contemporary law. For example, part of the rationale for the use of police powers for the emergency detention and civil commitment of suicides rests on this principle. This rationale is sometimes defended by appeal to the fact that fewer than 5 percent of persons who attempt suicide actually kill themselves within a 5-year period after the date of the attempted suicide, and that only roughly 10 percent of those who *attempt* suicide ever take their lives. Courts have therefore often held that the state can justifiably protect persons against attempted suicide.

But if we must respect the autonomy of those who choose to take their lives, is there not a *right* to commit suicide? Perhaps in devising preventive strategies and in intervening to stop suicides we act beneficently, but nonetheless violate the rights of persons. In the case of almost any similarly intrusive, liberty-limiting action, the person impeded could successfully sue those who intervene. A physician, for example, could be sued on grounds of malpractice for a similarly coercive treatment of patients.

But are these suicidal persons truly autonomous? Physicians and state officials often take the view that persons who attempt to commit suicide are under the strain of a temporary crisis, under the influence of drugs or alcohol, or beset with considerable ambivalence. Those who defend rights of autonomy to commit suicide do not deny this claim for many suicides; they hold that interference with persons of this description is appropriate, because they regard these suicidal actions as *non*autonomous. Accordingly, almost everyone agrees that suicide reporting, prevention, and intervention are justified in many instances in order to determine if a serious defect, encumbrance, misunderstanding, or mental constraint affects the person.

Nonetheless, once we get beyond this basic consensus many controversies appear. Many claims about reporting, preventing, or intervening in suicide are paternalistic toward autonomous persons as well as toward those with reduced or impaired autonomy, and these paternalistic views are particularly controversial. The term *paternalism* here refers to practices that restrict the autonomy of individuals without their consent in order to prevent some harm they might do to themselves or to produce some benefit for them they would not otherwise secure. It is vital to proper use of the term that the person's autonomy is limited. It is not paternalistic, for example, to put seriously injured and delirious persons in an ambulance and send them to the emergency room.

A supporter of a *general* paternalistic principle used to justify suicide intervention should carefully specify precisely which goods, needs, and interests warrant paternalistic protection for a person who has threatened suicide. In recent defenses of paternalism, several writers have maintained that such intervention with a person's liberty is justified if the person is protected against his or her (1) extremely and unreasonably risky actions, or (2) actions that are not in the person's known best interest, or (3) actions that are potentially both ruinous and irreversible in effect. Many acts of suicide fit one of these categories, and therefore those attracted to this form of paternalism believe that intervention would be justified in these cases.

Antipaternalism, rooted as it is in the principle of respect for autonomy, holds that it is legitimate to remonstrate with, to counsel, and to use other noncoercive measures to attempt to persuade the suicidal person not to perform the contemplated action, especially when that person approaches a friend or physician for help. It is also appropriate to arrange for counseling and health care that offer an opportunity for the person to reconsider a decision that may have been hasty. These are expressions of care and respect, and may engender a form of trust that will lead to a worthwhile reconsideration.

However, in other cases the antipaternalist believes that it is appropriate to step aside and allow persons to commit suicide and even to counsel or assist persons who are planning suicide (on this topic, see Chapter 4). Joel Feinberg presents some antipaternalistic arguments in this chapter, offering reasons against intervening to prevent rational suicides even with those who are not terminally ill. These arguments rest on the premise that one ought not to interfere with the free acts of sovereign persons if those actions do not harm persons other than the actors.

The major disagreement between paternalists and antipaternalists arises over cases in which the suicidal person is capable of deliberating and choosing a course of action, but at the same time is influenced in these deliberations by factors such as terminal illness and serious depression. The place of paternalism in such cases (if any) remains a matter of controversy. Paternalists contend that on at least some occasions we are morally obliged to intervene to prevent rational persons from doing harm to themselves. They think that we do not exhibit adequate moral concern about others unless we attempt to prevent or intervene. In this chapter, both Kate E. Bloch and Erwin Ringel offer vigorous defenses of forms of prevention and intervention. Bloch even envisions a legal duty to report suicide threats.

Although in today's psychiatry the person who commits suicide is no longer diagnosed by competent investigators as psychotic on the basis of the act of suicide alone, lively debates occur about the possibility of making a rational decision to commit suicide. On available theories of compulsion, the degree to which a given act of suicide is voluntary is usually difficult to evaluate. A typical example is found in students under academic pressure whose self-esteem has been shattered. These young people feel abandoned by old friends; their depression is penetrating, their adjustments in life radical. Many come to believe that their lives are behind them and no longer worth living, as do many others who must similarly adjust to tragedy and a radical new lifestyle. Suicide becomes attractive if they come to believe there is nothing left to live for.

Feinberg argues that suicide can be rational, or at least reasonable, even if a person is seriously ill or injured. However, many psychiatric and legal authorities believe that this view underestimates how suicides result from maladaptive attitudes that can only be handled if persons receive professional therapeutic attention. A version of this view is presented by Ringel. No party to these controversies doubts that we should intervene to prevent suicide attempts by incompetent persons. But if we accept an unrestricted, free-choice principle, the imprudent but competent suicide who would want to live under more favorable circumstances could not legitimately be prevented from committing suicide. Law, medicine, and philosophy continue to struggle with issues about the extent to which paternalism is justified in such cases, if it is.

NOTE

1. Peter M. Marzuk, et al. "Increased Risk of Suicide in Persons with AIDS," *Journal of the American Medical Association* 259 (March 4, 1988):1333–1337.

THE DEFINITION OF "SUICIDE"

Defining Suicide*

MANUEL G. VELASQUEZ

In the first selection in this chapter, Manuel Velasquez addresses the question, "What is suicide?" After a brief examination of the historical background of this problem, he argues that proper characterizations of suicidal intention and causation are essential to an adequate definition. He maintains that suicide occurs if a person intentionally causes his or her own death, either by an action or omission, for the purpose of bringing about death and by using the means to death that the person intended. In defense of this approach, and while objecting to the definition offered by Tom Beauchamp in the second selection in this chapter, Velasquez claims that death under the coercion of another person can be a suicide. For example, according to Velasquez, a person coerced by the threat of blackmail can properly be said to have committed suicide.

A growing number of courts are authorizing the withdrawal or withholding of nutrition and hydration from patients with nonterminal conditions.[1] The complex issues raised by these rulings and the legal and ethical implications involved have aroused concern and generated intense debate. Some of these court decisions have been interpreted by some as authorizations of suicide.[2] Others, however, have maintained that these cases need not be construed as suicide.[3] These debates have raised the question: *What is suicide?* . . .

HISTORICAL PERSPECTIVE

According to the *Oxford English Dictionary,* the word "suicide" is derived from the Latin word *"suicidium,"* meaning "to kill oneself," and was first used in 1651. Prior to the seventeenth century, the English terms for suicide included self-homicide, self-destruction, self-slaughter, and self-murder. These terms, in contrast to other terms of Semitic Indo-European origin, describe suicide as a kind of killing, rather than a mode of dying. In ancient Greece, for example, phrases used to convey the concept of suicide included "to grasp death," "to die voluntarily," and "to die by one's own hand." . . .

The influence of social attitudes toward suicide extends beyond its influence on the choice of terms used to denote it. The meaning imported to the term is also nuanced

*Source: Manuel G. Velasquez, "Defining Suicide," in *Issues in Law & Medicine,* Vol. 3 (1987), pp. 37–51.

by prevailing attitudes toward suicide. Consequently, a first step toward defining suicide would seem to require attention to contemporary attitudes toward suicide, which, in turn, necessitates an examination of the historical context from which they arose.

Public policy is one of the means through which a society translates its values and applies them to human conduct. In the United States today, public policy condemns suicide. It has been suggested that the condemnation of suicide which has characterized many Western societies can be traced to taboos associated with shedding blood and to an instinctive "fear of the ghost" in "primitive" cultures, . . .

CURRENT PHILOSOPHICAL DEBATE

Not surprisingly, then, a large number of philosophers have once again begun to address the problem of defining suicide and to discuss its morality. The definitions that appear in the literature they have produced range from broad definitions of suicide to narrow definitions. Broad definitions allow any act of self-destruction to count as suicide, as long as the act meets a very few minimal conditions. Broad definitions do not exclude much. Narrow definitions, on the other hand, place several additional restrictions on what counts as suicide. Because narrow definitions place several conditions on what counts as suicide, they restrict the term to a smaller range of candidates.

The most well-known broad definitions of suicide are those that are inspired by the work of Emile Durkeim. Durkeim defined suicide as any act that brings about the agent's own death, provided *only* that the agent knew the act would bring about his death. A suicide, he writes, is any "death resulting directly or indirectly from a positive or negative act of the victim himself, which he knows will produce this result." Thus, the only crucial requirement for suicide is knowledge of the result. Any self-destructive act counts as suicide so long as the agent had knowledge that the act would be self-destructive. . . .

A [relevant] moral premise seems to underlie . . . [a] definition recently advanced by Tom Beauchamp. Beauchamp notes that, when a person is forced or coerced into taking his life, it commonly is not classified as suicide. For example, Beauchamp argues, many do not say that Socrates committed suicide when he was forced to drink the hemlock in prison.[4] Consequently, Beauchamp's characterization of suicide is designed to exclude death by coercion. Although Beauchamp is unclear on this point, his reason for excluding deaths by coercion seems to be that such deaths are not blameworthy and so should not count as suicides.

Beauchamp also notes that, when a person's death is the result of a terminal disease that the person fails to treat, it also commonly is not classified as suicide. Take, for example, a person who is suffering from cancer who refuses to undergo any treatment, knowing death will result. Such is classified as a death from natural causes and not as suicide. Beauchamp's characterization of suicide excludes death that results from a condition, such as a disease, that the agent did not arrange as a means of death. Here, again, what seems to be operating is the moral intuition that, since it is not blameworthy to permit one's death from natural causes, such a death should not be counted as suicide. At any rate, Beauchamp's somewhat complicated definition of suicide is as follows: "An act is a suicide if a person brings about his or her own death

(1) in circumstances where others do not coerce him or her to the action, (2) except in those cases where death is caused by conditions not specifically arranged by the agent for the purpose of bringing about his or her own death."5 The first condition excludes death by coercion, while the second excludes death from an untreated terminal disease or mortal injury.

There is yet a third narrow definition of suicide that is influenced by the desire to exclude deaths that are not morally blameworthy. This third definition takes into account the fact that many self-destructive people are not rational because they are undergoing severe psychological disturbances. Germain Grisez and Joseph Boyle, Jr., have suggested that, when a nonrational person brings about his death, the death is not to be counted as suicide.6 Apparently underlying this approach, again, is the idea that self-destructive acts should be counted as suicides only if they are morally blameworthy. Since the acts of a nonrational person are not morally blameworthy, they should not be counted as suicide.

Each of these . . . definitions, unfortunately, fails to provide an adequate characterization of suicide. By excluding what is not morally blameworthy, they exclude too much. Consider . . . Margolis' view that killing oneself for an altruistic purpose is not suicide. Clearly this view is mistaken. If a man kills himself so that his impoverished family can collect the insurance, many would say that he committed suicide. The fact that he has a further purpose in taking his life does not mean that his act is not suicide. Second, consider Beauchamp's view that death resulting from coercion is not suicide. This claim, too, seems mistaken. A person who is coerced into self-destruction by the threat of blackmail will be said to have committed suicide.

Or, consider Beauchamp's view that, when a person's death is caused by some condition not specifically arranged for that purpose, the death is not a suicide. Imagine a skier who is racing down a mountain and has decided to commit suicide. Ahead, the skier sees an avalanche. If he stops, he can avoid the avalanche, but, instead, the skier seizes the chance and continues skiing down into the path of the avalanche. It seems appropriate to describe the skier as having committed suicide. Yet, because the avalanche was not "arranged" by the agent for the purpose of committing suicide, Beauchamp's definition would refuse to count it as suicide. Lastly, consider the view of Grisez that a nonrational person cannot commit suicide. If Grisez were right, then it would sound contradictory to describe some suicides as irrational suicides or as nonrational suicides. But, in fact, when persons who are mentally ill intentionally kill themselves, many say that they committed suicide. Nonrational suicides are still suicides.

Each of these narrow characterizations of suicide, then, are failures. Nevertheless, the attempts are instructive. Each characterization alerts us to some important questions that an adequate definition of suicide must address. First, why is it that some altruistically motivated self-killings are not counted as suicides? The soldier who throws himself on a grenade to save his companions is not said to have committed suicide. Second, why is it that some coerced self-killings are not counted as suicides? Most would agree that Socrates, who was forced to drink the hemlock, did not commit suicide. Third, why is it that the person who dies as a result of refusing to treat a deadly disease usually is not said to have committed suicide? And fourth, why is it that there is a reluctance to classify nonrational self-killing as suicide?

One might be tempted to try to answer these questions by simply pointing to a feature common to all of them: each refers to a class of self-killings which is not morally blameworthy. Thus, suicide could be defined as intentional self-killing that is morally blameworthy. There are three reasons for not pursuing this suggestion. First, such a definition would preclude discussion of the question whether suicide is ever morally permissible. Suicide, by definition, would be a morally blameworthy act. Second, such a definition would be wrong. Some acts of self-destruction are clearly acts of suicide, yet, one can argue that they are not morally blameworthy. For example, the persons who are mentally ill, who are not responsible for their actions, would not be said to have committed suicide should they kill themselves. Or, consider the example of the sick explorer whose illness is slowing down the rest of his party so that they are all in danger of dying since the others refuse to leave him behind. To save their lives, the sick explorer shoots himself, allowing them to hurry on without him and thus save their lives. He clearly committed suicide. But his act of suicide, one can argue, was heroic and not morally blameworthy. Thus, it would be a mistake to define suicide as the morally blameworthy act of killing oneself. Third, and most importantly, the cases that Margolis, Beauchamp, Grisez, and others want to exclude from the category of suicide should be excluded *not* because they are not blameworthy. Rather, they should be excluded because of the kind of *agency* or mental state that each case involves.

How, then, is suicide to be defined? The author proposes a characterization of suicide that answers the questions that have been raised. The proposed definition has two main components similar to the two main elements of the traditional legal definition of suicide: the element of intention and that of causation. The two-part definition will allow us to deal with many of those problems that the narrow definitions have tried to address, while incorporating the factors that the broad definitions emphasized. Suicide, then, can be characterized best as follows:

> Suicide is the act of bringing about a person's death, provided that: (1) death is brought about by that person's own acts or omissions, and (2) those acts or omissions are (a) intentionally carried out (b) for the purpose of bringing about death (c) by those concretely particular means that actually brought death about.

Let me explain now the rationale for advancing this definition. First, it provides a morally neutral definition of suicide. Given this definition, suicide might turn out to be an immoral or a moral act. In this respect the definition achieves one of the aims of the broad definitions: moral neutrality.

Second, the definition is designed to retain the idea that the person who commits suicide had to know or believe that his act would result in his death. This is part of what is meant by saying that the act that brings about death must be carried out for that purpose intentionally. Intention implies knowledge or belief that one's acts will have the intended effects.

Third, the definition is intended to capture the kernel of truth in the notion that a person who is forced to self-destruction, or a person who dies from a disease, usually is not considered to have committed suicide. As the definition makes clear, suicide requires that death be brought about by the person's own acts. To the extent, therefore, that a death is felt to have resulted from something other than the person's own agency, the death would not be classified as suicide. When one person forces another to act, the real agency is attributed to the person who exerts the force. For this reason, therefore, when a person's self-killing is perceived as being the result of force or coercion, the self-killing is attributed to an agency other than the person and, therefore, the act is not classified as suicide. For a similar reason, when a death is perceived as being the result of a disease, it is not seen as suicide because the death is attributed to the agency of the disease and not of the person. Suicide requires that persons be seen as the agents of their own death.

Fourth, the definition is intended to explain why there is sometimes a reluctance to classify the self-inflicted death of a person who is mentally disturbed as suicide. To the extent that an act is felt to have been caused by a mental affliction and to the extent that a person is felt not to be in control of himself or herself, to that extent there is reluctance to attribute genuine agency to that person. From this reluctance stems the reluctance to classify a person's self-inflicted death as suicide when the person is mentally ill. But that reluctance is only partial, there is also an intuition that even the acts of a person who is mentally ill are his own acts. To the extent that this intuition prevails, the self-inflicted death of a person who is mentally ill may be classified as suicide.

Fifth, the definition is intended to explain why some altruistically motivated self-killings may not be classified as suicides, while others are. When persons act or fail to act, knowing that their act or failure to act will result in death, they may or may not be aiming at death by their actions or omissions. The definition of suicide requires that one's actions be carried out for the purpose of bringing about death either as an end or as a means. The soldier who throws himself on the live grenade to save his companions, for example, is not aiming at death. That is, he does not intentionally jump on the grenade for the purpose of bringing about his death, but rather for the purpose of saving his companions. This is clear if one considers that, if he lives and his companions are saved, then he would have achieved his purpose without dying. For this reason, his act is not counted as suicide. On the other hand, consider the man who kills himself so his family can enjoy the proceeds from his life insurance. Clearly, he intentionally carries out his actions for the purpose of bringing about death. He is aiming at his death, albeit as a means to another end: if he lives, he would have failed in his purpose since, without his death, no inheritance will be forthcoming.

Sixth, the definition is also intended to deal with a little knot of technical problems that are raised by what are called "deviant causal chains."7 Consider the man who intends to kill himself by running out into a street of speeding cars. As he runs out into the street, however, he steps into the path of a bullet from the gun of a boy shooting at tin cans in an empty lot across the street. Here death is brought about by the man's own acts which were carried out for the purpose of bringing about his death, but the death did not occur quite by those means he intended it to occur. For that reason, we do not classify the death as suicide, but as accidental. Death was the result of (what philosophers call) a "deviant causal chain," and not by the intended means. If a person's death is to count as suicide, then, the particular concrete means that actually bring the death about must be those by which one was intentionally acting to bring death about. This match between actual means and intended means does not have to be exact: the means that actually bring death about need merely be reasonably close to the intended means. For example, if a person intends to kill himself with a shot in the head, but nervously shakes the gun so much that the person shoots himself in the heart instead, then, this is close enough to what the person intended to qualify the death as suicide.

Finally, the definition is intended to retain and explain some of the ambiguities that our concept of suicide carries with it. Sometimes, there is an uncertainty as to whether something should be called suicide. The definition identifies several sources of uncertainty. That uncertainty may be related to the inability to identify the agent of death. Thus, there is an uncertainty about element 1. Sometimes it is unclear whether the person's actions are intentional or accidental. Thus, there is an uncertainty about element 2(a). Sometimes it is difficult to discern the person's purpose for carrying out the act that resulted in death, thus there is an uncertainty about element 2(b). Finally, there may be uncertainty about whether the particular concrete means that actually brought death about were those by which death was intentionally being brought about. We are then unsure about element 2(c).

Given the proposed definition, it may appear that assisted suicide is a contradiction in terms. If one is assisted in killing oneself, then one's death seemingly is not brought about by one's own acts and so it does not appear to qualify as suicide. This appearance, however, is mistaken.

People can bring about their own deaths in many different ways. One way is by getting others to do their bidding. In assisted suicide, a person brings about death by getting others to act. Thus, an assisted suicide is indeed a death that is brought about by that person's own acts. The death is brought about by the person's own acts of bidding others to kill or to help kill.

Thus, this definition is perfectly adequate to serve as the basis for a discussion of assisted suicide, as indeed it was designed to be. But the definition is intended to do more than serve as a mere dictionary definition of a term. It is also intended to suggest how other pertinent concepts might relate to suicide in general and to assisted suicide in particular.

NOTES

1. See, e.g., *Bouvia v. Superior Court* (Glenchur), 225 Cal. Rptr. 297 (Cal. App. 2 Dist. 1986); *Corbett v. D'Alessandro,* 487 So. 2d 368 (Fla. App. 2 Dist. 1986); In re Jobes, 510 A. 2d 133 (N.J. Super. Ct. Ch. Div. 1986); *Brophy v. New England Sinai Hospital, Inc.,* 497 N.E. 2d 626 (Mass. 1986); In re Conroy, 486 A. 2d 1209 (N.J. 1985).
2. See, e.g., Dyck, *A Commentary on Brophy v. New England Sinai Hospital,* 2 BIOLAW U:172–74 (1986); Note, *Elizabeth Bouvia v. County of Riverside: Riverside General Hospital,* 1–2 BIOETHICS REP. 460–461 (1984); Kane, *Keeping Elizabeth Bouvia Alive for the Public Good,* 15 HASTINGS CENTER REP. 5–8 (Dec. 1985); Annas, *When Suicide Prevention Becomes Brutality: The Case of Elizabeth Bouvia,* 14 HASTINGS CENTER REP. 20–21, 46 (April 1984).

3. See, e.g., *Brophy,* 497 N.E. 2d at 626, 638; *Conroy,* 486 A. 2d at 1209–1210; O'Rourke, *The A.M.A. Statement on Tube Feeding: An Ethical Analysis,* 155 AMERICA 321–323, 331 (1986); Annas, *Elizabeth Bouvia: Who Should Prevail?,* 15 HASTINGS CENTER REP. 50 (April 1985).

4. The question of whether Socrates should be said to have committed suicide has been extensively discussed. *See* Frey, *Did Socrates Commit Suicide?,* 53 PHIL. 106–108 (1978); Smith, *Did Socrates Kill Himself Intentionally?,* 55 PHIL. 253–254 (1980); Walton, *"Socrates" Alleged Suicide,* 14 J. VALUE INQUIRY 287–299 (1980).

5. Tom Beauchamp, "Suicide," in MATTERS OF LIFE AND DEATH 77 (T. Regan ed. 1980).

6. G. Grisez and J. Boyle, LIFE AND DEATH WITH LIBERTY AND JUSTICE 407–412 (1979).

7. These problems are broadly discussed but not adequately resolved in Tolhurst, "Suicide, Self-Sacrifice and Coercion," 21 S. J. PHILOSOPHY 109–122 (1983).

The Problem of Defining Suicide

TOM L. BEAUCHAMP

In the following selection Tom L. Beauchamp argues that the term "suicide" is not amenable to simple definitional analysis because of several types of cases that we tend to view as not being suicidal acts. After treating cases of death by refusal of treatment and sacrificial deaths, Beauchamp formally defines suicide in terms of an intended, noncoerced death in circumstances in which an agent plays a role in arranging a situation so that death will occur. Beauchamp works primarily from the ordinary-language concept of suicide, but he notes that in ordinary language the act of suicide is tainted by a negative connotation of wrongfulness that we should try to set aside when doing moral analysis. Beauchamp also responds to Velasquez's criticisms—claiming that Velasquez's analysis misunderstands blackmail, likely misunderstands coercion, and certainly misunderstands Beauchamp's definition.

A death is commonly considered a suicide if it is an intentionally caused self-destruction. However, problems are presented by refusals of treatment with the intent to die, sacrificial deaths, and the like. Many problems about whether a death is a suicide result from incomplete evidence about a person's intentions and the role of those intentions in a circumstance in which the person died. We, therefore, should be prepared to encounter borderline cases of suicide and to find that it is an untidy concept.

STANDARD DEFINITIONS OF SUICIDE

Three general types of definition of suicide have been popular. The first, which might be called the *intentional-death definition,* is straightforward: Suicide occurs if and only if there is an intentional termination of one's life. Case law and several contemporary moral philosophers have used this definition. The second definition, by contrast, does not require a specific intent to terminate life. It has been used by courts in a few isolated legal cases, but its main influence has come from sociologist Emile Durkheim: "The term suicide is applied to all cases of death resulting directly or indirectly from a positive or negative act of the victim himself, which he knows will produce this result."[1] This *foreknowledge definition*—like the first definition—requires foreknowledge of death, but not an intention to produce death. The third definition is still broader and has fittingly been called *the omnibus definition:* Suicide occurs when an individual engages in a life-style that he knows might kill him (other than living another day)—and it does [kill him]."[2]

The primary problem with both the foreknowledge and the omnibus definitions is that they are too broad, allowing actions to be classified as suicides that should not be so classified. The third is far too broad: Those who frequently engage in waterfall rafting, hang gliding, police bomb-squad work, mountain diving (into

113

oceans), and space explorations of an adventuresome sort—and who die as a result of these activities—are suicides under this definition. Smokers, drug addicts, excessively fast drivers, and those who voluntarily serve in a dangerous division of the armed services and die as a result would similarly be suicides. Moreover, the definition fails to preserve the distinction between accidental death and suicide in cases in which high risks are commonly taken—for example, the risks taken by terrorists in hijacking airplanes, martyrs and ascetics who inflict intense privations on themselves and die, and military commanders who lead life-endangering charges into battle. Accordingly, the omnibus definition seems to require too much of a change in our ordinary notion of suicide, and for insufficient reasons.

Durkheim's foreknowledge definition is also too broad, as can be illustrated by the problem of the soldier who throws himself on a grenade in a sacrificial attempt to save his friends. He knows the act will bring about his death, so under the foreknowledge definition he is a suicide. Even the soldier who jumps from a trench in a hail of gunfire at his lieutenant's command knowing that he will die is a suicide under this definition. Similarly, a woman who resists a man's attempted rape with the knowledge that his threat to kill her will be carried out if she refuses is a suicide on Durkheim's definition, an absurd outcome.

Both the foreknowledge and the omnibus definitions suffer from a common defect: They overlook the difference between a suicide and what is sometimes loosely called suicidal conduct.

A problem with the intentional death and the foreknowledge definitions is that they omit all mention of the precise nature of the motivation, intention, or knowledge involved in a suicide. I agree that suicide must be an *intentional* self-killing, but more needs to be said both about what can or must cause the action and precisely what can or must be intended. Consider a captured soldier who, given the choice by an enemy of being executed or of executing himself, chooses self-execution. Because coercion to death underlies this self-killing, I am reluctant to classify the act as a suicide. The reason we exclude death by coercion from the category of suicide is that a coerced person does not act autonomously. Rather, the will of another deprives the person of autonomy. The act is intended, but not freely intended.

SHOULD CASES OF REFUSAL OF TREATMENT BE EXCLUDED?

Physicians and nurses have long worried that when they stop treatment and a patient dies, they will be accused of killing the patient. There has been a parallel concern that patients who withdraw from or forego treatment are killing themselves and that health professionals are assisting in the suicide. When death occurs by the patient's withdrawing from or withholding treatment, these acts *can* be suicides, because *any* means productive of death can be arranged to the end of killing oneself. This is so even if death is inevitable or the cause of death is natural. Pulling the plug on one's respirator is not relevantly different from plunging a knife into one's heart, if the conditions and the reason for putting an end to life are relevantly similar. Suicidal intent may occur in any circumstance of refusal of treatment.

Three features of such situations need to be distinguished:

1. whether *death is intended* by the agent;
2. whether an *active cause* of death is arranged by the agent;
3. whether a *nonfatal condition* is present (no terminal disease or mortal injury exists).

The closer we are to an unmistakable action that involves an *intentionally self-caused death* using an *active* means where there is a *nonfatal* condition, the more inclined we are to classify the act as a suicide; but the more these conditions are peeled away, the less inclined we are to classify the acts as suicides. For example, if a nonmortally wounded soldier in pain turns his rifle on himself and intentionally brings about his death, the act is a suicide. But what are we to say about the terminally ill patient who is ambivalent about whether he wishes to die, and refuses yet another blood transfusion knowing that death will ensue?

A passively allowed, natural death is typically excluded from the notion of suicide, but not all such naturally caused deaths can be eliminated from consideration as suicides, because of the agent's intention and causal role. The person might be using a passive means (for example, failing to take requisite drugs) as a socially acceptable and convenient way of ending it all. People who so intend to end their lives cannot be excluded as suicides merely because they select a passive means to this end. Given this mixture of elements, the following is an attractive hypothesis: An act is *not* a suicide if the person who dies suffers from a terminal disease or from a mortal injury that, by refusal of treatment, he or she allows to cause death. If the person intends to die and in refusing treatment arranges this outcome when the condition is treatable, the behavior does amount to suicide.

The precise causal role the agent plays in these cases is important, because it determines whether decisions made by the person who died were the relevant cause of death or whether some other cause was responsible. Suicide requires self-inflicted death, whereas in *pure* treatment-refusal cases death is disease inflicted or injury inflicted. The reason why in some refusal of treatment cases we categorize the death as suicide is that injury or disease is not the real cause, but rather a kind of manufactured cause used as a way to perform suicide. If, for example, a man is seriously burned but could by conventional treatment be restored to health, and if he refuses treatment because he prefers dying to living with such disfigurement, then this is a suicide despite its connection to refusal of treatment. We accept preexisting conditions such as disease and injury to be the relevant cause of death only if they are *not treatable* or *not controllable* so as to allow the person to go on living.

Clearly intention, not merely causation, plays a major role in our judgment. The more a person lacks a specific intention to cause death, and has only an intention such as relieving suffering, ending agony, or trying to live without dependence on a machine, the less are we inclined to classify the action as suicide. But the more the specific intent to cause death rises to the surface, the more we move in the direction of suicide. Thus far, then, the notion of suicide seems to require the conditions earlier mentioned (intended death and noncoercion), and *in addition* some form of causal arranging that exceeds mere refusal of treatment.

SHOULD CASES OF SELF-SACRIFICE BE EXCLUDED?

There remains the problem of whether altruistically motivated self-caused death should be excluded as suicide and, if so, which altruistic acts are excluded. Perhaps intentional self-sacrifice is excluded as suicide because the action has, from the suicide's point of view, plausible claim to justification for *other-regarding,* not *self-regarding,* reasons. We may not regard these acts as *actually* justified, but we can frame them as justified from the point of view of the agent. However, we need to be cautious with this claim, because a person with sacrificial intent may also have suicidal intent.

People who act from self-sacrificial motives are suicides if they intentionally arrange the life-threatening conditions that cause their deaths *for the purpose of bringing about death* (whether this purpose be primary or not). Because the monk who kills himself in protesting a war arranges the conditions, precisely for this purpose, he is a suicide, whereas because the soldier falling on the grenade does not hurl his body over the grenade for this purpose (of ending it all), he is *not* a suicide.

A good test case for my analysis is the classic case of Captain Oates, who walked into the Antarctic snow to die because he was suffering from an illness that hindered the progress of a party attempting to make its way out of a severe blizzard. According to the contemporary English philosopher R. F. Holland, Oates was not a suicide because: "in Oates's case I can say, 'No [he didn't kill himself]; the blizzard killed him.' Had Oates taken out a revolver and shot himself I should have agreed he was a suicide."[3] In contrast, I believe that Oates's heroic sacrifice is plausibly a suicide because of the active steps that he took to bring about his death. Although the fierce climatic conditions proximately caused his death, he knowingly and willingly brought about the relevant life-threatening condition causing his death with the intention that he die.

A FINAL DEFINITION OF SUICIDE

I can now formulate a definition of suicide:

An act or omission is a suicide if a person intentionally brings about his or her death, unless the death (a) is coerced or (b) is caused by conditions that are not specifically arranged by the agent for the purpose of bringing about the death.

Under this definition, a person must believe the act will result in self-caused death, and the death must occur in accordance with the agent's plan to produce his or her death. It is not suicide if disease or injury has not been arranged to be the cause, or if the person does not believe death will be caused by the action, or if death occurs in a way other than in accordance with the final plan selected by the agent.

My definition has several advantages over competing definitions. First, the definition is consistent with a long legal (and I think ordinary-language) tradition of determining when persons are or are not suicides by reference to their intentions. Second, the definition does not prejudge the morality of suicide. Unlike categories such as self-murder, this definition is morally neutral, and does not contain as a part of its *meaning* whether suicide is to be morally commended or condemned. Third, the definition takes account of our reluctance to categorize certain forms of coercion and treatment refusal as suicides.

Whatever the advantages of my definition, Manny Velasquez has objected to it, and I need to confront his objections. He writes as follows: "Beauchamp's view that death resulting from coercion is not suicide . . . seems mistaken. A person who is coerced into self-destruction by the threat of blackmail will be said to have committed suicide." This claim may misunderstand blackmail, likely misunderstands coercion, and certainly misunderstands my definition. *Blackmail* occurs only by extortion of money through a threat, not extortion of life, so Velasquez may be working with a faulty counterexample. Nonetheless, suppose there was an attempted blackmail, by, say, a threat of loss of reputation, and the person threatened *chose* self-caused death rather than the payment of money demanded (or after a revelation of corrupt activities). In this circumstance, the act is not a case of coercion to self-caused death and is a suicide on my definition.

Perhaps Velasquez is thinking of a circumstance in which one person coerces another person to suicide by threatening blackmail if he does not commit suicide. If the threat is credible, and such that the threatened person cannot reasonably resist the threat, which is required for coercion, then we do have a bona fide situation involving coercion to self-caused death, and the death is not a suicide. This case seems to me no different than the following: If a man threatens me with unbearable and prolonged torture that will eventuate in my dying unless I take a painless drug that will kill me, I am no more a suicide if I take the pill than if he forces the pill down my throat or if I do nothing and he tortures me to death. Similarly, the woman who kills herself under the credible threat of death to her children unless she kills herself does not commit suicide, in my view, any more than Socrates did. She does not freely aim at death; rather, under menace she takes the only course she has to save her children. In all these cases the person is deprived of autonomy because of the coercion. Velasquez's analysis would force us to the unacceptable conclusion that coerced acts are not merely intentional but also autonomous. Since Velasquez agrees with me that Socrates did not commit suicide, there seems to be an incoherence in his analysis unless he too accepts this conclusion.[4]

It is, however, difficult to capture precisely which intention is required for suicide, and what the right excluding conditions are. Suicide is an ill-ordered concept, and the linguistic intuitions of indigenous users of the language are inadequate to correct it. As we have seen, there are clear cases of suicide, clear cases of what is not suicide, and many cases where native speakers of the language find it difficult to reach a clear judgment. My definition does not eliminate all problems of imprecise boundaries. All one can ask from such an analysis is that most users of the language will find the definition congenial to the mainstream of their linguistic intuitions.

NOTES

1.   Emile Durkheim. *Suicide: A Study in Sociology,* translated by John A. Spaulding and George Simpson. New York: Free Press, 1966, p. 44.

2. Ronald Maris. "Sociology." In S. Perlin (ed.). *A Handbook for the Study of Suicide.* New York: Oxford University Press, 1975, p. 100.
3. R.F. Holland. "Suicide." In J. Rachels (ed.). *Moral Problems.* New York: Harper & Row, 1971, pp. 352–353.
4. Manuel G. Velasquez. "Defining Suicide." *Issues in Law and Medicine* 3 (1987): 48–49; this volume pp. 106–12.

CLASSICAL PROBLEMS IN THE MORALITY OF SUICIDE

Whether It Is Lawful to Kill Oneself*

ST. THOMAS AQUINAS

In the following selection, St. Thomas Aquinas discusses the morality of suicide. He claims that suicide is an offense against self, an offense against society, and a violation of God's sovereignty. It is therefore, "altogether unlawful to kill one-self." People belong to God, who is their creator; and suicide is, for that reason, analogous to theft: "Because life is God's gift to man . . . whoever takes his own life sins against God, even as he who kills another's slave, sins against that slave's master. . . . " Although Aquinas appeals to some statements in the Bible as au-thoritative, the core of his argument seems to be that suicide runs counter to the creator's general interest in human life and its flourishing. Aquinas defends an absolute prohibition of suicide, unless it is directly commanded by God.

Fifth Article

Objection 1. It would seem lawful for a man to kill himself. For murder is a sin insofar as it is contrary to justice. But no man can do an injustice to himself, as is proved in *Ethic*. v. 11. Therefore no man sins by killing himself.

Obj. 2. Further, it is lawful, for one who exercises public authority, to kill evildoers. Now he who exercises public authority is sometimes an evildoer. There-fore he may lawfully kill himself.

Obj. 3. Further, it is lawful for a man to suffer spontaneously a lesser dan-ger that he may avoid a greater: thus it is lawful for a man to cut off a decayed limb even from himself, that he may save his whole body. Now sometimes a man, by killing himself, avoids a greater evil, for example an unhappy life, or the shame of sin. Therefore a man may kill himself.

Obj. 4. Further, Samson killed himself, as related to Judges xvi., and yet he is numbered among the saints (Heb. xi). Therefore it is lawful for a man to kill himself.

Obj. 5. Further, it is related (2 Mach. xiv. 42) that a certain Razias killed himself, *choosing to die nobly rather than to fall into the hands of the wicked, and to*

*Source: From *Summa Theologica* (1925 trans.). Copyright 1947, Part II-II, Q, 64, Art. 5. Reprinted by permission of Benziger Brothers.

suffer abuses unbecoming his noble birth. Now nothing that is done nobly and bravely is unlawful. Therefore suicide is not unlawful.

On the contrary, Augustine says (*De Civ. Dei* i. 20): *Hence it follows that the words "Thou shalt not kill" refer to the killing of a man;—not another man; therefore, not even thyself. For he who kills himself, kills nothing else than a man.*

I answer that, It is altogether unlawful to kill oneself, for three reasons. First, because everything naturally loves itself, the result being that everything naturally keeps itself in being, and resists corruptions so far as it can. Wherefore suicide is contrary to the inclination of nature, and to charity whereby every man should love himself. Hence suicide is always a mortal sin, as being contrary to the natural law and to charity.

Secondly, because every part, as such, belongs to the whole. Now every man is part of the community, and so, as such, he belongs to the community. Hence by killing himself he injures the community, as the Philosopher declares (*Ethic.* v. 11).

Thirdly, because life is God's gift to man, and is subject to His power, Who kills and makes to live. Hence whoever takes his own life, sins against God, even as he who kills another's slave, sins against that slave's master, and as he who usurps to himself judgment of a matter not entrusted to him. For it belongs to God alone to pronounce sentence of death and life, according to Deut. xxxii. 39, *I will kill and I will make to live.*

Reply Obj. 1.   Murder is a sin, not only because it is contrary to justice, but also because it is opposed to charity which a man should have towards himself: in this respect suicide is a sin in relation to oneself. In relation to the community and to God, it is sinful, by reason also of its opposition to justice.

Reply Obj. 2.   One who exercises public authority may lawfully put to death an evildoer, since he can pass judgment on him. But no man is judge of himself. Wherefore it is not lawful for one who exercises public authority to put himself to death for any sin whatever: although he may lawfully commit himself to the judgment of others.

Reply Obj. 3.   Man is made master of himself through his free-will: wherefore he can lawfully dispose of himself as to those matters which pertain to this life which is ruled by man's free-will. But the passage from this life to another and happier one is subject not to man's free-will but to the power of God. Hence it is not lawful for man to take his own life that he may pass to a happier life, nor that he may escape any unhappiness whatsoever of the present life, because the ultimate and most fearsome evil of this life is death, as the Philosopher states (*Ethic.* iii.6). Therefore to bring death upon oneself in order to escape the other afflictions of this life, is to adopt a greater evil in order to avoid a lesser. In like manner it is unlawful to take one's own life on account of one's having committed a sin, both because by so doing one does oneself a very great injury, by depriving oneself of the time needful for repentance, and because it is not lawful to slay an evildoer except by the sentence of the public authority. Again it is unlawful for a woman to kill herself lest she be violated, because she ought not to commit on herself the very great sin of suicide, to avoid the lesser sin of another. For she commits no sin in being violated by force, provided she does not consent, since *without consent of the mind there is no stain on the body,* as the Blessed Lucy declared. Now it is evident that fornication and adultery are less grievous sins than taking a man's, especially one's own, life: since the latter is most grievous, because one injures oneself, to whom one owes the greatest love. Moreover it is most dangerous since no time is left wherein to expiate it by repentance. Again it is not lawful for anyone to take his own life for fear he should consent to sin, because *evil must not be done that good may come* (Rom. iii. 8) or that evil may be avoided, especially if the evil be of small account and an uncertain event, for it is uncertain whether one will at some future time consent to a sin, since God is able to deliver man from sin under any temptation whatever.

Reply Obj. 4. As Augustine says (*De Civ. Dei* i. 21), *not even Samson is to be excused that he crushed himself together with his enemies under the ruins of the house, except the Holy Ghost, Who had wrought many wonders through him, had secretly commanded him to do this.* He assigns the same reason in the case of certain holy women, who at the time of persecution took their own lives, and who are commemorated by the Church.

Reply Obj. 5. It belongs to fortitude that a man does not shrink from being slain by another, for the sake of the good of virtue, and that he may avoid sin. But that a man takes his own life in order to avoid penal evils has indeed an appearance of fortitude (for which reason some, among whom was Razias, have killed themselves thinking to act from fortitude), yet it is not true fortitude, but rather a weakness of soul unable to bear penal evils, as the Philosopher (*Ethic.* iii. 7) and Augustine (*De Civ. Dei* i. 22, 23) declare.

Of Suicide*

DAVID HUME

Aquinas's argument is deeply *theological*. The following essay by David Hume
significantly moves away from this commitment. Hume's views are antitheolog-
ical and in support of a right to commit suicide. Hume identified with a handful
of pre-Christian classical writers who considered suicide an honorable and sometimes praiseworthy act. He argues that if God is the creator of the world, his will
is expressed in all events. If all events equally reflect God's will, then suicide
cannot be a departure from that will. Hume further contends that suicide is not always harmful to society, may actually contribute to the public good, and sometimes is "laudable." He also believes that suicide may serve our interests and be
consistent with "our duty to ourselves."

. . . So great is our horror of death that when it presents itself, under any form,
besides that to which a man has endeavoured to reconcile his imagination, it acquires
new terrors and overcomes his feeble courage: But when the menaces of superstition
are joined to this natural timidity, no wonder it quite deprives men of all power over
their lives, since even many pleasures and enjoyments, to which we are carried by a
strong propensity, are torn from us by this inhuman tyrant. Let us here endeavour to
restore men to their native liberty by examining all the common arguments against
Suicide, and shewing that that action may be free from every imputation of guilt or
blame, according to the sentiments of all the ancient philosophers.

If Suicide be criminal, it must be a transgression of our duty either to God, our
neighbour, or ourselves. To prove that suicide is no transgression of our duty to God,
the following considerations may perhaps suffice. In order to govern the material
world, the almighty Creator has established general and immutable laws by which all
bodies, from the greatest planet to the smallest particle of matter, are maintained in
their proper sphere and function. To govern the animal world, he has endowed all living creatures with bodily and mental powers; with senses, passions, appetites, memory and judgment, by which they are impelled or regulated in that course of life to
which they are destined. These two distinct principles of the material and animal world
continually encroach upon each other, and mutually retard or forward each other's operations. The powers of men and of all other animals are restrained and directed by the
nature and qualities of the surrounding bodies; and the modifications and actions of
these bodies are incessantly altered by the operation of all animals. Man is stopped by
rivers in his passage over the surface of the earth; and rivers, when properly directed,
lend their force to the motion of machines, which serve to the use of man. But though
the provinces of material and animal powers are not kept entirely separate, there results from thence no discord or disorder in the creation; on the contrary, from the mixture, union and contrast of all the various powers of inanimate bodies and living

*Source: Originally published in Edinburgh, Scotland, 1777.

creatures, arises that surprising harmony and proportion which affords the surest argument of supreme wisdom. The providence of the Deity appears not immediately in any operation, but governs everything by those general and immutable laws, which have been established from the beginning of time. All events, in one sense, may be pronounced the action of the Almighty; they all proceed from those powers with which he has endowed his creatures. A house which falls by its own weight is not brought to ruin by his providence more than one destroyed by the hands of men; nor are the human faculties less his workmanship than the laws of motion and gravitation. When the passions play, when the judgment dictates, when the limbs obey; this is all the operation of God, and upon these animate principles, as well as upon the inanimate, has he established the government of the universe. Every event is alike important in the eyes of that infinite being, who takes in at one glance the most distant regions of space and remotest periods of time. There is no event, however important to us, which he has exempted from the general laws that govern the universe, or which he has peculiarly reserved for his own immediate action and operation. The revolution of states and empires depends upon the smallest caprice or passion of single men; and the lives of men are shortened or extended by the smallest accident of air or diet, sunshine or tempest. Nature still continues her progress and operation; and if general laws be ever broke by particular volitions of the Deity, 'tis after a manner which entirely escapes human observation. As, on the one hand, the elements and other inanimate parts of the creation carry on their action without regard to the particular interest and situation of men; so men are entrusted to their judgment and discretion, in the various shocks of matter, and may employ every faculty with which they are endowed, in order to provide for their ease, happiness, or preservation. What is the meaning then of that principle that a man, who, tired of life, and haunted by pain and misery, bravely overcomes all the natural terrors of death and makes his escape from this cruel scene; that such a man, I say, has incurred the indignation of his Creator by encroaching on the office of divine providence, and disturbing the order of the universe? Shall we assert that the Almighty has reserved to himself in any peculiar manner the disposal of the lives of men, and has not submitted that event, in common with others, to the general laws by which the universe is governed? This is plainly false; the lives of men depend upon the same laws as the lives of all other elements; and these are subjected to the general laws of matter and motion. The fall of a tower, or the infusion of poison, will destroy a man equally with the meanest creature; an inundation sweeps away every thing without distinction that comes within the reach of its fury. Since therefore the lives of men are for ever dependent on the general laws of matter and motion, is a man's disposing of his life criminal, because in every case it is criminal to encroach upon these laws, or disturb their operation? But this seems absurd; all animals are entrusted to their own prudence and skill for their conduct in the world, and have full authority, as far as their power extends, to alter all the operations of nature. Without the exercise of this authority they could not subsist a moment; every action, every motion of a man, innovates on the order of some parts of matter, and diverts from their ordinary course the general laws of motion. Putting together, therefore, these conclusions, we find that human life depends upon the general laws of matter and motion, and that it is no encroachment on the office of providence to disturb or alter these general laws: Has not everyone, of consequence, the free disposal of his own life? And may he not lawfully employ that power with which nature has endowed him? In order to destroy the evidence of this conclusion, we must shew a reason why this particular case is excepted; is it because human life is of so great importance, that 'tis a presumption for human prudence to dispose of it? But the life of a man is of no greater importance to the universe than that of an oyster. And were it of ever so great importance, the order of nature has actually submitted it to human prudence, and reduced us to a necessity in every incident of determining concerning it. Were the disposal of human life so much reserved as the peculiar province of the Almighty that it were an encroachment of his right for men to dispose of their own lives; it would be equally criminal to act for the preservation of life as for its destruction. If I turn aside a stone which is falling upon my head, I disturb the course of nature, and I invade the peculiar province of the Almighty by lengthening out my life beyond the period which by the general laws of matter and motion he had assigned it.

A hair, a fly, an insect is able to destroy this mighty being whose life is of such importance. Is it an absurdity to suppose that human prudence may lawfully dispose of what depends on such insignificant causes? It would be no crime in me to divert the Nile or Danube from its course, were I able to effect such purposes. Where then is the crime of turning a few ounces of blood from their natural channel? Do you imagine that I repine at providence or curse my creation, because I go out of life, and put a period to a being, which, were it to continue, would render me miserable? Far be such sentiments from me; I am only convinced of a matter of fact, which you yourself acknowledge possible, that human life may be unhappy, and that my existence, if further prolonged, would become ineligible: but I thank providence, both for the good which I have already enjoyed, and for the power with which I am endowed of escaping the ill that threatens me. To you it belongs to repine providence, who foolishly imagine that you have no such power, and who must still prolong a hated life, though loaded with pain and sickness, with shame and poverty. Do you not teach that when any ill befalls me, though by the malice of my enemies, I ought to be resigned to providence, and that the actions of men are the operations of the Almighty as much as the actions of inanimate beings? When I fall upon my own sword, therefore, I receive my death equally from the hands of the Deity as if it had proceeded from a lion, a precipice, or a fever. The submission which you require to providence in every calamity that befalls me excludes not human skill and industry, if possibly by their means I can avoid or escape the calamity: And why may I not employ one remedy as well as another? If my life be not my own, it were criminal for me to put it in danger, as well as to dispose of it; nor could one man deserve the appellation of *hero* whom glory of friendship transports into the greatest dangers, and another merit the reproach of *wretch* or *miscreant* who puts a period to his life for like motives. There is no being which possesses any power or faculty that it receives not from its Creator, nor is there any one which by ever so irregular an action can encroach upon the plan of his providence, or disorder the universe. Its operations are his works equally with that chain of events which it invades, and whichever principle prevails, we may for that very reason conclude it to be most favoured by him. Be it animate, or inanimate, rational, or irrational; 'tis all a case: Its power is still derived from the supreme creator, and is alike comprehended in the order of his providence. When the horror of pain prevails over the love of life; when a voluntary action anticipates the effects of blind causes; 'tis only in consequence of those powers and principles which he has implanted in his creatures. Divine providence is still inviolate and placed far beyond the reach of human injuries. 'Tis impious, says the old Roman superstition, to divert rivers from their course, or invade the prerogatives of nature. 'Tis impious, says the French superstition, to inoculate for the small-pox, or usurp the business of providence, by voluntarily producing distempers and maladies. 'Tis impious, says the modern European superstition, to put a period to our own life, and thereby rebel against our creator; and why not impious, say I, to build houses, cultivate the ground, or sail upon the ocean? In all these actions we employ our powers of mind and body to produce some innovation in the course of nature; and in none of them do we any more. They are all of them therefore equally innocent, or equally criminal. *But you are placed by Providence, like a sentinel in a particular station, and when you desert it without being recalled, you are equally guilty of rebellion against your Almighty Sovereign, and have incurred his displeasure.* I ask, why do you conclude that Providence has placed me in this station? For my part I find that I owe my birth to a long chain of causes, of which many depend upon voluntary actions of men. *But Providence guided all these causes, and nothing happens in the universe without its consent and cooperation.* If so, then neither does my death, however voluntary, happen without its consent; and whenever pain or sorrow so far overcome my patience as to make me tired of life, I may conclude that I am recalled from my station in the clearest and most express terms. 'Tis Providence surely that has placed me at this present moment in this chamber: But may I not leave it when I think proper, without being liable to the imputation of having deserted my post or station? When I shall be dead, the principles of which I am composed will still perform their part in the universe, and will be equally useful in the grand fabric, as when they composed this individual creature. The difference to the whole will be no greater than betwixt my being in a chamber and in the open air. The one change is of more importance to me than the other; but not more so to the universe.

'Tis a kind of blasphemy to imagine that any created being can disturb the order of the world or invade the business of providence! It supposes that that being possesses powers and faculties which it received not from its creator, and which are not subordinate to his government and authority. A man may disturb society no doubt, and thereby incur the displeasure of the Almighty: But the government of the world is placed far beyond his reach and violence. And how does it appear that the Almighty is displeased with those actions that disturb society? By the principles which he has implanted in human nature, and which inspire us with a sentiment of remorse if we ourselves have been guilty of such actions, and with that of blame and disapprobation, if we ever observe them in others. Let us now examine, according to the method proposed, whether Suicide be of this kind of action, and be a breach of our duty to our *neighbour* and to *society*.

A man who retires from life does no harm to society. He only ceases to do good; which, if it is an injury, is of the lowest kind. All our obligations to do good to society seem to imply something reciprocal. I receive the benefits of society and therefore ought to promote its interests, but when I withdraw myself altogether from society, can I be bound any longer? But, allowing that our obligations to do good were perpetual, they have certainly some bounds; I am not obliged to do a small good to society at the expense of a great harm to myself; why then should I prolong a miserable existence, because of some frivolous advantage which the public may perhaps receive from me? If upon account of age and infirmities I may lawfully resign any office, and employ my time altogether in fencing against these calamities, and alleviating as much as possible the miseries of my future life: Why may I not cut short these miseries at once by an action which is no more prejudicial to society? But suppose that it is no longer in my power to promote the interest of society; suppose that I am a burden to it; suppose that my life hinders some person from being much more useful to society. In such cases my resignation of life must not only be innocent but laudable. And most people who lie under any temptation to abandon existence are in some such situations those who have health, or power, or authority, have commonly better reason to be in humour with the world.

A man is engaged in a conspiracy for the public interest; is seized upon suspicion; is threatened with the rack; and knows from his own weakness that the secret will be extorted from him: Could such a one consult the public interest better than by putting a quick period to a miserable life? This was the case of the famous and brave Strozi of Florence. Again, suppose a malefactor is justly condemned to a shameful death; can any reason be imagined why he may not anticipate his punishment, and save himself all the anguish of thinking on its dreadful approaches? He invades the business of providence no more than the magistrate did, who ordered his execution; and his voluntary death is equally advantageous to society by ridding it of a pernicous member.

That suicide may often be consistent with interest and with our duty to ourselves, no one can question who allows that age, sickness, or misfortune may render life a burden, and make it worse even than annihilation. I believe that no man ever threw away life while it was worth keeping. For such is our natural horror of death that small motives will never be able to reconcile us to it; and though perhaps the situation of a man's health or fortune did not seem to require this remedy, we may at least be assured that any one who, without apparent reason, has had recourse to it, was curst with such an incurable depravity or gloominess of temper as must poison all enjoyment, and render him equally miserable as if he had been loaded with the most grievous misfortunes. If suicide be supposed a crime 'tis only cowardice can impel us to it. If it be no crime, both prudence and courage should engage us to rid ourselves at once of existence, when it becomes a burden. 'Tis the only way that we can then be useful to society, by setting an example, which, if imitated, would preserve to everyone his chance for happiness in life and would effectually free him from all danger or misery.

Moral Problems of Suicide Intervention

TOM L. BEAUCHAMP and JAMES F. CHILDRESS

Tom L. Beauchamp and James F. Childress provide an introduction to moral problems of suicide prevention and intervention in the next selection. They explore moral issues about whether principles of respect for life and beneficence create obligations to prevent suicide that override obligations based on the principle of respect for autonomy. They also look at reasons why courts have often held that the state can justifiably protect persons against attempted suicide. These authors are particularly concerned with paternalistic justifications for suicide intervention. The authors do not rule out justifications of intervention based on paternalism, but they do argue that such justifications are fraught with moral difficulties. In the end, they support a balancing model in which communal beneficence toward the suicidal person sometimes determines our obligations, whereas in other cases respect for autonomy suggests that nonintervention is appropriate even when the act is clearly a suicide that could be prevented.

Various forms and levels of paternalism are present in suicide intervention. The state, religious institutions, and health care facilities have all traditionally assumed some jurisdiction to intervene with suicide. Those who intervene do not always attempt to justify their actions on paternalistic grounds, but paternalism has been the primary justification. By "paternalism" we mean the intentional nonacquiescence or intervention in another person's preferences, desires, or actions with the goal of either avoiding harm to or benefiting the person.

The primary moral issue is the following: Do individuals have a moral right to decide about the acceptability of suicide and to act unimpeded on their convictions? If suicide is a protected moral right, then the state and other individuals such as health professionals have no legitimate grounds for intervention in autonomous suicide attempts. No one seriously doubts that we should intervene to prevent suicide by nonautonomous persons, and few people wish to return to the days when suicide was a criminal act. But if we accept an autonomy right, then the imprudent suicide who would want to live under more favorable circumstances could not legitimately be prevented from committing suicide.

A clear and relevant example of attempted suicide appears in the following case, involving John K., a thirty-two-year-old lawyer. Two neurologists independently confirmed that his facial twitching, which had been evident for 3 months, is an early sign of Huntington's disease, a neurological disorder that progressively worsens, leads to irreversible dementia, and is uniformly fatal in approximately 10 years. His mother suffered a horrible death from the same disease, and John K. had often said that he would prefer to die than to suffer the way his mother suffered. Over several years he had been anxious, had drunk heavily, and had sought psychiatric help for intermittent depression. Following a confirming diagnosis, John K. told his psychiatrist about his situation and asked for help in committing suicide. After the psychiatrist refused to help, he attempted to take his own life by ingesting his antidepressant medication, leaving a note of explanation to his wife and child.[1]

Several interventions occurred or were possible in this case. First, the psychiatrist refused to assist John K.'s suicide and would have sought to have him involuntarily committed if he had not assured the psychiatrist that he did not plan to attempt suicide anytime soon. The psychiatrist probably thought that he could provide appropriate psychotherapy over time. Second, John K.'s wife found him unconscious and rushed him to the emergency room. Third, the emergency room staff decided to treat him despite the suicide note. Which, if any, of these possible or actual interventions is justifiable?

One widely accepted account of our obligations is based on a modification of the strategy of temporary intervention defended by Mill: Intervention is justified to ascertain or to establish the quality of autonomy in the person; further intervention is unjustified once it is determined that the person's actions are substantially autonomous. Glanville Williams used this strategy in an influential statement:

> If one suddenly comes upon another person attempting suicide, the natural and humane thing to do is to try to stop him, for the purpose of ascertaining the cause of his distress and attempting to remedy it, or else of attempting moral dissuasion if it seems that the act of suicide shows lack of consideration for others, or else again from the purpose of trying to persuade him to accept psychiatric help if this seems to be called for. . . . But nothing longer than a temporary restraint could be defended. I would gravely doubt whether a suicide attempt should be a factor leading to a diagnosis of psychosis or to compulsory admissions to a hospital. Psychiatrists are too ready to assume that an attempt to commit suicide is the act of mentally sick persons.[2]

This antipaternalist stance is vulnerable to criticism on two grounds. First, failure to intervene symbolically communicates to potential suicides a lack of communal concern and works to diminish our sense of communal responsibility. Second, many persons who commit suicide are either mentally ill, clinically depressed, or destabilized by a crisis and are therefore not acting autonomously. From a clinical perspective, many suicidal persons are beset with ambivalence, simply wish to reduce or interrupt anxiety, or are under the influence of drugs, alcohol, or intense pressure.[3]

In a typical circumstance, the potential suicide plans how to end life while simultaneously holding fantasies about how rescue will occur, not only rescue from death but from the negative circumstances prompting the suicide. If the suicide springs from clinical depression or is a call for help, a failure to intervene seems to show disrespect for the person's deepest autonomous wishes, including his or her hopes for the future. Surface intentions do not always capture deeper desires or inclinations, and in a matter as serious as suicide, deeper motives should receive a heavy weighing in the justification of intervention.

Several public policy problems are connected to these claims. Many people are concerned that changes in suicide laws either to legalize physician-assisted suicide or to discourage suicide intervention will have the effect of encouraging suicides by persons who are not substantially autonomous, especially those who are terminally ill and in need of both care and resources. While recognizing the case for "rational suicide" by patients with AIDS, one physician contends that "from the clinical point of view, careful evaluations of suicides, even in terminally ill patients, almost invariably reveal evidence that the suicide occurred as a manifestation of a psychiatric disorder rather than as a rational choice."[4]

Another worry is that new suicide laws would have the effect of encouraging insensitive attitudes on the part of health care professionals and patients, especially in a medical system organized around cost reduction. Some institutions devoted to caring for the ill and elderly, such as the modern nursing home, already communicate a message of indifference to various forms of suffering that lead patients to end their lives. These institutions contrast sharply with the ethos of a hospice, which is a prime example of an institution established to care for suffering patients and to provide a supportive community.

However, caution is also needed in calls for communal beneficence, which may express itself paternalistically through forceful interventions or criminal sanctions. Suicide has been decriminalized, but a suicide attempt, irrespective of motive, almost universally provides a legal basis for intervention by public officers, as well as grounds for involuntary hospitalization.[5] Often the burden of proof is more appropriately placed on those who claim that the patient's judgment is not autonomous. For example, Ida Rollin, 74 years old, suffered from ovarian cancer, and her physicians told her that she had only a few months to live and that her dying would be very painful and upsetting. Rollin indicated to her daughter that she wanted to commit suicide and requested her assistance. The daughter secured some pills and conveyed a doctor's instructions about how they should be taken. When the daughter expressed reservations about these plans, her husband reminded her that they "weren't driving, she [Ida Rollin] was" and that they were only "navigators."[6]

This metaphor-laden reference to rightful authority is a reminder that those who propose suicide intervention require a solid moral justification that fits the context. There are occasions in health care (and elsewhere) when it is appropriate to step aside and allow a suicide, and even to assist in a person's suicide, just as there are occasions under which it is appropriate to intervene.

NOTES

1. This case has been adapted from Marc Basson, ed., *Rights and Responsibilities in Modern Medicine*. New York: Alan R. Liss, 1981, pp. 183–184.
2. Glanville Williams. "Euthanasia," *Medico-Legal Journal* 41 (1973):27.

3. See, e.g., three articles by psychiatrists Alan L. Berman, Robert E. Litman, and Sey-
    mour Perlin in *Non-Natural Death—Coming to Terms with Suicide, Euthanasia,
    Withholding or Withdrawing Treatment.* Denver: Center for Applied Biomedical
    Ethics at Rose Medical Center, 1986.
4. See Richard M. Glass, "AIDS and Suicide," *Journal of the American Medical Asso-
    ciation* 259 (March 4, 1988):1369–1370.
5. See President's Commission for the Study of Ethical Problems in Medicine and Bio-
    medical and Behavioral Research, *Deciding to Forego Life-Sustaining Treatment.*
    Washington: U.S. Government Printing Office, 1983, p. 37.
6. Betty Rollin. *Last Wish.* New York: Linden Press/Simon and Schuster, 1985.

The Role of Law in Suicide Prevention Beyond Civil Commitment— A Bystander Duty to Report Suicide Threats*

KATE E. BLOCH

Kate Bloch holds that it is a justified form of practical activity, to require legally (not just morally) that friends, school officials, parents, and the like report suicide threats of which they have firsthand knowledge to those who may be in a position to help prevent those acts. The implementation of this proposal would probably be impossible without some form of communal network such as a counseling or telephone service for reporting potential suicides. On her analysis, a law that gave legal immunity to one who made such a report would also be needed. Specification of the obligation would require a close look at the type of threats that merit reporting, at what kind of knowledge the bystander must have, and how to distinguish the obligation to report from the obligation to rescue. Bloch also analyzes the "limitations of the duty" that would have to be recognized in law.

Suicide is a societal ailment of tremendous proportion, and one for which there is no easy cure. The only practical approach to the problem is prevention: first, the immediate prevention of the attempt and second, treatment of the underlying problems that motivated that attempt. Such prevention will, of course, require the cooperative efforts of many disciplines. The analysis that follows explores a role that law can play in these prevention efforts. . . .

THE LIMITED REACH OF CURRENT COMMITMENT STATUTES

A. Problems of Scope: The Need to Enlist the Public's Help in Identifying Suicidal Individuals

Maggie Olsen

Fifty-eight days after her thirteenth birthday, Maggie Olsen hanged herself from a tree near her Morgan Hill home.[1] On the day of her suicide, Maggie was expelled from school for a second drug offense. Before leaving school, Maggie told the

*Source: Kate E. Bloch, "The Role of Law in Suicide Prevention: Beyond Civil Commitment—A Bystander Duty to Report Suicide Threats," *Stanford Law Review,* v. 39 (April 1987), pp. 929–953. © 1987 by the Board of Trustees of the Leland Stanford Junior University.

school nurse that she would kill herself rather than tolerate the punishment she believed was forthcoming. The school nurse reported the suicide threat to Maggie's mother and suggested that Maggie's mother get counseling for her daughter. When Maggie and her mother got home, Maggie went out to feed the chickens, returned to the house, and then left again to hang herself.

Mrs. B.

In a collection of letters written by people bereaved through suicide, a woman explained that she regretted never having paid heed to the repeated warnings of her mother's impending suicide:

> When Mom would be drinking heavily, she would always talk about suicide. This was the era when you were advised to disregard anyone threatening suicide; now, thank God, we know differently. We always told her not to talk about it, but she told everyone who would listen that she was going to kill herself. Sadly, no one took her seriously. . . . [2]

Before suicidal individuals like Maggie and Mrs. B. can benefit from current legal prevention mechanisms or be afforded psychiatric aid, generally someone must take their suicidal threat or behavior seriously. Almost 80% of those who kill themselves give definite verbal or behavioral warnings before taking their lives. But most people who hear such threats or see such behavior do not take them seriously. Active encouragement on the part of the law is particularly important in light of the popular, but erroneous, belief that people who threaten suicide do not attempt it. Unless suicide threats are given the attention they deserve, many suicidal individuals, like those discussed above, will never be reached by the existing suicide prevention apparatus.

Literature on bystander intervention in emergencies explains that an onlooker's "failure to intervene is not the result of a conscious decision but rather due to an unresolved internal conflict concerning whether to act. . . . "[3] "Once informed of the proper course of action, however, a bystander is more likely to intervene." Bystander hesitancy to respond is highly apparent in the suicide context. A panel of experts explained:

> Quite often, suicidal teen-agers will say something like "I'm tired of living, wouldn't it be better to be dead?" Or a suicidal teen-ager may make an overt declaration to a close friend, sworn to secrecy: "I'm going to kill myself." In a significant number of cases . . . close friends of adolescents considering suicide knew or strongly suspected their friends were considering ending their lives. The friends often said nothing, either out of confused loyalty, or because they did not believe the threat, and wanted to avoid getting friends into trouble.[4]

Obviously, not all suicides are preventable. But if the warnings given by almost four out of five suicidal individuals were recognized and taken more seriously by friends and relatives, the suicide rate could be substantially reduced.[5]

We do not know what percentage of those who threaten suicide actually attempt to take their own lives, but one expert estimates that "[t]hreats are followed by suicide attempts 70 percent of the time. . . . "[6] In many cases, the community has the opportunity to respond to the plea for assistance before the attempt, but only if someone recognizes and responds to the signs of a cry for help. If preventing suicide means identifying presuicidal individuals and making help available to them, then bystanders must be convinced of the urgency of taking threats seriously and, most importantly, must be required to respond immediately so that help can be made available.

B. "Extralegal" Efforts to Affect Bystander Behavior

Currently, the problem of suicide prevention is being considered in a number of different contexts. Congress has recognized the need for expansion of existing suicide prevention programs; school systems have begun to train their personnel in detecting suicidal behavior; and educational programs have increased public awareness of the suicide problem nationally. . . .

BEYOND EDUCATION AND CIVIL COMMITMENT: A BYSTANDER DUTY TO REPORT SUICIDE THREATS

A. Legal Encouragement: Convincing the Bystander to Act: The Imposition of a Duty to Report

In order to extend prevention efforts, states should motivate bystanders to take suicide threats seriously and notify the appropriate authorities of such threats. One way to extend suicide prevention efforts is to create a legal duty to report all suicide threats, whether verbal or written. For the purposes of this duty, a "bystander" would be a person who hears a threat of suicide or reads a written suicide threat.

1. A Duty to Report Suicide Threats

Specifically, a duty to report suicide threats would require bystanders who have firsthand knowledge of an individual's suicidal intentions, manifested in specific threats, to report such behavior to a crisis hotline as quickly as possible. The mental health professional on duty at the hotline center could then recommend the appropriate form of the response. The duty would accord civil immunity to those bystanders who reported in good faith.

With respect to the suicides described above, the duty would have directed the school nurse and Maggie's mother to call the hotline before Maggie went home. And all of the individuals to whom Mrs. B. confided her intent to end her life would have been responsible for telephoning the hotline for a professional's input and/or intervention.

2. Limitations of the Duty

Threats versus Behavior. The proposed duty to report should be limited to bystanders who have knowledge of actual verbal or written threats. This means that those suicidal individuals who do not make such threats are, at least for now, beyond the reach of the statute. Confining the duty to actual threats means that bystanders would not be responsible for interpreting often ambiguous presuicidal behavior. If, however, with the spread of the educatory measures described above, the public could be educated about the behaviors that constitute presuicide signals, the duty could then be expanded to include those behaviors that educated observers could identify.

Defining a Suicide Threat.   A further limitation on the bystander duty to report suicide threats stems from the difficulty of identifying a threat. How closely does the threat have to resemble "I'm going to kill myself?" Would "I'm tired of living and wish it were all over" constitute a reportable threat? Compared to a suicide attempt, language is inherently more ambiguous. A disadvantage of a duty to report threats is that it requires judgment on the part of the bystander, an interpretation of potentially ambiguous linguistic or physical symbols. But, at the very least, the duty should provoke the bystander to ask the speaker whether he seriously intends to take his own life, whether an apparent jest masks more serious intentions. Sometimes simply caring enough to respond is important to those individuals desperately crying out for help.

Nonetheless, there will be many cases in which the difficulties of interpreting language, facial expression or tone of voice leave the observer in doubt as to the threatener's intentions. In such cases, the observer must presume serious intent and report. This presumption will lead to an overreporting of threats or false alarms.

False alarms pose two problems. First they consume the time and energy of the hotline personnel. This, however, is the price of ensuring that serious threats are reported. The dangers of underreporting or of not reporting at all should outweigh the inconvenience of excessive reporting. The second difficulty is the problem of false positives or reports of nonsuicidal individuals claimed to be suicidal. In part to protect these individuals, the hotline should be manned by mental health professionals rather than lay volunteers. As professionals, it is their job to evaluate and weed out false positive reports. Such protection is, of course, not foolproof.

Firsthand Knowledge.   Finally, the duty to report should be imposed only if the observer has firsthand knowledge of a potential suicide.

Limitation of the duty to firsthand knowledge reflects a balance between the possibilities of suicide prevention through bystander reporting and the burden placed on the bystander. The goal is to oblige the bystander to report when he has knowledge of a threat but not to overburden the bystander by requiring detective or guesswork. The duty represents an effort to educate bystanders on the importance of taking suicide threats seriously, to require bystanders to respond quickly to these threats, to guide that response, and, when appropriate, to get immediate help for the suicidal individual.

3. Affirmative Duties Generally

Enacting a duty to report suicide threats transforms good samaritanism into a legal responsibility. Such transformations are no longer novel. Rather, there has been a general trend in American law toward requiring people to help one another in civil contexts. Of particular relevance here are statutory duties requiring either direct bystander intervention in emergencies or bystander reporting of the emergency to an appropriate authority. . . .

If linked to the threat rather than the actual attempt, a duty to report may promise widespread prevention possibilities for suicide. Because the immediate goal in suicide prevention is to prevent the life-endangering act, a duty to report threats focuses the bystander's and the state's attention on the would-be suicidal individual early in the suicidal episode—before the actual physical harm occurs. Moreover, since a threat is intended to have an audience while the actual attempt may be conducted in private, it is more likely that there will be a bystander to a suicide threat than to an attempt. Reporting of the threat enables the state to respond to ambivalent, cry-for-help suicides when such response is apt to be effective. Furthermore, the duty to report insures input from a mental health professional.

Enactment of a legal obligation to report suicide threats as opposed to a duty to rescue is not, however, intended to discourage a bystander from calling an ambulance once an attempt has been made or to discourage a bystander from trying to thwart an impending attempt. But the focus should be on interrupting the suicidal episode before it reaches the attempt stage.

4. Law Informing Behavior: Probable Impact of the Duty on Bystanders

The theory behind an affirmative duty in both the general rescue and the suicide contexts rests on the assumption that when the public knows a statutory duty to rescue or report exists, hesitant bystanders may be induced to render aid. Law serves to inform behavior on a large scale. It can shape attitudes and behaviors in crisis situations, directing bystanders to take action and choosing for the bystander the form the action shall take.

Opponents of affirmative duties question the effectiveness, desirability, and enforceability of a rescue statute. But the belief that an affirmative duty will inform bystander behavior and encourage modeling of the desired behavior finds support both in the practice of European countries where such duties already exist and in studies investigating the influence of affirmative legal duties on altruistic behavior and attitudes.

Approximately a dozen European countries recognize an affirmative legal duty to rescue.[7] Their statutes mandate that bystanders furnish reasonable assistance when they observe another person in peril. They generally impose prison sentences and/or fines for failure to provide such assistance. The acceptance and enforcement of such duties in Europe suggests that similar duties could be effectively implemented in this country.

In addition, research on altruism indicates that an expanded legal duty to aid may lead to more rescue behavior. The two theories preferred by social psychologists, the normative and social exchange theories, both predict that imposition of an expanded legal duty to aid would cause more persons to render aid. . . .

Finally, prosecution for a misdemeanor or imposition of a fine are not appropriate penalties for failure to report a suicide threat, particularly as the bystander who has failed to report will often be a friend, neighbor or family member, already suffering personal guilt as well as grief. Instead, violation of the duty might result in a specified number of hours of community service—perhaps even learning about and helping with crisis intervention. In this way, the bystander may use his tragic experience with suicidal behavior constructively, possibly helping to prevent a future suicide attempt.

5. Impact of the Bystander's Duty on the Suicidal Individual

The proposed duty to report applies to all suicide threats. It becomes not only incorrect but illegal for bystanders to second-guess or ignore a suicide threat. Reporting these threats to a hotline enables mental health professionals to perform triage on suicide threats. The professional is responsible for determining what form, if any, the intervention should take: It could be a recommendation to confront the threatener, to refer the suicidal individual to counseling at an appropriate agency, to contact a crisis team or other community service for onsite intervention, or whatever other response the professional determines is appropriate.

The call to the mental health professional increases the likelihood of an appropriate response to the suicide threat. If the attempt can be thwarted, the immediate danger is over and treatment for the underlying cause may permanently eliminate the urge toward self-destruction.

A bystander duty to report suicide threats could increase identification of suicidal individuals in need of help who are ambivalent about their desire for death and whose desire for death is itself temporary. Imposition of such a duty could also create more opportunities for the state to respond with appropriate prevention strategies before a life is endangered.

CONCLUSION

Historically, suicide was seen as a heinous crime against God and the state. Slowly, however, the criminal stigma abated. Suicide is now recognized as a complex behavior frequently involving extreme ambivalence and a desperate appeal for help. The duty to report suicide threats is intended particularly to facilitate prevention of the suicides of those individuals who are ambivalent about their desire for death, whose desire for death is temporary, and whose suicidal threats and/or behavior embody a cry for help.

One expert has labeled suicide, in particular suicide of the young, our "No. 1 preventable cause of death." It is time for every discipline to reassess its role in responding to suicidal cries for help and preventing such deaths.[8]

NOTES

1. *San Jose Mercury News,* Mar. 17, 1985, at 1A. col. 2.
2. *San Jose Mercury News,* Jan. 6, 1986, at 3C. col. 1 (the name used here is fictitious).

3. Wenik, *Forcing the Bystander to Get Involved: A Case for a Statute Requiring Witnesses to Report Crime,* 94 Yale L.J. 1787, 1789 (1985).

4. King, *Experts Describe "Epidemic" of Teen-Age Suicides, New York Times,* Dec. 15, 1984, at 8, col. 4.

5. Battin, M., *Ethical Issues in Suicide,* 12 (1982); N. St. John-Stevas, *Life, Death and the Law* 261 (1961).

6. *San Jose Mercury News,* Mar. 17, 1985, at 17A, col. 1 (quoting Meg Paris, Director, Suicide Prevention and Crisis Center of Santa Clara County).

7. See Rudinzinski, *The Duty to Rescue,* in *The Good Samaritan and the Law* 122 (J. Ratcliffe, ed. 1966). at 92. As of 1966, Czechoslovakia, Denmark.

8. DelBello, *Needed: A U.S. Commission on Teen-Age Suicide, New York Times,* Sept. 12, 1984, at A31, col. 1.

Whose Life Is It Anyway?*

JOEL FEINBERG

Joel Feinberg is a staunch defender of rights that protect personal autonomy. He sees those rights as a trump card to be played against authorities who would override autonomous decision making. In his extensive writing, Feinberg has tried to illuminate the importance of respecting autonomy and the connections between personal autonomy and personal integrity, independence, and self-reliance. He views autonomous persons as analogous to sovereign nations whose territory can be wrongly invaded. In the following selection he presents antipaternalistic arguments intended to show that intervening to prevent rational suicides is not justifiable even with some persons who are not terminally ill. The critical matter is not illness but autonomy. This is the reason for the title on his essay (borrowed from the title of a film he analyzes): Whose Life Is It Anyway? Feinberg sees continuing intervention to prevent a rational suicide as a denial of independence and a wrongful invasion of an inviolate right to control what is within one's own domain. In his analysis, respect for autonomy *always* takes precedence over protecting the person's welfare.

It stands to reason that occasionally a person who has been convicted of serious crimes and sentenced to incarceration for a large part or all of his natural life, who is loathed and mistreated by his guards, and distrusted and abused by his fellow prisoners, might genuinely prefer to die, and would kill himself if only he could find the means to do so cleanly. Can we be certain that a formal death request from such a person must have been coerced, ill-informed, or the product of impairment or distraction? Surely not; but prisons are highly coercive institutions, seething with barely contained violence, and founded on mutual distrust. Penal authorities always have an incentive to get rid of trouble-makers if they can. The suspicion of manipulation or intimidation would always be present, no matter how authentic the request might seem, and furthermore, once euthanasia of prisoners were approved in principle, the incentive for foul play would be all the greater. It is quite understandable why self-destruction in prisons should be prohibited absolutely.

The more likely place to look then for verifiably voluntary death requests from persons who are *not* in severe pain and *not* suffering from terminal illnesses is in the hospitals that sustain quadriplegics and others suffering from permanent and near totally disabling physical "handicaps." The best example for our purposes is a fictitious but highly believable one. On March 12, 1972, Granada TV in Great Britain produced an hour-long drama by Brian Clark called *Whose Life Is It Anyway?*[1] The television play was taped, replayed, and widely distributed. It was adapted for the stage and produced in London in 1978 and in New York a year later. In 1982 it was made into a motion picture and widely seen. The story is about Ken Harrison, a young man of great

---

*Joel Feinberg, "Whose Life Is it Anyway?" *Harm to Self,* 1986, pp. 351–362. New York: Oxford University Press.

wit and charm who is a sculptor who loves his work, a creative and sensual man in his late twenties. His spine has been ruptured in an automobile accident, and in the first scene he learns from Dr. Emerson that his paralysis from the neck down is incurable, and that he must remain hospitalized for the rest of his life. He has suspected that fearful fact for most of the six months that have elapsed since the accident. He has deliberated calmly and continuously over that period, and decided finally that he prefers to die now rather than live out his remaining four or five decades in a hospital. Since he is physically incapable of killing himself, and active euthanasia is forbidden by law, the only way he can satisfy his desire is to be released from the hospital and sent home where, without his sustaining treatments, he is sure to die within a week.2

Dr. Emerson, speaking for the hospital, will not permit it. It is his duty as a doctor, he says, to preserve life. Besides, Mr. Harrison is suffering from depression and is therefore "incapable of making a rational decision about life and death." Mr. Harrison, unimpressed by this argument, consults his solicitor who then petitions a court on his behalf for a writ of *habeas corpus,* alleging that his client has been deprived of liberty without proper cause. The writ is issued; the hospital accepts the challenge of showing that the detention is proper; and a judicial hearing is hastily arranged to be held in the petitioner's hospital room with a presiding judge, Mr. Harrison and his counsel, a "friendly" outside psychiatrist, Dr. Emerson, *his* counsel, and the hospital staff psychiatrist all in attendance.

The hearing is brief, the testimony terse but trenchant, the relevant philosophical arguments on both sides given their due. Dr. Emerson testifies about Harrison's physical injuries and the projected course of treatment. "It is common in these cases," he adds, "that depression and the tendency to make wrong decisions goes on for months, even years" (p. 132). But under cross-examination he admits that there are no objective tests or measurements that can be used to distinguish between a medical syndrome and a "sane, even justified, depression," and that he must rely simply on his "thirty years of experience as a physician dealing with both types" (p. 133). Dr. Barr, the consulting psychiatrist selected by Harrison's lawyer, testifies in rebuttal. He does not dispute that Harrison is depressed but judges that his attitude is not simply an expression of clinical depression; rather " . . . he is reacting in a perfectly rational way to a very bad situation" (p. 135). He too concedes that since the patient's physical condition masks the usual symptoms of clinical depression, there is no objective way of telling which sort of depression he has, save "by experience," and "by discovering when I talk to him that he has a remarkably incisive mind and is perfectly capable of understanding his position and of deciding what to do about it" (p. 136). Then comes the question with the dramatically surprising but philosophically stimulating answer: "One last thing, Doctor, do you think Mr. Harrison has made the right decision?" The psychiatrist answers without hesitation: "No, I thought he made the wrong decision."

Harrison himself is not called upon to testify, but he agrees to a brief interrogation by the judge who then concludes that he is satisfied that "Mr. Harrison is a brave and cool man who is in complete control of his mental faculties, and I shall therefore make an order for him to be set free" (p. 144). Harrison's only remaining life prospect now is "to get a room some place" and begin the gradual and inevitably messy dying process. One would think that by this point, when he has won every other victory, a painless lethal injection would be a humane favor, a decent thing to do, but of course that is impossible under the prevailing law. . . . Instead, Dr. Emerson offers the most that his conscience and the criminal law will permit, a room in the hospital with cessation of treatment and even feeding stopped if the patient wishes—a kind of supervised passive euthanasia. "You'll be unconscious in three days, dead in six at most" (p. 146). Dr. Emerson wants to be as kind as he can, but he also wants witnesses at hand in case the patient undergoes a last minute change of mind. And so the story ends with mutual respect between the antagonists, and British decency all around, but no ground given in the moral and philosophical debate.

This fictional tale serves as a much better test for the soft paternalist's position and its attendant theory of personal autonomy than do the more common cases of aged patients with painful terminal diseases, because it isolates the factor of voluntary choice and focuses our attention on it. . . . Its moral (if one can be attributed to it) is that respect for personal autonomy alone justifies our noninterference with a competent person's primarily self-regarding choice of death, quite independently of further humanitarian considerations. Mr. Harrison is not a terminal patient. He can expect to live on for another forty years or more if he stays in a hospital. (He becomes "terminal" only after the judge's release order). No rule is applied which limits the recognition of voluntariness to choices of death by persons whose whole reason is the desire to escape pain and who will die soon in any case. Whatever Mr. Harrison's reasons are, they are good enough, provided only they are *his* reasons. The soft paternalist, if he can be convinced that the choice is voluntary enough by reasonable tests, is firmly committed to a policy of noninterference with its implementation, for the life at stake is Mr. Harrison's life not ours. The person in sovereign control over it is precisely he.

In his final exchange with the judge, Harrison cites as the chief reason for his choice (and of course in his view the ground of its reasonableness or correctness) his desire for *dignity*. He is eloquent about the indignity of being forced to live in total dependence on others for even the basic primitive functions. In response to the judge, he then concedes that "many people with appalling physical handicaps have overcome them and lived essentially creative, dignified lives" (p. 142), but the point, he insists, is that "the dignity begins with their choice." It would be an indignity to force the others to die against their will, but an equal indignity to force him to remain alive, as a kind of "medical achievement," against his will. Human dignity is not possible without the acknowledgement of personal sovereignty. . . .

Mr. Harrison's reply (as he puts it later in the play) to the physician's diagnosis of "acute depression" is to concede the point, and then add "Is that surprising? I am almost totally paralyzed. I'd be insane if I *weren't* depressed" (p. 138). Some depression then is *understandable,* even proper, rational, and justifiable, a state of mind any normal person would experience if he were to suffer certain losses. "Depression" is also the name of a clinical syndrome marked by "affective disorders," involving "an accentuation in the intensity or duration of otherwise normal emotions."[3] Psychologists have not agreed on any simple criterion for distinguishing accentuated affective states that are "clinical" from those that are less extreme or less debillitating conditions, but they often speak of a plurality of symptoms, at least some of which are present in clinical depression, in addition to the depressed or "disphoric" mood (sadness, gloominess) that is common to both the clinical and nonclinical species. . . .

Mistaken inferences from depression to some specific incompetence are often profoundly unfair to the depressed person. Characteristically they deprive him, *a priori* as it were, of any opportunity to make a case for himself. Argumentatively, he is trapped in a destructive dilemma that defeats him from the start, leaving him no conceivable ground on which to stand. Mr. Harrison, at one point in the play (p. 97), complains that one of the justifications for refusing his request to die is a version of Catch-22. The term "Catch-22" comes from Joseph Heller's 1961 anti-military novel of that name,[4] in which it is used characteristically for a certain kind of military rule that places a petitioning soldier in an inescapable dilemma, in effect barring approval of his petition *a priori* in language that falsely suggest that there are conditions under which the request could be granted, when in fact those "conditions" are contradictory. . . .

Actually, there are as many as four Catch-22 arguments in *Whose Life Is It Anyway?* that beg the question against Mr. Harrison and make it *a priori* impossible for him to prove the voluntariness of his request. Consider Catch-22, number 1. This version focuses on suicide, a passive version of which is essentially that for which Harrison requests permission. Dr. Emerson and the friendly psychiatrist agree that the crucial question is whether or not Harrison's acknowledged clinical depression is the sort that impairs judgment. Dr. Emerson finds the answer self-evident. "You haven't understood," he says to Dr. Travers with ill-concealed impatience. "He's *suicidal*. He's determined to kill himself." The assumption apparently is that if a depressed person requests to die that *proves* that his depression impairs judgment, and his request therefore is insufficiently voluntary to be granted. This argument suggests that only persons who are happy are capable of voluntarily choosing suicide, and of course they are precisely the ones who won't apply. Thus if you are unhappy you *cannot* voluntarily choose suicide, and if you are happy you *will not* commit suicide. The conclusion: no suicide. Yet the context of discussion presupposes that the issue is initially an open question to be settled by discussion and evidence. Catch-22 rules out all evidence *a priori*. The assumption that no choice of suicide can be voluntary is the very question at issue in the case at hand, not one presumed to be settled in advance.

The second Catch-22 argument follows closely on the first, and is also concerned with the voluntariness of death requests. Another party takes up the argument against Dr. Emerson, one of his subordinate physicians, Dr. Scott, who reminds him that "It's *his* [Harrison's] life." Emerson replies "But my responsibility." "Only if he is incapable of making his own decision," rejoins Dr. Scott. "But he isn't capable," insists Emerson—"I refuse to believe that a man with a mind as quick as his, a man with enormous mental resources, would calmly choose suicide." Scott replies: "But he has done just that." "And therefore," interjects Emerson, "I say he is unbalanced" (pp. 91–92). Again the case is begged against the petitioner. His request cannot possibly be voluntary, not because it fails to satisfy independent formal tests of voluntariness, but entirely because of what it is a request *for*. . . .

Catch-22 number 3 is a closely related corollary of the preceding. The hospital staff psychiatrist, Dr. Travers, warns Harrison: "But your obvious intelligence

weakens your case. I'm not saying that you would find life easy, but you do have resources that an unintelligent person doesn't have." This is the observation that prompts
Harrison's remark about Catch-22: "If you're clever and sane enough to put up an in-
vincible case for suicide, it demonstrates that you ought not to die" (p. 97). The characterization of this requirement as "Catch-22" is perfectly apt. The authorities meet to
hear the petitioner's case. They invite him to present his arguments for their granting
his request. It is understood that if his arguments are weak, they will turn him down.
Better then that the arguments should be cogent, except for Catch-22, which declares
that if the arguments are convincing then the request cannot be granted, for in that case
the petitioner's obvious intellectual resources undermine the case for his death. However he argues, he cannot win. Why then have the hearing at all?

The final Catch-22 argument is put forward half-heartedly by the sympathetic
Dr. Scott, when she senses Harrison's excitement at the approach of his life-or-death
judicial hearing, and his zest for the debate. "I think you are enjoying all this," she
says. "I suppose I am in a way," he replies, "for the first time in six months I feel like
a human being again" (p. 108). This exchange underlines the paradox: Harrison is
never so alive as when he is staging and winning his fight for death. But to make too
much of the point is once again to put the petitioner in the position of Catch-22. If he
enjoys getting what he wants (permission to die), then he is not depressed and has
less reason to die, but if he is not pleased at his victory then he must not really have
wanted to die after all, and that casts doubt on the authenticity of his prior desire. . . .

Before leaving *Whose Life Is It Anyway?*, we should pay some heed to Dr.
Barr's surprising admission that Harrison's decision to die, while carefully reasoned
and voluntary, is nevertheless in his opinion the wrong decision. He might very well
have put the point . . . by saying that the decision is unreasonable (not one Dr. Barr
would have made in the circumstances) but not irrational, and hence not involuntary.
Why should a person be permitted to implement a "wrong" or "unreasonable" decision to die? The only answer possible is simply that it is *his* decision and *his* life, and
that the choice falls within the domain of *his* morally inviolate personal sovereignty.
But why does Dr. Barr think that the decision was the wrong one to make? In the play,
the question is left for our conjecture, but we may surmise that Dr. Barr's reason is
his anticipation that in the course of time, if only Harrison would wait more patiently,
his mind would change, and he would be happy that he had not chosen death earlier.
Harrison himself admits that possibility in an earlier discussion with the sympathetic
Dr. Scott (pp. 68–69):

H: I grant you, I may become lethargic and quiescent. Happy when a nurse comes to put
in a new catheter, or give me an enema, or to turn me over. These could become the
high spots of my day. I might even learn to do wonderful things like turn the pages
of a book with some miracle of modern science, or to type letters with flicking my
eyelids. And you would look at me and say: "Wasn't it worth waiting?" and I would
say: "Yes," and be proud of my achievements. Really proud. I grant you all that, but
it doesn't alter the validity of my present position.
S: But if you became happy?
H: But I don't want to become happy by becoming the computer section of a complex machine. And morally you must accept my decision.

Exactly so. . . . In order to become reconciled at a later date to his condition (a sculptor without the use of his hands, a sensualist without the use of his genitalia, a living tribute to the ingenuity of modern technology), he will have to become a very different person with very different values, and the person he is now, applying the values that he has now, prefers not to become the repugnant future person. The future self does not yet exist; the sovereign chooser is the clearheaded and determined present self. Whatever the hypothetical future self would say, it is only the actual present self who has the right to decide. The choice is squarely within the temporal boundaries of his sovereign domain.

NOTES

1. The stage version is now available in paperback: *Whose Life Is It Anyway? A Play by Brian Clark.* New York: Avon Books, 1978.
2. Harrison's solicitor tells him: "I am informed that without a catheter the toxic substance will build up in your bloodstream and you will be poisoned by your own blood." *Ibid.,* p. 115.
3. Gerald L. Klerman. "Affective Disorders," *The Harvard Guide to Modern Psychiatry.* Cambridge, MA, and London: Harvard University Press, 1978, Chapter 13, p. 255.
4. Joseph Heller. *Catch-22.* New York: Dell Publishing, 1961.

Suicide Prevention and the Value of Human Life*

ERWIN RINGEL

In the next selection, Erwin Ringel, an innovative leader in organizing programs of suicide intervention, resists liberal analyses such as that offered by Feinberg, and earlier by Hume. Ringel sees their views less as ways of respecting the autonomy of actors and more as ways of depreciating human lives. Ringel is particularly concerned by the more vulnerable members of society, such as the ill and those who are victims of social repression. Like Bloch, Ringel sees suicide prevention as a way of affirming the value of human life and transmitting one's sense of its value to suicidal persons. Thus, psychiatric and crisis intervention are warmly endorsed in his analysis, even if the motives and actions are paternalistic.

From time to time voices are heard accusing those who prevent suicide of inhumanity. One of man's fundamental rights, they say, is to put an end to his own life—that is, a right to suicide—and it is inhuman to want to take this right away from him. It is cruel, these voices say, to see men and women suffering abysmally, and in spite of this to encourage them to go on living. Eliot Slater, for instance, has claimed that it is inhuman to stand by and watch a patient's repeated attempts at suicide; he says that rather than repeatedly trying to save the patient, there is only one really humane solution: to give him the chance of an "honorable" death. I think Slater is right in just one point: to stand by and watch a series of suicide attempts without doing anything about them would indeed be inhuman.

It is an obvious human duty to grasp the hand which is extended in search of help. Anyone who has given serious scientific consideration to the problem of suicide knows that death—the state of not-being—is for the most part chosen under pathological circumstances or under the influence of diseased feelings. In fact, suicide cannot really be "chosen," since an intense, overwhelming inner compulsion renders any free "choice" null and void. The strongest human driving force is that of self-preservation. No one is ever, as Edwin Shneidman put it, 100 percent suicidal—no human being, no matter how determined he or she may seem to be to put an end to life, does not somewhere cherish the hope of being saved.

This is true even in the case of so-called planned death. In England some years ago, the Voluntary Euthanasia Bill of 1969 proposed that an individual suffering from a terminal illness should be able to decide the date of his own death: each individual would be encouraged to submit an application for painless death, said death to occur after a commission had met to examine and approve the application, provided the applicant continued to insist on this request. Fortunately, this proposal was turned down

*Erwin Ringel, "Suicide Prevention and the Value of Human Life," in M. P. Battin & D. Mayo, *Suicide*, 1980, pp. 205–211. New York: St. Martin's Press, Inc.

by an overwhelming majority. A physician who was a member of such a commission would, in carrying out such a function, be denying his true calling; he would be an accomplice, equally guilty, in the deadly outcome of such a request. Even nonmedical members of such a commission—people not bound by the Hippocratic Oath—would be faced with an insoluble task. Who can presume to judge with certainty and finality what any one man is likely to experience during the rest of his natural life—whether that life lasts for years, or days, or only hours? The future and the shape of that future remain for us all unforeseeable and unknowable, and we can only truly be humane if we do not try to exceed our limitations, or try to know the unknowable before the time is ripe.

Let me remind you of what happened to Konrad Adenauer when he was arrested after the attempt on Hitler's life on July 20, 1944. He was taken to a concentration camp. The camp commander had him brought up to his office and said to him, "Herr Adenauer, there is one thing you simply must not do—and that is to commit suicide!" Adenauer was taken by surprise, and asked him what on earth had given him this idea. The camp commander, surprised in turn, said, "Look, you are an old man, you are a prisoner, the future holds nothing for you. Isn't it obvious that you must be thinking of suicide?" As you know, of course, that "old man," that "prisoner without a future," was many years later to transform the face of his country, and with it, the face of Europe. This story is not just an example, but a warning.

But there are others who are threatened by suicide as well, and we who hope to prevent suicide must extend our efforts to these. Before the majesty of the law—in this case the law governing suicide prevention—all men are truly equal. It is precisely the despised, those people upon whom society heaps contempt, who are in particular need of special prophylactic treatment, because it is they who are particularly endangered. The crucial principle of suicide prevention, after all, is that *each* individual life is important! The aim of suicide prevention is not so much to reduce the suicide rates, after all (we know how unreliable the figures are anyway), but to help people: to make it possible for each individual person to take the road of self-realization rather than that of failure, of which the final consequence is suicide. We cannot value different people in different ways; each human life is equally valuable. There are no supermen and no subhuman beings; there are only human beings to whom one feels "incorrigibly drawn," as Morgenstern put it, and to whom one offers one's hand.

Labels like "psychopath," "drunkard," and "addict" have become invectives, and automatically call forth contempt and antipathy. But the people who bear these labels are human beings, urgently in need of special and specialized help. We need to give them understanding and therapy, not prejudice and contempt. And we need to recognize these labels as labels for disease, so that we can provide treatment and hope for therapeutic success.

We must also set more value on older people. In almost all countries in the world, the rates of suicide among persons over sixty are high and are steadily increasing. This may be no surprise: if we look at the behavior of many people toward the old and even toward the merely aging, we may begin to wonder just how sincere the wish of the community is to keep its older people alive. Unfortunately, we often hear the argument that people who commit suicide at a relatively advanced age would not have had very much longer to live. Worse, still, we hear the relatives of those who have died by suicide saying, comfortably, "Well, he didn't have much to expect of life anyway!" It is an impressive and important fact that in areas where the aged enjoy real esteem (as in certain Far Eastern countries), suicide among the old is actually a rare occurrence.

Suicide prevention must also have particular concern for people who have become criminals. Nobody has the right to differentiate between lives which are worth preserving and those which are not. The prisoner is isolated and his possibilities are restricted; when in addition attitudes towards prisoners are laden with contempt, this produces a suicidal climate, and sharply increases the prisoner's risk. Suicide prevention works to counteract this, and to show how important it is even for persons who have gone astray—the asocial elements—to maintain their human rights and their human dignity.

The slightest deviation from this principle—that *every* human life is important, and so *every* human life is to be saved—would not only undermine the entire idea of suicide prevention; it would be, as Grillparzer put it, "that first step from humanity to bestiality." We have of course seen tendencies to devalue human life again and again throughout history. Hegel talked of supermen, for whom "the litany of private virtues" such as modesty, humbleness, charity, and good-doing is not valid because, he argued, "such great figures must necessarily crush many an innocent flower and destroy many a thing along their way." Napoleon met the insistent demands of the Austrian chancellor Metternich to end a war costing innumerable human lives with the cynical reply, "A man like me doesn't care for the lives of a million people." But since the explorations of Sigmund Freud, we can no longer regard the rise of inhuman tyrants as accidental. We now know that "Führer personalities" achieve their power only because countless ordinary people project their own wishes, especially their own unconscious wish for self-punishment, onto these figures. A Hitler is no accident; we are all jointly responsible for the devaluation of human life carried out by some individuals. Our century has reached the climax of contempt for human life as such and for human beings in particular.

Let us not forget those people (and unfortunately, their names are legion in our times) who are persecuted for reasons of race, religion, or politics. The persecution of the Jews is the most conspicuous, perhaps, but certainly only one of many examples. Suicide prevention efforts must be particularly aware of the kinds of situations that arise under oppression of this sort, especially since the ruling powers tend to prohibit any kind of assistance for the endangered group. External factors can become so difficult under conditions of persecution that even people who do not, by and large, have tendencies toward suicide will nevertheless—as a last resort—kill themselves. For instance, during the period 1933–1945 the rate of Jewish suicide increased heavily under the pressure of Nazi persecution, although it is precisely the Jews who are normally not prone to suicide.

It is in these situations that suicide prevention can transcend itself into courageous humaneness. Life would not be worth living were one not able to observe, in situations like these, that miraculously there are always a few courageous individuals who may form into small groups or even larger communities to maintain and implement humane thinking. Among the persecuted, this may take the form of a compassionate turning toward one's fellow man. Jean-François Steiner, for instance, in his book about the uprising at Treblinka,[1] describes the way in which each inmate of the concentration camp was initially indifferent to the fate of the others. Gradually, though, it dawned upon them that each man's duty was to prevent the suicide of the others. In this, out of the mere aggregates of individuals or "series," as Sartre puts it, there arises the task of forming a human *community*. Here, as in other forms of human togetherness, we recognize this principle: only when the individual comes to feel responsible for the fate of the others, and for their remaining alive in the struggle against self-destruction, can the "series" become a group. After all, "no man is an island entire of itself; every man is a piece of the continent, a part of the main . . . "

Man is truly the only living creature who can choose to be, or not to be. But our endeavor must be to maintain and to keep this life, and all the implications and possibilities inherent in it, to the very last. Suicide prevention is the implementation of human responsibility toward one's fellow human beings. Thus, it is by no means inhuman to reject—decisively—any demand for suicide or for the planned termination of life.

Over and over again, those who support the idea of voluntary euthanasia present to us the picture of a patient suffering from incurable cancer and unbearable pain; this, they claim, is a perfect example of a psychologically understandable, justified suicide. But I think this is wrong. First, such "understandable" cases form only a very small percentage of all suicides. For most suicides, the situation was in no way hopeless, and often not even critical. More people take their own lives because they wrongly believe themselves to be suffering from cancer, than do those who actually have cancer. Carcinophobia is a psychic disease; and it is the mental and spiritual condition of the person, not the cancer, which is the actual cause for the suicide. In the great majority of all cases, suicide is based on transient psychic illnesses which can today be cured. About a third of all suicides, for instance, can be traced to depression, or "melancholia"—yet it is now possible, with appropriate administration of antidepressants, to shorten the phases of depression considerably and to help the patient to regain normal psychic condition.

Second, we must remain aware of the concept of the "mental crisis," during which there is intense psychic conflict and often, as a direct result of this, a false assessment of the situation. The tragic story of Romeo and Juliet shows how such a misinterpretation can lead to suicide. What suicide prevention practices is "crisis intervention," for all is won if the time of crisis can be overcome. Of course, it is not enough to keep people who have attempted suicide alive by medical measures, for example, detoxification; they also require intense psychiatric treatment and postclinical care. When both methods are put into action simultaneously, it is very often possible—as declining relapse rates have shown—to prevent a recurrence of a suicide attempt. In the face of these facts, would it not be inhuman to deprive those in need and sorrow of such medical, psychological, and social aid as have in the past proved their value?

Fortunately, psychiatry has made vast progress in recent years, and enables us to offer this help more and more effectively. An increasing number of crisis-intervention clinics for giving practical aid have been set up. But it is not only the retaining of human life that is the objective; it is to help and guide the despairing to enable them to make their lives happier and more worthwhile. It is in this way that we work to restore value to human life. Suicide prevention and humane thought go hand in hand, and suicide prevention must necessarily mobilize all available humaneness if it is to triumph over a wavering ethical background.

There is possibly no better way to sum up all the humanitarian impulses released in the most various fields and levels of suicide prevention than in the admirable words of Pope John XXIII, "I want to be good always, and to all!" This quotation serves to remind us that suicide prevention has contributed to the attempt of the Christian churches to go back to the values of early Christianity. The innumerable counseling centers of the churches do not practice suicide prevention merely in order to prevent this deadly sin, but first and foremost in order to practice the Christian call: "Behold how they love one another!"

Perhaps we can see this most clearly in the happiness and gratefulness of patients who have survived a crisis. These are the feelings experienced by those patients who have been saved after an attempted suicide; perhaps these feelings could also be described as gratitude for the gift of a new life.

No one can dispute the right of man to end his life. But it is also the case that no one can dispute our right to help, in whatever way we can, those who are in spiritual need, and who are at risk of suicide. The right to prevent suicide only dims when therapy cannot succeed in restoring to a person the feeling that his life is worth living; thanks to improved therapeutic possibilities, however, this is only very, very seldom the case.

NOTES

1. Jean-François Steiner, *Treblinka.* Preface by Simone de Beauvoir. Original French edition: Librairie Arthème Fayard, 1966; English translation by Helen Weaver, New York: Simon and Schuster, 1967.

SUGGESTED READINGS FOR CHAPTER 3

A. DEFINITION OF "SUICIDE"

DURKHEIM, EMILE. *Suicide: A Study in Sociology,* translated by John A. Spaulding and George Simpson. New York: Free Press, 1966.

HOLLAND, R. F. "Suicide," as reprinted in James Rachels (ed.). *Moral Problems,* 2nd ed. New York: Harper & Row, 1975.

MARGOLIS, JOSEPH. *Negativities: The Limits of Life.* Columbus, OH: Merrill, 1975, Chapter 2.

MAYO, DAVID J. "The Concept of Rational Suicide." *The Journal of Medicine and Philosophy* 11 (1986):143–155.

WREEN, MICHAEL. "The Definition of Suicide." *Social Theory and Practice* 14 (Spring 1988):1–23.

B. CLASSICAL ISSUES IN THE MORALITY OF SUICIDE

AUGUSTINE. *The City of God,* translated by Marcus Dods. New York: Random House, Modern Library, 1950. Bk. I, sections 17–27, esp. sections 21–22, 26.

BATTIN, M. PABST. *Ethical Issues in Suicide.* Englewood Cliffs, NJ: Prentice-Hall, 1982.

BATTIN, M. PABST, and DAVID J. MAYO (eds.). *Suicide: The Philosophical Issues.* New York: St. Martin's Press, 1980.

BEAUCHAMP, TOM L. "An Analysis of Hume's Essay On Suicide." *Review of Metaphysics* 30 (September, 1976):73–95.

BRODY, BARUCH A. (ed.). *Suicide and Euthanasia: Historical and Contemporary Themes.* Dordrecht, Holland: Kluwer Academic Publishers, 1989.

DONNE, JOHN. *Biathanatos.* In Michael Rudick and M. Pabst Battin, (eds.). New York: Garland Publishing, 1982.

DONNELLY, JOHN (ed.). *Suicide: Right or Wrong?* Buffalo, NY: Prometheus Books, 1991.

ENGELHARDT, H. TRISTRAM JR. "Suicide and the Cancer Patient." *CA-A Cancer Journal for Clinicians.* 1986 Mar–Apr; 36(2):105–109.

KANT, IMMANUEL. *Lectures on Ethics,* translated by Louis Infield. New York: Harper & Row, 1963, pp. 148–154.

LEBACQZ, KAREN, and H. TRISTRAM ENGELHARDT. "Suicide." In Horan, Dennis J., and David Mall (eds.). *Death, Dying, and Euthanasia.* Washington, DC: University Publications of America, 1977, pp. 669–705.

MATTHEWS, MARTHA ALYS. "Suicidal Competence and the Patient's Right to Refuse Lifesaving Treatment." *California Law Review* 75 (March 1987): 707–758.

NOVAK, DAVID. *Suicide and Morality: The Theories of Plato, Aquinas, and Kant and Their Relevance for Suicidology.* New York: Scholars Studies, 1975.

SENECA. "On Suicide." *Epistles,* translated by E. Barker. Oxford, England: Clarendon Press, 1932.

SHNEIDMAN, EDWIN S. "Rational Suicide and Psychiatric Disorders." *New England Journal of Medicine* 1992 Mar 26; 326(13):889–891.

SPROTT, S. E. *The English Debate on Suicide: From Donne to Hume.* LaSalle, IL: Open Court, 1961.

C. PREVENTION, INTERVENTION, AND PATERNALISM

BATTIN, MARGARET P. "Choosing the Time to Die: The Ethics and Economics of Suicide in Old Age." In S. F. Spicker, S. R. Ingman, and I. R. Lawson, (eds.). *Ethical Dimensions of Geriatric Care.* Boston: D. Reidel, 1987, pp. 161–189.

BRANDT, RICHARD B., ROBERT E. LITMAN, and MICHAEL JELLINEK. "A Suicide Attempt and Emergency Room Ethics." *Hastings Center Report* 9 (August 1979):12–13.

CHILDRESS, JAMES F. *Who Should Decide? Paternalism in Health Care.* New York: Oxford University Press, 1982.

GREENBERG, DAVID F. "Involuntary Psychiatric Commitments to Prevent Suicide." *New York University Law Review* 49 (1974): 227–269.

KLEINIG, JOHN. *Paternalism.* Totowa, NJ: Rowman and Allanheld, 1984. [Kleinig's book contains an outstanding bibliography.]

SLATER, ELIOT. "Choosing the Time to Die." In Battin and Mayo (eds.) op. cit., pp. 199–204.

SOBLE, ALAN. "Paternalism, Liberal Theory, and Suicide." *Canadian Journal of Philosophy* 12 (1982): 335–352.

Szasz, Thomas. "The Ethics of Suicide." *The Antioch Review* 31 (Spring 1971): 7–17. Reprinted in Battin and Mayo, op. cit.

Van De Veer, Donald. *Paternalistic Intervention: The Moral Bounds on Benevolence.* Princeton, NJ: Princeton University Press, 1986, Chapter 5.

Williams, Glanville. *The Sanctity of Life and the Criminal Law.* New York: Knopf, 1957.

D. EMPIRICAL STUDIES OF SUICIDE

Perlin, Seymour (ed.). *A Handbook for the Study of Suicide.* New York: Oxford University Press, 1975.

Shneidman, Edwin S. (ed.). *Suicidology: Contemporary Developments.* Seminars in Psychiatry, Milton Greenblatt (ed.). New York: Grune & Stratton, 1976.

BIBLIOGRAPHICAL SOURCES AND REFERENCE WORKS

Farberow, Norman L. *Bibliography on Suicide and Suicide Prevention, 1897–1957, 1958–1970.* DHEW Publication No. (HSM) 72-9080. Rockville, MD: National Institutes of Mental Health. Washington: U.S. Government Printing Office, 1972.

Lester, David, et al. *Suicide: A Guide to Information Sources.* Detroit: Gale Research, 1980.

Lineback, Richard H. (ed.). *Philosopher's Index.* Vols. 1–. Bowling Green, Ohio: Philosophy Documentation Center, Bowling Green State University. Issued Quarterly. See under "Active Euthanasia," "Death," "Dignity," "Dying," "Euthanasia," "Killing," "Letting Die," "Life," "Paternalism," "Sanctity of Life," and "Suicide."

Walters, LeRoy, and Tamar Joy Kahn (eds.). *Bibliography of Bioethics.* Vols. 1–. New York: Free Press. Issued annually. See under "Allowing to Die," "Euthanasia," "Killing," "Suicide," "Terminal Care," and "Treatment Refusal." (The information contained in the annual *Bibliography of Bioethics* can also be retrieved from BIOETHICSLINE, an on-line data base of the National Library of Medicine.)

Reich, Warren (ed.). *Encyclopedia of Bioethics.* New York: Macmillan, 1995, articles on:

Aging and the Aged
Pain and Suffering
Paternalism
Suicide

4

Physician-Assisted Suicide
and Euthanasia

INTRODUCTION

If competent patients have a right to refuse a life-sustaining treatment and per-haps even a right to commit suicide (as discussed in the previous chapter), it might seem that these rights permit patients and physicians to arrange for the patient's death and to choose the means by which the death will occur. However, no stronger or more enduring prohibition exists in medicine than the rule against *actively causing* the death of patients. Codes of health care ethics from the time of the Hippocratic oath to the present strictly prohibit direct assistance in causing death, even if a patient has good reasons for wanting to die.

Many writers in medical ethics are now challenging these traditional proscrip-tions. They propose to reform both law and medical practice by introducing more flexibility in the ways persons who are seriously or terminally ill can die. In the pre-sentation of these issues, various labels and slogans have been employed, including "death with dignity," "euthanasia," "allowing to die," "physician-assisted suicide," and "mercy killing." Several questions are addressed in this and the subsequent chap-ter about these notions and also about the distinction between killing and letting die.

THE MEANING AND TYPES OF EUTHANASIA

Conceptual confusion has long surrounded the meaning of the term *euthana-sia*. Originally, the word was derived from two Greek roots meaning "good death." The term subsequently came to have two distinct meanings: (1) the act or practice of painlessly putting to death those who suffer from terminal conditions (active eu-thanasia), and (2) intentionally not preventing death in those who suffer from termi-nal conditions (passive euthanasia). The second meaning came into usage when technological advances in medicine made it possible to prolong the lives of persons without hope of recovery. The requirement of a "terminal condition" was also dropped in many definitions, on grounds that some persons suffer from conditions that are not terminal.

Perhaps the most accurate general meaning of the term "euthanasia" today is the following: Euthanasia occurs if and only if: (1) The death is intended by at least one other person who is either the cause of death or a causally relevant factor in bringing the death about; (2) the person killed is either acutely suffering or irreversibly comatose (or soon will be), and this alone is the primary reason for intending the person's death; and (3) the means chosen to produce the death must be as painless as possible, or there must be a sufficient moral justification for a more painful method.

If a person who is capable of voluntary action requests the termination of his or her life, the action is called *voluntary euthanasia.* If the person is not mentally competent to make an informed request, the action is called *nonvoluntary euthanasia.* Both forms should be distinguished from *involuntary euthanasia,* which involves a person capable of making an informed request, but who has not done so. However, involuntary euthanasia is universally condemned and plays no role in current moral controversies.

Two subtypes of euthanasia were distinguished after the intentional omission of life-sustaining treatment came to be called euthanasia: *active* and *passive* euthanasia. This distinction was often, though misleadingly, equated with the distinction between *killing* and *letting die.* (Both distinctions are analyzed in Chapter 5.) When this distinction is combined with the voluntary-involuntary distinction, four general categories of euthanasia emerge, of which the second and third types have been particularly controversial.

1. Voluntary passive euthanasia. (See the *Bouvia* and *McAfee* cases in Chapter 6)
2. Nonvoluntary passive euthanasia (See the *Cruzan* and *Infant Doe* cases in Chapter 6)
3. Voluntary active euthanasia (See the *Quill* case that follows; some place *Bouvia* and *McAfee* here)
4. Nonvoluntary active euthanasia (Some place *Cruzan* and *Infant Doe* here)

Voluntary active euthanasia is the type primarily under discussion in this chapter. Timothy Quill and coauthors Christine Cassel and Diane Meier describe and defend one version of it, whereas Edmund Pellegrino and Richard Fenigsen reject it.

VOLUNTARY ACTIVE EUTHANASIA

Supporters of voluntary active euthanasia argue that some cases of relief from suffering justify doing what we otherwise would never do: intentionally bring about the death of patients. They argue that society is obligated to respect the decisions of autonomous persons to die and not to limit their liberty to end their lives; similarly, respect is owed to those who help them bring about death. It is not necessary to agree with their judgments, only to recognize their *rights* to choose and act. An argument espoused by Timothy Quill and others is the appropriateness of compassionate help by physicians if (and perhaps only if): (1) a condition has become overwhelmingly burdensome for a patient; (2) pain management for the patient is inadequate; and

(3) only a physician is capable of bringing proper relief. The third condition (3) has been challenged by some contemporary writers, who believe that assistance by *non-physicians* may actually be more appropriate than assistance by physicians, especially if the role of physicians would be corrupted or physicians would be given too much power and control over their patients by legalizing euthanasia.

However, voluntary active euthanasia in any form has rarely been recognized in law or traditional medical ethics, as Edmund Pellegrino and Richard Fenigsen note. They insist that practices of killing patients are inconsistent with the roles of nursing, caregiving, and healing, would introduce conflicts of interest into those roles, and would taint the roles. Another argument is more complex and has come to be the centerpiece of discussion. This argument is referred to as the wedge or slippery slope argument, and proceeds roughly as follows: Although particular acts of active killing are sometimes morally justified, the social consequences of sanctioning practices of killing would involve serious risk of abuse and misuse and, on balance, would cause more harm than benefit. The argument is not that these negative consequences will occur immediately, but that they will grow incrementally over time. Society might start by carefully restricting the number of patients who qualify for assistance in suicide or homicide, as appears to be the strategy in the law of Oregon reprinted in this chapter. But, the argument goes, these restrictions will be revised and expanded over time, with ever increasing possibilities in the system for unjustified killing. Unscrupulous persons would learn how to abuse the system, just as they do with methods of tax evasion that operate on the margins of the system of legitimate tax avoidance.

Slippery slope arguments are difficult both to defend and to refute because the success or failure of the arguments depends on speculative predictions regarding the likely or unlikely erosion of moral restraints. If the dire and unmanageable consequences that they predict actually will flow from the legal legitimation of assisted suicide or voluntary active euthanasia, then slippery slope arguments rightly show that such practices should be legally prohibited. But how good is the evidence that dire consequences will occur? Is there a sufficient reason to think that we cannot maintain control through strict public policies? Can such questions even be answered?

PHYSICIAN-ASSISTED SUICIDE

In some legal jurisdictions, *any* deliberate aiding, advising, or encouraging of suicide is illegal. But there is increasing pressure to reform these laws, so that physicians are allowed to play a more extensive role in facilitation. One initiative has been accepted by the majority of citizens in the state of Oregon (see below). However, in late December 1994, a federal judge in Eugene, Oregon, issued a preliminary injunction that prevented putting the new law into effect for an indefinite period of time. At the time, physicians' and pharmacists' groups in Oregon had not decided whether to participate under the new law. The AMA has declared that acts of assistance in suicide by doctors, including those allowed under the Oregon bill, are "immoral." How should we view the role of physicians in assisted suicide, and what role, if any, is there for such a law? Why should either law or medical ethics prevent a physician from assisting someone who has a good reason for dying?

The most widely discussed case about physician-assisted suicide in recent years has been Quill's report of his relationship with a leukemia patient, as reprinted in this chapter. Many believe that Quill's actions were justified because the patient was competent and informed, had a longstanding relationship with the physician, had a durable desire for death, and would eventually experience unbearable suffering (from the patient's perspective). Nonetheless, critics (including Pellegrino in this chapter) have found the action by Quill unsettling, unjustified, and against the traditions of physician ethics. His act violated a New York State law against assisted suicide and also opened the possibility of misconduct charges from the New York State Health Department.

One moral problem is whether physicians are justified in performing such actions; a second is whether public policies that legalize these acts are justified. It is one thing to justify particular acts of assisting a person in suicide, another to justify general practices or policies sanctioned by law. To maintain a viable practice that avoids undesirable consequences, it may be necessary to prohibit some acts that would not be wrong were it not for their far-reaching social consequences. Particular acts of assisted suicide may in particular circumstances be humane, compassionate, and in everyone's best interest, but a social policy that authorizes such acts in medicine, it is often argued (using the "wedge" or "slippery slope" argument), would weaken moral restraints that we cannot easily replace, threatening practices that provide a basis of trust between patients and health-care professionals. Thus, the focus of discussion is often on whether society can legalize assisted suicide without jeopardizing the lives of the vulnerable.

As these controversies have developed in North America and Europe, increasing attention has been devoted to the practices of physician-assisted suicide in The Netherlands, where each year a significant percentage of elderly deaths occurs from voluntary euthanasia. Under national legislation in this country, killing at the patient's informed request is allowed by state and medical authorities. The conditions of justified euthanasia consist of a voluntary, informed, stable request by the patient who is suffering unbearably, physician consultation with a second physician, and careful review of the patient's condition by the physician performing the euthanasia procedure. The *Remmelink Report,* authorized by the Dutch government, reports on the nature and scope of euthanasia in The Netherlands. Subsequent to this report, The Netherlands' supreme court found (in the Hilly Bosscher case, decided in November 1994) that intolerable psychological suffering is not relevantly different from intolerable physical suffering, and therefore that patients who are not terminally ill but suffer from deep psychological trauma also may exercise their right to die with dignity.

Many critics of Netherlands' practices see that country as dangerously down a slippery slope. For example, Fenigsen argues that the combination of voluntary and nonvoluntary euthanasia in Holland has led to a precarious slippery slope, has failed to deliver on its promise to spare the sick, has failed to recognize that there are painless alternatives, and constitutes a serious danger to medicine. Quill, Cassel, and Meier maintain that there are reasons to think such claims and fears overrated and that they generate inattentiveness to the needs of some patients.

Current public policy and legal debates in North America are centered on these issues, as several legal and public policy readings in the final section of the present chapter indicate. Physician-assisted suicide seemed to gain significant momentum in 1993–1994—as if the time for its serious public discussion had finally arrived. Besides the legislation in Oregon, three developments in particular were of far-reaching significance in North America. First, in 1993 the Canadian Supreme Court considered the case of Sue Rodriguez and her attempt to strike down a section of the Criminal Code of Canada prohibiting physician-assisted suicide. Although she lost, she gained national attention and a great deal of legislative sympathy. Second, a federal district court judge in the state of Washington ruled in April, 1994 (in *Compassion in Dying v. State of Washington*) that the 140-year-old legal prohibition of assisted suicide in that state is unconstitutional. Then, third, in the same month of the ruling in Washington, a court in Michigan acquitted Jack Kevorkian of charges that he violated the state's newly enacted law on physician-assisted suicide by administering carbon monoxide to a patient. A jury decision in this case found that Kevorkian did not have the relevant *intention* to be in violation of the Michigan law, which exempted physicians whose intent is to relieve pain or discomfort rather than to cause death. The jury found that Kevorkian had only intended to relieve the suffering of his patients.

These questions about the active-passive distinction, proper intentions, and legitimate ways of causing death dominate the readings in this chapter.

Death and Dignity: A Case of Individualized Decision Making*

TIMOTHY E. QUILL

Physician Timothy Quill discusses how and why he prescribed the barbiturates desired by a 45-year-old leukemia patient who had refused treatment but did not
want to let the matter rest with a mere refusal or omission of chemotherapy (which
offered a 25% chance of a long-term cure). She had been Quill's patient for many
years and had come to a decision to commit suicide with the counsel of Quill and
members of her family. Quill describes himself as a long-time advocate of active,
informed patient choice of treatment and nontreatment and of a patient's right to
die with as much control and dignity as possible. In effect, in prescribing barbiturates for his patient, Quill was acting as a civil disobedient, against established
canons of physician ethics, reporting rules, and the laws of the state of New York.
He discusses the patient's competence to make the decision, the nature of the
patient-physician relationship, the quality of informed decision making by the
patient and physician, the nature of the patient's desire for death, the patient's view
of suffering, who made the final decision, and the choice of a means to death.

Diane was feeling tired and had a rash. A common scenario, though there was
something subliminally worrisome that prompted me to check her blood count. Her
hematocrit was 22, and the white-cell count was 4.3 with some metamyelocytes and
unusual white cells. I wanted it to be viral, trying to deny what was staring me in the
face. Perhaps in a repeated count it would disappear. I called Diane and told her it
might be more serious than I had initially thought—that the test needed to be repeated
and that if she felt worse, we might have to move quickly. When she pressed for the
possibilities, I reluctantly opened the door to leukemia. Hearing the word seemed to
make it exist. "Oh, shit!" she said. "Don't tell me that." Oh, shit! I thought, I wish I
didn't have to.

Diane was no ordinary person (although no one I have ever come to know has
been really ordinary). She was raised in an alcoholic family and had felt alone for
much of her life. She had vaginal cancer as a young woman. Through much of her
adult life, she had struggled with depression and her own alcoholism. I had come to

know, respect, and admire her over the previous eight years as she confronted these problems and gradually overcame them. She was an incredibly clear, at times brutally honest, thinker and communicator. As she took control of her life, she developed a strong sense of independence and confidence. In the previous 3½ years, her hard work had paid off. She was completely abstinent from alcohol, she had established much deeper connections with her husband, college-age son, and several friends, and her business and her artistic work were blossoming. She felt she was really living fully for the first time.

Not surprisingly, the repeated blood count was abnormal, and detailed examination of the peripheral-blood smear showed myelocytes. I advised her to come into the hospital, explaining that we needed to do a bone marrow biopsy and make some decisions relatively rapidly. She came to the hospital knowing what we would find. She was terrified, angry, and sad. Although we knew the odds, we both clung to the thread of possibility that it might be something else.

The bone marrow confirmed the worst: acute myelomonocytic leukemia. In the face of this tragedy, we looked for signs of hope. This is an area of medicine in which technological intervention has been successful, with cures 25 percent of the time— long-term cures. As I probed the costs of these cures, I heard about induction chemotherapy (three weeks in the hospital, prolonged neutropenia, probable infectious complications, and hair loss; 75 percent of patients respond, 25 percent do not). For the survivors, this is followed by consolidation chemotherapy (with similar side effects; another 25 percent die, for a net survival of 50 percent). Those still alive, to have a reasonable chance of long-term survival, then need bone marrow transplantation (hospitalization for two months and whole-body irradiation, with complete killing of the bone marrow, infectious complications, and the possibility for graft-versus-host disease—with a survival of approximately 50 percent, or 25 percent of the original group). Though hematologists may argue over the exact percentages, they don't argue about the outcome of no treatment—certain death in days, weeks, or at most a few months.

Believing that delay was dangerous, our oncologist broke the news to Diane and began making plans to insert a Hickman catheter and begin induction chemotherapy that afternoon. When I saw her shortly thereafter, she was enraged at his presumption that she would want treatment, and devastated by the finality of the diagnosis. All she wanted to do was go home and be with her family. She had no further questions about treatment and in fact had decided that she wanted none. Together we lamented her tragedy and the unfairness of life. Before she left, I felt the need to be sure that she and her husband understood that there was some risk in delay, that the problem was not going to go away, and that we needed to keep considering the options over the next several days. We agreed to meet in two days.

She returned in two days with her husband and son. They had talked extensively about the problem and the options. She remained very clear about her wish not to undergo chemotherapy and to live whatever time she had left outside the hospital. As we explored her thinking further, it became clear that she was convinced she would die during the period of treatment and would suffer unspeakably in the process (from hospitalization, from lack of control over her body, from the side effects of chemotherapy, and from pain and anguish.) Although I could offer support and my best effort to minimize her suffering if she chose treatment, there was no way I could say any of this would not occur. In fact, the last four patients with acute leukemia at our hospital had died very painful deaths in the hospital during various stages of treatment (a fact I did not share with her). Her family wished she would choose treatment but sadly accepted her decision. She articulated very clearly that it was she who would be experiencing all the side effects of treatment and that odds of 25 percent were not good enough for her to undergo so toxic a course of therapy, given her expectations of chemotherapy and hospitalization and the absence of a closely matched bone marrow donor. I had her repeat her understanding of the treatment, the odds, and what to expect if there were no treatment. I clarified a few misunderstandings, but she had a remarkable grasp of the options and implications.

I have been a longtime advocate of active, informed patient choice of treatment or nontreatment, and of a patient's right to die with as much control and dignity as possible. Yet there was something about her giving up a 25 percent chance of long-term survival in favor of almost certain death that disturbed me. I had seen Diane fight and use her considerable inner resources to overcome alcoholism and depression, and I half expected her to change her mind over the next week. Since the window of time in which effective treatment can be initiated is rather narrow, we met several times that week. We obtained a second hematology consultation and talked at length about the meaning and implications of treatment and nontreatment. She talked to a psychologist she had seen in the past. I gradually understood the decision from her perspective and became convinced that it was the right decision for her. We arranged for home hospice care (although at that time Diane felt reasonably well, was active, and looked healthy), left the door open for her to change her mind, and tried to anticipate how to keep her comfortable in the time she had left.

Just as I was adjusting to her decision, she opened up another area that would stretch me profoundly. It was extraordinarily important to Diane to maintain control of herself and her own dignity during the time remaining to her. When this was no longer possible, she clearly wanted to die. As a former director of a hospice program, I know how to use pain medicines to keep patients comfortable and lessen suffering. I explained the philosophy of comfort care, which I strongly believe in. Although Diane understood and appreciated this, she had known of people lingering in what was called relative comfort, and she wanted no part of it. When the time came, she wanted to take her life in the least painful way possible. Knowing of her desire for independence and her decision to stay in control, I thought this request made perfect sense. I acknowledged and explored this wish but also thought that it was out of the realm of currently accepted medical practice and that it was more than I could offer or promise. In our discussion, it became clear that preoccupation with her fear of a lingering death would interfere with Diane's getting the most out of the time she had left until she found a safe way to ensure her death. I feared the effects of a violent death on her family, the consequences of an ineffective suicide that would leave her lingering in precisely the state she dreaded so much, and the possibility that a family member would be forced to assist her, with all the legal and personal repercussions that would follow. She discussed this at length with her family. They believed that they should respect her choice. With this in mind, I told Diane that information was available from the Hemlock Society that might be helpful to her.

A week later she phoned me with a request for barbiturates for sleep. Since I knew that this was an essential ingredient in a Hemlock Society suicide, I asked her to come to the office to talk things over. She was more than willing to protect me by participating in a superficial conversation about her insomnia, but it was important to me to know how she planned to use the drugs and to be sure that she was not in despair or overwhelmed in a way that might color her judgment. In our discussion, it was apparent that she was having trouble sleeping, but it was also evident that the security of having enough barbiturates available to commit suicide when and if the time came would leave her secure enough to live fully and concentrate on the present. It was clear that she was not despondent and that in fact she was making deep, personal connections with her family and close friends. I made sure that she knew how to use the barbiturates for sleep, and also that she knew the amount needed to commit suicide. We agreed to meet regularly, and she promised to meet with me before taking her life, to ensure that all other avenues had been exhausted. I wrote the prescription with an uneasy feeling about the boundaries I was exploring—spiritual, legal, professional, and personal. Yet I also felt strongly that I was setting her free to get the most out of the time she had left, and to maintain dignity and control on her own terms until her death.

The next several months were very intense and important for Diane. Her son stayed home from college, and they were able to be with one another and say much that had not been said earlier. Her husband did his work at home so that he and Diane could spend more time together. She spent time with her closest friends. I had her come into the hospital for a conference with our residents, at which she illustrated in a most profound and personal way the importance of informed decision making, the right to refuse treatment, and the extraordinarily personal effects of illness and interaction with the medical system. There were emotional and physical hardships as well. She had periods of intense sadness and anger. Several times she became very weak, but she received transfusions as an outpatient and responded with marked improvement of symptoms. She had two serious infections that responded surprisingly well to empirical courses of oral antibiotics. After three tumultuous months, there were two weeks of relative calm and well-being, and fantasies of a miracle began to surface.

Unfortunately, we had no miracle. Bone pain, weakness, fatigue, and fevers began to dominate her life. Although the hospice workers, family members, and I tried our best to minimize the suffering and promote comfort, it was clear that the end was approaching. Diane's immediate future held what she feared the most—increasing discomfort, dependence, and hard choices between pain and sedation. She called up her closest friends and asked them to come over to say goodbye, telling them that she would be leaving soon. As we had agreed, she let me know as well. When we met, it was clear that she knew what she was doing, that she was sad and frightened to be leaving, but that she would be even more terrified to stay and suffer. In our tearful goodbye, she promised a reunion in the future at her favorite spot on the edge of Lake Geneva, with dragons swimming in the sunset.

Two days later her husband called to say that Diane had died. She had said her final goodbyes to her husband and son that morning, and asked them to leave her alone for an hour. After an hour, which must have seemed like an eternity, they found her on the couch, lying very still and covered by her favorite shawl. There was no sign of struggle. She seemed to be at peace. They called me for advice about how to proceed. When I arrived at their house, Diane indeed seemed peaceful. Her husband and son were quiet. We talked about what a remarkable person she had been. They seemed to have no doubts about the course she had chosen or about their cooperation, although the unfairness of her illness and the finality of her death were overwhelming to us all.

I called the medical examiner to inform him that a hospice patient had died. When asked about the cause of death, I said, "acute leukemia." He said that was fine and that we should call a funeral director. Although acute leukemia was the truth, it was not the whole story. Yet any mention of suicide would have given rise to a police investigation and probably brought the arrival of an ambulance crew for resuscitation. Diane would have become a "coroner's case," and the decision to perform an autopsy would have been made at the discretion of the medical examiner. The family or I could have been subject to criminal prosecution, and I to professional review, for our roles in support of Diane's choices. Although I truly believe that the family and I gave her the best care possible, allowing her to define her limits and directions as much as possible, I am not sure the law, society, or the medical profession would agree. So I said "acute leukemia" to protect all of us, to protect Diane from an invasion into her past and her body, and to continue to shield society from the knowledge of the degree of suffering that people often undergo in the process of dying. Suffering can be lessened to some extent, but in no way eliminated or made benign, by the careful intervention of a competent, caring physician, given current social constraints.

Diane taught me about the range of help I can provide if I know people well and if I allow them to say what they really want. She taught me about life, death, and honesty and about taking charge and facing tragedy squarely when it strikes. She taught me that I can take small risks for people that I really know and care about. Although I did not assist in her suicide directly, I helped indirectly to make it possible, successful, and relatively painless. Although I know we have measures to help control pain and lessen suffering, to think that people do not suffer in the process of dying is an illusion. Prolonged dying can occasionally be peaceful, but more often the role of the physician and family is limited to lessening but not eliminating severe suffering.

I wonder how many families and physicians secretly help patients over the edge into death in the face of such severe suffering. I wonder how many severely ill or dying patients secretly take their lives, dying alone in despair. I wonder whether the image of Diane's final aloneness will persist in the minds of her family, or if they will remember more the intense meaningful months they had together before she died. I wonder whether Diane struggled in that last hour, and whether the Hemlock Society's way of death by suicide is the most benign. I wonder why Diane, who gave so much to so many of us, had to be alone for the last hour of her life. I wonder whether I will see Diane again, on the shore of Lake Geneva at sunset, with dragons swimming on the horizon.

Distortion of the Healing Relationship

EDMUND D. PELLEGRINO

In the next selection Edmund Pellegrino asks whether we are ready to intentionally kill patients when reasons of respect for self-determination and beneficence
suggest that it might be appropriate. Pellegrino defends a beneficence-oriented
model of medical ethics in which the patient-physician relationship begins when
a sick person seeks the expert knowledge and skill of a physician, whose job is
to heal or at least provide medical care. The relationship is driven by cure, containment, amelioration, or prevention of illness, pain, and disability. To introduce
killing into this type of relationship therefore distorts it, in his view, and eventually will lead to distortions of trust and respect for the patient's autonomy. Pellegrino's "beneficence model of the healing relationship" suggests that the patient
has a right to a good death, but not to the option of death by killing. Pellegrino
believes it is not clear that euthanasia is even a beneficent act, although he grants
that it can be a compassionate act (at least on the surface).

DISTORTIONS OF BENEFICENCE

The strongest arguments in favor of euthanasia and assisted suicide are based
in appeals to two basic principles of contemporary medical ethics—beneficence and
respect for autonomy. Protagonists of intentional death argue when the patient is
suffering intolerably, is ready to meet death, and able to give consent, that it is compassionate, merciful, and beneficent to kill the patient or assist him or her in killing
oneself. Not to do so would be to act maleficently, to violate the dignity and autonomy of the suffering person, and to inflict harm on another human—in effect, to
abandon a person in a time of greatest need. Since the doctor has the requisite
knowledge to make death easy and painless, it is not only cruel but immoral not to
accede to the patient's request.[1,2,3] Some would carry the argument further into the
realm of justice. They would make euthanasia a moral obligation. Not to "assist" an
incompetent patient is to act discriminatorily, for it deprives the comatose, the retarded, and infants the "benefit" of an early death. When the patient's intention cannot be expressed, the obligation, in justice, is to provide involuntary or nonvoluntary
access to the same benefit of death accessible to the competent patient.[4] The Dutch
Pediatric Society is already moving in this direction in the case of badly handicapped infants.[5]

It will not do to argue that one is not intending to kill but only to relieve suffering. This is a misuse of the principle of double effect. In this regard, it is interesting that the Remmelink Report shows that only 10 of the 187 cases of patients
studied who asked for active euthanasia in Holland did so for relief of pain alone,
while 46% mentioned pain in combination with loss of dignity, unworthy dying,
dependence, or surfeit with life.[6]

At this juncture, those who see euthanasia as beneficent may reply that, in fact, physicians do not manage pain optimally, that they are not educated to do so, and that they ignore contemporary methods of analgesia. It is concluded that we cannot realistically expect or trust physicians to control pain and this justifies killing the patient out of compassion. In this way, we make the victim of medical ineptitude a victim twice over. In fact, legitimating euthanasia in any form would relieve physicians of the time, effort, and care required to control *both* pain and suffering. The moral mandate is not to extinguish the life of the patient because doctors are inept at pain control but to better educate physicians in modern methods of analgesia.

A familiar argument used in many contexts today is that what is illegal or morally forbidden but desired by many should be "regularized" to keep it within respectable bounds. Examples of this kind of thinking include legalization of drug use, prostitution, commercialization of organ procurement, and so on. This argument misses the fact that the more decorous and regulated injection of a lethal dose of morphine or potassium chloride to bring about death in a hospital or one's own bedroom by one's family practitioner is not morally different from Kevorkian's crude methodology. The intention is the same—to kill or to help the patient kill oneself. Efficiency in the killing does not eradicate the unethical nature of the act.

Arguments based on euthanasia as a way to preserve the patient's dignity in dying are grounded in a misconception about dignity.[7] Patients do not lose their dignity as humans simply because they are suffering, in pain, perhaps disfigured by illness, incontinent, or comatose. A patient's dignity resides in his humanity. It cannot be lost, even through the ravages of disease. When proponents of euthanasia speak of loss of dignity, they are speaking more for their own reactions to seeing, living with, or treating terminally ill patients. When patients speak of their fear of a loss of "dignity," for the most part, they are speaking of the way they appear to, or are regarded by, others—by physicians, nurses, other patients, and even their families. This type of "dignity" is the fabrication of the observer, not a quality of the person observed.[8]

For the patient, this is not death with "dignity"; it is more like death as a remedy for the shame they feel, or are made to feel. Shame is a potent cause of suffering. It is far more human to treat that cause by treating the patient with true dignity. Acceding to the patient's request to die is not helping to restore his dignity. It is a confirmation of the loss of worth he has suffered in the eyes of those who behold him as an object of pity.

DISTORTION OF AUTONOMY

Protagonists of euthanasia and assisted suicide argue that assisting the patient to die is a beneficent act since it respects the principle of autonomy. On this view, those who refuse to comply with the autonomous request of a competent patient are in violation of respect for persons.[9] Such absolutization of autonomy has two serious moral limitations that make any form of euthanasia or assisted suicide a maleficent rather than a beneficent act. For one thing, the mere assertion of a request cannot, of itself, bind another person within, or outside the physician-patient relationship. When a demand becomes a command, it can violate another person's autonomy. Even more problematic is whether a person desperate enough to ask to be killed or assisted in killing herself can act autonomously. In the end, the person who opts for euthanasia uses her autonomy to give up her autonomy. She chooses to eradicate the basis on which autonomy is possible—consciousness and rationality.

At the other extreme, when death is imminent, the empirical questions of autonomy are equally problematic. The person who is fatally ill is a person, often in pain, anxious, and rejected by those who are healthy, afflicted with a sense of guilt and unworthiness, perceiving himself as a social, economic, and emotional burden to others. Can a person in this state satisfy the criteria for autonomous choice?[10] How well could these patients safeguard their autonomy if euthanasia were legalized? Chronically ill and dying patients are extremely sensitive to even the most subtle suggestions of unworthiness by their medical attendants, family, and friends. Any sign— verbal or nonverbal—that reinforces guilt or shame will be picked up as a subtle suggestion to take the "noble" way out.

The degree to which pain, guilt, and unworthiness may compromise autonomy is evident in the fact that when these are removed or ameliorated, patients do not ask to be killed.[11] Even if euthanasia were legalized, a first obligation under both principles of beneficence and autonomy would be to diagnose, ameliorate, or remove those causes of the patient's despondency and suffering that lead to a request for euthanasia in the first place.

DISTORTION OF TRUST

Trust plays an inescapable role in whatever model of physician-patient relationship one chooses.[12] The patient trusts the physician to do what is in the patient's best interests as it is indicated by the diagnosis, prognosis, and therapeutic possibilities. When patients know that euthanasia is a legitimate choice and that some physicians may see killing as healing, they know they are vulnerable to violations of trust.

A much more common danger at present is the possibility that the physician's values and acceptance of euthanasia may unconsciously shape how vigorously she treats the patient or presents the possibility of assisted suicide. How is the patient to know when his doctor is persuading or even subtly coercing him to choose death? The doctor's motives may be unconsciously to advance her own beliefs that euthanasia is a social good to relieve herself of the frustrating difficulties of caring for the patient, of her distress with the quality of life the patient is forced to lead, or promote her desire to conserve society's resources, etc. How will a patient ever be sure of the true motive for his doctor's recommendation? When is the doctor depreciating the value of available methods of pain relief or comprehensive palliative care because he believes the really "good" death is a planned death?

The power of physicians to shape their patient's choices is well-known to every experienced clinician. Physicians can get a patient to agree to almost any decision they want by the way they present the alternatives. All judgments may be influenced by the physician's attitude on euthanasia or her emotional and physical frustrations in treating a difficult patient. How realistic is patient autonomy in such circumstances? How effective can the criteria proposed to prevent abuses of legalized euthanasia really be?

ASSISTED SUICIDE: IS THERE A MORAL DIFFERENCE BETWEEN QUILL AND KEVORKIAN?

What I have attempted to show is the way in which intentional killing, if accepted into the body of medical ethics, would distort the ethics and purposes of the healing relationship in at least three of its dimensions—beneficence, protection of autonomy, and fidelity to trust. One may justifiably ask: Is the ethical situation different if the physician intends only to advise the patient on how to attain the goal of a "good" death by assisting the patient to kill oneself? Is not the causal and intentional relationship of the physician to the death of the patient essentially different?

I do not believe a convincing case can be made for a moral difference between the two. This is a classical instance of a distinction without a difference in kind. The intentional end sought in either case is the death of the patient: in active euthanasia, the physician is the immediate cause; in assisted suicide, the physician is the necessary cooperating cause, a moral accomplice without whom the patient could not kill oneself. In assisted suicide, the doctor fully shares the patient's intention to end his or her life. The doctor provides the lethal medication, advises on the proper dose, on how it should be taken to be most effective, and on what to do if the dose is regurgitated. The physician's cooperation is necessary if the act is to be carried out at all. The physician shares equal responsibility with the patient just as she or he would in active euthanasia.

This moral complicity is obvious in the cases reported by Dr. Timothy Quill and Dr. Jack Kevorkian. In both cases, the physician provided the means fully knowing the patient would use them and encouraging the patients to do so when they felt the time was right. Kevorkian's "death machine" was operated by the patient but designed and provided by Kevorkian. Quill's patient took the sedatives he prescribed. To be sure, Quill's account of his assistance in the death of a young woman with leukemia elicits more sympathy because the length and intensity of his professional relationship with her. Kevorkian's cases, in contrast, are remarkable for the brevity of the relationships, the absence of any serious attempt to provide palliative medical or psychiatric assistance, and the brusqueness with which the decisions are made and carried out. Kevorkian is the technician of death; Quill, its artist.

Quill's *modus operandi* is gentler and more deliberate, but this does not change the nature of the action in any essential way. Indeed, in some ways, Quill's approach is more dangerous to patient beneficence and autonomy because it compromises the patient more subtly and is conducted under the intention of "treatment." But when does the intention to treat become synonymous with the intent to assist in, or actively accelerate, death? Kevorkian's patients at least approach him with the intention already in their minds to commit suicide and to gain access to his machine. He is, after all, a pathologist, and his patients do not start out thinking he might be able to treat their illnesses. Quill's patients presumably come to him as a physician primarily, not as a minister of death. This may well change now that Quill has attained so much notoriety through his public zeal for assisted suicide.

NOTES

1. J.H. Van Den Berg. *Medical Power and Medical Ethics.* New York: W. W. Norton, 1978.
2. T.E. Quill. "Doctor, I Want to Die, Will You Help Me?" *Journal of the American Medical Association* 270(7): (1993):870–873.
3. C.K. Cassell and D.E. Meier. "Morals and Moralism in the Debate Over Euthanasia and Assisted Suicide." *New England Journal of Medicine* 323 (1990):750–752.
4. J. Lachs, "Active Euthanasia." *Journal of Clinical Ethics* 1(2) (1993):113–115.
5. E. Van Leeuwen and G.K. Kimsma. "Acting or Letting Go: Medical Decision Making in Neonatology in the Netherlands." *Cambridge Quarterly of Health Care Ethics* 2(3) (1993):265–269.
6. Commission on the Study of Medical Practice Concerning Euthanasia. "Medical Decisions Concerning the End of Life" (The Hague: Staatsuitgeverij, 1991). See also P.J. van der Maas, J.J.M. van Delden, et al. "Euthanasia and Other Medical Decisions Concerning the End of Life." *Lancet* 338 (1991):669–674.
7. T. Quill. *Death and Dignity: Making Choices and Taking Charge.* New York: W. W. Norton, 1992.
8. D.P. Sulmasy. "Death and Human Dignity." *Linacre Quarterly* 61(4) (1994):27–36.
9. J. Kevorkian. "The Goodness of a Planned Death: An Interview with Jack Kevorkian." *Free Inquiry* (Fall 1991):14–18.
10. Y. Conwell and E. Caine. "Rational Suicide and the Right to Die," *New England Journal of Medicine* 325 (Oct. 10, 1991):100–103.
11. N. Coyle. "The Last Weeks of Life." *American Journal of Nursing* (1990):75–78.
12. E.D. Pellegrino. "Trust and Distrust in Professional Ethics." In E.D. Pellegrino, et al. (eds.) *Ethics, Trust and the Professions.* Washington, DC: Georgetown University Press, 1991, pp. 69–92.

Care of the Hopelessly Ill
Proposed Clinical Criteria for
Physician-Assisted Suicide*

TIMOTHY E. QUILL, CHRISTINE K. CASSEL, AND DIANE E. MEIER

The authors of the next article have as their purpose to propose clinical criteria to allow physicians to help competent, incurably ill patients who request assisted suicide. They defend the legalization of physician-assisted suicide, but not voluntary active euthanasia. They argue that this way of drawing lines permits the best balance between human responsiveness to patients' requests and the social imperative to protect vulnerable persons. They advocate intensive comfort care for all incurably ill persons and use of all means to make their deaths tolerable. They insist that physician-assisted suicide should never be substituted for comprehensive care or for helping patients to resolve physical, personal, and social challenges posed by the dying process. But when an incurably ill patient rationally requests help in dying by suicide, these authors believe physicians are *obligated* to explore the request and, under appropriate circumstances, to comply with it.

One of medicine's most important purposes is to allow hopelessly ill persons to die with as much comfort, control, and dignity as possible. The philosophy and techniques of comfort care provide a humane alternative to more traditional, curative medical approaches in helping patients achieve this end.[1–6] Yet there remains instances in which incurably ill patients suffer intolerably before death despite comprehensive efforts to provide comfort. Some of these patients would rather die than continue to live under the conditions imposed by their illness, and a few request assistance from their physicians.

The patients who ask us to face such predicaments do not fall into simple diagnostic categories. Until recently, their problems have been relatively unacknowledged and unexplored by the medical profession, so little is objectively known about the spectrum and prevalence of such requests or about the range of physicians' responses.[7–10] Yet each request can be compelling. Consider the following patients: a former athlete, weighing 80 lb (36 kg) after an eight-year struggle with the acquired immunodeficiency syndrome (AIDS), who is losing his sight and his memory and is terrified of AIDS dementia; a mother of seven children, continually exhausted and bed-bound at home with a gaping, foul-smelling, open wound in her abdomen, who can no longer eat and who no longer wants to fight ovarian cancer; a fiercely independent retired factory worker, quadriplegic from amyotrophic lateral

*Source: Quill, T. E., Cassel, C. K., and Meier, D. E., "Care of the Hopelessly Ill: Proposed Clinical Criteria for Physician-Assisted Suicide," reprinted by permission of the *New England Journal of Medicine* 327, no. 19, Nov. 5, 1992, Massachusetts Medical Society, pp. 1380–1384.

sclerosis, who no longer wants to linger in a helpless, dependent state waiting and hoping for death; a writer with extensive bone metastases from lung cancer that has not responded to chemotherapy or radiation, who cannot accept the daily choice he must make between sedation and severe pain; and a physician colleague, dying of respiratory failure from progressive pulmonary fibrosis, who does not want to be maintained on a ventilator but is equally terrified of suffocation. Like the story of "Diane," which has been told in more detail,[11] there are personal stories of courage and grief for each of these patients that force us to take very seriously their requests for a physician's assistance in dying.

Our purpose is to propose clinical criteria that would allow physicians to respond to requests for assisted suicide from their competent, incurably ill patients. We support the legalization of such suicide, but not of active euthanasia. We believe this position permits the best balance between a humane response to the requests of patients like those described above and the need to protect other vulnerable people. We strongly advocate intensive, unrestrained care intended to provide comfort for all incurably ill persons.[1-6] When properly applied, such comfort care should result in a tolerable death, with symptoms relatively well controlled, for most patients. Physician-assisted suicide should never be contemplated as a substitute for comprehensive comfort care or for working with patients to resolve the physical, personal, and social challenges posed by the process of dying.[12] Yet it is not idiosyncratic, selfish, or indicative of a psychiatric disorder for people with an incurable illness to want some control over how they die. The idea of a noble, dignified death, with a meaning that is deeply personal and unique, is exalted in great literature, poetry, art, and music.[13] When an incurably ill patient asks for help in achieving such a death, we believe physicians have an obligation to explore the request fully and, under specified circumstances, carefully to consider making an exception to the prohibition against assisting with a suicide.

PHYSICIAN-ASSISTED SUICIDE

For a physician, assisting with suicide entails making a means of suicide (such as a prescription for barbiturates) available to a patient who is otherwise physically capable of suicide and who subsequently acts on his or her own. Physician-assisted suicide is distinguished from voluntary euthanasia, in which the physician not only makes the means available but, at the patient's request, also serves as the actual agent of death. Whereas active euthanasia is illegal throughout the United States, only 36 states have laws explicitly prohibiting assisted suicide.[14,15] In every situation in which a physician has compassionately helped a terminally ill person to commit suicide, criminal charges have been dismissed or a verdict of not guilty has been brought[14,15] (and Gostin L: personal communication). Although the prospect of a successful prosecution may be remote, the risk of an expensive, publicized professional and legal inquiry would be prohibitive for most physicians and would certainly keep the practice covert among those who participate.

It is not known how widespread physician-assisted suicide currently is in the United States, or how frequently patients' requests are turned down by physicians.

Approximately 6000 deaths per day in the United States are said to be in some way planned or indirectly assisted,[16] probably through the "double effect" of pain-relieving medications that may at the same time hasten death[3,12] or the discontinuation of or failure to start potentially life-prolonging treatments. From 3 to 37 percent of physicians responding to anonymous surveys reported secretly taking active steps to hasten a patient's death, but these survey data were flawed by low response rates and poor design.[7-10] Every public-opinion survey taken over the past 40 years has shown support by a majority of Americans for the idea of physician-assisted death for the terminally ill.[16-19] A referendum with loosely defined safeguards that would have legalized both voluntary euthanasia and assisted suicide was narrowly defeated in Washington State in 1991,[20] and more conservatively drawn initiatives are currently on the ballot in California, before the legislature in New Hampshire, and under consideration in Florida and Oregon.

A POLICY PROPOSAL

Although physician-assisted suicide and voluntary euthanasia both involve the active facilitation of a wished-for death, there are several important distinctions between them.[21] In assisted suicide, the final act is solely the patient's, and the risk of subtle coercion from doctors, family members, institutions, or other social forces is greatly reduced.[22] The balance of power between doctor and patient is more nearly equal in physician-assisted suicide than in euthanasia. The physician is counselor and witness and makes the means available, but ultimately the patient must be the one to act or not act. In voluntary euthanasia, the physician both provides the means and carries out the final act, with greatly amplified power over the patient and an increased risk of error, coercion, or abuse.

In view of these distinctions, we conclude that legalization of physician-assisted suicide, but not of voluntary euthanasia, is the policy best able to respond to patients' needs and to protect vulnerable people. From this perspective, physician-assisted suicide forms part of the continuum of options for comfort care, beginning with the forgoing of life-sustaining therapy, including more aggressive symptom-relieving measures, and permitting physician-assisted suicide only if all other alternatives have failed and all criteria have been met. Active voluntary euthanasia is excluded from this continuum because of the risk of abuse it presents. We recognize that this exclusion is made at a cost to competent, incurably ill patients who cannot swallow or move and who therefore cannot be helped to die by assisted suicide. Such persons, who meet agreed-on criteria in other respects, must not be abandoned to their suffering; a combination of decisions to forgo life-sustaining treatments (including food and fluids) with aggressive comfort measures (such as analgesics and sedatives) could be offered, along with a commitment to search for creative alternatives. We acknowledge that this solution is less than ideal, but we also recognize that in the United States access to medical care is currently too inequitable, and many doctor-patient relationships too impersonal, for us to tolerate the risks of permitting active voluntary euthanasia. We must monitor any change in public policy in this domain to evaluate both its benefits and its burdens.

We propose the following clinical guidelines to contribute to serious discussion about physician-assisted suicide. Although we favor a reconsideration of the legal and professional prohibitions in the case of patients who meet carefully defined criteria, we do not wish to promote an easy or impersonal process.23 If we are to consider allowing incurably ill patients more control over their deaths, it must be as an expression of our compassion and concern about their ultimate fate after all other alternatives have been exhausted. Such patients should not be held hostage to our reluctance or inability to forge policies in this difficult area.

PROPOSED CLINICAL CRITERIA FOR PHYSICIAN-ASSISTED SUICIDE

Because assisted suicide is extraordinary and irreversible treatment, the patient's primary physician must ensure that the following conditions are clearly satisfied before proceeding. First, the patient must have a condition that is incurable and associated with severe, unrelenting suffering. The patient must understand the condition, the prognosis, and the types of comfort care available as alternatives. Although most patients making this request will be near death, we acknowledge the inexactness of such prognostications24–26 and do not want to exclude arbitrarily persons with incurable, but not imminently terminal, progressive illnesses, such as amyotrophic lateral sclerosis or multiple sclerosis. When there is considerable uncertainty about the patient's medical condition or prognosis, a second opinion or opinions should be sought and the uncertainty clarified as much as possible before a final decision about the patient's request is made.

Second, the physician must ensure that the patient's suffering and the request are not the result of inadequate comfort care. All reasonable comfort-oriented measures must at least have been considered, and preferably have been tried, before the means for a physician-assisted suicide are provided. Physician-assisted suicide must never be used to circumvent the struggle to provide comprehensive care or find acceptable alternatives. The physician's prospective willingness to provide assisted suicide is a legitimate and important subject to discuss if the patient raises the question, since many patients will probably find the possibility of an escape from suffering more important than the reality.

Third, the patient must clearly and repeatedly, of his or her own free will and initiative, request to die rather than continue suffering. The physician should understand thoroughly what continued life means to the patient and why death appears preferable. A physician's too-ready acceptance of a patient's request could be perceived as encouragement to commit suicide, yet it is important not to force the patient to "beg" for assistance. Understanding the patient's desire to die and being certain that the request is serious are critical steps in evaluating the patient's rationality and ensuring that all alternative means of relieving suffering have been adequately explored. Any sign of ambivalence or uncertainty on the part of the patient should abort the process, because a clear, convincing, and continuous desire for an end of suffering through death is a strict requirement to proceed. Requests for assisted suicide made in an advance directive or by a health care surrogate should not be honored.

Fourth, the physician must be sure that the patient's judgment is not distorted. The patient must be capable of understanding the decision and its implications. The presence of depression is relevant if it is distorting rational decision making and is reversible in a way that would substantially alter the situation. Expert psychiatric evaluation should be sought when the primary physician is inexperienced in the diagnosis and treatment of depression, or when there is uncertainty about the rationality of the request or the presence of a reversible mental disorder the treatment of which would substantially change the patient's perception of his or her condition.[27]

Fifth, physician-assisted suicide should be carried out only in the context of a meaningful doctor-patient relationship. Ideally, the physician should have witnessed the patient's previous illness and suffering. There may not always be a preexisting relationship, but the physician must get to know the patient personally in order to understand fully the reasons for the request. The physician must understand why the patient considers death to be the best of a limited number of very unfortunate options. The primary physician must personally confirm that each of the criteria has been met. The patient should have no doubt that the physician is committed to finding alternative solutions if at any moment the patient's mind changes. Rather than create a new subspecialty focused on death,[28] assistance in suicide should be given by the same physician who has been struggling with the patient to provide comfort care, and who will stand by the patient and provide care until the time of death, no matter what path is taken.[23]

No physician should be forced to assist a patient in suicide if it violates the physician's fundamental values, although the patient's personal physician should think seriously before turning down such a request. Should a transfer of care be necessary, the personal physician should help the patient find another, more receptive primary physician.

Sixth, consultation with another experienced physician is required to ensure that the patient's request is voluntary and rational, the diagnosis and prognosis accurate, and the exploration of comfort-oriented alternatives thorough. The consulting physician should review the supporting materials and should interview and examine the patient.

Finally, clear documentation to support each condition is required. A system must be developed for reporting, reviewing, and studying such deaths and clearly distinguishing them from other forms of suicide. The patient, the primary physician, and the consultant must each sign a consent form. A physician-assisted suicide must neither invalidate insurance policies nor lead to an investigation by the medical examiner or an unwanted autopsy. The primary physician, the medical consultant, and the family must be assured that if the conditions agreed on are satisfied in good faith, they will be free from criminal prosecution for having assisted the patient to die.

Informing family members is strongly recommended, but whom to involve and inform should be left to the discretion and control of the patient. Similarly, spiritual counseling should be offered, depending on the patient's background and beliefs. Ideally, close family members should be an integral part of the decision-making process and should understand and support the patient's decision. If there is a major dispute between the family and the patient about how to proceed, it may require the involvement of an ethics committee or even of the courts. It is to be hoped, however, that most of these painful decisions can be worked through directly by the patient, the family, and health care providers. Under no circumstances should the family's wishes and requests override those of a competent patient.

THE METHOD

In physician-assisted suicide, a lethal amount of medication is usually prescribed that the patient then ingests. Since this process has been largely covert and unstudied, little is known about which methods are the most humane and effective. If there is a change in policy, there must be an open sharing of information within the profession, and a careful analysis of effectiveness. The methods selected should be reliable and should not add to the patient's suffering. We must also provide support and careful monitoring for the patients, physicians, and families affected, since the emotional and social effects are largely unknown but are undoubtedly far-reaching.

Assistance with suicide is one of the most profound and meaningful requests a patient can make of a physician. If the patient and the physician agree that there are no acceptable alternatives and that all the required conditions have been met, the lethal medication should ideally be taken in the physician's presence. Unless the patient specifically requests it, he or she should not be left alone at the time of death. In addition to the personal physician, other health care providers and family members should be encouraged to be present, as the patient wishes. It is of the utmost importance not to abandon the patient at this critical moment. The time before a controlled death can provide an opportunity for a rich and meaningful goodbye between family members, health care providers, and the patient. For this reason, we must be sure that any policies and laws enacted to allow assisted suicide do not require that the patient be left alone at the moment of death in order for the assisters to be safe from prosecution.

BALANCING RISKS AND BENEFITS

There is an intensifying debate within and outside the medical profession about the physician's appropriate role in assisting dying.[3,21,29–42] Although most agree that there are exceptional circumstances in which death is preferable to intolerable suffering, the case against both physician-assisted suicide and voluntary euthanasia is based mainly on the implications for public policy and the potential effect on the moral integrity of the medical profession.[35–42] The "slippery slope" argument asserts that permissive policies would inevitably lead to subtle coercion of the powerless to choose death rather than become burdens to society or their families. Access to health care in the United States is extraordinarily variable, often impersonal, and subject to intense pressures for cost containment. It may be dangerous to license physicians to take life in this unstable environment. It is also suggested that comfort care, skillfully applied, could provide a tolerable and dignified death for most persons and that physicians would have less incentive to become more proficient at providing such care if the option of a quick, controlled death were too readily available. Finally, some believe that physician-assisted death, no matter how noble and pure its intentions, could destroy the identity of the medical profession and its central ethos, protecting the sanctity of life. The question before policy makers, physicians, and voters is whether criteria such as those we have outlined here safeguard patients adequately against these risks.

The risks and burdens of continuing with the current prohibitions have been less clearly articulated in the literature.[21,29–34] The most pressing problem is the potential abandonment of competent, incurably ill patients who yearn for death despite comprehensive comfort care. These patients may be disintegrating physically and emotionally, but death is not imminent. They have often fought heroic medical battles only to find themselves in this final condition. Those who have witnessed difficult deaths in hospice programs are not reassured by the glib assertion that we can always make death tolerable, and patients fear that physicians will abandon them if their course becomes difficult or overwhelming in the face of comfort care. In fact, there is no empirical evidence that all physical suffering associated with incurable illness can be effectively relieved. In addition, the most frightening aspect of death for many is not physical pain, but the prospect of losing control and independence and of dying in an undignified, unesthetic, absurd, and existentially unacceptable condition.

Physicians who respond to requests for assisted suicide from such patients do so at substantial professional and legal peril, often acting in secret without the benefit of consultation or support from colleagues. This covert practice discourages open and honest communication among physicians, their colleagues, and their dying patients. Decisions often depend more on the physician's values and willingness to take risks than on the compelling nature of the patient's request. There may be more risk of abuse and idiosyncratic decision making with such secret practices than with a more open, carefully defined practice. Finally, terminally ill patients who do choose to take their lives often die alone so as not to place their families or care givers in legal jeopardy.[11]

CONCLUSIONS

Given current professional and legal prohibitions, physicians find themselves in a difficult position when they receive requests for assisted suicide from suffering patients who have exhausted the usefulness of measures for comfort care. To adhere to the letter of the law, they must turn down their patients' requests even if they find them reasonable and personally acceptable. If they accede to their patients' requests, they must risk violating legal and professional standards, and therefore they act in isolation and in secret collaboration with their patients. We believe that there is more risk for vulnerable patients and for the integrity of the profession in such hidden practices, however well intended, than there would be in a more open process restricted to competent patients who met carefully defined criteria. The medical and legal professions must collaborate if we are to create public policy that fully acknowledges irreversible suffering and offers dying patients a broader range of options to explore with their physicians.

NOTES

1. Wanzer S.H., Adelstein S.J. Cranford R.E., et al. The physician's responsibility toward hopelessly ill patients. *New England Journal of Medicine* 1984;310:955–999.
2. Wanzer S.H., Federman D.D., Adelstein S.J., et al. The physician's responsibility toward hopelessly ill patients: a second look. *New England Journal of Medicine* 1989;320:844–849.
3. Council on Ethical and Judicial Affairs, American Medical Association. Decisions near the end of life. *JAMA* 1992;267:2229–2233.
4. Rhymes J. Hospice care in America. *JAMA* 1990;264:369–372.
5. Broadfield L. Evaluation of palliative care: current status and future directions. *Journal of Palliative Care* 1988;4(3):21–28.
6. Wallston K.A., Burger C., Smith R.A., et al. Comparing the quality of death for hospice and non-hospice cancer patients. *Medical Care* 1988;26:177–182.
7. The National Hemlock Society. 1987 Survey of California physicians regarding voluntary active euthanasia for the terminally ill. Los Angeles: Hemlock Society, February 17, 1988.
8. Center for Health Ethics and Policy. Withholding and withdrawing life-sustaining treatment: a survey of opinions and experiences of Colorado physicians. Denver: University of Colorado Graduate School of Public Affairs, May 1988.
9. Heilig S. The SFMS Euthanasia Survey: results and analyses. San Francisco Med. May 1988:24–26, 34.
10. Overmyer M. National survey: physicians' views on the right to die. *Physicians Manage* 1991;31(7):40–45.
11. Quill T.E. Death and dignity—a case of individualized decision making. *New England Journal of Medicine* 1991;324:691–694.
12. Meier D.E., Cassel C.K. Euthanasia in old age: a case study and ethical analysis. *Journal of American Geriatrics Society* 1983;31:294–298.
13. Aries P. *The hour of our death.* New York: Vintage Books, 1982.
14. Newman S. A. Euthanasia: orchestrating "the last syllable of . . . time." *University of Pittsburgh Law Review* 1991;53:153–191.
15. Glantz L. H. Withholding and withdrawing treatment: the role of the criminal law. *Law Med Health Care* 1987/88;15:231–241.
16. Malcolm A. Giving death a hand: rending issue. *New York Times.* June 14, 1990:A6.
17. Gest T. Changing the rules on dying. *U.S. News & World Report.* July 9, 1990; 22–24.
18. The Hemlock Society. 1990 Roper poll on physician aid-in dying, allowing Nancy Cruzan to die, and physicians obeying the living will. New York: Roper Organization. April 24–25, 1990.
19. *Idem.* 1991 Roper poll of the West Coast on euthanasia. New York: Roper Organization, May 1991.
20. Misbin R.I. Physicians' aid in dying. *New England Journal of Medicine* 1991;325:1037–1311.
21. Weir R.F. The morality of physician-assisted suicide. *Law Med Health Care,* 1992: 20:116–126.

22. Glover J. *Causing death and saving lives.* New York: Penguin Books, 1977: 182–189.

23. Jecker N.S. Giving death a hand: when the dying and the doctor stand in a special relationship. *Journal of American Geriatrics Society* 1991;39:831–835.

24. Poses R.M., Bekes C., Copare F.J., Scott W.E. The answer to "What are my chances, doctor?" depends on whom is asked: prognostic disagreement and inaccuracy for critically ill patients. *Critical Care Medicine* 1989;17:827–833.

25. Charlson M.E. Studies of prognosis: progress and pitfalls. *J Gen Intern Med* 1987;2:359–361.

26. Schonwetter R.S., Teasdale T.A., Storey P., Luchi R.J. Estimation of survival time in terminal cancer patients: an impedance to hospice admissions? *Hospice Journal* 1990;6:65–79.

27. Conwell Y., Caine E.D., Rational suicide and the right to die—reality and myth. *New England Journal of Medicine* 1991;325:1100–1103.

28. Benrubi G.I. Euthanasia—the need for procedural safeguards. *New England Journal of Medicine* 1992;326:197–199.

29. Cassel C.K., Meier D.E. Morals and moralism in the debate over euthanasia and assisted suicide. *New England Journal of Medicine* 1990;323:750–752.

30. Reichel W., Dyck A.J. Euthanasia: a contemporary moral quandary. *Lancet* 1989;2:1321–1323.

31. Angell M. Euthanasia. *New England Journal of Medicine* 1988;319:1348–1350.

32. Rachels J. Active and passive euthanasia. *New England Journal of Medicine* 1975;292:78–80.

33. Lachs J. Humane treatment and the treatment of humans. *New England Journal of Medicine* 1976;294:838–840.

34. van der Maas P.J., van Delden J.J.M., Pijnenborg L., et al. Euthanasia and other medical decisions concerning the end of life. *Lancet* 1991;338:669–674.

35. Singer P.A., Siegler M. Euthanasia—a critique. *New England Journal of Medicine* 1990;322:1881–1883.

36. Orentlicher D. Physician participation in assisted suicide. *JAMA* 1898;262: 1844–1845.

37. Wolf S.M. Holding the line on euthanasia. *Hastings Center Report* 1989;19(1): Suppl:13–15.

38. Gaylin W., Kass L. R., Pellegrino E.D., Siegler M. "Doctors must not kill." *JAMA* 1988;259:2139–2140.

39. Vaux K. L. Debbie's dying: mercy killing and the good death. *JAMA* 1988;259: 2140–2141.

40. Gomez C.F. *Regulating death: euthanasia and the case of the Netherlands.* New York: Free Press, 1991.

41. Brahams D. Euthanasia in the Netherlands. *Lancet* 1990;335:591–592.

42. Leenen H.J.J. Coma patients in The Netherlands, *British Medical Journal* 1900;300:69.

A Case Against Dutch Euthanasia*

RICHARD FENIGSEN

The next article examines the growing acceptance of voluntary—and Richard Fenigsen thinks nonvoluntary—active euthanasia in The Netherlands. The author considers the use of plastic cards requesting active euthanasia, public opinion surveys, and the impact of support by leading physicians of legalized euthanasia. He condemns all practices of euthanasia, arguing that claims that autonomous choices are made by patients are often fraudulent or otherwise questionable. The author also believes that practices of euthanasia are and will be used to support nonvoluntary euthanasia, and that its hope to spare the sick person agony is empty. He is also concerned about the message these social practices send to the elderly, the sick, the weak, and the dependent and about the fallibility of medical judgments. Finally, the author is concerned about irreparable damage to the reputation of the medical profession.

Dutch general practitioners perform voluntary active euthanasia on an estimated 5,000 patients a year; the larger figure cited of 6,000 to 10,000 patients probably also includes hospital patients. However, figures as high as 18,000 or 20,000 cases a year have been mentioned. . . . Eighty-one percent of Dutch general practitioners have performed active euthanasia at some time during their professional careers; 28 percent perform active euthanasia on two patients yearly, and 14 percent on three to five patients every year. In Holland, the causes of death of people suffering from AIDS are different from those of patients with AIDS in other countries as 11.2 percent of Dutch AIDS patients die by active euthanasia.

Many people in The Netherlands carry a will requiring active euthanasia to be performed on them "in case of bodily injury or mental disturbance of which no recovery to reasonable and dignified existence is to be expected." Recently, the paper wills have begun to be replaced by small, handy plastic cards nicknamed "credit cards for easy death" by the Dutch press. In 1981 the number of people carrying such cards was reported to be 30,000, but is supposedly much higher now. . . .

Acceptance of "voluntary" active euthanasia by the Dutch people is growing. According to two consecutive polls, 70 percent of the Dutch people accepted active euthanasia in 1985, and 76 percent in 1986. This is interpreted by the media as a vote for human freedom (including the freedom of the individual to decide upon his or her life or death), but the reality is more complex. An analysis of public opinion reveals other, and quite different attitudes, in particular, views that oppose the individual's freedom of choice and support society's right to cut short a person's life. Thus, there is considerable public acceptance of the view that life-saving treatment should be denied to the severely handicapped, the elderly, and perhaps to persons

*Source: Richard Fenigsen, "A Case Against Dutch Euthanasia," *Hastings Center Report* Special Supplement (January/February 1989), pp. 22–30. Reproduced by permission. © The Hastings Center.

without families. Further, opinion polls show that a majority of the same public that proclaims support for voluntary euthanasia, freedom of choice, and the right to die, also accepts involuntary active euthanasia—that is, denial of free choice and of the right to live. . . .

EUTHANASIA IN THE COURTS

Of the 5,000 to 20,000 cases of active euthanasia occurring every year, an average of eleven prompt inquiries to be made by the offices of public prosecutors. The prosecutors act under a regulation issued by the Ministry of Justice which states that an inquiry should be launched only when it is suspected that the doctor performing euthanasia did not act in a careful manner. The legal authorities encourage doctors performing euthanasia to state active euthanasia as the cause of death to avoid their making false statements. In some cases, the doctors inform the public prosecutor beforehand that euthanasia is to be performed. The sentence passed by the court in Leeuwaarden in 1972 (one week of suspended arrest for a doctor who killed her mother) initiated the judicial trend now followed by all the courts, higher appellate courts, the Supreme Court, public prosecutors, and the Ministry of Justice. In the few cases of "voluntary" euthanasia brought to trial, the court declares the doctor guilty but does not impose punishment, whereupon the higher court overturns the "guilty" verdict on the grounds that the doctor acted out of higher necessity. The latter ruling is now being applied in every such case.

When a perpetrator of involuntary euthanasia is brought to trial, as in the case of the doctor who secretly committed the killings in *De Terp* nursing home in The Hague, punishment is imposed but abolished on a technicality by a higher court. . . .

WHY HOLLAND?

. . . The media have been virtually monopolized by the euthanasia proponents, and a whole generation of Dutch people has been raised without ever hearing any serious opposition to it.

Several features of Dutch public life seem to have enhanced the rapid expansion of the pro-euthanasia movement. First, Holland is a very democratic, liberated, and permissive society that highly values unlimited freedom of thought and expression, and encourages the rejecting of dogmas and the overthrowing of taboos. This has facilitated open discussion of euthanasia and the questioning of the "taboo" upholding the sacredness of human life. One peculiar feature (or side-effect) of the advanced democratization and liberalism of Dutch society is popular anti-medical feeling, which runs much higher here than in other European countries. There is great resentment against doctors who wield so much power without being elected, and who are seen as selfish, much too self-assured, devoid of common sense, and ignorant of people's needs. There is a strong link between this anti-medical public mood, nurtured by propaganda in the Dutch media, and the rush to euthanasia. Some people would rather die soon than be left to the mercy of doctors "and their machines." . . .

"VOLUNTARY" EUTHANASIA

. . . There are, and always have been, compelling reasons for which "voluntary" euthanasia was rejected by Western civilization in the past, and should be rejected now and in the future.

"Voluntary" euthanasia should be rejected *because its voluntariness is often counterfeit and always questionable.* In Holland, doctors have tried to coerce patients, and wives have coerced husbands and husbands wives to undergo "voluntary" euthanasia. But it is not these flagrant incidents that matter, it is all the others. For twenty years the population of Holland has been subjected to all-intrusive propaganda in favor of death. The highest terms of praise have been applied to the request to die: this act is "brave," "wise," and "progressive." All efforts are made to convince people that this is what they ought to do, what society expects of them, what is best for themselves and their families. The result is, as Attorney General T.M. Schalken stated in 1984, that "elderly people begin to consider themselves a burden to the society, and feel under an obligation to start conversations on euthanasia, or even to request it." Recently, the Dutch Patients' Association warned Parliament of reports showing how strongly a sick person's decision to request euthanasia is influenced by pressure from the family and the physician. It is striking that doctors who practice euthanasia have killed so many patients "at the latter's own request" (one doctor gives a figure of seventeen), while other, more traditional practitioners have yet to hear such a request from a patient. When evaluating the thousands of "voluntary" requests for euthanasia submitted every year in Holland, one should take into account the influence of propaganda and of the physician-provocateur.

"TAÏGETIAN" MEDICINE AND CRYPTHANASIA

"Voluntary" euthanasia must also be rejected because, contrary to the beliefs of some of its supporters, *it is inseparable from, and inherently linked to overtly involuntary forms of euthanasia.* . . .

There is now ample evidence that "voluntary" euthanasia is accompanied by the practice of crypthanasia (active euthanasia on sick people without their knowledge). Gunning was the first to report attempts to kill off elderly patients instead of admitting them to the hospital. In 1983, extensive information on crypthanasia became available with the publication of H.W.A. Hilhorst's well-researched book, *Euthanasia in the Hospital* (in Dutch), based on the results of a study conducted in eight hospitals. In this publication (sponsored by the Royal Dutch Academy of Science and the University of Utrecht) the author analyzed the practice of involuntary euthanasia and described cases of involuntary active euthanasia on adults and children. There followed, in 1985, reports on mass secret killings in the *De Terp* senior citizens' home in The Hague; my report about practices of crypthanasia at the internal department of a hospital in Rotterdam; estimates by Dessaur, Gunning, Dessaur and Rutenfrans, and van der Sluis that more people die in this country by involuntary than by voluntary euthanasia; and, in 1987, the discovery of serial killings of comatose patients by four nurses in the department of neurosurgery at the Free University Hospital in Amsterdam. . . .

Thus in Holland, "voluntary" and involuntary euthanasia are advocated by the same people and the same institutions, supported by the same public, practiced alongside each other and closely linked in the public mind. Both are manifestations of the same basic attitude, that is, the now widely shared conviction that people's lives may be cut short whenever there are good reasons for doing so. Those who contend that it is possible to accept and practice "voluntary" euthanasia and not allow involuntary totally disregard the Dutch reality.

SOCIAL IMPLICATIONS

"Voluntary" euthanasia should also be rejected *because of the ominous change it brings about in the society.* Instead of the message a humane society sends to its members—"Everybody has the right to be around, we want to keep you with us, every one of you"—the society that embraces euthanasia, even the "mildest" and most "voluntary" forms of it, tells people: "We wouldn't mind getting rid of you." This message reaches not only the elderly and the sick, but all the weak and dependent. Attorney General T.M. Schalken found that Dutch society has already undergone this transformation. As a consequence, some groups live in fear and uncertainty. The Dutch Patients' Association stated in 1985 that "in recent months the fear of euthanasia among people has considerably increased." A group of severely handicapped adults from Amersfoort stated in their letter to the Parliamentary Committees for Health Care and Justice:

> We feel our lives threatened . . . We realize that we cost the community a lot . . . Many people think we are useless . . . often we notice that we are being talked into desiring death . . . We will find it extremely dangerous and frightening if the new medical legislation includes euthanasia.

In their fears, people do not distinguish "voluntary" from involuntary euthanasia.

A study conducted among hospital patients showed that many fear their own families because these are people who could decide upon euthanasia or pressure them to request death. Out of fear of euthanasia some elderly people refuse to be placed in old-age or nursing homes, refuse to be hospitalized or to see doctors or take medicines. A study of the attitudes of the elderly showed that 47 percent of those living in their own homes, and 93 percent of those living in homes for senior citizens reject any active euthanasia "because later on, when they won't be in command of the situation any more, their lives, against their will, will be put to an end by others." Pathetic attempts are made to escape imposed medical death. The "Sanctuary Association" (*Schuilplaats*) printed "declarations of the will to live." This card "which anyone can carry on his person, states that the signer does not wish euthanasia performed on him." . . .

More change must be expected if the pro-euthanasia movement, having attained the legalization of "voluntary" euthanasia, is to achieve the rest of its proclaimed goals. Proposals calling for euthanasia of handicapped newborns mean that doctors acting, as they do everywhere, under state supervision, will issue some newborn citizens permits to live and destroy others. To exist, a human being will have to be approved by the government—a reversal of the democratic principle that governments, to exist, have to be approved by people. Such parts of the program as compulsory euthanasia for the demented elderly and limiting the lifespan of people by denying medical help to those above a certain age, as, in general, any measures to eliminate from society large numbers of citizens, voters, life-long taxpayers, living people, are incompatible with our present system of government. This does not mean that these programs will not be put into effect, but it does mean that the implementation of euthanasia programs will involve an essential change in the system of government now prevailing in Western nations.

FALSE PROMISE

"Voluntary" euthanasia should further be rejected *because its promise is false.* Euthanasia is supposed to spare the sick person the agony that precedes death or the sufferings of a prolonged illness. But this is not the case. When Wibo van den Linden filmed one patient's preparation for "voluntary" euthanasia, about a million Dutch television viewers watched the unfortunate lady's anguish and despair as the fixed day of execution approached. Millions die a human death, in uncertainty, fear, and hope, as cherished members of their family, of the human community, surrounded by those who won't let them go. But euthanasia causes extreme psychological suffering—the excommunication, the exclusion of a person from the community of the living while he is still alive. . . .

FALLIBILITY AND IRREVERSIBILITY

Voluntary euthanasia must also be rejected because of the *fundamental discrepancy between the uncertainty of human (and medical) judgments,* which are fallible, *and the deadly certainty of the act.*

Clinicians have traditionally rejected euthanasia because they realized that we all make mistakes, that diagnoses are uncertain and prognoses notoriously unreliable. Erroneous diagnosis of fatal disease remains a very real possibility. . . .

EUTHANASIA IS NEVER "NECESSARY"

"Voluntary" euthanasia is to be rejected *because it is totally unnecessary.* In my many years of work as a hospital doctor, I attended thousands of patients and, much to my regret, many hundreds of them died. They needed support, relief from pain, breathlessness, or nausea. Until their last conscious moments they needed to belong, to share with all of us our common destiny, fears, uncertainties, and hopes. None of them needed euthanasia, and with a single exception in thirty-six years, none asked for it.

It is a most demanding task of the doctor to assist his patient to the very end, one that is very different from what vocal supporters of euthanasia expect and demand. Suffering should be alleviated as effectively as possible. The drugs used to relieve pain, or the anticonvulsants used on patients who have suffered cardiac arrest, may shorten a person's life by suppressing respiration, but this is a risk we take; it should never be our intention. . . .

THE DANGER TO MEDICINE

"Voluntary" euthanasia should also be feared and rejected *because of the irreparable damage it causes to medicine.* It has become obvious that the practice of euthanasia interferes with doctors' performance as observers of nature and as helpers. The high occurrence of factual errors and oversights committed by doctors in the rush to euthanasia seems to be due to the excitement accompanying the socially and officially approved legalized killing. It has also been pointed out that it is the strong motivation of curative medicine that enables a doctor to grasp and memorize a great number of facts relevant to the case, while euthanasia dispenses the doctor from this necessity.

Desisting from potentially effective therapy because of the idea of euthanasia is a well-known phenomenon that is increasingly disabling the profession. Euthanasia does not just change medicine or extend its range; euthanasia *replaces* medicine. . . .

Euthanasia brings about the decline of medicine also by undermining the doctor-patient relationship. The old confidence of the public in the medical profession, the old certainty that a doctor would do everything in his power to help the patient, that he would abandon nothing that could be of help, that he would never consciously do anything injurious—this certainty has vanished. Patients realize, too, that some of those doctors prepared to put patients to death at their own request will also be capable of doing it without a patient's knowledge. In the era of euthanasia, patients' attitudes toward doctors are increasingly marked by distrust, suspicion, and fear. . . .

At present, however, a generation of doctors is being raised who learn that a doctor may treat a patient or, sometimes, kill him. The thought of what's happening to the most humane profession is terrifying. Every society has learned to coexist with several dozen criminal killers. But no society knows how to live with an army of benevolent or casual killers, thousands strong.

The Remmelink Report:
Medical Practice with Regard to Euthanasia and Related Medical Decisions in the Netherlands*

The next article is based on a study of euthanasia in the Netherlands mandated by the Dutch government. Popularly known as *The Remmelink Report,* the study was an attempt to provide an accurate assessment of the scope of euthanasia, the nature and number of requests by patients, the limits of medical duty, and other parts of the actual situation in the Netherlands. The report indicates that in most cases of ending life, the physician plays an active role in deciding that it is appropriate to hasten death. The report is focused on the nature of professional duties and the sociology of medical practice, rather than on the nature of the patient's request. It speaks of the actions taken as *medical* decisions with regard to the end of life.

COMMISSION, ASSIGNMENT AND RESEARCH

The commission of inquiry into medical practice with regard to euthanasia (Remmelink commission) was set up by the Minister of Justice, mr. E.M.H. Hirsch Ballin and the State Secretary of Welfare, Health and Cultural Affairs, drs. H.J. Simons on January 17, 1990. The commission was chaired by prof. mr. J. Remmelink, Attorney-General at the Supreme Court of the Netherlands.

The assignment of the commission was to report to the two members of government on the state of affairs regarding the practice of action and inaction by a doctor that may lead to the end of a patient's life at this patient's explicit and serious request or otherwise. . . .

DEFINITIONS

The following neutral, descriptive definition has been chosen: medical decisions with regard to the end of life. By this, all situations are meant in which doctors make decisions that are (also) intended to put a stop to suffering by precipitating the end of a patient's life, or in which a probable hastening of the patient's death is at least taken into account.

*Source: This brochure presents the outcome of a study on euthanasia and other medical decisions with regard to the end of life, mandated by the government of the Netherlands, Ministry of Welfare, Health and Cultural Affairs.

THE NATURE OF MEDICAL DECISIONS WITH REGARD TO THE END OF LIFE

From the research data the commission concludes that nearly all the doctors in the Netherlands who are involved in patient care, are faced with various medical decisions with regard to the end of life. Therefore these decisions belong to the normal field of activity of every doctor who is frequently confronted with deaths. The commission stresses that decisions to carry out euthanasia only make up a fraction of all these decisions. General practitioners are most frequently faced with requests for the termination of a life. That is why, in most cases, they are the ones who administer euthanasia. Least frequently euthanasia is carried out by doctors in nursing homes. However, the discontinuance of life-prolonging treatment or not starting one, without an explicit request by the patient, occurs relatively often in nursing homes. For the most part these cases involve very old or demented patients, when in consultation with relatives and the nursing staff the decision is made not to treat (any longer) a fatal disorder, such as cardiac arrest or pneumonia. In these instances one can speak of 'leaving nature to its own devices'. This course of action is generally regarded to be good and proper exercise of a doctor's professional duties. In foreign literature one comes across the assertion that in the Netherlands most cases of active termination of life occur in nursing homes. This assertion is contestable, as the research report shows.

EUTHANASIA (AND ASSISTANCE IN SUICIDE)

The data on the extent of euthanasia in the Netherlands, an extent that now has been determined scientifically (2300 cases: 1.8 percent of all deaths, 130,000 a year), disprove certain ideas that circulate in society. (The same goes for the small number of cases of assistance in suicide; approximately 400.) This extent does not warrant the assumption that euthanasia in the Netherlands occurs on an excessive scale and that it is used increasingly as an alternative to good palliative or terminal care. According to the commission, the assumption mentioned above is not only disproved by the self-evident number of 2300 cases a year, but also by the fact that doctors in the Netherlands are faced with about 9000 requests for the termination of a patient's life. In other words: it happens more often that a doctor does not comply with a request for the termination of a life, for example, because he finds an alternative to euthanasia, than that he actually carries out euthanasia. The research results show that doctors feel strongly about the decision to accede to a patient's request for the termination of his life, and that they regard this decision not in the least as a convenient alternative to good terminal care. All in all the commission sees no ground to suppose that this attitude is going to change in the future.

The commission points out that there is no proof whatsoever in the research results for the suggestion made from time to time that lack of funds in the health sector were (or will become) a cause for the administration of euthanasia. Unbearable suffering and/or the natural desire to die peacefully were the only reason for doctors in the Netherlands to carry out euthanasia. . . .

DELIBERATE LIFE-TERMINATING ACTIONS WITHOUT EXPLICIT REQUEST

The types of medical actions involved are indicated by the Commission as the following:

1. intensification of the treatment of pain and symptoms with a minor shortening of the patient's life as its side-effect.
2. to discontinue or never commence a life prolonging treatment.
3. active termination of life at a moment when vital functions already have begun to fail.
4. active termination of life at a moment when vital functions are still undamaged.

The actions referred to under 1, 2, and 3 are in the view of the Commission undisputed and are normal medical actions. As to both items 3 and 4, the commission points out that active intervention by the doctor in those cases where there is no request, is usually inevitable because of the patient's agony. That is why the commission has labelled the action in question as terminal care. The lack of a request for the termination of life under these circumstances only serves to make the decision process more difficult than in a situation in which there is indeed a sustained request, made freely and after careful consideration. The ultimate justification for the intervention is in both cases the patient's unbearable suffering. So, medically speaking, there is little difference between these situations and euthanasia, because in both cases patients are involved who suffer unacceptably. The absence of a special request for the termination of life stems partly from the circumstance that the party in question is not (any longer) able to express his will because he is already in the terminal stage, and partly because an explicit request is not in order when the treatment of pain and symptoms is intensified. The degrading condition the patient is in, confronts the doctor with a situation of force majeure. According to the commission, the intervention by the doctor can easily be regarded as an action that is justified by necessity, just like euthanasia. In a few dozen cases there were circumstances under which the doctor could have applied the procedure suitable for the decision process regarding the administration of euthanasia. According to the commission, situations like these must be avoided in the future. One means to this end is strict compliance with the scrupulous care that is necessary when euthanasia is carried out, including the requirement that all facts of the case are put down in writing.

Finally the commission remarks that the research report disproves the assertion often expressed, that nonvoluntary active termination of life occurs more frequently in the Netherlands than voluntary termination. . . .

The doctors who were interviewed indicated that not all forms of pain can be treated successfully. Some pain can only be stopped by bringing and keeping the patient in a state of total unconsciousness. When confronted with that possibility, many patients ask for the termination of their life. From this information the commission draws the conclusion that the opinion sometimes put forward, that more advanced techniques for the treatment of pain or symptoms would lead to fewer requests for euthanasia, is inaccurate, broadly speaking. In addition the commission points out that the patient can always decide that no (or no more) remedy against pain or symptoms is to be administered. . . .

THE DEATH CERTIFICATE

If there is a general awareness in society that, under certain, clearly defined circumstances and in accordance with the necessary scrupulous care, a doctor has the right to terminate the life of a patient, it follows that there must be an opportunity to review the doctor's action.

Each case in which euthanasia is carried out must, according to the committee, be reviewed by another doctor than the one in attendance. To that end it is necessary that cases of euthanasia are reported. The procedure for reporting euthanasia that has been in force since November 1990 makes such a review possible. This regulation is based upon the doctor's willingness to report a case of euthanasia to the municipal coroner who subsequently informs the public prosecutor. The commission has made a recommendation with regard to this procedure.

THE LIMITS OF MEDICAL DUTY

Doctors see it as their prime responsibility to guard the lives of their patients alive. That is what their medical duty is primarily aimed at. If there is no possibility for recovery left, they still consider it their duty to alleviate the suffering and to give adequate care. A moment may come when death has become inevitable and when the doctor is in view of a dignified end of life for his patient, must discontinue certain medical actions or never commence them at all, or, as part of the treatment of pain or symptoms, he may have to prescribe remedies that as a side-effect might shorten the patient's life. In extreme cases there will be no other option left but active interference. The commission acknowledges here that the research report contains, as a result of the researcher's choice to approach only doctors, no information concerning those situations in which patients who request the termination of their life, cannot depend upon actual assistance from their doctor. The committee believes that a doctor who thinks in good conscience that he will not be able to grant such a request, must refer the patient to a colleague.

RECOMMENDATIONS

The assignment of the commission was not to submit proposals for future legislation. Its task was to increase, to deepen and to specify the understanding of medical actions with regard to the end of life.

The commission has made some recommendations of a more or less general, technical nature at the end of its report. It is up to the members of government in question to decide what value they want to attach to these additional considerations.

A. It is advisable that the procedure for reporting that exists since November 1990, will also be applied to active interference by a doctor within the scope of care for the dying without an explicit request from the patient, apart from those situations in which the vital functions have already and irreversibly begun to fail, because in those cases a natural death would have followed anyhow. In the opinion of the commission there is no real justification for the current situation in which cases of euthanasia or of assistance in suicide are covered by the procedure for reporting, while the cases of active interference by the doctor in order to shorten the life of a patient whose vital functions are still intact, without an explicit request from the latter, are not. Medically speaking there is no difference between these actions. In view of a careful decision-making process, the requirements for scrupulous care must be observed. The current procedure that consists of a report to the municipal coroner and of a review by the public prosecutor, offers in the eyes of the commission a practicable procedure to which each medical decision with regard to the termination of life is unique.

B. With regard to the requirement that a colleague is to be consulted the commission notes the following: in order to get an independent judgment, primarily of a medical nature, the commission recommends that the general practitioner who is considering the administration of euthanasia, consults a specialist, preferably one who is already in attendance, and vice versa. All this for the sake of the quality of the decision-making process.

C. The commission believes that each doctor must strictly observe the requirements for scrupulous care in case of the administration of euthanasia. Especially the requirement of a written report is of paramount importance. The required procedure will have a positive effect upon the decision-making process and it enables the doctor to demonstrate his willingness to justify his conduct. This kind of public justification suits a democratic, constitutional state.

D. The commission endorses the expectation expressed in the research report that in the future doctors will be increasingly faced with important medical decisions with regard to the end of life. In the Netherlands the medical actions and decision process concerning the end of life are of high quality. Further forming of public opinion within the professional groups and sectors of health care would contribute to the increase of this quality. In consultation colleagues will be able to exchange expertise. Therefore the commission recommends a survey of the possibilities for the dissemination of knowledge concerning medical decisions with regard to the end of life.

E. The research report shows that the medical decision-making process with regard to the end of life demands more and more expertise in a number of different areas. First of all medical and technical know-how, especially in the field of the treatment of pain, of prognosis and of alternative options for the treatment of disorders that cause insufferable pain. In addition to that, the doctor must have social skills for his contact with a patient who is in the terminal stage, and with his next of kin. In real terms this consideration results in the recommendation that in the training for Medical Doctor, in the further stages of medical training and in continuing-education courses, there ought to be plenty of room (more than at present) for the issue of medical decisions with regard to the end of life. Especially doctors, but nurses as well, will have to be trained in terminal care. By terminal care the commission means the whole of assistance and care on behalf of dying humans and their next of kin. Optimal care for someone dying implies that the doctor has knowledge of adequate treatment for pain, of alternatives for the treatment of complaints about unbearable pain and awareness of the moment when he must allow the process of dying to run its natural course. Doctors still lack sufficient knowledge of this form of care that also includes ethical and legal aspects. In a country that is rated among the best in the world when it comes to birth care, knowledge with regard to care for the dying should not be lacking.

Sue Rodriguez v. Attorney General of Canada and Attorney General of British Columbia

Supreme Court of Canada

The following case of *Sue Rodriguez v. Attorney General of Canada* is a decision of the Supreme Court of Canada in a sensational case that received national attention for weeks in Canada. Rodriguez suffered from Lou Gehrig's disease (ALS) and attempted to strike down section 241 of the Criminal Code, which prohibits physician-assisted suicide. The court did not strike down section 241, but several justices delivered opinions that give strong support for Rodriguez's goal of dying with physician assistance. Even judges who denied her what she sought found merit in many of her arguments. In early 1994, shortly after this decision, Sue Rodriguez killed herself with the assistance of an anonymous physician.

THE CHIEF JUSTICE

I. Facts

The facts of this case are straightforward and well known. Sue Rodriguez is a 42-year-old woman living in British Columbia. She is married and the mother of an 8½-year-old son. Ms. Rodriguez suffers from amyotrophic lateral sclerosis (ALS), which is widely known as Lou Gehrig's disease; her life expectancy is between 2 and 14 months but her condition is rapidly deteriorating. Very soon she will lose the ability to swallow, speak, walk, and move her body without assistance. Thereafter, she will lose the capacity to breathe without a respirator, to eat without a gastrotomy and will eventually become confined to a bed.

Ms. Rodriguez knows of her condition, the trajectory of her illness, and the inevitability of how her life will end; her wish is to control the circumstances, timing, and manner of her death. She does not wish to die so long as she still has the capacity to enjoy life. However, by the time she no longer is able to enjoy life, she will be physically unable to terminate her life without assistance. Ms. Rodriguez seeks an order which will allow a qualified medical practitioner to set up technological means by which she might, by her own hand, at the time of her choosing, end her life.

Ms. Rodriguez applied to the Supreme Court of British Columbia for an order that s. 241(*b*) of the *Criminal Code*, R.S.C., 1985, c. C-46, to be declared invalid, pursuant to s. 24(1) of the *Canadian Charter of Rights and Freedoms,* on the ground that it violates her rights under ss. 7, 12 and 15(1) of the *Charter,* and was therefore, to the extent it prohibits a terminally ill person from committing "physician-assisted" suicide, of no force and effect by virtue of s. 52(1) of the *Constitution Act, 1982.* Melvin J. of the Supreme Court of British Columbia dismissed the appellant's application: (1992), 18 W.C.B. (2d) 279, [1993] B.C.W.L.D. 347. The British Columbia Court of

Appeal dismissed the appellant's appeal, McEachern C.J.B.C. dissenting: (1993), 76 B.C.L.R. (2d) 145 . . .

II. Relevant Statutory Provisions

The relevant provision of the *Criminal Code* is as follows:

241. Every One Who

(a) counsels a person to commit suicide, or
(b) aids or abets a person to commit suicide,

whether suicide ensues or not, is guilty of an indictable offence and liable to imprisonment for a term not exceeding fourteen years.

The relevant sections of the *Charter* are as follows:

1. The *Canadian Charter of Rights and Freedoms* guarantees the rights and freedoms set out in it subject only to such reasonable limits prescribed by law as can be demonstrably justified in a free and democratic society.
7. Everyone has the right to life, liberty, and security of the person and the right not to be deprived thereof except in accordance with the principles of fundamental justice.
12. Everyone has the right not to be subjected to any cruel and unusual treatment or punishment.
15. (1) Every individual is equal before and under the law and has the right to the equal protection and equal benefit of the law without discrimination and, in particular, without discrimination based on race, national or ethnic origin, colour, religion, sex, age or mental or physical disability.

III. Judgments Below

Supreme Court of British Columbia. . . . In the context of s. 7, Melvin J. noted that the appellant based her argument not on the "right to suicide," but on a right to "die with dignity." . . .

To grant Ms. Rodriguez a remedy under the *Charter,* would, in Melvin J.'s view, be tantamount to imposing a duty on physicians to assist patients who choose to terminate their own lives, which would be "diametrically opposed to the underlying hypothesis upon which a *Charter of Rights and Freedoms* is based, namely, the sanctity of human life." . . .

> Considering the nature of the rights protected by the *Charter* in other cases, I have no doubt that a terminally ill person facing what the Appellant faces qualifies under the value system upon which the *Charter* is based to protection under the rubric of either liberty or security of her person. This would include at least the lawful right of a terminally ill person to terminate her own life, and, in my view, to assistance under proper circumstances.

> It would be wrong, in my view, to judge this case as a contest between life and death. The *Charter* is not concerned only with the fact of life, but also with the quality and dignity of life. In my view, death and the way we die is a part of life itself. . . .

McEachern C.J. held that . . . the appellant could proceed to arrange for physician-assisted suicide, provided certain conditions were met. These conditions were set out in the following passage (at pp. 168–70):

First, the Appellant must be mentally competent to make a decision to end her own life. . . .

Secondly, in addition to being mentally competent, the physicians must certify that, in their opinion, (1) the Appellant is terminally ill and near death, and that there is no hope of her recovering; (2) that she is, or but for medication would be, suffering unbearable physical pain or severe psychological distress; (3) that they have informed her, and that she understands, that she has a continuing right to change her mind about terminating her life; and (4) when, in their opinion, the Appellant would likely die (a) if palliative care is being or would be administered to her, and (b) if palliative care should not be administered to her.

Thirdly . . . the Regional Coroner or his nominee, who must be a physician, may be present at the examination of the Appellant by a psychiatrist in order to be satisfied that the Appellant does indeed have mental competence to decide, and does in fact decide, to terminate her life.

Fourthly, one of the physicians giving any certificate as aforesaid, must re-examine the Appellant each day after the above-mentioned arrangements are put in place to ensure that she does not evidence any change in her intention to end her life. . . .

Fifthly, no one may assist the Appellant to attempt to commit suicide or to commit suicide after the expiration of thirty-one days from the date of the first mentioned certificate. . . .

Lastly, the act actually causing the death of the Appellant must be the unassisted act of the Appellant herself, and not of anyone else. . . .

In closing, McEachern C.J. emphasized once again that his remedy is directed specifically towards the appellant in her unique circumstances, and that other people in her situation would have to apply individually to a court to receive a similar order. . . .

Supreme Court of Canada.   That respect for human dignity is one of the underlying principles upon which our society is based is unquestioned. I have difficulty, however, in characterizing this in itself as a principle of fundamental justice within the meaning of s. 7. . . .

I cannot subscribe to the opinion expressed by my colleague, McLachlin J., that the state interest is an inappropriate consideration in recognizing the principles of fundamental justice in this case. This Court has affirmed that in arriving at these principles, a balancing of the interest of the state and the individual is required. . . .

Section 241(*b*) has as its purpose the protection of the vulnerable who might be induced in moments of weakness to commit suicide. This purpose is grounded in the state interest in protecting life and reflects the policy of the state that human life should not be depreciated by allowing life to be taken. This policy finds expression not only in the provisions of our *Criminal Code* which prohibit murder and other violent acts against others notwithstanding the consent of the victim, but also in the policy against capital punishment and, until its repeal, attempted suicide. This is not only a policy of the state, however, but is part of our fundamental conception of the sanctity of human life. . . .

[But] the principle of sanctity of life is no longer seen to require that all human life be preserved at all costs. Rather, it has come to be understood, at least by some, as encompassing quality of life considerations, and to be subject to certain limitations and qualifications reflective of personal autonomy and dignity. . . .

[W]hile both the House of Lords, and the Law Reform Commission of Canada have great sympathy for the plight of those who wish to end their lives so as to avoid significant suffering, neither has been prepared to recognize that the active assistance of a third party in carrying out this desire should be condoned, even for the terminally ill. The basis for this refusal is twofold it seems—first, the active participation by one individual in the death of another is intrinsically morally and legally wrong, and second, there is no certainty that abuses can be prevented by anything less than a complete prohibition. Creating an exception for the terminally ill might therefore frustrate the purpose of the legislation of protecting the vulnerable because adequate guidelines to control abuse are difficult or impossible to develop. . . .

The fact that doctors may deliver palliative care to terminally ill patients without fear of sanction, it is argued, attenuates to an even greater degree any legitimate distinction which can be drawn between assisted suicide and what are currently acceptable forms of medical treatment. The administration of drugs designed for pain control in dosages which the physician knows will hasten death constitutes active contribution to death by any standard. However, the distinction drawn here is one based upon intention—in the case of palliative care the intention is to ease pain, which has the effect of hastening death, while in the case of assisted suicide, the intention is undeniably to cause death. The Law Reform Commission, although it recommended the continued criminal prohibition of both euthanasia and assisted suicide, stated . . . that a doctor should never refuse palliative care to a terminally ill person only because it may hasten death. In my view, distinctions based upon intent are important, and in fact form the basis of our criminal law. While factually the distinction may, at times, be difficult to draw, legally it is clear. The fact that in some cases, the third party will, under the guise of palliative care, commit euthanasia or assist in suicide and go unsanctioned due to the difficulty of proof cannot be said to render the existence of the prohibition fundamentally unjust. . . .

Regardless of one's personal views as to whether the distinctions drawn between withdrawal of treatment and palliative care, on the one hand, and assisted suicide on the other are practically compelling, the fact remains that these distinctions are maintained and can be persuasively defended. To the extent that there is a consensus, it is that human life must be respected and we must be careful not to undermine the institutions that protect it.

This consensus finds legal expression in our legal system which prohibits capital punishment. This prohibition is supported, in part, on the basis that allowing the state to kill will cheapen the value of human life and thus the state will serve in a sense as a role model for individuals in society. The prohibition against assisted suicide serves a similar purpose. In upholding the respect for life, it may discourage those who consider that life is unbearable at a particular moment, or who perceive themselves to be a burden upon others, from committing suicide. To permit a physician to lawfully participate in taking life would send a signal that there are circumstances in which the state approves of suicide.

I also place some significance in the fact that the official position of various medical associations is against decriminalizing assisted suicide (Canadian Medical Association, British Medical Association, Council of Ethical and Judicial Affairs of the American Medical Association, World Medical Association and the American Nurses Association). Given the concerns about abuse that have been expressed and the great difficulty in creating appropriate safeguards to prevent these, it can not be said that the blanket prohibition on assisted suicide is arbitrary or unfair, or that it is not reflective of fundamental values at play in our society. I am thus unable to find that any principle of fundamental justice is violated by s.241(*b*). . . .

I agree with the sentiments expressed by the justices of the British Columbia Court of Appeal—this case is an upsetting one from a personal perspective. I have the deepest sympathy for the appellant and her family, as I am sure do all of my colleagues, and I am aware that the denial of her application by this Court may prevent her from managing the manner of her death. I have, however, concluded that the prohibition occasioned by s. 241(*b*) is not contrary to the provisions of the *Charter.*

In the result, the appeal is dismissed, but without costs.

The constitutional questions are answered as follows:

1. Does s. 241(*b*) of the *Criminal Code* of Canada infringe or deny, in whole or in part, the rights and freedoms guaranteed by ss. 7, 12 and 15(1) of the *Canadian Charter of Rights and Freedoms?*

    Answer. No, except as to s. 15 in respect of which an infringement is assumed.

2. If so, is it justified by s. 1 of the *Canadian Charter of Rights and Freedoms* and therefore not inconsistent with the *Constitution Act, 1982?*

    Answer. As to ss. 7 and 12, no answer is required. As to s. 15, the answer is yes.

McLACHLIN J. (DISSENTING):

I have read the reasons of the Chief Justice. Persuasive as they are, I am of the view that this is not at base a case about discrimination under s. 15 of the *Canadian Charter of Rights and Freedoms.* . . . I see this rather as a case about the manner in which the state may limit the right of a person to make decisions about her body under s. 7 of the *Charter.* I prefer to base my analysis on that ground. . . .

In my view, the denial to Sue Rodriguez of a choice available to others cannot be justified. The potential for abuse is amply guarded against by existing provisions in the *Criminal Code,* as supplemented by the condition of judicial authorization, and ultimately, it is hoped, revised legislation. I cannot agree that the failure of Parliament to address the problem of the terminally ill is determinative of this appeal. Nor do I agree that the fact that medically assisted suicide has not been widely accepted elsewhere bars Sue Rodriguez's claim. Since the advent of the *Charter,* this Court has been called upon to decide many issues which formerly lay fallow. If a law offends the *Charter,* this Court has no choice but to so declare. . . .

It is argued that the denial to Sue Rodriguez of the capacity to treat her body in a way available to the physically able is justified because to permit assisted suicide will open the doors, if not the floodgates, to the killing of disabled persons who may not truly consent to death. The argument is essentially this. There may be no reason on the facts of Sue Rodriguez' case for denying to her the choice to end her life, a choice that those physically able have available to them. Nevertheless, she must be denied that choice because of the danger that other people may wrongfully abuse the power they have over the weak and ill, and may end the lives of these persons against their consent. . . .

When one is considering whether a law breaches the principles of fundamental justice under s. 7 by reason of arbitrariness, the focus is on whether a legislative scheme infringes a particular person's protected interests in a way that cannot be justified having regard to the objective of this scheme. The principles of fundamental justice require that each person, considered individually, be treated fairly by the law. The fear that abuse may arise if an individual is permitted that which she is wrongly denied plays no part at this initial stage. In short, it does not accord with the principles of fundamental justice that Sue Rodriguez be disallowed what is available to others merely because it is possible that other people, at some other time, may suffer, not what she seeks, but an act of killing. . . .

Certain of the interveners raise the concern that the striking down of s. 241(*b*) might demean the value of life. But what value is there in life without the choice to do what one wants with one's life, one might counter. One's life includes one's death. Different people hold different views on life and on what devalues it. For some, the choice to end one's life with dignity is infinitely preferable to the inevitable pain and diminishment of a long, slow decline. Section 7 protects that choice against arbitrary state action which would remove it.

In summary, the law draws a distinction between suicide and assisted suicide. The latter is criminal, the former is not. The effect of the distinction is to prevent people like Sue Rodriguez from exercising the autonomy over their bodies available to other people. The distinction, to borrow the language of the Law Reform Commission of Canada, "is difficult to justify on grounds of logic alone": Working Paper 28, *Euthanasia, Aiding Suicide and the Cessation of Treatment* (1982), at p. 53. In short, it is arbitrary. . . .

It [has been] argued that if assisted suicide were permitted even in limited circumstances, then there would be reason to fear that homicide of the terminally ill and persons with physical disabilities could be readily disguised as assisted suicide and that, as a result, the most vulnerable people would be left most exposed to this grave threat. There may indeed be cause for such concern. Sadly, increasingly less value appears to be placed in our society on the lives of those who, for reason of illness, age or disability, can no longer control the use of their bodies. Such sentiments are often, unfortunately, shared by persons with physical disabilities themselves, who often feel they are merely a burden and expense to their families or on society as a whole. . . .

The principal fear is that the decriminalization of assisted suicide will increase the risk of persons with physical disabilities being manipulated by others. This "slippery slope" argument appeared to be the central justification behind the Law Reform Commission of Canada's recommendation not to repeal this provision. . . .

While I share a deep concern over the subtle and overt pressures that may be brought to bear on such persons if assisted suicide is decriminalized, even in limited circumstances, I do not think legislation that deprives a disadvantaged group of the right to equality can be justified solely on such speculative grounds, no matter how well intentioned. . . . The truth is that we simply do not and cannot know the range of implications that allowing some form of assisted suicide will have for persons with physical disabilities. What we do know and cannot ignore is the anguish of those in the position of Ms. Rodriguez. Respecting the consent of those in her position may necessarily imply running the risk that the consent will have been obtained improperly. The proper role of the legal system in these circumstances is to provide safeguards to ensure that the consent in question is as independent and informed as is reasonably possible. . . .

In my view, there is a range of options from which Parliament may choose in seeking to safeguard the interests of the vulnerable and still ensure the equal right to self-determination of persons with physical disabilities. The criteria for assuring the free and independent consent of Ms. Rodriguez set out in McEachern C.J.'s dissenting reasons in the Court of Appeal seem designed to address such concerns though they relate only to terminally ill persons. Regardless of the safeguards Parliament may wish to adopt, however, I find that an absolute prohibition that is indifferent to the individual or the circumstances in question cannot satisfy the constitutional duty on the government to impair the rights of persons with physical disabilities as little as reasonably possible. Section 241(*b*) cannot survive the minimal impairment component of the proportionality test, and therefore I need not proceed to the third component of the proportionality test. As a result, I find the infringement of s. 15 by this provision cannot be saved under s. 1. . . .

The remedy requested by Ms. Rodriguez, and that fashioned by McEachern C.J., can best be understood as constitutional exemptions. The appellant asks for "a declaration that the operation of s. 241(*b*) of the *Criminal Code* violates [her] constitutionally guaranteed rights and that, upon compliance with certain conditions, neither the Appellant nor any physician assisting her to attempt to commit, or to commit suicide, will by that means commit any offence against the law of Canada." . . .

The constitutional exemption I propose would be available only on the authority of a superior court order, granted on terms similar to those outlined by McEachern C.J. . . .

To summarize, then, I would make a constitutional exemption available to Ms. Rodriguez, and others, on the following conditions:

1. the constitutional exemption may only be sought by way of application to a superior court;
2. the applicant must be certified by a treating physician and independent psychiatrist, in the manner and at the time suggested by McEachern C.J., to be competent to make the decision to end her own life, and the physicians must certify that the applicant's decision has been made freely and voluntarily, and at least one of the physicians must be present with the applicant at the time the applicant commits assisted suicide;
3. the physicians must also certify:
   (i) that the applicant is or will become physically incapable of committing suicide unassisted, and (ii) that they have informed him or her, and that he or she understands, that he or she has a continuing right to change his or her mind about terminating his or her life;
4. notice and access must be given to the Regional Coroner at the time and in the manner described by McEachern C.J.;
5. the applicant must be examined daily by one of the certifying physicians at the time and in the manner outlined by McEachern C.J.;
6. the constitutional exemption will expire according to the time limits set by McEachern C.J.; and
7. the act causing the death of the applicant must be that of the applicant him or herself, and not of anyone else.

I wish to emphasize that these conditions have been tailored to the particular circumstances of Ms. Rodriguez. While they may be used as guidelines for future petitioners in a similar position, each application must be considered in its own individual context.

Disposition

I would answer the constitutional questions as follows:

1. Does s. 241(*b*) of the *Criminal Code* of Canada infringe or deny, in whole or in part, the rights and freedoms guaranteed by ss. 7, 12, and 15(1) of the *Canadian Charter of Rights and Freedoms*?

   Answer. Yes.

2. If so, is it justified by s. 1 of the *Canadian Charter of Rights and Freedoms* and therefore not inconsistent with the *Constitution Act, 1982*?

   Answer. No.

I would therefore allow the appeal, with costs to the appellant against the Attorneys General of British Columbia and Canada, and declare s. 241(*b*) to be of no force or effect.

People of the State of Michigan v. Jack Kevorkian

HONORABLE DAVID F. BRECK, CIRCUIT JUDGE

In this case, defendant Jack Kevorkian had been indicted by a Grand Jury on three counts, one of which was murder in the death of two women who had been suffering from uncontrollable pain and had contacted Kevorkian for help in committing suicide. Kevorkian discouraged both women for some months, but eventually helped both by using "suicide-machines." The court rules that assisted suicide is not a crime in Michigan and that no valid distinction can be drawn between a physician's disconnecting life-support and connecting equipment designed to cause death. The patient's right to control his or her medical treatment is held to outweigh any state interest in continued life.

INTRODUCTION

The Defendant, Jack Kevorkian, M.D., was indicted by the Grand Jury on two counts of Open Murder (MCLA 750.316) relating to Marjorie Wantz and Sherry Miller, and one count of Delivery of a Controlled Substance to Marjorie Wantz, to wit Methohexital (Brevital), a schedule IV controlled substance in violation of MCLA 7401 (1), (2)(c); 333.7218 (1). After a preliminary examination before Judge James Sheehy, the Defendant was bound over to stand trial on the open murder charges, and the Delivery of a Controlled Substance charge was dismissed. The Defendant has filed a motion to dismiss Counts I and II, and the Prosecutor has appealed the dismissal of Count III.

The preliminary examination testimony established that both Ms. Marjorie Wantz and Mrs. Sherry Miller were living lives of horrible desperation, both had contemplated suicide for a long period of time, and when they contacted Dr. Jack Kevorkian as a physician to give his aid in dying, he initially attempted to dissuade them from ending their lives.

William Wantz, Marjorie Wantz's husband, was called as prosecution witness and testified that he traveled to the Cleveland Clinic to seek advice about management of his wife's pain (115 to 116). Her medical records were furnished to Defendant (142). In 1990 she went into Sinai Hospital for surgery (143), but there was an effort (presumably by officials at Sinai) to commit her because she was suicidal (144). A doctor there did tell her suicide was one of her options (146). Eventually, a Kalamazoo state institution determined she was mentally competent (151). Her pain was in the vaginal area (164) and was not psychological (166). She even asked to have her spinal cord cut to stop the pain, but the physician at Cleveland Clinic advised there was no assurance that would eliminate the pain (167).

Besides the Cleveland Clinic, Mrs. Wantz contacted "numerous other places in the United States and nobody said they could do any good for her," including Mayo

Clinic, University of Indiana, where the examiner said, "I've never seen anybody this bad" (206), Detroit doctors, and the University of Michigan (167). Her medication was four times stronger than morphine (168).

In response to Mr. Fieger's questions, Mr. Wantz also testified that Mrs. Wantz took her own life after years of agonizing pain and only after undergoing nine or ten surgeries on her vagina (170). Further, he testified that for years his wife would scream from the pain and needed sleeping pills at night (172).

Despite her desire to commit suicide due to her constant pain, Dr. Kevorkian tried to dissuade her from suicide (173). He referred her to Cleveland and suggested acupuncture and hypnotism. Defendant also referred her to Dr. Finn at Southeastern Michigan Hospice for her pain, even though he knew that Dr. Finn did not subscribe to Defendant's position regarding physician-assisted suicide (174).

After medication failed, Dr. Finn's prognosis was "pain, pure and simple . . . that all the medicine he gave her wasn't taking care of it. His statement to me was it would be better off to be cancerous, at least in six months you might be dead" (meaning Mrs. Wantz) (175). She concluded finally that suicide was her only way out because no one could cure her pain (176). It was so bad even wearing her panties hurt her. She could rarely leave home, and when she rode in a car she had to lie down in the back seat (177). Mrs. Wantz described the vaginal pain as "like sitting on a bonfire all the time" (178). Ultimately, after unsuccessfully trying to shoot herself (190), Mrs. Wantz wrote Exhibit L, in which she said after three and one-half years, she could no longer go on with the pain and agony, only leaving the house to go to the doctor. She begged Dr. Kevorkian for two years. Her last thirteen months were spent living in "pure hell." She concluded, "No doctor can help me anymore. If God won't come to me, I'm going to God. Can't stand it no longer" (187).

As for Sherry Miller's condition, Sharon Welsh testified for the prosecution that Ms. Miller was diagnosed with multiple sclerosis in 1978 or 1979 (224). Around 1983 she was dragging one leg and then started using a cane (228), she "continually deteriorated" and went to a walker. Then her father carried her from place to place and in 1989, she went into a wheelchair, but she had to be put into it (231). A couple of years before talking about Defendant, Ms. Miller said she wished she were dead (232). In the spring of 1990 she wrote a letter to Dr. Kevorkian and spoke to him on the telephone (233). Ms. Miller told Mrs. Welsh that she felt she was becoming a burden on people (235). By 1991 she was either confined to a bed or wheelchair, did not have use of her legs and her right arm, only limited use of her left arm, and had problems talking and breathing (236), and said she probably would have to go into a nursing home although she did not want to (237).

In response to Mr. Fieger's questions, Mrs. Welsh testified that Ms. Miller's father had to put her on the toilet, that her food had to be cut into small pieces, and that she was getting rapidly worse (276). Due to the lack of joy in her life, she decided to commit suicide and contacted Dr. Kevorkian as a physician to assist her. For a number of years he encouraged her to seek treatment for multiple sclerosis and see a psychiatrist (278). When she made the decision to proceed, her siblings and parents supported her decision (288), as well as her psychiatrist (or psychologist) (293).

IS ASSISTED SUICIDE A CRIME IN MICHIGAN?

A. Campbell Is the Law

It is basic to our criminal law system that the public be advised of what behavior constitutes a crime. *People v. Wiegand,* 369 Mich. 204 (1963). As stated in *People v. Llewellyn,* 401 Mich. 314, 328 (1977):

> It is a long-standing rule in this state that criminal statutes must establish with reasonable certainty the elements of the offense so that all persons subject to their penalties may know what acts it is their duty to avoid.

There being no statute relating to suicide, the Court must look to the common law.

The first known Michigan case to address this issue is *People v. Roberts,* 211 Mich. 187 (1920). In that case the defendant, at his wife's request, placed poison within reach of his wife, who had expressed an intent to commit suicide because she had incurable multiple sclerosis. She drank the poison and died. Defendant was charged with murder under C. L. 1915, Section 15192, which in pertinent parts is identical to MCLA 750.316, and he pled guilty. Two issues presented themselves: What degree of murder was he guilty of (the judge determined it to be first degree) and whether there was "evidence of the commission of the crime charged." The court very clearly ruled that Defendant was guilty of murder by poisoning and in Section Two of the Opinion rejected the defense that assisted suicide was not a crime. . . .

It is commonly accepted law that patients have the right to insist they be removed from life support systems, even though to do so will hasten their deaths. *Cruzan v. Director, Missouri Department of Health,* 497 U.S_., 110 S. Ct. 2841, 111 L.Ed. 2d 224 (1990) and many cases cited therein. If a person can refuse life-sustaining treatment, then that person should have the right to insist on treatment which will cause death, providing the physician is willing to assist and the patient is lucid and meets rational criteria. While the interests of the State are different when suicide is involved, it appears to this Court that nevertheless the prevailing interest should be the constitutionally protected interests of the individual.

The distinction between assisted suicide and the withdrawal of life support is a distinction without merit. But for the doctor's act of disconnecting the life support system, or the act of inserting the I.V. needle, death would not have occurred. "There is no morally important difference. . . . " (Harvard L. Rev., *supra,* footnote 69). Dean Sheldon F. Kurtz, Dean and Foundation Professor of Law, Florida State University College of Law, concurs:

> Permitting the administration of a life-terminating drug, if intended by the patient, is morally indistinguishable from commonly accepted practices of withholding or withdrawing life-sustaining technologies, including food and hydration, from a terminally ill patient, an action that will also result in death. (Am. Med. News, Jan. 7, 1991, p. 13). . . .

It is this Court's conclusion that physician-assisted suicide is not a crime in Michigan, even when the person's condition is not terminal. . . .

THE APPLICABILITY OF MCLA 750.505 PUNISHMENT FOR INDICTABLE COMMON LAW OFFENSES

Historically, assisting a suicide fell within the common law definition of murder, *Michigan's "Uncommon Law" of Homicide,* 7 Cooley L. Rev. (1990). In Michigan, MCLA 750.316 and .317 provide the punishment for murder using the common law definition of murder. Therefore, any act defined as murder under the common law is properly prosecuted under MCLA 750.316 and .317. As the statutes have expressly provided punishment for those crimes defined as murder by the common law, MCLA 750.505 does not apply. Also, it does not apply because physician-assisted suicide was not a crime at common law. . . .

IS THERE A NEED FOR LEGISLATION?

Oakland County Prosecutor Richard Thompson, as well as other Michigan prosecutors, have encouraged legislative action. Judge Gerald McNally in his *Atkin's* Opinion, as well as Judge James Sheehy in his Opinion, recognized the need for legislation. Even now our Legislature is struggling with the issue of whether to make assisted suicide a crime, and the Michigan Medical Society is wisely urging the appointment of a commission to address the issue, prompted by the concerns of many physicians questioning the wisdom of making assisted suicide a crime.

This Court is uncertain whether legislation is the answer. Perhaps it is best to leave the solution to the Michigan Medical Society and the State Bar of Michigan.

CONCLUSION

While this Court has found that the physician-assisted suicide in this case is not a crime in Michigan, the prevalence of suicide can be kept to a minimum if doctors can be educated about, and the public be made aware of, the benefits of hospice. Many times a patient's pain can be relieved and the dedicated volunteers, nurses, physicians, and staffs can help the patient die in comfort and assist the family in their grief, thereby obviating the desire to commit suicide.

It must be recognized, though, that there are some people with intractable pain that cannot benefit from hospice treatment (*The Physician's Responsibility Toward Hopelessly Ill Patients,* New. Eng. J. Med., Mar. 30, 1989, p. 844, at 847). For those patients, whether terminal or not, who have unmanageable pain, physician-assisted suicide remains an alternative.

The following quotation seems especially appropriate at this point:

> Kevorkian's and Quill's desire for open debate, as well as that of the eight doctors who supported the role of physicians in assisting in rational suicide, is laudable. That collective social decisions are possible is evident in the Netherlands, where guidelines allow euthanasia under carefully regulated conditions. But if nothing more than legislated safeguards result from the debate in this country, we shall have failed in the goal of better meeting a patient's needs at death. For the discussion to proceed to the development of thoughtful and sensitive public policy, both the medical profession and legislators must be better able to distinguish between people whose suicidal intent is clearly

conceived and free of distorting mental disturbances and people who are in need of psychiatric care. As the debate proceeds, we must avoid romanticizing suicide, regarding it simplistically, or allowing negative attitudes toward aging to influence its course. Furthermore, the public controversy over euthanasia, suicide, and the right to die should not be confused with the equally important debate about allocating limited health resources to terminally ill patients. Additional research and education of the medical profession and the public about the nature of affective disorders and suicide late in life will lead to a more informed discussion and possibly to lower suicide rates resulting from the earlier recognition and treatment of people at risk. (*Rational Suicide and the Right to Die,* New Eng. J. Med., Oct. 10, 1991, at page 1102:)

This Court's opinion relies upon case law, but also includes mention of bioethics, philosophy, and references to medical texts and proposed legislation. These are not normally found in a legal opinion. However, because the parties have argued such matters in their briefs, and because this is case of first impression, the Court responded.

We must not lose sight of the two most important and sorrowful people who had such a crucial role in this case: Sherry Miller, whose life had no quality and who was so totally dependent upon others, and Marjorie Wantz, who suffered her excruciating pain probably longer than any of us would have endured. It is these sad women, whether terminal or not, for whom we must have compassion.

These final comments are addressed to Dr. Jack Kevorkian: you have brought to the world's attention the need to give this topic paramount concern. This Judge, however, respectfully requests that you forego any other activities in this field, including counseling, for the time being. To continue I fear hurts your cause, because you may force the Legislature to take hasty, and perhaps improvident, action. Give the Michigan Medical Society and the Michigan Bar Association more time to do right.

This case is dismissed. However, as this Opinion has limited precedential value, appeal is invited.

Dated: July 21, 1992

The Oregon Death With Dignity Act

The next selection derives from a ballot measure that was approved by voters in November 1994 in the state of Oregon. Under the provisions of "The Oregon Death with Dignity Act," physicians are legally allowed to hasten the death of terminally ill patients (so declared by two physicians) who wish to escape unbearable suffering and three times request a physician's prescription for lethal drugs. The doctor then must wait 15 days after the first request before writing a prescription for the requested lethal drugs. (See p. 153, regarding a preliminary injunction preventing the law.)

ALLOWS TERMINALLY ILL ADULTS TO OBTAIN PRESCRIPTION FOR LETHAL DRUGS

Question.   Shall law allow terminally ill adult patients voluntary informed choice to obtain physician's prescription for drugs to end life?

Summary.   Adopts law. Allows terminally ill adult Oregon residents voluntary informed choice to obtain physician's prescription for drugs to end life. Removes criminal penalties for qualifying physician-assisted suicide. Applies when physicians predict patient's death within 6 months. Requires:

15-day waiting period;
2 oral, 1 written request;
second physician's opinion;
counseling if either physician believes patient has mental disorder, impaired judgment
    from depression.

Person has choice whether to notify next of kin. Health care providers immune from civil, criminal liability for good faith compliance.

SECTION 1: GENERAL PROVISIONS

§ 1.01   Definitions

The following words and phrases, whenever used in this Act, shall have the following meanings:

1.   "Adult" means an individual who is 18 years of age or older.
2.   "Attending physician" means the physician who has primary responsibility for the care of the patient and treatment of the patient's terminal disease.
3.   "Consulting physician" means a physician who is qualified by specialty or experience to make a professional diagnosis and prognosis regarding the patient's disease.
4.   "Counseling" means a consultation between a state licensed psychiatrist or psychologist and a patient for the purpose of determining whether the patient is

suffering from a psychiatric or psychological disorder, or depression causing impaired judgment.

5. "Health care provider" means a person licensed, certified, or otherwise authorized or permitted by the law of this State to administer health care in the ordinary course of business or practice of a profession, and includes a health care facility.

6. "Incapable" means that in the opinion of a court or in the opinion of the patient's attending physician or consulting physician, a patient lacks the ability to make and communicate health care decisions to health care providers, including communication through persons familiar with the patient's manner of communicating if those persons are available. Capable means not incapable.

7. "Informed decision" means a decision by a qualified patient, to request and obtain a prescription to end his or her life in a humane and dignified manner, that is based on an appreciation of the relevant facts and after being fully informed by the attending physician of:

    (a) his or her medical diagnosis;
    (b) his or her prognosis;
    (c) the potential risks associated with taking the medication to be prescribed;
    (d) the probable result of taking the medication to be prescribed;
    (e) the feasible alternatives, including, but not limited to, comfort care, hospice care and pain control.

8. "Medically confirmed" means the medical opinion of the attending physician has been confirmed by a consulting physician who has examined the patient and the patient's relevant medical records.

9. "Patient" means a person who is under the care of a physician.

10. "Physician" means a doctor of medicine or osteopathy licensed to practice medicine by the Board of Medical Examiners for the State of Oregon.

11. "Qualified patient" means a capable adult who is a resident of Oregon and has satisfied the requirements of this Act in order to obtain a prescription for medication to end his or her life in a humane and dignified manner.

12. "Terminal disease" means an incurable and irreversible disease that has been medically confirmed and will, within reasonable medical judgment, produce death within six (6) months.

SECTION 2: WRITTEN REQUEST FOR MEDICATION TO END ONE'S LIFE IN A HUMANE AND DIGNIFIED MANNER

§ 2.01   Who May Initiate a Written Request for Medication

An adult who is capable, is a resident of Oregon, and has been determined by the attending physician and consulting physician to be suffering from a terminal disease, and who has voluntarily expressed his or her wish to die, may make a written request for medication for the purpose of ending his or her life in a humane and dignified manner in accordance with this Act.

§ 2.02   Form of the Written Request

1. A valid request for medication under this Act shall be in substantially the form described in Section 6 of this Act, signed and dated by the patient and witnessed by at least two individuals who, in the presence of the patient, attest that to the best of their

knowledge and belief the patient is capable, acting voluntarily, and is not being coerced to sign the request.

2. One of the witnesses shall be a person who is not:

   (a) A relative of the patient by blood, marriage or adoption;

   (b) A person who at the time the request is signed would be entitled to any portion of the estate of the qualified patient upon death under any will or by operation of law; or

   (c) An owner, operator or employee of a health care facility where the qualified patient is receiving medical treatment or is a resident.

3. The patient's attending physician at the time the request is signed shall not be a witness.

4. If the patient is a patient in a long term care facility at the time the written request is made, one of the witnesses shall be an individual designated by the facility and having the qualifications specified by the Department of Human Resources by rule.

SECTION 3: SAFEGUARDS

§ 3.01 Attending Physician Responsibilities

The attending physician shall:

1. Make the initial determination of whether a patient has a terminal disease, is capable, and has made the request voluntarily;

2. Inform the patient of:

   (a) his or her medical diagnosis;

   (b) his or her prognosis;

   (c) the potential risks associated with taking the medication to be prescribed;

   (d) the probable result of taking the medication to be prescribed;

   (e) the feasible alternatives, including, but not limited to, comfort care, hospice care and pain control.

3. Refer the patient to a consulting physician for medical confirmation of the diagnosis, and for a determination that the patient is capable and acting voluntarily;

4. Refer the patient for counseling if appropriate pursuant to Section 3.03;

5. Request that the patient notify next of kin;

6. Inform the patient that he or she has an opportunity to rescind the request at any time and in any manner, and offer the patient an opportunity to rescind at the end of the 15-day waiting period pursuant to Section 3.06;

7. Verify, immediately prior to writing the prescription for medication under this Act, that the patient is making an informed decision;

8. Fulfill the medical record documentation requirements of Section 3.09;

9. Ensure that all appropriate steps are carried out in accordance with this Act prior to writing a prescription for medication to enable a qualified patient to end his or her life in a humane and dignified manner.

§ 3.02 Consulting Physician Confirmation

Before a patient is qualified under this Act, a consulting physician shall examine the patient and his or her relevant medical records and confirm, in writing, the attending physician's diagnosis that the patient is suffering from a terminal disease, and verify that the patient is capable, is acting voluntarily and has made an informed decision.

§ 3.03   Counseling Referral

If in the opinion of the attending physician or the consulting physician a patient may be suffering from a psychiatric or psychological disorder, or depression causing impaired judgment, either physician shall refer the patient for counseling. No medication to end a patient's life in a humane and dignified manner shall be prescribed until the person performing the counseling determines that the patient is not suffering from a psychiatric or psychological disorder, or depression causing impaired judgment.

§ 3.04   Informed Decision

No person shall receive a prescription for medication to end his or her life in a humane and dignified manner unless he or she has made an informed decision as defined in Section 1.01(7). Immediately prior to writing a prescription for medication under this Act, the attending physician shall verify that the patient is making an informed decision.

§ 3.05   Family Notification

The attending physician shall ask the patient to notify next of kin of his or her request for medication pursuant to this Act. A patient who declines or is unable to notify next of kin shall not have his or her request denied for that reason.

§ 3.06   Written and Oral Requests

In order to receive a prescription for medication to end his or her life in a humane and dignified manner, a qualified patient shall have made an oral request and a written request, and reiterate the oral request to his or her attending physician no less than fifteen (15) days after making the initial oral request. At the time the qualified patient makes his or her second oral request, the attending physician shall offer the patient an opportunity to rescind the request.

§ 3.07   Right to Rescind Request

A patient may rescind his or her request at any time and in any manner without regard to his or her mental state. No prescription for medication under this Act may be written without the attending physician offering the qualified patient an opportunity to rescind the request.

§ 3.08   Waiting Periods

No less than fifteen (15) days shall elapse between the patient's initial oral request and the writing of a prescription under this Act. No less than 48 hours shall elapse between the patient's written request and the writing of a prescription under this Act.

§ 3.09   Medical Record Documentation Requirements

The following shall be documented or filed in the patient's medical record:

1. All oral requests by a patient for medication to end his or her life in a humane and dignified manner;
2. All written requests by a patient for medication to end his or her life in a humane and dignified manner;
3. The attending physician's diagnosis and prognosis, determination that the patient is capable, acting voluntarily and has made an informed decision;
4. The consulting physician's diagnosis and prognosis, and verification that the patient is capable, acting voluntarily and has made an informed decision;
5. A report of the outcome and determinations made during counseling, if performed;
6. The attending physician's offer to the patient to rescind his or her request at the time of the patient's second oral request pursuant to Section 3.06; and
7. A note by the attending physician indicating that all requirements under this Act have been met and indicating the steps taken to carry out the request, including a notation of the medication prescribed.

§ 3.10   Residency Requirement

Only requests made by Oregon residents, under this Act, shall be granted.

§ 3.11   Reporting Requirements

1. The Health Division shall annually review a sample of records maintained pursuant to this Act.
2. The Health Division shall make rules to facilitate the collection of information regarding compliance with this Act. The information collected shall not be a public record and may not be made available for inspection by the public.
3. The Health Division shall generate and make available to the public an annual statistical report of information collected under Section 3.11(2) of this Act.

§ 3.12   Effect on Construction of Wills, Contracts, and Statutes

1. No provision in a contract, will or other agreement, whether written or oral, to the extent the provision would affect whether a person may make or rescind a request for medication to end his or her life in a humane and dignified manner, shall be valid.
2. No obligation owing under any currently existing contract shall be conditioned or affected by the making or rescinding of a request, by a person, for medication to end his or her life in a humane and dignified manner.

§ 3.13   Insurance or Annuity Policies

The sale, procurement, or issuance of any life, health, or accident insurance or annuity policy or the rate charged for any policy shall not be conditioned upon or affected by the making or rescinding of a request, by a person, for medication to end his or her life in a humane and dignified manner. Neither shall a qualified patient's act of ingesting medication to end his or her life in a humane and dignified manner have an effect upon a life, health, or accident insurance or annuity policy.

§ 3.14   Construction of Act

Nothing in this Act shall be construed to authorize a physician or any other person to end a patient's life by lethal injection, mercy killing or active euthanasia. Actions taken in accordance with this Act shall not, for any purpose, constitute suicide, assisted suicide, mercy killing or homicide, under the law.

SECTION 4: IMMUNITIES AND LIABILITIES

§ 4.01   Immunities

Except as provided in Section 4.02:

1. No person shall be subject to civil or criminal liability or professional disciplinary action for participating in good faith compliance with this Act. This includes being present when a qualified patient takes the prescribed medication to end his or her life in a humane and dignified manner.
2. No professional organization or association, or health care provider, may subject a person to censure, discipline, suspension, loss of license, loss of privileges, loss of membership or other penalty for participating or refusing to participate in good faith compliance with this Act.
3. No request by a patient for or provision by an attending physician of medication in good faith compliance with the provisions of this Act shall constitute neglect for any purpose of law or provide the sole basis for the appointment of a guardian or conservator.
4. No health care provider shall be under any duty, whether by contract, by statute or by any other legal requirement to participate in the provision to a qualified patient of medication to end his or her life in a humane and dignified manner. If a health care provider is unable or unwilling to carry out a patient's request under this Act, and the patient transfers his or her care to a new health care provider, the prior health care provider shall transfer, upon request, a copy of the patient's relevant medical records to the new health care provider.

§ 4.02   Liabilities

1. A person who without authorization of the patient willfully alters or forges a request for medication or conceals or destroys a rescission of that request with the intent or effect of causing the patient's death shall be guilty of a Class A felony.
2. A person who coerces or exerts undue influence on a patient to request medication for the purpose of ending the patient's life, or to destroy a rescission of such a request, shall be guilty of a Class A felony.
3. Nothing in this Act limits further liability for civil damages resulting from other negligent conduct or intentional misconduct by any person.
4. The penalties in this Act do not preclude criminal penalties applicable under other law for conduct which is inconsistent with the provisions of this Act.

SECTION 5: SEVERABILITY

§ 5.01 Severability

Any section of this Act being held invalid as to any person or circumstance shall not affect the application of any other section of this Act which can be given full effect without the invalid section or application.

SECTION 6: FORM OF THE REQUEST

§ 6.01 Form of the Request

A request for a medication as authorized by this act shall be in substantially the [boxed] form (Fig. 1).

REQUEST FOR MEDICATION
TO END MY LIFE IN A HUMANE AND DIGNIFIED MANNER

I, _____ , am an adult of sound mind.

I am suffering from _____ , which my attending physician has determined is a terminal disease and which has been medically confirmed by a consulting physician.

I have been fully informed of my diagnosis, prognosis, the nature of medication to be prescribed and potential associated risks, the expected result, and the feasible alternatives, including comfort care, hospice care and pain control.

I request that my attending physician prescribe medication that will end my life in a humane and dignified manner.

INITIAL ONE:

_____ I have informed my family of my decision and taken their opinions into consideration.

_____ I have decided not to inform my family of my decision.

_____ I have no family to inform of my decision.

I understand that I have the right to rescind this request at any time.

I understand the full import of this request and I expect to die when I take the medication to be prescribed.

I make this request voluntarily and without reservation, and I accept full moral responsibility for my actions.

Signed: _____

Dated: _____

> ### DECLARATION OF WITNESSES
> We declare that the person signing this request:
> (a) Is personally known to us or has provided proof of identity;
> (b) Signed this request in our presence;
> (c) Appears to be of sound mind and not under duress, fraud or undue influence;
> (d) Is not a patient for whom either of us is attending physician.
>
> _____ Witness 1/Date
>
> _____ Witness 2/Date
>
> NOTE: one witness shall not be a relative (by blood, marriage or adoption) of the person signing this request, shall not be entitled to any portion of the person's estate upon death and shall not own, operate or be employed at a health care facility where the person is a patient or resident. If the patient is an inpatient at a health care facility, one of the witnesses shall be an individual designated by the facility.

SUGGESTED READINGS FOR CHAPTER 4

A. PROBLEMS IN THE MORALITY OF ACTIONS BY PHYSICIANS

American Geriatrics Society. Public Policy Committee. "Voluntary Active Euthanasia." *Journal of the American Geriatrics Society* 39(8, Aug. 1991):826.

American Medical Association. Council on Ethical and Judicial Affairs. "Physician Participation in Capital Punishment." *Journal of the American Medical Association* 21; 270(3, July 1993):365–368.

Anonymous. "It's Over, Debbie." *Journal of the American Medical Association* 259(2, Jan. 8, 1988):258–272.

BENDER, LESLIE, "A Feminist Analysis of Physician-Assisted Dying and Voluntary Active Euthanasia." *Tennessee Law Review* 59(3, Spring 1992):519–546.

BRODY, HOWARD, "Assisted Death—A Compassionate Response to a Medical Failure." *New England Journal of Medicine* 327(19, Nov. 5, 1992):1384–1388.

BROWNE, ALISTER. "Assisted Suicide and Active Voluntary Euthanasia." *Canadian Journal of Law and Jurisprudence* 2 (January 1989):35–55.

CALLAHAN, DANIEL. "Aid-in-Dying: The Social Dimensions." *Commonweal* 118(14, Suppl, Aug. 9, 1991):476–480.

CAPLAN, ARTHUR L. "The Doctors' Trial and Analogies to the Holocaust in Contemporary Bioethical Debates." In George J. Annas; Michael A. Grodin, (eds.). *The Nazi Doctors and the Nuremberg Code: Human Rights in Human Experimentation.* New York: Oxford University Press, 1992, pp. 258–275.

CASSEL, CHRISTINE K., and DIANE E. MEIER. "Morals and Moralism in the Debate over Euthanasia and Assisted Suicide." *New England Journal of Medicine* 323 (Sept. 13, 1990):750–752.

CASSEL, CHRISTINE K. "Physician-Assisted Suicide: Are We Asking the Right Questions?" *Second Opinion* 18(2, Oct. 1992):95–98.

CRANFORD, RONALD E. "The Contemporary Euthanasia Movement and the Nazi Euthanasia Program. Are There Meaningful Similarities?" In Arthur L Caplan, (ed.). *When Medicine Went Mad: Bioethics and the Holocaust.* Totowa, NJ: Humana Press, 1992, pp. 201–210, 345–346.

ENGELHARDT, H. TRISTRAM, and MICHELLE MALLOY. "Suicide and Assisting Suicide: A Critique of Legal Sanctions." *Southwestern Law Journal* 36 (1982):1003–1037.

GAYLIN, WILLARD, LEON KASS, EDMUND PELLEGRINO, and MARK SIEGLER. "Doctors Must Not Kill." *Journal of the American Medical Association* 259 (April 8, 1988):2139–2140.

GOSTIN, LAWRENCE O. "Drawing a Line Between Killing and Letting Die: The Law, and Law Reform, on Medically Assisted Dying." *Journal of Law, Medicine and Ethics* 21(1, Spring 1993):94–101.

HOWE, EDMUND G. "On Expanding the Parameters of Assisted Suicide, Directive Counseling, and Overriding Patients' Cultural Beliefs." *Journal of Clinical Ethics* 4 (Summer 1993):107–111.

HUMBER, JAMES M., ROBERT F. ALMEDER, and G. A. KASTING (eds.) *Physician-Assisted Death.* Totowa, NJ: Humana Press, 1993.

KASS, LEON R. "Suicide Mady Easy: The Evil of Rational Humaneness." *Commentary* 92(6, Winter 1989):19–24.

KASS, LEON R. "Neither for Love Nor Money: Why Doctors Must Not Kill." *Public Interest* (94, Winter 1989):25–46.

KOWALSKI, SUSAN. "Assisted Suicide: Where Do Nurses Draw the Line?" *Nursing and Health Care* 14(2, Feb. 1993):70–76.

LIFTON, ROBERT J. *The Nazi Doctors: Medical Killing and the Psychology of Genocide.* New York: Basic Books, 1986.

LYNN, JOANNE. "The Health Care Professional's Role When Active Euthanasia Is Sought." *Journal of Palliative Care* 4(1–2, May 1988):100–102.

MACKLIN, RUTH. "Which Way Down the Slippery Slope? Nazi Medical Killing and Euthanasia Today." In Arthur L. Caplan, (ed.) *When Medicine Went Mad: Bioethics and the Holocaust.* Totowa, NJ: Humana Press, 1992, pp. 173–200, 343–345.

MAYO, DAVID J., and MARTIN, GUNDERSON. "Physician Assisted Death and Hard Choices." *Journal of Medicine and Philosophy* 18(3, June 1993):329–341.

McCORMICK, RICHARD A., and NANCY HOOYMAN. "Support for Physician-Assisted Suicide Must Be Quelled." *Health Progress* 73 (July–August 1992):51–52.

MEIER, DIANE E. "Physician-Assisted Dying: Theory and Reality." *Journal of Clinical Ethics* 3(1, Spring 1992):35–37.

MILLER, FRANKLIN G., TIMOTHY QUILL, HOWARD BRODY, JOHN C. FLETCHER, LAWRENCE O. GOSTIN, DIANE E. MEIER. "Regulating Physician-Assisted Death." *New England Journal of Medicine* 331(1994): 119–123.

McCORMICK, RICHARD A. "Physician-Assisted Suicide: Flight from Compassion." *Christian Century* 4; 108(35, Dec. 4, 1991):1132–1134.

NOWELL-SMITH, PATRICK. "Euthanasia and the Doctors—A Rejection of the BMA's Report." *Journal of Medical Ethics* 15(3, Sept. 1989):124–128.

ORENTLICHER, DAVID. "Physician-Assisted Dying: The Conflict with Fundamental Principles of American Law." In Robert H. Blank, Andrea L. Bonnicksen, (eds.) *Medicine Unbound.* New York: Columbia University Press, 1994.

PELLEGRINO, EDMUND D. "Doctors Must Not Kill," *Journal of Clinical Ethics* 3(2, Summer 1992):95–102.

QUILL, TIMOTHY E. "Doctor, I Want to Die. Will You Help Me?" *Journal of the American Medical Association* 270(7, Aug. 18, 1993):870–873.

QUILL, TIMOTHY E. *Death and Dignity: Making Choices and Taking Charge.* New York: W. W. Norton, 1993.

QUILL, TIMOTHY E. "The Ambiguity of Clinical Intentions." *New England Journal of Medicine* 329(14, Sept. 30, 1993):1039–1040.

SCHAFFNER, KENNETH F., "Philosophical, Ethical, and Legal Aspects of Resuscitation Medicine. Recognizing the Tragic Choice: Food, Water, and the Right to Assisted Suicide." *Critical Care Medicine* 16 (October 1988):1063–1068.

TEN HAVE, HENK A. M. J., and JOS V. M. WELIE. "Euthanasia: Normal Medical Practice?" *Hastings Center Report* 22(2, Mar.–Apr., 1992):34–38.

UBEL, PETER A. "Assisted Suicide and the Case of Dr. Quill and Diane." *Issues in Law and Medicine* 8(4, Spring 1993):487–502.

WANZER, SIDNEY H., DAN D. FEDERMAN, S. T. EDELSTEIN, et al. "The Physician's Responsibility Toward Hopelessly Ill Patient: A Second Look." *New England Journal of Medicine* 320(13, Mar. 30, 1989):844–849.

WATTS, DAVID T. and TIMOTHY HOWELL "Assisted Suicide Is Not Euthanasia." *Journal of the American Geriatrics Society* 40(10, Oct. 1992):1043–1046.

WEIR, ROBERT F. "The Morality of Physician-Assisted Suicide." *Law, Medicine and Health Care* 20(1–2, Spring–Summer 1992):116–126.

B. PROBLEMS IN LAW AND PUBLIC POLICY

1. United States Law and Policy

BRODY, HOWARD. "Legislative Ban on Assisted Suicide: Impact on Michigan's Medical Practice." *Michigan Medicine* 92(2, Feb. 1993):32–34.

KAMISAR, YALE. "Are Laws Against Assisted Suicide Unconstitutional?" *Hastings Center Report* 23(3, May–June, 1993):32–41.

KASS, LEON R. "Death on the California Ballot: Giving Healers the Sanction to Kill." *American Enterprise* 3(5, Sept.–Oct., 1992):44–51.

KEVORKIAN, JACK. *Prescription Medicine: The Goodness of Planned Death.* Buffalo, NY: Prometheus Books, 1991.

McGOUGH, PETER M. "Washington State Initiative 119: The First Public Vote on Legalizing Physician-Assisted Death." *Cambridge Quarterly of Healthcare Ethics* 2(1, Winter 1993):63–67.

New York State Task Force on Life and the Law. *When Death Is Sought: Assisted Suicide and Euthanasia in the Medical Context.* New York: New York State Task Force, 1994.

PERSELS, JIM. "Forcing the Issue of Physician-Assisted Suicide: Impact of the Kevorkian Case on the Euthanasia Debate." *Journal of Legal Medicine* (1, Mar. 1993):93–124.

2. International Law and Policy

a. The Netherlands

ADMIRAAL, PIETER V. "Euthanasia in the Netherlands: Justifiable Euthanasia." *Issues in Law & Medicine,* 3(4, Spring 1988):361–370. Also *The Euthanasia Review* 1990 3(2, Fall–Winter, 1990):107–118.

BATTIN, MARGARET PABST. "Voluntary Euthanasia and the Risk of Abuse: Can We Learn Anything from the Netherlands?" *Law, Medicine and Health Care* 20(1–2, Spring–Summer 1992):133–143.

CAPRON, ALEXANDER MORGAN. "Euthanasia in the Netherlands: American Observations." *Hastings Center Report* 22(2, Mar.–Apr., 1992):30–33.

DE WACHTER, MAURICE A.M. "Euthanasia in the Netherlands." *Hastings Center Report* 22(2, Mar.–Apr., 1992):23–30.

FENIGSEN, RICHARD. "The Report of the Dutch Governmental Committee on Euthanasia." *Issues in Law and Medicine* 7(3, Winter, 1991):339–344.

PIJNENBORG, LOES; PAUL J. VAN DER MAAS; JOHANNES J. M. VAN DELDON; and CASPER W. N. LOOMAN. "Life Terminating Acts Without Explicit Request of Patient." *Lancet* 341(8854, May 8, 1993):1196–1199.

Royal Dutch Medical Association. "Report of the Royal Dutch Society of Medicine on Life-Terminating Actions with Incompetent Patients, Part I: Severely Handicapped Newborns." [Translated summary]. *Issues in Law and Medicine* 7(3, Winter, 1991):365–367.

VAN DELDEN, JOHANNES J. M.; LOES PIJNENBORG; and PAUL J. VAN DER MAAS. "The Remmelink Study: Two Years Later." *Hastings Center Report* 23(6, Nov Dec 1993): 24–27.

VAN DER MAAS, PAUL J., et al. "Euthanasia and Other Medical Decisions Concerning the End of Life." *Lancet* 338(8768, Sept. 14, 1991):669–674.

VAN DER MAAAS, PAUL J., et al. *Euthanasia and Other Medical Decisions Concerning the End of Life: An Investigation Performed Upon Request of the Commission of Inquiry into the Medical Practice Concerning Euthanasia.* Amsterdam: Elsevier Science Publishers, 1992.

VAN DER WAL, GERRIT. "Unrequested Termination of Life: Is it Permissible?" *Bioethics* 7(4, July 1993):330–339.

VAN LEEUWEN, E. and G. K. KIMSMA. "Acting or Letting Go: Medical Decision Making in Neonatology in the Netherlands." *Cambridge Quarterly of Healthcare Ethics* 2(3, Summer 1993):265–269.

WELIE, JOS V. M. "The Medical Exception: Physicians, Euthanasia and the Dutch Criminal Law." *Journal of Medicine and Philosophy* 17(4, Aug. 1992):419–437.

b. Canada

KLUGE, EIKE-HENNER. "Doctors, Death and Sue Rodriguez." *Canadian Medical Association Journal* 148(6, Mar. 1993):1015–1017.

Law Reform Commission of Canada. *Euthanasia Aiding Suicide and Cessation of Treatment* Ottawa, Canada, 1982.

BIBLIOGRAPHICAL SOURCES AND REFERENCE WORKS

McCARRICK, PATRICIA MILMOE. "Active Euthanasia and Assisted Suicide." *Kennedy Institute of Ethics Journal* 2(1, Mar. 1992):79–99.

WALTERS, LEROY and TAMAR JOY KAHN, (eds.). *Bibliography of Bioethics.* Vols. 1–. New York: Free Press. Issued annually. See under "Allowing to Die," "Euthanasia,"

"Killing," "Suicide," "Terminal Care," and "Treatment Refusal." (The information contained in the annual *Bibliography of Bioethics* can also be retrieved from BIOETHICSLINE, an on-line data base of the National Library of Medicine.)

REICH, WARREN. (ed.) *Encyclopedia of Bioethics.* New York: Macmillan, 1995, articles on:

Death and Dying: Euthanasia and Sustaining Life
Homicide
Suicide

5

Forgoing Treatment and Causing Death

INTRODUCTION

When patients, health professionals, or surrogate decision makers intentionally forgo treatment, do they sometimes *cause* the death of the patient, or is disease or illness alone the cause of deaths? If they cause death, do they *kill* the patient? Does it matter whether one *acts* to bring about someone's death or merely *forgoes acting* in the knowledge that the death will occur? Each of these questions is addressed in this chapter.

THE MORAL RELEVANCE OF THE KILLING-LETTING DIE DISTINCTION

In the previous chapter some conceptual issues were raised about the meaning and types of euthanasia and about distinctions such as those between killing and letting die, acting and omitting, and intention and the absence of intention. Even if clear definitions can be provided and sharp lines drawn between these very different notions, we can still ask whether these distinctions are *morally relevant* to problems of euthanasia and physician-assisted suicide. The primary question is the following: "Is the intentional action of killing in itself no different *morally* than the intentional inaction of allowing to die?" In thinking through this question, it is worth noting that the above mentioned distinctions can be combined to produce several different categories of killing and letting die, of which the following are the most important for purposes of the issues in this chapter:

1. intentional killing
   a. by commission (active)
   b. by omission (passive)
2. unintentional killing

3. intentional allowing to die
4. unintentional allowing to die

It would be too tedious here to define and analytically distinguish each of these categories (and other combinations that are possible, though less relevant). Nonetheless, the reader is encouraged to bear in mind these several different conceptual possibilities while reading the selections in this chapter, where they are often not distinguished.

Further, assume for a moment that "killing" is *not* a morally loaded term indicating wrongness, but rather a morally neutral term that identifies certain ways of causing death. Under this assumption, to assert that killing is no different morally than allowing to die is to say that correct labeling of actions as "killing" and as "letting die" does not determine whether one type of action is better or worse than the other, or whether either is acceptable. Some particular instance of killing (e.g., a callous murder) may be morally worse than some particular instance of allowing to die (e.g., forgoing treatment for a dying and comatose patient); but some particular instance of letting die (e.g., not resuscitating a patient who could easily be saved but who has refused treatment because of a series of mistaken assumptions) also may be morally worse than some particular instance of killing (e.g., mercy killing at the request of a seriously ill and suffering patient).

In this account, nothing about either killing or allowing to die entails judgments about the wrongness or rightness of either type of action. Rightness and wrongness depend on the merit of the *justification* underlying the action, not on the *type* of action it is. Neither killing nor letting die is per se wrongful, and in this regard they are to be distinguished from murder, which is per se wrongful. James Rachels pursues this line of argument in the present chapter, as do Tom Beauchamp and James Childress, who respond to Rachels.

Rachels is in part attacking an influential policy statement passed in 1973 (and revised in 1988 and 1991) by the American Medical Association's Council on Ethical and Judicial Affairs. This policy allows forgoing life-sustaining treatments but prohibits the "intentional termination of the life of one human being by another—mercy killing." Whether letting particular patients die is morally acceptable depends on several factors in this policy, but if the deaths involve killing—even in circumstances identical to those in which a patient is allowed to die—they are never justifiable. Rachels sternly rebukes the American Medical Association for this policy, but Beauchamp and Childress are less critical and argue that valid reasons exist for preserving some form of the killing/letting die distinction in the development of public policy.

Rachels also holds that if it is morally permissible to intend that a patient die, then acting directly to terminate a patient's life is justified if it causes less suffering to the patient than intentionally allowing him or her to die. By contrast, Beauchamp and Childress argue that killing may not be justified even if it causes less suffering for some patients, because seriously harmful consequences might occur if the killing/letting die distinction were publicly regarded as irrelevant. However, these apparently opposed views may not be inconsistent: One could argue that some particular acts of terminating a patient's life are morally justified, but that public policy should not legalize these actions (See Chapter 4, pp. 154-55).

FORGOING TREATMENT AND CAUSING DEATH

Physicians, lawyers, and moral philosophers have typically construed acts of forgoing treatment as letting die, not as acts of either causing death or killing. At the same time, physicians and nurses have worried that when they are involved in the decision to withdraw treatment and a patient dies, they will be involved in killing the patient and will be subject to criminal liability. They likewise worry that patients who withdraw or withhold treatment are killing themselves and that health professionals assist in suicide if they implement the refusal.

Many now believe that forgoing treatment to allow death cannot be meaningfully distinguished from taking active steps to end life when the motives, intentions, and projected consequences are identical. In both circumstances, the patient's death is intended and the central actors may be moved by compassion, mercy, and the like. Courts have usually tried to avoid this controversy by offering accounts of why, when an individual forgoes life-sustaining treatment, the cause of death should not be categorized as either suicide or homicide. They argue that, in acts of forgoing treatment, an underlying disease or injury is the cause of death and that medical technology—for example, a respirator—only delays the natural course of the disease or injury. When the technology is removed, a "natural death" occurs. Because disease or injury is the cause of death—not the physician's, surrogate's, or patient's action—the event is not homicide or suicide.

This legal premise helps to alleviate the fears of health professionals about moral blame and legal liability, but some critics in this chapter—notably Dan W. Brock and Justice Antonin Scalia—argue that this premise is not consistent with many of our beliefs about killing. They point out that the patient's decision and the physician's action do play important causal roles in the circumstance in which these deaths occur. The physicians' actions seem in many cases necessary, and perhaps sufficient conditions of death at the time and in the way it occurs. For example, to withhold nutrition and hydration so that a patient starves to death seems both a necessary and a sufficient condition of death by starvation at the time the death occurs. If the patient is suffering from a condition such as severe brain damage, pneumonia, cancer, or quadriplegia, these conditions (the real reason for refusing treatment) are neither necessary nor sufficient conditions of death by starvation. They are *not* in any respect the cause of death *as it occurs,* though they are the reason why the decision was made to bring about death.

Brock argues that if a nonphysician allows someone to die by removing medical technology that sustains life, the person clearly does more than release natural conditions. We could not rightly say, "He didn't kill the patient; he only allowed the patient to die." By intentionally "allowing" the patient to die, he killed him. Yet such a person's act seems to be exactly the same act that physicians typically perform (usually at a patient's or a family's request) in a case of "allowing to die." Brock and Scalia agree that, like typical suicides, patients who refuse treatment can intend to end their lives because of their grim prospects for the future.

A vigorous rejection of the idea that physicians cause death in refusal-of-treatment cases is found in the article by James Bernat, Bernard Gert, and Peter Mogielnicki. They argue that a rational patient's rejection of interventions alone places the physician in the position of allowing to die. If a rational refusal has occurred, the physician is never in the circumstance either of causing death or killing, and this is so even if the patient dies of starvation.

THE DOCTRINE OF DOUBLE EFFECT

A venerable attempt to resolve many of these problems about intending and causing death is the doctrine of double effect (DDE). This doctrine relies on a pivotal distinction between *intended effects* and merely *foreseen effects*. The DDE has the objective of justifying the claim that a single act having two foreseen effects, one good (such as relieving suffering) and one harmful (such as death), is not always morally prohibited. The key premise is that if the harmful effect is not intended, then the action can, under certain circumstances, be justified.

A well-known example of the use of the DDE is the seriously suffering, terminal patient who requests a physician's help in ending her life. If the physician directly kills her in order to end the suffering, her death is caused intentionally. Do matters change if the physician provides medication to relieve the patient's pain and suffering, knowing that a substantial risk exists that the patient's death will be hastened as a result of the medication? If the physician refuses to administer the toxic analgesia, the patient will suffer continuing pain; but if the physician provides the medication, the patient's death may be hastened. Under the DDE, the physician must intend to relieve the suffering in providing the medication and must not intend to hasten death. If a lethal effect is not intended and other double-effect conditions are met, then the act is not prohibited.

According to the mainstream formulation of the DDE, four conditions must be satisfied for an act with good and bad effects to be permissible. Each is a necessary condition and together they form jointly sufficient conditions of morally permissible action, despite the bad effect.

1. *Good* or *Neutral Act.* The act must be morally good or morally neutral, independent of its effects.
2. *Intention.* The agent must intend only the good effect. The bad effect can be foreseen and permitted, but not intended.
3. *Direct Means.* The bad effect must not be a means to the good effect (because the agent would have to intend the bad effect in pursuit of the good effect).
4. *Proportionality.* The good effect must proportionally outweigh the bad effect. This outweighing compensates for permitting the bad effect.

Critics contend that it is difficult and perhaps impossible in many cases through DDE conditions to establish what the relevant intention is—especially whether the intention is to give a patient additional pain-killing medication or, by contrast, intentionally to give a life-ending overdose. In neither case does the agent want or desire the death of the person, and the descriptions of the acts do not introduce morally relevant differences. It is not clear, say critics, why an overdose intentionally given to a patient is killing rather than medicating for pain with the *unintended* result that the patient dies. It is also not clear (either conceptually or empirically) whether in cases of administering additional pain-killing medication, the death is only foreseen, not intended. A proponent of the DDE must have a way to distinguish the intended from the merely foreseen, but it has proved difficult to draw defensible lines between the many possible cases.

It is a matter of ongoing controversy whether defenders of the DDE can resolve such problems. In the present chapter, Edmund Pellegrino defends the use of double effect in difficult medical circumstances in an essay that builds on the conclusions he reached in his essay in Chapter 4 (pp. 161-165 above).

Active and Passive Euthanasia*

JAMES RACHELS

In a widely discussed argument for rejecting both the distinction between active and passive euthanasia, James Rachels contends that killing as a type of act is not worse than letting die—although, of course, *some* killings are morally worse than *some* cases of allowing to die. Rachels employs two bathtub-drowning cases that differ only in that one involves killing while the other involves allowing to die. He contends that if there is no morally relevant difference between these cases, the bare difference between acts of killing and allowing to die cannot be morally relevant. In his view, the two acts are equally condemnable because of the agents' similar motives and actions, not because of the difference between killing and letting die. Therefore, if it is morally justified to act intentionally so that a person dies, then the morally important question is what makes the act justified, not what *type* of action it is (killing or letting die). Lengthening this logic, Rachels argues that if one finds acceptable an intentional omission of treatment that qualifies as passive euthanasia, then there will be parallel cases in which active euthanasia is likewise justified.

The distinction between active and passive euthanasia is thought to be crucial for medical ethics. The idea is that it is permissible, at least in some cases, to withhold treatment and allow a patient to die, but it is never permissible to take any direct action designed to kill the patient. This doctrine seems to be accepted by most doctors, and it was endorsed in a statement adopted by the House of Delegates of the American Medical Association on December 4, 1973:

> The intentional termination of the life of one human being by another—mercy killing—is contrary to that for which the medical profession stands and is contrary to the policy of the American Medical Association.
>
> The cessation of the employment of extraordinary means to prolong the life of the body when there is irrefutable evidence that biological death is imminent is the decision of the patient and/or his immediate family. The advice and judgment of the physician should be freely available to the patient and/or his immediate family.

However, a strong case can be made against this doctrine. In what follows I will set out some of the relevant arguments, and urge doctors to reconsider their views on this matter.

*Source: Rachels, J., "Active and Passive Euthanasia." Vol. 292, pp. 78–80, 1975. Copyright 1975. Massachusetts Medical Society. All rights reserved. Reprinted by permission of *The New England Journal of Medicine*.

To being with a familiar type of situation, a patient who is dying of incurable cancer of the throat is in terrible pain, which can no longer be satisfactorily alleviated. He is certain to die within a few days, even if present treatment is continued, but he does not want to go on living for those days since the pain is unbearable. So he asks the doctor for an end to it, and his family joins in the request.

Suppose the doctor agrees to withhold treatment, as the conventional doctrine says he may. The justification for his doing so is that the patient is in terrible agony, and since he is going to die anyway, it would be wrong to prolong his suffering needlessly. But now notice this. If one simply withholds treatment, it may take the patient longer to die, and so he may suffer more than he would if more direct action were taken and a lethal injection given. This fact provides strong reason for thinking that, once the initial decision not to prolong his agony has been made, active euthanasia is actually preferable to passive euthanasia, rather than the reverse. To say otherwise is to endorse the option that leads to more suffering rather than less, and is contrary to the humanitarian impulse that prompts the decision not to prolong his life in the first place.

Part of my point is that the process of being "allowed to die" can be relatively slow and painful, whereas being given a lethal injection is relatively quick and painless. Let me give a different sort of example. In the United States about one in 600 babies is born with Down's syndrome. Most of these babies are otherwise healthy— that is, with only the usual pediatric care, they will proceed to an otherwise normal infancy. Some, however, are born with congenital defects such as intestinal obstructions that require operations if they are to live. Sometimes, the parents and the doctor will decide not to operate, and let the infant die. Anthony Shaw describes what happens then.

> When surgery is denied [the doctor] must try to keep the infant from suffering while natural forces sap the baby's life away. As a surgeon whose natural inclination is to use the scalpel to fight off death, standing by and watching a salvageable baby die is the most emotionally exhausting experience I know. It is easy at a conference, in a theoretical discussion, to decide that such infants should be allowed to die. It is altogether different to stand by in the nursery and watch as dehydration and infection wither a tiny being over hours and days. This is a terrible ordeal for me and the hospital staff—much more so than for the parents who never set foot in the nursery.[1]

I can understand why some people are opposed to all euthanasia, and insist that such infants must be allowed to live. I think I can also understand why other people favor destroying these babies quickly and painlessly. But why should anyone favor letting "dehydration and infection wither a tiny being over hours and days"? The doctrine that says that a baby may be allowed to dehydrate and wither, but may not be given an injection that would end its life without suffering, seems so patently cruel as to require no further refutation. The strong language is not intended to offend, but only to put the point in the clearest possible way.

My second argument is that the conventional doctrine leads to the decisions concerning life and death made on irrelevant grounds.

Consider again the case of the infants with Down's syndrome who need operations for congenital defects unrelated to the syndrome to live. Sometimes there is no operation, and the baby dies, but when there is no such defect, the baby lives on. Now, an operation such as that to remove an intestinal obstruction is not prohibitively difficult. The reason why such operations are not performed in these cases is, clearly, that the child has Down's syndrome and the parents and doctor judge that because of that fact it is better for the child to die.

But notice that this situation is absurd, no matter what view one takes of the lives and potentials of such babies. If the life of such an infant is worth preserving, what does it matter if it needs a simple operation? Or, if one thinks it better that such a baby should not live on, what difference does it make that it happens to have an unobstructed intestinal tract? In either case, the matter of life and death is being decided on irrelevant grounds. It is the Down's syndrome, and not the intestines, that is the issue. The matter should be decided, if at all, on that basis, and not be allowed to depend on the essentially irrelevant question of whether the intestinal tract is blocked.

What makes this situation possible, of course, is the idea that when there is an intestinal blockage, one can "let the baby die," but when there is no such defect there is nothing that can be done, for one must not "kill" it. The fact that this idea leads to such results as deciding life or death on irrelevant grounds is another good reason why the doctrine should be rejected.

One reason why so many people think that there is an important moral difference between active and passive euthanasia is that they think killing someone is morally worse than letting someone die. But is it? Is killing, in itself, worse than letting die? To investigate this issue, two cases may be considered that are exactly alike except that one involves killing whereas the other involves letting someone die. Then, it can be asked whether this difference makes any difference to the moral assessments. It is important that the cases be exactly alike, except for this one difference, since otherwise one cannot be confident that it is this difference and not some other that accounts for any variation in the assessments of the two cases. So, let us consider this pair of cases:

In the first, Smith stands to gain a large inheritance if anything should happen to his six-year-old cousin. One evening while the child is taking his bath, Smith sneaks into the bathroom and drowns the child, and then arranges things so that it will look like an accident.

In the second, Jones also stand to gain if anything should happen to his six-year-old cousin. Like Smith, Jones sneaks in planning to drown the child in his bath. However, just as he enters the bathroom Jones sees the child slip and hit his head, and fall face down in the water. Jones is delighted; he stands by, ready to push the child's head back under if it is necessary, but it is not necessary. With only a little thrashing about, the child drowns all by himself, "accidentally," as Jones watches and does nothing.

Now Smith killed the child, whereas Jones "merely" let the child die. That is the only difference between them. Did either man behave better, from a moral point of view? If the difference between killing and letting die were in itself a morally important matter, one should say that Jones's behavior was less reprehensible than Smith's. But does one really want to say that? I think not. In the first place, both men acted from the same motive, personal gain, and both had exactly the same end in view when they acted. It may be inferred from Smith's conduct that he is a bad man, although that judgment may be withdrawn or modified if certain further facts are learned about him—for example, that he is mentally deranged. But would not the very same thing be inferred about Jones from his conduct? And would not the same further considerations also be relevant to any modification of this judgment? Moreover, suppose Jones pleaded, in his own defense, "After all, I didn't do anything except just stand there and watch the child drown. I didn't kill him; I only let him die." Again, if letting die were in itself less bad than killing, this defense should have at least some weight. But it does not. Such a "defense" can only be regarded as a grotesque perversion of moral reasoning. Morally speaking, it is no defense at all.

Now it may be pointed out, quite properly, that the cases of euthanasia with which doctors are concerned are not like this at all. They do not involve personal gain or the destruction of normal healthy children. Doctors are concerned only with cases in which the patient's life is of no further use to him, or in which the patient's life has become or will soon become a terrible burden. However, the point is the same in these cases: the bare difference between killing and letting die does not, in itself, make a moral difference. If a doctor lets a patient die, for humane reasons, he is in the same moral position as if he had given the patient a lethal injection for humane reasons. If his decision was wrong—if, for example, the patient's illness was in fact curable— the decision would be equally regrettable no matter which method was used to carry it out. And if the doctor's decision was the right one, the method used is not in itself important.

The AMA policy statement isolates the crucial issue very well; the crucial issue is "the intentional termination of the life of one human being by another." But after identifying this issue, and forbidding "mercy killing," the statement goes on to deny that the cessation of treatment is the intentional termination of a life. This is where the mistake comes in, for what is the cessation of treatment, in these circumstances, if it is not "the intentional termination of the life of one human being by another"? Of course it is exactly that, and if it were not, there would be no point to it.

Many people will find this judgment hard to accept. One reason, I think, is that it is very easy to conflate the question of whether killing is, in itself, worse than letting die, with the very different question of whether most actual cases of killing are more reprehensible than most actual cases of letting die. Most actual cases of killing are clearly terrible (think, for example, of all the murders reported in the newspapers), and one hears of such cases every day. On the other hand, one hardly ever hears of a case of letting die, except for the actions of doctors who are motivated by humanitarian reasons. So one learns to think of killing in a much worse light than of letting die. But this does not mean that there is something about killing that makes it in itself worse than letting die, for it is not the bare difference between killing and letting die that makes the difference in these cases. Rather, the other factors—the murderer's motive of personal gain, for example, contrasted with the doctor's humanitarian motivation—account for different reactions to the different cases.

I have argued that killing is not in itself any worse than letting die; if my contention is right, it follows that active euthanasia is not any worse than passive euthanasia. What arguments can be given on the other side? The most common, I believe, is the following:

"The important difference between active and passive euthanasia is that, in passive euthanasia, the doctor does not do anything to bring about the patient's death. The doctor does nothing, and the patient dies of whatever ills already afflict him. In active euthanasia, however, the doctor does something to bring about the patient's death: he kills him. The doctor who gives the patient with cancer a lethal injection has himself caused his patient's death; whereas if he merely ceases treatment, the cancer is the cause of the death."

A number of points needs to be made here. The first is that it is not exactly correct to say that in passive euthanasia the doctor does nothing, for he does do one thing that is very important: he lets the patient die. "Letting someone die" is certainly different, in some respects, from other types of action—mainly in that it is a kind of action that one may perform by way of not performing certain other actions. For example, one may let a patient die by way of not giving medication, just as one may insult someone by way of not shaking his hand. But for any purpose of moral assessment, it is a type of action nonetheless. The decision to let a patient die is subject to moral appraisal in the same way that a decision to kill him would be subject to moral appraisal: it may be assessed as wise or unwise, compassionate or sadistic, right or wrong. If a doctor deliberately let a patient die who was suffering from a routinely curable illness, the doctor would certainly be to blame for what he had done, just as he would be to blame if he had needlessly killed the patient. Charges against him would then be appropriate. If so, it would be no defense at all for him to insist that he didn't "do anything." He would have done something very serious indeed, for he let his patient die.

Fixing the cause of death may be very important from a legal point of view, for it may determine whether criminal charges are brought against the doctor. But I do not think that this notion can be used to show a moral difference between active and passive euthanasia. The reason why it is considered bad to be the cause of someone's death is that death is regarded as a great evil—and so it is. However, if it has been decided that euthanasia—even passive euthanasia—is desirable in a given case, it has also been decided that in this instance death is no greater an evil than the patient's continued existence. And if this is true, the usual reason for not wanting to be the cause of someone's death simply does not apply.

Finally, doctors may think that all of this is only of academic interest—the sort of thing that philosophers may worry about but that has no practical bearing on their own work. After all, doctors must be concerned about the legal consequences of what they do, and active euthanasia is clearly forbidden by the law. But even so, doctors should also be concerned with the fact that the law is forcing upon them a moral doctrine that may well be indefensible, and has a considerable effect on their practices. Of course, most doctors are not now in the position of being coerced in this matter, for they do not regard themselves as merely going along with what the law requires. Rather, in statements such as the AMA policy statement that I have quoted, they are endorsing this doctrine as a central point of medical ethics. In that statement, active euthanasia is condemned not merely as illegal but as "contrary to that for which the medical profession stands," whereas passive euthanasia is approved. However, the preceding considerations suggest that there is really no moral difference between the two, considered in themselves (there may be important moral differences in some cases in their *consequences*, but, as I pointed out, these differences may make active euthanasia, and not passive euthanasia, the morally preferable option). So, whereas doctors may have to discriminate between active and passive euthanasia to satisfy the law, they should not do any more than that. In particular, they should not give the distinction any added authority and weight by writing it into official statements of medical ethics.

NOTE

1. A. Shaw. "Doctor, Do We Have a Choice?" *The New York Times Magazine*, January 30, 1972, p. 54.

Rachels on Active
and Passive Euthanasia

TOM L. BEAUCHAMP AND JAMES F. CHILDRESS

Beauchamp and Childress agree with Rachels that nothing about either killing or allowing to die (or about commission and omission) entails wrongness or rightness, and they also agree that whether an act of either killing or letting die is justified or unjustified depends on the morally relevant features of the case at hand. However, they deny that Rachels' arguments and examples show that we have adequate reasons for altogether rejecting the killing-letting die distinction. Whereas Rachels's arguments focus on acts in isolation from their larger social consequences, Beauchamp and Childress focus on social practices, not merely the acts themselves. They bring slippery slope arguments into the picture, whereas Rachels's line of argument excluded such concerns. Beauchamp and Childress take seriously the AMA policy that Rachels rejects; they maintain that some forms of passive euthanasia are permissible, whereas active euthanasia may not be the best public policy.

James Rachels contends that killing is not, in itself, worse than letting die; the "bare difference" between acts of killing and acts of letting die is not in itself a morally relevant difference.[1] We agree with Rachels that the acts in his two cases are equally reprehensible because of the agents' motives and actions, and we agree that killing as a type of act is in itself no different *morally* than allowing to die as a type of act. However, we do not accept his conclusion that his examples and arguments show that the distinction between killing and letting die and passive and active euthanasia are morally irrelevant in the formulation of public policy. We also do not agree that his cases demonstrate what he claims.

PROBLEMS IN RACHELS'S ANALYSIS

First, Rachels's cases and the cessations of treatment envisioned by the AMA are so markedly disanalogous that Rachels's argument is misdirected. In some cases of unjustified acts, including both of Rachels's examples, we are not interested in moral distinctions between killing and letting die (per se). As Richard Trammell points out, some examples have a "masking" or "sledgehammer" effect; the fact that "one cannot distinguish the taste of two wines when both are mixed with green persimmon juice, does not imply that there is no distinction between the wines."[2] Because Rachels's examples involve two morally unjustified acts by agents whose motives and intentions are despicable, it is not surprising that some other features of their situations, such as killing and letting die, are not morally compelling considerations in the circumstances.

Second, Smith and Jones are morally responsible and morally blameworthy for the deaths of their respective cousins, even if Jones, who allowed his cousin to drown, is not causally responsible. The law might find only Smith, who killed his cousin, guilty of homicide (because of the law's theory of proximate cause), but morality condemns both actions alike because of the agents' commissions and omissions. We find Jones's actions reprehensible because he should have rescued the child. Even if he had no other special duties to the child, there is an affirmative obligation of beneficence in such a case.

Third, the point of the range of cases envisioned by the AMA is consistent with Rachels's arguments, though he thinks them inconsistent. The AMA's central claim is that the physician is always morally prohibited from killing patients but is not morally bound to preserve life in all cases. According to the AMA, the physician has a right and perhaps a duty to stop treatment if and only if three conditions are met: (1) the life of the body is being preserved by extraordinary means, (2) there is irrefutable evidence that biological death is imminent, and (3) the patient or the family consents. Whereas Rachels's cases involve two unjustified actions, one of killing and the other of letting die, the AMA statement distinguishes cases of unjustified killing from cases of justified letting die. The AMA statement does not claim that the moral difference is entirely predicated on the distinction between killing and letting die. It also does not imply that the bare difference between (passive) letting die and (active) killing is the major difference or a morally sufficient difference to distinguish the justified from the unjustified cases. The point is only that the justified actions in medicine are confined to letting die (passive euthanasia).

The AMA statement holds that "mercy killing" in medicine is unjustified in all circumstances, but it holds neither that letting die is right in all circumstances nor that killing outside medicine is always wrong. For an act that results in an earlier death for the patient to be justified, it is necessary that it be an act of letting die, but this condition is not sufficient to justify the act; nor is the bare fact of an act's being a killing sufficient to make the act wrong. This AMA declaration is meant to control conduct exclusively in the context of the physician-patient relationship. The rationale for the prohibition is not stated, but the scope of the prohibition is quite clear.

Even if the distinction between killing and letting die is morally irrelevant in many cases, it does not follow that it is morally irrelevant in all contexts. Although we quite agree that Rachels does effectively undermine all attempts to rest moral judgments about ending life on the "bare difference" between killing and letting die, his target may nonetheless be made of straw. Many philosophers and theologians have argued that there are independent moral, religious, and other reasons both for defending the distinction and for prohibiting killing while authorizing allowing to die in some circumstances or based on some motives.

One theologian has argued, for example, that we can discern the moral significance of the distinction between killing and letting die by "placing it in the religious context out of which it grew."[3] That context is the biblical story of God's actions toward his creatures. In that context it makes sense to talk about "placing patients in God's hands," just as it is important not to usurp God's prerogatives by desperately struggling to prolong life when the patient is irreversibly dying. But even if the distinction between killing and letting die originated within a religious context, and even if it makes more sense in that context than in some others, it can be defended on non-theological grounds without being reduced to a claim about a "bare difference." We turn next to this defense of the distinction.

HOW AND WHERE TO DEFEND THE DISTINCTION BETWEEN KILLING AND LETTING DIE

Even if there are sufficient reasons in some cases to warrant mercy killing, there may also be good reasons to retain the distinction between killing and letting die and to maintain our current practices and policies against killing *in medicine*, albeit with some clarifications and modifications.

Acts and Practices. The most important arguments for the distinction between killing and letting die depend on a distinction between acts and practices.4 It is one thing to justify an act; it is another to justify a general practice. Many beliefs about principles and consequences are applied to rules rather than directly to acts. For example, we might justify a rule of confidentiality because it encourages people to seek therapy and because it promotes respect for persons and their privacy, although such a rule might lead to undesirable results in particular cases where confidentiality should not be maintained.

Similarly, a rule that prohibits "active killing" while permitting some "allowed deaths" may be justifiable, even if it excludes some particular acts of killing that in themselves are justifiable. For example, the rule would not permit us to kill a patient who suffers from terrible pain, who will probably die within three weeks, and who rationally asks for a merciful-assisted death. In order to maintain a viable practice that expresses our principles and avoids seriously undesirable consequences, it may be necessary to prohibit some acts that are not otherwise wrong and in some cases may be morally justified. Thus, although particular *acts* of killing may be humane and compassionate, a *policy* or *practice* that authorizes killing in medicine—in even a few cases—might create a grave risk of harm in many cases and a risk that we find it unjustified to assume.

The prohibition of killing even for "mercy" expresses principles and supports practices that provide a basis of trust between patients and health-care professionals. When we trust these professionals, we expect them to ask our consent and to do us no harm without a prospect of correlative benefit. The prohibition of killing is an attempt to promote a solid basis for trust in the role of caring for patients and protecting them from harm. This prohibition is both instrumentally and symbolically important, and its removal could weaken a set of practices and restraints that we cannot easily replace.

Wedge or Slippery Slope Arguments. This last argument—an incipient wedge or slippery slope argument—is plausible but needs to be stated carefully. Because of the widespread misuses of such arguments in biomedical ethics, there is a tendency to dismiss them whenever they are offered. However, as expressions of the principle of nonmaleficence, they are defensible in some cases. They also force us to consider whether unacceptable harms may result from attractive and apparently innocent first steps. Legitimation of acts such as active voluntary euthanasia run the risk of leading to other acts or practices that are morally objectionable even if some individual acts of this type are acceptable in themselves. The claim made by those who defend these arguments is that accepting the act in question would cross a line that has already been drawn against killing; and once that line has been crossed, it will not be possible to draw it again to preclude unacceptable acts or practices.

However, wedge arguments of some types may not be as damaging as they may seem at first. As Rachels correctly contends, "there obviously are good reasons for objecting to killing patients in order to get away for the weekend—or for even more respectable purposes, such as securing organs for transplantation—which do not apply to killing in order to put the patient out of extreme agony."5 In other words, the counterreply is that relevant distinctions can be drawn, and we are not subject to uncontrollable implications from general principles. Some versions of the wedge argument, therefore, do not assist supporters of the distinction between killing and letting die as much as they might suppose.

Indeed, the argument can be used against them: If it is rational and morally defensible to allow patients to die under conditions X, Y, and Z, then it is rational and morally defensible to kill them under those same conditions. If it is in their best interests to die, it is (*prima facie*) irrelevant how death is brought about. Rachels makes a similar point when he argues that reliance on the distinction between killing and letting die may lead to decisions about life and death made on irrelevant grounds—such as whether the patient will or will not die without certain forms of treatment—instead of being made in terms of the patient's best interests.

In the now famous Johns Hopkins Hospital case, an infant with Down syndrome and duodenal atresia was placed in a back room and died eleven days later of dehydration and starvation. This process of dying, which senior physicians had recommended against, was extremely difficult for all the parties involved, particularly the nurses. If decision makers legitimately determine that a patient would be better off dead (we think the parties mistakenly came to this conclusion in this case), how could an act of killing violate the patient's interests if the patient will not die when artificial treatment is discontinued? A morally irrelevant factor would be allowed to dictate the outcome.

The lack of empirical evidence to determine the adequacy of slippery slope arguments is unfortunate, but it is not a sufficient reason to reject them. Some arguments of this form should be taken with the utmost seriousness. They force us to think carefully about whether unacceptable harm is likely to result from attractive and apparently innocent first steps.

NOTES

1. James Rachels. "Active and Passive Euthanasia," *New England Journal of Medicine* 292 (1975):78–80.
2. Richard L. Trammell. "Saving Life and Taking Life," *Journal of Philosophy* 72 (1975):131–137.

3. Gilbert Meilaender. "The Distinction between Killing and Allowing to Die," *Theological Studies* 37 (1976):467–470.

4. This distinction and our arguments are indebted to John Rawls, "Two Concepts of Rules," *Philosophical Review* 64 (1955):3–32.

5. James Rachels. "Medical Ethics and the Rule against Killing: Comments on Professor Hare's Paper." S. F. Spicker and H. T. Engelhardt (eds.). p. 65. In *Philosophical Medical Ethics*, Dordrecht, Holland: D. Reidel, 1977.

Cruzan v. Director, Missouri Dept. of Health

JUSTICE ANTONIN SCALIA, CONCURRING IN UNITED STATES SUPREME COURT

The next selection is another part of the *Cruzan* case discussed in the previous chapter. Justice Scalia argues that withdrawing or withholding of treatment sometimes constitutes suicide, because *any* means productive of death (by omission as well as commission) can be arranged to the end of killing oneself—even if death is inevitable or the causes of death are natural. Pulling the plug on one's respirator is not relevantly different from plunging a knife into one's heart, if the conditions and the reason for putting an end to life are relevantly similar. There may, from this perspective, be suicidal intent in any circumstance of refusal of life-sustaining treatment (a case of intentional killing by omission). A withdrawing or withholding of treatment does sometimes constitute suicide or homicide, then, and a physician who supports the omission can be involved in assisted suicide or homicide, which under law can qualify as murder. Scalia argues for moral recognition of "the irrelevance of the action–inaction distinction" and legal recognition that the U.S. Constitution has nothing to say about the right to die.

Justice SCALIA, concurring.

While I agree with the Court's analysis today, and therefore join in its opinion, I would have preferred that we announce, clearly and promptly, that the federal courts have no business in this field; that American law has always accorded the State the power to prevent, by force if necessary, suicide—including suicide by refusing to take appropriate measures necessary to preserve one's life; that the point at which life becomes "worthless," and the point at which the means necessary to preserve it become "extraordinary" or "inappropriate," are neither set forth in the Constitution nor known to the nine Justices of this Court any better than they are known to nine people picked at random from the Kansas City telephone directory; and hence, that even when it *is* demonstrated by clear and convincing evidence that a patient no longer wishes certain measures to be taken to preserve her life, it is up to the citizens of Missouri to decide, through their elected representatives, whether that wish will be honored. . . .

At common law in England, a suicide—defined as one who "deliberately puts an end to his own existence, or commits any unlawful malicious act, the consequence of which is his own death," 4 W. Blackstone, Commentaries 189—was criminally liable. *Ibid.* Although the States abolished the penalties imposed by the common law (i.e., forfeiture and ignominious burial), they did so to spare the innocent family, and not to legitimize the act. Case law at the time of the Fourteenth Amendment generally held that assisting suicide was a criminal offense. . . .

Petitioners rely on three distinctions to separate Nancy Cruzan's case from ordinary suicide: (1) that she is permanently incapacitated and in pain; (2) that she would bring on her death not by any affirmative act but by merely declining treatment that provides nourishment; and (3) that preventing her from effectuating her presumed wish to die requires violation of her bodily integrity. None of these suffices. Suicide was not excused even when committed "to avoid those ills which [persons] had not the fortitude to endure." 4 Blackstone, *supra*, at 189. "The life of those to whom life has become a burden—of those who are hopelessly diseased or fatally wounded—nay, even the lives of criminals condemned to death, are under the protection of the law, equally as the lives of those who are in the full tide of life's enjoyment, and anxious to continue to live." *Blackburn v. State*, 23 Ohio St. 146, 163 (1873). Thus, a man who prepared a poison, and placed it within reach of his wife, "to put an end to her suffering" from a terminal illness was convicted of murder, *People v. Roberts*, 211 Mich. 187, 178 N.W. 690, 693 (1920); the "incurable suffering of the suicide, as a legal question, could hardly affect the degree of criminality. . . . " Note, 30 Yale L.J. 408, 412 (1921) (discussing *Roberts*). Nor would the imminence of the patient's death have affected liability. "The lives of all are equally under the protection of the law, and under that protection to their last moment. . . . [Assisted suicide] is declared by the law to be murder, irrespective of the wishes or the condition of the party to whom the poison is administered. . . . " *Blackburn, supra*, at 163. . . .

The second asserted distinction—suggested by the recent cases canvassed by the Court concerning the right to refuse treatment, *ante*, at 2846–2850—relies on the dichotomy between action and inaction. Suicide, it is said, consists of an affirmative act to end one's life; refusing treatment is not an affirmative act "causing" death, but merely a passive acceptance of the natural process of dying. I readily acknowledge that the distinction between action and inaction has some bearing upon the legislative judgment of what ought to be prevented as suicide—though even there it would seem to me unreasonable to draw the line precisely between action and inaction, rather than between various forms of inaction. It would not make much sense to say that one may not kill oneself by walking into the sea, but may sit on the beach until submerged by the incoming tide; or that one may not intentionally lock oneself into a cold storage locker, but may refrain from coming indoors when the temperature drops below freezing. Even as a legislative matter, in other words, the intelligent line does not fall between action and inaction but between those forms of inaction that consist of abstaining from "ordinary" care and those that consist of abstaining from "excessive" or "heroic" measures. Unlike action *vs.* inaction, that is not a line to be discerned by logic or legal analysis, and we should not pretend that it is.

But to return to the principal point for present purposes: the irrelevance of the action-inaction distinction. Starving oneself to death is no different from putting a gun to one's temple as far as the commonlaw definition of suicide is concerned; the cause of death in both cases is the suicide's conscious decision to "pu[t] an end to his own existence." 4 Blackstone, *supra*, at 189. . . .

The third asserted basis of distinction—that frustrating Nancy Cruzan's wish to die in the present case requires interference with her bodily integrity—is likewise inadequate, because such interference is impermissible only if one begs the question whether her refusal to undergo the treatment on her own is suicide. It has always been lawful not only for the State, but even for private citizens, to interfere with bodily integrity to prevent a felony. . . . That general rule has of course been applied to suicide. At common law, even a private person's use of force to prevent suicide was privileged. . . .

Insofar as balancing the relative interests of the State and the individual is concerned, there is nothing distinctive about accepting death through the refusal of "medical treatment," as opposed to accepting it through the refusal of food, or through the failure to shut off the engine and get out of the car after parking in one's garage after work. Suppose that Nancy Cruzan were in precisely the condition she is in today, except that she could be fed and digest food and water *without* artificial assistance. How is the State's "interest" in keeping her alive thereby increased, or her interest in deciding whether she wants to continue living reduced? . . .

What I have said above is not meant to suggest that I would think it desirable, if we were sure that Nancy Cruzan wanted to die, to keep her alive by the means at issue here. I assert only that the Constitution has nothing to say about the subject. To raise up a constitutional right here we would have to create out of nothing (for it exists neither in text nor tradition) some constitutional principle whereby, although the State may insist that an individual come in out of the cold and eat food, it may not insist that he take medicine; and although it may pump his stomach empty of poison he has ingested, it may not fill his stomach with food he has failed to ingest. Are there, then, no reasonable and humane limits that ought not to be exceeded in requiring an individual to preserve his own life? There obviously are, but they are not set forth in the Due Process Clause. . . . Our salvation is the Equal Protection Clause, which requires the democratic majority to accept for themselves and their loved ones what they impose on you and me. This Court need not, and has no authority to, inject itself into every field of human activity where irrationality and oppression may theoretically occur, and if it tries to do so it will destroy itself.

Deciding to Forego
Life-Sustaining Treatment

PRESIDENT'S COMMISSION FOR THE STUDY
OF ETHICAL PROBLEMS IN MEDICINE AND
BIOMEDICAL AND BEHAVIORAL RESEARCH

The next selection by the President's Commission comes from *Deciding to Forego Life-Sustaining Treatment,* a monograph of policy recommendations made in 1983 by this government-appointed commission. Commissioners found that no morally or legally appropriate distinction exists between withholding or withdrawing any treatment and that no particular treatments, including nutrition or hydration, antibiotics, and transfusions, are universally warranted and obligatory. The Commission also found that we do not well understand the extent to which families or guardians and physicians act or fail to act to pursue the best interests of infants, minors, or incompetent individuals, thus rendering it morally appropriate to require internal committee review whenever parents, families, or guardians decide that life-sustaining therapy should be forgone.

In the selection in this chapter, Commissioners maintain that the distinction between actions and omissions is insufficient to explain wrongful killing, but they try to explain both why fatal actions are usually worse than fatal omissions and what makes them worse. They also try to distinguish the causes of death that are wrongful from those that are not wrong, which leads them to discuss the conditions under which a physician who plays some causal role in a death is morally or legally blameworthy. Finally, Commissioners conclude that, from a public policy perspective, the current legal prohibition of active killing should be sustained.

Lawyers, health care professionals, and policymakers today are in general accord that treatment refusals by dying patients should be honored. Physicians commonly acquiesce in the wishes of competent patients not to receive specified treatments, even when failure to provide those treatments will increase the chance— or make certain—that the patient will die soon. . . . Courts have sanctioned such decisions by guardians for incompetent patients, as well as by competent patients who might have lived for an indefinite period if treated. Although declining to start or continue life-sustaining treatment is often acceptable, health care providers properly refuse to honor a patient's request to be directly killed. Not only would killing, as by violence or strychnine, be outside the bounds of accepted medical practice, but as murder it would be subject to a range of criminal sanctions, regardless of the provider's motives.

In both scholarly and policy discussions, "killing" is often equated with an action causing death, and "allowing to die" is with an omission causing death.[1] Killing and allowing to die are then used as merely descriptive terms, leaving open which actual actions that cause death (that is, killings) are morally wrong. Certainly some actions that cause death, such as self-defense, are morally justified. However, particularly in medicine, "killing" is often understood to mean actions that *wrongfully* cause death, and so is never justifiably done by health care providers. Likewise, "allowing to die" is often used to communicate *approval* of accepting that death will occur rather than simply to describe the behavior. In an attempt to avoid confusion that stems from these conflicting usages and to present the important issues clearly, the Commission's discussion employs the descriptive terms—actions that lead to death and omissions that lead to death—rather than mixing the normative and descriptive connotations of the terms killing and allowing to die.

Although the Commission believes that most omissions that lead to death in medical practice are acceptable, it does not believe that the moral distinction between that practice and wrongful killing lies in the difference between actions and omissions per se. Not only is this distinction often difficult to draw in actual practice, it fails to provide an adequate foundation for the moral and legal evaluation of events leading to death. Rather, the acceptability or unacceptability of conduct turns upon other morally significant factors, such as the duties owed to patients, the patients' prospects and wishes, and the risks created for someone who acts or who refrains from acting.

The Difference between Actions and Omissions That Lead to Death.   The distinction between acts and omissions is often easy to draw. A person acts in a way that results in another's death, for example, by fatally poisoning an otherwise healthy person. On the other hand, a person's omission leads to the death of another if the first person knows he or she has the ability and opportunity to act so as to prevent the other dying (at a particular time and in a particular way) but refrains from doing so. For example, an omission leads to death when a person could, but does not, rescue a nearby child who is drowning. The difference, then, is that when A acts to cause B to die, the course of events into which A's action intervenes is otherwise one in which B is not likely to die, whereas when A omits to act and thus causes B to die, the course of events already under way (into which A fails to intervene) includes B's imminent death. Thus, the distinction between a fatal act and a fatal omission depends both upon the difference between a person physically acting and refraining from acting and upon what might be called the background course of events.

If a patient's death is imminent (for example, death is expected within a matter of days) failing to treat and thus hastening death is seen by some not even to be a case of an omission that leads to death—failing to treat is said to be merely "avoiding prolonging the dying process."[2] To hold that such a failure to treat is neither a fatal act nor an omission is wrong and misleading. No one can prevent a person's ever dying: death can only be postponed by preventing it at the moment. Usually, though not always, to postpone death for only a very short time is less important, but that is relevant to whether an omission is wrong and how serious the wrong is, not to whether it is an omission that leads to a patient's death.

Sometimes deciding whether a particular course involves an act or an omission is less clear. Stopping a respirator at the request of a competent patient who could have lived with it for a few years but who will die without it in just a few hours is such an ambiguous case. Does the physician omit continuing the treatment or act to disconnect it? Discontinuing essential dialysis treatments or choosing not to give the next in a sequence of antibiotic doses are other events that could be described either as acts or omissions.

The Moral Significance of the Difference.   Actual instances of actions leading to death, especially outside the medical context, are more likely to be seriously morally wrong than are omissions that lead to death, which, in the medical context, are most often morally justified. Usually, one or more of several factors make fatal actions worse than fatal omissions.

1. The motives of an agent who acts to cause death are usually worse (for example, self-interest or malice) than those of someone who omits to act and lets another die.
2. A person who is barred from acting to cause another's death is usually thereby placed at no personal risk of harm; whereas, especially outside the medical context, if a person were forced to intercede to save another's life (instead of standing by and omitting to act), he or she would often be put at substantial risk.
3. The nature and duration of future life denied to a person whose life is ended by another's act is usually much greater than that denied to a dying person whose death comes slightly more quickly due to an omission of treatment.
4. A person, especially a patient, may still have some possibility of surviving if one omits to act, while survival is more often foreclosed by actions that lead to death.

Each of these factors—or several in combination—can make a significant moral difference in the evaluation of any particular instance of acting and omitting to act. Together they help explain why most actions leading to death are correctly considered morally worse than most omissions leading to death. Moreover, the greater stringency of the legal duties to refrain from killing than to intervene to save life reinforces people's view of which conduct is worse morally.[3]

However, the distinction between omissions leading to death and acts leading to death is not a reliable guide to their moral evaluation. In the case of medical treatment, the first and third factors are not likely to provide grounds for a distinction: family members and health professionals could be equally merciful in their intention—either in acting or omitting—and life may end immediately for some patients after treatment is withdrawn. Likewise, the second factor—based on the usual rule that people have fairly limited duties to save others with whom they stand in no special relation—does not apply in the medical context. Health professionals have a special role-related duty to use their skills, insofar as possible, on behalf of their patients, and this duty removes any distinction between acts and omissions.

Only the final factor—turning the possibility of death into a certainty—can apply as much in medical settings as elsewhere. Indeed, this factor has particular relevance here since the element of uncertainty—whether a patient really will die if treatment is ceased—is sometimes unavoidable in the medical setting. A valid distinction may therefore arise between an act causing certain death (for example, a poisoning) and an omission that hastens or risks death (such as not amputating a gangrenous limb). But sometimes death is as certain following withdrawal of a treatment as following a particular action that is reliably expected to lead to death.

Consequently, merely determining whether what was done involved a fatal act or omission does not establish whether it was morally acceptable. Some actions that lead to death can be acceptable: very dangerous but potentially beneficial surgery or the use of hazardous doses of morphine for severe pain are examples. Some omissions that lead to death are very serious wrongs: deliberately failing to treat an ordinary patient's bacterial pneumonia or ignoring a bleeding patient's pleas for help would be totally unacceptable conduct for that patient's physician.

Not only are there difficult cases to classify as acts or omissions and difficulties in placing moral significance on the distinction, but making the distinction also presupposes an unsound conception of responsibility, namely (1) that human action is an intervention in the existing course of nature, (2) that not acting is not intervening, and (3) that people are responsible only for their interventions (or, at least, are much more responsible for deliberate interventions than for deliberate omissions). The weaknesses of this position include the ambiguous meaning of "intervention" when someone takes an action as part of a plan of nonintervention (such as writing orders not to resuscitate), the inability to define clearly the "course of nature," and the indefensibility of not holding someone responsible for states of affairs that the person could have prevented.

In sum, then, actions that lead to death are likely to be serious wrongs, while many omissions in the medical context are quite acceptable. Yet this is not a fixed moral assessment based on the mere descriptive difference between acts and omissions, but a generalization from experience that rests on such factors as whether the decision reflects the pursuit of the patient's ends and values, whether the health care providers have fulfilled their duties, and whether the risk of death has been appropriately considered.

The Cause of Death.   Sometimes acts that lead to death seem to be more seriously wrong than omissions that likewise lead to death because the cause of death in the first instance is seen to be the act while the cause of death in an omission is regarded as the underlying disease. For example, were a physician deliberately to inject a patient with a lethal poison, the physician's action would be the cause of the patient's death. On the other hand, if an otherwise dying patient is not resuscitated in the event of cardiac arrest, or if a pneumonia or kidney failure goes untreated, the underlying disease process is said to be the cause of death. Since people ordinarily feel responsible for their own acts but not for another person's disease, this is a very comforting formulation.

The difference in this common account of causation does not actually explain the different moral assessment—rather, the account of causation *reflects* an underlying assessment of what is right or wrong under the circumstances. Commonly, many factors play some causal role in a person's death. . . . In some situations, although one person's action is unquestionably a factual cause of another's death, holding the person responsible for the death is unfair because the death could not reasonably have been foreseen or because the person was under no obligation to prevent the death.

Beyond selecting "the cause" of death from among the many factors empirically determined to have causally contributed to a patient's death, both the legal and the moral inquiry presuppose that some kinds of causal roles in a death are wrong, and then ask whether any person played any of those roles. Therefore, a determination of causation ordinarily must presuppose, and cannot itself justify, the sorts of decisions that ought to be permissible. For example, in a death following nontreatment, designating the disease as the cause not only asserts that a fatal disease process was present but also communicates acceptance of the physician's behavior in foregoing treatment. Conversely, if an otherwise healthy patient who desired treatment died from untreated pneumonia, the physician's failure to treat would be considered to have caused the patient's death. . . . As this example shows, the action/omission distinction does not always correspond to the usual understanding of whether the physician or the disease is the cause of death, and so the attribution of what caused a death cannot make acts morally different from omissions.

In addition, the physician's behavior is among the factual causes of a patient's death both in acting and in omitting to act. This is clear enough if a physician were to give a lethal injection—the patient would not have died at that time and in that way if the physician had not given the injection. But exactly the same is true of a physician's omission of treatment: had a physician not refrained from resuscitating or from treating a pneumonia or a kidney failure, a patient would not have died at that time and in that way. In either case, a different choice by the physician would have led to the patient living longer. To refrain from treating is justifiable in some cases—for example, if the patient does not want the treatment, is suffering, and will die very soon whatever is done. But the justification rests on these other reasons, rather than on not classifying a physician's omission as a cause of the patient's death. Thus, calling the disease the cause of death can be misleading but does reflect a sound point: that a physician who omits treatment in such a case is not morally or legally blameworthy.

The Role of the Distinction in Public Policy.   It is common to make decisions that one knows risk shortening patients' lives and that sometimes turn out to do so. As a result, there is a strong motivation to interpret the actions decided upon and carried out, especially if by people other than the patient, as something other than acts of killing. Thus, the concerned parties very much want these to be regarded as cases of "allowing to die" (rather than "killing"), of "not prolonging the dying process" (instead of "hastening death"), or of "failing to stop a disease from causing death" (rather than "someone's action was the cause of death"). Consequently, these distinctions, while often conceptually unclear and of dubious moral importance in themselves, are useful in facilitating acceptance of sound decisions that would otherwise meet unwarranted resistance. They help people involved to understand, in ways acceptable to them, their proper roles in implementing decisions to forgo life-sustaining treatment.

Law, as a principal instrument of public policy in this area, has sought an accommodation that adequately protects human life while not resulting in officious overtreatment of dying patients. The present general legal prohibition against deliberate, active killing, reinforced by a strong social and professional presumption in favor of sustaining life, serves as a public affirmation of the high value accorded to each human life. The law, and public policy in general, has not interpreted the termination of life-sustaining treatment, even when it requires active steps such as turning off a respirator, as falling under this general prohibition. For competent patients, the principle of self-determination is understood to include a right to refuse life-sustaining treatment, and to place a duty on providers and others to respect that right. Providers, in turn, are protected from liability when they act to aid a patient in carrying out that right. . . .

Although there are some cases in which the acting-omitting distinction is difficult to make and although its moral importance originates in other considerations, the commonly accepted prohibition of active killing helps to produce the correct decision in the great majority of cases. Furthermore, weakening the legal prohibition to allow a deliberate taking of life in extreme circumstances would risk allowing wholly unjustified taking of life in less extreme circumstances. Such a risk would be warranted only if there were substantial evidence of serious harms to be relieved by a weakened legal protection of life, which the Commission does not find to be the case. Thus the Commission concludes that the current interpretation of the legal prohibition of active killing should be sustained.

One serious consequence of maintaining the legal prohibition against direct killing of terminally ill patients could be the prolongation of suffering. In the final stages of some diseases, such as cancer, patients may undergo unbearable suffering that only ends with death. Some have claimed that sometimes the only way to improve such patients' lot is to actively and intentionally end their lives. If such steps are forbidden, physicians and family might be forced to deny these patients the relief they seek and to prolong their agony pointlessly.

If this were a common consequence of a policy prohibiting all active termination of human life, it should force a reevaluation of maintaining the prohibition. Rarely, however, does such suffering persist when there is adequate use of pain-relieving drugs and procedures. Health care professionals ought to realize that they are already authorized and obligated to use such means with a patient's or surrogate's consent, even if an earlier death is likely to result. The Commission endorses allowing physicians and patients to select treatments known to risk death in order to relieve suffering as well as to pursue a return to health.

Policies prohibiting direct killing may also conflict with the important value of patient self-determination. This conflict will arise when deliberate actions intended to cause death have been freely chosen by an informed and competent patient as the necessary or preferred means of carrying out his or her wishes, but the patient is unable to kill him or herself unaided, or others prevent the patient from doing so. The frequency with which this conflict occurs is not known, although it is probably rare. The Commission finds this limitation on individual self-determination to be an acceptable cost of securing the general protection of human life afforded by the prohibition of direct killing.

NOTES

1.   See, e.g., James Rachels, "Active and Passive Euthanasia," 292 *New England Journal of Medicine* 78 (1975); Tom Beauchamp, "A Reply to Rachels on Active and Passive Euthanasia," in Tom Beauchamp and Seymour Perlin, eds., *Ethical Issues in Death and Dying*, Prentice-Hall, Inc., Englewood Cliffs, NJ (1978) at 246; Sisella

Bok, "Death and Dying: Euthanasia and Sustaining Life: Ethical Views," in 1 *Encyclopedia of Bioethics*, at 268.

2. See, e.g., Jonathan Glover, *Causing Death and Saving Lives*, Penguin Books, New York (1977) at 92. James B. Nelson, *Human Medicine: Ethical Perspectives on New Medical Issues*, Augsburg Pub. House, Minneapolis, MN (1973) at 125; Natural Death statutes for Alabama, the District of Columbia, and Kansas, *reprinted in* Appendix D, pp. 318–323, 335–340, 345–349 *infra*.

3. See A. D. Woozley, "Law and the Legislation of Morality," in Arthur L. Caplan and Daniel Callahan, eds., *Ethics in Hard Times*, Plenum Press, New York (1981) at 143.

Cause of Death*

DAN W. BROCK

Dan Brock considers whether it is killing to intentionally forgo hydration and nutrition, stop life-support treatments, and the like. Relying on what he calls a "but-for" conception of causality, Brock argues that if a lay person off the street detaches someone from a respirator, he or she does more than release natural conditions and cause a natural death. Yet this person's act seems to be the same act that the physician typically performs (usually at a family's request) in a case of "allowing to die." In both cases, but-for their act the patient's death would not have occurred. What the physician does is *causally* no different than what the person off the street does: Machinery is removed and the patient dies as a result. Brock concludes that physicians often do cause death when they stop life-sustaining nutrition or respirators. He maintains that the withdrawal of life-sustaining treatment is killing in more cases than medicine and law now acknowledge. Generally, the motives *are* proper and there *is* both moral and legal justification for the action. But whether the motive is evil and reprehensible or noble and laudable, the act remains a killing.

Many persons hold that to stop a life-support process such as feeding is to kill, because one directly causes the patient's death; whereas, when one allows to die, it is the underlying disease process, not the physician, that causes the patient's death.

Questions of causality are exceedingly difficult and complex, but I will try at least briefly to illuminate two important confusions about causing death prominent in discussions about life-sustaining treatment generally, and relevant to forgoing food and water in particular. Consider what can be called a "but-for" sense of causality: but for this, that wouldn't have occurred; but for Jones poisoning the food Smith later ate, Smith would not have died. Consider [a] greedy nephew. . . . But for his turning off the respirator, his uncle wouldn't have died: the nephew, therefore, causes the uncle's death. . . . It would be absurd for the nephew to assert, "No, not I but the underlying disease caused my uncle's death." Now consider the physician who seemingly does the same thing and stops the patient's respirator: he too satisfies the "but-for" condition for the patient's death. But for the physician's stopping the respirator, the patient would not have died; the physician causes the patient's death. Finally, consider stopping feeding. But for that, the patient would not have died; the physician's withholding food and water causes the patient's death.

What I have called a "but-for" sense of causality is *not* by itself an adequate account of ordinary attributions of causality. There, one who kills another (e.g., by giving poisoned food) is considered the cause of the other's death, whereas one who allows another to die (e.g., by not providing food to a famine victim) is not generally said to have caused the other's death. The point is that the broader "but for" sense of

*Source: Brock, D., "Cause of Death," in Rynn, ed. *By No Extraordinary Means.* 1986. pp. 126–129. Bloomington, Indiana: Indiana University Press.

causality seems to provide the necessary control over the outcomes of what a person does ("does" interpreted broadly to include both acts and omissions) to allow ascription of at least prima facie moral responsibility to the person for the outcomes. And the "but-for" causality condition for the death is satisfied both when one kills and when one allows to die, and equally by the greedy nephew, the physician stopping the respirator, and the physician stopping feeding. Why then should we mark any moral difference in these cases because of supposed causal differences when the "but-for" sense of causality is equally satisfied in all of them?

I will consider two responses to my claim that there is no morally important causal difference in these cases, each of which, I think, brings out something interesting about causing death, and about why causal talk is often confusing in this area. The first response is associated with talk of "merely prolonging the dying process," and goes like this: If a patient is terminally ill, then a physician who stops the patient's life-sustaining treatment neither kills nor allows him to die. The physician doesn't kill him; rather, the fatal disease does (more on this shortly). Nor does the physician allow him to die, because to allow someone to die it has to be possible for you to save the person; if the patient is terminally ill, you couldn't save him. So on this response, there's nothing the physician does that causes death, nothing that but for doing it the patient would live. There is more than one confusion in this response. Surely one *can* either kill or not save a terminally ill person. When one either kills or allows to die, what one does causes death in the "but-for" sense of causality. This can only mean that one causes a patient to die *at a particular time* (and, to avoid certain complications of causal overdetermination, in a particular way). No one ever prevents someone's death completely, without any qualifications to its being at a particular time (or in a particular way), because we can't make anyone immortal. What we do is to make or allow death to occur earlier than it otherwise would have done, and in that sense what we do does causally affect the person's death, whether or not the person was terminally ill.

It is worth noting that the claim that a physician is never a "but-for" cause of the patient's death would not help in some important cases of stopping food and water even if it was itself sound. I have in mind, especially, permanently unconscious patients who are usually not terminally ill in any plausible sense of "terminally ill." These patients can, and often do, survive for many years in that state. This ought to give some pause to the many commentators who seem prepared to agree that stopping food and water, or for that matter stopping other life-sustaining treatment, can only be justified if the patient is terminally ill. If one believes, as I do, that stopping life-sustaining treatment, including food and water, can be morally permissible with permanently unconscious patients, then one should not endorse a restriction to stopping that treatment only with terminally ill patients.

Let me turn to a second response to my suggestions that it is a broad "but-for" sense of causality that is relevant to moral responsibility for outcomes, and that on this account physicians *do* cause death when they stop life-sustaining food and water or respirators. Consider the legal inquiry into the patient's cause of death. In the case of stopping a life-sustaining respirator, the cause of death would commonly be identified as the underlying disease which resulted in death once the patient was taken off the respirator. Doesn't this suggest that I am mistaken in identifying the physician and what he does as causing death? I think not, and that is because the inquiry into the cause of death is somewhat more complex that it may look at first. It is not simply an empirical inquiry into what conditions played a causal role in the death. It is in part an empirical or factual inquiry of this sort, but it is shaped as well by normative concerns; these are legal concerns when it is a legal inquiry, moral concerns when it is a moral inquiry.

The inquiry into the cause of death is, roughly, something like this: We take all the factors which are "but-for" causes, but for these factors the patient would not have died in that way and at that time. There will be a great many such factors, and we do not actually assemble them all, but rather restrict our selection of the cause from among them. On what basis do we select *the* cause of death from among all the "but-for" causes? We do not do it solely on empirical or factual grounds, we also consider normative grounds. We ask, for example, in the legal inquiry: Among the "but-for" causes, is there anyone who acted in a legally prohibited role with whom the law then wants to concern itself? And we can ask an analogous question in a moral inquiry: Among the "but-for" causes, is there anyone whose action was morally impermissible? This helps to explain "cause of death talk" in our earlier two cases in which respirators were stopped by a physician and by a greedy nephew. The action of each is a "but-for" cause of the patient's death. The physician's action, however, is within a legally protected role. He acts in accordance with a competent patient's right to refuse even life-sustaining treatment, and so the law does not single him out for further concern when he stops the respirator. The greedy nephew, on the other hand, acts in a legally prohibited role, since (among other things) he acted without the patient's consent, and so the law is concerned further with him. This difference is reflected in our holding the greedy nephew to be the cause of death, while in the case of the physician who also stopped a life-sustaining respirator, the patient's underlying disease is held to be the cause of death.

If this is correct, then it should be no surprise that there is uncertainty and controversy about whether the physician who withholds food and water is the cause of the patient's death. That is a reflection of the uncertainty and controversy that exists about whether stopping food and water is legally and/or morally permissible. If we reach greater agreement on those questions, then it will become clearer whether the physician who stops food and water should be held to be *the* cause of the patient's death. But then it will be the legal and moral permissibility helping determine what or who is *the* cause of death, not whether the physician is the cause being a determinant of legal and moral permissibility.

Intending to Kill and the Principle of Double Effect

EDMUND D. PELLEGRINO

Consistent with the views he expressed in Chapter 4 in defense of professional role obligations that prohibit bringing about death, Edmund Pellegrino argues in the next selection that in many cases a physician distorts the healing relationship by intending the death of a patient. Pellegrino believes that intentional killing, whether by omission or commission, is never warranted and that the issue of intentional killing touches medicine at its core. Using double effect theory, Pellegrino explains precisely when it is morally defensible to withhold or withdraw treatments. Pellegrino is urging health professionals to repudiate intentional killing of patients and, at the same time, to recognize and focus on when treatments are futile and can be omitted.

Some might construe ending the life of the patient as a social obligation of the profession resulting from its possession of knowledge that the patient both needs and is entitled to, and for which the physician is licensed. A weaker view would use the same arguments but would not impose an ethical obligation on the physician. It would, however, provide a warrant for legalization of euthanasia and assisted suicide which would empower those physicians who see no moral harm in killing, or helping to kill, patients who requested it. (See my essay in chapter 4.)

But, in either case, it will not do to argue that one is not intending to kill but only to relieve suffering. This is a misuse of the principle of double effect which has as one of its key requirements for legitimate use the proviso that the morally permissible intention and act (relief of pain) should not be caused by a directly intended, morally impermissible act (killing the patient). Obviously, if one denies that killing is a morally wrong act, then one will not worry much about intention or double effects.

Moreover, the patient's own intention or decision to die may be less motivated by intolerable suffering than by a conscious or unconscious attempt to act beneficently towards family, doctor, or society. The "benefit" sought may be relief of guilt for being the "cause" of distress and trouble to others or the wish to die "nobly."

The moral status of the patient's intention in asking for discontinuance of treatment is not something the physician can ascertain with precision unless the patient clearly states death to be her intention. In most cases, the question is how best to fulfill our obligation in medical ethics to assist the patient with a good death, but one which does not include intentional killing or assisted suicide. This means providing all the support of palliative care, desisting from futile or excessively burdensome treatment, and allowing the patient to die as a result of the disease process.

I am obviously invoking here the principle of double effect which covers this and the many other clinical situations in which some things which should never be done (intentional killing) and some things that should be done (relief of pain, saving life) are intermingled so that both might occur as the result of a clinical decision. On this principle, such an action is morally defensible if the harms are not intended but are side-effects or accidental, if there are sufficiently weighty moral reasons for taking the foreseen risks, and if the good effect is not the result of a morally wrong action and intention. This is not the place to define or defend this moral principle and its current status in moral philosophy.[1] Suffice it to say here that a morally valid concept of intention is crucial if this principle is to be applied properly.

In general terms, withholding and withdrawing treatments are morally defensible if: (1) The patient is fully competent or is represented by a morally valid surrogate or valid advance directive and (2) the intervention, itself, meets certain moral criteria, that is, (a) the patient has a serious disease which may terminate in death with reasonable certitude in a foreseeable period of time; (b) the relations of effectiveness, benefit, and burden are disproportionate, that is, treatment is futile both from the medical point of view and that of the patient; (c) "quality of life" is used as a criterion as judged by the competent patient or his valid surrogate, not the physician; (d) the cost of care, similarly, as a criterion is judged by the patient or his surrogate, not the physician; (e) age is not a criterion by itself; (f) HIV infection, social status, merit, and so on are not criteria; (g) some system for resolution of conflicts is in place which protects the moral values of all participants and provides mechanisms of decision if irreconcilable differences persist. I have detailed my reasons for each of these criteria elsewhere.[2]

One need not intend the death of the patient when withholding or withdrawing life sustaining treatment under the conditions outlined. The physician might even find the patient's death a desirable outcome. But desire is not equivalent either to intention nor to choice. Rather, in these situations, the physician's intention can sincerely be to refrain from or withdraw treatment that is futile and, thus, not indicated. This is not the same as the intention which leads the physician to inject a lethal dose of morphine to end the life of the patient summarily. Marginal, futile, or unwanted treatment constitutes harmful intervention which the physician is obligated to remove. Removal is the primary intention. This is a morally required act since futile treatment does not promote the patient's well-being. The patient dies as a result because the futile treatment was only prolonging life without benefitting the patient. The patient dies not by the doctor's hand but by progression of the natural history of the disease.

The most difficult situations involve vegetative states in which the patient is kept alive by artificial feeding and hydration for prolonged periods. In such states, patients are unaware of self or environment although brain stem and hypothalamic autonomic functions are preserved. Such patients are not dead but they quickly die if life support measures are withdrawn. Vegetative states become "persistent" when they last beyond a given period of time defined in terms of the type and cause of brain damage.[3] All vegetative states, therefore, are not persistent. Withdrawal of life support can be considered licitly only when the criteria for futility or persistence are fulfilled.

The decision-makers in these situations are the morally valid surrogate (informed, competent, and without conflict of interest) and the physicians and nurses attending the patient. If the criteria outlined in the preceding paragraphs are met, withdrawal of life support may be considered when the vegetative state is unquestionably permanent. If this is done, the question of intention will arise. Are we not intending death since it will occur by our act of omission of treatment?

On the view I have been taking, to intend death would be morally inadmissible. To remove futile treatment would be admissible, even though the probability of death can be foreseen. To foresee an event is not the same as intending to cause that event. The close union of the agent with the act depends on the active, willful choice of the death of the patient and of the means that will bring about that intention. This union is missing in events we foresee as possible or probable but do not actively intend.

NOTES

1. J. Boyle. "The Roman Catholic Tradition and Bioethics," *Bioethics Yearbook Volume I, 1988–1990: Theological Developments in Bioethics*. Boston: Kluwer Academic Publishers, 1991, pp. 14–18, and many other sources.
2. E.D. Pellegrino. "Doctors Must Not Kill." In R. Misbin (ed.). *Euthanasia: The Good of the Patient, the Good of Society*. Frederick, MD: University Publishing Group, 1992, pp. 27–41.
3. The Multi-Society Task Force on PVS. "Medical Aspects of the Persistent Vegetative State," *New England Journal of Medicine* 1994; 330:1499–1508 and 1572–1579.

Patient Refusal of Hydration and Nutrition: An Alternative to Physician-Assisted Suicide or Voluntary Active Euthanasia*

JAMES L. BERNAT, BERNARD GERT,
AND R. PETER MOGIELNICKI

The next three writers argue that no one is constrained to stay alive, because every patient can refuse hydration and nutrition, which will ultimately cause death. Even patients who are not terminally ill have a right to refuse treatment. All patients therefore already have the power to control their own destinies, and there is therefore no need to rush to physician-assisted suicide or voluntary active euthanasia. These authors offer a "preferable alternative" based entirely on the right to refuse treatment. Somewhat like Rachels, they maintain that all the key questions in these debates turn on whether a competent patient has rationally refused treatment, not on whether it is a case of acting or omitting. What makes something a case of letting a competent person die is the patient's refusal, not an "inaction" or "omission" by the physician. Similarly, they deny that questions of *causation* are as important as Scalia, Brock, and others seem to think. They maintain that the only important matter is whether a patient has made a rational decision, leaving the physician without any authority to override that refusal. Therefore, the distinction between killing and letting die should be retained and based on patients' requests vs. patients' refusals. Paradoxically, dying by starvation is, on this analysis, a case of letting die, not of killing.

Public and scholarly debates on legalizing physician-assisted suicide (PAS) and voluntary active euthanasia (VAE) have increased dramatically in recent years.[1-5] These debates have highlighted a significant moral controversy between those who regard PAS and VAE as morally permissible and those who do not. Unfortunately, the adversarial nature of this controversy has led both sides to ignore an alternative that avoids moral controversy altogether and has fewer associated practical problems in its implementation. In this article, we suggest that educating chronically and terminally ill patients about the feasibility of patient refusal of hydration and nutrition (PRHN) can empower them to control their own destiny without requiring physicians to reject the taboos on PAS and VAE that have existed for millennia. . . .

*Source: Bernat, J. L., Bernard Gert, and R. Peter Mogielnicki, "Patient Refusal of Hydration and Nutrition," *Archives of Internal Medicine* (December 1993), Vol. 153, pp. 2723–2728. Copyright 1993, American Medical Association.

CONFUSION CONCERNING KILLING VS. LETTING DIE

Three areas of terminologic confusion that have clouded clear thinking about the morality of physician involvement in the care of the dying patient are (1) requests vs. refusals by patients, (2) acts vs. omissions by physicians, and (3) "natural" vs. other causes of death.

PATIENTS' REQUESTS VS. REFUSALS

. . . The distinction between requests and refusals has a critical importance in understanding the distinction between voluntary passive euthanasia (letting die) and VAE (killing). Patient *refusals* must be honored when they represent the rational decisions of competent patients even when physicians know death will result. There is no moral requirement to honor patient *requests* when physicians know death will result and there may be legal prohibitions against doing so.

PHYSICIANS' ACTS VS. OMISSIONS

Some philosophers have misunderstood the definitions of VAE (killing) and passive euthanasia (letting die, including PRHN) and their moral significance by basing the distinction between killing and letting die on the distinction between acts and omissions.[6,7] In so doing, they have followed many physicians who have concentrated solely on what they themselves do (acts) or do not do (omissions) in distinguishing between killing and letting die. This way of distinguishing between killing and letting die creates a false moral distinction between a physician turning off intravenous feeding (act) and not replacing the intravenous solution container when it is empty (omission). When the distinction between killing and letting die is made in this way, it undermines legitimate medical and legal practice that permits allowing to die and does not permit killing.

This mistaken narrow focus on what the physician does or does not do without taking into account the larger context in which the physician acts or does not act can lead to the mistaken conclusion that PAS and VAE are really no different from voluntary passive euthanasia or "letting die." Recognition of the key role of whether or not the action is in response to the *patient's request* or the *patient's refusal* casts the issue in a clearer light.

As a matter of medical and legal practice, on the basis of a rational refusal of a competent patient, it is permitted either not to begin ventilatory therapy or to stop it; not to start treatment with antibiotics or to discontinue antibiotics; and not to start artificial hydration and nutrition or to cease them. All of these acts and omissions are morally and legally permitted when they result from a rational refusal by a competent patient. Indeed, it is misleading to say that these acts are morally and legally permitted, for they are morally and legally *required*. It is the rational refusal by a competent patient that is decisive here, not whether the physician acts or omits acting. It is the patient's refusal that makes the physician's acts and omissions "letting die" rather than "killing." Whether honoring this refusal requires the physician to act or omit acting is irrelevant. That is why those who base the distinction between killing and letting die on the distinction between acts and omissions mistakenly conclude that no morally relevant distinction exists.

"NATURAL" VS. OTHER CAUSES OF DEATH

The term *natural*, as in "death by natural causes," has been another source of confusion. *Natural* is often used as a word of praise or, more generally, as a way of condoning something that otherwise would be considered unacceptable. Thus, voluntary passive euthanasia is often presented as acceptable because it allows the patient to "die a natural death." Because the death was caused by the disease process, no person is assigned responsibility for the death. The freedom from responsibility for the patient's death is psychologically helpful for the physician. To make some state laws authorizing advance directives more acceptable to the public, they even have been labeled "natural death acts."

When death results from lack of hydration and nutrition, however, it is less plausible to say that "the death was caused by the disease process." Thus, someone must be assigned responsibility for the patient's death, and physicians wish to avoid this responsibility. A partial explanation for the misuse of technology to prolong dying unjustifiably may be an attempt by physicians to avoid this psychological responsibility. Physicians who recognize that patients have the authority to refuse any treatment, including hydration and nutrition, are more likely to avoid unjustified feelings of responsibility for their deaths.

Just as it is erroneous to think that the distinction between acts and omissions has any moral relevance, so it is erroneous to think that anything morally significant turns on the use of the terms *natural* or *cause*. What is morally significant is that the terminally ill patient is competent and has made a rational decision to refuse further treatment. Indeed, it is not even important whether what the patient has refused counts as treatment. If the patient has refused, the physician has no moral or legal authority to overrule that refusal. It is morally and legally irrelevant whether or not the resulting death is considered natural.

PATIENT REFUSAL OF HYDRATION AND NUTRITION

We maintain that a preferable alternative to legalization of PAS and VAE is for physicians to educate patients that they may refuse hydration and nutrition and that physicians will help them do so in a way that minimizes suffering. Chronically or terminally ill patients who wish to gain more control over their deaths can then refuse to eat and drink and refuse enteral or parenteral feedings or hydration. The failure of the present debate to include this alternative may be the result of the confusion discussed above, an erroneous assumption that thirst and hunger remain strong drives in terminal illness, and a misconception that failure to satisfy these drives causes intractable suffering. . . .

It is the consensus of experienced physicians and nurses that terminally ill patients dying of dehydration or lack of nutrition do not suffer if treated properly. In fact, maintaining physiologic hydration and adequate nutrition is difficult in most seriously ill patients because intrinsic thirst and hunger are usually diminished or absent. . . .

However, if the distinction between killing and letting die is based as it should be on patients' requests vs patients' refusals, these latter considerations lose their force. Now the crucial consideration becomes the degree of suffering associated with lack of hydration and nutrition. If the associated suffering is trivial, PRHN clearly has major advantages over PAS or VAE. Only if this suffering is unmanageable does the choice become more difficult. Scientific studies and anecdotal reports both suggest that dehydration and starvation in the seriously ill do not cause significant suffering. Physicians and particularly nurses have written many observational pieces describing peaceful and apparently comfortable deaths by starvation and dehydration.[8–10] Lay observers have corroborated these reports.[11] . . .

A handful of laboratory studies and clinical trials are consistent with these older observational comments, but the picture is far from complete.

Observational data on the experience of terminally ill patients dying of dehydration have been recorded most recently in the hospice literature. This evidence suggests that the overwhelming majority of hospice deaths resulting from lack of hydration and nutrition can be managed such that the patients remain comfortable.[8,12–15] In a 1990 survey of 826 members of the (US) Academy of Hospice Physicians, 89% of hospice nurses and 86% of hospice physicians reported that their terminal patients who died by cessation of hydration and nutrition had peaceful and comfortable deaths.[16]

Taken in toto, the anecdotal reports, laboratory studies, and the observations of nurses and physicians who care for terminally ill patients suggest that lack of hydration and nutrition does not cause unmanageable suffering in terminally ill patients and may even have an analgesic effect. Clinical experience with severely ill patients suggests that the major symptom of dry mouth can be relieved by ice chips, methyl cellulose, artificial saliva, or small sips of water insufficient to reverse progressive dehydration.

BENEFITS OF PRHN OVER PAS AND VAE

Unlike PAS and VAE, PRHN is recognized by all as consistent with current medical, moral, and legal practices. It does not compromise public confidence in the medical profession because it does not require physicians to assume any new role or responsibility that could alter their roles of healer, caregiver, and counselor. It places the proper emphasis on the duty of physicians to care for dying patients, because these patients need care and comfort measures during the dying period. It encourages physicians to engage in educational discussions with patients and families about dying and the desirability of formulating clear advance directives.

Legalization of PAS or VAE would likely create unintended and harmful social pressures and expectations. Many elderly or chronically ill patients could feel "the duty to die." They would request euthanasia not on the basis of personal choice but because they believed that their families considered them a burden and expected them to agree to be killed. Furthermore, patients might sense pressure from their physicians to consider VAE as an alternative and agree because the physicians must know what is best for them.[17] The meaning of "voluntary" euthanasia thus could become corrupted, causing the elderly and chronically ill to become victimized.

Unlike the "duty to die" resulting from legalizing PAS or VAE, it is unlikely that patients choosing to die by PRHN would feel as much social pressure or expectations from family members to die earlier because of the duration of the process and the opportunity therein for reconsideration and family interaction. . . .

THE PHYSICIAN'S ROLE IN PRHN

The current interest in legalizing PAS and VAE misplaces the emphasis of physicians' duties to their dying patients. Physicians should be more concerned about providing patients optimal terminal care than killing them or helping them kill themselves. Legalizing PAS would make it unnecessary for physicians to strive to maximize comfort measures in terminally ill patients and unnecessary for society to support research to improve the science of palliation. By comparison, PRHN appropriately encourages the physician to attend to the medical treatment of dying patients. . . .

NOTES

1. Crigger B.J., ed. Dying well? a colloquy on euthanasia and assisted suicide. *Hastings Center Report* 1992;22:6–55.
2. Campbell C.S., Crigger B.J., eds. Mercy, murder, and morality: perspectives on euthanasia. *Hastings Center Report* 1989;19(suppl 1):1–32.
3. Pellegrino E.D. Doctors must not kill. *Journal of Clinical Ethics* 1992;3:95–102.
4. Quill T.E., Cassel C.K., Meier D.E. Care of the hopelessly ill: proposed clinical criteria for physician-assisted suicide. *New England Journal of Medicine* 1992;327:1380–1384.
5. Brody H. Assisted death: a compassionate response to a medical failure. *New England Journal of Medicine* 1992;327:1384–1388.
6. Rachels J. Active and passive euthanasia. *New England Journal of Medicine* 1975;292:78–80.
7. Brock D.W. Voluntary active euthanasia. *Hastings Center Report* 1992;22:10–22.
8. Andrews M., Levine A. Dehydration in the terminal patient: perception of hospice nurses. *American Journal of Hospice Care* 1989;3:31–34.
9. Zerwekh J. The dehydration question. *Nursing* 1983;13:47–51.
10. Printz L.A. Terminal dehydration: a compassionate treatment. *Archives of Internal Medicine* 1992;152:697–700.
11. Nearing H. *Loving and Leaving the Good Life.* Post Mills, Vt: Chelsea Green Publishing Co, 1992.
12. Miller R.J., Albright P.G. What is the role of nutritional support and hydration in terminal cancer patients? *American Journal of Hospice Care* 1989;6:33–38.
13. Cox S.S. Is dehydration painful? *Ethics Medicine* 1987;12:1–2.
14. Lichter I., Hunt E. The last 48 hours of life. *Journal of Palliative Care* 1990;6:7–15.
15. Miller R.J. Hospice care as an alternative to euthanasia. *Law Med Health Care* 1992;20:127–132.

16. Miller R.J. Nutrition and hydration in terminal disease. *Journal of Palliative Care* In press.
17. Kamisar Y. Some non-religious views against proposed 'mercy-killing' legislation. *Minneapolis Law Review* 1958;42:969–1042.

SUGGESTED READINGS FOR CHAPTER 5

A. ACTIVE AND PASSIVE EUTHANASIA

American Medical Association. Council on Ethical and Judicial Affairs. "Decisions Near the End of Life." *Journal of the American Medical Association* 267(16, Apr. 22/29, 1992):2229–2233.

AMUNDSEN, DARREL W. "The Physician's Obligation to Prolong Life: A Medical Duty Without Classical Roots." *Hastings Center Report* 8(4, Aug. 1978):23–30.

ARRAS, JOHN. "The Right to Die on the Slippery Slope." *Social Theory and Practice* 8(3, Fall 1982):285–328.

BATTIN, MARGARET PABST. "Euthanasia: The Way We Do It, the Way They Do It." *Journal of Pain and Symptom Management* 6(5, July 1991):298–305.

BATTIN, MARGARET PABST. "Euthanasia." In Donald VanDeVeer and Tom Regan (eds.) *Health Care Ethics: An Introduction*. Philadelphia: Temple University Press, 1987, pp. 58–97.

BEAUCHAMP, TOM L. "A Reply to Rachels on Active and Passive Euthanasia." In T. Beauchamp and T. Pinkard (eds.). *Ethics and Public Policy*. 2nd ed. Englewood Cliffs, NJ: Prentice-Hall, 1982, pp. 318–329.

BEAUCHAMP, TOM L., AND ARNOLD DAVIDSON. "The Definition of Euthanasia." *Journal of Medicine and Philosophy* 4(3, Sept. 1979):294–312.

BLEICH, J. D. "Life As an Intrinsic Rather Than Instrumental Good: The 'Spiritual' Case Against Euthanasia." *Issues in Law and Medicine* 9(2, Fall 1993):139–149.

BROCK, DAN W. "Voluntary Active Euthanasia." *Hastings Center Report* 22(2, Mar.–Apr., 1992):10–22.

CHILDRESS, JAMES F. "Non-heart-beating Donors: Are the Distinctions between Direct and Indirect Effects and between Killing and Letting Die Relevant and Helpful?" *Kennedy Institute of Ethics Journal* 3(2, June 1993):203–216.

DWORKIN, RONALD. *Life's Dominion: An Argument about Abortion, Euthanasia, and Individual Freedom*. New York: Vintage Books, 1994.

FOOT, PHILIPPA. "Euthanasia." *Philosophy & Public Affairs*. 6(2, Winter 1977):85–112.

FYE, W. B. "Active Euthanasia: An Historical Survey of Its Conceptual Origins and Introduction into Medical Thought." *Bulletin of the History of Medicine* 52(4, Winter 1978):492–502.

GLOVER, JONATHAN. *Causing Death and Saving Life*. Harmondsworth, England: Penguin Books, 1977.

HAMEL, RONALD P. (ed.). *Active Euthanasia, Religion, and the Public Debate*. Chicago: Park Ridge Center for the Study of Health, Faith, and Ethics, 1991.

HUMPHRY, DEREK. *Lawful Exit: The Limits of Freedom for Help in Dying*. Junction City, OR: Norris Lane Press, 1993.

HUMPHRY, DEREK, AND ANN WICKETT. *The Right to Die: Understanding Euthanasia*. New York: Harper and Row, 1986.

KLUGE, EIKE-HENNER. "Euthanasia and Related Taboos." *Canadian Medical Association Journal* 144(3, Feb. 1, 1991):359–360.

KOHL, MARVIN. "Euthanasia." In Lawrence C. Becker, and Charlotte B. Becker (eds.). *Encyclopedia of Ethics.* Volume I. New York: Garland, 1992, pp. 335–339.

KOOP, C. EVERETT. "The Challenge of Definition." *Hastings Center Report* 19(1, Jan.–Feb. 1989):S2–S3.

KOTTOW, M.H. "Euthanasia After the Holocaust—Is It Possible? A report from the Federal Republic of Germany." *Bioethics* 2(1, Jan. 1988):58–59.

KUHSE, HELGA. *The Sanctity-of-Life Doctrine in Medicine: A Critique.* Oxford: Clarendon Press, 1987.

KUHSE, HELGA, AND PETER SINGER. "Euthanasia: A Survey of Nurses' Attitudes and Practices." *Australian Nurses' Journal* 21(8, Mar. 1992):21–22.

LECSO, PHILLIP A. "Euthanasia: A Buddhist Perspective." *Journal of Religion and Health* 25(1, Spring 1992):51–57.

LIFTON, ROBERT. *The Nazi Doctors: Medical Killing and the Psychology of Genocide.* New York: Basic Books, 1986.

MALM, H.M. "Killing, Letting Die, and Simple Conflicts." *Philosophy and Public Affairs* 18(3, Summer 1989):238–258.

MEILAENDER, GILBERT. "The Distinction between Killing and Allowing to Die." *Theological Studies.* 37(3, Sept. 1976):467–470.

MENZEL, PAUL J. "Are Killing and Letting Die Morally Different in Medical Contexts?" *Journal of Medicine and Philosophy* 4 (September 1979):269–293.

MILLER, FRANKLIN G., AND JOHN C. FLETCHER. "The Case for Legalized Euthanasia." *Perspectives in Biology and Medicine* 36(2, Winter 1993):159–176.

MISBIN, ROBERT I. (ed.). *Euthanasia: The Good of the Patient, the Good of Society.* Frederick, MD: University Publishing Group, 1992, pp. 43–51.

QIU, REN-ZONG. "Chinese Medical Ethics and Euthanasia." *Cambridge Quarterly of Healthcare Ethics* 2(1, Winter 1993):69–76.

RACHELS, JAMES. *The End of Life: Euthanasia and Morality.* Oxford: Oxford University Press, 1986.

REICHENBACH, BRUCE R. "Euthanasia and the Active-Passive Distinction." *Bioethics* 1(1, Jan. 1987):51–73.

Sacred Congregation for the Doctrine of the Faith. "Declaration on Euthanasia" (May 5, 1980). *Vatican Council II.* 1982; vol. 2: 510–516.

SHERLOCK, RICHARD. *Preserving Life: Public Policy and the Life Not Worth Living.* Chicago: Loyola University Press, 1987.

SHUMAN, CAROLYN R., GLENN P. FOURNET, PAUL F. ZELHART, BILLY C. ROLAND, AND ROBERT E. ESTES. "Attitudes of Registered Nurses toward Euthanasia." *Death Studies* 1992 Jan-Feb; 16(1):1–15.

SINGER, PETER A., AND MARK SIEGLER. "Euthanasia—A Critique." *New England Journal of Medicine* 322(26, June 28, 1990):1881–1883.

STEINBOCK, BONNIE (ed.). *Killing and Letting Die.* Englewood Cliffs, NJ: Prentice-Hall, 1980.

TENO, JOAN, AND JOANNE LYNN. "Voluntary Active Euthanasia: The Individual Case and Public Policy." *Journal of the American Geriatrics Society* 39(8, Aug. 1991): 827–830.

THOMASMA, DAVID C., AND GLENN C. GRABER. *Euthanasia: Toward an Ethical Social Policy.* New York: Continuum Publishing, 1990.

THOMSON, JUDITH JARVIS. "Killing, Letting Die and the Trolley Problem." *The Monist* 59 (April 1976):204–217.

WOLF, SUSAN M. "Holding the Line on Euthanasia." *Hastings Center Report* 19(1, Jan.–Feb., 1989):S13–S15.

B. INTENDING AND CAUSING DEATH

1. Cruzan

ANGELL, MARCIA. "Prisoners of Technology: The Case of Nancy Cruzan. [Editorial]." *New England Journal of Medicine* 322(17, Apr. 26, 1990):1226–1228.

ANNAS, GEORGE J. "Bioethicists' Statement on the U.S. Supreme Court's Cruzan Decision." *New England Journal of Medicine* 323(10, Sept. 6, 1990):686–687.

ANNAS, GEORGE J. "Nancy Cruzan and the Right to Die." *New England Journal of Medicine* 323(10, Sept. 6, 1990):670 –673.

ARRAS, JOHN D. "Beyond <Cruzan>: Individual Rights, Family Autonomy and the Persistent Vegetative State." *Journal of the American Geriatrics Society* 39(10, Oct. 1991):1018–1024.

BOPP, JAMES. "Choosing Death for Nancy Cruzan." *Hastings Center Report* 20(1, Jan./Feb. 1990):42–44.

EMANUEL, EZEKIEL J. "Securing Patients' Right to Refuse Medical Care: In Praise of the <Cruzan> Decision." *American Journal of Medicine* 92(3, Mar. 1992):307–311.

GLOVER, JACQUELINE J., AND JOANNE LYNN. "After Cruzan—The Work to be Done." *Journal of the American Geriatrics Society* 39(4, Apr. 1991):423–424.

HADDAD, MARK E. "Cruzan and the Demands of Due Process." *Issues in Law and Medicine* 8(2, Fall 1992):205–228.

Journal of Medicine and Philosophy. 1992; 17. Special issue on the "Cruzan Case."

Law, Medicine and Health Care. 19 (No. 1-2, Spring-Summer 1991) [Special Issue on Cruzan].

LO, BERNARD, AND ROBERT STEINBROOK. "Beyond the Cruzan Case: the U.S. Supreme Court and Medical Practice." *Annals of Internal Medicine* 114(10, May 15, 1991):895–901.

MEISEL, ALAN. "A Retrospective on <Cruzan>." *Law, Medicine and Health Care* 20(4, Winter 1992):340–353.

MEISEL, ALAN. "Lessons from Cruzan." *Journal of Clinical Ethics* 1(3, Fall 1990): 245–250.

ORENTLICHER, DAVID. "Cruzan v. Director of Missouri Department of Health: An Ethical and Legal Perspective." *Journal of the American Medical Association* 262(20, Nov. 24, 1989):2928–2930.

ROBERTSON, JOHN A. "Cruzan and the Constitutional Status of Nontreatment Decisions for Incompetent Patients." *Georgia Law Review* 25(5, Summer 1991):1139–1202.

SCHNEIDER, CARL E. "Cruzan and the Constitutionalization of American Life." *Journal of Medicine and Philosophy* 17(6, Dec. 1992):589–604.

VEATCH, ROBERT M. "Nancy Cruzan and the Best Interest Standard." *Midwest Medical Ethics* 6 (Fall 1990):17–19.

WOLF, SUSAN M. "Nancy Beth Cruzan: In No Voice at All." *Hastings Center Report* 20(1, Jan./Feb. 1990):38–41.

2. Conroy

ANNAS, GEORGE J. "When Procedures Limit Rights: From Quinlan to Conroy." *Hastings Center Report* 15(2, Apr. 1985):24–26.

BURT, ROBERT A. "Withholding Nutrition and Mistrusting Nurturance: The Vocabulary of <In re Conroy>." *Issues in Law and Medicine* 2(4, Jan. 1987):317–330.

CANTOR, NORMAN L. "<Conroy>, Best Interests, and the Handling of Dying Patients." *Rutgers Law Review* 37(3, Spring 1985):543–577.

CONNERY, JOHN R. "In the Matter of Claire Conroy." *Linacre Quarterly* 52(4, Nov. 1985):321–328.

LYNN, JOANNE. "Brief and Appendix for <amicus curiae>: The American Geriatrics Society. [In re Conroy]." *Journal of the American Geriatrics Society* 32(12, Dec. 1984):915–922.

MARZEN, THOMAS J. "In the matter of Claire C. Conroy. [Note]." *Issues in Law and Medicine* 1 (1, July 1985): 77–84.

MCCORMICK, RICHARD A. "Caring or Starving? The Case of Claire Conroy." *America* 152(13, April 6, 1985):269–273.

NEVINS, MICHAEL A. "Analysis of the Supreme Court of New Jersey's Decision in the Claire Conroy Case." *Journal of the American Geriatrics Society* 34(2, Feb. 1986): 140–143.

PARIS, JOHN J., AND FRANK E. REARDON. "Court Responses to Withholding or Withdrawing Artificial Nutrition and Fluids." *Journal of the American Medication Association* 253(15, Apr. 1985):2243–2245.

SOMERS, THOMAS H. "<In re Conroy>: Self Determination—Extending the Right to Die. [Note]." *Journal of Contemporary Health Law and Policy* 2(Spring 1986):351–363.

3. Nutrition and Hydration

CALLAHAN, DANIEL. "On Feeding the Dying." *The Hastings Center Report* 13(5, 1983):22.

CHILDRESS, JAMES F. "When Is It Morally Justifiable to Discontinue Medical Nutrition and Hydration?" In Joanne Lynn (ed.). *By No Extraordinary Means: The Choice to Forgo Life-Sustaining Food and Water.* Bloomington, IN: Indiana University Press, 1986, pp. 67–83.

CONNERY, JOHN R. "The Ethical Standards for Withholding/Withdrawing Nutrition and Hydration." *Issues in Law and Medicine* 2(2, Sept. 1986):87–97.

DERR, PATRICK, G. "Why Food and Fluids Can Never Be Denied." *Hastings Center Report* 16 (February 1986):28–30.

LYNN, JOANNE (ed.). *By No Extraordinary Means: The Choice to Forgo Life-Sustaining Food and Water.* Bloomington, IN: Indiana University Press, 1986.

MAY, WILLIAM E., et al. "Feeding and Hydrating the Permanently Unconscious and Other Vulnerable Persons." *Issues in Law and Medicine* 3(3, 1987):203–217.

POPE JOHN XXIII. Medical-Moral Research and Education Center. "Can a Catholic Hospital Tolerate Refusal of Ethically Ordinary Treatment?" *Hospital Progress* 65(1984):72–74.

SIEGLER, MARK, AND ALAN J. WEISBARD. "Against the Emerging Stream: Should Fluids and Nutritional Support Be Discontinued?" *Archives of Internal Medicine* 145(1, Jan. 1985):129–131.

SMITH, WILLIAM B. "Is a Decision to Forgo Tube Feeding for Another a Decision to Kill?" *Issues in Law and Medicine* 6(4, Spring 1991):385–394.

4. Double Effect

BOYLE, JOSEPH. "Toward Understanding the Principle of Double Effect." *Ethics.* 90(1980):527–538.

DAVIS, NANCY. "The Doctrine of Double Effect: Problems of Interpretation." *Pacific Philosophical Quarterly* 65(1984):107–123.

DEVETTERE, RAYMOND J. "Sedation Before Ventilator Withdrawal: Can It Be Justified by Double Effect and Called Allowing a Patient to Die?" *Journal of Clinical Ethics* 2(2, Summer 1991):122–124.

EDWARDS, BARBARA SPRINGER, AND WINSTON M. UENO. "Sedation Before Ventilator Withdrawal." [Case presentation]. *Journal of Clinical Ethics* 2(2, Summer 1991): 118–122.

FRANKENA, WILLIAM K. "McCormick and the Traditional Distinction." In Richard McCormick and Paul Ramsey (eds.). *Doing Evil to Achieve Good.* Chicago: Loyola University Press, 1978, pp. 145–164.

GRABER, GLENN C. "Some Questions about Double Effect." *Ethics in Science and Medicine* 6(1, 1979):65–84.

MARQUIS, DONALD B. "Four Versions of Double Effect." *Journal of Medicine and Philosophy* 16(5, Oct. 1991):515–544.

MCCORMICK, RICHARD A., AND PAUL RAMSEY (eds.). *Doing Evil to Achieve Good: Moral Choice in Conflict Situations.* Chicago: Loyola University Press, 1978.

QUINN, WARREN S. "Actions, Intentions, and Consequences: The Doctrine of Double Effect." *Philosophy and Public Affairs* 18(4, Fall 1989):334–351.

SCHNEIDERMAN, LAWRENCE J. "Is It Morally Justifiable *Not* to Sedate This Patient Before Ventilator Withdrawal?" *Journal of Clinical Ethics* 2(2, Summer 1991):129–130.

TRUOG, ROBERT D., JOHN H. ARNOLD, AND MARK A. ROCKOFF. "Sedation Before Ventilator Withdrawal: Medical and Ethical Considerations." *Journal of Clinical Ethics* 2(2, Summer 1991):127–129.

BIBLIOGRAPHICAL SOURCES AND REFERENCE WORKS

BAILEY, DON V. *The Challenge of Euthanasia: An Annotated Bibliography on Euthanasia and Related Subjects.* Lanham, MD: University Press of America, 1990.

BUEHLER, DAVID A. "CQ Sources: Suicide and Euthanasia." [Bibliography]. *Cambridge Quarterly of Healthcare Ethics* 2(1, Winter 1993):77–80.

MCCARRICK, PATRICIA MILMORE. "Active Euthanasia and Assisted Suicide." *Kennedy Institute of Ethics Journal* 2 (March 1992):79–99.

REICH, WARREN (ed.). *Encyclopedia of Bioethics.* New York: Macmillan, 1995, articles on:

Death and Dying: Euthanasia and Sustaining Life
Double Effect
Homicide

6

Decisions to Forgo Treatment Involving (Once) Competent Persons

INTRODUCTION

Under what conditions, if any, is it permissible for patients, health professionals, and surrogate decision makers to forgo treatment with the foreknowledge that the patient will die? This question is addressed in this chapter with respect to both presently competent and formerly competent patients; never-competent patients are treated in Chapter 7.

DECISION MAKING BY COMPETENT ADULTS

It is now generally agreed, in both law and ethics, that a competent patient has the right to forgo treatment at any time, including the right to refuse medical nutrition and hydration. This right gives some patients the opportunity to control the time of their death, and a refusal is legally unproblematic in the typical case if the person is competent at the time of the decision. However, in some cases competent persons exercise their rights in a way inconsistent with the commitments of a health care institution; in other cases, a once-competent, but now-incompetent person has left instructions that seem to demand poor medical practice. What are the obligations of health professionals under these circumstances?

Several cases of problematic refusals of treatment have reached the courts in recent years, despite the widespread acceptance of the right to refuse treatment. Two are considered in this chapter: the cases of Larry McAfee and Elizabeth Bouvia. First, in *McAfee*, we encounter a competent adult patient paralyzed from the neck down as the result of an automobile accident. He asked for a physician's assistance in administering a sedative just before he attempted to disconnect himself from a ventilator. The Georgia court absolved physicians of criminal and civil liability and crudely hinted that McAfee has a right to the sedative. However, as Nat Hentoff points out in his article, there are different ways to interpret why McAfee wanted to refuse treatment and whether he would have done so under different conditions.

In the case of 28-year-old quadriplegic Elizabeth Bouvia, an appellate court pushed matters further. Since birth Bouvia suffered from cerebral palsy that left her with virtually no motor function in her limbs or skeletal muscles. She was bedridden, entirely dependent on others, and in constant, uncontrollable pain. She was unaffected cognitively. The court asserts that patients have a moral and constitutional right to refuse treatment even if its exercise creates a "life-threatening condition" of which physicians disapprove. This opinion urges courts and physicians to protect this right so that physicians can assist patients in bringing about the end of their lives in dignity and comfort. In a particularly vigorous concurring opinion, Associate Justice Compton exhorts physicians to rethink their traditional objections to assisting such patients to die.

The article by Steven H. Miles, Peter A. Singer, and Mark Siegler in this chapter acknowledges the trends present in these cases, but the authors maintain that institutional commitments and interests must be considered in addition to the interests of patients.

The final two articles in this first section consider an increasingly popular procedure in which a competent person either writes a directive for health care professionals or selects a surrogate to make decisions about life-sustaining treatments during periods of incompetence. Here we need to distinguish two types of *advance directive:* (1) *substantive directives,* sometimes called *living wills,* which specify medical procedures that should be provided or foregone in specific circumstances, and (2) *durable powers of attorney* (DPA) for health care—a legal document in which one person assigns another person authority to perform specified actions on behalf of the signer.

The medical directive proposed by Linda and Ezekiel Emanuel in this chapter sketches several different possible circumstances of illness and allows the person filling out the form to choose among treatment options in each situation. The essay by Dan Brock points to problems in the practical implementation of these medical directives.

DECISION MAKING ON BEHALF OF FORMERLY COMPETENT ADULTS

A hospital, a physician, or a family member may justifiably assume a decision making role if a patient is not competent to choose or refuse treatment. Courts and legislatures have been actively involved in this area since the Karen Quinlan decision in 1976, but much remains undecided, particularly with regard to patients who are incompetent and debilitated, yet conscious. Celebrated legal cases have centered on formerly competent patients, including Quinlan, Claire Conroy, and Nancy Cruzan. Several issues that emerged from these cases are discussed in this chapter, beginning with *Cruzan*—the only case of its type ever to reach the Supreme Court of the United States.

The 25-year-old Ms. Cruzan was in a persistent vegetative state for over 3 years. Her parents then petitioned for permission to remove the feeding tube, knowing that, by doing so, their daughter would die. A lower court's authorization of termination of treatment was reversed by the Missouri Supreme Court, which ruled that no one may order an end to life-sustaining treatment for an incompetent person in the absence of a valid living will or clear and convincing evidence of the patient's wishes. This decision was appealed to the United States Supreme Court, which handed down its decision in 1990. The majority opinion holds that a state may constitutionally require "clear and convincing evidence" whenever surrogates claim to represent a patient's desires about continuing or refusing life-sustaining treatment. The dissenting justices express a particularly vigorous disagreement with this majority opinion. The essays by Lawrence Gostin and John Robertson respond, in diverse ways, to this Supreme Court opinion.

This Supreme Court decision was followed by another hearing before a County probate judge at which three friends of Nancy Cruzan provided sufficient additional evidence that she had expressed a clear and convincing preference not to live "like a vegetable" connected to machines. This new evidence led the judge to accept the parents' request to remove the feeding tube, and 13 days after removal, and 8 years in a coma, Nancy Cruzan died.

STANDARDS FOR SURROGATE DECISION MAKING

Either prior to or subsequent to *Cruzan,* almost all states in the United States have adopted statutes that allow advance directives and erect standards of decision making by surrogates for incompetent patients. Two questions are apparent in all cases that require surrogate decision making: (1) What standards should be used in making the decisions? and (2) Who should make the decisions? We will consider each question in turn.

Three standards are available for surrogate decision makers in such cases: *substituted judgment, pure autonomy,* and the *patient's best interests.*

1. *The Substituted Judgment Standard.* The standard of substituted judgment uses the premise that decisions about treatment properly belong to the incompetent or non-competent patient because they have rights of autonomy and privacy. This standard requires a surrogate decision maker to reach the decision the incompetent person would make if the person were competent. This is an onerous and difficult standard unless a relevant, competent decision or preference has already been stated by the patient (see #2 that follows), and one it may not be possible to implement in actual decision making for patients whose competent views are not known or only poorly understood.
2. *The Pure Autonomy Standard.* The second standard eliminates the mere *presumption* of autonomy found in substituted judgment. It applies exclusively to formerly competent patients who actually expressed a relevant competent decision or preference, perhaps through an advance directive. Whether or not there exists a formal advance directive, this standard asserts that prior judgments by competent persons should be accepted. However, the Cruzan and Conroy cases both point to practical difficulties that can arise by using this standard when only weak evidence fits the case at hand.
3. *The Best Interests Standard.* Under the best interests standard a surrogate decision maker must determine the most substantial benefit among the available options, assigning different weights to interests the patient has in each option and discounting

or subtracting inherent risks or costs. The obligation is to maximize benefit through a comparative assessment. This standard protects another's well-being by assessing risks and benefits of various treatments and alternatives to treatment, by considering pain and suffering, and by evaluating restoration and loss of functioning. It is a quality-of-life criterion.

In addition to moral problems about the respective merit of these three standards, many questions concern *who* should decide for the incompetent patient. Conventionally, we have designated next-of-kin or families as the appropriate decision makers, but in doing so we assume families that care deeply about their elderly and incompetent members. This focus is often too narrow. Many incompetent persons lack family members or are residents of nursing homes, psychiatric hospitals, and facilities for the disabled and mentally retarded. Many of these patients rarely, if ever, see a family member.

Four classes of decision makers have been proposed and used in cases of withholding and terminating treatment for incompetent patients who have not explicitly designated a surrogate: families, physicians and other health care professionals, institutional committees, and courts. It is now widely agreed that the patient's closest family member is presumptively the first choice, because of expectable identification with the patient's interests and intimate knowledge of his or her wishes. However, in some relatively rare cases, surrogates or parents refuse treatments that are in the interests of those they should protect, and physicians then acquiesce in their decisions. Here a mechanism or procedure is needed to help make a decision or to break a closed, private circle of refusal and acquiescence. A similar need exists for assistance in decisions regarding residents of nursing homes and hospices, psychiatric hospitals, and residential facilities in which families often play no significant role. Possible participants in decisions about life-sustaining treatment include hospital administrators, hospital ethics committees, attorneys, and public officials acting to protect the interests of society.

DECISIONS BY COMPETENT ADULTS

Bouvia v. Superior Court*

CALIFORNIA COURT OF APPEALS, SECOND DISTRICT

The first selection is a court opinion in the case of Elizabeth Bouvia. Since birth Bouvia suffered from cerebral palsy that left her with virtually no functioning limbs or skeletal muscles and in constant, uncontrollable pain. She was unaffected cognitively and found her pain difficult to endure and her dependence on others "humiliating" and "disgusting." At first, she directed her father to take her to a hospital where, after admission, she disclosed her intention to refuse all treatment and starve herself to death—apparently a *suicide* attempt by a person who was not terminally ill. Later she changed her mind and decided to continue living until "nature took its course."

The *Bouvia* court's opinion is notable for several reasons: (1) its analysis of the difference between complying with a refusal of treatment and assisting in suicide, (2) the issues of paternalism it treats, and (3) its strong interpretation of the right to refuse medical treatment. This appellate court suggested not only that there is a right of privacy to refuse treatments, including nutrition and hydration, but that courts and physicians morally should make it possible for physicians to assist patients in bringing about the end of their lives in dignity and comfort. The concurring opinion written by Associate Justice Compton is even stronger; he exhorts physicians to rethink their traditional objections to assisting such patients to die.

DECIDED APRIL 16, 1986

Elizabeth BOUVIA, Petitioner.

v.

SUPERIOR COURT of the State of California For
the County of Los Angeles, Respondent
(Glenchur)

OPINION AND ORDER FOR A PEREMPTORY WRIT OF MANDATE

BEACH, ASSOCIATE JUSTICE

Petitioner, Elizabeth Bouvia, a patient in a public hospital seeks the removal from her body of a nasogastric tube inserted and maintained against her will and

---

*Source: Reprinted from the *California Reporter,* 225 Cal.Rptr. 297 (Cal.App. 2 Dist.).

without her consent by physicians who so placed it for the purpose of keeping her alive through involuntary forced feeding. . . .

The trial court denied petitioner's request for the immediate relief she sought. It concluded that leaving the tube in place was necessary to prolong petitioner's life, and that it would, in fact, do so. With the tube in place petitioner probably will survive the time required to prepare for trial, a trial itself and an appeal, if one proved necessary. The real party physicians also assert, and the trial court agreed, that physically petitioner tolerates the tube reasonably well and thus is not in great physical discomfort. . . .

Factual Background

Petitioner is a 28-year-old woman. Since birth she has been afflicted with and suffered from severe cerebral palsy. She is quadriplegic. She is now a patient at a public hospital maintained by one of the real parties in interest, the County of Los Angeles. . . . Petitioner's physical handicaps of palsy and quadriplegia have progressed to the point where she is completely bedridden. Except for a few fingers of one hand and some slight head and facial movements, she is immobile. She is physically helpless and wholly unable to care for herself. She is totally dependent upon others for all of her needs. These include feeding, washing, cleaning, toileting, turning, and helping her with elimination and other bodily functions. She cannot stand or sit upright in bed or in a wheelchair. She lies flat in bed and must do so the rest of her life. She suffers also from degenerative and severely crippling arthritis. She is in continual pain. Another tube permanently attached to her chest automatically injects her with periodic doses of morphine which relieves some, but not all of her physical pain and discomfort.

She is intelligent, very mentally competent. She earned a college degree. She was married but her husband has left her. She suffered a miscarriage. She lived with her parents until her father told her that they could no longer care for her. She has stayed intermittently with friends and at public facilities. A search for a permanent place to live where she might receive the constant care which she needs has been unsuccessful. She is without financial means to support herself and, therefore, must accept public assistance for medical and other care.

She has on several occasions expressed the desire to die. In 1983 she sought the right to be cared for in a public hospital in Riverside County while she intentionally "starved herself to death." A court in that county denied her judicial assistance to accomplish that goal. She later abandoned an appeal from that ruling. Thereafter, friends took her to several different facilities, both public and private, arriving finally at her present location. . . .

Petitioner must be spoon fed in order to eat. Her present medical and dietary staff have determined that she is not consuming a sufficient amount of nutrients. Petitioner stops eating when she feels she cannot orally swallow more, without nausea and vomiting. As she cannot now retain solids, she is fed soft liquid-like food. Because of her previously announced resolve to starve herself, the medical staff feared her weight loss might reach a life-threatening level. Her weight since admission to real parties' facility seems to hover between 65 and 70 pounds. Accordingly, they inserted the subject tube against her will and contrary to her express written instruction. . . .

The Right to Refuse Medical Treatment

"[A] person of adult years and in sound mind has the right, in the exercise of control over his own body, to determine whether or not to submit to lawful medical treatment." (*Cobbs v. Grant* (1972) 8 Cal.3d 229, 242, 104 Cal.Rptr. 505, 502 P.2d 1.) It follows that such a patient has the right to refuse *any* medical treatment, even that which may save or prolong her life. (*Barber v. Superior Court* (1983) 147 Cal. App.3d 1006, 195 Cal.Rptr. 484; *Bartling v. Superior Court* (1984) 163 Cal.App.3d 186, 209 Cal.Rptr. 220.) In our view the foregoing authorities are dispositive of the case at bench. Nonetheless, the County and its medical staff contend that for reasons unique to this case, Elizabeth Bouvia may not exercise the right available to others. Accordingly, we again briefly discuss the rule in the light of real parties' contentions.

The right to refuse medical treatment is basic and fundamental. It is recognized as a part of the right of privacy protected by both the state and federal constitutions. . . . Its exercise requires no one's approval. It is not merely one vote subject to being overridden by medical opinion.

In *Barber v. Superior Court, supra,* 147 Cal.App.3d 1006, 195 Cal.Rptr. 484, we considered this same issue although in a different context. Writing on behalf of this division, Justice Compton thoroughly analyzed and reviewed the issue of withdrawal of life-support systems beginning with the seminal case of the *Matter of Quinlan* (N.J. 1976) 355 A.2d 647, *cert. den.* 429 U.S. 922, 97 S.Ct. 319, 50 L.Ed.2d 289, and continuing on to the then recent enactment of the California Natural Death Act (Health & Saf. Code. §§ 7185–7195). His opinion clearly and repeatedly stresses the fundamental underpinning of its conclusion, i.e., the patient's right to decide: 147 Cal.App.3d at page 1015, 195 Cal.Rptr. 484, "In this state a clearly recognized legal right to control one's own medical treatment predated the Natural Death Act. A long line of cases, approved by the Supreme Court in *Cobbs v. Grant* (1972) 8 Cal.3d 229 [104 Cal. Rptr. 505, 502 P.2d 1] . . . have held that where a doctor performs treatment in the absence of an informed consent, there is an actionable battery. The obvious corollary to this principle is that *a competent adult patient has the legal right to refuse medical treatment.*" . . .

Bartling v. Superior Court, supra, 163 Cal.App.3d 186, 209 Cal.Rptr. 220, was factually much like the case at bench. Although not totally identical in all respects, the issue there centered on the same question here present: i.e., "May the patient refuse even life continuing treatment?" Justice Hastings, writing for another division of this court, explained: "In this case we are called upon to decide whether a competent adult patient, with serious illnesses which are probably incurable but have not been diagnosed as terminal, has the right, over the objection of his physicians and the hospital, to have life-support equipment disconnected despite the fact that withdrawal of such devices will surely hasten his death." (At p. 189, 209 Cal.Rptr. 220.) . . .

The description of Mr. Bartling's condition fits that of Elizabeth Bouvia. The holding of that case applies here and compels real parties to respect her decision even though she is not "terminally" ill. . . .

The Claimed Exceptions to the Patient's Right to Choose Are Inapplicable

. . . At bench the trial court concluded that with sufficient feeding petitioner could live an additional 15 to 20 years; therefore, the preservation of petitioner's life for that period outweighed her right to decide. In so holding the trial court mistakenly attached undue importance to the *amount of time* possibly available to petitioner, and failed to give equal weight and consideration for the *quality* of that life; an equal, if not more significant, consideration.

All decisions permitting cessation of medical treatment or life-support procedures to some degree hastened the arrival of death. In part, at least, this was permitted because the quality of life during the time remaining in those cases had been terribly diminished. In Elizabeth Bouvia's view, the quality of her life has been diminished to the point of hopelessness, uselessness, unenjoyability and frustration. She, as the patient, lying helplessly in bed, unable to care for herself, may consider her existence meaningless. . . .

Here Elizabeth Bouvia's decision to forego medical treatment or life-support through a mechanical means belongs to her. It is not a medical decision for her physicians to make. Neither is it a legal question whose soundness is to be resolved by lawyers or judges. It is not a conditional right subject to approval by ethics committees or courts of law. It is a moral and philosophical decision that, being a competent adult, is hers alone. . . .

Here, if force fed, petitioner faces 15 to 20 years of a painful existence, endurable only by the constant administrations of morphine. Her condition is irreversible. There is no cure for her palsy or arthritis. Petitioner would have to be fed, cleaned, turned, bedded, toileted by others for 15 to 20 years! Although alert, bright, sensitive, perhaps even brave and feisty, she must lie immobile, unable to exist except through physical acts of others. Her mind and spirit may be free to take great flights but she herself is imprisoned and must lie physically helpless subject to the ignominy, embarrassment, humiliation, and dehumanizing aspects created by her helplessness. We do not believe it is the policy of this State that all and every life must be preserved against the will of the sufferer. It is incongruous, if not monstrous, for medical practitioners to assert their right to preserve a life that someone else must live, or, more accurately, endure, for "15 to 20 years." We cannot conceive it to be the policy of this State to inflict such an ordeal upon anyone.

It is, therefore, immaterial that the removal of the nasogastric tube will hasten or cause Bouvia's eventual death. Being competent she has the right to live out the remainder of her natural life in dignity and peace. It is precisely the aim and purpose of the many decisions upholding the withdrawal of life-support systems to accord and provide as large a measure of dignity, respect and comfort as possible to every patient for the remainder of his days, whatever be their number.

This goal is not to hasten death, though its earlier arrival may be an expected and understood likelihood. . . .

It is not necessary to here define or dwell at length upon what constitutes suicide. Our Supreme Court dealt with the matter in the case of *In re Joseph G.* (1983) 34 Cal.3d 429, 194 Cal.Rptr. 163, 667 P.2d 1176, wherein declaring that the State has an interest in preserving and recognizing the sanctity of life, it observed that it is a crime to aid in suicide. But it is significant that the instances and the means there discussed all involved affirmative, assertive, proximate, direct conduct such as furnishing a gun, poison, knife, or other instrumentality or usable means by which another could physically and immediately inflict some death producing injury upon himself. Such situations are far different than the mere presence of a doctor during the exercise of his patient's constitutional rights.

This is the teaching of *Bartling* and *Barber*. No criminal or civil liability attaches to honoring a competent, informed patient's refusal of medical service.

We do not purport to establish what will constitute proper medical practice in all other cases or even other aspects of the care to be provided petitioner. We hold only that her right to refuse medical treatment even of the life-sustaining variety, entitles her to the immediate removal of the nasogastric tube that has been involuntarily inserted into her body. The hospital and medical staff are still free to perform a substantial, if not the greater part of their duty, i.e., that of trying to alleviate Bouvia's pain and suffering.

Petitioner is without means to go to a private hospital and, apparently, real parties' hospital as a public facility was required to accept her. Having done so it may not deny her relief from pain and suffering merely because she has chosen to exercise her fundamental right to protect what little privacy remains to her. . . .

IT IS ORDERED

Let a peremptory writ of mandate issue commanding the Los Angles Superior Court immediately upon receipt thereof, to make and enter a new and different order granting Elizabeth Bouvia's request for a preliminary injunction, and the relief prayed for therein; in particular to make an order (1) directing real parties in interest forthwith to remove the nasogastric tube from petitioner, Elizabeth Bouvia's, body, and (2) prohibiting any and all of the real parties in interest from replacing or aiding in replacing said tube or any other or similar device in or on petitioner without her consent. . . .

Compton, Associate Justice, Concurring Opinion

I have no doubt that Elizabeth Bouvia wants to die; and if she had the full use of even one hand, could probably find a way to end her life—in a word—commit suicide. In order to seek the assistance which she needs in ending her life by the only means she sees available—starvation—she has had to stultify her position before this court by disavowing her desire to end her life in such a fashion and proclaiming that she will eat all that she can physically tolerate. Even the majority opinion here must necessarily "dance" around the issue.

Elizabeth apparently has made a conscious and informed choice that she prefers death to continued existence in her helpless and, to her, intolerable condition. I believe she has an absolute right to effectuate that decision. This state and the medical profession instead of frustrating her desire, should be attempting to relieve her suffering by permitting and in fact assisting her to die with ease and dignity. The fact that she is forced to suffer the ordeal of self-starvation to achieve her objective is in itself inhumane.

The right to die is an integral part of our right to control our own destinies so long as the rights of others are not affected. That right should, in my opinion, include the ability to enlist assistance from others, including the medical profession, in making death as painless and quick as possible. . . .

Conflicts Between Patients' Wishes to Forgo Treatment and the Policies of Health Care Facilities*

STEVEN H. MILES, PETER A. SINGER, AND MARK SIEGLER

The authors in the next selection explore how the rights of patients to refuse life-sustaining treatments can be reconciled with a hospital's or nursing home's contrasting views about appropriate care. They consider three related court cases, examine whether officials representing a health care facility may refuse to comply with refusals of life support, and examine the alternatives available in these circumstances. They conclude that in pluralistic societies diversity in health care facilities should be promoted and that patients should be able to and be encouraged to seek care from facilities and practitioners that openly disclose their treatment policies.

The right of patients to forgo life-sustaining treatment has been well established in health law and medical ethics. But do patients also have a right to compel health care facilities or their staffs to participate in carrying out such a decision? What happens when an institution has enunciated a treatment philosophy that is incompatible with a patient's or family's request to discontinue life support? If institutions and their staffs refuse to execute a patient's request, how can that patient's right to forgo life-sustaining treatment be effectuated? In recent cases involving decisions to forgo artificial feeding, courts have held that the rights of individual patients to refuse a treatment prevail over the objections of a hospital or nursing home. This article reviews three recent court cases addressing this issue, considers whether the administration of a health care facility may decline to comply with a patient's request to forgo life-sustaining treatment, and examines the options in such situations.

THREE RECENT CASES

Beverly Requena, a competent 55-year-old woman hospitalized with amyotrophic lateral sclerosis in a church-owned hospital,[1,2] became dependent on a ventilator in April 1985. In July 1986 she stated that she would refuse tube feeding. The hospital administration objected, maintaining that food and fluids were fundamental forms of care, but arranged to transfer Requena to a nearby facility willing to honor her request. She refused the transfer, and the hospital sued to compel her to leave. The

---

judge ruled that her wish to decline tube feeding must be honored by the hospital staff, who had voiced moral objections to this change in her treatment plan. The judge suggested that "by rethinking more carefully their own attitudes, the health care workers at the Hospital might find it possible to be more fully accepting and supportive of Ms. Requena's decision." The decision was affirmed on appeal.

Nancy Jobes, a 31-year-old nursing home patient, had been in a persistent vegetative state[3] for five years when her family requested that tube feeding be stopped. In 1985 a lower court upheld the family's request over objections of the nursing home, but it allowed the home to continue the tube feeding until the patient could be transferred elsewhere. In 1987 the New Jersey Supreme Court affirmed that feeding could be discontinued, but it also ordered the facility to continue to care for Jobes until she died. The court noted that the nursing home had not informed the family of its policy against the withdrawal of artificial feeding until after the family requested that feeding be withdrawn.

Marcia Gray, a 49-year-old woman, had been hospitalized in a persistent vegetative state since 1986, after a cerebral hemorrhage and subsequent neurosurgery.[4] In 1987 her family requested that artificial feeding be ended. When the hospital objected, the family sought court authorization, and in October 1988 the Federal District Court of Rhode Island ruled that feeding be stopped. The court found that Gray's right to forgo artificial feeding was protected by a constitutional right of privacy, that artificial feeding was a form of medical treatment that she could refuse, that her previously expressed wishes clearly supported her decision, and that her right to refuse treatment outweighed competing governmental interests with regard to the preservation of life, the prevention of suicide, the protection of innocent third parties, and the integrity of medical ethics. The court also found that if Gray could not be "promptly transferred to a health care facility that will respect her wishes, the [hospital] must accede to her requests."

In the Requena, Jobes, and Gray cases, the courts upheld the rights of the individual patients and dismissed the objections of the health care facilities. Even so, the prerogative of health care facilities to pursue particular treatment philosophies may serve an important purpose in our morally pluralistic society. These cases suggest that it is time to review the standing of institutional policies in the ethics of medical decisions.

HOSPITALS AS MORAL AGENTS

George Annas, a prominent medical ethicist, has framed the debate over the role of institutions in the ethics of medical decisions as follows: "Hospitals are corporations that have no natural personhood, and hence are incapable of having moral or ethical objections to actions. . . . Hospitals don't practice medicine, physicians do."[5]

According to this view, health care facilities have no institutional responsibility for the morality of the medical decisions made inside their walls. Yet in many ways society articulates expectations of the moral obligation of such facilities.[6,7] For example, the Joint Commission on the Accreditation of Health Care Organizations requires that health care facilities adopt policies governing decisions to withhold resuscitation.[8] Similarly, the Health Care Financing Administration requires hospitals to abstain from "dumping" medically unstable persons who cannot pay for their care. The recent emergence of ethics committees and ethics consultants represents a further expansion of institutional responsibilities to consider the ethical dimensions of the health care transaction.

As Annas notes, people, not institutions, actually carry out health care. The courts should hesitate to force health care facilities to carry out morally controversial treatment requests. Some nurses and physicians have profound moral objections to participating in certain treatment plans, such as those that require caring for a patient who has refused feeding. The right of individual providers of health care to refuse to participate in treatment plans that they find morally objectionable has been well established.[9] As the President's Commission noted, a health professional is not "obligated to accede to the patient in a way that violates . . . the provider's own deeply held moral beliefs."[10] If the courts cannot compel people to violate their own conscientiously held moral standards, then it follows that on occasion institutions may be unable to comply with court-ordered directives to carry out certain actions, because no one in the institution is willing to do so.

MISSION STATEMENTS

The treatment philosophy of a health care facility or its staff is sometimes expressed in a statement of mission. Mission statements define the "purpose, philosophy, values, and services of a health care facility."[11] They may affirm an institutional commitment to a sectarian philosophy of treatment, express a general commitment to "quality health care," restate constitutional guarantees such as nondiscrimination,[12] or define areas of expertise, such as cancer research and treatment[13] or palliative care.[14] Or they may distinguish morally between actions that are permitted and those that are unacceptable, such as the passive and active forms of euthanasia.[15] They may also proscribe treatment plans that, although legal, are not consonant with the philosophy of the facility—for example, elective abortion in Catholic hospitals.

The mission statements of health facilities may best be seen as part of a dialogue with potential patients. As such, the statements should describe the facility's purpose and the implications with respect to specific treatment issues. The statement may outline how moral diversity can be accommodated within the facility and what kinds of treatment plans are unacceptable in the context of the overall mission. The statement should provide procedures for appeal, so that individual circumstances not anticipated by the general rules may be addressed. Mission statements should be available to patients at admission. As institutions providing total, long-term care, nursing homes have a special duty and opportunity to review the implications of their mission with potential residents.

Mission statements are important because our society respects personal choices. Many people choose to affiliate in distinct moral communities—voluntary associations of people who share a common view of the moral good.[16] The mission statements of health care facilities may express the philosophy of such communities. A presidential commission[10] and the American Hospital Association have affirmed that each facility has "the prerogative to develop a mission reflecting its historical roots and philosophy."[17] The view that each facility should embrace a moral vision is a longstanding tradition of the American hospital system.[18] A critical task in bioethics is to promote social policies that tolerate the diversity of moral communities and allow the coexistence of public expressions of communal differences.[16,19]

Mission statements play a constructive part in the health care system. Health professionals are able to work in facilities that promote a particular vision of good health care. Health care workers are encouraged to regard their work as a moral enterprise, thereby strengthening the foundation of professional integrity.

Patients may also prefer to obtain care from a facility with a particular mission. In such facilities, patients can obtain care from a staff that is explicitly committed to a philosophy of health care that resembles the patient's own. This may explain why elderly patients often seek nursing homes affiliated with their faith, and why patients who are terminally ill and seeking palliative care choose a hospice. Institutional missions offer the promise that treatment proposals begin from shared fundamental beliefs. Statements of institutional mission are important because "good" health care is complex—too complex to be reduced to the aggregate of consents to individual treatments.[20]

PATIENTS' REQUESTS AND INSTITUTIONAL MISSIONS

Conflicts between a patient's request to forgo life-sustaining treatment and an institutional mission or the views of individual health care providers admit no easy resolution. Patients have a preeminent right to decline any life-prolonging treatment.[10,21] The patient's right may be encumbered temporarily to allow an accommodation with the comparably important rights of others who should not be compelled to violate personal moral sentiments. The rights of members of communities to create institutions that express diverse health care philosophies are also fundamentally related to the principle of respect for autonomy.

Many such conflicts do not involve an institution's mission statement about treatment philosophy, but arise because of institutional policy that staff members not be compelled to violate their deeply held moral views.[22] Some of these situations can be resolved by negotiation between patients and medical staff. Thus, a difference over discontinuing life-sustaining therapy might be resolved by an agreement to limit new interventions or to continue the therapy for a limited time to clarify clinical uncertainty. In some cases, the staff and directors will be able to find other staff members willing to accommodate the patient's preferences. An ethics committee or consultant might facilitate such negotiations.

The requests of some patients may be irreconcilable with an institution's treatment philosophy. In a pluralistic society, health care facilities must act swiftly so that a patient's rights are accommodated, even as the institution's treatment philosophy is affirmed. In some cases, the courts have said that it may be appropriate to end the therapeutic relationship and transfer the patient to another provider.[4,23] Such transfers, as a last resort, may be the lesser of two evils if the alternative is to override the treatment philosophy of the institution. This inconvenience accommodates the patient's request while preserving the ability of health providers to work in, and patients to seek care in, facilities with specific missions. In the case of William Bartling, a man dependent on a respirator in a "Christian, prolife" hospital, the court noted that the unwanted ventilator should have been removed as the patient requested, but that the hospital also might transfer him to the care of another facility.[24]

There are circumstances in which facilities should not be permitted to transfer a patient because they do not wish to honor a request to withhold treatment. Public hospitals may not promote sectarian views and should respond affirmatively to any legal and medically appropriate preference on the part of the patient. If alternative providers cannot be found, even sectarian facilities may be obligated to yield to a patient's directive. A facility that did not inform a patient in advance that its mission was incompatible with possible future requests for treatment might lose the option of restricting its treatment options later.

CONCLUSION

Our pluralistic society should go to some lengths to promote diversity among health care facilities. As the available treatment options have expanded, accommodation between the irreconcilable moral views of providers and patients with respect to the attendant ethical issues has become more problematic. By embodying the views of distinct moral communities, health care facilities play an important part in expanding the health care options for patients and health care professionals. As society upholds the rights of patients to forgo treatment, it should also avoid encroaching on these missions and on the moral sentiments of individual health care professionals. Patients should be able to seek care from facilities and professionals who affirm their preferences rather than blandly or begrudgingly tolerate them.

NOTES

1. In the matter of Beverly Requena. 213 N.J. Super. Ch. 475 (1986).
2. In the matter of Beverly Requena. 213 N.J. super. A.D. 443 (1986).
3. In the matter of Nancy Ellen Jobes, Supreme Court of New Jersey A-108/109 (1987).
4. Marcia Gray vs. Thomas D. Romeo et al., U.S. District Court for the District of Rhode Island. 87-0573B (1988).
5. Annas G.J. Transferring the ethical hot potato. *Hastings Center Report* 1987; 17(1):20–1.
6. Kapp M. Can hospitals have moral objections? *Hastings Center Report* 1987; 17(5):43–44.
7. Helsper S.T., McCarthy J.J. Can hospitals have moral objections? *Hasting Center Report* 1987; 17(5):43.
8. Accreditation manual for hospitals. Chicago: Joint Commission on Accreditation of Hospitals, 1988:50, 90.
9. Hastings Center. Guidelines on the termination of life-sustaining treatment and the care of the dying: a report. Briarcliff Manor, NY: Hastings Center, 1987:32.
10. President's Commission for the Study of Ethical Problems in Medicine and Biomedical and Behavioral Research. Making health care decisions: A report on the

ethical and legal implications of informed consent in the patient-practitioner relationship. Washington, DC: Government Printing Office, 1982:48.

11. Reeves P.N., ed. Strategic planning for hospitals. Chicago: American College of Hospital Administrators, 1983.

12. Limited treatment policies and guidelines: a model for hospitals and nursing homes. Minneapolis: Minnesota Hospital Association and Biomedical Ethics Committee of Fairview Riverside Hospital, 1986:3.

13. van Eys J., Bowen, J.M., Alt J., et al. Creating a code of ethics: Report of The University of Texas System Cancer Center M.D. Anderson Hospital and Tumor Institute. CA 1986; 36:115–119.

14. Task Force On Supportive Care. The supportive care plan: Its meaning and application: recommendations and guidelines. *Law Med Health Care* 1984; 12:97–102.

15. Saint Joseph Hospital Board of Trustees. Principles and guidelines for the treatment of a patient for whom a no-code order has been written. In: Doudera A.E., Peters J.D. (eds.) *Legal and ethical aspects of treating critically and terminally ill patients.* Ann Arbor, MI: Health Administration Press, 1982:296–297.

16. Engelhardt H.T. *The foundations of bioethics.* New York: Oxford University Press, 1986.

17. Special Committee on Biomedical Ethics. Values in conflict: resolving ethical issues in hospital care. Chicago: American Hospital Association, 1985:36–37.

18. Rosenberg C.E. *The care of strangers: The rise of America's hospital system.* New York: Basic Books, 1987.

19. Paris J.J. Personal autonomy over institutional considerations. *New Jersey Law Journal* 1987; 120:23–24.

20. Pellegrino E.D., Thomasma D.C. *A philosophical basis of medical practice: Toward a philosophy and ethic of the healing professions.* New York: Oxford University Press, 1981:244–265.

21. In re Bouvia. 1986; 179 Cal. App. 3d 1127:297–308.

22. Uhlmann R.F., Clark H. Pearlman R.A., Downs J.C., Addison J.H., Haining R.G. Medical management decisions in nursing home patients: Principles and policy recommendations. *Annals of Internal Medicine* 1987; 106:879–885.

23. *Brophy v. New England Sinai Hospital Inc.,* 497 N.E. 2nd 626 (Mass. 1986).

24. In re Bartling. 1984; 163 Cal. App. 3d 186:220–227.

State of Georgia v. McAfee

SUPREME COURT OF GEORGIA

In the next selection, the Georgia Supreme Court analyzes legitimate forms of assistance to Larry McAfee, a competent adult paralyzed from the neck down from an automobile accident. He was not terminally ill, but found his life as a quadriplegic intolerable. A professional engineer, McAfee devised a self-disconnecting, mouth-controlled mechanism that would separate him from his ventilator, thereby causing his death. The Georgia court found that McAfee's right to refuse treatment and disconnect himself outweighed the state's interest in the preservation of life and in preventing suicide. In its opinion, the court treated more than the right to *refuse* treatment. McAfee had previously attempted to disconnect himself from the respirator, but had been unable to do so because he suffered severe pain from loss of oxygen in the attempt. He therefore asked for a physician's assistance in administering a sedative just before attempting to disconnect himself. The court found that no criminal or civil liability would attach to any physician who helped him by administering the sedative, but the court hinted that physicians could not be ordered to administer the sedative. Nevertheless, the court found that McAfee's "right to have a sedative . . . administered before the ventilator is disconnected is a part of his right to control his medical treatment."

Gregory, Justice

Larry James McAfee suffered a severe injury to his spinal cord in a motorcycle accident in 1985 which left him quadriplegic. Mr. McAfee is incapable of spontaneous respiration, and is dependent upon a ventilator to breathe. According to the record there is no hope that Mr. McAfee's condition will improve with time, nor is there any known medical treatment which can improve his condition.

In August 1989 Mr. McAfee filed a petition in Fulton Superior Court, seeking a determination that he be allowed to turn off his ventilator, which will result in his death. He also prayed that the ventilator not be restarted once it is disconnected. Through the assistance of an engineer, Mr. McAfee has devised a means of turning off the ventilator himself by way of a timer. He has requested that he be provided a sedative to alleviate the pain which will occur when the ventilator is disconnected.

It is not disputed that Mr. McAfee is a competent adult who has been counseled on the issues involved in this case and has discussed these issues with his family. According to the record, his family supports his decision to refuse medical treatment.

The trial court granted Mr. McAfee's petition for declaratory relief, finding his constitutional rights of privacy and liberty, *Griswold v. Connecticut,* 381 U.S. 479, 85 S.Ct. 1678, 14 L.Ed.2d 510 (1965); 1983 Georgia Constitution, Art. I, Sec. I, Par. I, and the concomitant right to refuse medical treatment outweigh any interest the state has in this proceeding. The trial court concluded that it could not order a medical professional to administer a sedative to Mr. McAfee, but held that no civil or criminal liability would attach to anyone who did so.

1.   In *In re L.H.R.,* 253 Ga. 439, 446, 321 S.E.2d 716 (1984), this court stated that "[i]n Georgia, as elsewhere, a competent adult patient has the right to refuse medical treatment in the absence of conflicting state interest." The parties have identified four generally recognized interests of the state which must be balanced against a competent, adult patient's right to refuse medical treatment: the state's interest in preserving life; its interest in preventing suicide; preservation of the integrity of the medical profession; and protection of innocent third parties. . . . The parties agree that the only interest of the state implicated in this case is the general interest in preserving life. The state concedes that its interest in preserving life does not outweigh Mr. McAfee's right to refuse medical treatment. Analyzing most of the decisions cited above, the state takes the position that, "there is simply no basis in this case upon which the State may intervene and oppose the exercise of Mr. McAfee's right to refuse treatment." We note that we do not have before us a case where the state's interest is in preserving the life of an innocent third party, such as the unborn child of a woman who wishes to refuse medical treatment. See generally, *Jefferson v. Griffin etc. Hospital Auth.,* 247 Ga. 86, 274 S.E.2d 457 (1981). Therefore we hold that under the circumstances of this case the trial court was correct in granting Mr. McAfee's petition for declaratory relief.

2.   We further hold that Mr. McAfee's right to be free from pain at the time the ventilator is disconnected is inseparable from his right to refuse medical treatment. The record shows that Mr. McAfee has attempted to disconnect his ventilator in the past, but has been unable to do so due to the severe pain he suffers when deprived of oxygen. His right to have a sedative (a medication that in no way causes or accelerates death) administered before the ventilator is disconnected is a part of his right to control his medical treatment.

3.   We point out that the legislature has enacted the Living Will Act, OCGA § 31–32–1 et seq., which allows a competent adult to execute a document directing that should he have a terminal condition as defined by the Act, life-sustaining procedures will be withheld. A "terminal condition" is defined as an "incurable condition caused by disease, illness or injury, which regardless of the application of life-sustaining procedures, would produce death." OCGA §31–32–2(10). Subsection (B) imposes the requirement that death from the terminal condition be "imminent." We held in *In re L.H.R.,* supra, that the right afforded by the Act to execute a Living Will "rises to the level of a constitutional right which is not lost because of the incompetence or youth of the patient." However, the Living Will Act does not apply where the patient, as here, does not have a "terminal condition" because death is not imminent and will not result regardless of the use of a life-sustaining procedure. As such the legislature might well choose to legislate in this area to provide appropriate non-judicial procedures for competent adult patients who do not have "terminal conditions," but who wish to exercise their rights to refuse medical treatment by the withdrawal of life-sustaining procedures.

Judgment affirmed.

All the Justices concur.

Helping Larry James McAfee Die*

NAT HENTOFF

In the next brief article, taken from a nationally syndicated newspaper column, Nat Hentoff argues that the judges in the McAfee case have opened the door to "lawful assisted suicide," even though it is illegal and disapproved by medical societies. In defense of this widely accepted view of the unacceptability of assisted suicide, Hentoff paradoxically rejects widely accepted views that the injury that left McAfee in his condition would be the cause of death (it would be "nature taking its course") if he removed the ventilator, rather than McAfee's and the physician's actions being the cause of death. Hentoff also hints that McAfee's decision (and those of many persons with disabilities) might have been different if he had had more resources at his disposal.

SWEET LAND OF LIBERTY

Paralyzed from the neck down in a 1985 motorcycle accident, Larry James McAfee, 33, wants to be removed from the ventilator that keeps him alive. When those responsible for his treatment refused to abide by his wishes, McAfee went to Georgia Superior Court Judge Edward H. Johnson for permission to turn the ventilator off.

McAfee could do this by himself, having helped design a mouth-activated timing device by which he can divert air intended for his lungs away from him. But that procedure would be painful and very frightening during those final minutes when he would be without air. Therefore, McAfee asked the court both for permission to turn off the ventilator and for someone to give him a sedative to ease his end.

Johnson ruled that McAfee is competent and therefore has the common law right—and the right under the Constitution of the state of Georgia—to refuse any further medical treatment, including the use of the ventilator. McAfee, moreover, had very clearly stated his conviction that life no longer had any enjoyment for him. He finds total dependency "demeaning" and utterly "draining."

But how far could the judge go to help McAfee accomplish his purpose? In his decision, Johnson said it was "highly problematical" that any court has "the authority to order a physician or other health care giver" to disconnect the ventilator or "compel a physician to administer a sedative."

True, McAfee is able to shut off the ventilator by himself, so that should be no problem. But what about the sedative? At this point Johnson did something that apparently no other court in the country has yet done.

He declared that any doctor who gives McAfee a sedative—or, for that matter, helps him disconnect his ventilator if it turns out McAfee can't do it himself—will not be "subject to any adverse legal consequences." The same immunity from civil

*Source: Hentoff, N., "Helping Larry James McAfee Die," *Washington Post* (November 25, 1989). p. A23, col. 1. © The Washington Post.

or criminal liability will apply to workers in health care facilities and anyone else "who merely assists Larry McAfee in exercising his constitutional and statutory right to refuse medical treatment."

This would seem to open the door to lawful assisted suicide, which is illegal elsewhere and is disapproved by most medical societies and even by some bioethicists. The fear of the objectors is that once it is lawful to help someone commit suicide, it will eventually be lawful to end the lives of those who have not asked for death but whose "quality of life" is considered no longer worth sustaining.

Johnson, however, insists that McAfee—if he does end his life—would not be committing suicide. The judge cites friend-of-the-court briefs from the Roman Catholic Archdiocese of Atlanta and the Medical Association of Georgia. Both groups say that McAfee's shutting off his ventilator would not be the cause of his death but rather, as the medical association puts it, "the natural consequences of his motorcycle accident" would be the cause of his death.

The accident, you see, resulted in McAfee's inability to breathe on his own, and that inability would cause his death.

This has become a standard mechanical way of avoiding the fact that if, for instance, a feeding tube were removed and the person starved to death, the cause of death would be starvation. Most secular and religious bioethicists insist, however, that once these means of treatment are removed, death results not from starvation but from "nature taking its course." Nonetheless, if those means, including "extraordinary" ones, had not been removed, life would have continued.

In any case, McAfee, using his mouth to mark an X on a document that was part of his petition to the court, certified he knew full well that he would die if his ventilator were turned off. And that is what he wanted to do—end his life.

Meanwhile, disability rights activists in Atlanta have been pointing out that McAfee, once his health insurance money ran out, became a ward of the state of Georgia, which then denied him the kind of support that enables other quadriplegics to work and live independently with home aides, as McAfee had begun to do when he had insurance money. "Maybe if I had had more control of things," he told Newsday, "maybe things would have been different."

Paul Longmore, a historian and a quadriplegic who has used a ventilator for 25 years, notes mordantly, "The only people who are telling Larry McAfee they want him to try to live are other disabled people." They take Johnson's message to be that if your quality of life makes able-bodied people shake their heads in pity, you're better off dead.

The Medical Directive*

LINDA L. EMANUEL AND EZEKIEL J. EMANUEL**

"The Medical Directive" is an unusual article in which Linda and Ezekiel Emanuel both clarify the nature of advance directives and propose a standard, and perhaps ideal, form of directive. It provides six illness situations and allows the person executing the directive to select treatment options and to specify a goal of treatment for each situation. The authors provide distinct sections for a personal statement, for stating a preference among settings for terminal care, for specifying a decision about organ donation, and for selecting ways of designing a surrogate decision maker.

INTRODUCTION

As part of a person's right to self-determination, every adult may accept or refuse any recommended medical treatment. This is relatively easy when people are well and can speak. Unfortunately, during serious illness they are often unconscious or otherwise unable to communicate their wishes—at the very time when many critical decisions need to be made.

The Medical Directive allows you to record your wishes regarding various types of medical treatment in several representative situations so that your desires can be respected. It also lets you appoint someone to make medical decisions for you if you should become unable to make them on your own.

The Medical Directive comes into effect only if you become incompetent (unable to make decisions or to express your wishes), and you can change it at any time until then. As long as you are competent, you should discuss your care directly with your physician. (See Fig. 2.)

MY MEDICAL DIRECTIVE

This Medical Directive expresses, and shall stand for, my wishes regarding medical treatments in the event that illness should make me unable to communicate them directly. I make this Directive, being 18 years or more of age, of sound mind, and appreciating the consequences of my decisions.

*Source: Emanuel, L. L. and E. J. Emanuel, "The Medical Directive," in Cate and Gill, *The Patient Self-Determination Act: Implementation Issues and Opportunities,* 1991, pp. 58–64.

**Copyright 1990 by Linda L. Emanuel and Ezekiel J. Emanuel. The authors of this form advise that it should be completed pursuant to a discussion between the principal and his or her physician, so that the principal can be adequately informed of any pertinent medical information, and so that the physician can be appraised of the intentions of the principal and the exsitence of such a document which may be made part of the principal's medical records.

This form was originally published as part of an article by Linda L. Emanuel and Ezekiel J. Emanuel, "The Medical Directive: A New Comprehensive Advance Care Document" in *Journal of the American Medical Association* June 9, 1989;261:3290. It does not reflect the official policy of the American Medical Association.

SITUATION A

If I am in a coma or a persistent vegetative state and, in the opinion of my physician and two consultants, have no known hope of regaining awareness and higher mental functions no matter what is done, then my wishes—if medically reasonable—for this and any additional illness would be:

	I want	I want treatment tried. If no clear improvement, stop.	I am undecided	I do not want
1. **Cardiopulmonary resuscitation** (chest compressions, drugs, electric shocks, and artificial breathing aimed at reviving a person who is on the point of dying), **or major surgery** (for example, removing the gall bladder or part of the colon)		Not applicable		
2. **Mechanical breathing** (respiration by machine, through a tube in the throat), **or dialysis** (cleaning the blood by machine or by fluid passed through the belly)				
3. **Blood transfusions or blood products**		Not applicable		
4. **Artificial nutrition and hydration** (given though a tube in a vein or in the stomach)				
5. **Simple diagnostic tests** (for example, blood tests or x-rays), **or antibiotics** (drugs to fight infection)		Not applicable		
6. **Pain medications, even if they dull consciousness and indirectly shorten my life**		Not applicable		

THE GOAL OF MEDICAL CARE SHOULD BE (check one):

_____ prolong life; treat everything
_____ choose quality of life over longevity
_____ provide comfort care only
_____ other (*please specify*): _____

Figure 2

SITUATION B

If I am in a coma and, in the opinion of my physician and two consultants, have a small but uncertain chance of regaining higher mental functions, a somewhat greater chance of surviving with permanent brain damage, and a much greater chance of not recovering at all, then my wishes—if reasonable—for this and any additional illness would be:

	I want	I want treatment tried. If no clear improve-ment, stop.	I am undecided	I do not want
1. **Cardiopulmonary resuscitation** (chest compressions, drugs, electric shocks, and artificial breathing aimed at reviving a person who is on the point of dying), **or major surgery** (for example, removing the gall bladder or part of the colon)		Not applicable		
2. **Mechanical breathing** (respiration by machine, through a tube in the throat), **or dialysis** (cleaning the blood by machine or by fluid passed through the belly)				
3. **Blood transfusions or blood products**		Not applicable		
4. **Artificial nutrition and hydration** (given though a tube in a vein or in the stomach)				
5. **Simple diagnostic tests** (for example, blood tests or x-rays), **or antibiotics** (drugs to fight infection)		Not applicable		
6. **Pain medications, even if they dull consciousness and indirectly shorten my life**		Not applicable		

THE GOAL OF MEDICAL CARE SHOULD BE (*check one*):

____ prolong life; treat everything
____ attempt to cure, but reevaluate often
____ choose quality of life over longevity
____ provide comfort care only
____ other (*please specify*): _____

Figure 2   (cont.)

SITUATION C

If I have brain damage or some brain disease that in the opinion of my physician and two consultants cannot be reversed and that makes me unable to recognize people, to speak meaningfully to them, or to live independently, *and I also have a terminal illness*, then my wishes—if medically reasonable—for this and any additional illness would be:

	I want	I want treatment tried. If no clear improvement, stop.	I am undecided	I do not want
1. Cardiopulmonary resuscitation (chest compressions, drugs, electric shocks, and artificial breathing aimed at reviving a person who is on the point of dying), **or major surgery** (for example, removing the gall bladder or part of the colon)		Not applicable		
2. Mechanical breathing (respiration by machine, through a tube in the throat), **or dialysis** (cleaning the blood by machine or by fluid passed through the belly)				
3. Blood transfusions or blood products		Not applicable		
4. Artificial nutrition and hydration (given though a tube in a vein or in the stomach)				
5. Simple diagnostic tests (for example, blood tests or x-rays), **or antibiotics** (drugs to fight infection)		Not applicable		
6. Pain medications, even if they dull consciousness and indirectly shorten my life		Not applicable		

THE GOAL OF MEDICAL CARE SHOULD BE (*check one*):

_____ prolong life; treat everything
_____ attempt to cure, but reevaluate often
_____ choose quality of life over longevity
_____ provide comfort care only
_____ other (*please specify*): _____
_____

Figure 2   (cont.)

SITUATION D

If I have brain damage or some brain disease that in the opinion of my physician and two consultants cannot be reversed and that makes me unable to recognize people, to speak meaningfully to them, or to live independently, *but I have no terminal illness*, then my wishes—if medically reasonable—for this and any additional illness would be:

	I want	I want treatment tried. If no clear improvement, stop.	I am undecided	I do not want
1. **Cardiopulmonary resuscitation** (chest compressions, drugs, electric shocks, and artificial breathing aimed at reviving a person who is on the point of dying), **or major surgery** (for example, removing the gall bladder or part of the colon)		Not applicable		
2. **Mechanical breathing** (respiration by machine, through a tube in the throat), **or dialysis** (cleaning the blood by machine or by fluid passed through the belly)				
3. **Blood transfusions or blood products**		Not applicable		
4. **Artificial nutrition and hydration** (given though a tube in a vein or in the stomach)				
5. **Simple diagnostic tests** (for example, blood tests or x-rays), **or antibiotics** (drugs to fight infection)		Not applicable		
6. **Pain medications, even if they dull consciousness and indirectly shorten my life**		Not applicable		

THE GOAL OF MEDICAL CARE SHOULD BE (*check one*):

_____ prolong life; treat everything
_____ attempt to cure, but reevaluate often
_____ choose quality of life over longevity
_____ provide comfort care only
_____ other (*please specify*): _____

Figure 2   (cont.)

SITUATION E

If, in the opinion of my physician and two consultants, I have an incurable chronic illness that involves mental disability or physical suffering and ultimately causes death, and in addition I have an illness that is immediately life threatening but reversible, and I am temporarily unable to make decisions, and then my wishes—if medically reasonable—would be:

	I want	I want treatment tried. If no clear improvement, stop.	I am undecided	I do not want
1. **Cardiopulmonary resuscitation** (chest compressions, drugs, electric shocks, and artificial breathing aimed at reviving a person who is on the point of dying), **or major surgery** (for example, removing the gall bladder or part of the colon)		Not applicable		
2. **Mechanical breathing** (respiration by machine, through a tube in the throat), **or dialysis** (cleaning the blood by machine or by fluid passed through the belly)				
3. **Blood transfusions or blood products**		Not applicable		
4. **Artificial nutrition and hydration** (given though a tube in a vein or in the stomach)				
5. **Simple diagnostic tests** (for example, blood tests or x-rays), **or antibiotics** (drugs to fight infection)		Not applicable		
6. **Pain medications, even if they dull consciousness and indirectly shorten my life**		Not applicable		

THE GOAL OF MEDICAL CARE SHOULD BE (*check one*):

____ prolong life; treat everything
____ attempt to cure, but reevaluate often
____ choose quality of life over longevity
____ provide comfort care only
____ other (*please specify*): _____

Figure 2 (cont.)

SITUATION F

If I am in my current state of health (*describe briefly*): _____

_____

and then have an illness that, in the opinion of my physician and two consultants, is life threatening but reversible, and I am temporarily unable to make decisions, then my wishes—if medically reasonable—would be:

	I want	I want treatment tried. If no clear improvement, stop.	I am undecided	I do not want
1. Cardiopulmonary resuscitation (chest compressions, drugs, electric shocks, and artificial breathing aimed at reviving a person who is on the point of dying), **or major surgery** (for example, removing the gall bladder or part of the colon)		Not applicable		
2. Mechanical breathing (respiration by machine, through a tube in the throat), **or dialysis** (cleaning the blood by machine or by fluid passed through the belly)				
3. Blood transfusions or blood products	Not applicable			
4. Artificial nutrition and hydration (given though a tube in a vein or in the stomach)				
5. Simple diagnostic tests (for example, blood tests or x-rays), **or antibiotics** (drugs to fight infection)	Not applicable			
6. Pain medications, even if they dull consciousness and indirectly shorten my life	Not applicable		·	

THE GOAL OF MEDICAL CARE SHOULD BE (*check one*):

_____ prolong life; treat everything
_____ attempt to cure, but reevaluate often
_____ choose quality of life over longevity
_____ provide comfort care only
_____ other (*please specify*): _____

_____

Figure 2 (cont.)

WHAT TO DO WITH THE FORM

Once you have completed the form, you and two adult witnesses (other than your proxy) who have no interest in your estate need to sign and date it.

Many states have legislation covering documents of this sort. To determine the laws in your state, you should call the office of its attorney general or consult a lawyer. If your state has a statutory document, you may wish to use the Medical Directive and append it to this form.

You should give a copy of the completed document to your physician. His or her signature is desirable but not mandatory. The Directive should be placed in your medical records and flagged so that anyone who might be involved in your care can be aware of its presence. Your proxy, a family member, and/or a friend should also have a copy. In addition, you may want to carry a wallet card noting that you have such a document and where it can be found.

MY PERSONAL STATEMENT

(*use another page if necessary*)

Please mention anything that would be important for your physician and your proxy to know. In particular, try to answer the following questions: (1) What medical conditions, if any, would make living so unpleasant that you would want life-sustaining treatment *withheld*? (Intractable pain? Irreversible mental damage? Inability to share love? Dependence on others? Another condition you would regard as intolerable?) (2) Under what medical circumstances would you want to *stop* interventions that might already have been started?

Should there be any difference between my preferences detailed in the illness situations and those understood from my goals or from my personal statement, I wish my treatment selections/my goals/my personal statement (*please delete as appropriate*) to be given greater weight.

When I am dying, I would like—if my proxy and my health-care team think it is reasonable—to be cared for:

- ☐ at home or in a hospice
- ☐ in a nursing home
- ☐ in a hospital
- ☐ other (*please specify*): _____

ORGAN DONATION
(*please check all boxes and fill in blanks where appropriate*)

—I hereby make this anatomical gift, to take effect after my death:

I give ☐ my body
       ☐ any needed organs or parts
       ☐ the following parts: _____

Figure 3

to   ☐   the following person or institution: _____
        ☐   the physician in attendance at my death
        ☐   the hospital in which I die
        ☐   the following physician, hospital storage bank, or other medical institution: _____

for   ☐   any purpose authorized by law
        ☐   therapy of another person
        ☐   medical education
        ☐   transplantation
        ☐   research
—I do not wish to make any anatomical gift from my body.

DURABLE POWER OF ATTORNEY FOR HEALTH CARE
I appoint as my proxy decision-maker(s):

_____
Name and address

and (*optional*)

_____
Name and Address

I direct my proxy to make health-care decisions based on his/her assessment of my personal wishes. If my personal desires are unknown, my proxy is to make health-care decisions based on his/her best guess as to my wishes. My proxy shall have the authority to make all health-care decisions for me, including decisions about life-sustaining treatment, if I am unable to make them myself. My proxy's authority becomes effective if my attending physician determines in writing that I lack the capacity to make or to communicate health-care decisions. My proxy is then to have the same authority to make health-care decisions as I would if I had the capacity to make them, EXCEPT (*list the limitations, if any, you wish to place on your proxy's authority*):

Should there be any disagreement between the wishes I have indicated in this document and the decisions favored by my above-named proxy, I wish my proxy to have authority over my written statements / I wish my written statements to bind my proxy. (*Please delete as necessary.*) If I have appointed more than one proxy and there is disagreement between their wishes, _____
shall have final authority.

Signed: _____
        Signature   Printed Name

_____
Address   Date

Figure 3   (cont.)

Witness: _____
        Signature   Printed Name

_____
        Address   Date

Witness: _____
        Signature   Printed Name

_____
        Address   Date

Physician (*optional*):

I am _____'s physician. I have seen this advance care document and have had an opportunity to discuss his/her preferences regarding medical interventions at the end of life. If _____ becomes incompetent, I understand that it is my duty to interpret and implement the preferences contained in this document in order to fulfill his/her wishes.

_____
        Signature   Printed Name

_____
        Address   Date

Figure 3   (cont.)

Trumping Advance Directives*

DAN W. BROCK

In the next article Dan Brock points out that advance directives will face practical difficulties when they are implemented. He argues that these directives do not reflect what patients really would want in many circumstances and have other limitations imposed by special, unforeseen circumstances and by third parties. He points to problems of vagueness, misunderstanding, limited knowledge, disagreements expressed by persons in positions of authority, questions about the authoritativeness of the decision made by the patient, and conflicts that occur with the interests of others. Brock argues that these problems present a sharp challenge for those who frame public policies that govern advance directives.

When, if ever, should a patient's advance directive not be followed? Since it is widely accepted that a competent patient's treatment choice must be respected, and an advance directive can reasonably be understood as the treatment choice of a patient while still competent, some believe that informed, voluntary advance directives should always be followed. However, there are several reasons for special doubts about whether an advance directive accurately reflects what the patient would have wanted.

Uncertainty as to how closely an advance directive reflects what a patient actually would want may arise from any of several sources. Advance directives typically require individuals to predict what they would want well in advance of the use of the directive in treatment decisionmaking, and so treatment choices in advance directives often inevitably are less well informed than competent patients' contemporaneous choices. For example, new, highly beneficial treatment may have been developed of which the patient was unaware; or if the directive is very old there may be evidence that the patient's wishes about treatment have changed. Also, advance directives must often be formulated without knowing what it will be like to experience the radically different conditions in which later treatment choices must be made. Further, advance directives are often formulated in somewhat vague or general terms, which inevitably leaves significant discretion in applying them to later treatment choices and, in turn, uncertainty about whether they have been correctly interpreted.

Moreover, when competent patients make choices that appear to be seriously in conflict with their well-being or settled preferences and values, these choices will typically be questioned, explored, and even opposed by their physicians, family members, and others who care for them to insure that the patients fully understand the nature and implications of their choices, and that the choices are what they "really" want. Directives executed by no longer competent patients obviously cannot be similarly clarified. Finally, advance directives are often framed with implicit as-

*Source: Brock, D. W., "Trumping Advance Directives," *Hastings Center Report,* September/October 1991, pp. S5–S6. Reproduced by permission. © The Hastings Center.

sumptions about the conditions in which the directive will be applied. For example, an advance directive declining CPR may be intended by the patient to apply to circumstances where her overall condition has so deteriorated that she is virtually certain not to survive the attempt. The patient may not have meant her directive to apply, however, should a cardiac arrest be caused by a medical procedure or in reaction to a drug, and in circumstances where CPR is highly likely to succeed and to leave the patient unimpaired.

In the second kind of case in which an advance directive might be trumped, what the individual executing the directive really wanted need not be in doubt. Instead, the issue is the moral authority of that individual's advance directive to determine the patient's treatment. That authority can be called into question when the directive appears to be seriously in conflict with important interests of the present patient or the patient has suffered such profound cognitive changes—for example, being now in a persistent vegetative state or severely demented—that there are doubts whether personal identity is maintained between the person who executed the advance directive and the present patient. The strongest cases of this sort for trumping advance directives will be when both these conditions obtain, with directives requesting either the forgoing of treatment or maximally aggressive treatment. For example, a person with some cognitive impairment from a stroke may have issued an advance directive that all life-sustaining treatments be forgone if he becomes significantly cognitively impaired. Though mentally handicapped, he is now otherwise healthy and with support leads a pleasant life. If he develops pneumonia that would be easily treatable with antibiotics, forgoing treatment appears contrary to his current interests.

The third general kind of case in which an advance directive might be trumped is when the interests of others warrant not honoring it, just as they can limit the decisionmaking authority of a competent patient. In the more common scenario of a directive refusing certain forms of care, only in a very few cases should the interests of others override the patient's advance directive. For example, in treating patients very near death physicians sometimes say that they are principally treating the family, not the patient. What is often meant is that the treatment being provided will have little effect one way or the other on the interests of the patient, who will die very soon whatever is done, but may have a great effect on the surviving family and how they are able to deal with the patient's dying and death. Stopping treatment might then be very briefly delayed to help the family accept the patient's death. In the case of an advance directive asking *for* particular treatments, limits on the authority of advance directives can apply: when the treatment requested will be funded by the resources of others and exceeds the just level of health care that should be provided from those sources, public procedures might justly deny that care. So too it may be ethical not to honor the patient's directive asking for treatment if doing so would seriously violate the moral or professional integrity of the treating physician; for example, if the patient's directive requests treatment that would now be certainly and completely futile. However, in many such conflicts transfer of the patient's care to others who can honor the advance directive is appropriate.

The issue for public policy, then, is what procedures should be required before an advance directive is set aside or overridden. Because of reasonable fears about abuse by physicians or family members of any authority not to honor advance directives, some believe they should always be binding. A better alternative, I think, is to develop institutional and judicial procedures and safeguards to reduce the risk of abuse to tolerable levels. These procedures might require going to court for some, or even nearly all cases, and consultation with ethics committees or other intra-institutional bodies in others. Though advance directives may not be ethically binding in all cases, they should be honored in the vast majority, and should only be set aside after careful consideration and by following procedures adequate to limit abuse.

DECISIONS ON BEHALF OF FORMERLY COMPETENT ADULTS

Cruzan v. Director, Missouri Department of Health*

UNITED STATES SUPREME COURT

In the following contribution, the U.S. Supreme Court affirms (5-4) a Missouri Supreme Court decision holding that an incompetent person does not have the same rights as a competent person to refuse life-sustaining technologies. The Court says a state is permitted but not required to recognize a family's decision making role. A state is also permitted to require "clear and convincing evidence" of patient preferences if third parties claim to represent the preferences of a patient regarding refusal of life-sustaining treatment. The majority insists that its findings rest on a judgment by society that it is better to err in preserving life in a vegetative state than to err through a decision that leads directly to death.

The concurring and dissenting opinions in the *Cruzan* case add additional perspectives on these issues. In a concurring opinion, Justice O'Connor limits her support. She notes that artificial modes of medical nutrition and hydration cannot be sharply distinguished from other types of medical treatments and that the court's decision in this case does not necessarily apply to cases in which a "patient's duly appointed surrogate" is refusing life-sustaining treatment. Justices Brennan, Marshall, and Blackmun then find that "Nancy Cruzan has a fundamental right to be free of unwanted artificial nutrition and hydration"—a direct challenge to the line of argument in the majority opinion.

ARGUED DECEMBER 6, 1989.
DECIDED JUNE 25, 1990.

OPINION OF THE COURT

Chief Justice **Rehnquist** delivered the opinion of the Court.

Petitioner Nancy Beth Cruzan was rendered incompetent as a result of severe injuries sustained during an automobile accident. Co-petitioners Lester and Joyce

*Source: From *United States* [*Supreme Court*] *Reports* 497 (1990), 261–357 (excerpts). Some footnotes and references omitted.

Cruzan, Nancy's parents and co-guardians, sought a court order directing the withdrawal of their daughter's artificial feeding and hydration equipment after it became apparent that she had virtually no chance of recovering her cognitive faculties. The Supreme Court of Missouri held that because there was no clear and convincing evidence of Nancy's desire to have life-sustaining treatment withdrawn under such circumstances, her parents lacked authority to effectuate such a request. . . .

She now lies in a Missouri state hospital in what is commonly referred to as a persistent vegetative state: generally, a condition in which a person exhibits motor reflexes but evinces no indications of significant cognitive function.[1] The State of Missouri is bearing the cost of her care.

After it had become apparent that Nancy Cruzan had virtually no chance of regaining her mental facilities her parents asked hospital employees to terminate the artificial nutrition and hydration procedures. All agree that such a removal would cause her death. The employees refused to honor the request without court approval. The parents then sought and received authorization from the state trial court for termination. The court found that a person in Nancy's condition had a fundamental right under the State and Federal Constitutions to refuse or direct the withdrawal of "death prolonging procedures." App to Pet for Cert A99. The court also found that Nancy's "expressed thoughts at age twenty-five in somewhat serious conversation with a housemate friend that if sick or injured she would not wish to continue her life unless she could live at least halfway normally suggest that given her present condition she would not wish to continue with her nutrition and hydration." Id., at A97–A98.

The Supreme Court of Missouri reversed by a divided vote. The court recognized a right to refuse treatment embodied in the common-law doctrine of informed consent, but expressed skepticism about the application of that doctrine in the circumstances of this case. Cruzan v Harmon, 760 SW2d 408, 416–417 (Mo 1988) (en banc). The court also declined to read a broad right of privacy into the State Constitution which would "support the right of a person to refuse medical treatment in every circumstance," and expressed doubt as to whether such a right existed under the United States Constitution. Id., at 417–418. It then decided that the Missouri Living Will statute, Mo Rev Stat § 459.010 et seq. (1986), embodied a state policy strongly favoring the preservation of life. 760 SW2d, at 419–420. The court found that Cruzan's statements to her roommate regarding her desire to live or die under certain conditions were "unreliable for the purpose of determining her intent," id., at 424, "and thus insufficient to support the co-guardians claim to exercise substituted judgment on Nancy's behalf." Id., at 426. It rejected the argument that Cruzan's parents were entitled to order the termination of her medical treatment, concluding that "no person can assume that choice for an incompetent in the absence of the formalities required under Missouri's Living Will statutes or the clear and convincing, inherently reliable evidence absent here." Id., at 425. The court also expressed its view that "[b]road policy questions bearing on life and death are more properly addressed by representative assemblies" than judicial bodies. Id., at 426. . . .

[The] notion of bodily integrity has been embodied in the requirement that informed consent is generally required for medical treatment. Justice Cardozo, while on the Court of Appeals of New York, aptly described this doctrine: "Every human being of adult years and sound mind has a right to determine what shall be done with his own body; and a surgeon who performs an operation without his patient's consent commits an assault, for which he is liable in damages." Schloendorff v Society of New York Hospital, 211 NY 125, 129–30, 105 NE 92, 93 (1914). The informed consent doctrine has become firmly entrenched in American tort law. . . .

The common-law doctrine of informed consent is viewed as generally encompassing the right of a competent individual to refuse medical treatment. Beyond that, [court] decisions demonstrate both similarity and diversity in their approach to decision of what all agree is a perplexing question with unusual strong moral and ethical overtones. State courts have available to them for decision a number of sources—state constitutions, statutes, and common law—which are not available to us. In this Court, the question is simply and starkly whether the United States Constitution prohibits Missouri from choosing the rule of decision which it did. This is the first case in which we have been squarely presented with the issue of whether the United States Constitution grants what is in common parlance referred to as a "right to die." . . .

The Fourteenth Amendment provides that no State shall "deprive any person of life, liberty, or property, without due process of law." The principle that a competent person has a constitutionally protected liberty interest in refusing unwanted medical treatment may be inferred from our prior decisions. . . .

But determining that a person has a "liberty interest" under the Due Process Clause does not end the inquiry; "whether respondent's constitutional rights have been violated must be determined by balancing his liberty interests against the relevant state interests." Youngberg v Romeo, 457 US 307, 321 (1982). See also Mills v Rogers, 457 US 291, 299 (1982).

Petitioners insist that under the general holdings of our cases, the forced administration of life-sustaining medical treatment, and even of artificially delivered food and water essential to life, would implicate a competent person's liberty interest. . . . The dramatic consequences involved in refusal of treatment would inform the inquiry as to whether the deprivation of the interest is constitutionally permissible. But for purposes of this case, we assume that the United States Constitution would grant a competent person a constitutionally protected right to refuse lifesaving hydration and nutrition.

Petitioners go on to assert that an incompetent person should possess the same right in this respect as is possessed by a competent person. . . .

The difficulty with petitioners' claim is that in a sense it begs the question: an incompetent person is not able to make an informed and voluntary choice to exercise a hypothetical right to refuse treatment or any other right. Such a "right" must be exercised for her, if at all, by some sort of surrogate. Here, Missouri has in effect recognized that under certain circumstances a surrogate may act for the patient in electing to have hydration and nutrition withdrawn in such a way as to cause death, but it has established a procedural safeguard to assure that the action of the surrogate conforms as best it may to the wishes expressed by the patient while competent. Missouri requires that evidence of the incompetent's wishes as to the withdrawal of treatment be proved by clear and convincing evidence. The question, then, is whether the United States Constitution forbids the establishment of this procedural requirement by the State. We hold that it does not.

Whether or not Missouri's clear and convincing evidence requirement comports with the United States Constitution depends in part on what interests the State may properly seek to protect in this situation. Missouri relies on its interest in the protection and preservation of human life, and there can be no gainsaying this interest. . . .

But in the context presented here, a State has more particular interests at stake. The choice between life and death is a deeply personal decision of obvious and overwhelming finality. We believe Missouri may legitimately seek to safeguard the personal element of this choice through the imposition of heightened evidentiary requirements. It cannot be disputed that the Due Process Clause protects an interest in life as well as an interest in refusing life-sustaining medical treatment. Not all incompetent patients will have loved ones available to serve as surrogate decision-makers. And even where family members are present "[t]here will, of course, be some unfortunate situations in which family members will not act to protect a patient." . . . Finally, we think a State may properly decline to make judgments about the "quality" of life that a particular individual may enjoy, and simply assert an unqualified interest in the preservation of human life to be weighed against the constitutionally protected interests of the individual.

In our view, Missouri has permissibly sought to advance these interests through the adoption of a "clear and convincing" standard of proof to govern such proceedings. "The function of a standard of proof, as that concept is embodied in the Due Process Clause and in the realm of factfinding, is to 'instruct the factfinder concerning the degree of confidence our society thinks he should have in the correctness of factual conclusions for a particular type of adjudication.'" . . .

There is no doubt that statutes requiring wills to be in writing, and statutes of frauds which require that a contract to make a will be in writing, on occasion frustrate the effectuation of the intent of a particular decedent, just as Missouri's requirement of proof in this case may have frustrated the effectuation of the not-fully-expressed desires of Nancy Cruzan. But the Constitution does not require general rules to work faultlessly; no general rule can. . . .

The Supreme Court of Missouri held that in this case the testimony adduced at trial did not amount to clear and convincing proof of the patient's desire to have hydration and nutrition withdrawn. In so doing, it reversed a decision of the Missouri trial court which had found that the evidence "suggest[ed]" Nancy Cruzan would not have desired to continue such measures, App to Pet for Cert A98, but which had not adopted the standard of "clear and convincing evidence" enunciated by the Supreme Court. The testimony adduced at trial consisted primarily of Nancy Cruzan's statements made to a housemate about a year before her accident that she would not want to live should she face life as a "vegetable," and other observations to the same effect. The observations did not deal in terms with withdrawal of medical treatment or of hydration and nutrition. We cannot say that the Supreme Court of Missouri committed constitutional error in reaching the conclusion that it did. . . .

No doubt is engendered by anything in this record but that Nancy Cruzan's mother and father are loving and caring parents. If the States were required by the United States Constitution to repose a right of "substituted judgment" with anyone, the Cruzans would surely qualify. But we do not think the Due Process Clause requires the State to repose judgment on these matters with anyone but the patient herself. Close family members may have a strong feeling—a feeling not at all ignoble or unworthy, but not entirely disinterested, either—that they do not wish to witness the continuation of the life of a loved one which they regard as hopeless, meaningless, and even degrading. But there is no automatic assurance that the view of close family members will necessarily be the same as the patient's would have been had she been confronted with the prospect of her situation while competent. All of the reasons previously discussed for allowing Missouri to require clear and convincing evidence of the patient's wishes lead us to conclude that the State may choose to defer only to those wishes, rather than confide the decision to close family members.

The judgment of the Supreme Court of Missouri is affirmed.

SEPARATE OPINIONS

Justice O'Connor, concurring.

[T]he Court does not today decide the issue whether a State must also give effect to the decisions of a surrogate decisionmaker. . . . In my view, such a duty may well be constitutionally required to protect the patient's liberty interest in refusing medical treatment. Few individuals provide explicit oral or written instructions regarding their intent to refuse medical treatment should they become incompetent.[1] States which decline to consider any evidence other than such instructions may frequently fail to honor a patient's intent. Such failures might be avoided if the State considered an equally probative source of evidence: the patient's appointment of a proxy to make health care decisions on her behalf. Delegating the authority to make medical decisions to a family member or friend is becoming a common method of planning for the future. . . .

Today's decision, holding only that the Constitution permits a State to require clear and convincing evidence of Nancy Cruzan's desire to have artificial hydration and nutrition withdrawn, does not preclude a future determination that the Constitution requires the States to implement the decisions of a patient's duly appointed surrogate. Nor does it prevent States from developing other approaches for protecting an incompetent individual's liberty interest in refusing medical treatment. As is evident from the Court's survey of state court decisions, . . . no national consensus has yet emerged on the best solution for this difficult and sensitive problem. Today we decide only that one State's practice does not violate the Constitution; the more challenging task of crafting appropriate procedures for safeguarding incompetents' liberty interests is entrusted to the "laboratory" of the States, New State Ice Co. v Liebmann, 285 US 262, 311 (1932) (Brandeis, J., dissenting), in the first instance. [For excerpts of Justice Scalia's concurring opinion see Chapter 5.]

Justice Brennan, with whom Justice Marshall and Justice Blackmun join, dissenting.

A grown woman at the time of the accident, Nancy had previously expressed her wish to forgo continuing medical care under circumstances such as these. Her family and her friends are convinced that this is what she would want. A guardian ad litem appointed by the trial court is also convinced that this is what Nancy would want. See 760 SW2d, at 444 (Higgins, J., dissenting from denial of rehearing). Yet the Missouri Supreme Court, alone among state courts deciding such a question, has determined that an irreversibly vegetative patient will remain a passive prisoner of medical technology—for Nancy, perhaps for the next 30 years. . . . Because I believe that Nancy Cruzan has a fundamental right to be free of unwanted artificial nutrition and hydration, which right is not outweighed by any interests of the State, and because I find that the improperly biased procedural obstacles imposed by the Missouri Supreme Court impermissibly burden that right, I respectfully dissent. Nancy Cruzan is entitled to choose to die with dignity. . . .

I

The starting point for our legal analysis must be whether a competent person has a constitutional right to avoid unwanted medical care. Earlier this Term, this Court held that the Due Process Clause of the Fourteenth Amendment confers a significant liberty interest in avoiding unwanted medical treatment. Washington v Harper, 108 L Ed 2d 178 (1990). Today, the Court concedes that our prior decisions "support the recognition of a general liberty interest in refusing medical treatment." The Court, however, avoids discussing either the measure of that liberty interest or its application by assuming, for purposes of this case only, that a competent person has a constitutionally protected liberty interest in being free of unwanted artificial nutrition and hydration. . . .

The right to be free from medical attention without consent, to determine what shall be done with one's own body, *is* deeply rooted in this Nation's traditions, as the majority acknowledges. . . . This right has long been "firmly entrenched in American tort law" and is securely grounded in the earliest common law. . . . " 'Anglo-American law starts with the premise of thoroughgoing self determination. It follows that each man is considered to be master of his own body, and he may, if he be of sound mind, expressly prohibit the performance of lifesaving surgery, or other medical treatment.' " Natanson v Kline, 186 Kan 393, 406–407, 350 P2d 1093, 1104 (1960). . . .

No material distinction can be drawn between the treatment to which Nancy Cruzan continues to be subject—artificial nutrition and hydration—and any other medical treatment. . . .

Artificial delivery of food and water is regarded as medical treatment by the medical profession and the Federal Government. According to the American Academy of Neurology, "[t]he artificial provision of nutrition and hydration is a form of medical treatment . . . analogous to other forms of life-sustaining treatment, such as the use of the respirator. When a patient is unconscious, both a respirator and an artificial feeding device serve to support or replace normal bodily functions that are compromised as a result of the patient's illness." . . .

II

A

The right to be free from unwanted medical attention is a right to evaluate the potential benefit of treatment and its possible consequences according to one's own values and to make a personal decision whether to subject oneself to the intrusion. For a patient like Nancy Cruzan, the sole benefit of medical treatment is being kept metabolically alive. . . .

There are also affirmative reasons why someone like Nancy might choose to forgo artificial nutrition and hydration under these circumstances. Dying is personal. And it is profound. For many, the thought of an ignoble end, steeped in decay, is abhorrent. A quiet, proud death, bodily integrity intact, is a matter of extreme consequence. "In certain, thankfully rare, circumstances the burden of maintaining the corporeal existence degrades the very humanity it was meant to serve." Brophy v New England Sinai Hospital, Inc. 398 Mass 417, 434, 497 NE2d 626, 635–636 (1986). . . .

Such conditions are, for many, humiliating to contemplate, as is visiting a prolonged and anguished vigil on one's parents, spouse, and children. A long, drawn-out death can have a debilitating effect on family members. . . .

B

Although the right to be free of unwanted medical intervention, like other constitutionally protected interests, may not be absolute, no State interest could outweigh the rights of an individual in Nancy Cruzan's position. Whatever a State's possible interests in mandating life-support treatment under other circumstances, there is no good to be obtained here by Missouri's insistence that Nancy Cruzan remain on life-support systems if it is indeed her wish not to do so. Missouri does not claim, nor could it, that society as a whole will be benefited by Nancy's receiving medical treatment. No third party's situation will be improved and no harm to others will be averted. Cf. nn 6 and 8, supra.

The only state interest asserted here is a general interest in the preservation of life. But the State has no legitimate general interest in someone's life, completely abstracted from the interest of the person living that life, that could outweigh the person's choice to avoid medical treatment. . . . Thus, the State's general interest in life must accede to Nancy Cruzan's particularized and intense interest in self-determination in her choice of medical treatment. There is simply nothing legitimately within the State's purview to be gained by superseding her decision.

Moreover, there may be considerable danger that Missouri's rule of decision would impair rather than serve any interest the State does have in sustaining life. Current medical practice recommends use of heroic measures if there is a scintilla of a chance that the patient will recover, on the assumption that the measures will be discontinued should the patient improve. When the President's Commission in 1982 approved the withdrawal of life support equipment from irreversibly vegetative patients, it explained that "[a]n even more troubling wrong occurs when a treatment that might save life or improve health is not started because the health care personnel are afraid that they will find it very difficult to stop the treatment if, as is fairly likely, it proves to be of little benefit and greatly burdens the patient." President's Commission 75. . . .

III

Missouri may constitutionally impose only those procedural requirements that serve to enhance the accuracy of a determination of Nancy Cruzan's wishes or are at least consistent with an accurate determination. The Missouri "safeguard" that the Court upholds today does not meet that standard. The determination needed in this context is whether the incompetent person would choose to live in a persistent vegetative state on life-support or to avoid this medical treatment. Missouri's rule of decision imposes a markedly asymmetrical evidentiary burden. Only evidence of specific statements of treatment choice made by the patient when competent is admissible to support a finding that the patient, now in a persistent vegetative state, would wish to avoid further medical treatment. Moreover, this evidence must be clear and convincing. No proof is required to support a finding that the incompetent person would wish to continue treatment. . . .

Even more than its heightened evidentiary standard, the Missouri court's categorical exclusion of relevant evidence dispenses with any semblance of accurate factfinding. The court adverted to no evidence supporting its decision, but held that no clear and convincing, inherently reliable evidence had been presented to show that Nancy would want to avoid further treatment. In doing so, the court failed to consider statements Nancy had made to family members and a close friend. The court also failed to consider testimony from Nancy's mother and sister that they were certain that Nancy would want to discontinue artificial nutrition and hydration, even after the court found that Nancy's family was loving and without malignant motive. See 760 SW2d, at 412. The court also failed to consider the conclusions of the guardian ad litem, appointed by the trial court, that there was clear and convincing evidence that Nancy would want to discontinue medical treatment and that this was in her best interests. Id., at 444 (Higgins, J., dissenting from denial of rehearing); Brief for Respondent Guardian Ad Litem 2–3. The court did not specifically define what kind of evidence it would consider clear and convincing, but its general discussion suggests that only a living will or equivalently formal directive from the patient when competent would meet this standard. See 760 SW2d, at 424–425. . . .

The Missouri court's disdain for Nancy's statements in serious conversations not long before her accident, for the opinions of Nancy's family and friends as to her values, beliefs and certain choice, and even for the opinion of an outside objective factfinder appointed by the State evinces a disdain for Nancy Cruzan's own right to choose. The rules by which an incompetent person's wishes are determined must represent every effort to determine those wishes. The rule that the Missouri court adopted and that this Court upholds, however, skews the result away from a determination that as accurately as possible reflects the individual's own preferences and beliefs. It is a rule that transforms human beings into passive subjects of medical technology. . . .

That Missouri and this Court may truly be motivated only by concern for incompetent patients makes no matter. As one of our most prominent jurists warned us decades ago: "Experience should teach us to be most on our guard to protect liberty when the government's purposes are beneficient. . . . The greatest dangers to liberty lurk in insidious encroachment by men of zeal, well meaning but without understanding." Olmstead v United States, 277 US 438, 479 (1928) (Brandeis, J., dissenting).

I respectfully dissent.

NOTE

1. See 2 President's Commission for the Study of Ethical Problems in Medicine and Biomedical and Behavioral Research, Making Health Care Decisions 241–242 (1982) (36% of those surveyed gave instructions regarding how they would like to be treated if they ever became too sick to make decisions: 23% put those instructions in writing) (Lou Harris Poll, September 1982); American Medical Association Surveys of Physicians and Public Opinion on Health Care Issues 29–30 (1988) (56% of those surveyed had told family members their wishes concerning the use of life-sustaining treatment if they entered an irreversible coma; 15% had filled out a living will specifying those wishes).

Life and Death Choices
After *Cruzan**

LARRY GOSTIN

In the following article, Lawrence Gostin argues that the state has no bona fide interests in preserving the life of a PVS patient and that all of the burden must be borne by the family. Gostin would have us focus more on whether an abuse is occurring by a family's decisions than on whether the patient has stated some prior preference about treatments of this type. Gostin believes the Court's opinion does little to protect the interests of these patients, while doing much to harm those interests. He finds the "clear and convincing evidence" criterion far too strenuous. His only apparent sympathy with the Court is found in his partial agreement with the opinion of Justice O'Connor. Gostin then lays out a series of alternatives that could displace the ruling in *Cruzan* as better public policy.

The state interests used by the court to justify denial of Nancy Cruzan's right to decline artificial feeding are hardly persuasive. The state interest in preserving the life of a person in PVS is purely theoretical. The state's authority to preserve "life" has become a magical concept, often driven by blind ideology rather than by any thoughtful appreciation of the unique characteristics of human life. When an individual has no meaningful interaction with her environment, no recognition of familiar persons or objects, nor any human feelings or experience of any kind, the state's interest in life is a mere abstraction.

To assert an interest in the outcome of a decision to abate life-sustaining treatment requires some demonstrable burden. All of the burden is borne by the family who suffers from the refusal of the law to allow a decision to dignify a natural death process. Whether the burden of continued life is measured by emotional suffering, by economic cost,[1] or by any other standard, it is not society, the medical profession, or the state that has to pay the cost. The family must live with the consequences.

The right of a person in PVS to be allowed to die is now well grounded in biomedical ethics. What greater purpose could a moral right to liberty—or a constitutional right to privacy—achieve than to reject unwarranted state intrusion into such an intimate moment as death? The essence of the right to liberty (or privacy) is that the decision is deeply personal and critically important in the ordering of a patient's life. It is a decision which uniquely involves the individual, and in which the outcome matters little to third parties—no one else is harmed by the decision, affected by it, or is properly interested. A family's decision to abate treatment of a loved one in PVS is supremely a private decision.

*Source: Gostin, L. "Life and Death Choices After *Cruzan*," *Law, Medicine & Health Care*, 19, nos. 1–2 (1991): 9–12. Reprinted with the permission of the American Society of Law, Medicine & Ethics and Professor Gostin.

No one doubts the validity of the state interests in preventing abuse by a surrogate and in ensuring accurate fact finding. But these interests are not reasonably achieved by requiring clear and convincing evidence of the incompetent patient's prior wishes. Some review process, perhaps by a hospital ethics committee, to ensure that the diagnosis of PVS is reliable and that the family is properly motivated may be appropriate. The state can reasonably ensure that surrogates do not abuse their authority, not by removing their power of substitute judgment as occurred in *Cruzan,* but by ensuring that they are not unduly motivated by economic or other personal benefit.

Nor does a clear and convincing standard best ensure accurate fact finding. Justice Brennan's dissent in *Cruzan* explains the markedly asymmetrical evidentiary burden of the Missouri rule. All of the burden rests on the incompetent patient and her family to prove unequivocally that she would not want to be treated. The proxy must adduce specific statements by the patient that foresaw the precise technological shackles she now endures. The state, on the other hand, need not submit any proof to support a finding that the patient would want to continue treatment.

The fact is that the Supreme Court has removed an entire class of people from the protection of the federal constitution. The Court accepted a high evidentiary standard that only a few previously foresighted nonautonomous patients will be able to meet. The *Cruzan* opinion does not constitutionally protect the never-autonomous (e.g., the severely mentally retarded and young children who cannot express any view); the once-autonomous who failed to express a view about their future treatment; and the once-autonomous who expressed views insufficiently exact to meet the rigorous clear and convincing evidence standard. . . .

The *Cruzan* decision shows how far out of touch the Supreme Court has become with regard to how people think and behave. The overwhelming majority of people do not anticipate the circumstances of their death with the exactness required under a clear and convincing evidence standard and do not plan their lives by creating formal legal instruments.[2] Even if a person dwells on the remote possibility of loss of cognition, she may not marshal the formal evidence of her preferences or may not be sufficiently precise in enunciating the exact medical circumstances under which treatment should be abated.[3] When a person tells a family member or close friend that she does not want her life sustained artificially, she is "express[ing] her wishes in the only terms familiar to her, and . . . as clearly as a lay person should be asked to express them."[4]

What is more important, the Court creates a presumption that a person would want technological support to sustain an unconscious, non-purposeful life. Exactly the opposite presumption is warranted. When asked, very few people would choose to be kept physically alive when all conscious life is over.

Finally, the Court reasons that since *some* family members are improperly motivated, *all* family members may be precluded from making substitute decisions in the absence of a durable power or other legally sufficient evidence of intent. Again, most people prefer close relatives or friends who know them well to make proxy decisions. Patients certainly do not wish to have their family's hands tied because they neglected to execute the proper legal instrument.

The insistence on "clear and convincing evidence" imposes a particular burden on persons without sufficient education or means. Legal formalities in drafting adequate advance directives or complying with statutory requirements can be complicated and vary from state to state. Those who are poor, illiterate, or have inadequate access to legal or other advice simply will be foreclosed from exercising their rights. . . .

One obvious method of ensuring that a person's wishes are respected after *Cruzan* is to provide assistance in complying with state evidentiary requirements in writing a power of attorney and/or an advance directive. State agencies could publish and distribute simple advance directive forms. Alternatively, states could fund charitable or community organizations to provide forms and advice in completing them. . . .

Some states may still fail to recognize the constitutional importance of advance directives. We can expect to see future federal court cases under the constitutional theory that durable powers of attorney have binding force even in restrictive states like Missouri. Justice O'Connor's concurrence opens the door to the argument that durable powers give patients a constitutional right to have the decisions of their proxies respected.

While states should make every effort to encourage persons to prepare advance directives, the greater challenge is to devise legal mechanisms to respect patient choices with a minimum of legal formality. State legislatures have a number of policy options. First, the state could establish a low threshold of proof. A person's desire to have treatment abated could be demonstrated by a preponderance of evidence (i.e., the balance of evidence)—not merely by legal instrument, but by informal communication. . . .

Second, states could create a presumption favoring substitute decisions by family members. By relying primarily on family evaluation of a patient's statements and values, states could at once avoid the burden of a lengthy process of judicial review, and designate the proxy decision-maker most likely to be intimately familiar with the patient. Only in cases where the family has a conflict of interest or is divided itself would an alternative process of evaluation be necessary. . . .

Third, states could enact laws which require health care facilities to inform patients of the right to make an advance directive and to record their treatment preferences. Reasonable opportunities for persons to reflect on treatment alternatives arise when they are admitted to a hospital, nursing home, or hospice, or even when they apply for health insurance, Medicaid, or Medicare. . . .

The federal Patient Self-Determination Act, enacted within the Omnibus Budget Reconciliation Act of 1990, provides a good illustration of a "routine offering" requirement.[5] The Act requires health care providers, as a condition of the receipt of Medicare or Medicaid dollars, to provide written information at the time of admission about the patient's rights under state law to accept or refuse medical treatment and to formulate advance directives. Health care providers will be responsible for documenting in each person's medical record whether she has executed an advance directive. States are required to develop a written description of state law on advance directives, and health care providers must undertake public education programs for staff and the community on the subject of advance directives.

A wide chasm exists between people's desires to express their wishes and their failure to draft written advance directives.6 The most probable reason is that people are simply not asked. "Routine offering" statutes will ensure that, long after *Cruzan* has been forgotten by most citizens, patients will be informed of their rights and provided assistance in exercising them.

Experience dictates that even considerable efforts to encourage patients to plan for their deaths are not always successful. . . . In the absence of known preferences, the state should assume that individuals would wish to be treated in their best interests and would trust their families to make decisions on their behalf. Decisions to abate treatment, therefore, could be made by loved ones in the cases in which this would best serve the patient's interests.

Life and death choices across the country could sink to such a low level that people would be required to deliberatively marshall their legal evidence in the fear that their government will fail to respect their wishes and privacy with regard to medical treatments. Alternatively, states can enact creative laws to encourage meaningful dialogue with family and physicians on final care, assist people in making clear and simple statements of their preferences, and adopt legal presumptions about the closeness of family life which best reflect the value systems and behavior of most Americans.

NOTES

1. The Supreme Court, however, was careful to observe that in Nancy Cruzan's case the state was paying for the costs of her continued treatment. The Court did not indicate, however, that it would have altered its decisions if the family were bearing the financial burden.
2. S.V. McCrary and J.R. Botkin, "Hospital Policy on Advance Directives," *Journal of the American Medical Association* 1989, 262:2411–14; L. Emanuel and E. Emanuel, "The Medical Directive: A New Comprehensive Advance Care Document," *Journal of the American Medical Association* 1989, 261:3288.
3. Cruzan v. Director, Missouri Department of Health, 110 S.Ct. 2841 (1990).
4. In re O'Connor, 72 N.Y.2d 517, 551 (1988) (Simons J, dissenting).
5. The implementation date of the Act is December 1, 1991.
6. J.C. Danforth, "Opening Statement to Subcommittee on Medicare and Long-term Care of the Committee on Finance Hearing on the Patient Self-Determination Act," July 20, 1990.

Cruzan: No Rights Violated*

JOHN A. ROBERTSON

In the next article, John Robertson argues that the Supreme Court's decision violates no constitutional right of Nancy Cruzan or of her family, because the protected liberty interest in refusing medical treatment can only be exercised by competent patients, not by either incompetent patients or surrogates. Robertson even argues that sustaining PVS patients never harms them because they do not "have interests that can be harmed." Certainly, he says, Cruzan's right to refuse treatment is not being denied, because she has not refused treatment. Robertson fully agrees with the Court that a state can maintain strict standards of the sort Missouri envisages and that, in any event, states should have wide discretion in setting these standards.

Cruzan was correctly decided. Not because persons in persistent vegetative state should be sustained indefinitely, but because sustaining them does not violate their own or their family's constitutional rights.

Gastrostomy feeding of Nancy Cruzan does not harm her. A permanently vegetative patient does not have interests that can be harmed. Even critics of the decision agree that she does not feel pain and is unaware of her situation. Thus she cannot be harmed by medical treatment. The state is not violating her right to refuse treatment because, in her present condition, she has not refused treatment. Indeed, she is incapable of refusing.

Nor does treatment violate a right to decline treatment in advance. If such a right exists, it is a right to choose—to direct—that treatment not occur. A state could violate such a right only if the person when competent had clearly directed that no treatment occur. Surmising that the person probably would have refused, or that nontreatment is consistent with her previous values does not itself establish a violation of the right to decide in advance. Inferences that the patient would have issued such a directive are not evidence that the directive was issued. To trump a state law mandating treatment, the patient must have in fact issued a directive against treatment.

The nub of *Cruzan* is this: May the state require that the past directive be clearly established if treatment is to be withheld on the basis of that directive? The Supreme Court correctly says yes. Surely a state may require reliable evidence that a past directive was knowingly made. Requiring that it be written or otherwise explicitly made is not an undue burden on persons who wish to issue directives against medical care when incompetent.

What if clear evidence of a past directive is lacking (as often occurs)? Treatment in that case does not violate a right to direct future care, for there is no evidence that the patient so directed. Nor does it violate a present right to refuse treatment when

*Source: Robertson, J. A., "*Cruzan*: No Rights Violated," *Hastings Center Report* 20 (September/October 1990), pp. 8–9. Reproduced by permission. © The Hastings Center.

the patient lacks the capacity to refuse. Since the patient is comatose treatment would not violate any other constitutional interest.

One could argue that an incompetent patient has a right to have a proxy decide for the patient on the basis of her previous values. But that claim cannot be based on the comatose patient's current interests (there are none), nor on a past exercise of autonomy, for no directive against treatment has been issued. Surely there is no constitutional right to be treated "like one once was" now that one is so radically different.

The claim in *Cruzan* thus becomes the family's right to decide the matter because of the impact of continued treatment on their own, not Nancy's interests. Does family privacy, recognized by the Court to include decisions about having children and how they are reared, include the right to terminate medical treatment that is not harming (or helping) their daughter? Parents have never had the right to deny their children medical care that the state deems necessary. For example, parents are free to terminate their custody of handicapped newborns but not necessarily to terminate treatment. The Supreme Court should not expand family privacy when harm to the comatose ward from the disputed treatment does not exist.

Critics of *Cruzan* ignore these important distinctions, and fallaciously conclude that an undesirable state policy is necessarily unconstitutional. Treating Nancy over her parents' objections may be unwise, but it does not follow that anyone's constitutional rights are thereby violated.

In some respects, however, *Cruzan* is a significant victory for a constitutional "right to die." The competent patient's right to refuse treatment has been explicitly recognized (though called a liberty interest rather than a fundamental right). Logical development of this interest could extend beyond refusing medical treatment to suicide, assisted suicide, and consensual active euthanasia. The right to be free of state mandated medical intrusions could be taken to require that a competent person also be free of state interference with his or her other efforts to end the bodily burdens of disease.

The Court also seems prepared to accept a right to make explicit directives concerning treatment when incompetent. Such an extension, however, does not necessarily follow. The interest in being free of present bodily burdens that underlies the right to refuse treatment does not exist when one is issuing a directive about a hypothetical future state in which one's interests will be drastically altered from how they appear to the now competent person. There are no bodily burdens being imposed at the time the directive is issued. There may be none when the directive would take effect.

Moreover, recognizing a constitutional right to make binding directives against medical treatment would logically lead to constitutionalizing a whole range of prior directives, from living wills and testamentary dispositions to surrogate mother contracts and agreements to dispose of frozen embryos. If autonomy gives the right to refuse treatment in advance, why should it not give the right to consent to termination of child custody or abortion in advance as well? The fact that the person is competent when these future situations occur should not matter—it is the prior exercise of autonomy that is the claimed right. Indeed, since other persons will have relied on prior reproductive directives, the case for enforcing them is even stronger.

The Court in *Cruzan* rightfully leaves states wide discretion to resolve difficult questions of life and death decisionmaking. Missouri, like most other states, *should* permit the family to stop Nancy's treatment and their own ordeal. But Missouri violates no constitutional rights in choosing otherwise.

SUGGESTED READINGS FOR CHAPTER 6

A. DECISIONS BY COMPETENT ADULTS

1. Bouvia

ANNAS, GEORGE J. "Elizabeth Bouvia: Whose Space Is This Anyway?" *Hastings Center Report* 16(2, Apr. 1986):24–25.

BAYLEY, CORRINE. "The Case of Elizabeth Bouvia: A Strain on Our Ethical Reasoning." *Health Progress* 67(6, July–Aug. 1986):40–47, 86.

Bouvia v. County of Riverside, No. 159780 (Cal. Super. Ct. Dec. 16, 1983).

Bouvia v. Superior Court (Glenchur). California Reporter. Apr 16, 1986 (date of decision); 225, 297–308.

Elizabeth Bouvia vs. County of Riverside In the Superior Court of the State of California in and for the County of Riverside. "Reporter's Transcript of Proceedings," December 16, 1983.

GOODMAN, WALTER. "Quadriplegic's Efforts to Die Stir Deep Legal and Ethical Issues." *New York Times* Jan 3, 1984; p. A16.

HERR, STANLEY S., BARRY A. BOSTROM, AND REBECCA S. BARTON. "No Place to Go: Refusal of Life-Sustaining Treatment by Competent Persons with Physical Disabilities." *Issues in Law and Medicine* 8(1, Summer 1992):3–36.

KANE, FRANCIS I. "What Nurses Profess: The Elizabeth Bouvia Case." *Health Progress* 1985 July–Aug; 66(6):52–54, 68.

STEINBROOK, ROBERT, AND BERNARD LO. "The Case of Elizabeth Bouvia: Starvation, Suicide, or Problem Patient?" *Archives of Internal Medicine* 146 (1986): 161–164.

2. McAfee

ANDERSON, CHARLES EDWARD. "The Right to Choose Death." *ABA Journal* 75 (Dec., 1989):18.

ANONYMOUS. "Georgia Man Asks to Turn Off Life-Supporting Ventilator." *Origins* 19(17, Sept. 28, 1989):273, 275–279.

BOURKE, LEON H. "State of Georgia v. McAfee. [Note]." *Issues in Law and Medicine* 6(1, Summer 1990):77.

HERR, STANLEY S., BARRY A. BOSTROM, AND REBECCA S. BARTON. "No Place to Go: Refusal of Life-Sustaining Treatment by Competent Persons with Physical Disabilities." *Issues in Law and Medicine* 8(1, Summer 1992):3–36.

3. Criteria for Forgoing Treatment (Ordinary Means)

American Thoracic Society. "Withholding and Withdrawing Life-Sustaining Therapy." *Annals of Internal Medicine* 115(6, Sept. 15, 1991):478–485.

CALLAHAN, DANIEL. "When Self-Determination Runs Amok." *Hastings Center Report* 22(2, Mar.–Apr. 1992):52–55.

CALLAHAN, DANIEL. *The Troubled Dream of Life: Living with Mortality.* New York: Simon and Schuster, 1993.

EMANUEL, EZEKIEL J. *The Ends of Human Life: Medical Ethics in a Liberal Polity.* Cambridge, MA: Harvard University Press, 1991.

FEINBERG, JOEL. "Voluntary Euthanasia and the Inalienable Right to Life." *Philosophy and Public Affairs* 7 (Winter 1978):93–123.

KAMISAR, YALE. "When Is There a Constitutional Right to Die? When Is There *No* Constitutional Right to Live?" *Georgia Law Review* 25(5, Summer 1991): 1203–1242.

McCARTNEY, JAMES J. "The Development of the Doctrine of Ordinary and Extraordinary Means of Preserving Life in Catholic Moral Theology Before the Karen Quinlan Case." *Linacre Quarterly* 47 (1980):215–224.

McCORMICK, RICHARD A., AND ROBERT M. VEATCH. "The Preservation of Life and Self-Determination." *Theological Studies* 41 (June 1980):390–396.

National Center for the State Courts [and] Coordinating Council on Life-Sustaining Medical Treatment Decision Making by the Courts (Thomas Hafemeister, Project Director). *Guidelines for State Court Decision Making in Authorizing or Withholding Life-Sustaining Medical Treatment.* Williamsburg, VA: National Center for State Courts, 1991.

ROBERTSON, JOHN A. "Assessing Quality of Life: A Response to Professor Kamisar." *Georgia Law Review* 25(5, Summer 1991):1243–1252.

VEATCH, ROBERT M. "An Ethical Framework for Terminal Care Decisions: A New Classification of Patients." *Journal of the American Geriatrics Society* 32 (September 1984):665–669.

WEIR, ROBERT F. *Abating Treatment with Critically Ill Patients: Ethical and Legal Limits to the Medical Prolongation of Life.* New York: Oxford University Press, 1989.

4. Advance Directives

Advance Directives Seminar Group. "Advance Directives: Are They an Advance?" *Canadian Medical Association Journal* 146 (January 15, 1992): 127–134.

CANTOR, NORMAN L. "My Annotated Living Will." *Law, Medicine & Health Care* 18 (Spring-Summer 1990):114–122.

CANTOR, NORMAN L. *Advance Directives and the Pursuit of Death with Dignity.* Bloomington, IN: Indiana University Press, 1993.

CANTOR, NORMAN L. *Legal Frontiers of Death and Dying.* Bloomington, IN: Indiana University Press, 1987.

DAVIDSON, KENT W., CHRIS HACKLER, DELBRA CARADINE et al. "Physicians' Attitudes on Advance Directives." *Journal of the American Medical Association* 262(17, Nov. 3, 1989):2415–2419.

DOUKAS, DAVID J., AND LAURENCE B. McCULLOUGH. "The Values History: The Evaluation of the Patient's Values and Advance Directives." *Journal of Family Practice* 32(2, 1991):145–153.

EMANUEL, EZEKIEL J., AND LINDA L. EMANUEL. "Living Wills: Past, Present, and Future." *Journal of Clinical Ethics* 1(1, 1991):9–19.

GAMBLE, E. R., et al. "Knowledge, Attitudes, and Behavior of Elderly Persons Regarding Living Wills." *Archives of Internal Medicine* 151 (1991):277–280.

KIELSTEIN, RITA, AND HANS-MARTIN SASS. "Using Stories to Assess Values and Establish Medical Directives." *Kennedy Institute of Ethics Journal* 3 (Sept. 1993):303–318.

KING, NANCY. *Making Sense of Advance Directives.* Dordrecht, the Netherlands: Kluwer Academic Publishers, 1991.

New York State Task Force on Life and the Law. *Life-Sustaining Treatment: Making Decisions and Appointing a Health Care Agent.* New York: New York State Task Force, 1987.

OLICK, ROBERT. "Approximating Informed Consent and Fostering Communication: The Anatomy of an Advance Directive." *Journal of Clinical Ethics* 2 (1991): 181–195.

Society for the Right to Die. *Refusal of Treatment Legislation, 1991: A State by State Compilation of Enacted and Model Statutes.* [Looseleaf binder]. New York: The Society, Mar. 1, 1991.

5. Vegetative State

American Neurological Association. Committee on Ethical Affairs. "Persistent Vegetative State: Report." *Annals of Neurology* 33(4, Apr. 1993):386–390.

BRODY, BARUCH A. "Special Ethical Issues in the Management of PVS Patients." *Law, Medicine and Health Care* 20(1–2, Spring–Summer 1992):104–115.

WILDES, KEVIN WM. "Life as a Good and Our Obligations to Persistently Vegetative Patients." In Wildes, et al. (eds.). *Birth, Suffering, and Death: Catholic Perspectives at the Edges of Life.* Boston: Kluwer Academic, 1992, pp. 145–154.

6. Reviews and Compilations of Laws Pertaining to Competent Patient Decision Making

Choice in Dying, Inc. *Right to Die Law Digest Statutes.* New York: Choice in Dying, Inc., ND.

KUTNER, LUIS. "Due Process of Euthanasia: The Living Will, a Proposal." *Indiana Law Journal* 44 (1969):539–554.

B. DECISIONS ON BEHALF OF FORMERLY COMPETENT ADULTS

1. Brophy

ANNAS, GEORGE J. "Do Feeding Tubes Have More Rights Than Patients?" *Hastings Center Report* 16(1, Feb. 1986):26–28.

ANONYMOUS. "Brophy v. New England Sinai Hospital, Inc.: Brief Amicus Curiae, Society for the Right to Die, Inc. on Behalf of Appellant." *Journal of the American Geriatrics Society* 35(7, July 1987):669–678.

BERESFORD, H. RICHARD. "The Brophy Case: Whose Life Is It?" *Neurology* 37(8, 1987): 1357–1358.

BOYLE, PHILIP, LARRY KING, AND KEVIN O'ROURKE. "The Brophy Case: The Use of Artificial Hydration and Nutrition." *Linacre Quarterly* 54 (1987, May):63–72.

CRANFORD, RONALD E. "Brophy and Heresford: More Questions Than Answers." *Neurology* 37(8, 1987):1359–1360.

DRINAN, ROBERT F. "Should Paul Brophy Have Been Allowed to Die?" *America* 155(15, Nov. 22, 1986):324–325, 332.

NIMZ, MARY M. "Brophy v. New England Sinai Hospital. [Note]." *Issues in Law and Medicine* 2(3, Nov. 1986):221–234.

PARIS, JOHN J. "When Burdens of Feeding Outweigh Benefits." *Hastings Center Report* 16(1, Feb. 1986):30–32.

ROTHENBERG, LESLIE STEVEN. "The Dissenting Opinions: Biting the Hands That Won't Feed." *Health Progress* 67(10, Dec. 1986):38–45, 99.

2. Cruzan (See bibliography in Chapter 5, B. 1.)

3. Substituted Judgment and the Theory of Deciding for Formerly Competent Patients

BUCHANAN, ALLEN E., AND DAN W. BROCK. *Deciding for Others: The Ethics of Surrogate Decision Making.* Cambridge, MA: Cambridge University Press, 1989.

FORTE, DAVID F. "The Role of the Clear and Convincing Standard of Proof in Right to Die Cases." *Issues in Law and Medicine* 8(2, Fall 1992):183–203.

PEARLMAN, ROBERT A., RICHARD F. UHLMANN, AND NANCY S. JECKER. "Spousal Understanding of Patient Quality of Life: Implications for Surrogate Decisions." *Journal of Clinical Ethics* 3(2, Summer 1992):114–121.

SECKLER, ALLISON B., DIANE E. MEIER, MICHAEL MULVIHILL, AND PARIS, BARBARA E. CAMMER. "Substituted Judgment: How Accurate Are Proxy Predictions?" *Annals of Internal Medicine* 115 (July 15, 1991):92–98.

4. Do-Not-Resuscitate Decisions

BEDELL, SUSANNA E., AND THOMAS L. DELBANCO. "Choices About Cardiopulmonary Resuscitation in the Hospital: When Do Physicians Talk with Patients?" *New England Journal of Medicine* 310(17, Apr. 26, 1984):1089–1093.

BEDELL, SUSANNA E., DENISE PELLE, PATRICIA L. MAHER, AND PAUL D. CLEARY. "Do-Not-Resuscitate Orders for Critically Ill Patients in the Hospital: How Are They Used and What Is Their Impact?" *Journal of the American Medical Association* 256(2, July 11, 1986):233–237.

Clinical Care Committee of the Massachusetts General Hospital. "Optimum Care for Hopelessly Ill Patients." *New England Journal of Medicine* 295 (August 12, 1976): 362–364.

KELLERMANN, ARTHUR L., BELA B. HACKMAN, AND GRANT SOMES. "Predicting the Outcome of Unsuccessful Prehospital Advanced Cardiac Life Support." *Journal of the American Medical Association* 270(12, 1993):1433–1436.

SULMASY, DANIEL P., GAIL GELLER, RUTH FADEN, AND DAVID M. LEVINE. "The Quality of Mercy: Caring for Patients With 'Do Not Resuscitate' Orders." *Journal of the American Medical Association* 267(5, Feb. 5, 1992):682–686.

YOUNGNER, STUART J. "Do-Not-Resuscitate Orders: No Longer Secret, But Still a Problem." *Hastings Center Report* February 17(1, 1987):24–33.

BIBLIOGRAPHICAL SOURCES AND REFERENCE WORKS

REICH, WARREN (ed.). *Encyclopedia of Bioethics.* New York: Macmillan, 1995, articles on:

Competency
Informed Consent
Paternalism
Patients' Rights

7

Decisions to Forgo Treatment Involving Never-Competent Persons

INTRODUCTION

In the previous chapter we considered the conditions under which it is permissible to forgo treatment for now-competent and once-competent patients. In this chapter similar questions are asked about never-competent patients. This group of patients includes infants, young children, and persons who have throughout their lives had a seriously disabling mental disorder. Once-competent patients who have left no indication of their preferences often must be treated in circumstances of medical decision making as if they were never competent.

DECISIONS ON BEHALF OF CHILDREN

Prenatal obstetric management and neonatal intensive care can now salvage the lives of many anomalous fetuses and disabled newborns with physical conditions that would have been fatal only two decades ago. However, the resultant quality of life is sometimes so low that questions arise about whether the aggressive obstetric management or intensive care has produced more harm than benefit for the patient. For example, infants with severe congenital abnormalities or low birth weights are sometimes treated at a large financial expense, despite a poor prognosis for survival. If they do survive, it may only be with severe disabilities or a profoundly impaired quality of life. These problems for the patient—and related problems for the family, health professionals, and society—have led some to conclude that the omission of treatment for never-competent patients is ethically acceptable under some conditions.

Three competing approaches have been formulated to address these problems. The first is that every person with a life-threatening condition should receive all treatments necessary to save the person's life whenever it is possible to save the life. Treatment should be as aggressive as necessary, and both allowing to die and killing a rescuable person are deemed morally wrong. The primary justifications for this position are, negatively, that no one should be authorized to make life-and-death decisions on behalf of never-competent individuals and, positively, that every patient, regardless of his or her physical or mental condition, has a right to life.

A second approach is that life-and-death decisions should be made entirely on the basis of the patient's best interests. Treatment should be limited only if it does nothing to promote the patient's interests—including cases in which sustained suffering or a drastically diminished quality of life would make existence a burden to the person. Here "best interests" is to be judged by the best estimate of what reasonable persons would consider the highest net benefit for the patient among the available options. These quality-of-life judgments need to be governed by justifiable criteria of benefits and burdens, so that quality of life is not reduced to arbitrary and partial judgments of personal preference or of the social worth of a person.

A third approach allows decisions concerning treatment to be determined, or at least strongly influenced, by familial burdens and broader social considerations. If, say, an infant's continued existence would be likely to undermine a marriage, adversely affect other family members, or claim an undue share of society's resources (consuming resources that might be used to save or improve the lives of others), then a decision to allow the patient to die would be morally justified. A benefit-harm calculus is involved in the implementation of this strategy, as in the second. However, factors other than patient benefit could legitimately be included in the calculations.

With respect to infants and young children, the major problem is whether it is justifiable to withhold or to withdraw treatment when quality of life is so low that aggressive intervention or intensive care produces more harm than benefit for the patient. Some reports in the mid-1970s in the United States led to a public debate that continued for almost a decade without government intervention. However, during the early years of the Reagan administration a case in Indiana led to efforts by the U.S. government to protect handicapped infants from abuse or neglect. In this case, as reported in the first reading in this section of the chapter, Infant Doe died 6 days after he was born with Down's syndrome and cardiac, respiratory, and digestive complications requiring major surgery, which his parents refused to authorize.

Subsequently, Congress passed amendments to the Child Abuse and Treatment Act that designated the "withholding of medically indicated treatment" from children as child abuse. The final version of the new federal rules on "Child Abuse and Neglect Prevention and Treatment," published in April 1985 (and still in effect today), required the administration of "appropriate nutrition, hydration, and medication" to virtually all infants. This law and subsequent regulations define "medically indicated treatment" as that which in the physician's "reasonable medical judgment will be most likely to be effective in ameliorating or correcting all" life-threatening conditions. Only three conditions are recognized under which life-sustaining treatment is optional.

1. The infant is chronically and irreversibly comatose.
2. Provision of such treatment would merely prolong dying or not be effective in ameliorating or correcting the infant's life-threatening conditions.
3. Provision of such treatment would be futile and the treatment would be inhumane.

This framework has been interpreted by some government officials as involving reasonable *medical* judgments, rather than *quality-of-life* judgments. This interpretation attempts to keep judgments in line with sound professional practice, but it has been sharply criticized on grounds, for example, that "medically indicated treatments" themselves presuppose values and, often, standards of quality of life. Critics have argued that conditions 1 through 3 cannot be reduced to nonevaluative, medically indicated treatments. Rather, these conditions express the government's view of ethically indicated exceptions, and they incorporate quality-of-life judgments regarding which lives should be saved. The American Medical Association expresses its conclusions, also critical, in a brief policy statement reprinted in this chapter. In addition, the essays by Amnon Goldworth and Alan Fleischman in this chapter provide moral analyses of these problems.

The remaining essay in this section deals not with newborns but with a 6-month-old infant, Samuel Linares, who swallowed a balloon and nearly died. Medical efforts succeeded in restoring his vital functions; however, during 9 months of intensive care he did not return to consciousness. His father's repeated requests to disconnect his son from the respirator were not honored by the health care team, in part because of questionable legal advice given by the hospital attorney. In desperation, the father disconnected the respirator from his son, and held the staff of the unit at bay with a handgun. Within 30 minutes Samuel Linares died in his father's arms. John Lantos, Steven Miles, and Christine Cassel provide a summary of and commentary on the Linares case. In particular, the authors explore the option of judicial review and assess the hospital attorney's opinion in the decision-making process.

DECISIONS ON BEHALF OF ADULTS

Many judgments about terminating or continuing treatment must be made for mature persons who have never been competent (or never expressed preferences while competent) and are now suffering from life-threatening conditions. Approximately 80 percent of those who die each year in the United States die in nursing homes or hospitals under the care of strangers, often at considerable cost to their families and to society. Some of these patients, such as long-term care patients, are highly vulnerable.

A celebrated legal case centered on 67-year-old Joseph Saikewicz, who had an IQ of ten and a mental age of approximately 2 years and 8 months. He suffered from acute myeloblastic monocytic leukemia. Chemotherapy would have produced extensive suffering and possibly serious side effects. Remission under chemotherapy occurs in only 30 to 50 percent of cases and typically only for between 2 and 13 months. Without chemotherapy, Saikewicz could be expected to live for several weeks or perhaps several months, during which he would not experience severe pain or suffering. In not ordering treatment, a lower court considered "the quality of life available to him [Saikewicz] even if the treatment does bring about remission."

The Supreme Judicial Court of Massachusetts, however, rejected this formulation when construed to equate the value of a life with the quality of that life—in particular, with Saikweicz's lower quality of life because of mental retardation. The court held that mental retardation was irrelevant, but that "the 'best interests' of an incompetent person are not necessarily served by imposing on such persons results not mandated as to competent persons similarly situated." The court balanced prospective benefit against pain and suffering, finally determining that the patient's interests supported a decision not to provide chemotherapy. This court invoked the standard of substituted judgment (see the Introduction to Chapter 6) to decide that Saikewicz would not have chosen treatment had he been competent.

But can an incompetent person literally be said to have the right to make medical decisions if the right can only be exercised by competent persons? The seemingly fictional quality of substituted judgment makes it controversial: It seems conceptually and normatively dubious to treat never-autonomous patients as if they were autonomous. Some have therefore argued that what the court was really seeking in this case was a best-interest judgment. Allen Buchanan and Dan Brock argue in their essay that severely and permanently demented persons like Saikewicz may have no interest in life-sustaining treatment or in continued life, although they do have interests in the avoidance of pain and suffering. C. Everett Koop and Edward Grant react vigorously to approaches of this sort.

Quality of life *for the patient* is sometimes confused in these discussions with the quality of life or the value of life *for others*. Quality of life is not to be understood in the latter way, but as the balance of benefits and burdens to the patient. It is now widely, though not universally believed that surrogates should not refuse treatment against the incompetent patient's interests in order to avoid burdens to the family or costs to society. From this perspective, the incompetent patient's best medical interests should be the decisive criterion for a surrogate, even if these interests conflict with familial interests. However, as some authors point out in this chapter, the patient's *overall* welfare may be more important for surrogate decision making than a narrower medical view of the best *treatment* for the patient.

In the Matter of the Treatment and Care of Infant Doe

CIRCUIT COURT FOR THE COUNTY OF MONROE, STATE OF INDIANA

The "Infant Doe" case began when the parents of a Down's syndrome infant born in Indiana in 1982 decided not to permit surgery to repair the baby's tracheo-esophageal fistula (an opening between the trachea and esophagus that makes it impossible to consume food normally). The infant starved to death in the hospital. The parents and physicians maintained that survival was not in this infant's best interests because the child could not have a minimally acceptable quality of life. The parents decided to let the infant die rather than perform an operation available at Riley Hospital in Indianapolis to repair the fistula—a repair that had been recommended by two physicians in Bloomington. The parents did not consider their *omission* of treatment an act of killing the infant, nor did their physician, Walter L. Owens; but others did consider it a form of killing. In this court opinion, Judge Baker finds that the parents have the right to determine the course of treatment.

This matter came to be heard by the Court under certain extraordinary conditions concerning the emergency care and treatment of a minor child born at the Bloomington Hospital.

The Court was contacted at his residence by representatives of the Bloomington Hospital. On the basis of representations made by those representatives, the Court quickly determined that an extreme emergency existed.

The Court further determined that the Judge of the Monroe Circuit Court had been contacted concerning this matter and was unable to attend the emergency hearing, and the Court personally contacted the Judge of the Monroe Circuit Court who directed this Court to proceed with hearing. Thereafter, hearing was held on the Sixth Floor of the Bloomington Hospital at approximately 10:30 p.m., Saturday, the 10th day of April, 1982.

The following persons were present: John Doe, natural father of Infant Doe, with counsel, Andrew C. Mallor, Esquire; Maggie Keller, Gene Perry, Administrative Vice-Presidents of Bloomington Hospital; Len E. Bunger, counsel for Bloomington Hospital; Dr. Walter L. Owens, Dr. William R. Anderson, Dr. Brandt L. Ludlow, obstetricians admitted to practice in the State of Indiana with privileges at Bloomington Hospital; Doctor Owens being the obstetrician in attendance at delivery of Infant

Doe; Dr. Paul J. Wenzler, family practitioner with pediatric privilege at Bloomington Hospital and who has attended to Mr. and Mrs. Doe's other two children after their birth; Dr. James J. Schaffer and Dr. James J. Laughlin, pediatricians holding pediatric privileges at Bloomington Hospital. (Mrs. Doe was physically unable to attend.)

The Court thereafter heard evidence. Doctor Owens spoke for and on behalf of the obstetric group that delivered the Infant Doe, advising the Court that at approximately 8:19 p.m. on the evening of April 9, Infant Doe was born to Mary Doe in an uneventful delivery, but that shortly thereafter it was very apparent that the child suffered from Down's syndrome, with the further complication of tracheoesophageal fistula, meaning the passage from the mouth to the stomach had not appropriately developed and, in fact, were the child to be fed orally, substances would be taken into the lungs and the child most likely would suffocate.

Doctor Owens further stated that he had been previously advised that Doctor Wenzler would serve as practitioner for Infant Doe and that he was further advised that Doctor Wenzler, when faced with extraordinary cases, routinely consulted with Doctor Schaffer. Doctor Schaffer was at the Bloomington Hospital at that time and was called by Doctor Owens and was requested to examine the baby. Doctor Wenzler was notified. Doctors Owens, Schaffer, and Wenzler consulted; Doctors Wenzler and Schaffer indicated that the proper treatment for Infant Doe was his immediate transfer to Riley Hospital for corrective surgery. Doctor Owens, representing the concurring opinions of himself, Drs. Anderson and Ludlow, recommended that the child remain at Bloomington Hospital with full knowledge that surgery to correct tracheoesophageal fistula was not possible at Bloomington Hospital and that within a short period of time the child would succumb due to inability to receive nutriment and/or pneumonia.

His recommended course of treatment consisted of basic techniques administered to aid in keeping the child comfortable and free of pain. Doctor Owens testified that, even if surgery were successful, the possibility of a minimally adequate quality of life was nonexistent due to the child's severe and irreversible mental retardation.

Doctor Schaffer testified that Doctor Owen's prognosis regarding the child's mental retardation was correct, but that he believed the only acceptable course of medical treatment was transfer to Riley Hospital in Indianapolis for repair of tracheoesophageal fistula.

Doctor Wenzler concurred in Doctor Schaffer's proposed treatment. Doctor Laughlin testified that he concurred in the opinions of Doctors Schaffer and Wenzler, and he differed with Doctor Owen's opinion in that he knew of at least three instances in his practice where a child suffering from Down's syndrome had a reasonable quality of life. However, he related no knowledge of treatment of children with co-existent maladies of Down's syndrome and tracheosesophageal fistula.

Doctor Owens testified that he presented Mr. and Mrs. Doe with the two recommended courses of treatment and requested that they come to a decision. Doctor Owens understood that Doctors Schaffer and Wenzler also discussed their recommendations with Mr. and Mrs. Doe.

Mr. Doe testified that he had been a licensed public school teacher for over seven years and had on occasion worked closely with handicapped children and children with Down's syndrome and that he and his wife felt that a minimally acceptable quality of life was never present for a child suffering from such a condition. Mr. Doe was lucid and able to make an intelligent, informed decision.

Mr. Doe further testified that, after consulting with Doctors Owens, Schaffer, Wenzler and Laughlin, he and his wife have determined that it is in the best interest of the Infant Doe and the two children who are at home and their family entity as a whole, that the course of treatment prescribed by Doctor Owens should be followed, and at approximately 2:45 p.m., he and his wife, in the presence of each other and witnesses, signed a statement directing Doctor Owens to proceed with treatment of the infant, the content of said statement, omitting names and dates, is as follows:

> The undersigned being the parents of Infant _____, born _____, at Bloomington Hospital, have had explained to them and they acknowledge that they understand, the course of this treatment for Infant _____, as indicated appropriate for Infant _____ by Doctors Walter E. Owens, James J. Laughlin, James J. Schaffer and Paul J. Wenzler.
>
> Acknowledging their understanding and the consequences of all of the above proposals made by all the above four physicians, that they direct that the course of treatment shall proceed as directed by Dr. Walter E. Owens, M.D., who does not have privilege to practice pediatrics at Bloomington Hospital.

Mr. Len E. Bunger, on behalf of Bloomington Hospital made a statement that it was the hospital's primary function to reduce morbidity and mortality and that the hospital did not have the knowledge or the authority to make diagnoses or to prescribe treatment and, for that reason, had requested the Court to make a ruling in this matter.

The Court, having heard evidence, recesses and thereafter determines as follows:

1. All qualified persons available to present evidence in this matter were present and thus appointment of a guardian ad litem for Infant Doe was not required to proceed further in this hearing.
2. The Court appeared solely as a representative of the State of Indiana and the laws of the State of Indiana require that the parents be sufficiently informed, as they are in this instance, and any personal feelings of the Court should not intervene.

ISSUE

Do Mr. and Mrs. Doe, as the natural parents of Infant Doe have the right, after being fully informed of the consequences, to determine the appropriate course of treatment for their minor child?

CONCLUSION

It is the opinion of the Court that Mr. and Mrs. Doe, after having been fully informed of the opinions of two sets of physicians, have the right to choose a medically recommended course of treatment for their child in the present circumstances.

ORDER

The Court, being sufficiently advised, now directs the Bloomington Hospital to allow treatment prescribed by Dr. Walter L. Owens, as directed by the natural parents, Mr. and Mrs. Doe, for the Infant Doe.

The Court further directs that the Clerk of this Court assign a cause number and enter this cause upon the guardianship docket and fee book of this Court.

The Court further appoints the Monroe County Department of Public Welfare as guardian ad litem for the Infant Doe to determine whether the judgment of this Court should be appealed.

DATED this 12th day of April, 1982.

(signed)
JOHN G. BAKER
Judge, Monroe Superior Court
Division III, and as
Special Judge, Monroe Circuit Court

(copies to)
Len E. Bunger
Andrew C. Mallor
Betty K. Mintz, Counsel
  Monroe County Department of Public Welfare

Child Abuse and Neglect Prevention and Treatment*

U.S. DEPARTMENT OF HEALTH AND HUMAN SERVICES, OFFICE OF HUMAN DEVELOPMENT SERVICES

A public outcry occurred over the Infant Doe case, and critics charged that the parents and physicians had *killed* the child by (negligently) *allowing the child to die*. This controversy led to intense efforts by the U.S. federal government to protect handicapped infants from abuse or neglect. The Secretary of the Department of Health and Human Services proposed federal regulations to require that hospitals post notices that health care could not be withheld from infants on the basis of mental or physical impairments. This regulation took effect early in 1984, and evolved thereafter. Under the final rule, reprinted here, treatments of infants with life-threatening conditions must include providing appropriate nutrition, hydration, and medication. Only when treatments are futile in terms promoting the infant's survival, the infant is "chronically and irreversibly comatose, or the treatment would be virtually futile and inhumane" can life-prolonging interventions be withheld, and even then appropriate nutrition and hydration must be provided.

§ 1340.15 Services and treatment for disabled infants.

a. *Purpose.* The regulations in this section implement certain provisions of the Child Abuse Amendments of 1984, including section 4(b)(2)(K) of the Child Abuse Prevention and Treatment Act governing the protection and care of disabled infants with life-threatening conditions.

b. *Definitions.* (1) The term "medical neglect" means the failure to provide adequate medical care in the context of the definitions of "child abuse and neglect" in section 3 of the Act and § 1340.2(d) of this part. The term "medical neglect" includes, but is not limited to, the withholding of medically indicated treatment from a disabled infant with a life-threatening condition.

2. The term "withholding of medically indicated treatment" means the failure to respond to the infant's life-threatening conditions by providing treatment (including appropriate nutrition, hydration, and medication) which, in the treating physician's (or physicians') reasonable medical judgment, will be most likely to be effective in ameliorating or correcting all such conditions, except that the term does not include the failure to provide treatment (other than appropriate nutrition, hydration, or medication) to an infant when, in the treating physician's (or physicians') reasonable medical judgment any of the following circumstances apply:

   i. The infant is chronically and irreversibly comatose:

   ii. The provision of such treatment would merely prolong dying, not be effective in ameliorating or correcting all of the infant's life-threatening conditions, or otherwise be futile in terms of the survival of the infant; or

*Source: Reprinted from *Federal Register* 50 (April 15, 1985), pp. 14887–14888.

      iii. The provision of such treatment would be virtually futile in terms of the survival of the infant and the treatment itself under such circumstances would be inhumane.

3. Following are definitions of terms used in paragraph (b)(2) of this section:

      i. The term "infant" means an infant less than one year of age. The reference to less than one year of age shall not be construed to imply that treatment should be changed or discontinued when an infant reaches one year of age, or to affect or limit any existing protections available under State laws regarding medical neglect of children over one year of age. In addition to their applicability to infants less than one year of age, the standards set forth in paragraph (b)(2) of this section should be consulted thoroughly in the evaluation of any issue of medical neglect involving an infant older than one year of age who has been continuously hospitalized since birth, who was born extremely prematurely, or who has a long-term disability.

      ii. The term "reasonable medical judgment" means a medical judgment that would be made by a reasonably prudent physician, knowledgeable about the case and the treatment possibilities with respect to the medical conditions involved . . .

Treatment Decisions for Seriously Ill Newborns: Ethical Critique of Baby Doe Rule*

AMERICAN MEDICAL ASSOCIATION, COUNCIL ON ETHICAL AND JUDICIAL AFFAIRS

The AMA subsequently drafted its own guidelines on these issues, which are printed below. The AMA believes that the government rules are drawn too narrowly, fail to adequately consider quality of life, and undermine parental decisionmaking. The AMA offers several "Recommendations" to overcome these problems.

A survey of neonatologists indicates that there is serious discontent with the current Baby Doe rule among physicians who are involved in the care of seriously ill newborns. The survey found that 76% of the neonatologists that responded to the survey believed the regulations were not necessary to protect the rights of handicapped infants. Sixty-six percent believed that the rule interfered with parents' right to make treatment decisions that are in the best interests of their children. Sixty percent believed that the regulations did not allow adequate consideration of the infants' suffering. In three vignettes presented in the survey, up to 32% felt that maximal treatment was not in the best interests of the children described, but such treatment was required by the Baby Doe regulations.

Based on ethical principles, the Council has similar objections to the current rule.

A. **Range of Situations Where Treatment Is Not Required Is Too Narrow**   The current Baby Doe Rule lists a number of exceptions where failure to provide medically indicated treatment is not considered medical neglect: 1) if the infant is chronically and irreversibly comatose, 2) the treatment will prolong dying, 3) the treatment is futile "in terms of survival of the infant," and 4) the treatment is virtually futile and the treatment itself would be inhumane. These exceptions, however, fail to encompass many of the situations in which the ethical guidelines above do permit physicians to respect parents' decisions to forgo life-sustaining treatment for their newborns.

The exception for a newborn who is chronically and irreversibly comatose is too narrow. First, technically, an irreversible coma is a terminal condition, and therefore cannot be chronic. Second, a coma is a neurological condition distinct from a persistent vegetative state. Both are states of permanent unconsciousness. However, a coma is a sleeplike unarousability, while a persistent vegetative state is a state of

*Source: American Medical Association, Council on Ethical and Judicial Affairs, "Treatment Decisions for Seriously Ill Newborns: Ethical Critique of Baby Doe Rule." *Reports of the Council,* No. 43. Chicago: American Medical Association. 1992 July, pp. 71–74.

unconsciousness where the patient exhibits sleep-wake cycles and other responses controlled by the brain stem. Therefore, a strict interpretation of the Baby Doe rule would require that a newborn who is in a persistent vegetative state always be treated. Although one court has ruled that an infant who was in a persistent vegetative state met the rule's exception even though it was not comatose, there still exists much confusion over how broadly the exception should be interpreted. The Council believes life-sustaining treatment may be ethically withheld or withdrawn from any newborn who is so neurologically damaged such that he or she will never possess any of the capabilities that give life meaning.

The rule also requires that nutrition, hydration and medication always be provided. The Council concluded in Report B and D (A-91) that artificial nutrition and hydration as well as medication, are forms of life-sustaining treatment that may be forgone if their provision is not in the best interests of a patient that has never been competent. Although life-sustaining treatment including artificial nutrition and hydration and medication may ethically be withheld or withdrawn, comfort care must not be discontinued.

B.   **Rejects Use of Quality of Life Considerations**   The Amendment to the Child Abuse Prevention Act noticeably omits reference to quality of life considerations. Furthermore, in its nonbinding interpretive guidelines for the Amendment, the DHHS explicitly rejects the legitimacy of quality of life considerations. The Council, however, believes that it is important to consider the quality of life the infant will likely have with and without treatment from the infant's perspective.

C.   **Undermines Parental Decisionmaking**   The DHHS' discussion accompanying its nonbinding interpretive guidelines states that in most cases the parents should have the authority to make treatment decisions for their infant. However, the discretion that parents have is considerably limited by the rule itself. In particular parents cannot decide to refuse consent for a medically indicated treatment because they believe that the life their child will have if treated will be so overwhelmed by suffering that it is in the best interests of the infant not to have his or her life prolonged.

Circumstances where decisions about whether to provide life-sustaining treatment to seriously ill newborns can be extremely complicated. While there must be every effort made to be objective, the values of the decisionmaker will occasionally unavoidably enter into these decisions. Reasonable persons may disagree as to whether a particular infant's life holds enough promise for benefit to the infant that treatment should be provided despite the suffering that the child will also have to experience.

The President's Commission recognized a gray area of situations for which treatment decisions must be made for seriously ill newborns. In such cases the Commission concludes, parents should have the authority to make decisions for their newborn including a decision for nontreatment. This framework is helpful and better represents the complex nature of these decisions than does the current Baby Doe Rule. The Baby Doe Rule does not recognize this gray area of decision making, primarily because it rejects the use of quality of life considerations.

RECOMMENDATIONS

The Council recommends that physicians should play an active role in advocating for changes in the Child Abuse Prevention Act as well as state laws that require physicians to violate the following ethical guidelines:

1. The primary consideration for decisions regarding life-sustaining treatment for seriously ill newborns should be what is best for that newborn. Factors that should be weighed are: 1) the chance that therapy will succeed, 2) the risks involved with treatment and nontreatment, 3) the degree to which the therapy, if successful, will extend life, 4) the pain and discomfort associated with the therapy, and 5) the anticipated quality of life for the newborn with and without treatment.

2. Care must be taken to evaluate the newborn's expected quality of life from the child's perspective. Life-sustaining treatment may be withheld or withdrawn from a newborn upon the parents' request when the pain and suffering expected to be endured by the child will overwhelm any potential for joy during his or her life. When an infant suffers extreme neurological damage, and is consequently not capable of experiencing either suffering or joy a decision may be made to withhold or withdraw life-sustaining treatment upon the parents' request. When life-sustaining treatment is withheld or withdrawn, comfort care must not be discontinued.

3. When an infant's prognosis is largely uncertain, as is often the case with extremely premature newborns, all life-sustaining and life-enhancing treatment should be initiated. Decisions about life-sustaining treatment should be made once the prognosis becomes more certain. It is not necessary to attain absolute or near absolute prognostic certainty before life-sustaining treatment is withdrawn, since this goal is often unattainable and risks unnecessarily prolonging the infant's suffering.

4. Physicians must provide full information to parents of seriously ill newborns regarding the nature of treatments, therapeutic options and expected prognosis with and without therapy, so that parents can make informed decisions for their children about life-sustaining treatment. Counseling services and an opportunity to talk with persons who have had to make similar decisions should be available to parents. Ethics committees or infant review committees should also be utilized to facilitate parental decisionmaking for these decisions. These committees should help mediate resolutions of conflicts that may arise among parents, physicians and others involved in the care of the infant. These committees should also be responsible for referring cases to the appropriate public agencies when it is concluded that the parents' decision is not a decision that could reasonably be judged to be in the best interests of the infant.

Human Rights and the Omission or Cessation of Treatment for Infants*

AMNON GOLDWORTH

In the following essay, Amnon Goldworth considers questions of the minimal quality of life that must be met to justify the continued existence of children who suffer serious pain and psychosocial deficits that cannot be significantly alleviated by modern medicine. After rejecting some standard approaches, Goldworth argues that infants, like all persons, have a right to die in desperate circumstances and that cessation of treatment on their behalf is sometimes morally required, not merely morally permitted.

All medical procedures are invested with moral significance. This fact is generally overlooked because medical interventions serve as means to ends which are commonly valued: everyone wants to be healthy; no one wants to suffer pain. Thus, the right thing to do—which medicine aims to do—is to help and not harm the patient.

But medicine has both helped and harmed. For instance, neonatal intensive care, which has reduced infant mortality and repaired the damage done by genetic and congenital anomalies, has also salvaged those whose lives are painful and deprived. It has created choices and accompanying moral problems and dilemmas where none existed before.

Given the relationship between the medical and the moral, the identification and application of appropriate moral criteria, which are a part of the economy of moral decision making, are part of medical decision making as well. Such criteria help to locate areas of moral concern and to guide us in our assessments of particular moral states of affairs. They are of particular importance in the intensive care nursery in which the unprecedented is encountered, and in which every action taken on behalf of fragile lives weighs heavily on the scales of life and death, health and illness.

As Munson[1] has movingly observed:

> If we could speak of nature in human terms, we would often say that it is cruel and piti-less. Nowhere does it seem more heartless than in the case of babies born into the world with severe physical defects and deformities. The birth of such a child transforms an occasion of expected joy into one of immense sadness. It forces the child's parents to make a momentous decision at a time they are least prepared to reason clearly. Shall they insist that everything be done to save the child's life? Or shall they request that the child be allowed an easeful death? Nor can physicians and nurses escape the burden the birth

---

*Source: Goldworth, A., "Human Rights and the Omission or Cessation of Treatment for Infants," *Journal of Perinatology* 9(1) March 1989, pp. 79–82.

of such a child delivers. Committed to saving lives, can they condone the death of the child? . . . No one involved in the situation can escape the moral agonies that it brings.[1]

Munson asked whether parents or health professionals can ask for or condone the death of a child who is born with serious physical defects and deformities. It is my belief that in some circumstances, the death of such a child is not merely to be condoned but is morally required.

On April 9, 1982, a child was born in Bloomington, Indiana, whose short life and painful death set loose a dramatic series of public and legal events that culminated in the Child Abuse and Neglect Prevention and Treatment Program.*

Although the U.S. Supreme Court invalidated the so-called Baby Doe regulations of 1984, the Child Abuse rule, like the Baby Doe rule, stipulates that treatment options are not to be based on quality-of-life judgments and that withdrawal of treatment (except appropriate hydration, nutrition, and medication) is called for only when:

> (1) the infant is chronically and irreversibly comatose; or (2) the provision of such treatment would merely prolong dying or not be effective in ameliorating or correcting all the infant's life-threatening conditions, or otherwise be futile in terms of the survival of the infant; or (3) the provision of such treatment would be virtually futile in terms of the survival of the infant and the treatment itself under such circumstances would be inhumane.[2]

The Federal Government's position is that quality-of-life assessments cannot be employed in deciding on treatment or nontreatment, because they are subjective and the only relevant consideration is the survivability of the infant.

This insistence that quality-of-life judgments are not to be employed does not entirely eliminate such judgments. For it is a quality-of-life judgment on the part of the government to claim that an infant's life is worth living and therefore worth saving, no matter what its quality is or may be. What the government is opposed to is the view that there is a minimal quality-of-life below which life is not worth living.

Yet, one might support the government's position by observing that there is no agreement among doctors, lawyers, and ethicists as to what a reasonable alternative should be. Disagreement alone, however, is not sufficient to show that no alternative criterion is satisfactory. To do this requires the sort of systemic analysis provided by Robertson.[3]

Robertson is critical of two sorts of arguments that favor the withdrawal of treatment from defective infants. The first states that treatment is not morally required for such infants because they are not persons and therefore do no possess a right to life. The second argument states that we are not morally required to treat when the costs of maintaining the infant's life outweigh the benefits. Although costs and benefits are experienced by parents, health care providers and the general public, as well as infants, we will deal with Robertson's critique as it applies only to the latter.

Robertson argues cogently against the position stated by Michael Tooley[4] that defective infants are not persons by pointing out that his characterization of

*Intended to implement the Child Abuse Amendments of 1984, which are supplements to the Child Abuse Prevention and Treatment Act, which became law in 1974.

personhood as requiring self-consciousness would also justify the nontreatment of the unconscious, the suicidal, and the deranged.3 Unless we are prepared to deny personhood to such individuals, Tooley's definition is flawed.

With reference to the second argument, there are two general circumstances in which the costs of treatment so outweigh its benefits that omission or cessation of treatment appears justified. One circumstance involves the experiencing of severe physical pain; the other involves psychosocial suffering generated by a life devoid of social interaction. As Robertson observes,

> Many defective children never can walk even with prosthesis, never interact with normal children, never appreciate growth, adolescence, or the fulfillment of education and employment, and seldom are even able to care for themselves. In cases of severe retardation, they may be left with a vegetative existence in a crib, incapable of choice or the most minimal response to stimuli. Parents or others may reject them, and much of their time will be spent in hospitals, in surgery, or fighting the many illnesses that beset them.3

With reference to the first situation, Robertson says that pain may not be a constant and may be controlled by analgesics. Thus, unless the pain is unmanageable, there is not sufficient reason to conclude that life is not worth living. With reference to the second situation, Robertson claims that there are two possible responses. The first is to accept the premises but to question the amount of suffering experienced in particular cases. This, he holds, would eliminate the justification of death except in the most extreme cases of psychosocial deprivation. The second is to repudiate the quality-of-life argument entirely.

In keeping with the first approach, Robertson points out that lack of opportunities for schooling and social interaction may be caused by a failing in social attitudes on the part of healthy individuals. Many defective individuals who are nonambulatory can be trained to do satisfying work, and even if they cannot, one must not assume that a nonproductive life is necessarily an unhappy one. Thus the conclusion that the lives of those who suffer from psychosocial deprivations are not worth living cannot, in most instances, be justified.

But, there are those infants who suffer from such gross malformation or such extreme retardation that their ability to interact with others is minimal. In response to this, Robertson introduces the second approach. He challenges one's judgments of the quality-of-life of another by way of the following remarks.

> . . . in what sense can the proxy validly conclude that a person with different wants, needs, and interests, if able to speak, would agree that such a life were worse than death? . . . Compared with the situation and life prospects of a "reasonable man," the child's potential quality of life indeed appears dim. Yet a standard based on healthy, ordinary development may be entirely inappropriate to the situation. One who has never known the pleasures of mental operation, ambulation, and social interaction surely does not suffer from that loss as much as one who has. While one who has known these capacities may prefer death to a life without them, we have no assurance that the handicapped person, with no point of comparison, would agree. Life, and life alone, whatever its limitations, might be of sufficient worth to him.3

Robertson's central point is that we cannot make proxy judgments of the quality of life of defective children. Life alone, whatever its character, may be of worth to the defective individual. Therefore we cannot justifiably omit or withdraw life-supporting treatment. However, Robertson's argument can be taken in two ways. If we cannot make the appropriate quality-of-life judgments, then it is also possible that life may *not* be of worth to the defective individual. Thus, no judgment is possible as to which is the better course of action: treatment or nontreatment. Under these circumstances, the only rational procedure for deciding what to do in terms of the interests of the infant is to randomize the giving or withdrawing of treatment.

Why does Robertson, in the face of uncertainty concerning pain and psychosocial defects, favor treatment? Because he presumes that infants are persons and as such have rights that include the human right to life. I accept this presumption because, as English has observed, "There is no single core of necessary and sufficient features which we can draw upon with the assurance that they constitute what really makes a person; these are only features that are more or less typical."[5]

But personhood not only confers the right to live, it also confers the right to die. The latter has, until recently, not been claimed because the natural course of dying was not radically interfered with. However, modern medicine's ability to prolong or artificially sustain life has brought the right to die to the fore. What, then, is a human right and what does the human right to die tell us about the omission or cessation of life-supporting treatment for infants?

A human right is a justified claim against the world. It is recognized as protecting essential human needs or interests. However, one may make a claim to a human right and fail for two reasons to have it honored. First, it may not be morally justified, or if it is so justified then the objective conditions by which it can be satisfied do not exist. Second, there may be an arbitrary refusal to honor the claim even though it is morally justified and the objective conditions by which it can be satisfied do exist.

What sort of human rights claim is morally justified? Put differently, what informs us that we have a human right? Social existence involves a compromise between the advantages provided by society and the disadvantages that society produces by the constraints it places on our freedom of action. We are willing to forgo the satisfying of some interests because we are adequately compensated for their absence or loss. But we are unwilling to forgo the satisfying of other interests. For example, we cannot adequately compensate healthy, normal individuals for the loss of their lives or for the loss of their freedom, because no adequate compensation is possible. Thus, a human right is one which if not honored deprives a person of the satisfying of a fundamental need or interest for which there is no adequate compensation. (Jean-Jacques Rousseau understood this when, in his book *The Social Contract,* he pointed out that human freedom cannot be forfeited because nothing can adequately compensate for a life of servitude.)

What is essential to the concept of a human right needs the following qualifications. First, the range of human rights is restricted to universal human needs or interests. A concert violinist may have a compelling need for a particular violin; no other will satisfy his musical demands as fully as this one. Thus, nothing can adequately compensate him for its loss. But this need does not extend to all or most persons and is therefore not a universal human need. Second, the concept of a human right is not time-dependent or community-dependent. But, what is time- or community-dependent is how human rights come to be satisfied.

The right to die, given the proper circumstances, satisfies a universal human need or interest. Furthermore, the objective conditions by which this right can be satisfied exist. What are the circumstances in which an infant's right to die supersedes its right to live? The answer is: When a failure to honor the infant's right to die results in the infant being deprived of the fundamental need *not* to suffer chronic pain or *not* to be alienated from other human beings because of psychosocial deficits, and there is nothing in the infant's continued existence to adequately compensate it for this pain or alienation. To sustain such a life medically constitutes a violation of its right to die.

There is one obvious objection that could be raised against this analysis which is derived from John Robertson's claim that we are not justified in judging the inner states of another individual and therefore, we cannot know that someone is deprived of his fundamental needs or interests.

In fact, such assertions as "He is feeling depressed," "She has a toothache," and "The child is unhappy" indicate that we judge the inner states of others constantly. And, each, as well as all such judgments, is based on verbal and nonverbal behavioral evidence. To deny the authority of such evidence leads to an absurd solipsism in which the only human being that can be said to exist is oneself.

Skepticism concerning our ability to assess the inner states of others comforts the physician with the facile but false assumption that he always does the morally right thing when he treats. Doubt seems to lend moral support to the normal impulse on the part of the physician to intervene in the presence of illness. But once it is recognized, as it should be, that to treat and save may create the conditions for a deeply deprived life, then the physician cannot hide behind the view that his life-rescuing efforts are always for the best, for they may not be. Does this leave us with no means by which to determine whether treatment or nontreatment is best? No, not if one takes into account our human rights which include the right to die. However, to acknowledge this latter right requires that one also acknowledge the corresponding moral obligation to omit or cease life-supporting treatment.

NOTES

1. Munson R. *Intervention and Reflection: Basic Issues in Medical Ethics.* Belmont, C: Wadsworth Publishing, 1983, p. 103.
2. Fed. Reg. vol 50, No. 72, p. 14878, 1985.
3. Robertson J. A. Involuntary euthanasia of defective newborns: A legal analysis. *Stanford Law Review* 27 (January):249–250, 253, 254, 1975.
4. Tooley M. Abortion and infanticide: Philosophy. *Public Affairs* 2 (Fall), 1972.
5. English J. Abortion and the concept of a person. *Canadian Journal Philosophy* 5:2, 1975.

The Right to Die vs. Death in the Best Interests of the Infant*

ALAN R. FLEISCHMAN

The following essay by Alan R. Fleischman is a direct response to Goldworth. Fleischman expresses reservations about the language of a right to die and looks to ways of protecting the infant's interests, such as procedural requirements of committee review by an infant bioethics committee. Fleischman prefers a more traditional formulation in terms of the obligation to act in the best interests of the infant.

The author of the article "Human Rights and the Omission or Cessation of Treatment for Infants" makes an impassioned plea that infants have the "right to die" when they are suffering chronic pain or when they have been alienated from other human beings because of psychosocial deficits. The author further asserts that "in some circumstances the death of such a child [a child born with serious physical defects and deformities] is not merely to be condoned but is morally required."

This attempt at moral persuasion is motivated by the present environment of federal regulations and the massive overtreatment of neonates as perceived and practiced by America's neonatologists.[1] Maybe it is time to empower the neonate with the "right to die," but rights language in this regard can be divisive and result in the inappropriate duty to ensure the death of a child. Who is to articulate this right and how will we enforce the duty to fulfill that right?

Perhaps a more reasoned approach moves away from the adversarial language of rights and looks toward the language of interests. Treatment remains appropriate for a child as long as it is in the child's best interests. This standard is a child-centered one, albeit potentially vague and in need of interpretation. It is certainly in the child's best interests to be free from pain that has no compensating benefit. However, because few children suffer unrelenting physical pain, one might ask how nonexistence can be preferable to impaired existence without pain, from the view of the child. McCormick, in a classic article published in 1974,[2] adds the concept of "relational potential" to the best interests standard. He argues that when a patient lacks the present capacity or future potential for human relationships, that patient can be said to have no interests at all, except the interest in being free from pain and discomfort.

When continued treatment is clearly against the best interests of a patient, it is obligatory that it be discontinued. In contrast, when the relational potential standard is being utilized, it is obligatory only to withdraw painful treatments and it is acceptable to withdraw other treatments. Assuming the patient is not in pain, continued

*Source: Fleischman, A. R., "The Right to Die vs. Death in the Best Interests of the Infant," *Journal of Perinatology* 9(1), March 1989. pp. 86–87.

treatment would neither benefit nor harm the patient who is severely neurologically impaired and lacks the potential for human relationships.[3] Therefore, it becomes a procedural matter to decide whether the treatment ought to be discontinued.

Regardless of the philosophical basis upon which one can condone the withdrawing of inappropriate treatments from neonates, there must be a procedural mechanism by which this occurs. Invoking a child's "right to die" requires some other party to determine when that right should be respected and a corresponding duty to ensure it is fulfilled. This principle only speaks to actions to be taken to withdraw treatments that will result in the death of the child. In contrast, utilizing the framework of "best interests" obligates the caregivers to make all decisions for the infant in a manner consistent with the infant's interests and future quality of life, not just the decisions that may result in his death.

In conclusion, although I, too, am concerned about the overtreatment of infants and the need to empower their parents and caregivers with a rationale for terminating burdensome treatments, I do not believe that empowering infants with the "right to die" will result in benefiting these critically ill infants. Rather, obligating caregivers to act in the best interests of the child is more likely to result in compassionate assessment of the appropriate level of treatment to be rendered.

NOTES

1. Kopelman I. M., Irons T. G., Kopelman A. E. Neonatologists judge the "Baby Doe" regulations. *New England Journal of Medicine* 318:677–683, 1988.
2. McCormick R. To save or let die: The dilemma of modern medicine. *JAMA* 229:2, 172–176, 1974.
3. Arras J. D. Ethical principles for the care of imperiled newborns: Toward an ethic or ambiguity. In Murray T. H., Caplan A. L. (eds.) *Which Babies Shall Live? Humanistic Dimensions of the Care of Imperiled Newborns*. Humana Press, Clifton, NJ, 1985, pp. 83–135.

The Linares Affair*

JOHN D. LANTOS, STEVEN H. MILES, AND CHRISTINE K. CASSEL

The next article by Lantos, Miles, and Cassel, provides a summary of and commentary on the Linares case. As noted, Rudolfo Linares detached his 15-month-old, permanently unconscious son, Samuel, from a ventilator knowing that he would die. The district attorney said he also killed Samuel, and therefore, brought a homicide complaint, although a grand jury refused to issue a homicide indictment. The authors explore the history of the case and problems in relying on the family for the critical decisions, discuss the option of judicial review, and offer a framework for treatment withdrawal decisions.

INTRODUCTION

On August 2, 1988, 6-month-old Samuel Linares aspirated a balloon at a birthday party and was unconscious and blue when his father, Rudolfo, found him. Nine months later, his father used a gun to keep medical staff at bay while he disconnected the respirator keeping his comatose son alive. Mr. Linares ignited much soul-searching among pediatricians, lawyers, and ethicists about treatment decisions for profoundly damaged children.

Public discussion of the ethics of forgoing life support in pediatric care moves like a pendulum between fear of inappropriately allowing children to die and fear of unrestrained life-supporting technology. In the early 1970s, physicians[1] and theologians[2] challenged accepted tenets of law and ethics by proposing that pediatricians should allow critically ill or severely disabled babies to die without the most aggressive use of technology. By 1982, Baby Doe caught the nation's moral imagination and raised the possibility that withholding or withdrawing life-sustaining procedures amounted to sanctioned infanticide.[3] This concern led to restriction on the right of parents and doctors to decide to discontinue treatment. Public sympathy for Mr. Linares suggests that the pendulum may be swinging back toward a less restrictive public policy about forgoing life-sustaining treatment in children.

This paper . . . consider[s] the ambiguities and lessons of the Linares case that have bearing on how such cases can be addressed in the future.

CASE HISTORY

When Mr. Linares found his unconscious son, he attempted mouth-to-mouth resuscitation but could not ventilate the child. He called 911, and then, impatient with the paramedics, ran with the child half a block to a neighborhood fire station. Firemen were unable to perform mouth-to-mouth resuscitation, discovered the balloon in

*Source: John D. Lantos, Steven H. Miles, and Christine K. Cassel, "The Linares Affair," *Law, Medicine, & Health Care,* 17, no. 4 (Winter, 1989):308–15. Reprinted with the permission of the American Society of Law, Medicine & Ethics and Drs. Lantos, Miles, and Cassel.

the child's throat, and removed it with a forceps. The boy was rushed to the MacNeal Hospital Emergency Room where he had no spontaneous respirations, no heartbeat and no pulse. Advanced cardiac life-support established a pulse and blood pressure after the child had had no vital signs for at least 20 minutes. He had fixed and dilated pupils, no deep tendon reflexes, and no reaction to painful stimuli. Two tertiary care hospitals refused to accept the child in transfer—one saying that it sounded like the boy was already dead. Finally, Rush-Presbyterian-St. Luke's Medical Center accepted the boy for admission to the pediatric intensive care unit (PICU).

PICU staff initially expected the boy to die during that night. Three days later, Samuel remained unstable and a conference was held with Mr. and Mrs. Linares, Samuel's primary nurse, and the medical director of the PICU.[4] Mr. Linares said he wanted Samuel removed from the ventilator. Mrs. Linares' preferences are not known. PICU staff said that, without a court order, they could not disconnect the ventilator unless the child was brain dead. A do-not-resuscitate order was agreed upon.

Days passed with no improvement. Samuel remained ventilator dependent. Electroencephalograms (EEGs) showed minimal brain activity. A pediatric neurologist diagnosed the child as being in a persistent vegetative state (PVS). Dr. Gil Goldman, the head of the PICU, became convinced that the child had no reasonable chance for recovery of neurologic function. Dr. Goldman was later to write, "I have disconnected ventilators from vegetative or brain dead children dozens of times," but undisclosed elements of this case led him to defer to the recommendations of the hospital lawyer.[5]

Max Brown, a ten year veteran as Rush hospital's legal counsel, told the physicians that discontinuing the ventilator would create civil and criminal liability for the doctors and the hospital. He based his conclusion on the lack of statutory authority or case law precedent in Illinois for removing life-support from a child. He insisted that the ventilator could not be withdrawn without a declaratory judgment or court order. He felt that the parents, rather than the hospital, were the most appropriate petitioners for such a process. The hospital might be perceived as having a conflict of interest, he thought, due to its ongoing financial losses secondary to inadequate Medicaid reimbursement for care of the child. By April, hospital charges were over $600,000 and the hospital had been paid $100,000.

During the first few months, Mr. Linares visited frequently, usually alone and late at night. He repeatedly requested that life-support be discontinued. Sympathetic members of the PICU staff helped Mr. Linares contact a lawyer for help. In December, while visiting his son in the middle of the night, Mr. Linares took his child off the ventilator. Security guards wrestled him to the ground and PICU staff reconnected the ventilator. After that incident, Mr. Linares' visits to the hospital decreased.

Plans were made to transfer the child to a nursing home. Although the Linares parents visited the nursing home and consented to the transfer, family members describe their deep misgivings about a prolonged vegetative existence in a nursing home. Complicating the family's social problems, the Illinois Department of Welfare, on April 22, informed the Linares that, as a result of alleged welfare fraud, the family would lose its medical benefits.

On April 25, a hospital nurse left a recording on the Linares' telephone answering machine telling them that Samuel was to be transferred the next day. Shortly thereafter, a neighbor warned the hospital that Mr. Linares was on his way to the hospital and appeared quite upset. Security guards met the couple and after a brief discussion permitted them to go to the PICU. After visiting the PICU together, Mr. Linares sent his wife to the car. Brandishing a handgun, he disconnected the respirator, using the weapon to hold the staff at bay. He told the staff that "I'm not here to hurt anyone" and allowed hospital staff to remove the three other patients in the PICU. Within 30 minutes, the boy died in his father's arms. After confirming the death with a stethoscope that a physician slid across the floor, Mr. Linares surrendered to police. He told authorities that "I did it because I love my son and wife." Mrs. Linares stated that she "pretty much agreed" with what her husband had done. Months later she stated, "I only wanted him to be at rest."

The incident generated intense public discussion. Health care professionals, lawyers, ethicists, and editorialists were generally sympathetic with the anguished Linares family and critical of the hospital's handling of the case. Criticism focused on how the hospital informed the family of the transfer and on the prolonged support of the comatose boy over parental objections. There were several opinions about how the case should have been handled. Leon Kass, a physician-ethicist, was among those who thought that properly informed and motivated physicians could have discussed this issue and removed the respirator within the existing legal framework regarding forgoing life-sustaining treatment (*Chicago Tribune,* 4/28, page 1,24). Others, like Ila Rothschild of the American Hospital Association's Office of Legal and Regulatory Affairs, stressed the role of hospital policies to "determine the appropriate time to consult with family members and who among the medical and support staff should talk with family" (*American Hospital Association News,* 5/15, page 8). The appropriate role of ethics committees in such cases was hotly debated (see *Medical Ethics Advisor,* June 1989).

Mr. Brown insisted that, although people might prefer extrajudicial mechanisms to make treatment withdrawal decisions, the disparity between the law in Illinois and public sentiment makes such mechanisms useless. He stated, "What we're dealing with here is a legal problem. Ethics committees are fine so long as what is ethically being contemplated is legally acceptable. When you have an ethical alternative that is by all accounts illegal, an ethics committee cannot do much to make it legal." (*Medical Ethics Advisor,* June 1989). The hospital claimed that the family declined to meet with an ethics consultant. Rush does not have an ethics committee but has a philosopher-ethicist who was not involved in the management of this case. Given Brown's view of the discretional scope of an ethics committee in this case, the meaning of such an offer from the hospital is opaque.

Asserting that "the facts of this case clearly dictate the filing of first degree murder charges," State's Attorney Cecil Partee filed a homicide complaint as a first step to obtaining an indictment. Linares was given a public defender and underwent psychiatric evaluation as a condition of his bond. After the coroner found the balloon to be the primary cause of death but failed to conclude whether the "manner of death" was an accident or homicide, a Grand Jury refused to issue a homicide indictment. Opining that Mr. Linares "suffered quite enough," Mr. Partee declined to press charges. Mr. Linares received a suspended sentence on a misdemeanor weapon charge.

On May 19, after reviewing the Grand Jury decision, the coroner ruled that the death was accidental and that the child was dead at the time of admission to the hospital (*NY Times,* May 22, 1989, A8). The coroner later said that the application of brain death criteria for a child this age was unclear. He said that at autopsy he found Samuel Linares' brainstem to be intact. He personally believed that the child was "dead" at admission, and he said that he had assigned no official time of death (phone conversation with S. H. Miles, 7/26/89). . . .

In the *Linares* case, hospital staff expressed reservations about the family's ability to participate in [serious] discussions. The family was a troubled one. Mr. Brown contends that Mr. Linares drank before hospital visits, including the night he came into the PICU with the gun (*Medical Ethics Advisor,* June 1989, 72). Hospital staff allege (and family lawyers deny) that the family was unwilling to fully discuss their views with the health care providers. If true, this may reflect an unwillingness to participate in a process of shared decision-making. Conversely, the family may have perceived that the hospital had come to a final position that it would not remove the respirator and justifiably concluded that further discussion would be useless.

Where parents are unable to participate in discussions, or where discussions break down, legal procedures may be necessary to determine who may authorize treatment withdrawal decisions on a child's behalf. There are no easily applicable standards for determining when family decisions are appropriate. . . .

A FRAMEWORK FOR TREATMENT WITHDRAWAL DECISIONS

Extrajudicial Procedures

Decisions to withhold or withdraw life-sustaining therapy are frequently made in pediatrics units. Rarely do such cases involve court intervention. Generally, such decisions are made in discussions between parents and doctors,[6] or after review by ethics committees,[7] or ethics consultants [8] who may work with hospital legal staff.

Each of these approaches involves some degree of legal risk. Holder notes that the legal risk to physicians and parents in decisions to withhold treatment from a comatose infant is small but cautions, "In the current political climate, however, (a manslaughter or child abuse) charge cannot be entirely ruled out, particularly if a prosecutor wants to generate some favorable publicity for himself as a savior of innocent babies."[9] She counsels that intra-institutional procedural review mechanisms might provide an extra layer of protection in such situations: "Enlightened self-interest in the current political climate would indicate that at a minimum, departments of pediatrics should have procedural guidelines for situations in which a decision is made to allow an infant to die." Such intra-hospital review does not directly confer immunity; rather it demonstrates a reflective, noncapricious patient-centered decision-making process which offers a plausible defence against negligence. The small but recognizable risk of legal liability highlights the need for informed clinical advice by hospital counsel. . . .

The Role of the Hospital Attorney

Though Illinois case law does not address this issue, precedents from other states suggest that state courts will support decisions to terminate treatment of children in a persistent vegetative state. This impression is further supported by the absence of adverse action against providers in similar cases. In fact, no physician has ever been convicted of any crime for withholding or withdrawing treatment from such a patient, in spite of much evidence in the medical literature that such decisions take place. Mr. Brown's assertion that theoretical liability existed in regard to the treatment withdrawal decision is inarguable, but its relevance is questionable.

The second issue concerns Mr. Brown's management of his conflict of interest in the case. Mr. Brown asserts that his concern was to protect the physicians from prosecution and the hospital from unfavorable publicity, either because it was willing to withdraw treatment or because of its potential conflict of interest with regard to inadequate reimbursement for Samuel's care. These concerns are proper for a hospital lawyer who designs institutional risk management strategies or who represents physicians after a clinical event has occurred.

When acting in the context of an ongoing clinical relationship, however, a hospital lawyer, like a physician, is obliged to accept ethical responsibility for clinical outcomes. In such cases, the lawyer must consider not only his or her responsibility to the hospital, but also the impact of decisions on a particular patient. The idea that there are ethical obligations, inherent in patient care, regardless of whether that care is being directed by a physician or a lawyer, and that these obligations may supercede traditional lawyer-client obligations may jar traditional legal sensibilities. Nevertheless, if lawyers and physicians participate together in particular clinical decisions, these obligations are present and their implications must be dealt with. . . .

We cannot eliminate legal risks. We can, however, take steps to manage such risks by documentation, staff education, and appropriate consent and decision-making procedures. In the case of treatment withdrawal decisions for children, we may empower an expert, patient-centered intrahospital ethics review of parental decisions. If questions remain about parental motives, we may seek child protection agency or court involvement. None of these steps were taken in the Linares case. Instead, the hospital requested that the family obtain a court order to withdraw the respirator, a request that this family was ill-equipped and financially unable to undertake, and that Illinois courts were unlikely to address expeditiously.

This approach reveals either an unfamiliarity with the medicolegal literature on the standard of care in forgoing treatment or an unrealistic and ultimately insensitive standard of institutional and professional risk management. The undue weight given to the remote risk of liability and the demand for the least practical modes of addressing this liability represent improper projection of institutional interest into what must have been a particularly fragile physician-family dialogue. Mr. Linares' final outraged response was, if not praiseworthy, at least understandable.

NOTES

1. J. Lorber, "Results of treatment of myelomeningcocele." *Developmental Medicine and Child Neurology* 13: 279–303, 1971; R. S. Duff, A. G. M. Campbell, "Moral and ethical dilemmas in the special care nursery." *New England Journal of Medicine* 289:890–894, 1973.
2. R. A. McCormick, "To save or let die: The dilemma of modern medicine." *JAMA,* 1974:229:172–176.
3. N. Hentoff, "The awful privacy of Baby Doe." *The Atlantic Monthly,* January, 1985:54–61.
4. K. Stratton, L. Stark, "Linares: The untold story." *The Nursing Spectrum,* 1989; 2:15,20.
5. American Hospital Association, "The Linares Case." *Hospital Ethics,* 1989;5(4): 11–14.
6. R. S. Duff, A. G. M. Campbell, "On deciding the care of severely handicapped or dying persons: With particular reference to infants." *Pediatrics,* 1976:57:487–491; R. H. Gross, A. Cox, R. Tatyrek, M. Pollay, W. A. Barnes, "Early management and decision making for the treatment of myelomeningocele." *Pediatrics,* 1983;72: 450–458.
7. R. H. Michaels, T. K. Oliver, "Human rights consultation: A 12-year experience of a pediatric bioethics committee." *Pediatrics* 1986;78:566–572; R. Kliegman, M. Mahowald, S. Youngner, "In our best interests: Experience and workings of an ethics review committee." *Journal of Pediatrics* 1986;108:178–187.
8. J. D. Lantos, S. H. Miles, "Autonomy in adolescence: A framework for decisions about end of life care." *Journal Adolescent Medicine,* 1989, In Press.
9. A. Holder, *Legal Issues in Pediatrics and Adolescent Medicine.* Yale University Press, 1985.

DECISIONS ON BEHALF OF ADULTS

Superintendent of Belchertown State School v. Saikewicz

SUPREME JUDICIAL COURT OF MASSACHUSETTS, HAMPSHIRE*

The following is a landmark case in surrogate decision making for the never-competent. Sixty-seven-year-old Joseph Saikewicz had lived in state institutions for more than 40 years. His IQ was ten, his mental age approximately 2 years and 8 months. He could communicate only by gestures and grunts, and he responded only to gestures or physical contacts. He appeared to be unaware of risks in his environment and became disoriented when removed from familiar surroundings. His health was generally good until April, 1976, when he was diagnosed as having acute myeloblastic monocytic leukemia, which is invariably fatal. At the petition of the Belchertown State School where Saikewicz lived, the probate court appointed a guardian *ad litem* with authority to make the necessary decisions concerning the patient's care and treatment. The guardian *ad litem* noted that Saikewicz's illness was incurable, that chemotherapy had significant adverse side effects and discomfort, and that Saikewicz could not understand the treatment or the resulting pain. For all these reasons, he concluded "that not treating Mr. Saikewicz would be in his best interests." The Supreme Judicial Court of Massachusetts upheld this decision in the following opinion, which is generally considered the leading case using a balancing approach to array and assess all of the competing interests at stake in the case, including any interests of the state.

LIACOS, Justice.

On April 26, 1976, William E. Jones, superintendent of the Belchertown State School (a facility of the Massachusetts Department of Mental Health), and Paul R. Rogers, a staff attorney at the school, petitioned the Probate Court for Hampshire County for the appointment of a guardian of Joseph Saikewicz, a resident of the State school. Simultaneously they filed a motion for the immediate appointment of a guardian *ad litem,* with authority to make the necessary decisions concerning the care and treatment of Saikewicz, who was suffering with acute myeloblastic monocytic leukemia. The petition alleged that Saikewicz was a mentally retarded person in urgent need of medical treatment and that he was a person with disability incapable of giving informed consent for such treatment.

*Source: From 370 *North Eastern Reporter, 2d Series* 417, pp. 420–423, 428–432, and 435. Decided November 28, 1977.

On May 5, 1976, the probate judge appointed a guardian *ad litem.* On May 6, 1976, the guardian *ad litem* filed a report with the court. The guardian *ad litem*'s report indicated that Saikewicz's illness was an incurable one, and that although chemotherapy was the medically indicated course of treatment it would cause Saikewicz significant adverse side effects and discomfort. The guardian *ad litem* concluded that these factors, as well as the inability of the ward to understand the treatment to which he would be subjected and the fear and pain he would suffer as a result, outweighed the limited prospect of any benefit from such treatment, namely, the possibility of some uncertain but limited extension of life. He therefore recommended "that not treating Mr. Saikewicz would be in his best interests."

A hearing on the report was held on May 13, 1976. Present were the petitioners and the guardian *ad litem.* . . . After hearing the evidence, the judge entered findings of fact and an order that in essence agreed with the recommendation of the guardian *ad litem.* The decision of the judge appears to be based in part on the testimony of Saikewicz's two attending physicians who recommended against chemotherapy. The judge then reported to the Appeals Court the two questions set forth in the margin. An application for direct appellate review was allowed by this court. On July 9, 1976, this court issued an order answering the questions reported in the affirmative with the notation "rescript and opinion . . . will follow." We now issue that opinion.

I

The judge below found that Joseph Saikewicz, at the time the matter arose, was sixty-seven years old, with an I.Q. of ten and a mental age of approximately two years and eight months. He was profoundly mentally retarded. The record discloses that, apart from his leukemic condition, Saikewicz enjoyed generally good health. He was physically strong and well built, nutritionally nourished, and ambulatory. He was not, however, able to communicate verbally—resorting to gestures and grunts to make his wishes known to others and responding only to gestures or physical contacts. In the course of treatment for various medical conditions arising during Saikewicz's residency at the school, he had been unable to respond intelligibly to inquiries such as whether he was experiencing pain. It was the opinion of a consulting psychologist, not contested by the other experts relied on by the judge below, that Saikewicz was not aware of dangers and was disoriented outside his immediate environment. As a result of his condition, Saikewicz had lived in State institutions since 1923 and had resided at the Belchertown State School since 1928. Two of his sisters, the only members of his family who could be located, were notified of his condition and of the hearing, but they preferred not to attend or otherwise become involved.

On April 19, 1976, Saikewicz was diagnosed as suffering from acute myeloblastic monocytic leukemia. Leukemia is a disease of the blood. . . . The disease is invariably fatal.

Chemotherapy, as was testified to at the hearing in the Probate Court, involves the administration of drugs over several weeks, the purpose of which is to kill the leukemia cells. This treatment unfortunately affects normal cells as well. One expert testified that the end result, in effect, is to destroy the living vitality of the bone marrow. Because of this effect, the patient becomes very anemic and may bleed or suffer infections—a condition which requires a number of blood transfusions. In this sense, the patient immediately becomes much "sicker" with the commencement of chemotherapy, and there is a possibility that infections during the initial period of severe anemia will prove fatal. Moreover, while most patients survive chemotherapy, remission of the leukemia is achieved in only thirty to fifty per cent of the cases. Remission is meant here as a temporary return to normal as measured by clinical and laboratory means. If remission does occur, it typically lasts for between two and thirteen months although longer periods of remission are possible. Estimates of the effectiveness of chemotherapy are complicated in cases, such as the one presented here, in which the patient's age becomes a factor. According to the medical testimony before the court below, persons over age sixty have more difficulty tolerating chemotherapy, and the treatment is likely to be less successful than in younger patients. This prognosis may be compared with the doctors' estimates that, left untreated, a patient in Saikewicz's condition would live for a matter of weeks or, perhaps, several months. According to the testimony, a decision to allow the disease to run its natural course would not result in pain for the patient, and death would probably come without discomfort.

An important facet of the chemotherapy process, to which the judge below directed careful attention, is the problem of serious adverse side effects caused by the treating drugs. Among these side effects are severe nausea, bladder irritation, numbness and tingling of the extremities, and loss of hair. The bladder irritation can be avoided, however, if the patient drinks fluids, and the nausea can be treated by drugs. It was the opinion of the guardian *ad litem,* as well as the doctors who testified before the probate judge, that most people elect to suffer the side effects of chemotherapy rather than to allow their leukemia to run its natural course.

Drawing on the evidence before him, including the testimony of the medical experts, and the report of the guardian *ad litem,* the probate judge issued detailed findings with regard to the costs and benefits of allowing Saikewicz to undergo chemotherapy. The judge's findings are reproduced in part here because of the importance of clearly delimiting the issues presented in this case. The judge below found:

5. That the majority of persons suffering from leukemia who are faced with a choice of receiving or forgoing such chemotherapy, and who are able to make an informed judgment thereon, choose to receive treatment in spite of its toxic side effects and risks of failure.

6. That such toxic side effects of chemotherapy include pain and discomfort, depressed bone marrow, pronounced anemia, increased chance of infection, possible bladder irritation, and possible loss of hair.

7. That administration of such chemotherapy requires cooperation from the patient over several weeks of time, which cooperation said JOSEPH SAIKEWICZ is unable to give due to his profound retardation.

8. That, considering the age and general state of health of said JOSEPH SAIKEWICZ, there is only a 30–40 percent chance that chemotherapy will produce a remission of said leukemia, which remission would probably be for a period of time of from 2 to 13 months, but that said chemotherapy will certainly not completely cure such leukemia.

9. That if such chemotherapy is to be administered at all it should be administered immediately, inasmuch as the risks involved will increase and the chances of successfully bringing about remission will decrease as time goes by.

10. That, at present, said JOSEPH SAIKEWICZ'S leukemia condition is stable and is not deteriorating.

11. That said JOSEPH SAIKEWICZ is not now in pain and will probably die within a matter of weeks or months a relatively painless death due to the leukemia unless other factors should intervene to themselves cause death.

12. That it is impossible to predict how long said JOSEPH SAIKEWICZ will probably live without chemotherapy or how long he will probably live with chemotherapy, but it is to a very high degree medically likely that he will die sooner without treatment than with it.

Balancing these various factors, the judge concluded that the following considerations weighed *against* administering chemotherapy to Saikewicz: "(1) his age, (2) his inability to cooperate with the treatment, (3) probable adverse side effects of treatment, (4) low chance of producing remission, (5) the certainty that treatment will cause immediate suffering, and (6) the quality of life possible for him even if the treatment does bring about remission."

The following considerations were determined to weigh in *favor* of chemotherapy: "(1) the chance that his life may be lengthened thereby, and (2) the fact that most people in his situation when given a chance to do so elect to take the gamble of treatment."

Concluding that, in this case, the negative factors of treatment exceeded the benefits, the probate judge ordered on May 13, 1976, that no treatment be administered to Saikewicz for his condition of acute myeloblastic monocytic leukemia except by further order of the court. The judge further ordered that all reasonable and necessary supportive measures be taken, medical or otherwise, to safeguard the well-being of Saikewicz in all other respects and to reduce as far as possible any suffering or discomfort which he might experience.

Saikewicz died on September 4, 1976, at the Belchertown State School hospital. Death was due to bronchial pneumonia, a complication of the leukemia. Saikewicz died without pain or discomfort.

II

The question what legal standards govern the decision whether to administer potentially life-prolonging treatment to an incompetent person encompasses two distinct and important subissues. First, does a choice exist? That is, is it the unvarying responsibility of the State to order medical treatment in all circumstances involving the care of an incompetent person? Second, if a choice does exist under certain conditions, what considerations enter into the decision-making process?

We think that principles of equality and respect for all individuals require the conclusion that a choice exists . . . We recognize a general right in all persons to refuse medical treatment in appropriate circumstances. The recognition of that right must extend to the case of an incompetent, as well as a competent, patient because the value of human dignity extends to both.

This is not to deny that the State has a traditional power and responsibility, under the doctrine of *parens patriae,* to care for and protect the "best interests" of the incompetent person. Indeed, the existence of this power and responsibility has impelled a number of courts to hold that the "best interests" of such a person mandate an unvarying responsibility by the courts to order necessary medical treatment for an incompetent person facing an immediate and severe danger to life. Whatever the merits of such a policy where life-saving treatment is available—a situation unfortunately not presented by this case—a more flexible view of the "best interests" of the incompetent patient is not precluded under other conditions. . . .

The "best interests" of an incompetent person are not necessarily served by imposing on such persons results not mandated as to competent persons similarly situated. It does not advance the interest of the State or the ward to treat the ward as a person of lesser status or dignity than others. To protect the incompetent person within its power, the State must recognize the dignity and worth of such a person and afford to that person the same panoply of rights and choices it recognizes in competent persons. If a competent person faced with death may choose to decline treatment which not only will cure the person but which substantially may increase suffering in exchange for a possible yet brief prolongation of life, then it cannot be said that it is always in the "best interests" of the ward to require submission to such treatment. Nor do statistical factors indicating that a majority of competent persons similarly situated choose treatment resolve the issue. The significant decisions of life are more complex than statistical determinations. Individual choice is determined not by the vote of the majority but by the complexities of the singular situation viewed from the unique perspective of the person called on to make the decision. To presume that the incompetent person must always be subjected to what many rational and intelligent persons may decline is to downgrade the status of the incompetent person by placing a lesser value on his intrinsic human worth and vitality.

The trend in the law has been to give incompetent persons the same rights as other individuals. Recognition of this principle of equality requires understanding that in certain circumstances it may be appropriate for a court to consent to the withholding of treatment from an incompetent individual. This leads us to the question of how the right of an incompetent person to decline treatment might be best exercised so as to give the fullest possible expression to the character and circumstances of that individual. . . .

Evidence that most people would or would not act in a certain way is certainly an important consideration in attempting to ascertain the predilections of any individual, but care must be taken, as in any analogy, to ensure that operative factors are similar or at least to take notice of the dissimilarities. With this in mind, it is profitable to compare the situations presented in the *Quinlan* case and the case presently before us. Karen Quinlan, subsequent to her accident, was totally incapable of knowing or appreciating life, was physically debilitated, and was pathetically reliant on sophisticated machinery to nourish and clean her body. Any other person suffering from similar massive brain damage would be in a similar state of total incapacity, and thus it is not unreasonable to give weight to a supposed general, and widespread, response to the situation.

Karen Quinlan's situation, however, must be distinguished from that of Joseph Saikewicz. Saikewicz was profoundly mentally retarded. His mental state was a cognitive one but limited in his capacity to comprehend and communicate. Evidence that most people choose to accept the rigors of chemotherapy has no direct bearing on the likely choice that Joseph Saikewicz would have made. Unlike most people, Saikewicz had no capacity to understand his present situation or his prognosis. The guardian *ad litem* gave expression to this important distinction in coming to grips with this "most troubling aspect" of withholding treatment from Saikewicz: "If he is treated with toxic drugs he will be involuntarily immersed in a state of painful suffering, the reason for which he will never understand. Patients who request treatment know the risks involved and can appreciate the painful side-effects when they arrive. They know the reason for the pain and their hope makes it tolerable." To make a worthwhile comparison, one would have to ask whether a majority of people would choose chemotherapy if they were told merely that something outside of their previous experience was going to be done to them, that this something would cause them pain and discomfort, that they would be removed to strange surroundings and possibly restrained for extended periods of time, and that the advantages of this course of action were measured by concepts of time and mortality beyond their ability to comprehend.

To put the above discussion in proper perspective, we realize that an inquiry into what a majority of people would do in circumstances that truly were similar assumed an objective viewpoint not far removed from a "reasonable person" inquiry. While we recognize the value of this kind of indirect evidence, we should make it plain that the primary test is subjective in nature—that is, the goal is to determine with as much accuracy as possible the wants and needs of the individual involved. This may or may not conform to what is thought wise or prudent by most people. The problems of arriving at an accurate substituted judgment in matters of life and death vary greatly in degree, if not in kind, in different circumstances. . . .

The "substituted judgment" standard which we have described commends itself simply because of its straightforward respect for the integrity and autonomy of the individual. . . . We believe that both the guardian *ad litem* in his recommendation and the judge in his decision should have attempted (as they did) to ascertain the incompetent person's actual interests and preferences. In short, the decision in cases such as this should be that which would be made by the incompetent person, if that person were competent, but taking into account the present and future incompetency of the individual as one of the factors which would necessarily enter into the decision-making process of the competent person. Having recognized the right of a competent person to make for himself the same decision as the court made in this case, the question is, do the facts on the record support the proposition that Saikewicz himself would have made the decision under the standard set forth. We believe they do. . . .

A reading of the entire record clearly reveals the judge's concern that special care be taken to respect the dignity and worth of Saikewicz's life precisely because of his vulnerable position. The judge, as well as all the parties, were keenly aware that the supposed ability of Saikewicz, by virtue of his mental retardation, to appreciate or experience life had no place in the decision before them. Rather than reading the judge's formulation in a manner that demeans the value of the life of one who is mentally retarded, the vague, and perhaps ill-chosen, terms "quality of life" should be understood as a reference to the continuing state of pain and disorientation precipitated by the chemotherapy treatment. Viewing the term in this manner, together with the other factors properly considered by the judge, we are satisfied that the decision to withhold treatment from Saikewicz was based on a regard for his actual interests and preferences and that the facts supported this decision.

III

Finding no State interest sufficient to counterbalance a patient's decision to decline life-prolonging medical treatment in the circumstances of this case, we conclude that the patient's right to privacy and self-determination is entitled to enforcement. Because of this conclusion, and in view of the position of equality of an incompetent person in Joseph Saikewicz's position, we conclude that the probate judge acted appropriately in this case. For these reasons we issued our order of July 9, 1976, and responded as we did to the questions of the probate judge.

Deciding for Others:
The Permanently Unconscious and the Severely and Permanently Demented*

ALLEN E. BUCHANAN AND DAN W. BROCK

According to Allen Buchanan and Dan Brock, persons who lack *self*-consciousness or have permanently lost their capacities to form plans for their future are in important respects more like animals than intact adult persons, because they cannot have plans and desires about their future that would be frustrated by death. The permanently unconscious and the severely and permanently demented typically satisfy this conception, and therefore have "minimal" or "truncated" interests, in their view. They therefore have no claims of distributive justice on social resources, and often they have no interest in life-sustaining treatment or, more generally, in continued life.

A. THE PERMANENTLY UNCONSCIOUS: MINIMAL INTERESTS

A proper understanding of the limits of the best interest principle makes it clear that the continued support of permanently unconscious patients is *not* ethically required, and that withdrawal of support constitutes no injury to them. For even if, in subscribing to the whole-brain concept of death, one concludes that such patients are not dead, one can nonetheless exclude them as legitimate claimants for scarce resources because they do not, as permanently unconscious beings, have any experiential interests nor any reasonable prospects of regaining any. Thus, they lack interests of the sort that can compete for scarce resources with the claims of others who can genuinely benefit from the social resources in question. . . .

There is, however, as we have already noted, an alternative route by which permanently unconscious patients as such may be excluded from the domain of problems of distributive justice. It is far from inconceivable that the process of conceptual change in response to technological advances that led from the cardiopulmonary concept of death to the whole-brain concept should eventually push us to a higher-brain function concept of death. If this change—which has already been advocated by a number of ethicists—does occur, then permanently unconscious individuals will be declared dead and thus as such will no longer be viewed as having claims on social resources. . . .

Use of social resources to sustain the permanently unconscious is irrational and, it could be argued, poor medical practice as well, if there are other, less costly ways of dealing humanely with the family's denial. The most obvious alternative is to coun-

---

*Source: Allen E. Buchanan and Dan W. Brock, "Deciding for Others: The Permanently Unconscious and the Severely and Permanently Demented," from *Deciding for Others*, Allen E. Buchanan and Dan Brock, Cambridge University Press, 1990, pp. 194–200. Reprinted with the permission of Cambridge University Press.

sel the family during the recommended period of two- to three-week waiting period in which the prognosis of persistent vegetative state is confirmed, utilizing the expertise of social workers, psychologists, psychiatrists, or chaplains, if necessary, to enable the family to come to terms with the fate of their loved one.

B. THE SEVERELY AND PERMANENTLY DEMENTED: TRUNCATED INTERESTS

These patients, . . . are unlike the permanently unconscious in one morally crucial respect: they are capable of pain and simple pleasures. Unlike the permanently unconscious, they have an interest in experiencing pleasure and in avoiding pain. It was also seen, however, that at least the most severely brain-damaged members of this group lack one or more of those cognitive capacities that are widely thought to be the necessary conditions for personhood. Finally, we also noted that even if it can be said that these beings have an interest in a continued existence that includes a favorable balance of pleasure over pain, any obligation we might be said to have to use social resources to continue such an existence is of lesser weight than our important obligations to persons. The same would appear to hold true for whatever obligations we might be thought to have to provide pleasure to sentiment nonpersons. In other words, if a conflict occurred between an obligation to give pleasure to a nonperson (or to continue a nonperson's on-balance pleasurable existence) and important obligations toward persons, we could forego the former in order to fulfill the latter, without injustice. Indeed, it is only because these nonpersons were once persons, embedded in relationships with others, that it is plausible to argue that there is *any* significant obligation to continue a pleasurable existence for them. Other nonpersons, such as many animals, are not commonly believed to have claims on social resources to continue their pleasurable lives, though it remains wrong to cause them gratuitous suffering.

It is plausible to hold that a severely demented individual in whom the psychological continuity necessary for personhood has been destroyed has no current, as opposed to surviving, interest in life-sustaining treatment. He or she does, however, have a current interest while alive in palliative care to relieve pain or suffering and to produce pleasure.

To see why such severely demented individuals have interests in pleasure and in minimizing pain and suffering, but no interest as such in continued life, it may help to consider how we would or should regard beings that *never* had advanced beyond the mental life of the severely demented. While wishing not to offend those who care deeply for those who have now become severely demented, we believe the comparison with some animals is instructive. It is widely agreed, for example, that mice and chickens are not persons. Presumably, this is not simply because they are not members of the human species, since it is at least possible that there are nonhuman persons, but because they lack some important properties or capacities that humans normally possess. Animals such as dogs and horses surely are sentient beings—they are conscious and capable of experiencing pleasure and pain, and in particular they can be made to suffer. What they presumably lack is the capacity for or experience of *self*-consciousness, a conception of themselves as, and experience of being, a single self-conscious individual who persists through time. Thus, while they can experience pain and suffer here and now in the present, and can be conditioned to associate pain and suffering with experiences not themselves painful, they lack capacities for hopes and fears, dreads and longing for their future. For this, they would require what it is commonly believed they lack, a belief that they themselves are beings that persist through time with a continuity of self-consciousness over time.

This may go some way toward explaining what otherwise appears an anomalous feature of many persons' moral views about the treatment of animals. Many persons hold that causing gratuitous pain or suffering to animals such as mice and chickens is seriously wrong, although painlessly killing such animals is not wrong. The apparent anomaly is that with persons it is commonly believed that killing them against their will is one of the, if not the, most serious wrongs that can be done to them, and specifically is a more serious wrong than causing them pain or suffering. Why then for animals is the more serious wrong of killing commonly held not to be a wrong at all, while causing them pain or suffering remains a wrong? We believe the explanation lies in the difference between humans and animals just noted—while each can be caused pain, which is immediately experienced as unpleasant and unwanted, only humans but not animals can have plans and desires about their future, and indeed have desires to have or experience that possible future, which can all be frustrated, or at least left unsatisfied, by being killed. It is this capacity to envisage and desire a future for oneself that best explains why killing a normal adult human wrongs that person.

The severely demented, while of course remaining members of the human species, approach more closely the condition of animals than normal adult humans in their psychological capacities. In some respects the severely demented are even worse off than animals such as dogs and horses, which have a capacity for integrated and goal-directed behavior that the severely demented substantially lack. The severe dementia that destroys memory undermines the individual's psychological capacities to forge links across time that establish a sense of personal identity across time, and for this reason robs him or her of personhood. This means in turn that such individuals lose the fundamental basis for persons' interest in continued life and in measures which sustain life—that their future life is a necessary condition for satisfying all of a person's desires about and plans for the future.

The priority of interests of persons has significant implications for problems of distributive justice. It implies that in choosing public policies that will ration health care by withholding life-support resources from the severely and permanently demented in order to fulfill our obligations to persons who can benefit from those resources we would not be failing to honor any legitimate distributive claims of the severely and permanently demented. This way of understanding our obligations to the severely and permanently demented who are nonpersons captures and renders coherent two strong elements of commonsense morality. The first is the belief that the distinction between persons and nonpersons marks a fundamental difference between two kinds of moral status. The second is that those nonpersons who have the capacity for pain and pleasure have some rights, although these rights are limited due to the inferior moral status of nonpersons.

Commonsense morality, at least upon reflection, generally resists attempts to introduce any *further* distinction of basic moral status *within* the class of persons. It is, of course, true that we do not ascribe a general right of self-determination (or more specific agency rights such as the right to enter into legal contracts or the right to refuse medical care or treatment) to those persons whose mental disabilities prevent them from meeting the appropriate threshold of competence. But the withholding of *these* rights does not affect the moral weight of those rights we do ascribe to such beings.

The 'Small Beginnings' of Euthanasia: Examining the Erosion in Legal Prohibitions Against Mercy-Killing*

C. EVERETT KOOP and EDWARD R. GRANT

In the following essay, C. Everett Koop, former Surgeon General of the United States, and Edward R. Grant denounce practices of allowing newborns to die as infanticide by starving a child. They likewise condemn such practices for adults as intentional acts of killing that amount to active euthanasia because they cause a preventable death. From this perspective, although it is legitimate to omit some forms of treatment from incompetent patients, life-saving treatment cannot justifiably be omitted. They advance a version of the wedge or slippery slope argument. Their claim is that policies of not providing treatment sow the seeds of potential abuse. Their fears about the removal of an important clinical, psychological, and social barrier center on a slide from "small beginnings" of acting in the patient's interests to acting in the society's interests, from considering the patient's quality of life to considering the patient's value for society, from decisions about dying patients to decisions about nondying patients, from letting die to killing, and from cessation of artificial feeding to cessation of natural feeding. Unlike several previous authors, they support government provisions such as the federal Child Abuse Amendments.

America is aging more rapidly than at any time in her history. Modern health care, especially through its technological advances, has expanded our life expectancies, but cannot deliver life-affirming care to the long-term elderly and disabled. The potential impact of these factors upon public policy may be illustrated by comparison to another medico-legal controversy of recent vintage. Each year, approximately 50,000 infants are born with life-threatening handicaps, and thus, are potentially subject to the "Baby Doe" amendments made to the federal child abuse statue. By the year 2000, in comparison, there will be 35 million Americans over the age of sixty-five, and by the year 2020, that number will soar to over 50 million.[1] Each of these elderly persons may at some time require extensive (and expensive) medical care. In short, for every potential Baby Doe, there will be approximately 15,000 "Granny Does." The impact of this demographic fact is likely to wield greater influence on the debate over euthanasia than jurisprudential concerns over the appropriate extent of personal liberty, patient autonomy, and the state interest in preserving life.

*Source: C. Everett Koop and Edward R. Grant, "The 'Small Beginnings' of Euthanasia: Examining the Erosion in Legal Prohibitions against Mercy-Killing," *Notre Dame Journal of Law, Ethics, and Public Policy* 2 (1986), pp. 588–590, 595, 616–618, & 621–622.

This article will examine whether the legislation and court decisions . . . in recent years have strengthened or weakened existing legal prohibitions against euthanasia. We will commence with a brief explanation of the legal definition of
euthanasia. Our substantive discussion will concern three categories of legal developments: the legislative definition of death, legislation regarding the "living will,"
and recent judicial opinions. Within each of these categories, we will focus on a specific, representative development for our detailed analysis.

Our thesis is that changes in the obligation to provide medical treatment to seriously ill and incompetent patients have created a legal climate that is favorable to
euthanasia, which is the *intentional* killing, by omission or direct action, of those
whose lives are considered of insufficient value to maintain. The consequences of fostering such a climate were compellingly stated by the late Dr. Leo Alexander, a
Boston psychiatrist and professor of medicine who died in 1985. Dr. Alexander
served as a medical consultant at the war-crimes trials of physicians who participated
in the atrocities of the Nazi regime in Germany. His witness to a depraved aspect of
twentieth-century history is more salient in the America of 1986 than it was in the
America of 1948.

> Whatever proportions these crimes finally assumed, it became evident to all who in-
> vestigated them that they had started *from small beginnings.* The beginnings at first were
> merely a subtle shift in emphasis in the basic attitude of physicians. It started with the
> acceptance of the attitude, basic in the euthanasia movement, that there is such a thing
> as life not worthy to be lived. This attitude in its early stages concerned itself merely
> with the severely and chronically sick. Gradually, the sphere of those to be included in
> this category was enlarged to encompass the socially unproductive, the ideologically un-
> wanted, and finally all non-Germans. But it is important to realize that the infinitely
> small wedged-in lever from which this entire trend of mind received its impetus *was the
> attitude toward the nonrehabilitable sick.*[2]

The legal developments that have taken place in the past decade offer convincing evidence that American legal institutions in the 1980s are examining precisely the
same question that was addressed so tragically by the legal profession in Germany in
the 1920s; society's attitude towards those who are chronically sick and infirm. . . .

This is particularly so in the case of passive euthanasia, since the potential tar-
gets are those who are most dependent upon others for basic means of support. Legal
doctrines which diminish the obligation to provide these means of support, even if
they do not explicitly endorse euthanasia, lead to an erosion of the jurisprudential
principles under which passive euthanasia is prohibited. Even if it were possible to
permit these forms of passive euthanasia, while drawing a firm line against active euthanasia, a possibility we do not admit, the likely outcome would be widespread death
by neglect. Under these conditions, it would be hypocritical to maintain a prohibition
against active euthanasia. . . .

One area of social change which has been inadequately addressed by legislation is the phenomenon of elderly, impaired patients, lacking frequent family contact,
who reside in nursing homes. This is a problem that did not exist in its current pro-
portions a generation ago, and one that will expand by the turn of the century and

beyond. Such persons are vulnerable medically because they are seen by physicians infrequently, vulnerable socially because they are cut off from a family environment and other stimuli, and vulnerable politically because they have no capacity of their own to influence the many governmental decisions which affect their lives.

Although legislation to reform the nursing home industry is helpful, our proposal is that states go further to establish offices for the protection of individual nursing home patients, and other vulnerable adults. The Minnesota Vulnerable Adults Protection Act[3] might be considered as a model of such legislation. Under this legislation, private complainants may initiate an investigation of suspected abuse of adults.[4] Such procedures may be effective ways of deterring medical abuse without resort to adversarial proceedings. A similar approach has been enacted by Congress with respect to the medical treatment of handicapped infants. An alternative to the Minnesota legislation is that highlighted by the New Jersey Supreme Court in its *Conroy* opinion: an office of ombudsman for the institutionalized elderly. Under *Conroy,* the office of ombudsman, created by statute several years earlier, was granted a new authority: to investigate and file a report in cases where life-prolonging medical treatment is sought to be withdrawn from terminally ill nursing home patients.[5]

Conceivably, such legislation could be used not only to reinforce legal protection for the elderly, but to investigate, and deter, true instances of over-treatment of the elderly. If a patient's bodily integrity or dignity were being violated by overly aggressive medical treatment, an appropriate complaint could be filed with an ombudsman, who would then investigate and make recommendations. Contested cases could be resolved in court, or through an "ethics committee" mechanism similar to that recommended for infant treatment controversies. . . .

The lack of consensus should not stay the legislature's hand; a similar circumstance prevailed on the issue of treatment for handicapped infants and was resolved largely as a result of the public interest stirred by the case of Infant Doe in Bloomington, Indiana.

The Child Abuse Amendments of 1984, pertaining to the Infant Doe issue, offer guidance for creating a base standard of medical care. Under these amendments, beneficial medical treatment must be provided to any infant unless 1) the infant is chronically and irreversibly comatose; 2) the provision of such treatment would merely prolong dying or be otherwise futile in terms of survival; and 3) the provision of treatment would be futile and the treatment itself would be inhumane under the circumstances.[6] Even under these exceptions, however, a patient cannot be denied "appropriate nutrition, hydration and medication." This standard provides a workable foundation for a proper standard of care towards terminally ill adults. . . .

In order to draw the line against euthanasia by starvation, the law should insist that any decision to forego nutrition and hydration be strictly justifiable by medical criteria: impossibility, imminent death which makes surgical intervention inappropriate, futility due to inability to metabolize or otherwise benefit from nutrition.[7] In addition to appropriate nutrition and medication, such legislation ought to mandate other measures needed for the comfort and personal dignity of patients: personal hygiene care, turning to prevent bedsores, adequate warmth. . . .

Whether or not the treatment of Karen Quinlan constituted euthanasia, or was otherwise improper, there is increasing support for the conclusion that, on balance, the *Quinlan* opinion has weakened legal and ethical prohibitions against euthanasia. . . . *Quinlan* forged [a] link between the "right to die" and the "right to kill" by defining the incompetent patient's constitutional rights of personal autonomy to include a right to refuse life-preserving medical treatment, by ruling that this right could be exercised on behalf of the incompetent patient by a family member or guardian, and by holding that in cases of severe disability, such as Miss Quinlan's, the state interest in preserving life could not check the guardian's exercise of the patient's "privacy" rights.

The implications of this series of rulings for existing laws against euthanasia are self-evident. If a "right to die" is given constitutional protection, and if that right can be "exercised on behalf of" an incompetent patient by imputing to that patient the desire to die, then all persons have a right to receive "voluntary" euthanasia— whether or not they actually request it. *Quinlan,* therefore provides a legal scheme by which the legalization of voluntary euthanasia will inevitably lead to the practice of all forms of euthanasia. Qualms regarding the practice of euthanasia could be satisfied, in each case, by completing the ritual of "imputing" the will of the patient to choose euthanasia. In that way, every act of euthanasia could be considered "voluntary," at least by those willing to be so comforted.

Further evidence of the danger *Quinlan* poses to existing laws against euthanasia may be surmised from the court's discussion of whether the death of Karen Quinlan upon removal of the respirator would constitute a homicide. The court answered that insofar as the death resulted from existing natural causes—Karen's inability to breathe—it would not constitute homicide. "[E]ven if it were regarded as homicide," the court continued, "it would not be unlawful,"[8] presumably because it would be exonerated under the constitutional right to privacy.[9] The court's reading of the right to privacy, therefore, encompasses constitutional protection for intentional acts of killing. Accordingly, the avenue of constitutional rights emerged from *Quinlan* as the most direct route to avoid the application of homicide laws to acts of euthanasia.

NOTES

1. 1985 Annual Report of the Board of Trustees Federal Old-Age and Survivors Insurance and Disability Insurance Trust Funds, H.R. Doc. No. 46, 99th Cong., 1st Sess. 77 (1985).
2. Leo Alexander, "Medical Science under Dictatorship," *New England Journal of Medicine* 39 (1949), at 44 (emphasis supplied).
3. Minn. Stat. Ann. § 626.557 (West 1983).
4. *Id.* § 626.557 Subd. 3.
5. 98 N.J. at 378-85, 486 A.2d at 1239–42.

6. 45 C.F.R. § 1340.15(b)(2) (1985).
7. This is virtually identical to the standard enunciated by the trial court in *Brophy v. New England Sinai Hosp. Inc.,* No. 85E0009-G1 (Mass. Probate Ct. Norfolk, Oct. 21, 1985), *rev'd in relevant part,* No. 4152 (Mass. Sup. Jud. Ct. Sept. 11, 1986).
8. 70 N.J. at 51, 355 A.2d at 670.
9. *Id.* at 51-52, 355 A.2d at 670.

SUGGESTED READINGS FOR CHAPTER 7

A. DECISIONS ON BEHALF OF CHILDREN

American Academy of Pediatrics. "Special Report: Comments on the 'Baby Doe II' Regulations." *New England Journal of Medicine* 309 (August 18, 1983):443–444.

American Medical Association. Council on Ethical and Judicial Affairs. "Treatment Decisions for Seriously Ill Newborns." *Reports of the Council,* No. 43. Chicago: American Medical Association, Jun 1992, pp. 66–75.

ANONYMOUS. "Nondiscrimination on the Basis of Handicap Relating to Health Care for Handicapped Infants." *Federal Register* 48 (July 5, 1983):30846–30852. Proposed rules.

DUFF, RAYMOND S., AND A.G.M. CAMPBELL. "Moral and Ethical Dilemmas in the Special-Care Nursery." *New England Journal of Medicine* 289 (October 25, 1973):890–894.

FLETCHER, JOHN. "Abortion, Euthanasia, and Care of Defective Newborn." *New England Journal of Medicine* 292 (January 9, 1975):75–77.

FOST, NORMAN. "Putting Hospitals on Notice: Baby Doe and Federal Funding." *Hastings Center Report* 12 (August 1982):5–8.

GUSTAFSON, JAMES M. "Mongolism, Parental Desires, and the Right to Life." *Perspectives in Biology and Medicine* 16 (Spring 1973):529–557.

HEYMANN, PHILIP B., AND SARA HOLTZ. "The Severely Defective Newborns: The Dilemma and the Decision Process." *Public Policy* 23 (Fall 1975):381–417.

JONSEN, ALBERT R., AND MICHAEL J. GARLAND (eds.). *Ethics of Newborn Intensive Care.* Berkeley, CA: University of California, 1976.

KOHL, MARVIN(ed.). *Infanticide and the Value of Life.* Buffalo, NY: Prometheus Books, 1978.

KOOP, C. EVERETT. "Ethical and Surgical Considerations in the Care of the Newborn with Congenital Abnormalities." In D.J. Horan and M. Delahoyde (eds.). *Infanticide and the Handicapped Newborn,* Provo, UT: Brigham Young University Press, 1982.

KUHSE, HELGA, AND PETER SINGER. *Should the Baby Live?: The Problem of Handicapped Infants.* Oxford: Oxford University Press, 1985.

Law, Medicine and Health Care. 17(4, Winter 1989). Special issue on the "Linares Case."

McCORMICK, RICHARD A. "To Save or Let Die: The Dilemma of Modern Medicine." *Journal of the American Medical Association* 229 (July 8, 1974):172–176.

McMILLAN, RICHARD C., H. TRISTRAM ENGELHARDT, JR., AND STUART F. SPICKER (eds.). *Euthanasia and the Newborn: Conflicts Regarding Saving Lives.* Dordrecht, The Netherlands: D. Reidel, 1987.

"Nondiscrimination on the Basis of Handicap, Procedures and Guidelines Relating to Health Care for Handicapped Infants, Final Rule." *Federal Register* 49(No. 8, January 12, 1984 (Part 84)):1622–54.

RHODEN, NANCY. "Treatment Dilemmas for Imperiled Newborns: Why Quality of Life Counts." *Southern California Law Review* 58(6, Sept. 1985):1283–1347.

ROBERTSON, JOHN. "Involuntary Euthanasia of Defective Newborns: A Legal Analysis." *Stanford Law Review* 27 (January 1975):213–267.

SHAW, ANTHONY. "Dilemmas of 'Informed Consent' in Children." *New England Journal of Medicine* 289 (October 25, 1973):885–894.

SHELP, EARL E. *Born to Die? Deciding The Fate of Critically Ill Newborns.* New York: Free Press, 1986.

STRAIN, JAMES E. "The American Academy of Pediatrics Comments on the 'Baby Doe II' Regulations." *New England Journal of Medicine* 309 (August 18, 1983): 443–444.

SWINYARD, CHESTER. *Decision Making and the Defective Newborn.* Springfield, IL: Charles C. Thomas, 1978.

TOOLEY, MICHAEL. *Abortion and Infanticide.* Oxford: Oxford University Press, 1983.

U.S. Department of Health and Human Services. "Infant Care Review Committees— Model Guidelines." *Federal Register* 50(72, Apr. 15, 1985):14893–14901.

WEIR, ROBERT. *Selective Nontreatment of Handicapped Newborns.* New York: Oxford University Press, 1983.

B. DECISIONS ON BEHALF OF ADULTS

[NB: See also section on formerly competent adults in Chapter 6]

AREEN, JUDITH. "The Legal Status of Consent Obtained from Families of Adult Patients to Withhold or Withdraw Treatment." *Journal of the American Medical Association* 258:July 10, 1987, 229–235.

C. GENERAL

American Medical Association. Council on Ethical and Judicial Affairs. "Decisions to Forgo Life-Sustaining Treatment for Incompetent Patients." *Reports of the Council,* No. 34. Chicago: American Medical Association. Jul 1991, pp. 65–77.

BARON, C. H. "Assuring 'Detached but Passionate Investigation and Decision': The Role of Guardians Ad Litem in Saikewicz-type Cases." *American Journal of Law and Medicine* 4 (1978):111–130.

BERNSTEIN, ARTHUR H. "Incompetent's Right to Die: Who Decides?" *Hastings Center Report* 10 (June 1980):20–21.

BUCHANAN, ALLEN. "Medical Paternalism or Legal Imperialism: Not the Only Alternatives for Handling Saikewicz-type Cases." *American Journal of Law and Medicine* 5 (Summer 1979):97–117.

BUCHANAN, ALLEN E., AND DAN W. BROCK. *Deciding for Others: The Ethics of Surrogate Decision Making.* Cambridge, MA: Cambridge University Press, 1989.

EMANUEL, EZEKIEL J., AND LINDA L. EMANUEL. "Proxy Decision Making for Incompetent Patients: An Ethical and Empirical Analysis." *Journal of the American Medical Association* 267(15, Apr. 15, 1992):2067–2071.

EMANUEL, LINDA L., AND EZEKIEL J. EMANUEL. "Decisions at the End of Life: Guided by Communities of Patients." *Hastings Center Report* 23(5, Sept.–Oct. 1993):6–14.

KING, PATRICIA. "The Authority of Families to Make Medical Decisions for Incompetent Patients after the *Cruzan* Decision." *Law, Medicine and Health Care.* 19(1–2, Spring–Summer 1991):76–79.

New York State Task Force on Life and the Law. *When Others Must Choose: Deciding for Patients Without Capacity.* New York: New York State Task Force, 1992.

VEATCH, ROBERT M. "Limits of Guardian Treatment Refusal: A Reasonableness Standard." *American Journal of Law and Medicine* 9(4, Winter 1984):427–468.

BIBLIOGRAPHICAL SOURCES AND REFERENCE WORKS

REICH, WARREN, (ed.). *Encyclopedia of Bioethics.* New York: Macmillan, 1995, articles on:

Abuse, Interpersonal: Child Abuse
Children: Rights of Children
Infants: History of Infanticide
Infants: Ethical Issues
Infants: Public Policy and Legal Issues
Paternalism

8

Futile Treatment and Terminal Care

INTRODUCTION

Until the 1980s the debate over the ethics of terminal care almost always involved patients or their surrogates who were attempting to get life-prolonging medical treatment stopped. They had reached the conclusion that the treatment, on balance, could not be expected to offer a benefit. The dynamic of the interaction between health care provider, on the one hand, and patient or family, on the other, was one in which the provider felt a moral obligation to prolong life while the patient or family was ready to stop prolonging life. This created a situation in which the health care provider was convinced that some good (or at least some moral purpose) was served by the medical intervention while the patient or family believed the effort was not worth it.

As the movement to permit forgoing life-sustaining treatment progressed more and more physicians came to understand the limits of medical intervention. They joined the death-with-dignity movement, so to speak. They increasingly acknowledged that sometimes medical interventions serve no purpose. They began accepting patient and family decisions to forgo treatment. In fact, some began counseling patients that the wiser and more humane course would be to stop. By the end of the 1980s this view emerged as a consensus.

This consensus was widely accepted. It was reflected in the report from The President's Commission for the Study of Ethical Problems in Medicine and Biomedical and Behavioral Research, a federal government commission on bioethics. It was in accord with the long-held views of the Catholic Church. It was supported by almost all court decisions. As long as the patient and family accepted this advice, there was a meeting of the minds and quiet decisions to forgo further life-sustaining treatment were accepted by all. But once in a while the patient or family has not seen the decision the same way. They have differed in the evaluative judgment about when life was worth preserving.

The difficult cases have been those in which aggressive medical intervention can prolong life indefinitely (or at least for a long period), but will preserve it in a state that many people consider of no value. Some patients are in a permanent vegetative state. They lack all mental function and cannot ever recover it. They are permanently unconscious. Other patients are infants with severe, incurable brain defects such as anencephaly. They lack major portions of the brain and, like the permanently vegetative, no amount of medical treatment will produce consciousness. Still others are suffering from metastatic cancers, AIDS, or other conditions that are inevitably going to take the patient's life fairly soon. In all of these cases, medical intervention can change the way these patients die. They can be kept alive, at least for a while, with medical treatment, but the underlying condition cannot be changed.

Some of these patients (or family members acting as surrogates) have begun insisting that life should be preserved for as long as possible. They may have done so for religious reasons—believing that life is a gift from God and precious in its every moment. They may have done so for secular reasons—believing that any human life is of infinite value regardless of its quality. Holders of these views have begun to insist that life support be provided. They insist on ventilators, dialysis, blood transfusions, and chemotherapy, even though they understand that the underlying condition cannot be cured.

Physicians and others who are skeptical of the value of this kind of life prolongation have begun referring to these interventions as *futile care*. It is futile in the sense that, from the perspective of the medical provider, it offers no medical benefit. Some have gone along with patients and family demanding such treatment, especially if they realized that the effect will only be temporary. But others are resisting demands by patients for life prolongation with an insistence equal to that of the physicians who in an earlier era insisted that it was the physicians prerogative and moral duty to prolong life to the last gasp.

Sometimes physicians have claimed that deciding whether medical treatment is beneficial is a "medical" decision. If the physician determines that the treatment will provide no benefit, then he or she has the prerogative to decide to stop. They point to physician decisions to cease CPR on a patient who has suffered cardiac arrest or to a decision not to prescribe antibiotics for an infection that is almost certainly viral and therefore not amenable to the drug.

A conceptual distinction is now being made by many analysts. If the treatment will not produce the effect desired by the patient or surrogate, the term *physiological futility* is sometimes applied. Deciding that a treatment will or will not produce a specified effect surely requires the kind of technical medical expertise that physicians should possess. It would seem strange for the physician to yield to a lay person in deciding whether an antibiotic would cure an infection.

But others point out that often the disagreements are typically not about whether the treatment will produce a specified effect. In the case of the vegetative patient, the clinician can agree that the ventilator will increase the probability of the patient continuing to live. In the case of the metastatic cancer patient, the clinician can agree that chemotherapy could produce a brief extension of life. In the case of anemia associated with untreatable end stage renal failure, the clinician can agree that a blood transfusion will add a day or two of extra life. In these cases the dispute is sometimes over whether there is any value in these extra days of life.

In the earlier era, the patient often insisted that these days were of no value while the clinician insisted that they should be pursued even if there was no chance of a cure. Now clinicians are the ones insisting the temporary life-prolongation is of no value while patients or surrogates are convinced of the value. Deciding that temporary life-prolongation is achievable, but of no value is different from deciding that the extra days cannot be achieved. If the treatment is judged futile, the judgment is a normative one, not one that can be derived from medical science. For this reason, this kind of futility judgment is sometimes called *normative futility*. Normative futility judgments rely on value judgments; they cannot be deduced directly from beliefs about medical facts.

The focus of current controversy is on whether clinicians should have the authority to decide to forgo some treatments deemed futile, and, if so, which ones. We shall see in the selections that follow that different reasoning may apply in cases of physiological futility and in cases of normative futility.

Many clinicians and professional organizations are claiming the right to have the clinician unilaterally decide to forgo futile treatments. They offer two general kinds of reasons. First, many of these treatments can be expensive. If the benefit is so marginal that many people decline the treatment when it is offered and many physicians consider them useless, this is surely a place to consider eliminating expenditures if health resources need to be conserved. This concern for limiting the use of scarce, expensive, inefficient resources is a major concern, but some people doubt that rationing should be the responsibility of the bedside clinician or that "futility" is the basis of the decision. Rationing is taken up in Chapter 9; only the issue of futility is taken up here.

The second reason why clinicians might feel justified in unilaterally excluding treatments they consider futile is more personal. Clinicians consider themselves professionals who should act in accord with their own understanding of the ends and standard operating procedures of medicine. They resist casting themselves in the role of business persons who will deliver whatever the patient demands. A term that is now often used in this debate over futile care is *professional integrity*. Some physicians feel that as professionals they are morally obliged to act with integrity and cooperate in providing medical services only when it is consistent with their understanding of the purposes and standards of medicine. Perpetual biological support of a permanently vegetative or anencephalic patient seems to them a violation of their integrity.

The argument from integrity is not without its challengers. It is pointed out that physicians are in a real sense public servants. They are professionals who are licensed. They have certain obligations to provide services even if they happen to have personal objections to the services. They have obligations to render emergency treatment that extend to the hypothetical situation in which an emergency room physician has religious or moral objections to delivering the care, say, because of unusual views about race or gender or objections to particular treatments. For example, a Jehovah's Witness emergency room physician who objected to transfusing blood for accident victims would appear to have a moral and legal obligation to provide the blood that would still be binding if he or she had a conscientious, religious objection to doing so. By accepting a license to practice medicine and accepting assignment to be on duty in the emergency room, the physician has taken on a public commitment to deliver certain services to patients in need. The fact that the physician's objection was deeply held and religiously based seems irrelevant. It would seem not to be sufficient to claim that providing blood violated the physician's integrity. If physicians have made certain implied promises to deliver services as part of their contract with the public that accompanies licensure, then in some cases they would have obligations to provide those services that would not be overcome by personal moral objections. Surely, this obligation is limited to special conditions. For example, life-saving treatments and those that relieve severe suffering would seem particularly weighty. Exactly which treatments patients would have a right to in the face of a physician's belief that the treatment was futile requires considerable work to establish. Identifying the criteria that establish this right is the task of the readings in this chapter.

The first group of readings examine conceptual issues: what is meant by futility, the difference between physiological and normative futility, and the role of clinicians and patients in defining futility. Then two of the most famous futile care cases are presented: that of an elderly woman in a permanent vegetative state, Helga Wanglie, who purportedly held a life-long belief that she would want ventilatory support so she could continue living under these circumstances and that of Baby K, an infant born with anencephaly whose mother for religious reasons wanted ventilatory support to preserve her life.

The final group of readings looks at the moral and public policy issues raised by these cases. They consider what role, if any, bedside clinicians should have in limiting such treatments, and whether the principle of respect for autonomy in medical ethics provides a basis for a right of access to care deemed futile by clinicians in the same way it provides a basis for a patient's right of refusal. These selections examine criteria for limiting care and for granting a right of access. They set the stage for debates over limiting such care for the purposes of conserving scarce social resources, the topic to be taken up in more detail in Chapter 9.

THE CONCEPT OF FUTILITY

Who Defines Futility?*

STUART J. YOUNGNER

Donald Murphy, a clinician who studies the outcomes of cardiopulmonary resuscitation (CPR) published a proposal in 1988 that, in cases in which a physician believes intervention would be of no benefit, the clinician should have the
authority unilaterally to decide against resuscitation and omit telling patients and
families about the decision. Stuart Youngner responds to this proposal in the selection that follows. In the process he explores the concept of *futility* and distinguishes between treatments that physiologically cannot produce the effect sought
by the patient and treatments that will produce some effect, but are judged by the
clinician to be of no benefit based on the clinician's value judgments. Youngner
claims that, except for physiological futility, all judgments that lead to the conclusion that a treatment is of no benefit involve value judgments.

For the past two decades, our society has struggled to identify the proper circumstances under which life-sustaining medical treatment should be limited. In fact,
we seem to have reached a consensus on some aspects of the problem. It is generally
agreed that a competent patient has the right to refuse life-sustaining treatment; when
the patient is not competent, family members may limit treatment to serve the patient's best interests.

Donald Murphy[1] . . . examines a more controversial question that is currently
at the forefront of the treatment-limitation debate—i.e., under what circumstances
can life-sustaining interventions be limited *without* the informed consent of the patient or family?

Murphy notes correctly that cardiopulmonary resuscitation (CPR) is "rarely effective and in many cases futile" in the setting of a long-term-care facility, where
many elderly patients are chronically ill or severely demented. He proposes a policy
that "enables health care providers to make ethically sound, *unilateral* [emphasis
mine] decisions regarding CPR. . . . " Physicians should only discuss the resuscitation decision with patients and families if resuscitation offers "some level of benefit"
or the patient's prognosis is "at all equivocal."

Murphy argues that such a policy would avoid "futile" therapy that "can be
harmful" because it prevents "a timely death." By acting unilaterally, physicians
would avoid causing unnecessary suffering for the patient as well as an unfair "burden of guilt" for the family. Moreover, he argues, families' treatment decisions may

*Source: Youngner, Stuart J. "Who Defines Futility?" *JAMA* 260(1988): 2094–2095. Copyright ©1988, American Medical Association.

be based on factors (e.g., guilt over not visiting the patient or fear of death) that have little to do with what the patient desired. (He believes, I assume, that health professionals are less likely than family members to have interests or values that potentially conflict with those of the patient.) Finally, he raises the question of whether society should provide the "substantial resources" that aggressive treatment of long-term-care patients would require.

Murphy justifies these claims with two ethical arguments. First, physicians' scientific knowledge and clinical experience enable them to recognize when a life-sustaining treatment is "futile." At this point, they should "reconsider the emphasis on autonomy" and exercise a strong paternalism that promotes patient (and family) well-being by limiting such treatment unilaterally and without even informing the patient and/or family. The second argument involves the broader social issue of the proper allocation of our nation's resources. . . .

The word "futile" has a categorical ring that masks a more subtle complexity. To delineate its meaning in specific situations, we must first examine the potential goals of the medical intervention in question.[2] For example, we can understand futility in purely *physiological* terms. . . . In the case of resuscitation, will CPR reestablish spontaneous heartbeat? We can also understand futility in terms of *postponing death.* We might, with diligent attention, be able to keep the serum sodium level within normal limits in a patient whose condition is rapidly deteriorating, but still fail to postpone death by even a few minutes. According to one standard, our efforts were futile; according to another, they were quite effective. *Length of life* represents another standard for judging futility. If our attention to fluid and electrolyte balance manages to postpone the patient's death for 24 hours, were our efforts futile? . . . Using this standard, CPR was futile if the patient lived a week, but died before discharge. And what about the *quality of life?* An intervention that kept a patient alive for six months might well be judged futile because it did not achieve an important goal of the patient—e.g., being able to walk and take care of his or her own personal hygiene. Finally, we might think of futility in terms of *probability.* A given intervention could be judged futile if the chance of achieving one or more of the goals just examined is not entirely absent, but is highly unlikely. . . . Should statisticians define futility? When is an outside chance a chance worth taking?

Physicians are in the best position to know the empirical facts about the many aspects of futility. I would argue, however, that all, except for physiological futility and an absolute inability to postpone death, also involve value judgments. Physicians may be best suited to frame the choices by describing prognosis and quality of life—as well as the odds for achieving them. Physicians should not offer treatments that are physiologically futile or certain not to prolong life, and they could ethically refuse patient and family requests for such treatments. Beyond that, they run the risk of "giving options disguised as data."[3]

Living for five more days might give some patients the opportunity to say goodbyes, to wait for the arrival of a loved one from another city, or to live to see the birth of a grandchild. . . .

Nonetheless, the aggressive intervention of CPR in the event of cardiac arrest seems intuitively contraindicated in the long-term-care population described by Murphy. . . . He provided patients and family members with accurate descriptions of their medical conditions, poor prognoses, and the grisly realities of dying in a critical care unit. He presented the options as objectively as he could. The results were gratifying: 23 of 24 patients opposed resuscitation. None refused to discuss the tough issues because they felt uncomfortable. When patients were incompetent, all but one relative indicated that the patient would not have opted for resuscitation.

Why then does Murphy propose excluding patients and families from the decision-making process, and the even more radical step of not informing them of the do-not-resuscitate decision made unilaterally by the physician? Such a policy seems unnecessary; by communicating frankly with patients and families, he achieved the desired outcome. Why take the next step? Murphy seems to lapse back into an outdated (but perhaps yearned for) notion of paternalism. After giving ample evidence to the contrary, he worries that families will feel too guilty or will fail to "fully understand the implications of resuscitation despite detailed explanations." He goes on to say that making do-not-resuscitate decisions unilaterally and not informing patients and families will enable us to save time "better spent discussing other therapies and plans . . . that may have potential benefit." Acceptance of this position would also provide a justification for having physicians make unilateral and secret decisions about other "useless" therapies.

This latter reasoning becomes even more alarming when Murphy shifts from a paternalistic concern about what is best for the patient and family to a worry about how society should use its resources. He is not the first to be concerned about the massive resources consumed by the elderly in their final months, weeks, and even days of life—a problem that has been likened to a medical "avalanche."[4] As more and more elderly patients with chronic illnesses and severe dementia fill beds in long-term-care facilities in the decades ahead, the problem may become monumental.

While everyone seems to agree that the avalanche is coming, there is little consensus in our society about a national policy to handle the situation. Responsible persons, such as philosophers Daniel Callahan and Norman Daniels, as well as former Colorado Governor Lamm, have suggested that care to the elderly be limited; their ideas have met with loud and often harsh criticism. . . .

These are issues that must be decided at the public policy level. Americans may well choose explicitly to ration medical resources by denying them to those persons with the least chance of deriving benefit; other countries have chosen this course implicitly, by tradition. While rationing is always a painful process, the potential success of treatment may be a more ethically acceptable criterion than others, such as social worth or ability to pay.[5,6] . . .

As professionals, we are there to serve our patients. As citizens, we can vote or lobby for policies that limit individual choice in the interests of a broader social good.

Murphy's proposal is a regressive step. Under the guise of medical expertise and concern for proper resource allocation, it encourages physicians to substitute their own value judgments for those of their patients. He urges physicians to cut off communication with patients and families about the futility of resuscitation, an intervention imbued with complex and powerful symbolism.[7]

His actions were much more appealing. By engaging in honest communication, he was able to use his clinical knowledge and judgment to help families and patients make wise choices about painful but inescapable issues. Physicians would do well to follow Dr. Murphy's example—not his proposal.

NOTES

1. Murphy D. J. Do-not-resuscitate orders: Time for reappraisal in long-term-care institutions. *JAMA* 1988;260:2098–2101.
2. Tomlinson T., Brody H. Ethics and communication in do-not-resuscitate orders. 1988;318:43–46.
3. McQuillen M. P. Ethics of life support and resuscitation. *New England Journal of Medicine* 1988;318:1756.
4. Callahan D. *Setting Limits: Medical Goals in an Aging Society.* New York, Simon & Schuster Inc. Publishers, 1987.
5. Rescher N. The allocation of exotic medical lifesaving therapy. *Ethics* 1969;79: 173–186.
6. Childress J. Who shall live when not all can live? *Soundings* 1970;53:339–355.
7. Nolan K. In death's shadow: The meanings of withholding resuscitation. *Hastings Center Report* 1987:17:9–14.

Futility: A Concept in Search of a Definition*

RONALD CRANFORD AND LAWRENCE GOSTIN

Ronald Cranford and Lawrence Gostin continue the process of defining the concept of futility. They rely on the distinction between physiological futility and judgments made by clinicians that certain treatments produce no benefit even though they produce an effect. By 1992, however, the claim that judgments about physiological futility are value-free was being called into question. Cranford and Gostin refer to the judgment of physiological futility as "virtually a value-free decision." They emphasize that labeling a treatment futile very frequently serves as a device for permitting the clinician to make evaluative decisions based on quality of life. They expand the concept of futility to apply to treatments regarded as harmful to patients and those that utilize scarce resources that could go to more needy patients. Others have argued that, while these may be good reasons to limit medical care, treatments that produce burdens to patients and treatments that consume resources that could benefit others should not be labeled *futile*. Rather, that term should be limited to treatments that produce no benefit—either because they produce no physiological effect or because the effect they produce is considered of no value. Cranford and Gostin also enter the normative debate by raising the question of whether the principle of autonomy, which permits patients to refuse treatment, can also provide a basis for insisting on a right of access. They appear to assume that if patients have such a right, it must be grounded in autonomy. They conclude that physicians should not make social choices on the false assumption that they are purely scientific, and that patients and their surrogates cannot have a right to receive all possible services.

In the landmark case of *Cruzan v. Director, Missouri Department of Health,*[1] the United States Supreme Court went out of its way to emphasize that the state was paying for Nancy Cruzan's care. The court refused to allow removal of the artificial nutrition and hydration that was maintaining Nancy Cruzan in a persistent vegetative state (PVS). What if, instead of the state's paying for the care, the parents had to "spend down" in order to be eligible for Medicaid? Could the state opt for life and require the family to pay for the care? If not, do constitutional rights depend on who can or will pay the cost of care?

Now turn the facts of *Cruzan* around and assume that the parents want to keep the child alive. Could the parents force the state to bear the cost of keeping a PVS patient alive indefinitely? If not, why should the state, but not the parents, have a constitutional right to preserve life? Do constitutional rights boil down to dollars?

*Source: Ronald Cranford and Lawrence Gostin, "Futility: A Concept in Search of a Definition," *Law, Medicine & Health Care,* 20, no. 4 (1992):307-309. Reprinted with the permission of the American Society of Law, Medicine & Ethics and Professor Gostin & Dr. Cranford.

357

Finally, assume the patient has left a living will to say she wants to be kept alive in PVS at any cost. But the patient is penniless when she lapses into PVS and all the costs need to be borne by her parents. Should America's over-abiding belief in absolute autonomy compel a family to bear any burden?

We do not have convincing ethical or legal answers to these difficult questions, but we can observe that their analysis requires a reconciliation or amalgamation of various societal values. Answers to these tortuous questions cannot simply be derived from the predominantly medical concept of "futility," the legal concept of "consent" or "substituted consent," or the ethical concept of "autonomy."

Shortly after *Cruzan*, the Minnesota case of Helga Wanglie emerged as the paradigm for the concept of "futility." Mrs. Wanglie was an 86-year-old woman in a persistent vegetative state. Her husband insisted that her biological life should be maintained at any cost. Her physicians, however, regarded mechanical ventilation and intensive care as futile. Unable to find any hospital or physician in Minnesota willing to take Mrs. Wanglie in transfer, her care-givers at the Hennepin County Medical Center in Minneapolis requested that the court appoint an independent conservator. The court denied the petition, reaffirming the authority of her husband as the appropriate legal surrogate.

The Wanglie case and the modern debate over futility, however, should not obscure one central fact. The medical profession has for many years thwarted the wishes of patients and their families to withhold or withdraw life sustaining treatment. In almost every landmark right-to-die case in the U.S. courts—from *Quinlan* in 1975 through *Cruzan* in 1990—the situation was the reverse of *Wanglie;* in the face of an overwhelmingly poor prognosis for the patient, the family wanted to stop treatment, but the physicians objected. Thus, in the past, the profession rarely claimed that sustaining the biological life of persons in PVS was futile. It is difficult now to take seriously the claim that termination of treatment is a mere medical judgment devoid of social values and ethical conduct.

FUTILITY

The concept of "futility" can be reasonably defined only in its most limited sense. The Hastings Center Guidelines define "physiologic futility" as applying to treatment that is "clearly futile in achieving its physiological objective and so offers no physiologic benefit to the patient. . . . "[2] Truog and colleagues properly see physiologic futility in very narrow terms. Where an intervention stands very little chance of achieving its physiologic objective, it becomes virtually a value-free decision; thus, it may be made principally by the health care team. Even here, serious questions arise as to the level of certainty needed to claim physiological futility, for few interventions have *no* chance of succeeding.[3]

Apart from the very narrow definition of physiological futility, all other uses of the term appear to mask different agendas. The term "futility" allows the profession to medicalize a difficult personal, familial, and social decision. Once a decision is framed by the term "futility," it provides a justification for physicians to either 1) override the wishes of the patient, family, or other surrogates, or 2) make a nontreatment decision without even obtaining informed consent by not discussing the unilateral decision with the patient, family, or surrogate at all. This promise of objectivity, as suggested by the empirical research of Solomon and her colleagues, is deceptive.4 "Almost invariably, when futility arguments were invoked, they were used to support evaluative judgments based on quality-of-life considerations; only rarely were they used to designate treatments that were medically inefficacious."5

We suggest several value-laden ways in which the term "futility" has been applied. First, . . . physicians understandably set therapeutic goals for interventions based on fundamental goals of medicine such as promoting or preserving health, minimizing disability, and minimizing pain and suffering. If medical intervention is unlikely to provide an overall improvement in the physical or mental condition of the patient, it is often regarded as outside the boundaries of appropriate medical practice. . . . For someone who is permanently and completely unconscious . . . medical treatment cannot minimize suffering for one who experiences no consciousness and therefore no suffering.

While such interventions may not serve the goal of improved quality of life, they still remain subject to societal judgment. The sharply drawn political and social conflict regarding the right to life for persons in PVC (which includes physicians on both sides) illustrates vividly how ethical, personal, and social choices play significant roles in such decisions. The religious, personal and moral views of many Americans include the belief that biological life is essential to maintain even if the quality of that life is negligible. Many physicians now feel that preservation of "life," when "life" is defined only in terms of vegetative functions of heartbeat, respiration, etc., is not and never was a fundamental goal of medical treatment when all possibility of restoring conscious life has been extinguished. If society is to hold that treatment is inappropriate in these or other circumstances, the choice must be based upon a clear, public resolution of the social issues, and not driven by a falsely framed medical judgment called "futility."

A second value-laden use of the term futility occurs when health care professionals regard treatment as harmful to the patient. A decision to use CPR on a terminally ill patient who would "recover" with gross disabilities is sometimes perceived as harmful to the patient. While most patients would not wish to survive for a short period of time in a painful or dependent condition, some would. The judgment as to whether a short existence with severe disability is a life worth living is a personal, and value-laden, not merely medical judgment. The concept of futility implies that the physician is capable of judging the value of a certain kind of life for a patient; the physician, of course, is not usually in a position to make that subjective judgment for her patient. . . .

Other uses of futility are even more morally problematic because they involve other considerations which have nothing to do with the best interests of the individual patient.

A third use of the term "futility" occurs when the patient is utilizing scarce health care resources that should be available for other "more needy" patients. The allocation of scarce resources implicitly undergirds many medical decisions that treatment is futile. When a physician, for example, argues that maintaining a person in PVS or resuscitating a person at the end of life is futile, she may actually mean that it would deprive another patient of a hospital bed or a high cost medical intervention.

The United States has no clear policy about the allocation of scarce health care resources either at the institutional or national level. . . .

Again, the sharp clash of beliefs among legislators, policy makers, ethicists, and advocates over the Oregon plan shows that withdrawing or withholding treatment from *any* group in society is fraught with value assumptions. If it is understandably so difficult for a state legislature to make such a decision after exhaustive public discussion and debate, what right would a single physician claim to make a unilateral choice behind closed doors, especially when it is based on broad social policy allocation of resources?

AUTONOMY: CONSENT AND SUBSTITUTED CONSENT

Patients and their families or surrogates often state that it is *their* decision whether to refuse or receive medical treatment. Competent patients or their legal surrogates have the right to refuse medical treatment of any kind—even if the abatement of treatment will result in the patient's death.[6] It is tempting to assume that, if patients or surrogates have the right to refuse, they also have the right to insist on whatever treatment they want. This simple symmetrical statement, however, is not supported by law or logic.

The right to refuse treatment is premised on the patient's entitlement to be free from bodily interference. Treatment imposed without the consent of the patient is a battery, according to the same legal doctrine that applies to any unwanted touching.

While citizens have a right not to have others invade their bodily integrity without permission, they have no corresponding right to insist on receiving any and all services they may desire. Once a doctor-patient relationship is formed, to be sure, the physician may not precipitously abandon the patient if it would cause irreversible harm. But neither patients nor their families have a general right to insist on receiving every possible treatment irrespective of cost, efficacy, risk, possible outcome or future quality of life.

Persons may have a reasonable expectation of basic primary and secondary health care. In America, however, even the most fundamental rights of access to health care, nutrition and housing are frequently unmet. What legal or ethical rule would hold that persons have the right to have their biological life maintained irrespective of the quality of that life or the cost, while others have no entitlement to the most fundamental primary care? If a line needs to be drawn (we presume that a society cannot afford to have truly unlimited access), then it is for society to draw it. The physician cannot make that social choice based upon the false assumption that it is purely a scientific judgment; nor can the patient or her surrogate make that choice based on the false claim of an absolute right to receive any and all possible services.

The simplistic concepts of futility and autonomy, then, cannot adequately inform society about the kinds of health care services that are appropriately provided to patients. Health care professionals, patients, and their surrogates are left with the arduous but necessary task of communicating effectively and of searching for an equitable resolution to the treatment conflict. With these introductory remarks to help frame the discussion, we invite you to read LMHC's mini-symposium on futility, and to decide for yourself about this relatively new, extremely important, but also highly dangerous, concept of medical futility.

NOTES

1. 110 S.Ct. 2841 (1990).
2. Hastings Center, *Guidelines on the Termination of Life-Sustaining Treatment and the Care of the Dying.* Bloomington: Indiana University Press, 1987; p. 32.
3. R.D. Truog, A.S. Brett, J. Frader. "The Problem with Futility," *New England Journal of Medicine* 1992; 326:1560–1564.
4. M.Z. Solomon. *Life and Death Decisions: Physician Perspectives and Their Implications for Professional Education.* Ann Arbor, MI: U. Michigan Intl. 1991.
5. M.Z. Solomon. "Futility as a Criterion in Limiting Treatment," (letter) *New England Journal of Medicine.* 1992; 327(17):1239.
6. R.F. Weir. *Abating Treatment with Critically Ill Patients: Ethical and Legal Limits to the Medical Prolongation of Life.* Oxford University Press, 1989.

In Re: The Conservatorship of Helga M. Wanglie

STATE OF MINNESOTA, DISTRICT COURT, PROBATE COURT DIVISION, COUNTY OF HENNEPIN, FOURTH JUDICIAL DISTRICT

FINDINGS OF FACT, CONCLUSIONS OF LAW AND ORDER

One of the two major legal cases often thought of as raising the question of futility arose in Minneapolis, Minnesota. It involved Helga M. Wanglie, an 87-year-old woman who was in a persistent vegetative state being maintained on a ventilator. Her physicians came to the conclusion that further ventilation was futile since it could not restore consciousness. Nevertheless, Mrs. Wanglie's husband, Oliver, concluded that it would be best if ventilatory support continued.

The case became a public controversy in 1991 when Steven Miles, a physician and member of the Hennepin County Medical Center Ethics Committee who consulted with the physicians treating physicians, sought to have a conservator appointed who might consent to the removal of the ventilator. The judicial proceeding that denied this request and supported Mr. Wanglie's request to continue as his wife's guardian is presented here. Mrs. Wanglie died three days after the court ruling despite continuation of aggressive medical care.

This matter was heard commencing May 28, 1991, and through May 31, 1991, by the Honorable Patricia L. Belois, Judge of the District Court, Probate Court Division. Hearing was held upon the Second Amended Petition for Appointment of Terrence Larpenteur as General Conservator (Person Only) filed on May 14, 1991, by Steven H. Miles, M.D., Petitioner, and upon the Amended Petition for Appointment of a Guardian (Person and Estate) filed May 2, 1991, by Oliver Wanglie, Petitioner. . . .

Based upon the file and record herein, the Court makes the following:

Findings of Fact with Regard to Helga Wanglie

1. The proposed Conservatee/Ward, Helga Wanglie, is 87 years old. She has been married to Oliver Wanglie for 53 years and is the mother of two adult children, David Wanglie and Ruth Wanglie.
2. Helga Wanglie is a well-educated woman, a graduate of St. Olaf College, with advanced certification from the Minnesota Business College and a master's degree from St. Thomas College.

3. Helga Wanglie is a devout Lutheran and a dedicated churchwoman who served her congregation for many years as a Sunday school teacher, a member of the library board, and a participant in Operation Love.
4. The religious beliefs of Helga Wanglie and her husband are congruent, of long standing, firmly held, and consistent.
5. Until December, 1989, when she tripped over a rug in her home and broke her hip, Helga Wanglie drove a car, kept house, prepared meals, read the newspaper, and otherwise enjoyed life with her husband and family to the fullest.
6. From time to time, Helga Wanglie had discussions with her husband and son about the meaning of life and the use of life-sustaining medical treatments which were triggered by something one of them read or by news about the illness of a friend or acquaintance. No evidence suggests Helga Wanglie considered the possibility that she would be afflicted exactly as she now is, or that she would ever become ventilator-dependent.
7. Helga Wanglie is incapable of interacting with other people at this time. She is unable to establish new relationships.
8. Helga Wanglie does not have a living will. She no longer has the capacity to express a preference for one person or another to become her Conservator.
9. Helga Wanglie is not a patient in a state hospital for the mentally ill or a mentally retarded or dependent or neglected ward of the Commissioner of Human Services or under the temporary custody of the Commissioner of Human Services.

Findings of Fact with Regard to Petitioner Steven H. Miles, MD.

1. Steven H. Miles, M.D., (Miles) is a physician licensed to practice medicine in the State of Minnesota. He is a board certified internist and a geriontologist. He is a member of the Hennepin County Medical Center Ethics Committee.
2. He has been a consultant to the physicians treating Helga Wanglie on issues of medical ethics since October, 1990. He was also an ethical consultant to physicians caring for her in June, 1990, when the feasibility of cardiopulmonary resuscitation for Helga Wanglie was discussed. Other medical ethicists have also consulted with the treating physicians during Helga Wanglie's extensive hospitalization.
3. At no time when Helga Wanglie was conscious and able to express her own wishes did any physician or staff member at the Hennepin County Medical Center discuss her treatment preferences with her.
4. Other than proving that Oliver Wanglie does not accept the advice and counsel of the physicians treating Helga Wanglie and refuses to consent to remove the ventilator which breathes for her, Miles has offered no evidence that Oliver Wanglie is incompetent to discharge the trust as Conservator of the Person of his wife.
5. Miles has petitioned the Court to appoint an independent conservator to make medical care and abode choices for Helga Wanglie.

Findings of Fact with Regard to Terrence Larpenteur

1. Miles has nominated Terrence Larpenteur (Larpenteur) to be the Conservator of Helga Wanglie's Person for the limited purposes of determining her place of abode and consenting to or refusing necessary medical care for her.
2. Larpenteur is qualified to be the conservator for Helga Wanglie. He is an experienced, professional conservator. Among his 80 clients, he has two ventilator-dependent clients at this time.

3. Larpenteur is willing to accept the Court's order appointing him as Conservator in this case.
4. Larpenteur has deliberately, and appropriately, avoided learning about the particulars of this case and is, in every sense, a stranger to Helga Wanglie, her family, her medical situation and her physicians.

Findings of Fact with Regard to Oliver Wanglie

1. Oliver Wanglie is the closest person to Helga Wanglie, and he knows her conscientious, religious, and moral beliefs intimately.
2. Oliver Wanglie has a well-established pattern of conferring with family members in matters involving serious decisions; however, he reserves the making of the decisions to himself.
3. Oliver Wanglie is fully able to maintain a current understanding of Helga Wanglie's mental and physical needs.
4. Oliver Wanglie is dedicated to promoting his wife's welfare. He has consistently followed the recommendations of her treating physicians with regard to her general medical care, the place where she should receive care and treatment, and the decision not to resuscitate her from future cardiopulmonary arrests. He carefully considers the quality of medical care Helga Wanglie will receive in the various places that are available to her, and he has appropriate concerns about the availability of third-party payment for her care in different settings.
5. Oliver Wanglie's children are in agreement that he should be the person to make decisions for their mother's medical care.

Other Findings of Fact

1. The stipulation of the parties filed May 14, 1991, is adopted by the Court and by this reference is included among these Findings of Fact. A copy of the Stipulation is attached to this order as Exhibit A.
2. The proposed Conservatee has property which will be dissipated without proper management.
3. The attached Memorandum is incorporated herein by this reference.

CONCLUSIONS OF LAW

1. Helga Wanglie is an incapacitated person. . . .
2. No protective arrangement or other transaction . . . nor other alternative to guardianship would provide adequate protection for Helga Wanglie.
3. Helga Wanglie requires the continuing protection of a guardian of her person and estate, which guardian would have all the powers described in Minn. Stat. 525.56, Subds. 3 and 4.
4. It is in Helga Wanglie's best interest that Oliver Wanglie, her husband, be appointed as the guardian of her person and estate.
5. Oliver Wanglie is the most suitable and best qualified person among those nominees who are now available.

ORDER

1. The amended petition of Oliver Wanglie filed May 2, 1991, is granted.
2. The amended petition of Steven B. Miles, M.D., filed May 14, 1991, is denied.

3. Oliver Wanglie be and hereby is appointed Guardian of the Person and Estate of Helga Wanglie, and possesses all the powers enumerated in Minn. Stat. 525.56, Subds. 3 and 4.
4. Letters of Guardianship shall issue to Oliver Wanglie upon the filing of his oath, acceptance of trust, and bond in the amount of $5,000.00
5. The Guardian shall give notice . . . before any sale or disposition of the Ward's clothing, furniture, vehicles or other personal effects. . . .

BY THE COURT

Patricia L. Belois
Judge of District Court
Probate Court Division

Dated: June 28, 1991

EXHIBIT A

FILE NO. PX-91-283

STIPULATION OF FACTS

WHEREAS, counsel for all parties deem it to be in the interest of judicial economy to simplify and agree upon certain medical facts in this case; and

WHEREAS, Mrs. Wanglie's medical condition has been thoroughly documented since May 31, 1990, at Hennepin County Medical Center;

NOW, THEREFORE, it is hereby agreed and stipulated as follows:

1. Helga Wanglie is 86 years old, having been born on October 20, 1904;
2. In December, 1989, Mrs. Wanglie sustained a hip fracture, causing her to be hospitalized at North Memorial Hospital and subsequently placed at a nursing home;
3. On January 1, 1990, while being transferred from a nursing home to Hennepin County Medical Center (HCMC) by ambulance, she suffered an acute respiratory arrest;
4. Following the respiratory arrest, she was placed on a respirator at HCMC, and over time it was determined that she was ventilator dependent;
5. On May 7, 1990, Mrs. Wanglie was transferred to Bethesda Lutheran Hospital in St. Paul, Minnesota;
6. On May 23, 1990, Mrs. Wanglie suffered a cardiorespiratory arrest, and was transferred to St. Joseph's Hospital in St. Paul after being resuscitated;
7. On May 31, 1990, Mrs. Wanglie was transferred to HCMC, where she has remained until the present time;
8. As a result of the cardiorespiratory arrest on May 23, 1990, Mrs. Wanglie suffered severe anoxic encephalopathy and has not regained consciousness since that time;
9. Since readmission to HCMC on May 31, 1990, Mrs. Wanglie has been respirator dependent (via tracheotomy tube); has been given nourishment only by intubation; has been on a Kinn-Air bed, which shifts her position and weight periodically because she cannot move herself, in order to prevent decubitus ulcers; and has received repeated courses of antibiotics for recurrent lung infections;

10. Mrs. Wanglie has the following medical conditions:

   a. Aortic insufficiency murmur;

   b. Congestive heart failure;

   c. Chronic, recurrent pneumonias secondary to underlying lung disease, unconsciousness and recumbency;

   d. Bilateral atelectasis and calcified lung disease;

   e. Chronic respiratory insufficiency with dependence on mechanical ventilation, which her physicians have concluded is irreversible;

   f. Persistent vegetative state with no change in one year, i.e. unconsciousness since her cardiorespiratory arrest on May 23, 1990, which her physicians have concluded is irreversible.

11. Mrs. Wanglie is incapacitated within the meaning of Minn. Stat. § 525.54, Subds. 1 and 2 (1990).

WILLIAM L. H. LUBOV (64762)
Attorney for Helga Wanglie
2445 Park Avenue
Minneapolis, MN 55404
Dated: 5/13/91   Telephone: (612) 870-7400

BARRY WILLIAM MCKEE (70877)
Attorney for Oliver Wanglie
324 South Main Street, Suite 220
Stillwater, MN 55082
Dated: 5/13/91   Telephone: (612) 430-1717

MICHAEL O. FREEMAN
Hennepin County Attorney

By: _____
MICHAEL B. MILLER (73349)
Sr. Assistant County Attorney
Attorneys for Petitioner
2000A Government Center
Minneapolis, MN 55487
Dated: 5/13/91   Telephone: (612) 348-5488

MEMORANDUM

The Court is asked whether it is in the best interest of an elderly woman who is comatose, gravely ill, and ventilator-dependent to have decisions about her medical care made by her husband of 53 years or by a stranger.

Minnesota guardianship law requires the guardian to be the individual whose appointment is in the best interest of the incapacitated person. . . . Further, Minn. Stat. . . . instructs that: "Kinship is not a conclusive factor in determining the best interests of the ward . . . but should be considered to the extent that it is relevant to the other factors contained in this subdivision." . . . The parties acknowledge that a consideration of these factors often results in the appointment of a family member, unless the relative is unable to perform the duties of the office.

Petitioner Miles does not contest that Oliver Wanglie is a suitable person to be the guardian of Helga Wanglie's estate. Similarly, Miles does not dispute that Oliver Wanglie is qualified to be guardian with regard to providing food and clothing, fulfilling her social and emotional requirements, and arranging training, education and rehabilitation. Miles believes that Oliver Wanglie is not competent to be Helga Wanglie's conservator with regard to making decisions about her shelter, medical care, and religious requirements. Oliver Wanglie disagrees.

Except for unconvincing testimony from some physicians and health care providers at the Hennepin County Medical Center, there is no evidence that Oliver Wanglie is unable to perform the duties and responsibilities of a guardian. The evidence overwhelmingly supports the conclusion that Oliver Wanglie can understand the medical issues involving his wife.

In view of the Ward's comatose condition and the positions of the parties, the language of Minn. Stat. Sec. 525.539, Subd. 7 (1990), pertinent to this case reads: " 'Best interests of the ward . . . ' means all relevant factors to be considered or evaluated by the Court in nominating a guardian, . . . including but not limited to: (3) the interest and commitment of the proposed guardian or conservator in promoting the welfare of the ward . . . and the proposed guardian's ability to maintain a current understanding of the ward's . . . physical and mental status and needs. In the case of a ward . . . , welfare includes: (i) . . . shelter, and appropriate medical care . . . (ii) religious . . . requirements. . . . "

Oliver Wanglie has shown himself to be dedicated to his wife's proper medical care. He visits her regularly, although the frequency is in dispute. He expresses the belief that the nurses caring for his wife are skilled professionals and compassionate people. Except with regard to the issue of removing the ventilator, he has thoughtfully agreed with the treating physicians about every major decision in his wife's care. He is in the best position to investigate and act upon Helga Wanglie's conscientious, religious and moral beliefs and he has indicated that he will do so. . . .

No Court order to continue or stop any medical treatment for Helga Wanglie has been made or requested at this time. Whether such a request will be made, or such an order is proper, or this Court would make such an order, and whether Oliver Wanglie would execute such an order are speculative matters not now before the Court.

Oliver Wanglie believes that he is the best person to be the guardian for his wife. Their children agree with him. The evidence clearly and convincingly supports their position.

Informed Demand for "Non-Beneficial" Medical Treatment*

STEVEN H. MILES

Soon after the court ruled in favor of Mr. Wanglie's request to continue as his wife's guardian and against Steven Miles' request to have a conservator appointed, Miles presented his case for removal of the ventilator from Mrs. Wanglie in an article in the *New England Journal of Medicine*. Throughout the debate over the case, Miles has claimed that since the ventilator could prolong life, it was not characterized as "futile." Nevertheless, it is this case, and cases like it, that have been the focus of the futile care debate.

Miles focuses his discussion on the claim that physicians are not obliged to provide all treatments that patients or their surrogates request. As was argued by Ronald Cranford, a colleague of Miles at Hennepin County, Miles stresses that a right of access cannot be grounded in autonomy. He argues for cessation of the ventilator based on the lack of any clear benefit, community standards, and fair use of collective medical care resources.

An 85-year-old woman was taken from a nursing home to Hennepin County Medical Center on January 1, 1990, for emergency treatment of dyspnea from chronic bronchiectasis. The patient, Mrs. Helga Wanglie, required emergency intubation and was placed on a respirator. She occasionally acknowledged discomfort and recognized her family but could not communicate clearly. In May, after attempts to wean her from the respirator failed, she was discharged to a chronic care hospital. One week later, her heart stopped during a weaning attempt; she was resuscitated and taken to another hospital for intensive care. She remained unconscious, and a physician suggested that it would be appropriate to consider withdrawing life support. In response, the family transferred her back to the medical center on May 31. Two weeks later, physicians concluded that she was in a persistent vegetative state as a result of severe anoxic encephalopathy. She was maintained on a respirator, with repeated courses of antibiotics, frequent airway suctioning, tube feedings, an air flotation bed, and biochemical monitoring.

In June and July of 1990, physicians suggested that life-sustaining treatment be withdrawn since it was not benefiting the patient. Her husband, daughter, and son insisted on continued treatment. They stated their view that physicians should not play God, that the patient would not be better off dead, that removing life support showed moral decay in our civilization, and that a miracle could occur. Her husband told a physician that his wife had never stated her preferences concerning life-

*Source: Miles, Steven H. "Informed Demand for 'Non-Beneficial' Medical Treatment." *The New England Journal of Medicine* 325 (1991):512-515.

sustaining treatment. He believed that the cardiac arrest would not have occurred if she had not been transferred from Hennepin County Medical Center in May. The family reluctantly accepted a do-not-resuscitate order based on the improbability of Mrs. Wanglie's surviving a cardiac arrest. In June, an ethics committee consultant recommended continued counseling for the family. The family declined counseling, including the counsel of their own pastor, and in late July asked that the respirator not be discussed again. In August, nurses expressed their consensus that continued life support did not seem appropriate, and I, as the newly appointed ethics consultant, counseled them.

In October 1990, a new attending physician consulted with specialists and confirmed the permanence of the patient's cerebral and pulmonary conditions. He concluded that she was at the end of her life and that the respirator was "non-beneficial," in that it could not heal her lungs, palliate her suffering, or enable this unconscious and permanently respirator-dependent woman to experience the benefit of the life afforded by respirator support. Because the respirator could prolong life, it was not characterized as "futile."[1] In November, the physician, with my concurrence, told the family that he was not willing to continue to prescribe the respirator. The husband, an attorney, rejected proposals to transfer the patient to another facility or to seek a court order mandating this unusual treatment. The hospital told the family that it would ask a court to decide whether members of its staff were obliged to continue treatment. A second conference two weeks later, after the family had hired an attorney, confirmed these positions, and the husband asserted that the patient had consistently said she wanted respiratory support for such a condition.

In December, the medical director and hospital administrator asked the Hennepin County Board of Commissioners (the medical center's board of directors) to allow the hospital to go to court to resolve the dispute. In January, the county board gave permission by a 4-to-3 vote. Neither the hospital nor the county had a financial interest in terminating treatment. Medicare largely financed the $200,000 for the first hospitalization at Hennepin County; a private insurer would pay the $500,000 bill for the second. From February through May of 1991, the family and its attorney unsuccessfully searched for another health care facility that would admit Mrs. Wanglie. Facilities with empty beds cited her poor potential for rehabilitation.

The hospital chose a two-step legal procedure, first asking for the appointment of an independent conservator to decide whether the respirator was beneficial to the patient and second, if the conservator found it was not, for a second hearing on whether it was obliged to provide the respirator. The husband cross-filed, requesting to be appointed conservator. After a hearing in late May, the trial court on July 1, 1991, appointed the husband, as best able to represent the patient's interests. It noted that no request to stop treatment had been made and declined to speculate on the legality of such an order.[2] The hospital said that it would continue to provide the respirator in the light of continuing uncertainty about its legal obligation to provide it. Three days later, despite aggressive care, the patient died of multisystem organ failure resulting from septicemia. The family declined an autopsy and stated that the patient had received excellent care.

DISCUSSION

This sad story illustrates the problem of what to do when a family demands medical treatment that the attending physician concludes cannot benefit the patient. Only 600 elderly people are treated with respirators for more than six months in the United States each year.[3] Presumably, most of these people are actually or potentially conscious. It is common practice to discontinue the use of a respirator before death when it can no longer benefit a patient.[4,5]

We do not know Mrs. Wanglie's treatment preferences. A large majority of elderly people prefer not to receive prolonged respirator support for irreversible unconsciousness.[6] Studies show that an older person's designated family proxy overestimates that person's preference for life-sustaining treatment in a hypothetical coma.[7-9] The implications of this research for clinical decision making have not been cogently analyzed.

A patient's request for a treatment does not necessarily oblige a provider or the health care system. Patients may not demand that physicians injure them (for example, by mutilation), or provide plausible but inappropriate therapies (for example, amphetamines for weight reduction), or therapies that have no value (such as laetrile for cancer). Physicians are not obliged to violate their personal moral views on medical care so long as patients' rights are served. Minnesota's Living Will law says that physicians are "legally bound to act consistently within my wishes within limits of reasonable medical practice" in acting on requests and refusals of treatment.[10] Minnesota's Bill of Patients' Rights says that patients "have the right to appropriate medical . . . care based on individual needs . . . [which is] limited where the service is not reimbursable."[11] Mrs. Wanglie also had aortic insufficiency. Had this condition worsened, a surgeon's refusal to perform a life-prolonging valve replacement as medically inappropriate would hardly occasion public controversy. . . .

Disputes between physicians and patients about treatment plans are often handled by transferring patients to the care of other providers. In this case, every provider contacted by the hospital or the family refused to treat this patient with a respirator. These refusals occurred before and after this case became a matter of public controversy and despite the availability of third-party reimbursement. We believe they represent a medical consensus that respirator support is inappropriate in such a case.

The handling of this case is compatible with current practices regarding informed consent, respect for patients' autonomy, and the right to health care. Doctors should inform patients of all medically reasonable treatments, even those available from other providers. Patients can refuse any prescribed treatment or choose among any medical alternatives that physicians are willing to prescribe. Respect for autonomy does not empower patients to oblige physicians to prescribe treatments in ways that are fruitless or inappropriate. Previous "right to die" cases address the different situation of a patient's right to choose to be free of a prescribed therapy. This case is more about the nature of the patient's entitlement to treatment than about the patient's choice in using that entitlement.

The proposal that the family's preference for this unusual and costly treatment, which is commonly regarded as inappropriate, establishes a right to such treatment is ironic, given that preference does not create a right to other needed, efficacious, and widely desired treatments in the United States. We could not afford a universal health care system based on patients' demands. Such a system would irrationally allocate health care to socially powerful people with strong preferences for immediate treatment to the disadvantage of those with less power or less immediate needs.

After the conclusion was reached that the respirator was not benefiting the patient, the decision to seek a review of the duty to provide it was based on an ethic of "stewardship." Even though the insurer played no part in this case, physicians' discretion to prescribe requires responsible handling of requests for inappropriate treatment. Physicians exercise this stewardship by counseling against or denying such treatment or by submitting such requests to external review. This stewardship is not aimed at protecting the assets of insurance companies but rests on fairness to people who have pooled their resources to insure their collective access to appropriate health care. Several citizens complained to Hennepin County Medical Center that Mrs. Wanglie was receiving expensive treatment paid for by people who had not consented to underwrite a level of medical care whose appropriateness was defined by family demands. . . .

I believe that the grieving husband was simply mistaken about whether the respirator was benefiting his wife. A direct request to remove the respirator seems to center procedural oversight on the soundness of the medical decision making rather than on the nature of the patient's need. Clearly, the gravity of these decisions merits openness, due process, and meticulous accountability. The relative merits of various procedures need further study. . . .

Each case must be evaluated individually. In this case, the husband's request seemed entirely inconsistent with what medical care could do for his wife, the standards of the community, and his fair share of resources that many people pooled for their collective medical care. This case is about limits to what can be achieved at the end of life.

NOTES

1. Tomlinson T., Brody H. Futility and the ethics of resuscitation. *JAMA* 1990; 264:1276–1280.
2. In re Helga Wanglie, Fourth Judicial District (Dist. Ct., Probate Ct. Div.) PX-91-283. Minnesota, Hennepin County.
3. Office of Technology Assessment Task Force. Life-sustaining technologies and the elderly. Washington, DC: Government Printing Office, 1987.
4. Smedira, N.G., Evans B.H., Grais L.S., et al. Withholding and withdrawal of life support from the critically ill. *New England Journal of Medicine* 1990; 322:309–315.
5. Lantos J.D., Singer P.A., Walker R.M. et al. The illusion of futility in clinical practice. *American Journal of Medicine* 1989; 87:81–84.

6. Emanuel L.L., Barry M.J., Stoeckle J.D., Ettelson L.M., Emanuel E.J. Advance directives for medical care—a case for greater use. *New England Journal of Medicine* 1991; 324:889–895.

7. Zweibel N.R., Cassel C.K. Treatment choices at the end of life: a comparison of decisions by older patients and their physician-selected proxies. *Gerontologist* 1989; 29:615–621.

8. Tomlinson T., Howe K., Notman M., Rossmiller D. An empirical study of proxy consent for elderly persons. *Gerontologist* 1990; 30:54–64.

9. Danis M., Southerland L.I., Garrett J.M., et al. A prospective study of advance directives for life-sustaining care. *New England Journal of Medicine* 1991; 324: 882–888.

10. Minnesota Statutes. Adult Health Care Decisions Act. 145b.04.

11. Minnesota Statutes. Patients and residents of health care facilities; Bill of rights. 144.651:Subd. 6.

The Case of Helga Wanglie
A New Kind of "Right to Die" Case*

MARCIA ANGELL

Miles's argument for forgoing ventilatory support of Mrs. Wanglie was accompanied by an editorial by Marcia Angell, the Executive Editor of the *New England Journal of Medicine,* in which she provides a quite different analysis. She focuses on the emerging consensus that it is the right of the family to make decisions about life-sustaining treatment when the patient is no longer able to do so. Whenever earlier cases of persistent vegetative state have supported forgoing ventilators, these have been cases in which the family has wanted the treatment stopped. In this case the patient and the family apparently wanted the ventilator to continue. Angell points out that Mrs. Wanglie was incapable of suffering. Angell agrees that there are some cases, including those in which an incompetent patient would be made to suffer from continued treatment, in which the family should not have the right to demand continued life-support, but she considers it wrong for physicians such as Miles to intervene in family decisions in cases like Mrs. Wanglie's.

. . . The Wanglie case differed in a crucial way from earlier right-to-die cases, beginning with the case of Karen Quinlan 16 years ago. In the earlier cases, the families wished to withhold life-sustaining treatment and the institutions had misgivings. Here it was the reverse; the family wanted to continue life-sustaining treatment, not to stop it, and the institution argued for the right to die. Mr. Wanglie believed that life should be maintained as long as possible, no matter what the circumstances, and he asserted that his wife shared this belief.

In one sense, the court's opinion in the Wanglie case would seem to be at odds with most of the earlier opinions in that it resulted in continued treatment of a patient in a persistent vegetative state. In another sense, however, the opinion was quite consistent, because it affirmed the right of the family to make decisions about life-sustaining treatment when the patient was no longer able to do so. By granting guardianship of Mrs. Wanglie to her husband, the judge indicated that the most important consideration was who made the decision, not what the decision was. I believe that this was wise; any other decision by the court would have been inimical to patient autonomy and would have undermined the consensus on the right to die that has been carefully crafted since the Quinlan case. . . .

The well-publicized legal disputes involving the right to die—such as the Quinlan case, the Brophy case in Massachusetts,[1] and the Cruzan case in Missouri—have reached the courts either because the institution believed it improper to withhold life-sustaining treatment at the family's request or because the institution wanted legal

*Source: Angell, Marcia. "The Case of Helga Wanglie: A New Kind of 'Right to Die' Case." *The New England Journal of Medicine* 325(1991): 511-512.

immunity before doing so. Until the Wanglie case, there was only one well-publicized case of the reverse situation—that is, of a family wishing to persist in treatment over the objections of the institution. This was the poignant case of Baby L, described last year in the *Journal*.2 The case involved a two-year-old child, profoundly retarded and completely immobile, who required repeated cardiopulmonary resuscitation for survival. Baby L's mother insisted that this be done as often as necessary, despite the fact that there was no hope of recovery. Representatives of the hospital challenged her decision in court on the grounds that the continued treatment caused great suffering to the child and thus violated its best interests. Before the court reached a decision, however, the mother transferred the child to a hospital that agreed to continue the treatment, and the case became legally moot.

Unlike the case of Baby L, the Wanglie case did not involve a course that would cause the patient great suffering. Because she was in a persistent vegetative state, Mrs. Wanglie was incapable of suffering. Therefore, a compelling case could not be made that her best interests were being violated by continued use of the respirator. Instead, representatives of the institution invoked Mrs. Wanglie's best interests to make a weaker case: that the use of the respirator failed to serve Mrs. Wanglie's best interests and should therefore not be continued. It was suggested that a victory for Mr. Wanglie would mean that patients or their families could demand whatever treatment they wished, regardless of its efficacy. Many commentators also emphasized the enormous expense of maintaining a patient on life support when those resources are needed to care for people who would clearly benefit. Elsewhere in this issue, Steven H. Miles, M.D., the ethics committee consultant at the Hennepin County Medical Center who was the petitioner in the Wanglie case, presents the arguments of the institution.3 They are strong arguments that deserve to be examined, but I believe that they are on balance not persuasive.

It is generally agreed, as Miles points out, that patients or their surrogates do not have the right to demand any medical treatment they choose.4,5 For example, a patient cannot insist that his doctor give him penicillin for a head cold. Patients' rights on this score are limited to refusing treatment or to choosing among effective ones. In the case of Helga Wanglie, the institution saw the respirator as "non-beneficial" because it would not restore her to consciousness. In the family's view, however, merely maintaining life was a worthy goal, and the respirator was not only effective toward that end, but essential.

Public opinion polls indicate that most people would not want their lives maintained in a persistent vegetative state. Many consider life in this state to be an indignity, and care givers often find caring for such patients demoralizing. It is important, however, to acknowledge that not everyone agrees with this view and it is a highly personal issue. For the decision to rest with the family is the most sensitive and workable approach, and it is the generally accepted one. Furthermore, a system in which life-sustaining treatment is discontinued over the objections of those who love the patient, on a case-by-case basis, would be callous. It can be argued on medical grounds that the definition of brain death should be legally extended to include a persistent vegetative state, but unless that is done universally we have no principled basis on which to override a family's decision in this kind of case. It is dismaying, of course, that resources are spent sustaining the lives of patients who will never be sentient, but we as a society would be on the slipperiest of slopes if we permitted ourselves to withdraw life support from a patient simply because it would save money.

Since the Quinlan case it has gradually been accepted that the particular decision is less important than a clear understanding of who should make it, and the Wanglie case underscores this approach. When self-determination is impossible or an unambiguous proxy decision is unavailable, the consensus is that the family should make the decision. To be meaningful, this approach requires that we be willing to accept decisions with which we disagree. Only if a decision appears to violate the best interests of a patient who left no guidance or could provide none, as in the case of Baby L, should it be challenged by the institution. Thus, the sources of decisions about refusing medical treatment are, in order of precedence, the patient, the patient's prior directives or designated proxy, and the patient's family. Decisions from each of these sources should reflect the following standards, respectively: immediate self-determination, self-determination exercised earlier, and the best interests of the patient. Institutions lie outside this hierarchy of decision making and should intervene by going to court only if they believe a decision violates these standards. Although I am sympathetic with the view of the doctors at the Hennepin County Medical Center, I agree with the court that they were wrong to try to impose it on the Wanglie family.

NOTES

1. Brophy v. New England Sinai Hospital, Inc., (Mass, Probate County Ct., Oct. 21, Nov. 29, 1985) 85E0009-G1.
2. Paris J.J., Crone R.K., Reardon F. Physicians' refusal of requested treatment: the case of Baby L. *New England Journal of Medicine* 1990; 322:1012–1015.
3. Miles S.H. Informed demand for "non-beneficial" medical treatment. *New England Journal of Medicine* 1991; 325:512–515.
4. Brett A.S., McCullough L.B. When patients request specific interventions: defining the limits of the physician's obligation. *New England Journal of Medicine* 1986; 315:1347–1351.
5. Blackhall L.J. Must we always use CPR? *New England Journal of Medicine* 1987; 317:1281–1285.

THE CASE OF BABY K

In the Matter of BABY K.*

The second major case often referred to as a futile care case involved a baby who had been diagnosed prenatally as having a condition known as anencephaly. Although the term literally means "without a brain" such babies actually may have some lower brain centers including that responsible for controlling respiratory and other reflex functions. The mother was advised of the condition—that it would mean her baby could never have any consciousness and would almost certainly die soon after birth if it were not stillborn. Unlike many women told of this diagnosis, she chose not to abort the fetus and after the birth insisted that ventilatory support be provided if necessary to support life.

The clinicians responsible for providing medical care continued to see aggressive life-support as inappropriate. They consulted with the hospital's ethics committee and eventually asked the court to approve of omission of any further ventilator support in the event the baby had trouble breathing. The lower court refused to grant the request and its decision was sustained by the Court of Appeals. Eventually, the United States Supreme Court refused to review the decision. Two years after Baby K's birth, she remained alive, in a nursing home. The court order providing for emergency ventilation if necessary to sustain life was in place.

United States District Court, E.D. Virginia, Alexandria Division.

Civ. A. No. 93-68-A (filed under seal).

July 1, 1993.

FINDINGS OF FACT AND CONCLUSIONS OF LAW

HILTON, DISTRICT JUDGE

This case was tried before the court, and upon the evidence presented and argument of counsel, the court makes the following Findings of Fact and Conclusions of Law.

Findings of Fact

1. Plaintiff Hospital is a general acute care hospital located in Virginia that is licensed to provide diagnosis, treatment, and medical and nursing services to the public as

*Source: In the Matter of Baby K. 832 F. Supp. 1022 (E.D. Va. 1993).

provided by Virginia law. Among other facilities, the Hospital has a Pediatric Intensive Care Department and an Emergency Department.

2. The Hospital is a recipient of federal and state funds including those from Medicare and Medicaid and is a "participating hospital" pursuant to 42 U.S.C. § 1395cc.

3. The Hospital and its staff (including emergency doctors, pediatricians, neonatologists and pediatric intensivists) treat sick children on a daily basis.

4. Defendant Ms. H, a citizen of the Commonwealth of Virginia, is the biological mother of Baby K, an infant girl born by Caesarean section at the Hospital on October 13, 1992. Baby K was born with anencephaly.

5. Anencephaly is a congenital defect in which the brain stem is present but the cerebral cortex is rudimentary or absent. There is no treatment that will cure, correct, or ameliorate anencephaly. Baby K is permanently unconscious and cannot hear or see. Lacking a cerebral function, Baby K does not feel pain. Baby K has brain stem functions primarily limited to reflexive actions such as feeding reflexes (rooting, sucking, swallowing), respiratory reflexes (breathing, coughing), and reflexive responses to sound or touch. Baby K has a normal heart rate, blood pressure, liver function, digestion, kidney function, and bladder function and has gained weight since her birth. Most anencephalic infants die within days of birth.

6. Baby K was diagnosed prenatally as being anencephalic. Despite the counseling of her obstetrician and neonatologist that she terminate her pregnancy, Ms. H refused to have her unborn child aborted.

7. A Virginia court of competent jurisdiction has found defendant Mr. K, a citizen of the Commonwealth of Virginia, to be Baby K's biological father.

8. Ms. H and Mr. K have never been married.

9. Since Baby K's birth, Mr. K has, at most, been only distantly involved in matters relating to the infant. Neither the Hospital nor Ms. H ever sought Mr. K's opinion or consent in providing medical treatment to Baby K.

10. Because Baby K had difficulty breathing immediately upon birth, Hospital physicians provided her with mechanical ventilator treatment to allow her to breathe.

11. Within days of Baby K's birth, Hospital medical personnel urged Ms. H to permit a "Do Not Resuscitate Order" for Baby K that would discontinue ventilator treatment. Her physicians told her that no treatment existed for Baby K's anencephalic condition, no therapeutic or palliative purpose was served by the treatment, and that ventilator care was medically unnecessary and inappropriate. Despite this pressure, Ms. H continued to request ventilator treatment for her child.

12. Because of Ms. H's continued insistence that Baby K receive ventilator treatment, her treating physicians requested the assistance of the Hospital's "Ethics Committee" in overriding the mother's wishes.

13. A three person Ethics Committee subcommittee, composed of a family practitioner, a psychiatrist, and a minister, met with physicians providing care to Baby K. On October 22, 1992, the group concluded that Baby K's ventilator treatment should end because "such care is futile" and decided to "wait a reasonable time for the family to help the caregiver terminate aggressive therapy." If the family refused to follow this advice, the committee recommended that the Hospital should "attempt to resolve this through our legal system."

14. Ms. H subsequently rejected the committee's recommendation. Before pursuing legal action to override Ms. H's position, the Hospital decided to transfer the infant to another health care facility.

15. Baby K was transferred to a nursing home ("Nursing Home") in Virginia on November 30, 1992 during a period when she was not experiencing respiratory distress and thus did not need ventilator treatment. A condition of the transfer was that the

Hospital agreed to take the infant back if Baby K again developed respiratory distress to receive ventilator treatment which was unavailable at the Nursing Home. Ms. H agreed to this transfer.

16. Baby K returned to the Hospital on January 15, 1993 after experiencing respiratory distress to receive ventilator treatment. Hospital officials again attempted to persuade Ms. H to discontinue ventilator treatment for her child. Ms. H again refused. After Baby K could breathe on her own, she was transferred back to the Nursing Home on February 12, 1993.

17. Baby K again experienced breathing difficulties on March 3, 1993 and returned to the Hospital to receive ventilator treatment.

18. On March 15, 1993, Baby K received a tracheotomy, a procedure in which a breathing tube is surgically implanted in her windpipe, to facilitate ventilator treatment. Ms. H agreed to this operation.

19. After no longer requiring ventilator treatment, Baby K was transferred back to the Nursing Home on April 13, 1993 where she continues to live.

20. Baby K will almost certainly continue to have episodes of respiratory distress in the future. In the absence of ventilator treatment during these episodes, she would suffer serious impairment of her bodily functions and soon die.

21. Ms. H visits Baby K daily. The mother opposes the discontinuation of ventilator treatment when Baby K experiences respiratory distress because she believes that all human life has value, including her anencephalic daughter's life. Ms. H has a firm Christian faith that all life should be protected. She believes that God will work a miracle if that is his will. Otherwise, Ms. H believes, God, and not other humans, should decide the moment of her daughter's death. As Baby K's mother and as the only parent who has participated in the infant's care, Ms. H believes that she has the right to decide what is in her child's best interests.

22. On the Hospital's motion, a guardian *ad litem* to represent Baby K was appointed pursuant to Virginia Code § 8.01-9.

23. Both the guardian *ad litem* and Mr. K share the Hospital's position that ventilator treatment should be withheld from Baby K when she experiences respiratory distress.

24. The Hospital has stipulated that it is not proposing to deny ventilator treatment to Baby K because of any lack of adequate resources or any inability of Ms. H to pay for the treatment.

Conclusions of Law

Pursuant to the Declaratory Judgment Act, 28 U.S.C. § 2201, the Hospital has sought declaratory and injunctive relief under four federal statutes and one Virginia statute: the Emergency Medical Treatment and Active Labor Act, 42 U.S.C. § 1395dd; the Rehabilitation Act of 1973, 29 U.S.C. § 794; the Americans with Disabilities Act of 1990, 42 U.S.C. § 12101 *et seq.;* the Child Abuse Amendments of 1984, 42 U.S.C. § 5102 *et seq.;* and the Virginia Medical Malpractice Act, Va.Code § 8.01-581.1 *et seq.* This court has federal question jurisdiction under the four federal statutes and supplemental jurisdiction regarding the Virginia statute. 28 U.S.C. §§ 1331, 1367.

I. EMERGENCY MEDICAL TREATMENT AND ACTIVE LABOR ACT

[1] Plaintiff seeks a declaration that its refusal to provide Baby K with life-supporting medical care would not transgress the Emergency Medical Treatment and Active La-

bor Act, 42 U.S.C. § 1395dd ("EMTALA"). EMTALA requires that participating hospitals provide stabilizing medical treatment to any person who comes to an emergency department in an "emergency medical condition" when treatment is requested on that person's behalf. An "emergency medical condition" is defined in the statute as "acute symptoms of sufficient severity . . . such that the absence of immediate medical attention could reasonably be expected to result in . . . serious impairment to bodily functions, or serious dysfunction of any bodily organ or part." 42 U.S.C. § 1395dd(e)(1)(A). "Stabilizing" medical treatment is defined as "such medical treatment of the condition as may be necessary to assure, within reasonable medical probability, that no material deterioration of the condition" will result. Id. § 1395dd(e)(3)(A). The statute's legislative history includes a position paper by the American College of Emergency Physicians stating that "stabilization" should include "[e]stablishing and assuring an adequate airway and adequate ventilation." H.R.Rep. No. 241 (Pt. 3), 99th Cong., 1st Sess. 26 (1985).

The Hospital admits that Baby K would meet these criteria if she is brought to the Hospital while experiencing breathing difficulty. As stated in the Hospital's complaint, when Baby K is in respiratory distress, that condition is "such that the absence of immediate medical attention could reasonably be expected to cause serious impairment to her bodily functions"—i.e., her breathing difficulties constitute an "emergency medical condition." The Hospital also concedes in its complaint that ventilator treatment is required in such circumstances to assure "that no material deterioration of Baby K's condition is likely to occur"—i.e., a ventilator is necessary to "stabilize" the baby's condition. These admissions establish that the Hospital would be liable under EMTALA if Baby K arrived there in respiratory distress (or some other emergency medical condition) and the Hospital failed to provide mechanical ventilation (or some other medical treatment) necessary to stabilize her acute condition.

The Hospital would also have an obligation to continue to provide stabilizing medical treatment to Baby K even if she were admitted to the pediatric intensive care unit or other unit of the Hospital and to provide the treatment until she could be transferred back to the Nursing Home or to another facility willing to accept her. . . .

Despite EMTALA's clear requirements and in the face of the Hospital's admissions, the Hospital seeks an exemption from the statute for instances in which the treatment at issue is deemed "futile" or "inhumane" by the hospital physicians. The plain language of the statute requires stabilization of an emergency medical condition. The statute does not admit of any "futility" or "inhumanity" exceptions. Any argument to the contrary should be directed to the U.S. Congress, not to the Federal Judiciary.

Even if EMTALA contained the exceptions advanced by the Hospital, these exceptions would not apply here. The use of a mechanical ventilator to assist breathing is not "futile" or "inhumane" in relieving the *acute* symptoms of respiratory difficulty which is the emergency medical condition that must be treated under EMTALA. To hold otherwise would allow hospitals to deny emergency treatment to numerous classes of patients, such as accident victims who have terminal cancer or AIDS, on the grounds that they eventually will die anyway from those diseases and that emergency care for them would therefore be "futile."

II. REHABILITATION ACT

[2, 3]   Section 504 of the Rehabilitation Act prohibits discrimination against an "otherwise qualified" handicapped individual, solely by reason of his or her handicap, under any program or activity receiving federal financial assistance. Hospitals such
as plaintiff that accept Medicare and Medicaid funding are subject to the Act. . . .

   [4]   Section 504's plain text spells out the necessary scope of inquiry: Is Baby K otherwise qualified to receive ventilator treatment and is ventilator treatment being
threatened with being denied because of an unjustified consideration of her anencephalic handicap? The Hospital has admitted that the sole reason it wishes to
withhold ventilator treatment for Baby K over her mother's objections, is because
of Baby K's anencephaly—her handicap and disability.

   To evade this textual mandate, the Hospital relies on two cases which held that
a hospital's decision not to override the desire of the parents of babies with congenital defects to withhold treatment did not violate section 504. *Johnson v. Thompson,*
971 F.2d 1487, 1493, (10th Cir.1992), *cert. denied,*—U.S.—, 113 S.Ct. 1255, 122
L.Ed.2d.654 (1993); *United States v. University Hospital, State U. of New York,* 729
F2d 144, 156–57 (2d Cir.1984). Because the parents in *Johnson* and *University Hospital* consented to the withholding of treatment, the two cases are factually distinguishable from this case.[1]

   When the Rehabilitation Act was passed in 1973, Congress intended that discrimination on the basis of a handicap be treated in the same manner that Title VI of
the Civil Rights Act treats racial discrimination. *University Hospital,* 729 F.2d at
161–163 (Winter, J., dissenting). This analogy to race dispels any ambiguity about the
extent to which Baby K has statutory rights not to be discriminated against on the basis of her handicap. It also shatters the Hospital's contention that ventilator treatment
should be withheld because Baby K's recurring breathing troubles are intrinsically
related to her handicap. No such distinction would be permissible within the context
of racial discrimination. In addition, the Hospital was able to perform a tracheotomy
on Baby K. This surgery was far more complicated than linking her to a ventilator to
allow her to breathe. . . . Just as an AIDS patient seeking ear surgery is "otherwise
qualified" to receive treatment despite poor long term prospects of living, Baby K is
"otherwise qualified" to receive ventilator treatment despite similarly dismal health
prospects. . . . Thus, the Hospital's desire to withhold ventilator treatment from Baby
K over her mother's objections would violate the Rehabilitation Act.

III. AMERICANS WITH DISABILITIES ACT

   [5]   Section 302 of the Americans with Disabilities Act ("ADA") prohibits discrimination against disabled individuals by "public accommodations." 42 U.S.C. § 12182.
A "disability" is "a physical or mental impairment that substantially limits one or
more of the major life activities" of an individual. 42 U.S.C. § 12102(2). This includes any physiological disorder or condition affecting the neurological system,
musculoskeletal system, or sense organs, among others. 28 C.F.R. § 36.104 (definition of "physical or mental impairment"). Anencephaly is a disability, because it

affects the baby's neurological functioning, ability to walk, and ability to see or talk. "Public accommodation" is defined to include a "professional office of a health care provider, hospital, or other service establishment." 42 U.S.C. § 12181(7). The Hospital is a public accommodation under the ADA. 28 C.F.R. § 36.104.

[6] Section 302(a) of the ADA states a general rule of nondiscrimination against the disabled:

> General rule. No individual shall be discriminated against on the basis of disability in the full and equal enjoyment of the goods, services, facilities, privileges, advantages, or accommodation of any place of public accommodations by any person who owns, leases (or leases to), or operates a place of public accommodation.

42 U.S.C. § 12182(a). In contrast to the Rehabilitation Act, the ADA does not require that a handicapped individual be "otherwise qualified" to receive the benefits of participation. Further, section 302(b)(1)(A) of the ADA states that "[i]t shall be discriminatory to subject an individual or class of individuals on the basis of a disability . . . to a denial of the opportunity of the individual or class to participate in or benefit from the goods, services, facilities, privileges, advantages, or accommodations of an entity." 42 U.S.C. § 12182(b)(1)(A)(i).

The Hospital asks this court for authorization to deny the benefits of ventilator services to Baby K by reason of her anencephaly. The Hospital's claim is that it is "futile" to keep alive an anencephalic baby, even though the mother has requested such treatment. But the plain language of the ADA does not permit the denial of ventilator services that would keep alive an anencephalic baby when those life-saving services would otherwise be provided to a baby without disabilities at the parent's request. The Hospital's reasoning would lead to the denial of medical services to anencephalic babies as a class of disabled individuals. Such discrimination against a vulnerable population class is exactly what the American with Disabilities Act was enacted to prohibit. The Hospital would therefore violate the ADA if it were to withhold ventilator treatment from Baby K.

IV. CHILD ABUSE ACT

[7] Plaintiff seeks a declaration that it may refuse to provide life-supporting medical care to Baby K without incurring liability under the Child Abuse Amendments of 1984, 42 U.S.C. § 5101 *et seq.* ("Child Abuse Act"). This request for relief must be denied because the Hospital has failed to join a necessary party—the Virginia Child Protective Services.

[8] There is no private right of action against a health care provider under the Child Abuse Act. . . . The Act only authorizes states which receive federal grants for child abuse and neglect programs to bring legal action through their child protective services agencies to prevent the medical neglect of disabled infants. 42 U.S.C. § 5106a(b)(10)(C); 45 C.F.R. § 1340.15(c)(2)(iii).

Because the Virginia Child Protective Services has an interest in a declaratory judgment regarding the Child Abuse Act and is the only party that can enforce the Act, it is a necessary party. This court must have the sole enforcing authority party before it before considering the declaratory judgment. . . . Thus, the Hospital's request for declaratory and injunctive relief under the Child Abuse Amendments must be denied. . . .

V. VIRGINIA MEDICAL MALPRACTICE ACT

[9, 10] The Hospital seeks a declaration that its refusal to provide Baby K with ventilator treatment does not constitute malpractice under the Virginia Medical Malpractice Act, Va.Code § 8.01-581.1 *et seq.* Under the Declaratory Judgment Act, 28 U.S.C. § 2201, a federal court has discretion to assert jurisdiction to render a declaration. . . . Because of the significant state interests manifested by this review process as well as the Commonwealth's interest in resolving this contentious and unsettled social issue for itself, this court declines to "elbow its way" into Virginia medical malpractice standards. . . .

VI. CONSTITUTIONAL AND COMMON LAW ISSUES

[11, 12] Baby K's parents disagree over whether or not to continue medical treatment for her. Mr. K and Baby K's guardian *ad litem* join the Hospital in seeking the right to override the wishes of Ms. H, Baby K's mother. Regardless of the questions of statutory interpretation presented in this case, Ms. H retains significant legal rights regarding her insistence that her daughter be kept alive with ventilator treatment. A parent has a constitutionally protected right to "bring up children" grounded in the Fourteenth Amendment's due process clause. . . . Parents have the "primary role" in the "nurture and upbringing of their children." . . . Decisions for children can be based in the parent's free exercise of religion, protected by the First Amendment. . . .

[13] These constitutional principles extend to the right of parents to make medical treatment decisions for their minor children. Absent a finding of neglect or abuse, parents retain plenary authority to seek medical care for their children, even when the decision might impinge on a liberty interest of the child. . . . Indeed, there is a "presumption that the parents act in the best interests of their child" because the "natural bonds of affection lead parents to act in the best interests of their children. . . . "

[14] Based on Ms. H's "natural bonds of affection," and the relative noninvolvement of Baby K's biological father, the constitutional and common law presumption must be that Ms. H. is the appropriate decision maker. "[W]hen parents do not agree on the issue of termination of life support . . . this Court must yield to the presumption in favor of life." *In re Jane Doe, A Minor,* Civ. No. D—93064, mem. op. at 18 (Super.Ct. Fulton Co., Ga., October 17, 1991), *aff'd,* 262 Ga. 389, 418 S.E.2d 3 (1992). This presumption arises from the explicit guarantees of a right to life in the United States Constitution, Amendments V and XIV, and the Virginia Constitution, Article 1, Sections I and II.

[15] The presumption in favor of life in this case is also based on Ms. H's religious conviction that all life is sacred and must be protected, thus implicating her First Amendment rights. When an individual asserts "the Free Exercise Clause in conjunction with other constitutional protections, such as . . . the right of parents," only a clear and compelling governmental interest can justify a statute that interferes with the person's religious convictions. . . .

[16, 17]   The Hospital cannot establish any "clear and compelling" interest in this case. The Supreme Court has not decided whether the right to liberty encompasses a right to refuse medical treatment, often called a "right to die." . . . Parents have standing to assert the constitutional rights of their minor children. . . . When one parent asserts the child's explicit constitutional right to life as the basis for continuing medical treatment and the other is asserting the nebulous liberty interest in refusing life-saving treatment on behalf of a minor child, the explicit right to life must prevail. . . .

[18]   Reflecting the constitutional principles of family autonomy and the presumption in favor of life, courts have generally scrutinized a family's decision only where the family has sought to terminate or withhold medical treatment for an incompetent minor or incompetent adult. . . . In a recent case in which a hospital sought to terminate life-supporting ventilation over the objections of the patient's husband, a Minnesota state court refused to remove decisionmaking authority from the husband. *In re Wanglie*, No. PX-91-283 (Prob.Ct., Hennepin Co., Minn., June 28, 1991). Likewise, where parents disagreed over whether to continue life-supporting mechanical ventilation, nutrition, and hydration for a minor child in an irreversible stupor or coma, a Georgia state court gave effect to the decision of the parent opting in favor of life support. *In re Jane Doe, supra.*[2]

At the very least, the Hospital must establish by clear and convincing evidence that Ms. H's treatment decision should not be respected because it would constitute abuse or neglect of Baby K. This clear and convincing evidence standard has been adopted by numerous courts and was upheld by the Supreme Court in *Cruzan* in authorizing the withdrawal of life-supporting treatment from an incompetent patient. . . . In this case, where the choice essentially devolves to a subjective determination as to the quality of Baby's K's life, it cannot be said that the continuation of Baby K's life is so unreasonably harmful as to constitute child abuse or neglect.

For the foregoing reasons, the Hospital's request for a declaratory judgment that the withholding of ventilator treatment from Baby K would not violate the Emergency Medical Treatment and Active Labor Act, the Rehabilitation Act of 1973, the Americans with Disabilities Act, the Child Abuse Amendments of 1984, and the Virginia Medical Malpractice Act should be DENIED. Under the Emergency Medical Treatment and Active Labor Act, the Rehabilitation Act of 1973, and the Americans with Disabilities Act, the Hospital is legally obligated to provide ventilator treatment to Baby K. The court makes no ruling as to any rights or obligations under the Child Abuse Amendments of 1984 and under the Virginia Medical Malpractice Act.

An appropriate order shall issue.

NOTES

1.   Department of Health and Human Services guidelines addressing hospital reporting obligations under the Act if parents seek to withhold treatment from anencephalic infants are similarly inapplicable because of their silence regarding whether hospitals are allowed to terminate care in spite of a parent's wishes to the contrary. See 45 C.F.R. Part 84, App. C., paragraph (a)(5)(iii) (1992).

2. Although the court in *Jane Doe* had appointed a guardian *ad litem* because of the parents' disagreement, the guardian's view (if any) was not discussed in the court's ruling. This is consistent with the limited role of a guardian *ad litem* as an independent fact finder and not a surrogate decisionmaker where family members are involved. Under Virginia law, the role of a guardian *ad litem* appointed under Va.Code § 8.01-9(A) is to "investigate thoroughly the facts" and "carefully examine[ ] the facts surrounding the case." *Ruffin v. Commonwealth,* 10 Va.App. 488, 393 S.E.2d 425 (Va.App.1990). The recommendation of Baby K's court-appointed guardian *ad litem* is thus irrelevant to the disposition of this case.

The Concept of Futility
Patients Do Not Have a Right to
Demand Medically Useless Treatment*

JAMES F. DRANE AND JOHN L. COULEHAN

Reflecting on cases like that of Helga Wanglie and Baby K, James Drane and John Coulehan argue for limits on the patient's right to choose (or refuse) treatment based on the physician's right (and duty) to practice medicine responsibly. They define futility in such a way that the term includes treatments that are physiologically effective but nonbeneficial. They claim that physicians should be able to decide when a particular treatment is futile based on their knowledge of the treatment's effects and likely impact on a patient's quality of life.

I will use the dieta [treatment] to help the sick according to my ability and judgement, but never with a view to injury and wrong-doing.

—From the Hippocratic Oath

The norm of beneficence, which directs physicians to apply their insights and techniques for patients' good, has been a basic principle of medical ethics for 2,500 years. Under this principle, physicians do not provide treatments when the interventions at their disposal do not produce medical benefits.

Traditionally, when medical treatment was provided in a paternalistic style (i.e., when physicians made treatment choices without asking their patients' permission), the application of the norm of beneficence was relatively straightforward. Today, however, an ethic of patient autonomy and informed consent has replaced the traditional paternalistic approach that gave maximum authority (as well as responsibility) to the physician. Thus the principle of beneficence must now be balanced with the principle of patient self-determination.

The question we address here is whether the patient self-determination requirement can compel physicians to make futile interventions—treatments they know provide no benefits and therefore violate the beneficence principle. The

*Source: Drane, James F., and John L. Coulehan. "The Concept of Futility: Patients Do Not Have a Right to Demand Medically Useless Treatment," *Health Progress* 74 (December 1993 No. 10): 28–32.

futility issue can be a key ethical consideration in cases in which the principles of physician beneficence and patient autonomy appear to conflict.

PHYSICIAN BENEFICENCE AND PATIENT AUTONOMY

Patient autonomy, or self-determination, is first a right to refuse treatment and then a right to choose from among medically justifiable options. It is *not* a right to demand treatment. Put differently, a patient's right to choose or refuse treatment is limited by the physician's right (and duty) to practice medicine responsibly. The belief that medical professionals ought to respect the informed choices of patients or their surrogates arises, first, out of respect for autonomy. But it is also a consequence of the realization that beneficence is ordinarily best served when patients can judge for themselves the impact of various treatment options on their life plans and personal goals.

Although patients ordinarily choose a course of action they judge to be in their best interests, sometimes they make bizarre and destructive choices. Such irrational choices are not sacrosanct simply because the patient made them. Commitment to beneficence demands at least that physicians try to understand patients' intent and motivation and to influence them to make a rational decision. In some cases, physicians may choose not to act on patient decisions that appear to be unreasonably destructive.[1]

Professional discretion and judgment are always part of the clinical decision-making process. Physicians should communicate with patients throughout the treatment process and must monitor patient participation in medical decision making. Physicians, in effect, make judgments about the nature and relevance of patient values, in addition to making value judgments about medical issues. They evaluate patient competency based on patients' responses to medical interventions, their thoughts about their medical situations, and their reasons for deciding one way or the other.

To suggest that doctors abandon all such judgments and then ignore the personal harm resulting from a risky or useless intervention "because the patient asked for it" is to subvert the core of medical professionalism.[2] Medical judgments are never value free. However, physicians should be aware of the value components of their decisions and be able to justify them.[3]

Value commitments (e.g., relieve suffering, do not assist in suicide, do not harm patients, do not cause suffering without proportionate benefit) inform most physician decisions. These professional standards reflect medical values and guide judgments about the appropriateness of a medical intervention for a particular patient. Among these standards should be the following: Do not offer futile treatments as medical options.[4]

THE CONCEPT OF FUTILITY

The concept of futility has had historic importance in medicine. For Hippocratic physicians, attempting a futile treatment was a display of ignorance.[5] Contemporary ethical standards published by the Council on Ethical and Judicial Affairs of the American Medical Association (AMA) show continuity with this tradition:

"Physicians should not provide or seek compensation for services that are known to be unnecessary or worthless."[6]

Because the concept of futility has been consistently confused with other concepts and categories, some distinctions are in order. A futile intervention is different from one that is *harmful* (e.g., poison), *ineffective* (like cough drops for a lymphoma), or *impossible* (like a self-administered coronary bypass). Nor is a futile intervention the same as a treatment whose goal is to achieve *uncommon* or *unusual* outcomes, like the long-term survival of a patient with metastatic pancreatic cancer. The issue of whether a situation is deemed *hopeless* is also irrelevant to the issue of futility, since hope is a subjective disposition that can be maintained even in the face of impossible situations. Finally, while certain treatments in certain situations are simply too expensive for a family or a society, it does not help to refer to these as economically futile.[7] Much of the confusion about futility arises when authors claim to be talking about this concept but are actually addressing very different issues.

Some clarity can be achieved by distinguishing futility from ineffectiveness. In contemporary medicine, ineffectiveness is determined statistically on the basis of accepted scientific standards. A 0 percent success rate in 1,000 trials, for example, would constitute an ineffective treatment. Categorizing a treatment as ineffective, however, does not imply 100 percent certainty about its outcome, because the next trial might reveal an effect not evident in the previous 1,000. Another closely related category is *highly improbable*. In this case, a given treatment may have been successful on a few occasions, but its success can neither be scientifically explained nor reliably predicted.

A futile treatment differs from an ineffective or highly improbable treatment in that it is always somewhat effective (e.g., a temperature is lowered or raised, lung function is sustained). However, futile treatments are fruitless because they do not achieve "worth" in the sense of meeting a patient's medical goal or providing a true personal benefit.[8] Doctor-patient communication is sometimes required to know that personal patient benefit cannot be attained, but at other times it is obvious (with the permanently unconscious or dying).

In light of the above distinctions, a medically futile treatment can be more accurately defined as an action, intervention, or procedure that might be physiologically effective in a given case, but cannot benefit the patient, no matter how often it is repeated. A futile treatment is not ineffective, but it is worthless, either because the medical action itself is futile (no matter what the patient's condition) or the condition of the patient makes it futile.[9]

FUTILITY AND PATIENT CONSENT

Attempts to determine personal patient benefit or acceptable quality of life ordinarily depend on patient input. Should all futility questions then be left up to patients or surrogates? Do futility decisions fall outside physician discretion?

Some medical ethicists think so.[10] We take the opposite position. Determining futility entails evaluations of a medical intervention and a patient's medical status that only a physician can make. Physicians know, for example, that cardiopulmonary resuscitation (CPR) can do no good for terminal patients whose cardiac arrest relates to the natural progression of their disease.[11] Even if the patient is incompetent and no family is available to provide input about his or her preferences, physicians in consultation with other team members can decide that a particular treatment cannot achieve medical goals, values, or objectives.

The discussion of futile treatments with patients and family is altogether appropriate,[12] except when such a discussion would cause added and unbearable burden to an already difficult situation. The objective of such discussions is to help patients and families understand the clinical situation and why a particular intervention is not an option. The physician should be as responsive as possible to the patient's physical, emotional, and spiritual needs, but neither consent nor refusal should be requested.

The AMA's Council on Ethical and Judicial Affairs upheld this view in deciding that physicians need not seek consent for a do-not-resuscitate order when CPR is deemed futile.[13] Informed consent is a process by which competent patients make judgments about real options and, as such, supposes socially sanctioned standards of rationality. Although some individuals may operate outside these rational limits (e.g., by demanding what is useless or futile), they cannot insist that professional standards and public policies support their preferences.

Beneficence requires that doctors do only what is medically helpful. Individual autonomy cannot be so inflated in importance as to destroy the principle of beneficence. The key to the futility debate is identifying what constitutes legitimate medical help. Like most contemporary medical ethics problems, determining futility requires balancing the values and goals of medicine with the goals and values of patients, taking into consideration the uncertainty inherent in making predictive medical judgments.[14] Inevitably there will be some differences among physicians in judging uncertainty and the helpfulness of specific treatments.[15]

ETHICAL RULES, RATIONALITY, AND BENEFICENCE

Ethical rules covering futility can be developed based on socially sanctioned standards of rationality and on traditional physician-based values. Several such rules are suggested in the Box.

Some ethicists argue that allowing physicians to not offer futile treatment to patients would constitute an unacceptable return to paternalistic medical practice. They hold, in effect, that physician assessments of benefit are always suspect, and that benefit is so inherently subjective that even the most idiosyncratic patient or surrogate choices must be honored.

Obviously, a physician's decision will reflect his or her values. A professional physician's value judgment, however, will be neither random nor individualistic. If doubt is raised about an instance of physician decision making, the decision can be reviewed by an ethics committee to make sure that beneficence and not some selfish value is operating.

An extreme autonomy position ignores the fact that a well-established "best interest" standard assumes both a connectedness of the patient to family and physi-

Ethical Guidelines for Determining Futility

- A treatment is futile and the physician should not present it to a patient or surrogate as an option when, for example, the treatment:
  1. Does not alter a person's persistent vegetative state
  2. Does not alter diseases or defects that make a baby's survival beyond infancy impossible
  3. Leaves permanently unrestored a patient's neurocardiorespiratory capacity, capacity for relationship, or moral agency
  4. Will not help free a patient from permanent dependency on total intensive care support

- Because they require assessment of medical interventions and their relation to medical goals, decisions about futility are made by physicians, even though they involve considerations of patient benefit or patient quality of life. Some quality-of-life judgments are linked with traditional medical goals and values and assume public standards of rationality.
- Because medicine is directed to patient benefit, not everything a doctor can do falls within the ethical goals of medicine.
- Futility always involves a failure to achieve a medical goal or a personal good. If patients do not benefit in a medical sense, even temporarily effective treatments are futile and physicians have a right (indeed a duty) based on the principles of beneficence and nonmaleficence not to offer them.

---

cian and a communication process that allows surrogates to decide based on objective, community-based best interest standards.[16] The existence of such standards and their relevance to medical decision making can be seen from the fact that five state courts recently permitted forgoing life supports for incompetent patients who had never expressed a previous preference.[17] Without available subjective preference, the decisions were made on physicians' and families' objective evaluations of a patient's best interest.

The current situation, in which patients or their surrogates are commonly (but falsely) led to believe that futile treatments are medically acceptable, actually does violence to the principle of autonomy, as well as to beneficence. It creates a sphere of decision making where (rationally) none exists and, thus, seems intrinsically deceptive.

Frequently, physicians believe they have done their duty when they allow patients or families to make difficult treatment decisions, even when they have not explained sufficiently the medical and human consequences of the options. In such cases the focus on patient choice diminishes the physician's commitment to professional duty and patient well-being. Thus we believe that respect for autonomy and beneficence is impaired by allowing patients to choose futile treatments or by claiming that the concept of futility is so inherently subjective that it is useless.

Weakening futility as a workable category has other ill effects. Aggressive treatments that override considerations of futility are frequently justified by standards requiring absolute certainty and by fear of malpractice. Clarifying the concept of futility and establishing defensible ethical policies covering futility are important steps toward eliminating unhelpful, medically inappropriate practices. Even the famous Baby Doe regulations of the Reagan administration, which advocated aggressive medical interventions for infants in almost all situations, recognized an exception for futility and virtual futility, when medical goals could not be achieved and quality of life had slipped below what is considered acceptably human.[18] . . .

FOR TRADITIONAL STANDARDS

Futility and physician discretion arguments will increasingly be crowded out by another influence on physician discretion—cost. The need to control medical costs will require that strict statistical measures of effectiveness be used to limit the options physicians can offer.

But independent of limitations on treatment options that might be imposed by considerations of justice and public policy, we have shown that an analysis based on beneficence allows physicians to refuse to offer—in fact, makes it their duty *not* to offer—futile or ineffective treatments. Futile and ineffective treatments are not acceptable or advisable even if they can be afforded.

The idea that a right exists to futile treatments is absurd, especially when there is not enough money for basic care for millions. Physicians and health-care institutions need to make a stand for traditional medical rights and professional standards.

NOTES

1. Harry Yeide, Jr., "The Many Faces of Autonomy," *Journal of Clinical Ethics* Winter 1992; 269–273.
2. Tom Tomlinson and Howard Brody. "Futility and the Ethics of Resuscitation," *JAMA* September 12, 1990: 1,276–1,280.
3. Allan S. Brett and Lawrence B. McCullough. "When Patients Request Specific Interventions: Defining the Limits of the Physician's Obligation," *New England Journal of Medicine* November 20, 1986; 1,347–1,351.
4. Ronald B. Miller. "Medical Futility: A Value-dependent Concept," *Update* 7, 1991; 3–5.
5. Albert R. Jonsen. *The New Medicine and the Old Ethics,* Harvard University Press, Cambridge, MA, 1990, p. 52.
6. Council on Ethical and Judicial Affairs of the AMA, *Current Opinions,* American Medical Association, Chicago, 1989, p. 13.
7. Tomlinson and Brody.
8. Some literature on futility assumes that futility means the absence of any effect. If an intervention produces any effect or any goal, then it is presumed not to be futile. See J. D. Lantos et al., "The Illusion of Futility in Clinical Practice," *American Journal of Medicine* 87, 1989:81–84.
9. Lawrence J. Schneiderman and Nancy S. Jecker. "Futility in Practice," *Archives of Internal Medicine* vol. 153, 1993; 437–440.
10. Stuart J. Youngner. "Who Defines Futility?" *JAMA* vol. 260, 1988; 2,094–2,095. Youngner argues that except for obviously inane, "physiologically futile," "empirically factual," ineffective treatments, physicians have to defer to patients and fam-

ily lest they "run the risk of giving opinions disguised as data." He confuses "opinion" with values and assumes the latter are inappropriate for physicians.

11. L.J. Blackhall. "Must We Always Use CPR? *New England Journal of Medicine* 317, 1987; 1,281–1,285; Donald J. Murphy, "Do-Not-Resuscitate Orders: Time for Reappraisal in Long-Term-Care Institutions," *JAMA* October 14, 1988; 2,098–2,101.

12. Howard Brody and Tom Tomlinson. "In-Hospital Cardiopulmonary Resuscitation," *JAMA* 261, 1989; 1,581.

13. Council on Ethical and Judicial Affairs, "AMA Guidelines for Appropriate Uses of DNR Orders," *JAMA* April 10, 1991; 1,868–1,871.

14. K. Faber-Langendoen, "Medical Futility: Values, Goals, and Certainty," *Journal of Laboratory and Clinical Medicine,* December 1990; 831–835.

15. F. Rosner, et al., "Medical Futility," *New York State Journal of Medicine* November 1992; 485–488.

16. Jane M. Trau and James J. McCartney. "In the Best Interest of the Patient," *Health Progress* April 1993; 50–56.

17. A. Meisel. "The Legal Consensus about Forgoing Life-sustaining Treatment: Its Status and Its Prospects," *Kennedy Institute of Ethics Journal* December 1992; 309–345.

18. U.S. Department of Health and Human Services, Office of Human Development Services, "Child Abuse and Neglect Prevention and Treatment," *Federal Register* 50, 1985; 14,887–14,888.

Futile Care
Physicians Should Not Be Allowed to
Refuse to Treat*

ROBERT M. VEATCH AND CAROL MASON SPICER

Acknowledging that physicians can be presumed to judge certain treatments are
expendable because they cannot produce the effects desired, Robert Veatch and
Carol Spicer argue that certain treatments that really will prolong life should not
be unilaterally excluded on the basis of the physician's value judgment that the
life-prolongation is not beneficial. They do not base their conclusion on any patient or surrogate autonomy. Rather they argue that there is an implied promise
or contract that attaches to medical licensure. That promise requires that clinicians in an ongoing relation with a patient are obliged to use potentially effective
treatments to attempt to extend life when the patient or surrogate desires it,
provided certain conditions are met. They claim that reasonable people who
did not know whether they would have unusual desires to have their lives prolonged would fear they might be in the minority. To protect against that possibility they would insist that clinicians who are granted monopoly control over
life-prolonging technologies must promise to use them for patients who desire them.

MEDICALLY INAPPROPRIATE: A MISNOMER

On December 14, 1989, 86-year-old Helga Wanglie slipped on a rug and broke
her hip.[1] The healthcare team's unanimous conclusion was that the treatment was futile and "medically inappropriate."

But what can *medically* inappropriate mean here? It is morally reasonable to
support the withdrawal of ventilators or even feeding tubes in such cases. But calling
the inappropriateness "medical" tells us absolutely nothing and, in fact, perpetuates
a serious philosophical mistake that has horrendous implications.

If continuing treatment is inappropriate, it is inappropriate religiously, philosophically, or morally, but medically the treatment has a definite effect. It clearly prolongs her life and is therefore efficacious.

TWO BASIC DISTINCTIONS

To understand the debate over futile care, two basic distinctions must be made:

- A critical distinction between physiologically futile care and "normatively futile care"
- A distinction between denying so-called futile care on the basis of allocating scarce resources and denying it on the grounds that it violates care givers' integrity

*Source: Veatch, Robert M., and Carol Mason Spicer. "Futile Care: Physicians Should Not
Be Allowed to Refuse to Treat." *Health Progress* 74 (December 1993, No. 10):22–27.

Physiological Versus Normative Futility. Some interventions labeled futile are really without physical effect. This is what Stuart J. Youngner has called "physiologically futile treatment."[2] Such treatment will not produce the effect sought by the one insisting on it. This must be distinguished from care that has the anticipated effect but is believed by someone to be of no net benefit. We will call this second kind of futility "normative futility" because it involves a value judgment that the effect is of no benefit.

Physiological futility is more or less a question of medical science. We say "more or less" because every scientific question involves some value judgments (e.g., a choice of p values and a choice of the concepts used to describe the effects). In rare instances, clinicians will disagree over the facts because of these hidden value disputes. Laypersons may also disagree with clinicians over such matters. To the extent that they do, it is not irrational for society to require care that physicians have deemed physiologically futile. That occurs only in unusual circumstances, however. In virtually all cases of so-called futile care, the real disagreement is not over whether a treatment will produce an effect; it is over whether some agreed-on potential effect is of any value.

To distinguish physiological from normative futility, ask the question, Is the disagreement over the science (the judgment about what the effect will be) or over the value of the agreed-on outcome? We can presume that clinicians are correct on the science, but also that they have no special claim to expertise on the value of the outcomes.

Rationing Versus Clinician Integrity. A second distinction is also important. There are two separate reasons to be concerned about patient demands for care deemed futile: issues of rationing and of care givers' integrity.

First, an obvious reason to resist providing care believed to be futile (in either sense) is that it appears to consume scarce resources and therefore burden others. Our communal resources are inevitably scarce. Surely, if a treatment's benefits are so debatable that most of us consider them to be nonexistent, that is an obvious place to cut. But that does not mean it is a clinician's role to do the cutting.

We have acknowledged the legitimacy and necessity of rationing healthcare,[3] provided it is done equitably and with full public participation in decisions. But historically the clinician's job has been to help patients, not to act as society's cost-containment agent. This gatekeeping role must be someone else's task. Just like a defense attorney's role in the legal system is to advocate for a client, even an unworthy client, a clinician's job in the medical system is to advocate for his or her patient.

We agree that care without effect should not be funded on scientific grounds. A clinician should not be permitted to authorize treatments that he or she is convinced will not produce the effect a patient or surrogate seeks. In fact, insurers who receive requests for reimbursement for such care ought not to pay for it. However, for care that affects the dying trajectory but seems to most of us to offer no benefit, the proper course is for society—not clinicians—to cut patients off. Subscribers to insurance should have a strong interest in limiting care that offers little or no benefit and should agree to exclude such coverage from their plans.

For example, most Americans apparently believe that providing continued, long-term life support serves no purpose for a patient who is in a PVS. Insurers or health maintenance organizations (HMOs) should ask whether subscribers want to include long-term support for PVS patients in their coverage. Insurers should be able to explain what premiums would be if coverage for PVS treatment is and is not included. Insurers should not care whether subscribers vote PVS treatment in or out as long as they set an appropriately larger premium if such treatment is included.

We believe that most subscribers would vote PVS treatment out. The minority of subscribers who have an interest in such care can decide to buy supplemental insurance (a PVS rider) or to pay for the care out of pocket. If the insured group votes to include the coverage, or if individuals self-fund or buy supplemental coverage, then there is no unfairness to society as a whole. We can call this "equitable funding."

Helga Wanglie was an HMO member. HMO administrators should have asked her and her fellow subscribers whether they wanted to fund care for PVS patients. However, the HMO was explicit in its willingness to provide the funding for the care. There was thus no economic reason why the hospital or the individual physician responsible for Helga Wanglie's care should have felt compelled to resist on grounds of allocation or resources. Also, at the time there were no noneconomic demands—a scarcity of time or of beds—that would force a rationing decision. Had there been such scarcities, the institution would have had a moral obligation to make allocational choices.

Concern about a scarcity of resources, however, is increasingly not the reason physicians want to limit care they deem futile. More commonly physicians want to protect the "integrity" of the physician who feels that it violates professional norms to deliver care that will do no good. We argue that under certain circumstances patients should have a right to receive life-prolonging care from their clinicians, provided it is equitably funded, even if the clinicians believe the care is futile and even if it violates their consciences to provide it.

This is a serious conflict, and we do not endorse such a position lightly. But clearly in some cases a physician must be obliged to violate his or her conscience. Consider, for example, someone raised as a racist who sincerely believes that it is wrong to provide medical treatment for racial minorities. The mere fact that the prejudiced belief is held sincerely surely would not permit the physician to refuse to treat all members of minority groups.

It is similarly clear that patients cannot be allowed to receive any medical treatment that they happen to crave. Certain conditions will have to be met before the duty to provide care deemed futile will prevail. We will detail these conditions later in this article, but first we will explain the moral reasons why some patients may have a legitimate claim to care that physicians believe will do no good.

MORAL COMPLEXITIES SURROUNDING A DUTY TO TREAT

Let us return to the case of Helga Wanglie. She and her husband were members of the right-to-life movement. Previously she had told family members that she would never want anything done to shorten her life. Her husband is quoted as saying, "I'm a pro-lifer; I take the position that human life is sacred."[4] He said that his wife of 53 years felt the same way. Their daughter agreed.

There was no dispute about the medical facts. The physicians and the Wanglie family agreed that she was permanently unconscious, that providing a ventilator and nasogastric tube would prolong her life, albeit in a vegetative state. The only question was the value of vegetative life.

A Comparison with Quinlan.   Compare this "futile care" case with the classic treatment refusal case of Karen Ann Quinlan, the young woman who in 1975 suffered a respiratory arrest that left her in a PVS.[5] Her physician, Robert Morse, was absolutely convinced that a ventilator believed necessary to preserve her life was providing benefit. He considered it "medically appropriate," claiming, probably incorrectly, that letting a permanently vegetative patient die violated the professional standard of the time.

The most critical issue in the court battle was whether a clinician's judgment about benefit for a patient could take precedence over a patient's or surrogate's assessment of benefit. Karen Quinlan's family and lawyer successfully argued that a professional consensus about whether an effective treatment was beneficial was irrelevant. Her father was, in effect, given the power to decide whether his daughter would consider this treatment beneficial.

The *Quinlan* and *Wanglie* cases, despite the seemingly opposite values of the decision makers, are similar in that both involved an assessment of the value of vegetative life. This assessment is fundamentally not a technical medical matter. Different people with different beliefs and values can come to different conclusions about whether ventilating a permanently vegetative patient is a benefit. When a patient is competent, he or she has the right to decide. When the patient is not competent, then the designated surrogate has the responsibility to try to determine what is best.

The two types of cases differ, however, in that the moral issue confronting physicians in futile care cases is whether patients or surrogates who make the decision that such care serves a worthwhile purpose have a right to insist that it be provided and, if so, on what basis.

Autonomy Problem.   Some defenders of the right to access make the mistake of claiming that the moral principle of autonomy confers that right. Autonomy gives a patient a right to refuse treatment. By extension, it even gives family members a limited right to decline treatment on a patient's behalf. But that does not imply that autonomy can give the patient a right of access. There is a lack of symmetry. Autonomy is a liberty right. A patient has a right to cancel the patient-physician relationship and at least metaphorically walk away. But in so far as autonomy is relevant, it also should give a provider the right to sever the relationship. Autonomy cannot be the basis of the claim to a right to access.

Burden of Futile Care.   A second complexity in the argument concerns the possibility that acting on the demand for care deemed futile might impose excessive burdens on a patient. Clinicians evaluate some care not only as providing no benefit, but as actually harming a patient. But if harm refers to pain and suffering, a patient must at least be conscious for harm to occur. It is difficult to understand how Helga Wanglie or Karen Quinlan can be burdened by continued life support. There may well be moral offense if, for example, the life support is administered against a patient's wishes but a patient must be conscious to be burdened in any real sense.

FUTILE CARE FOR PATIENTS WHO ARE NOT BEING HARMED

Cases involving burden to incompetent patients are really not the essence of the futile care debate, however. The real issue is futile care for patients who are not being harmed. This is true futile care (i.e., care that produces neither benefits nor burdens for a patient). For the moment let us simplify the analysis by limiting the discussion to interventions that will predictably prolong life.

Clinicians always have the right to withdraw from a case, just as a competent patient might, provided someone else is willing to take the case. It is in neither a patient's nor a physician's interest to insist that the original physician continue. But if no colleague is willing to step forward, the treatment is life prolonging, and the treatment will not be burdensome, then a licensed professional responsible for and capable of providing the care has a duty to provide it even if he or she is morally opposed. Otherwise that clinician would have to argue that the patient is better off dead even though the patient is not being injured and even though the patient or surrogate disagrees. Effective, nonburdensome, life-prolonging care is always morally required if a patient or surrogate desires it.

But why should physician autonomy be violated in this one case when generally patient autonomy should not be violated? Two arguments can be offered: the argument from offense and the argument from contract.

Argument from Offense. If a patient or surrogate is demanding life-prolonging care that his or her clinician believes is futile and a violation of his or her integrity to provide, we have a head-on clash between a patient's or surrogate's choice for life and the provider's autonomy. A society that forces people to die against their will produces more offense than one that forces healthcare providers to provide services that violate their consciences. If society must offend, the lesser offense is preferred.

Argument from Contract. The second argument rests on the notion of the social contract or covenant between medical professionals and society. Licensed professionals are the only members of society licensed to control the use of medical, life-prolonging technologies. When they accept licensure, they accept a public trust to use their monopoly on medical knowledge to preserve lives when the appropriate decision makers want them preserved.

Imagine that society is contemplating creating monopoly control over certain life-prolonging technologies. Further, imagine that there will be cases in which a minority desperately wants these technologies used while a majority does not see any value in their use. Finally, imagine that we cannot know whether we will be in the majority or the minority. We believe a rational society will extract, as a condition of licensure, a promise that the clinician will use these technologies for people who want them.

Of course, some conditions would be attached to such a promise. These might include:

1. An ongoing patient-physician relationship
2. No colleague capable and willing to take the case
3. A clinician competent to provide the desired service
4. Equitable funding
5. The care being predictably life prolonging.

At least if all these conditions were met, we believe clinicians would be obliged to render the desired care. All these conditions were met in the *Wanglie* case. Once the court determined that Helga Wanglie's husband was the proper surrogate, physicians wisely acknowledged their duty to provide the care they believed was futile even though it violated their sense of professional integrity. Once one realizes that the decision to forgo effective, life-prolonging care is a moral choice rather than a technical one, it seems hard to deny the right of the minority to access. If we have created a monopoly in the use of that technology, we would be wise to insist that minority interests be protected by ensuring that holders of minority views can have their lives prolonged. The alternative is to permit physicians to decide that a patient would be better off dead even though the patient is not being burdened and even though the patient or surrogate believes the life should be preserved.

NON-LIFE-PROLONGING FUNDAMENTAL CARE

What we have said thus far is limited to care that can be expected to prolong life effectively, at least for a length of time that a patient or surrogate considers worthwhile. The argument for the duty to provide care deemed futile clearly does not extend to all non-life prolonging treatments that may be of interest to the patient. Some patients' demands are too offensive or too trivial to make them part of the contract between professionals and society. For example, a patient's demand that a surgeon amputate a healthy limb would not have to be honored.

On the other hand, some care that does not prolong life may still be considered so fundamental that physicians would have a duty to provide it. Consider, for example, medication to relieve severe chronic pain. Some physicians may sincerely believe that providing such medication is wrong, for instance, because it may shorten a patient's life. A physician may consider the use of such risky medication immoral, even though Catholic moral theology and much secular thought acknowledges the legitimacy of risking the indirect side effects in such cases. Even if a physician is sincerely opposed, however, he or she may well be expected by society to administer the pain relief, provided no other physician will take the case.

The key is that some interests of patients and surrogates may be recognized as fundamental. Even if a majority would not consider the treatment worth pursuing, that majority might recognize the importance of the minority's claim. Life-prolonging care is fundamental in this way; certain non-life-prolonging care may be as well. If the care is perceived as fundamental, then it should be part of the social covenant between society and the profession. In such cases, as in ones involving life-prolonging treatment, if (1) there is an ongoing patient-physician relationship, (2) no other physician will take the case, (3) the clinician is competent to provide the care, and (4) the funding is equitable, the licensed professional who is given a monopoly over the control of life should be expected to promise to use that technology when patients or surrogates ask for it.

NOTES

1. Steven H. Miles, "Informed Demand for 'Nonbeneficial' Medical Treatment," *New England Journal of Medicine* August 15, 1991: 512–515.
2. Stuart J. Youngner, "Who Defines Futility?" *JAMA* 260, 1988: 2,094–2095.
3. Robert M. Veatch and Carol Mason Spicer, "Medically Futile Care: The Role of the Physician in Setting Limits," *American Journal of Law and Medicine,* 18(1 and 2) 1992: 15–36; Robert M. Veatch, "DRGs and the Ethical Reallocation of Resources," *Hastings Center Report* June 1986; 32–40.
4. B.D. Colen, "Fight over Life," *Newsday,* January 29, 1991, p. S64.
5. *In re Quinlan,* 70 N.J. 10, 355 A.2d 647 (1976), *cert. denied sub nom.; Garger v. New Jersey,* 429 U.S. 922 (1976), overruled in part; *In re Conroy,* 98 N.J. 321, 486 A.2d 1209 (1985).

SUGGESTED READINGS FOR CHAPTER 8

A. THE CONCEPT OF FUTILITY

CALLAHAN, DANIEL. "Medical Futility, Medical Necessity: The-Problem-Without-a-Name." *Hastings Center Report* 21 (4, July-Aug. 1991):30–35.

CRANFORD, RONALD E. "Medical Futility: Transforming a Clinical Concept into Legal and Social Policies." *Journal of the American Geriatrics Society* 42(8, 1994): 894–898.

JECKER, NANCY S., AND ROBERT A. PEARLMAN. "Medical Futility: Who Decides?" *Archives of Internal Medicine* 152 (June 1992):1140–1144.

LANTOS, JOHN D., PETER A. SINGER, ROBERT M. WALKER, GREGORY P. GRAMELSPACHER, GARY R. SHAPIRO, MIGUEL A. SANCHEZ-GONZALEZ, CAROL B. STOCKING, STEVEN H. MILES, AND MARK SIEGLER. "The Illusion of Futility in Clinical Practice." *American Journal of Medicine* 87 (1989):81–84.

PARIS, JOHN J. "Pipes, Colanders, and Leaky Buckets: Reflections on the Futility Debate," *Cambridge Quarterly for Healthcare Ethics* 2 (1993):147–149.

SCHNEIDERMAN, LAWRENCE J., NANCY S. JECKER, AND ALBERT R. JONSEN. "Medical Futility: Its Meaning and Ethical Implications." *Annals of Internal Medicine* 112 (1990):949–954.

VEATCH, ROBERT M. "Why Physicians Cannot Determine If Care Is Futile." *Journal of the American Geriatrics Society* 42(8, 1994):871–874.

YOUNGNER, STUART J. "Futility in Context. [Editorial]." *Journal of the American Medical Association* 264(10, Sept. 12, 1990):1295–1296.

B. THE CASE OF HELGA WANGLIE

CAPRON, ALEXANDER MORGAN. "In re Helga Wanglie." *Hastings Center Report* 21(5, Sept.–Oct. 1991):26–28.

CRANFORD, RONALD E. "Helga Wanglie's Ventilator." *Hastings Center Report* 21(4, July–Aug. 1991):23–24.

GOLENSKI, JOHN D., AND LAWRENCE J. NELSON, "The Wanglie Case: A Demand for Treatment Clashes with Medical Integrity. [Introduction and case analysis]." *Clinical Ethics Report* 6(1, 1992):1–8.

MILES, STEVEN H. "Interpersonal Issues in the Wanglie case." *Kennedy Institute of Ethics* 2(1, Mar. 1992):61–72.

MILES, STEVEN H. "Legal Procedures in <Wanglie>: A Two-Step, not a Sidestep." *Journal of Clinical Ethics* 2(4, Winter 1991):285–286.

THE CASE OF BABY K

ANNAS, GEORGE J. "Asking the Courts to Set the Standard of Emergency Care—The Case of Baby K." *New England Journal of Medicine* 330(21, 1994):1542–1545.

PEABODY, JOYCE L. "When a Parent Demands What Health Care Providers Deem Foolish." *Clinical Ethics Report* 7(4, 1993):1–12.

D. THE MORAL DEBATE

BLACKHALL, LESLIE J. "Must We Always Use CPR?" *New England Journal of Medicine* 317 (1987):1281–1285.

BLUSTEIN, JEFFREY. "Doing What the Patient Orders: Maintaining Integrity in the Doctor-Patient Relationship." *Bioethics* 7(4, July 1993):290–314.

BRODY, HOWARD. "The Physician's Role in Determining Futility." *Journal of the American Geriatrics Society* 42(8, 1994):875–878.

BROWN, CRYSTAL. "Limiting Care: Is CPR for Everyone?" *AACN Clinical Issues in Critical Care Nursing* 1(1, May 1990):161–168.

CALLAHAN, DANIEL. "Necessity, Futility, and the Good Society." *Journal of the American Geriatrics Society* 42(8, 1994):866–867.

FINS, JOSEPH J. "Futility in Clinical Practice: Report on a Congress of Clinical Societies." *Journal of the American Geriatrics Society* 42(8, 1994):861–865.

JECKER, NANCY S., LAWRENCE J. SCHNEIDERMAN. "Futility and Rationing." *American Journal of Medicine* 92(2, Feb. 1992):189–196.

LANTOS, JOHN D. "Futility Assessments and the Doctor-Patient Relationship." *Journal of the American Geriatrics Society* 42(8, 1994):868–870.

LANTOS, JOHN D., STEVEN H. MILES, MARC D. SILVERSTEIN, AND CAROL B. STOCKING. "Survival After Cardiopulmonary Resuscitation in Babies of Very Low Birth Weight: Is CPR Futile Therapy?" *New England Journal of Medicine* 318(2, 1988): 91–95.

MURPHY, DONALD J. "Do-Not-Resuscitate Orders: Time for Reappraisal in Long-term-Care Institutions." *Journal of the American Medical Association* 250 (1988): 2098–2101.

NELSON, JAMES LINDEMANN. "Families and Futility." *Journal of the American Geriatrics Society* 42(8, 1994):879–882.

PARIS, JOHN J., FRANK E. REARDON. "Physician Refusal of Requests for Futile or Ineffective Interventions." *Cambridge Quarterly of Healthcare Ethics* 1(2, Spring 1992):127–134.

SADLER, JOHN Z., THOMAS WM. MAYO. "The Parkland Approach to Demands for "Futile" Treatment." *HEC (HealthCare Ethics Committee) Forum* 5(1, Jan. 1992):35–38.

SCHIEDERMAYER, DAVID L. "The Decision to Forgo CPR in the Elderly Patient." *Journal of the American Medical Association* 260 (1988):2096–2097.

SCHNEIDERMAN, LAWRENCE J. "The Futility Debate: Effective vs. Beneficial Intervention." *Journal of the American Geriatrics Society* 42(8, 1994):883–886.

Society of Critical Care Medicine Ethics Committee. "Consensus Statement on the Triage of Critically Ill Patients." *Journal of the American Medical Association* 271(1994): 1200–1203.

TOMLINSON, TOM, AND HOWARD BRODY. "Ethics and Communication in Do-Not-Resuscitate Orders." *New England Journal of Medicine* 318 (1988):43–46.

VEATCH, ROBERT M., AND CAROL MASON SPICER. "Medically Futile Care: The Role of the Physician in Setting Limits. *American Journal of Law and Medicine* 18(1&2, 1992):15–36.

YOUNGNER, STUART J. "Applying Futility: Saying No Is Not Enough." *Journal of the American Geriatrics Society* 42(8, 1994):887–889.

9

Social Reasons for Limiting Terminal Care

INTRODUCTION

As early as the 1960s medical economists were reporting that 22 percent of all Medicare funds were going to the 5 percent of patients who died within the calendar year.[1] That percentage of funds spent on those who would soon die has even increased since that time.[2] Of course, some would say that it is only to be expected that the patients who were critically ill were using a substantial portion of the medical resources. On the other hand, if many of these resources were being used on desperate, last-ditch efforts merely to prolong the dying process in patients who were known to be dying imminently, it could be argued that they neither served the interests of these patients nor used scarce resources responsibly.

Many of those interventions might have been inflicted on patients who would have declined them had they had the opportunity. Others, however, might have been approved by and actually desired by the patients or their surrogates. Even though rational, self-interested patients might desire these services, some might offer only minimal benefit or minimal chance of success and offer that marginal benefit at great cost. Since public Medicare funds were being used for those questionable treatments, it is reasonable that people would ask whether the interests of society or of other patients who could be helped with those resources would justify limiting care to the terminally ill.

Since that time these questions of social reasons for limiting care to the terminally ill have arisen with increasing urgency. As medical costs skyrocketed and the patients' rights movement became more prominent, decisions about terminal care have become more public and more controversial. Many of these treatments have been judged by patients or their surrogates to offer no net benefit. These treatments can now be declined based on the principles and policies discussed in earlier chapters. The important cases for a social ethics of terminal care are those that offer what patients or surrogates (and sometimes others) perceive as marginal net benefit, but offer that small benefit at significant cost.

We have increasingly recognized that assessment of both benefits and harms of medical treatments have inherently subjective dimensions. An intervention that is perceived to be of potentially great value to one person may be of very limited value or no value at all to another. In fact, to some that intervention may be seen as a net burden. Medical science, by itself, may be able to tell what the outcome of a treatment will be (or at least provide an estimate of the probability of a particular outcome). What it cannot do is establish whether that outcome is a benefit and, if it is a benefit, how beneficial it is. This means that outcomes research, empirical studies of expected results, and clinical judgment cannot be decisive in establishing how much benefit an intervention will offer to a particular patient. In some cases, a significant majority of people may consider an outcome of no value, while a minority sees it as worth pursuing. Maintaining irreversibly unconscious life, such as that of Karen Quinlan or Nancy Cruzan, is an example. Many thought that no purpose was served whereas some saw their lives as worth preserving. When interventions will produce marginal benefits or effects whose value is in dispute, important social policy issues arise.

Some such care goes to patients whose clinicians cannot predict accurately whether the patient will die soon. Even though the care is provided to patients who die soon, there is no way to know in advance that the treatment would provide so little benefit. Thus, not all this treatment can be known in advance to be wasted. Also, even for patients who are known to be dying soon, some care is intended to provide comfort. That treatment is important; it also cannot be thought of as wasted. Nevertheless, billions of dollars of medical care in the United States is devoted to last ditch, heroic efforts on patients who are dying and who receive no benefit from the treatment—not even palliation. Other care offers benefit that is very marginal. Ethical controversy has arisen over proposals to limit such care to the terminally ill for the purpose of avoiding waste and conserving scarce medical resources.

This chapter opens with a case study that reveals the role economics is playing in decisions about limiting medical care to the terminally ill. Following that opening case, the selections in the next section of this chapter present the empirical debate over how much could be saved from policies designed to limit care to the terminally ill in order to benefit society. Some have limited their attention to specific policies, such as decisions not to resuscitate. Some research, such as the studies by Maksoud, Jahnigen, and Skibinski,[3] by Chambers and his colleagues,[4] by Weeks and his colleagues,[5] and the article by Murphy and Finucane presented here,[6] lead authors to conclude that so-called DNR (do not resuscitate) orders could lower costs significantly. Other analyses, however, such as those by Schneiderman and his colleagues,[7] the articles by Teno and her colleagues,[8] and by the Emanuels,[9] as presented here, suggest that the savings may be much more limited.

Even the studies that are skeptical about the extent of the savings suggest that some care is nearly useless and that some can be identified in advance. Especially if some of the larger estimates of potential savings are correct, serious moral questions are raised.

Some ethical theories, such as utilitarianism, conclude that the social policy that can be expected to produce the most good for the population as a whole is morally preferred. If these medical resources could do more good by saving them for healthier patients, then, according to utility-maximizing ethical theories, such restrictions should be made. Since, by definition, the terminally ill are going to die soon regardless of medical interventions, it stands to reason that often more good can be done by utilizing society's resources for others. One device that is now being used to make these comparisons of benefit is the quality-adjusted life-year (QALY). It is a unit that takes into account both the number of years the anticipated benefit is likely to last and the quality of life of the person during that time. Thus, if the goal is to divert resources from the terminally ill when more benefit will come from other uses of the resources, health planners can compare QALYs to determine which use is more beneficial in terms of adding quality-adjusted years of life.

Others are not convinced that increasing the aggregate benefit to the society as a whole is a sufficient reason to limit care to terminally ill patients. For instance, theories that stress the principle of justice, at least justice of the egalitarian sort, favor social policies that benefit the least well off. Particularly in medicine it may turn out to be inefficient to benefit the least well off. Even extensive resources could turn out to do little or no good. Egalitarians who believe the terminally ill are among the worst off may resist the proposal to restrict care to the dying, even if they concede that some of their care is predictably inefficient. The egalitarian's goal is to do what is possible to help the worst off even if using the resources for the more fortunate would produce more substantial results.

Other ethical theories emphasize ethical principles that challenge the utilitarian's conclusion. Some terminally ill patients have insurance policies that include commitments to fund certain kinds of care. If they have been promised the care, then those who believe there is a *prima facie* duty to keep promises will insist that there are ethical reasons to provide the care, even if giving it to the better off would do more good. The selections in the third section of this chapter examine these ethical claims of the terminally ill to care.

The fourth and final section examines a closely related controversy over the role of age in allocating medical resources. Some are proposing that some expenditures for the elderly be limited soley on the basis of age. Although the elderly are often thought of as facing their final days, especially if they are critically ill, not all elderly people are terminally ill if *terminal illness* is defined as declining rapidly toward death *regardless of treatment*. Technically, according to many definitions of terminal illness, one is only dying if one would be declining relatively rapidly toward death even if treatment were provided. By this definition many of the ill elderly are not terminal, but they are nevertheless facing life-and-death decisions. They will soon be dead if they do not get appropriate treatments, but not if that treatment is provided. The elderly who are the focus of the current debate are candidates for receiving significant medial resources. They are candidates for organ transplants, hemodialysis, joint replacement, cardiac surgery, or chronic ventilatory support. If they do not receive these interventions, they will die.

Many, including former Governor Richard Lamm of Colorado, have been claiming that the elderly have had their chance at life. In his unguarded moments he has spoken of the elderly as having a "duty to die." Generally, he appeals to our sense of fairness in suggesting that the time has come to give the younger generations a chance.

Many who reject utilitarian arguments for limiting care to the elderly nevertheless have concluded that there are other moral bases for imposing such limits. Daniel Callahan has spoken of people who have completed their life projects who should be provided with basic medical care and with palliative services, but should consider whether high technologies that battle inevitable death make sense. He sometimes implies that insurance policies should limit such care on the basis of age. When the life span is complete, that is, when life's reasonable projects have been completed, there is less reason to use these technologies.

Some ethical analysts, such as Kilner,[10] Jecker,[11] and Harris,[12] whose views are presented here, object to these age-based limits. They often cast their objections in terms of a right to equal access to treatment. They believe that young and old people with similar diagnoses should not be denied a right to equal treatment.

Norman Daniels presses us to examine carefully exactly what is meant by "equality" and "the principle of justice." He introduces the notion of age-specific normal opportunity ranges. He argues that people have normal functions that differ at different points in the life span. Medical treatments that are needed to function normally at one stage are not the same as those needed to function normally at another stage. He suggests that how we allocate our health care among different stages in the life cycle is a matter of prudence. We need not allocate exactly the same services at each stage. As long as everyone similarly situated at a particular stage of life is entitled to the same medical services, then equals will be treated equally regardless of whether all persons have the same entitlement at each stage of the life cycle. What was at first thought to be a problem of interpersonal competition for scarce resources—that is, one among different persons—is turned into an intrapersonal allocation—deciding how to spread one's share of the resources over one's lifespan—that can be resolved on the basis of prudence.

That suggests, however, that there may not be a morally preferable way to allocate resources to the different stages of the life cycle. Others have asked whether prudential decision making is always fair to all persons. For example, we know that some people will die early in life. If resources are allocated prudentially toward different stages of the life span based on the assumption that persons will live through all the stages, then those who will not survive through all those stages might consider the allocation unfair. They would have preferred an allocation with their resources devoted to the earlier stages. Some are suggesting that not all prudent arrangements of resources are fair or just. Giving the elderly resources to treat some medical problems has been labeled unjust by some commentators. In what is sometimes called a "fair innings" argument, these commentators claim that justice requires giving people their fair chance to survive to later stages before we devote resources to efforts to prolong the lives of those who have already had a long life. This could mean that if a youngster and an elderly person are equally in need of a scarce organ for transplant and only one organ were available, justice would require giving it to the young person who otherwise would die rather than giving it to the octogenarian. Even though each has equal need for the organ a the present moment, the octogenarian has already had his "fair inning" and therefore has less claim to the scarce resources.

A true egalitarian who takes this perspective would favor the allocation to the younger patient even if the older person would receive more benefit from the treatment. This reveals a clear distinction between egalitarians and utilitarians. The former are willing to tolerate inefficiencies in order to give priority to the worst off, whereas the latter are willing to tolerate unequal treatment in order to maximize aggregate net utility.

The readings in this chapter make clear that the ethics of terminal care, which were once thought to pose moral problems limited to the rights and duties of the patient, family, and care-giving team, are now being thought of as raising larger social policy questions. The ethics of terminal care increasingly is a matter of community concern, not just the concern of individuals.

NOTES

1. Piro, P. A., and T. Lutins. *Utilization and Reimbursement Under Medicare for Persons who Died in 1967 and 1968.* Washington, DC: Social Security Administration, 1973.
2. Lubitz, J., and R. Prihoda. "The Use and Costs of Medicare Services in the Last Two Years of Life. *Health Care Financing Review* 5 (1984):117–131; Lubitz, J. D., and G. F. Riley. "Trends in Medicare Payments in the Last Year of Life." *New England Journal of Medicine* 328 (1993):1092–1096.
3. Maksoud, Alfred, Dennis W. Jahnigen, and Christine I. Skibinski. "Do Not Resuscitate Orders and the Cost of Death." *Archives of Internal Medicine* 153 (May 24, 1993):1249–1253.
4. Chambers, Christopher V., James J. Diamond, Robert L. Perkel, and Lori A. Lasch. "Relationship of Advance Directives to Hospital Charges in a Medicare Population." *Archives of Internal Medicine* 154 (1994):541–547.
5. Weeks, William B., Lial L. Kofoed, Amy E. Wallace, and H. Gilbert Welch. "Advance Directives and the Cost of Terminal Hospitalization." *Archives of Internal Medicine* 154 (1994):2077–2083.
6. Murphy, Donald J., and Thomas E. Finucane. "New Do-Not-Resuscitate Policies: A First Step in Cost Control." *Archives of Internal Medicine* 153 (July 26, 1994): 1641–1647.
7. Schneiderman, Lawrence J., Richard Kronick, Robert M. Kaplan, John P. Anderson, and Robert D. Langer. "Attitudes of Seriously Ill Patients toward Treatment that Involves High Costs and Burdens on Others." *The Journal of Clinical Ethics.* 5 (Summer 1994):109–112; Schneiderman, Lawrence J., Richard Kronick, Robert M. Kaplan, John P. Anderson, and Robert D. Langer. "Effects of Offering Advance Directives on Medical Treatments and Costs." *Archives of Internal Medicine* 117 (1992):599–606.
8. Teno, Joan M., Donald Murphy, Joanne Lynn, Anna Tosteson, Norman Desbiens, Alfred F. Connors, Jr., Mary Beth Hamel, Albert Wu, Russell Phillips, Neil Wenger,

Frank Harrell, Jr., and William A. Knaus for the SUPPORT Investigators. "Prognosis-Based Futility Guidelines: Does Anyone Win? *Journal of the American Geriatrics Society* 42 (Nov. 1994):1202–1207.

9. Emanuel, Ezekiel J., and Linda L. Emanuel. "The Economics of Dying: The Illusion of Cost Savings at the End of Life. *New England Journal of Medicine* 330 (Feb. 24, 1994):540–544.

10. Kilner, John F. "Age Criteria in Medicine: Are the Medical Justifications Ethical?" *Archives of Internal Medicine* 149 (1989):2343–2346.

11. Jecker, Nancy S. "Toward a Theory of Age-Group Justice." *Journal of Medicine and Philosophy* 14 (1989):655–676.

12. Harris, John. *The Value of Life: An Introduction to Medical Ethics.* London: Routledge & Kegan Paul, 1985, Chapter 5.

AN OPENING CASE

When Is Patient Care
Not Costworthy?*

DAN W. BROCK

The paradigm case of a social reason for limiting terminal care involves a patient who is facing almost certain death, but whose life can be prolonged for a brief period through the use of an expensive therapeutic effort. Often the patients themselves decide that such efforts are not of enough value to justify the intervention. In other cases, the patient may decide the treatment would be desired from a personal point of view, but decide to forgo it in order to preserve resources for their family or others. But in some cases, as in the case with which this chapter begins, the patient has insurance to cover the financial costs and desires the marginal benefit from the expensive treatment. Dan Brock, in the commentary that follows, argues that the clinicians are not the ones who should be making these decisions.

The following dialogue occurred during Grand Rounds: . . .

Gertrude Handel, a sixty-year-old woman, has had cancer of the pancreas for six months. The cancer has metastasized despite her participation in an experimental chemotherapy program. Currently, 95 percent of her liver is cancerous, she has metastases in her lungs, and her peritoneal cavity is filled with malignant ascites [cancerous fluid]. The patient has become anuric [her kidneys have stopped functioning], and she is encephalopathic [has suffered severe brain damage] due to kidney and liver failure.

The family has been told that she is dying and that there is nothing further that medical science can do for her. They have been advised that the present aim should be to keep the patient free from pain and as comfortable as possible. However, the family refuses to accept this and insists on placing the patient in the Intensive Care Unit to receive all available aggressive treatment. . . .

Intensive care would prolong the patient's life for a few days at most. The patient has no chance of recovering from the brain damage. Further, this is a particularly unresponsive form of cancer. Studies indicate that those who have it, even those who have participated in experimental protocols, invariably die. . . . The beds in the ICU are all occupied. . . . there is [no] other patient who could be safely discharged to make room for the patient.

[The family says] that the patient has told them on several occasions that she would want everything possible done to keep her alive if she should ever become terminally ill. . . . Dr. Bernstein said, "The patient has catastrophic health care insurance, and the effect of the costs of her care would not be felt by the family. It seemed the wrong time to bring up costs with them, as they were very upset, and the costs do

*Source: Reprinted from Cynthia Cohen (Ed.) *Casebook on Termination of Life-Sustaining Treatment and the Care of the Dying.* Bloomington: Indiana University Press, 1988.

not directly affect them. . . . Although the expenses incurred by additional treatment won't financially devastate the patient and her family, they *do* affect the costs of medical care to others who are in the patient's insurance pool. This has been overlooked by patients and physicians and is one reason why the costs of medical care have been rising so rapidly. Another reason is that we don't stop to consider whether some of the medical care we are providing is worth its high cost—or whether it is wasteful or useless. Some expensive medical treatments should be carried out . . . because they can restore patients to a meaningful life. But in this case, further treatments cannot do that. They would be futile, and it seems wrong to ask others to pay for them." . . .

Dr. Lean replied, "I believe that [another physician] is way off base if he thinks that doctors should consider the costs of care that they provide to patients. It is essential to the ethic of medicine that physicians ignore costs. Once we begin to talk about whether money should be spent on some patients and not others, we get into a devilish kind of reasoning that ends in allowing elderly people to die because their care is too expensive and that dumps poor people out of ERs because they have no insurance coverage. No one has a right to put a price on a patient's life. I know that I could never consider how much money each procedure costs when making a treatment decision for my patients. It would be contrary to everything that I stand for as a doctor. . . . I must admit that I, too, am bothered by the idea of giving the patient treatment that will only keep her alive for a few more days at great expense. I just want someone else, not me, to decide when treatment is too costly to provide. We shouldn't make these kinds of decisions at the bedside. We need some kind of policy that we know is ethical for determining when treatment is just not worth its costs." . . .

Should Mrs. Handel be denied admission to the ICU because her care would not be costworthy? If so, should her family be apprised of this?

COMMENTARY BY DAN W. BROCK

The central issue raised by this case is what role, if any, physicians should play in rationing health care when benefits seem not worth its costs. More specifically, should Mrs. Handel's physicians make decisions "at the bedside" about whether particular health care for her is worth its cost? It is easy to sympathize with Dr. Bernstein's concern about the social bill for expensive care such as that which Mrs. Handel's family seeks for her, since it appears to be both wasteful and inappropriate. At the same time, it is also easy to sympathize with Dr. Lean's concern that if physicians ever begin to decide whether care for their patients is worth its cost, they will inevitably be carried down a slippery slope toward clearly wrongful denials of care to the old or poor. Any plausible response for limiting use of noncostworthy care must be sensitive to both these concerns.

It is sometimes said that for so important a good as health care, cost should never be a consideration in whether a particular patient receives it. I believe it is easy to see that this cannot be correct. There is wide agreement that it is ethically permissible for a competent patient to decide to forgo any life-sustaining care that he or she judges to be unduly burdensome. One of the burdens of care is the financial cost that it imposes on the patient or others about whom the patient cares. Patient resources used for health care will not be available for other uses. Thus, a patient might freely choose not to undergo some forms of even life-sustaining treatment in order, for example, to preserve an inheritance for his family. Few would find such a choice based on consideration of financial costs ethically objectionable.

When a patient is incompetent to make treatment choices for him or herself, a surrogate, commonly a family member who knows the patient best, must decide for the patient. The widely accepted substituted judgment principle requires that surrogates attempt to decide as the patient would have decided in the circumstances if he or she had capacity. If there is clear and compelling evidence that the patient would not have wanted a particular treatment, in part because of its expense, respecting the patient's self-determination strongly supports the decision of the patient's surrogate against the costly care. Thus, there is nothing intrinsically unethical in either patients or their surrogates sometimes deciding to forgo treatment because of its cost.

The specific issue this case raises, however, is whether Mrs. Handel's physicians should take it upon themselves to deny care to her that she and her surrogates want solely on grounds that its benefits do not warrant its costs. I believe there are several important reasons why they should not. First, Mrs. Handel has obtained catastrophic health care insurance presumably in order to be able to pay the costs of care in circumstances like these. While this does not obligate her physicians to offer whatever care her surrogates might demand for her, it probably does obligate them not to deny her care on grounds of its cost. Her insurance, in effect, creates both an entitlement and a legitimate expectation that any medically appropriate care covered by her policy will be paid for by the insurance. While the insurance payments for her care will come from the pooled funds largely of others, all members of a private insurance pool join together to pool their funds precisely in order to fund members' entitlements to reimbursement for catastrophic health care costs. Even if the insurance comes from a government program funded by general tax revenues, that program would have the same democratic legitimacy as would other government spending programs, and the entitlements the program establishes should be honored, not surreptitiously undermined, by Mrs. Handel's physicians.

Institutions such as the government, employers, and health insurers all have an interest in holding down their bill for health care. They should not expect or pressure physicians, however, to deny care to patients in circumstances like Mrs. Handle's in which patients have an entitlement to be reimbursed for the financial costs of care. That would be to put the physicians in an ethically unacceptable position. It *is* ethically acceptable for physicians to help patients or their surrogates weigh the true costs of care against its benefits when the patients or surrogates wish to do so. I believe it is also ethically acceptable for the incentive structures of reimbursement systems to encourage patients or surrogates to weigh the true costs of care against its benefits more than is now common, so long as that does not result in denying patients an adequate level of care. The main reason this is so notoriously difficult to do is that health care insurance, the means of reimbursement for most health care in our country today, reduces or eliminates both out-of-pocket costs to the patient for care utilized, and in turn, the patient's economic incentive to consider or even learn the true costs of care. Yet the unpredictability and great variability in the amount and cost of health care that an individual may need provide powerful reasons to have insurance for health care costs.

A second important reason why Mrs. Handel's physicians should not take it upon themselves to decide whether her care is too costly to the other members of her insurance pool is that they lack any social, moral, or legal authorization to do so. If there is to be a serious public debate in this country about limiting utilization of non-costworthy care, particularly if that is life-sustaining care, then we are now only in the early stages of that debate. Any authorization for physicians to act as health care rationers with their individual patients should come as a result of such a debate, and not merely from pressures from third party payors to reduce their health care outlays. These pressures would be likely to fall most heavily on the vulnerable and powerless and would perhaps end up realizing Dr. Lean's worst fears.

When cost containment measures are openly adopted in financially closed health care systems like HMO's, then both physicians and patients can have reason-able assurance that cost savings will be passed on in the form of lower rates, improved quality of care, or new available forms of care to members who have forgone care to produce the savings. In such settings, it is possible for patients and physicians to co-operate together with the shared goal of providing good quality health care while lim-iting health care costs. When physicians instead only reduce "society's" overall health care cost by denying care that may benefit or be wanted by their patients, their justi-fication cannot be that the savings are returned to those denied the care for them to spend in alternative ways.

A third serious concern about physicians assuming the role of health care ra-tioners with their individual patients is whether denials of noncostworthy care would be equitably or fairly applied to different patients. If physicians are left to determine without further guidance what care is costworthy for individual patients at the bed-side, then almost certainly the effects of these attempts to control health care costs will *not* be equitable. This is because physicians, in the absence of clear standards of costworthy care, would inevitably reach differing conclusions about what care is cost-worthy and would also be susceptible to allowing ethically irrelevant factors, such as the social worth of the patient, subtly to influence their judgments. The relatively vul-nerable and powerless could be expected to suffer a disproportionate share of the ef-fects of such rationing.

A fourth major concern about physicians becoming "bedside rationers" is that this will create new conflicts of interest between patients and their physicians and so be likely to undermine the trust necessary for well-functioning physician/patient relationships. If physicians come to think of themselves as responsible for ensur-ing that society's resources are prudently spent, patients' trust that the treatment rec-ommendations and decisions of their physicians are guided first and foremost by concern for their patients' well-being will quite justifiably erode. I think that this concern lies behind Dr. Lean's view that physicians should remain unconstrained advocates for their patients and that "someone else . . . should decide when treat-ment is too costly to provide."

These various worries about physicians becoming bedside rationers do not im-ply that economic considerations should never play any role in decisions concerning life-sustaining treatment. Instead, they support an ethical case: (1) that decisions about standards and/or procedures for identifying care that will not be provided to patients because it is not costworthy be arrived at through public processes that allow substantial input to those who will be affected; (2) that health care institutions limiting access to noncostworthy care inform current and potential patients of those limitations; (3) that procedures be put in place to monitor the application of limitations on provision of noncostworthy care to insure that it is done equitably and without denying patients access at least to an adequate level of health care.

The appropriate decisionmaking bodies for defining limitations on noncostworthy care will vary depending on the context. For example, in an HMO these issues might be addressed by a committee within the HMO with substantial patient member representation. For government insurance programs, open debate at relevant points in the political process such as legislatures, public hearings, and so forth, would be appropriate. In other cases, participant input may be fostered by employers and health insurers that provide their employees and insurees with a greater range of alternative insurance plans that attempt to define and limit reimbursement for noncostworthy care to varying extents. There is no single institutional mechanism or group of persons that should address and make decisions about what care is costworthy. Nor is there any single correct definition of costworthy care, or any ethical necessity for societal uniformity in the definitions arrived at.

These several reasons for Mrs. Handel's physicians not to deny her the aggressive care she seems to have wanted because it is too costly do not mean she must go to the ICU.

THE ECONOMICS OF TERMINAL CARE

New Do-Not-Resuscitate Policies
A First Step in Cost Control*

DONALD J. MURPHY AND THOMAS E. FINUCANE

The movement to limit treatments for the terminally ill in order to save resources needed by others has been built on the assumption that these treatments
involve major costs that could be reduced or eliminated. Only recently have investigators begun to document the treatments that generate these costs and calculate the potential savings. Physicians Donald J. Murphy and Thomas E.
Finucane have focused on so-called orders "not to resuscitate patients." Murphy
and Finucane claim that only a small portion of patients in certain classes stand
to benefit significantly from cardiopulmonary resuscitation in the event of a
cardiac or respiratory arrest. They say that 2 percent or less of these patients
survive and are discharged and even fewer return to a "minimal level of functioning." They propose establishing limits on CPR, but they admit that some
patients will die sooner without CPR. They believe that, in the end, more good
will be done, which, for them, apparently provides a utilitarian justification for
the limits.

To control the cost of health care and to improve access to care for the un-
insured, our society will have to set limits on health care use. We believe that new
do-not-resuscitate (DNR) policies would be just and relatively painless ways of beginning to set these limits. . . . We suggest a DNR policy that eliminates cardiopulmonary resuscitation (CPR) for certain groups of people who are near death and that
CPR no longer be considered part of standard care for these patients. The major rationale for this policy change is cost control. Our society cannot achieve real cost
control until we agree to set limits. This new policy would have many additional advantages. It would help to (1) protect many patients who are near death from overtreatment, (2) operationalize the concept of futility, (3) reflect the majority's view of
marginally beneficial life sustaining care, and (4) protect professionals who care for
patients who are dying. The policy would have some disadvantages in that it would
limit individual patient autonomy, be legally risky, depend on imprecise data, be difficult to communicate, and result in an earlier death for some patients who would have
wanted CPR and who would have survived as a result of CPR. We believe the advantages outweigh the disadvantages.

*Source: Murphy, D.J. and Thomas E. Finucane, "New Do-Not-Resuscitate Policies: A First
Step in Cost Control." *Archives of Internal Medicine* 153 (July 26, 1994). pp. 1641–1648. Copyright
1994, American Medical Association.

We present data about outcomes of CPR and propose a change in policy for its use. The data identify three groups of patients for whom the probability of surviving to hospital discharge after CPR is less than 3%. The policy we propose is that CPR (i.e., advanced cardiac life support in the setting of a cardiopulmonary arrest) should not be considered standard medical care for patients in these groups. . . .

The following is a summary of patients who are extremely unlikely to survive after CPR. For these groups of patients, hospitals should consider new DNR policies.

PATIENTS WITH POOR PROGNOSES AFTER CPR

Patients with any of the following three conditions have an extremely poor prognosis after CPR: (1) advanced, progressive, ultimately lethal illnesses; (2) acute near-fatal illness or injury without improvement shortly after hospitalization; and (3) out-of-hosptial CPR without restoration of pulse rate or blood pressure in the field. The chance of survival to hospital discharge after CPR in these patients is approximately 2% or less; the chance of returning to even a minimal level of function after hospital discharge is probably less than 1%. . . .

CONTROLLING COSTS: ARE LIMITS REALLY NECESSARY?

Critics of our proposed DNR policy might argue that such limits are not necessary because we can achieve cost control by other means. . . . However, we do not believe that solutions to these problems alone will suffice. A more fundamental change in society's expectations will be necessary to obtain—and sustain—cost control. . . .

We agree with Lundberg,[1] whose first suggestion for "producing real cost control" is that "clearly futile care should cease."

DEFINING FUTILITY

The first question is, Who should define futility? The public should help define futile care if they are to accept limits on such care.[2–5] However, to expect the public to take the initiative in solving this problem is unrealistic. The health care profession must take the lead if society is to make progress in this debate. Our proposed policy would help define futile care by presenting a change that can be critiqued by the public. . . .

The cost-conscious physician of the twenty-first century must be comfortable in limiting other therapies and diagnostic tests that rarely lead to desirable outcomes. They will need to work with guidelines and policies, and their patients will need to expect them to do so. New DNR policies are a start in this direction, and we believe that the indirect monetary savings will be substantial. . . .

DISADVANTAGES OF NEW DNR POLICIES

New Policies Would Restrict Patient Autonomy

Restricted autonomy is the major disadvantage of new DNR policies. Our society may consider this too great a price to pay for the benefits of these policies.

However, we believe that the public should be able to compare this sacrifice with other sacrifices necessary for cost control.

Some Patients Will Die Sooner Without CPR

Some patients will correctly understand the decision they are being asked to make, will want CPR, and will be an individual who would have survived, but they well be refused CPR. They will die sooner under the proposed policy than they would have if their request had been honored under current policy. The rarity of this event needs to be emphasized. We estimate that the probability that a patient in any of the categories we define would understand the outcomes of CPR and would genuinely desire CPR is between .1 and .25.[6] The probability of surviving to hospital discharge after CPR is less than .03. Based on these estimates, the probability that a patient who has provided genuine informed consent would survive to hospital discharge is in the range of .001 (.1 $\times$ .01) to .0075 (.25 $\times$ .03). Current policies are designed to prevent this rare outcome. The policy we suggest would prevent the more common outcome of inappropriate and fruitless CPR (*New York Times*. October 4, 1990; sect B:20). . . .

New DNR Policies Are Risky

Special interest groups might make acceptance of this policy politically diffi-cult and, if it were accepted, legally risky. The risk of adverse public relations ("be careful at that hospital because they won't resuscitate your grandmother") may pre-vent hospital administrators from trying new and different policies. Both kinds of risks, legal and public relations, could be reduced significantly if hospitals collabo-rate (at city, county, or state levels) and include the public in changing the standard of care.[7] A more appropriate standard of care, one that sets limits on futile care as a matter of policy, may help prevent court cases that are emerging because of dis-agreements about futile care.[8–10] Public debate, not adjudication, is preferable for solving the problem of futility.[11] Furthermore, no policy provides perfect protection from liability.[12]

Informing the Public Will Be Difficult

Communicating changes in policy would be difficult. People expect that everything will be done to preserve their lives. We believe that any exception to these expectations needs to be communicated clearly to patients. The Patient Self-Determination Act may provide an ideal opportunity to communicate policy changes and involve the public in the dialogue.

New DNR Policies May Not Accommodate Certain Religious Beliefs

Certain philosophic and religious beliefs would not be well accommodated by the new policy.[13,14] If an individual insists on therapy that is thought to be inappro-priate by the larger community,[15] the burden of arranging this therapy should be on the individual, not on society.[16] Furthermore, it seems fair that such individuals pay out of pocket for care that is deemed inappropriate by society. A patient who believes in miracles, for example, should not expect the public or private insurance policy holders to support that belief with taxes or higher insurance premiums. . . .

CONCLUSIONS

We believe that our society must set explicit limits to allocate health care more justly in our society. Explicit limits will mean that a small number of 65-year-olds with pancreatic cancer or 19-year-olds with severe head trauma will die months or weeks earlier than they would have with CPR. Patients who are near death and who are unlikely to survive after CPR are an identifiable group. We believe that limits based on probability of benefit are more fair—and less painful—than the current limits in health care that are based on ability to pay. . . .

As the political debate evolves and prognostication improves, the details of our proposal will change. The essence of the proposal—optimal care of a person who is almost certainly dying should not include CPR—will not. Explicit debate about such policies, eg, where death occurs after technology is withheld, may lead to a clearer public understanding of the limits of medical care and the potential costs of its misapplication.

NOTES

1. Lundberg G.D. National health care reform: The aura of inevitability intensifies. *JAMA* 1992; 267:2521–2524.
2. Veatch R.M., Spicer C.M. Medically futile care: The role of the physician in setting limits. *American Journal Law Med* 1992; 18:15–36.
3. Scofield G.R. Is consent useful when resuscitation isn't? *Hasting Center Report* 1991;21:28–36.
4. Jecker N.S., Pearlman R. A. Medical futility: Who decides? *Archives of Internal Medicine* 1992;152:1140–1144.
5. Callahan D. Medical futility, medical necessity: The-problem-without-a-name. *Hastings Center Report* 1991;21:30–35.
6. Murphy D.J., Burrows D., Santilli S., et al. Older patients' preferences for CPR: The effect of likelihood of survival. *J Am Geriatr Soc* 1992;40:SA16. Abstract.
7. Morreim E.H. Stratified scarcity: Redefining the standard of care. *Law Med Health Care* 1989;17:356–367.
8. Miles S.H. Informed demand for 'non-beneficial' medical treatment. *N Engl J Med* 1991;325:512–515.
9. Paris J.J. Crone, R.K., Reardon F. Physicians' refusal of requested treatment: the case of Baby L. *N Engl J Med* 1990;332:1012–1015.
10. Paris J.J., Crone R.K., Reardon F.E. Ethical context for physician refusal of requested treatment. *J Perinatol* 1991;11:273–275.
11. Callahan D. Not out of court. *Hastings Cent Rep* 1991;21:43.
12. Kapp M.B. 'Cookbook' medicine: A legal perspective. *Arch Intern Med* 1990;150: 496–500.

13. Feldman L.J. A Halakhic/ethical view of 'no CPR' orders. *Journal Ageing Judaism* 1989;4:113–118.

14. Ackerman F. The significance of a wish. *Hastings Center Report* 1991;21:27–29.

15. Murphy D.J., Matchar D.B. Life-sustaining therapy: A model for appropriate use. *JAMA* 1990;264:2103–2108.

16. Weir R.F., Gostin L. Decisions to abate life-sustaining treatment for nonautonomous patients: Ethical standards and legal liability for physicians after *Cruzan*. *JAMA* 1990;264:1846–1853.

Prognosis-Based Futility Guidelines
Does Anyone Win?*

JOAN M. TENO, DONALD MURPHY, JOANNE LYNN,
ANNA TOSTESON, NORMAN DESBIENS,
ALFRED F. CONNORS, JR. MARY BETH HAMEL,
ALBERT WU, RUSSELL PHILLIPS, NEIL WENGER,
FRANK HARRELL, JR., AND WILLIAM A. KNAUS
FOR THE *SUPPORT* INVESTIGATORS

The claims that large amounts could be saved by eliminating certain life supports from the terminally ill have recently been challenged by medical investigators who are pressing for more specific documentation. One such study has been conducted by the SUPPORT investigators. "SUPPORT" stands for the Study to Understand Prognoses and Preferences for Outcomes and Risks of Treatments. These investigators have examined many empirical claims about the care of the terminally ill, including whether resources would be saved if treatments were limited. They studied 4301 patients, 115 of which were believed to have less than 1 percent chance of living more than 2 months. They found that patients who will soon die can be identified, but that implementation of strict, prognosis-based limits on terminal care would result in savings that would only be modest.

Guidelines for decision-making about life-sustaining treatment recommend that choices be based on the patient's informed preferences. In the past decade, however, debate has focused on whether physicians should not offer and, if asked, should deny requests for treatment deemed futile. Disagreements over the definition of futility and over the authority to make this judgment have fueled the debate over futility. However, the desire for cost control gives the debate a sense of urgency.

Lundberg estimated that our society could save billions of dollars annually by limiting futile care.[1] He argued that by implementing " . . . guidelines to prevent futile care, everyone wins—the patient, the family, and society as a whole." Such a proposal requires a social consensus on the definition of futile care. This definition should be unambiguous in order to avoid unjustifiable biases based on considerations like race, socioeconomic status, or disability. Furthermore, the definition will have to be able to be applied prospectively and equitably. With such a guideline, health care providers would not be obliged to offer or provide treatments deemed to be futile. According to one definition, which might meet these criteria, a treatment is futile when, despite treatment, the prognosis for short term survival falls below a specific threshold (here referred to as "prognosis-based futility guideline"). Schneiderman and colleagues have suggested a quantitative threshold: " . . . in the last 100 cases, a medical treatment has been useless . . . "[2]

*Source: Teno, J.M., D. Murphy, J. Lynn et al. "Prognosis-Based Futility Guidelines: Does Anyone Win?" *Journal of the American Geriatrics Society,* 42 (November 1994). 1202–1207. Reprinted with the permission of Williams & Wilkins, a Waverly Company.

Would elimination of such futile care result in better care and/or substantial cost savings? Few empirical studies shed light on this issue.[3] We describe the impact of a prognosis-based futility guideline by describing the treatments, decisions, and outcomes of seriously ill adults who would have been excluded from receiving life-sustaining treatment because they had ≤ 1% chance of 2-month survival.

METHODS

Study Population

The data collection methods used in the Study to Understand Prognoses and Preferences for Outcomes and Risks of Treatments (SUPPORT) have been reported previously.[4] . . . Entry criteria required that patients be in an advanced stage of one of the following conditions: nontraumatic coma, acute respiratory failure, multiple organ system failure with sepsis or malignancy, chronic obstructive lung disease, congestive heart failure, cirrhosis, metastatic colon cancer, or inoperable non-small cell lung cancer.[5] . . .

Patients, their surrogates, and physicians were interviewed between the second and sixth study day about patients' quality of life, physical functioning, preferences for resuscitation, and the influence of religion on treatment decisions. . . .

Analytic Approach

After describing the characteristics, decisions, and outcomes of patients who met each of the proposed prognosis-based futility guidelines, we examined the actual survival time for subjects who would have qualified for each prognostic cutpoint. We then simulated the potential impact of prognosis-based futility guidelines by assuming that life-sustaining treatment (i.e., a mechanical ventilator, vasopressors, or the use of dialysis) would be stopped or not initiated after the third day following study entry. This timing reflects the usual clinical needs for an initial period (here 2 days) for diagnosis and negotiation of a plan of care. We assumed that seriously ill patients would not survive more than 1 day without a mechanical ventilator or vasopressor or more than 2 days after the withdrawal of hemodialysis. These assumptions were affirmed by analysis of the time to death after the deliberate withdrawal of these treatments in SUPPORT. The potential savings were approximated by a count of the number of days of hospitalization that would be forgone with these assumptions. As a crude estimate of hospital charge savings, we multiplied the average daily hospital charges for that patient by the days of hospitalization forgone because the guideline led to earlier death.

RESULTS

Study Population

A total of 4301 subjects were enrolled from the five institutions. Subjects' average age was 62 (SD 16, range 18–100 years). . . .

Simulation of Futility Guidelines

We simulated the impact of a strict futility guideline that directed that life-sustaining treatment (ie, mechanical ventilator, vasopressors, or dialysis) be withdrawn on the third day after study entry or not be initiated after that day. All but 14 of the subjects with an expected 2-month prognosis ≤ 1% were receiving one or more of these three life-sustaining treatments. We then calculated the total number of hospital days that actually occurred after the day the futility guideline would have mandated stopping treatment. Of the total of 1688 hospital days, 199 (10.8%) would have been forgone. If a futility guideline had been in place, only 32 subjects would have died at an earlier time, with their deaths occurring between 1 and 310 days earlier. The vast majority ($n = 83$) of the subjects, however, would not have died earlier, because so many died on study Day 3 or 4 with their current-decision making and medical care.

For patients with ≤ 1% chance for 2-month survival, we estimate stopping treatment with a prognosis-based futility guideline would have saved $1.2 of the $8.8 million dollars in total charges (13.2%). Nearly three-fourths of the decrease in total hospital days would be accounted for by 12 patients. Six of these subjects were less than age 51. One 46-year-old patient with cirrhosis received a liver transplant on this admission and died 10 months later.

If the prognosis cutpoint for the futility guidelines were expanded to ≤10% expected survival at 2 months, 252 persons would have qualified, and 95% of those would have died by the second month. Median life expectancy for those 252 patients was 2 days beyond the day on which prognosis was assessed. We estimate that 1073 of 4528 hospital days would be saved by earlier death (potentially $5.0 out of $20.3 million in hospital charges). This would result in earlier death for 13 patients who did survive 2 months and nine who survived 6 months or longer.

DISCUSSION

The public believes that valuable resources are "wasted" on terminally ill patients, although some claim the data to support this conclusion are frail at best.[3,6–10] Nevertheless, some have proposed futility guidelines as one means of ensuring more appropriate care while also saving resources on care at the end of life.[1,11,12] To implement such a policy, the following four claims would need to be met. First, patients meeting the proposed definition of futility would have to be identifiable prospectively. Second, they would have to receive treatment that prolongs their lives somewhat but does not otherwise yield substantial benefits. Third, stopping or forgoing such care would have to result in sizable potential savings of resources. Finally, society would have to approve the principle of stopping life-sustaining treatment in these patients. . . .

Despite widespread public concern about overtreatment of terminally ill patients, the time course to death was quite short, in part, because so few had life support treatments continued. For those with 1% or less chance of 2-month survival, 90% died within 1 week of becoming so ill. Nearly 85% had a resuscitation effort withheld at the time of death, and about one-third had a life-sustaining mechanical ventilator withdrawn.

Among those with ≤ 1% chance of survival to 2 months, for example, virtually all died within a few days. Only four such patients survived 20 or more hospital days. . . .

Are Potential Savings Substantial?

With the assumptions about the timing of death after withdrawal of life-
sustaining treatment, we found that 199 days of hospitalization (10.8%) could have
been saved in the cohort where expected survival ≤1% at 2 months.

Examining the 12 cases that comprise the majority of the 199 hospital days savings with a 1% statistical threshold for 2-month survival illuminates some concerns.
In three cases, the patients were said to desire resuscitation, and their religious beliefs
were said to underlie treatment preferences. One of these cases, a 46-year-old man,
survived 10 months. In response to a structured interview at 6 months, he noted no
functional impairment and responded that his quality of life was good. We can only
speculate as to whether a societal consensus could be achieved to deny care in situations such as this one. Some will surely find it quite unsettling to foreclose the possibility of survival for these patients, especially since they voice a strong desire for
aggressive treatment to try to survive, often buttressed by religious claim. Others may
find it inequitable or otherwise improper to use this amount of resources on many patients to obtain less than 1 year of survival for one person. . . .

Alternatives to a Prognosis-Based Futility Guideline

If, as this analysis has suggested, strict application of a one-time ≤1% survival at 2 months futility guideline would result in only modest savings, what are the
alternatives? . . . An approach aimed at comfort may develop as the standard of care
for the patient with poor prognosis; only under unusual circumstances would aggressive care be pursued. This might lead to substantial cost savings. One can only
speculate about those potential savings. Whether professionals and the public would
be able to agree on such a definition of futility for the purposes of public policy remains uncertain.[13] . . .

CONCLUSION

In our health care system, we are faced with the paradox of plentiful, expensive
intensive care, while 37 million persons lack health insurance and many more can't
afford preventive or maintenance health services. In 1992, $62 billion (of $809 bil-
lion spent for health care in the United States) was spent on ICU services alone.[14,15]
If a large portion of these resources was being spent upon those with virtually no
chance of survival, and if ways could be devised to preclude that use, then we would
almost certainly should take the steps necessary to do so. However, persons in SUP-
PORT who met this one-time, quantitative definition of futility rarely lingered in an
ICU on vasopressors, mechanical ventilators, or dialysis. Rather, families and physicians quickly made decisions, and the potential savings from further acceleration of
forgoing aggressive treatment would be modest. A better alternative may be to ensure

that decision-making is informed by the patient's preferences and likely outcomes of care. In the second phase of SUPPORT, we will explicitly test whether providing health care providers with better information on prognosis and more opportunity for discussion of values and outcomes will enhance decision-making and reduce resource utilization in seriously ill patients. . . .

NOTES

1. Lundberg G.D. National health care reform: The aura of inevitability intensifies. *JAMA* 1992;267:2521–2524.
2. Schneiderman L.J., Jecker N.S., Jonsen A.R. Medical futility: Its meaning and ethical implications. *Annals of Internal Medicine* 1990;112:949–954.
3. Emanuel E.J., Emanuel L.L. The economics of dying: The illusion of cost savings at the end of life. *New England Journal of Medicine* 1994;330:540–544.
4. Lynn J., Knaus W.A. Background for SUPPORT. *Journal of Clinical Epidemiology* 1990;43 (suppl):1–4S.
5. Murphy D.J., Knaus W.A., Lynn J. Study population in SUPPORT: Patients (as defined by disease categories and mortality projections), surrogates, and physicians. *Journal of Clinical Epidemiology* 1990;43(suppl):11–285.
6. Ginzberg E. High-tech medicine and rising health care costs. *JAMA* 1990;263:1820–1822.
7. Bayer R., Callahan D., Fletcher J., et al. The care of the terminally ill: Morality and economics. *New England Journal of Medicine* 1983;309:1490–1494.
8. Schroeder S.A., Showstack J.A., Schwartz J. Survival of adult high-cost patients. Report of a follow-up study from nine acute-care hospitals. *JAMA* 1981;245:1446–1449.
9. Scitovsky A.A., Capron A.M. Medical care at the end of life: The interaction of economics and ethics. *Annual Review of Public Health* 1986;7:59–75.
10. Scitovsky A.A. Medical care in the last twelve months of life: The relation between age, functional status, and medical care expenditures. *Milbank Quarterly* 1988;66:640–660.
11. Murphy D.J., Finucane T.E. New Do-Not-Resuscitate policies: A first step in cost control. *Archives of Internal Medicine* 1993;153:1641–1648.
12. Fries J.F., Koop C.E., Beadle C.E., et al. Reducing health care costs by reducing the need and demand for medical services. *New England Journal of Medicine* 1993;329:321–325.
13. Youngner S.J. Who defines futility. *JAMA* 1988;260:2094–2095.
14. Hack M., Fanaroff A.A. Outcomes of extremely immature infants—a perinatal dilemma. *New England Journal of Medicine* 1993;329:1649–1650.
15. Oye R. K., Bellamy P. E. Patterns of resource consumption in medical intensive care. *Chest* 1991;99:685–689.

MORAL REFLECTION ON THE ECONOMICS OF TERMINAL CARE

Medical Care at the End of Life
The Interaction of Economics and Ethics*

A. A. SCITOVSKY AND A. M. CAPRON

Dispute remains regarding how much could be saved by eliminating aggressive life support from patients who are known to be dying and whose lives are prolonged only briefly by that intervention. Everyone agrees, however, that at least some scarce medical resources are used for this purpose. The real moral issue being debated is how much of this treatment can justifiably be eliminated without the consent of the patient or a valid surrogate. In the following reading, an economist and a health lawyer provide one of the first sustained moral analyses of efforts to set such limits. They point out that determining what will produce the most good for the society is itself a controversial issue and that doing what is just or fair may not lead to the same limits as doing what will do the most good in aggregate for the society as a whole.

INTRODUCTION

The rising cost of medical care in the United States over the past quarter century has become a matter of growing concern for both private citizens and government at all levels. . . . Only a small part of this increase is attributable to the increase in the population, which grew by only about 30% during this period. The major factors accounting for the increase in spending for medical care are the steady rise in medical care prices, . . . and . . . increase in the number and proportion of persons aged 65 years and older, who have higher medical care expenses per capita than younger persons.

It is this last problem, the high medical expenses of the elderly, which has been receiving special attention in recent years. One reason for this concern is the drain these expenses are putting on the Medicare Hospital Insurance Trust Fund, which is in danger of a deficit by the end of the century unless changes are made in its benefit structure or financing or both. . . .

In this article we review the . . . ethical and legal aspects of medical care of terminal patients as well as the more complex ethical problems posed by the growing number of elderly patients who are frail and sick but—despite the apparent assumptions of some studies—are not necessarily terminally ill.

*Source: Scitovsky, A. A., and A. M. Capron. "Medical Care at the End of Life: The Interaction of Economics and Ethics." *Annual Review of Public Health* 7(1986):59–75. Reproduced, with permission, from the *Annual Review of Public Health,* Vol. 7, © 1986, by Annual Reviews, Inc.

HEALTH CARE AND THE ELDERLY

The Aging of the Population

More Americans are living to age 65 and over than ever before. . . . During the first half of this century the major cause of the aging of the population was the decline in fertility, which reduced the proportion of young persons to older persons. In the second half of the century, the leading factor has been the decline in mortality across all age groups, resulting from improved living standards and medical advances in the prevention and treatment of infectious diseases that formerly were often fatal.[1] . . .

The elderly also are the principal users of nursing home services. . . . Almost 5% of persons aged 65 and over were in nursing homes, accounting for almost 90% of all nursing home residents.[2] . . .

Health Care Expenditures of the Elderly

. . . [T]he aging of the population, and especially the increase in the number and proportion of the very old, has been an important cause of the increase in national health care expenditures in the United States and is largely responsible for the financial difficulties of the Medicare program. Because Medicare reimbursements increase with age, average annual reimbursements per enrollee have increased; and because elderly people live longer, Medicare payments per enrollee continue over a longer period of years than when the program was introduced in 1965.

THE ECONOMICS OF CARING FOR PATIENTS WHO DIE

Just as concern over the growing proportion of national expenditures devoted to health care often focuses on the major contribution made by the aging of the population, concern about the high cost of care for the elderly is heightened by the evidence from several studies that shows that a large part of these expenses is incurred in the last year or months of life. . . . In fact, as Fuchs has pointed out, the high medical expenses of persons who die are the principal reason that medial care expenditures of the elderly rise with age.[3] . . .

To determine whether medical resources are being misused for the dying, a review and evaluation of the data on medical care use and expenditures at the end of life are essential. Studies of medical care at the end of life have been classified into two broad categories: (*a*) studies dealing specifically with use and costs of care at the end of life, and (*b*) studies of high-cost illness in general, which also provide some information about high-cost patients who died during the period under study.[4]

Evaluating the Studies

None of the studies tell the whole story of medical care use and costs at the end of life. Some of the studies cover only hospital care, others only one specific cause of death, cancer. . . . Nevertheless, taken together the studies leave little doubt that medical care expenditures at the end of life are indeed high. . . . The greater concern about these costs today than 15 or 20 years ago is tied to the general concern over constantly rising medical care expenses. . . . As one public official opined, "We've got a duty to die and get out of the way with all our machines and artificial hearts and everything else like that and let the other society, our kids, build a reasonable life."[5] However, although studies establish that medical care costs at the end of life are high, this by no means proves that a "disproportionate" amount is being spent on terminally ill patients.

The assertion that the "dying elderly" are receiving "too much" health care could mean several different things. First, those concerned with controlling health care expenditures may mean that elderly patients who die absorb an "excessive" amount of the total public (and/or private) resources available for health care. . . .

Alternatively, the claim of "too much" care may be that these patients are receiving care that is neither desired by, nor appropriate for, them. Rather than being an economic argument, this conclusion is explicitly framed in ethical terms. An analysis of the philosophical principles by which this assertion can be evaluated demonstrates, however, that the first version of the "disproportionality" claim also rests—and should be judged—on ethical as well as economic presuppositions.

ETHICAL IMPLICATIONS AND PROBLEMS

Among the teleological and deontological theories that might bear on the subject, three merit special attention. The funding of care at the end of life can be evaluated based upon principles of (*a*) justice, (*b*) utility, or (*c*) beneficence and autonomy.

Just Allocation

Justice is a complex concept, with meanings that range in different contexts from procedural fairness to the distribution of benefits and burdens by desert.[6] Health care financing raises issues of comparative justice, that is, the fairness of one person or group receiving a resource at the expense of another person or group.

In a society in which most goods are distributed through marketplace mechanisms, the claim that a particular good (such as health care) is distributed unfairly could be collapsed into a complaint about the basic distribution of wealth and income. However, given the large role that public funding plays in health care, especially for the elderly, the claim that it is unfairly distributed need not be seen as an invitation to a wide-ranging debate about the entire organization of American society. What, then, are the criteria by which the fairness of health care's distribution might be judged? Three—equality, need, and equity—require examination.

Equal Allocation.   In many settings, justice is served by treating people equally (i.e., "one person, one . . . "). If this standard were applied to health care, it might mean that each person would be entitled to an equal amount of care over the course of a year or perhaps over the person's lifetime. Given the wide variations in health status among individuals, such a standard would almost certainly have unacceptable results: If the amount of care guaranteed were set high (so as to encompass those whose health is chronically poor), an enormous drain would be imposed on resources that could be used to meet other, nonhealth care needs; if, to avoid this problem, the level were set low (merely enough to meet the needs of persons in average health or better), services that could preserve life or restore health would be unavailable for some sick people. Indeed, if the equality standard were strictly applied, such services would have to be withheld from patients who wished to use their own resources to purchase health care rather than other goods and services. Thus, the fact that health care expenditures are not even among individuals or among groups in the population—such as the elderly versus the nonelderly—is not grounds for concluding that the distribution of care is unjust.

Distribution by Need. To remedy the perverse effects of an equality standard, distribution according to need has been suggested as a preferable criterion for justice. Under this standard, the high incidence of chronic illness among the elderly would justify the greater proportion of health care provided to this group, just as a large percentage of education dollars is appropriately spent on the young. The problem with using need as the basis of an ethical theory of health care distribution is that it opens the door to unlimited spending on this one good, to the potential exclusion of many other individual and social goods.

Equitable Access. In light of the weaknesses in need and equality as standards, the President's Commission for the Study of Ethical Problems in Medicine and Biomedical and Behavioral Research concluded that the principle of justice required that everyone have *equitable* access to health care, which was interpreted to mean that society has an ethical obligation to ensure access to an adequate level of care for all without imposing undue burdens on anyone in obtaining that care.[7] Thus, to decide whether an unfair amount of care was being provided to patients who die, one would have to determine . . . whether the provision of that care went beyond the adequate level. . . . Millions of Americans are not ensured access to an adequate level of care, while public funds help secure far more than merely adequate care for others.[7]

> In the long run, a societal consensus about access to health care, including life-sustaining care, is needed. Rather than beginning with restrictions on life-sustaining care, however, it would be better to develop principles for equitable and acceptable limits on the use of health care generally, and then to apply those principles to issues at the end of life[8] (p. 100).

The second aspect of equity—whether the allocation of resources to one deprives others of an adequate level of care—reveals that adequacy is a comparative concept. . . . If one concentrates solely on the physical aspects of health care (i.e., preserving life and restoring functioning), then resources would be most sensibly applied to younger rather than older patients, since the former will enjoy the prospect of benefitting from the results of successful treatment much longer than the latter. . . . If there are problems of distributional justice in the system, they are likely to be exacerbated rather than solved by the Draconian step of cutting off high cost care for older "dying patients."

Utilitarian Analysis

An alternative analysis of the concern over excessive expenditures at the end of life would turn to the principle of utility, under which the distribution of health care is examined in terms of its relative efficacy in producing the greatest net benefit for all persons affected. . . . It is extremely difficult to make valid comparisons: Is restoration of function in a 12-year-old valued the same as in a 72-year-old?

Prognostic Limitations.   Even if (for the purposes of argument) continued life is taken to be an absolute value, a basic problem with a utilitarian evaluation remains: To be applicable, such a method would have to be able accurately to predict which patients will live (i.e., should be treated) and which will die (i.e., where treatment—beyond palliation of pain—would be "wasted"). . . .

Practically all the studies dealing with medical care costs at the end of life fail to face the problem of how to determine in advance who will die. . . . How many of those who died, one wonders, were recognized as being terminal patients, and how long before death was their status clear? Conversely, how many of the survivors were regarded as hopelessly ill according to the best judgment of their physicians but surprised them by recovering? One has to be cautious, therefore, not to equate the high medical costs at the end of life with the high costs of terminal care.

Beneficence and Autonomy

As this analysis suggests, ethical analysis is needed to evaluate the concerns voiced about a disproportionate percentage of health care (and especially public) funds being expended for patients who die. . . . Dr. Alexander Leaf, the chief of medicine at the Massachusetts General Hospital, spoke for many concerned physicians when he observed that in acute-care hospitals, the elderly "are too often subjected to the same management that might offer hope of benefitting a younger person with less extensive disease"[9] (p. 888). . . .

Improving Decisions.   The means developed in recent years to further the interests of all patients have particular importance for very sick or dying patients whose condition prevents them from participating in decisions about their own care. The objective of most of these mechanisms is to promote goals associated with the ethical principle of autonomy—namely, that all treatments be based upon the patient's individual value preferences and definition of what serves his or her goals.

The first of these mechanisms, under the title of the "Living Will," provides a means for a person, while still competent, to instruct his or her physician, family, and other advisors about the limits of treatment if the person becomes incompetent and there is no reasonable prospect of recovery from extreme physical or mental disability. . . .

Recently, another alternative—a patient's appointment of someone to make choices on his or her behalf—has been recommended as a more realistic and flexible tool to ensure that the patient receives treatment of a type and scope desired, even when the patient has lost the capacity to participate in decision making.[8] . . . Thus, it provides a means (much simpler and more expeditious than judicial appointment of a guardian) to serve the goals both of autonomy and beneficence. Further, some hospitals have recently appointed Institutional Ethics Committees to improve the quality of decisions made in certain difficult cases and to ensure that the best interests of very sick (and usually incapacitated) patients are served.

Remaining Problems. Such mechanisms are not widely employed by patients and physicians, nor yet incorporated into the ethos of the medical profession; therefore, practical questions about the extent and vigor appropriate in treating acute illness in elderly patients remain. . . .

CONCLUSION

In sum, although the available data are not conclusive, it appears unlikely that more than a relatively small part of the high medical expenses at the end of life, and of the elderly in general, are due to excessively aggressive care of terminally ill patients. Most of these expenses seem to be for the care of very ill but not necessarily dying patients, care that, especially in the case of the very old and chronically ill, is relatively conservative yet expensive. . . .

Moreover, the fact that this second group of patients is not "dying" raises grave questions in the minds of many about the application to them of the substantive standards for withdrawal of "life-sustaining" treatment that have recently come to be widely accepted regarding more gravely ill patients. Many people may share the sentiments of the respected journalist, Alan Otten, who publicly expressed concern over the fate of his 90-year-old mother and others like her in nursing homes, "enduring barren year after barren year, with chronic diseases that unfortunately do not kill but merely irrevocably waste the body and destroy the mind."[10]

> Doctors, nursing homes and hospitals work to keep these old people alive with tube feeding, nutritional supplements, antibiotics at the first sign of infection. For what? Are we really doing these people any favor by fighting so hard to prolong their lives?

Yet, despite the prevalence of such views[11] society has only just begun to address this problem. . . . Until medical prognostic powers improve substantially and ethical and legal standards emerge to allay fears that any failure to "do everything possible" for these patients would send the country sliding into the abyss of active euthanasia, medical treatment will continue to be provided that possibly wastes resources and that may harm rather than help some patients.

NOTES

1. Fingerhut, L.A. 1982. Changes in mortality among the elderly: United States, 1940–79. *Vital and Health Statistics,* Ser. 3, No. 22, Hyattsville, MD: Natl. Cent. Health Stat. DHHS Publ. No. (PHS) 82–1406.
2. DHEW, Natl. Cent. Health Stat. 1979. The National Nursing Home Survey: 1977 Summary for the United States. *Vital and Health Statistics, Ser.* 13, No. 43. Hyattsville, MD: DHEW, Natl. Cent. Health Stat. DHEW Publ. No. (PHS) 79–1794.
3. Fuchs, V.R. 1984. Though much is taken: Reflections on aging, health, and medical care. *Milbank Memorial Fund Quarterly* 62:151–154.
4. Scitovsky, A.A. 1984. "The high cost of dying": What do the data show? *Milbank Memorial Fund Quarterly.* 62:591–608.

5. Lamm, R.D., Governor of Colorado, 1984. Speech before Colorado Health Lawyers Association, Denver CO, March 27, 1984 (corrected transcript, *Denver Post*).
6. Beauchamp, T.L., Childress, J.F. 1983. *Principles of Biomedical Studies,* pp. 183–220. New York/Oxford: Oxford Univ. Press. p. 364.
7. President's Commission for the Study of Ethical Problems in Medicine and Biomedical and Behavioral Research. 1983. *Securing Access to Health Care.* Washington DC: US GPO. p. 223.
8. President's Commission for the Study of Ethical Problems in Medicine and Biomedical and Behavioral Research. 1983. *Deciding to Forego Life-Sustaining Treatment.* Washington DC: US GPO. 554 pp.
9. Leaf, A. 1977. Medicine and the aged. *New England. Journal of Medicine* 297: 887–90.
10. Otten, A.L. 1985. Can't we put my mother to sleep? *Wall St. Journal,* June 5, p. 34, col. 3.
11. Malcolm, A.H. 1984. Many see mercy in ending empty lives. *NY Times,* Sept. 23, p. 1, col. 3.

Quality of Life and Resource Allocation*

MICHAEL LOCKWOOD

Beginning in the mid-1970s those concerned about the social limits of medical care became concerned about the fact that the goal of medicine is not only the preservation of life, but also the relief of suffering. If systematic planning leading to choices about which care to fund for the terminally ill was to take place, some unit of comparison of alternative uses of resources was needed. One approach has been to measure health care benefits in "quality-adjusted life-years." Now often abbreviated QALYs, these units measure the expected number of years of life added by alternative uses of resources, but in each case the number of years is adjusted for the quality of life during those years. For example, if someone would consider 12 years with a handicap to be of equal value to 10 years without it, the 12 years would be discounted to be the equivalent of 10 quality-adjusted life years. This approach, which permits measuring the expected benefits of all medical interventions in QALYs, makes possible comparison of the benefits of highly diverse uses of resources some of which may extend life, but extend it at poor quality while others may have little effect on length of life, but more significant effects on the quality of life. Having a common unit permits comparisons. The possibility of comparisons, in turn, raises important moral issues. If the goal is maximizing the number of QALYs per dollar invested, the approach has utilitarian philosophical underpinnings. This essay examines those underpinnings and explores the potential conflict between maximizing benefits produced and distributing the benefit fairly.

I

. . . Now a natural response to allocation problems, both at macro and micro levels, is to say simply: one should put one's resources where they will do the most good. Well, yes, perhaps one should. But that then raises the further question: what does one mean by "the most good"? One kind of good, arguably the most important kind of good, that health care may achieve is the saving of lives, or more precisely (if less optimistically) postponing death. So one measure—albeit a very crude and one-sided measure—of the good that health care does would be the overall extension of live expectancy that it generates: years of life gained. Some writers have argued that we should give a very high priority to this aim of maximizing aggregate years of life gained; and that, moreover, this aim morally requires an allocation of resources, both within and outside medicine, that is radically at odds with the present allocation pattern in developed countries. . . .

*Source: Lockwood, Michael. "Quality of Life and Resource Allocation." In J.M. Bell and Susan Mendus, eds. *Philosophy and Medical Welfare.* Cambridge, England: Cambridge University Press, 1988, pp. 33–55.

Most of what is done in the name of health care is directed towards the allevi-ation of pain, discomfort and disability, rather than the extension of life, but is surely no less valuable on that account. Moreover, things which rank equal in terms of the threat to life that they pose, may well rank unequal in terms of their effect on the qual-ity of life, or in terms of the typical quality of the lives that they threaten to cut short; both sorts of consideration are surely relevant to the question of the relative priority to be given to their prevention or cure.

Thus, judgments about which of several forms of health care expenditure does the most good calls, in general, for one to balance against each other the life-enhancing and the life-extending aspects of health care: quality and quantity of life have some-how to be rendered mutually commensurable. This is where [quality-adjusted life-years] QALYs come in. I quote from Alan Williams, of the University of York, who has done most to develop this approach.

> The essence of a QALY is that it takes a year of health life expectancy to be worth 1, but regards a year of unhealthy life expectancy as worth less than 1. Its precise value is lower the worse the quality of life of the unhealthy person (which is what the "quality ad-justed" bit is all about). If being dead is worth zero, it is, in principle, possible for a QALY to be negative, i.e., for the quality of someone's life to be judged worse than be-ing dead.
>
> The general idea is that a beneficial health care activity is one that generates a pos-itive amount of QALYs, and that an efficient health care activity is one where the cost per QALY is as low as it can be. A high-priority health care activity is one where the cost-per-QALY is low, and a low priority activity is one where cost-per QALY is high.[1]

The assumption here is that there is some rational way of trading off length of life against quality of life, so that one could say, for example, that three years of life with some specified degree of discomfort, loss of mobility or whatever was worth two years of normal life. Such tradeoffs are, of course, often inescapable in medical practice. . . .

What economists who favour the QALY approach do, in a macroallocation con-text, is take a checklist of health factors that are likely to affect the perceived quality of life of normal people, and assign weightings to them. (Most work done in Britain has been based on the *Rosser distress and disability index,* which health economists would be the first to admit provides only rather a crude measure of quality, but one which they would hope to improve upon in time.[2]) There is, of course, an inescapable element of arbitrariness here, both in the choice of factors to be taken into account and in the relative weightings that are attached to them, which, as already pointed out, would differ markedly from patient to patient. (Immobility, for example, is likely to prove far more irksome to the athlete than to the philosopher.) But the factors and their associated weightings are mostly so chosen as to reflect the feelings and con-sidered judgments which the average or representative patient is likely to evince in practice, when faced with various forms of disability or discomfort, either in prospect or, better, having actually experienced them. On this basis, a given form of treat-ment is assigned a QALY value, corresponding to the number of QALYs such a pa-tient can look forward to with the treatment minus the number of QALYs the patient can look forward to if untreated. One then calculates what each QALY gained by these means actually costs.

Whatever philosophical reservations one might have about such an exercise (and I will turn to these in due course), it has yielded some interesting, indeed surprising, results. In Britain there is (or certainly was in the recent past) a widespread feeling that heart transplants represent a wasteful use of medical resources, that the benefits yielded are simply not sufficiently great to justify the cost. But on the other hand, people who say this will usually argue that not enough funds are, in Britain, allocated to long-term renal dialysis. It is widely regarded as a scandal that a treatment that is so effective in extending life should not be made universally available. Williams, evaluating these and other forms of treatment using the notion of a QALY, has come to a very different conclusion. Williams assigns to heart transplantation a QALY value of 4.5 (the point, neglected by most critics of heart transplants, being that their effect, when successful, on the quality of life is dramatic), whereas home and hospital dialysis receive QALY values of 6 and 5 respectively (the neglected point here being that, for most people, long-term dialysis represents a considerable ordeal).[3] Nevertheless, dialysis, so far, comes out somewhat ahead of heart transplants. But now the cost per patient of long-term dialysis is considerably greater than that of a heart transplant. So the cost per QALY is only £5,000 in the case of heart transplants, as compared to £11,000 and £14,000 respectively, in the case of home and hospital dialysis.[4]

Actually, all three figures turned out to be very high as compared with, say, hip replacement or heart valve replacement and pacemaker implantation, whereas Williams assesses the costs per QALY gained as, respectively, £750, £900 and £700;[5] in these latter operations one gets far more QALYs for one's money. In most parts of Britain there are waiting lists for all these operations; in the case of hip replacement operations the average waiting list under the National Health Service is three years (and in some areas is as high as five years)—it is not in the least unusual for people to die before they reach the head of the queue! Someone who believed that macroallocation in health care should be determined wholly on the basis of directing funds to where they can generate the maximum number of QALYs might well conclude from these figures that given a fixed health care budget, it would be rationally appropriate actually to transfer funds from such relatively high cost-per-QALY, albeit life-saving, forms of treatment as renal dialysis, to such things as hip-replacement operations, right up to the point at which the waiting lists had been eliminated—even if this meant providing no long-term dialysis at all! A pretty startling conclusion. . . .

II

Appealing to QALYs in a macroallocation context, despite the fact that, as we have just seen, it is likely to result in recommendations wildly at odds with present practice, tends to raise fewer hackles than its application to problems of microallocation. Indeed, the advocates of this approach themselves tend to talk less about microallocation than macroallocation. But the approach has clear implications for microallocation too. It implies, for example, that life-saving treatment should, other things being equal, go to those who, with the treatment, will have a longer life expectancy; thus, generally speaking, it will favour younger over older patients. This is in line with actual policy within the British National Health Service with regard to renal dialysis: most centres operate an effective 65-year cut-off. It also implies that, if there appeared, on other grounds, to be nothing to choose between two rival candidates for some life-saving treatment, but one was suffering from a condition, whether or not related to whatever it was that threatened his life, that detracted from its quality, then one should prefer to treat the other candidate. . . .

These health-care economists have, it appears, rediscovered utilitarianism. Indeed the QALY approach has a pleasantly nostalgic air, for those familiar with Jeremy Bentham's 'felicific calculus'.6 Most of the philosophical doubts one might have about the QALY approach would be particular instances of familiar charges that have been laid against utilitarianism. It should be emphasized, however, that the use of QALYs does not commit one to *classical* or *eudaimonic* utilitarianism: that is to say, there is no suggestion that the good is to be equated with happiness. If we adopt a terminology recently advocated by Amartya Sen,7 the QALY approach to allocation is, strictly speaking, *welfarist* rather than utilitarian—welfarism being the doctrine that we should so act as to maximize aggregate benefit. Classical utilitarianism is thus a particular form of welfarism, characterized by its equation of benefit with happiness. The concept of a QALY is, of course, committed to no such equation. Indeed, it is in one sense only a framework, requiring to be fleshed out by some substantive conception of what contributes to or detracts from the intrinsic value or worthwhileness of a life, and to what degree—a conception, that is, of what it is about a life that determines of how much benefit it is to the person whose life it is. . . .

III

Any sane moral theory is bound, it seems to me, to incorporate a welfarist element: other things being equal, it should be regarded as morally preferable to confer greater aggregate benefit than less. To this extent, it seems to me that QALY calculations, or something equivalent to them, should certainly be regarded as highly germane to the resolution of allocation problems within medicine. And, as I have just indicated, the fact that any assignment of precise QALY values is bound, in practice, to involve a degree of arbitrariness need not invalidate the qualitative conclusions that emerge, to the extent that the latter prove robust. But of course, it is one thing to say that welfarist considerations deserve to be given weight (great weight, even) in decisions regarding allocation, quite another to say that they should invariably be regarded as decisive. . . .

IV

But I mention welfarist consideration[s] mainly to put them to one side. For what I really want to focus on here is the philosophically more fundamental objection that can be levelled against the QALY approach: namely, that, precisely *because* it is uncompromisingly welfarist, it is in principle liable to result in forms of allocation that are *unjust* or *unfair*. . . .

One reason, then, why the QALY approach can strike one as intuitively unjust is that the principle "To each according to what will generate the most QALYs" is potentially in conflict with the principle 'To each according to his need'. A patient suffering from end-stage renal failure may be said to *need* dialysis or a kidney transplant, just as a patient with an arthritic hip *needs* a hip replacement. But the first patient's need is clearly the greater. Following David Wiggins,[8] one can think of the degree to which a person, P, needs something, X, as a function of the degree to which his lack of X compromises P's capacity to flourish as a human being ("flourishing" now being, in British philosophical circles, the most favoured translation of Aristotle's *eudaimonia*). Someone, then, who will die without some particular treatment needs it in the strongest possible sense; for one cannot flourish at all if one is dead. Other things being equal, one would think, the greater the need the weightier the claim on available resources. But the QALY arithmetic is inherently insensitive to differences in degree of need, except in so far as they happen to correlate with the degree of benefit per unit cost that treatment can confer. It attaches just as much value to the QALYs generated by treating those in a state of lesser need as it does to those generated by treating those in a state of greater need.

Indeed, it is arguable that some forms of medical treatment, whilst they confer a genuine benefit, do not minister to any *need,* as such, at all. I have in mind, for example, cosmetic surgery designed to remove normal wrinkles from the faces of middle-aged ladies. A model or an actress might, to be sure, need such an operation if she was to flourish, if the wrinkles compromised her ability to find employment (and so might a woman who was neurotically obsessed with her looks, if the operation could remove the obsession). But for the rest, the wrinkles do not compromise their capacity to flourish; it is merely that, with the operation, they may be enabled to flourish at a higher level. Such operations are, in short, a luxury. Suppose, then, as seems to me entirely possible, that some health care economist were able to show that facelifts, say, generated even more QALYs per unit cost than do hip-replacement operations. Would anyone really think that was sufficient reason for switching resources from hip replacements towards such cosmetic surgery?

Surely not. And if not, then by the same token it is far from clear that the QALY calculations cited by Williams constitute a sufficient reason for transferring resources from renal dialysis to hip replacements. One could plausibly argue that someone who will die, if he or she doesn't receive a certain form of treatment, has an intrinsically much stronger claim on available resources than someone whose life is not at stake, even if there is a sense in which greater aggregate benefit could be achieved by neglecting those whose life was threatened in favour of those suffering from reduced mobility or discomfort. And if so, then the greater moral weight that attaches to the claim could be held to outweigh the greater cost of the life-saving treatment per unit QALY generated. . . .

NOTES

1. Alan Williams. "The Value of QALYs," *Health and Social Service Journal* July (1985), 3.
2. P. Kind, R. Rosser, and A. Williams. "Valuation of quality of life: Some Psychometric Evidence," in M. W. Jones-Lee, *The Value of Life and Safety.* Amsterdam: Elsevier/North-Holland, 1982.
3. Alan Williams. "Economics of Coronary Bypass Grafting." *British Medical Journal* 291 (3 August 1985), 328.
4. Ibid.
5. Ibid.
6. Jeremy Bentham. *The Principles of Morals and Legislation* (1789), Chapters 1–5.
7. See Amartya Sen, "Utilitarianism and Welfarism," *Journal of Philosophy* 76 (September 1979).
8. David Wiggins. "Claims of Need," in Ted Honderich (ed.). *Morality and Objectivity.* London: Routledge & Kegan Paul, 1984, pp. 149–202.

AGE AND THE ALLOCATION
OF RESOURCES

The Value of Life*

JOHN HARRIS

The writings of Richard Lamm and others proposing to limit care on the basis of age have produced a significant backlash. In the following essay John Harris accuses proponents of such limits of being "ageist." He considers it an injustice to cut life short regardless of age. Harris presents a version of what is sometimes called the "fair-innings" argument and then offers his opposition to it. The "fair-innings" argument he considers is based on the view that some span of years constitutes a reasonable, complete life. He presents problems with this position, holding that it has limited application in the selection of patients for medical treatment. He opposes the use of the fair-innings argument except in special cases in which a forced choice must be made because resources are inherently limited.

Suppose that only one place is available on a renal dialysis programme or that only one bed is vacant in a vital transplantation unit or that resuscitation could be given in the time and with the resources available to only one patient. Suppose further that of the two patients requiring any of these resources, one is a 70-year-old widower, friendless and living alone, and the other a 40-year-old mother of three young children with a husband and a career. . . .

I THE MORAL SIGNIFICANCE OF AGE

Many, perhaps most, people feel that, in cases like the one with which we began, there is some moral reason to save the 40-year-old mother rather than the 70-year-old widower. A smaller, but perhaps growing, group of people would see this as a sort of "ageist" prejudice which, in a number of important areas of resource allocation and care, involves giving the old a much worse deal than the younger members of society. This is an exceptionally difficult issue to resolve. A number of the ways of thinking about the issue of the moral relevance of age yield opposed conclusions or seem to tug in opposite directions.

I want first to look at an argument which denies that we should prefer the young mother in our opening example. It is an anti-ageist argument so that is

*Source: Harris, John. *The Value of Life: An Introduction to Medical Ethics.* London: Routledge and Kegan Paul, 1985, pp. 87–101.

what I will call it, but it is not perhaps the usual sort of argument used to defend the rights of the old.

The Anti-Ageist Argument

All of us who wish to go on living have something that each of us values equally although for each it is different in character, for some a much richer prize than for others, and we none of us know its true extent. This thing is of course "the rest of our lives." So long as we do not know the date of our deaths then for each of us the 'rest of our lives' is of indefinite duration. Whether we are 17 or 70, in perfect health or suffering from a terminal disease we each have the rest of our lives to lead. So long as we each fervently wish to live out the rest of our lives, however long that turns out to be, then if we do not deserve to die, we each suffer the same injustice if our wishes are deliberately frustrated and we are cut off prematurely. Indeed there may well be a double injustice in deciding that those whose life expectation is short should not benefit from rescue or resuscitation. Suppose I am told today that I have terminal cancer with only approximately six months or so to live, but I want to live until I die, or at least until I decide that life is no longer worth living. Suppose I then am involved in an accident and because my condition is known to my potential rescuers and there are not enough resources to treat all who could immediately be saved I am marked among those who will not be helped. I am then the victim of a double tragedy and a double injustice. I am stricken first by cancer and the knowledge that I have only a short time to live and I'm then stricken again when I'm told that because of my first tragedy a second and more immediate one is to be visited upon me. Because I have once been unlucky I'm now no longer worth saving.

The point is a simple but powerful one. However short or long my life will be, so long as I want to go on living it then I suffer a terrible injustice when that life is prematurely cut short. Imagine a group of people all of an age, say a class of students all in their mid-20s. If fire trapped all in the lecture theatre and only twenty could be rescued in time should the rescuers shout "youngest first!"? Suppose they had time to debate the question or had been debating it "academically" before the first? It would surely seem invidious to deny some what all value so dearly merely because of an accident of birth? It might be argued that age here provides no criterion precisely because although the lifespans of such a group might be expected to vary widely, there would be no way of knowing who was most likely to live longest. But suppose a reliable astrologer could make very realistic estimates or, what amounts to the same thing, suppose the age range of the students to be much greater, say 17 to 55. Does not the invidiousness of selecting by birth-date remain? Should a 17-year-old be saved before a 29-year-old or she before the 45-year-old and should the 55-year-old clearly be the last to be saved or the first to be sacrificed?

Our normal intuitions would share this sense of the invidiousness of choosing between our imaginary students by reason of their respective ages, but would start to want to make age relevant at some extremes, say if there were a 2-day-old baby and a 90-year-old grandmother. We will be returning to discuss a possible basis for this intuition in a moment. However, it is important to be clear that the anti-ageist argument denies the relevance of age or life expectancy as a criterion absolutely. It argues that even if I know for certain that I have only a little space to live, that space, however short, may be very precious to me. Precious, precisely because it is all the time I have left, and just as precious to me on that account as all the time you have left is precious to you, however much those two timespans differ in length. So that where we both want, equally strongly, to go on living, then we each suffer the same injustice when our lives are cut short or are cut further short.

It might seem that someone who would insist on living out the last few months of his life when by "going quietly" someone else might have the chance to live for a much longer time would be a very selfish person. But this would be true only if the anti-ageist argument is false. It will be true only if it is not plausible to claim that living out the rest of one's life could be equally valuable to the individual whose life it is irrespective of the amount of unelapsed time that is left. And this is of course precisely the usual situation when individuals do not normally have anything but the haziest of ideas as to how long it is that they might have left.

I think the anti-ageist argument has much plausibility. It locates the wrongness of ending an individual's life in the evil of thwarting that person's desire to go on living and argues that it is profoundly unjust to frustrate that desire merely because some of those who have exactly the same desire, held no more strongly, also have a longer life expectancy than the others. However, there are a number of arguments that pull in the opposite direction and these we must now consider.

The Fair-Innings Argument

One problem with the anti-ageist argument is our feeling that there is something unfair about a person who has lived a long and happy life hanging on grimly at the end, while someone who has not been so fortunate suffers a related double misfortune, of losing out in a lottery in which his life happened to be in the balance with that of the grim octogenarian. It might be argued that we could accept the part of the anti-ageist argument which focusses on the equal value of unelapsed time, if this could be tempered in some way. How can it be just that someone who has already had more than her fair share of life and its delights should be preferred or even given an equal chance of continued survival with the young person who has not been so favoured? One strategy that seems to take account of our feeling that there is something wrong with taking steps to prolong the lives of the very old at the expense of those much younger is the fair-innings argument.

The fair-innings argument takes the view that there is some span of years that we consider a reasonable life, a fair innings. Let's say that a fair share of life is the traditional three score and ten, seventy years. Anyone who does not reach 70 suffers, on this view, the injustice of being cut off in their prime. They have missed out on a reasonable share of life; they have been short-changed. Those, however, who do make 70 suffer no such injustice, they have not lost out but rather must consider any additional years a sort of bonus beyond that which could reasonably be hoped for. The fair innings argument requires that everyone be given an equal chance to have a fair innings, to reach the appropriate threshold but, having reached it, they have received their entitlement. The rest of their life is the sort of bonus which may be cancelled when this is necessary to help others reach the threshold.

The attraction of the fair innings argument is that it preserves and incorporates many of the features that made the anti-ageist argument plausible, but allows us to preserve our feeling that the old who have had a good run for their money should not be endlessly propped up at the expense of those who have not had the same chance. We can preserve the conclusion of the anti-ageist argument, that so long as life is equally valued by the person whose life it is, it should be given an equal chance of preservation, and we can go on taking this view until the people in question have reached a fair innings.

There is, however, an important difficulty with the fair innings argument. It is that the very arguments which support the setting of the threshold at an age which might plausibly be considered to be a reasonable lifespan, equally support the setting of the threshold at any age at all, so long as an argument from fairness can be used to support so doing. Suppose that there is only one place available on the dialysis pro-gramme and two patients are in competition for it. One is 30, and the other 40 years of age. The fair innings argument requires that neither be preferred on the grounds of age since both are below the threshold and are entitled to an equal chance of reaching it. If there is no other reason to choose between them we should do something like toss a coin. However, the 30-year-old can argue that the considerations which support the fair innings argument require that she be given the place. After all, what's fair about the fair innings argument is precisely that each individual should have an equal chance of enjoying the benefits of a reasonable lifespan. The younger patient can argue that from where she's standing, the age of 40 looks much more reasonable a span than that of 30, and that she should be given the chance to benefit from those ten extra years.

This argument generalised becomes a reason for always preferring to save younger rather than older people, whatever the age difference, and makes the origi-nal anti-ageist argument begin to look again the more attractive line to take. For the younger person can always argue that the older has had a fairer innings, and should now give way. It is difficult to stop whatever span is taken to be a fair innings col-lapsing towards zero under pressure from those younger candidates who see their in-nings as less fair than that of those with a larger share.

But perhaps this objection to the fair innings argument is mistaken? If seventy years is a fair innings it does not follow that the nearer a span life approaches seventy years, the fairer an innings it is. This may be revealed by considering a different sort of threshold. Suppose that most people can run a mile in seven minutes, and that two people are given the opportunity to show that they can run a mile in that time. They both expect to be given seven minutes. However, if one is in fact given only three minutes and the other only four, it's not true that the latter is given a fairer running time: for people with average abilities four minutes is no more realistic a time in which to run a mile than is three. Four minutes is neither a fair threshold in itself, nor a fairer one than three minutes would be.

Nor does the argument that establishes seven minutes as an appropriate thresh-old lend itself to variation downwards. For that argument just is that seven is the number of minutes that an average adult takes to run a mile. Why then is it different for lifespans? If three score and ten is the number of years available to most people for getting what life has to offer, and is also the number of years people can reasonably expect to have, then it is a misfortune to be allowed anything less however much less one is allowed, if nothing less than the full span normally suffices for getting what can be got out of life. It's true that the 40-year-old gets more time than the 30-year-old, but the frame of reference is not time only, but time normally required for a full life.

This objection has some force, but its failure to be a good analogy reveals that two sorts of considerations go to make an innings fair. For while living a full or complete life, just in the sense of experiencing all the ages of man, is one mark of a fair innings, there is also value in living through as many ages as possible. Just as completing the mile is one value, it is not the only one. Runners in the race of life also value ground covered, and generally judge success in terms of distance run.

What the fair innings argument needs to do is to capture and express in a workable form the truth that while it is always a *misfortune* to die when one wants to go on living, it is not a *tragedy* to die in old age; but it is on the other hand, both a tragedy and a misfortune to be cut off prematurely. Of course ideas like "old age" and " premature death" are inescapably vague, and may vary from society to society, and over time as techniques for postponing death improve. We must also remember that while it may be invidious to choose between a 30- and a 40-year-old on the grounds that one has had a fairer innings than the other, it may not be invidious to choose between the 30- and the 65-year-old on those grounds.

If we remember, too, that it will remain wrong to end the life of someone who wants to live or to fail to save them, and that the fair innings argument will only operate as a principle of selection where we are forced to choose between lives, then something workable might well be salvaged.

While "old age" is irredeemably vague, we can tell the old from the young, and even the old from the middle-aged. So that without attempting precise formulation, a reasonable form of the fair innings argument might hold; and might hold that people who had achieved old age or who were closely approaching it would not have their lives further prolonged when this could only be achieved at the cost of the lives of those who were not nearing old age. These categories could be left vague, the idea being that it would be morally defensible to prefer to save the lives of those who "still had their lives before them" rather than those who had "already lived full lives." The criterion to be employed in each case would simply be what reasonable people would say about whether someone had had a fair innings. Where reasonable people would be in no doubt that a particular individual was nearing old age *and* that the person's life could only be further prolonged at the expense of the life of someone that no reasonable person would classify as nearing old age, then the fair innings argument would apply, and it would be justifiable to save the younger candidate. . . .

Fair Innings or No Ageism?

We have then two principles which can in hard cases pull in opposite directions. What should we do in the sorts of hard cases we have been considering? First, we should be clear that while the very old and those with terminal conditions are alike, in that they both have a short life expectancy, they may well differ with respect to whether or not they have had a fair innings. I do not believe that this issue is at all clear cut but I am inclined to believe that where two individuals both equally wish to go on living for as long as possible our duty to respect this wish is paramount. It is, as I have suggested, the most important part of what is involved in valuing the lives of others. Each person's desire to stay alive should be regarded as of the same importance and as deserving the same respect as that of anyone else, irrespective of the quality of their life or its expected duration.

This would hold good in all cases in which we have to choose between lives, except one. And that is where one individual has had a fair innings and the other not. In this case, while both equally wish to have their lives further prolonged one, but not the other, has had a fair innings. In this case, although there is nothing to choose between the two candidates from the point of view of their respective will to live and both would suffer the injustice of having their life cut short when it might continue, only one would suffer the further injustice of being deprived of a fair innings—a benefit that the other has received. . . .

Limiting Health Care for the Old*

DANIEL CALLAHAN

Many people easily grasp the utilitarian benefits of limiting medical treatments to the elderly. However, in response to arguments presented by John Harris and others, there have been efforts to develop nonutilitarian defenses of age-based allocations. The following three essays present different versions of these positions. Daniel Callahan's approach is grounded in the idea that there is a natural lifespan, that is, a series of life stages, which, when completed constitute a full lifespan. He claims that there is no point in continuing to pursue more days of life once one's lifespan has been completed. He does not favor a cruel cutoff of all benefits to those who have completed their lifespan, but would provide only humane nursing care and palliation, not advanced life-support technologies that simply extend life in old age.

. . . Our culture has worked hard to redefine old age as a time of liberation, not decline, a time of travel, of new ventures in education and self-discovery, of the ever-accessible tennis court or golf course, and of delightfully periodic but thankfully brief visits from well behaved grandchildren. That is, to be sure, an idealized picture, but it arouses hopes that spur medicine to wage an aggressive war against the infirmities of old age. As we have seen, the costs of such a war would be prohibitive. No matter how much is spent, the ultimate problem will still remain: people will grow old and die. Worse still, by pretending that old age can be turned into a kind of endless middle age, we rob it of meaning and significance for the elderly.

There is a plausible alternative: a fresh vision of what it means to live a decently long and adequate life, what might be called a "natural lifespan." Earlier generations accepted the idea that there was a natural lifespan—the biblical norm of three score and ten captures that notion (even though, in fact, that was a much longer lifespan than was typical in ancient times). It is an idea well worth reconsidering, and would provide us with a meaningful and realizable goal. Modern medicine and biology have done much, however, to wean us from that kind of thinking. They have insinuated the belief that the average lifespan is not a natural fact at all, but instead one that is strictly dependent on the state of medical knowledge and skill. Also, there is much to that belief as a statistical fact: The average life expectancy continues to increase, with no end in sight.

However, that is not what I think we ought to mean by a natural lifespan. We need a notion of a full life that is based on some deeper understanding of human needs and possibilities, not on the state of medical technology or its potential. We should think of a natural lifespan as the achievement of a life that is sufficiently long to take advantage of those opportunities life typically offers and that we ordinarily regard as

*Source: Daniel Callahan "Limiting Health Care for the Old" in N. Jecker, *Aging and Ethics;* Clifton, NJ: The Humana Press, 1991.

its prime benefits—loving and "living," raising a family, engaging in work that is satisfying, reading, thinking, cherishing our friends and families. People differ on what might be a full natural lifespan; my view is that it can be achieved by the late 70s or early 80s.

A longer life does not guarantee a better life. No matter how long medicine enables people to live, death at any time—at age 90 or 100 or 110—would frustrate some possibility, some as-yet-unrealized goal. The easily preventable death of a young child is an outrage. Death from an incurable disease of someone in the prime of young adulthood is a tragedy. However, death at an old age, after a long and full life, is simply sad, but it is a part of life itself.

As it confronts aging, medicine should have as its specific goals the averting of premature death, that is, death prior to the completion of a natural lifespan, and thereafter, the relief of suffering. It should pursue those goals so that the elderly can finish out their years with as little needless pain as possible—and with as much vitality as can be generated in contributing to the welfare of younger age groups and to the community of which they are a part. Above all, the elderly need to have a sense of the meaning and significance of their stage in life, one that is not dependent on economic productivity or physical vigor.

What would medicine oriented toward the relief of suffering rather than the deliberate extension of life be like? We do not have a clear answer to that question, so long standing, central, and persistent has been medicine's preoccupation with the struggle against death. However, the hospice movement is providing us with much guidance. It has learned how to distinguish between the relief of suffering and the lengthening of life. Greater control by elderly persons over their own dying—and particularly an enforceable right to refuse aggressive life-extending treatment—is a minimal goal.

What does this have to do with the rising cost of health care for the elderly? Everything. The indefinite extension of life combined with an insatiable ambition to improve the health of the elderly is a recipe for monomania and bottomless spending. It fails to put health in its proper place as only one among many human goods. It fails to accept aging and death as part of the human condition. It fails to present to younger generations a model of wise stewardship.

How might we devise a plan to limit the costs of health care for the aged under public entitlement programs that is fair, humane, and sensitive to their special requirements and dignity? Let me suggest three principles to undergird a quest for limits. First, government has a duty, based an our collective social obligations, to help people live out a natural lifespan, but not to help medically extend life beyond that point. Second, government is obliged to develop under its research subsidies, and to pay for, under its entitlement programs, only the kind and degree of life-extending technology necessary for medicine to achieve and serve the aim of a natural lifespan. Third, beyond the point of a natural lifespan, government should provide only the means necessary for the relief of suffering, not those for life-extending technology.

A system based on those principles would not immediately bring down the cost of care of the elderly; it would add cost, but it would set in place the beginning of a new understanding of old age, one that would admit of eventual stabilization and limits. The elderly will not be served by a belief that only a lack of resources, better financing mechanisms, or political power stands between them and the limitations of their bodies. The good of younger age groups will not be served by inspiring in them a desire to live to an old age that maintains the vitality of youth indefinitely, as if old age were nothing but a sign that medicine has failed in its mission. The future of our society will not be served by allowing expenditures on health care for the elderly to escalate endlessly and uncontrollably, fueled by the false altruistic belief that anything less is to deny the elderly their dignity. Nor will it be aided by the pervasive kind of self-serving argument that urges the young to support such a crusade because they will eventually benefit from it also.

We require, instead, an understanding of the process of aging and death that looks to our obligation to the young and to the future, that recognizes the necessity of limits and the acceptance of decline and death, and that values the old for their age and not for their continuing youthful vitality. In the name of accepting the elderly and repudiating discrimination against them, we have succeeded mainly in pretending that, with enough will and money, the unpleasant part of old age can be abolished. In the name of medical progress, we have carried out a relentless war against death and decline, failing to ask in any probing way if that will give us a better society for all.

A Lifespan Approach to Health Care*

NORMAN DANIELS

Norman Daniels attempts to convert problems of allocation to the elderly from a
conflict among different people in different generations into a set of prudential
choices about how one will allocate personal resources to different stages of one's
own life. He suggests that we view health resource allocation as a problem of deciding how we would distribute a lifetime's health resources over different stages
of the life span. He has elsewhere argued that health care claims should be related
to what is needed to perform functions typical of the species. In dealing with problems of age and allocation, Daniels applies this idea by proposing age-specific
species typical functioning. He claims it is a matter of prudence how people want
to allocate their lifetime's health resources over different stages of the lifespan.

Some general theories of justice, most notably Rawls', provide foundations for
a principle protecting fair equality of opportunity. If such a principle is indeed a requirement of an acceptable general theory of justice, then I believe we have a natural
way to extend such general theories to govern the distribution of health care. We
should include health care institutions among those basic institutions of a society that
are governed by the fair equality of opportunity principle. If this approach to a theory of just health care is correct, it means that there are social obligations to provide
health care services that protect and restore normal functioning. In short, the principle of justice that should govern the design of health care institutions is a principle
that calls for guaranteeing fair equality of opportunity.

This principle of justice has implications for both access and resource allocation. It implies that there should be no financial, geographical, or discriminatory bar-
riers to a level of care that promotes normal functioning. It also implies that resources
be allocated in ways that are effective in promoting normal functioning. That is, since
we can use the effect on normal opportunity range as a crude way of ranking the moral
importance of health care services, we can guide hard public policy choices about
which services are more important to provide. Thus, the principle does not imply that
every technology that might have a positive impact on normal functioning for some
individuals should be introduced: we must weigh new technologies against alternatives to judge the overall impact of introducing them on fair equality of opportunity—
this gives a slightly new sense to the term "opportunity cost." The point is that social
obligations to provide just health care must be met within the conditions of moderate
scarcity that we face. This is not an approach that gives individuals a basic right to
have all their health care needs met. There are social obligations to provide individuals only with those services that are part of the design of a system that, on the whole,
protects equal opportunity.

*Source: Daniels, N., "A Lifespan Approach to Health Care," in N. Jecker, ed., *Aging and
Ethics*. Clifton, N.J.: The Humana Press, 1991. pp. 235–238.

We must refine this account so that it applies more directly to the problem of allocating health care over the lifespan—among different age groups. I draw on three basic observations. First, there is the banal fact we have all noticed: we age. By contrast, we do not change sex or race. This contrast has important implications for the problem of equality. If I treat blacks and whites or men and women differently, than I produce an inequality, and such inequalities raise questions about justice. If I treat the old and the young differently, I may or may not produce an inequality. If I treat them differently just occasionally and arbitrarily, then I will treat different persons unequally, but if I treat as a matter of policy the old one way and the young another, and I do so over their whole lives, then I treat all persons the same way. No inequality is produced. Thus, the fact that we all notice, that we age, means age is different from race or sex when we think about distributive justice.

Second, as we age, we pass through institutions that redistribute wealth and income in a way that performs a "savings" function. The observation is trivial with regard to income support institutions, such as the Social Security system. It is not often noticed that our health care system does the same thing. When we reach age 65, we consume health care resources at about 3.5 times the rate (in dollars) that we do prior to age 65. However, we pay, as working people, a combined health care insurance premium—through private premiums, through employee contributions, and through Social Security taxes—that covers not just our actuarially fair costs, but the costs of the elderly and of children as well. If this system continues as we age, others will pay "inflated premiums" that will cover our higher costs when we are elderly. In effect, the system allows us to defer the use of resources from one stage of our lives to a later one. It "saves" health care for our old age—when we need more of it.

Third, our health care system is not prudently designed, given that it plays this role as a savings institution. It lavishes life-extending resources on us as we are dying, but it withholds other kinds of services, such as personal care and social support services, which may be crucial to our well-being when our lives are not under immediate threat. The system could be far more prudently designed. It could pay better attention to matching services to needs at different stages of our lives and, thus, be more effective in its savings function.

Earlier, I claimed that the just design of our health care institutions should rest on a principle protecting fair equality of opportunity. Imagine that each of us has a lifetime allocation of health care services, which we can claim only if the appropriate needs arise, as a result of appealing to such a principle. Our task now is to allocate that fair share over the lifespan—and to do so prudently. In this exercise, we will find out what is just or fair between age groups by discovering what it is prudent to do between stages of life, over the whole lifespan. One way to make sure we do not bias this allocation, favoring one stage of life and, thus, one age group over another is to pretend that we do not know how old we are. We must allocate these resources imagining that we must live our whole lives with the result of our choices. One way we would refine our earlier principle of justice is to conclude that we should protect our fair shares of the normal opportunity range at each stage of life. Since we must live through each stage, we will not treat any one stage as less important than another.

   Notice what this rather abstract perspective—I call it the Prudential Lifespan Account—accomplishes: it tells us that we should not think of age groups as competing with each other, but as sharing a whole life. We want to make that life go as well as possible, and we must therefore make the appropriate decisions about what needs it is most important to meet at each stage of life. If we do this prudently, we will learn how it is fair to treat each age group. Instead of focusing on competition, we have a unifying perspective or vision. I am suggesting that, as individuals and as a society, we must think through the decisions we must make about our health care system from this perspective.

How Age Should Matter
Justice as the Basis for Limiting Care to the Elderly*

ROBERT M. VEATCH

While Callahan would relate health-care allocations to the elderly to a notion of a completed life span and Daniels would relate it to prudent allocations based on age-specific, species-typical functioning, the following essay attempts to build a justification for age-based allocation grounded in the moral principle of justice. It suggests that there are two ways of determining who is worst off and therefore has a justice-based claim to health care. Sometimes we should determine who is worst off at a "moment in time." In other cases we should ask who is worst off "over-a-lifetime." For health services properly based on over-a-lifetime well-being comparisons, this essay claims that two people who are equally well-off at a given moment may nevertheless be positioned differently. In particular, persons who have had more opportunity for life experiences are better off—they have lives we would prefer if we could choose. The thesis of this essay is that justice may require allocating scarce health-care resources in these cases to the younger patient.

THE ROLE OF AGE IN AGE-BASED ALLOCATION

It is not as easy as one might think to figure out exactly what the role of age is in apparently age-based allocation policies. It could be that age is used as a crude predictor of the benefit from treatment. A policy committed to using resources where they will do the most good might include the view that in cases where older people will not do as well with an intervention, age should be used as an indirect, approximating measure of where resources will do the most good. Even if the medical benefit measured in terms of cure rates or incidence of side effects is the same for older patients, the benefit measured in years will predictably not be as great. The elderly will not benefit as long, if the treatment is a success. Allocators might argue that it would be impractical to assess outcomes on a case-by-case basis and choose, instead, to use chronological age as a predictor of benefit.

This raises the ethical issue of the use of sociological measures as predictors of outcome. In the United States, in many situations, it is considered unethical (as well as illegal) in allocating goods to use sociological categories to predict expected outcome. . . . We cannot use sex, race, or other sociological measures as a basis for excluding individual members of their groups even if we can show that the group as a whole will use the resource less efficiently. We need evidence for the individual.

*Source: Veatch, Robert M. "How Age Should Matter: Justice as the Basis for Limiting Care to the Elderly." In Gerald R. Winslow and James W. Walters, eds. *Facing Limits: Ethics and Health Care for the Elderly.* Boulder, CO: Westview Press, 1993, pp. 211–229.

Then can we insist that age be used only when we can show that age is a predictor of a poor outcome in the case of the individual elderly person? If so, that would be almost impossible to show.

CONSEQUENTIALIST ARGUMENT PERTAINING TO THE USE OF AGE

Consequentialist Arguments for Age-Based Allocation

The arguments that appear most readily are grounded in appeals to the consequences of allocating on the basis of age. These appeals necessarily look at the benefits and social costs of using age as a criterion in allocation. The argument begins with the conclusion we have just reached: Resources are inevitably scarce. Those committed to one or another version of utilitarian, normative ethical theory hold that in such cases the ethical imperative is to do the greatest good for the greatest number; we need to maximize the net good in aggregate. For health care the ethical imperative is the use of health planning and cost-benefit analyses to make sure we use our health-care dollars to do the most good possible. As we have seen, it is impossibly inefficient to measure the benefits for each individual patient. The process itself would have great disutilities. The prudent, efficient thing to do would be to opt for the allocation formula that will do the greatest good overall. If age is a reasonably good predictor of good, then it morally must be used according to utilitarian theory. The welfare of individuals may have to be sacrificed in certain cases in order to produce the greatest aggregate benefit. A true consequentialist would not be dissuaded from this conclusion by concern that such a policy might be unfair to certain elderly persons.

Many American health planners find this persuasive. They assume that if we must ration—and we must—then the rationing must be on the basis of maximizing the common or aggregate good. There are reasons, however, why these utilitarian reasons for using age as a basis for allocating health resources should be resisted.

Consequentialist Arguments Against Using Age

Some critics of the use of age buy the principle, but reject the moral calculation. They accept that the goal is to serve the aggregate good, but then reject the claim that using age as a criterion will maximize the aggregate good. Their arguments are as follows:

First, some elderly can be very productive citizens. . . . That consequentialist argument against the use of age, however, overlooks the fact that statistically the elderly are not as productive as the young. . . . Statistically, it seems clear that more good will be done if the younger patients get the resources. Even the process of figuring out who is physiologically young could have severe disutilities both in terms of cost and in terms of inevitable conflicts.

Second, critics of the use of age might argue that the psychological burden of anticipating reaching old age without life-sustaining medical care would be a serious disutility of using age as a criterion.

But one must also take into account the psychological burdens that would result from knowing that younger people might not get the benefits of needed medical care if resources are going to the elderly.

Third, utilitarian critics of the use of age as a criterion might appeal to the psychological and economic burdens on families whose elderly members were excluded from health care that could offer at least marginal benefits. Once again, however, these would be offset by the psychological and economic burdens on families whose younger members would be deprived of care if resources went to the elderly.

On balance, the consequentialist case for using age as a criterion in allocating resources seems to be convincing, provided the utilitarian principle of maximizing aggregate net outcome is morally legitimate in the first place. To the surprise of many, however, it may turn out that even if we move to nonconsequentialist (or deontological) ethical theory, age may be a legitimate basis for allocating health resources.

NONCONSEQUENTIALIST CONSIDERATIONS

Some ethical systems hold that morality is not just a matter of producing good and avoiding evil consequences. This characteristic is shared by the ethics of Kant, the Jewish ethics of the Ten Commandments, and by much Protestant thought. It is central to secular, liberal political philosophy that places the rights of the individual over against the aggregate welfare at least in some cases. In the Ten Commandments, for instance, the command is "Thou shalt not." There is no clause added "except when it would produce good consequences."

One nonconsequentialist principle is the principle of justice. It is social and allocational but, as an independent ethical principle, does not focus on the aggregate amount of consequences produced. It is the nature of morally interesting allocational problems that the pattern that produces the greatest aggregate good is not the same as the one that distributes the good most justly. The criterion for what is a just or equitable pattern of distribution is itself a controversy among those who are committed to justice as a patterned principle. One particularly appealing formulation recognizes distributions as just when they provide opportunities for net welfare that are equal among people. The policy implication is that resources should be allocated in such a way as to give people an opportunity for equality of well being.[1]

Often the conflict between utility and justice is an uninteresting one since distributing resources to those who are worst off will do the most good. That is what economists refer to as decreasing marginal utility. However, often in health care the worst off—the ones who have the strongest claims of justice—are the sickest and, as such, they are just the ones whom it is most difficult to benefit. They are chronically ill with incurable, perhaps hopeless conditions. Here spending resources on the worst off will do the least good rather than the most good. Thus in health care the conflict between utility and justice is often a real one. This is particularly true with the elderly. Thus it will be critical to see whether the principle of justice militates against using age as a criterion for allocating health resources.

Justice-Based Arguments Against the Use of Age

It seems at first like justice weighs in against the use of age as an allocation criterion. A number of commentators who are committed to justice as an allocational principle have criticized the use of age as a criterion.[2] The logic is that justice requires that resources be used to provide opportunities to have needs met. Elderly people are often precisely the ones who are most needy medically. Therefore, they deserve priority. They at least deserve to be treated identically to those younger people who are medically in equal need.

This appears to set a battle between consequentialists and nonconsequentialists, with consequentialists arguing for the use of an age-based allocation criterion to promote efficient use of resources and nonconsequentialists wringing their hands, screaming it is unfair and unjust.

Justice-Based Arguments for the Use of Age

There is, of course, one other possibility. One might mount a justice-based argument in favor of the use of age as a criterion. That is precisely what I believe is called for and shall attempt to do in the remainder of this essay.

It should be noted that there have been other efforts along these lines recently. Philosophers Daniel Callahan and Norman Daniels have both made important attempts to argue for limits on health care for the elderly that have not been grounded exclusively in considerations of utility. I am now convinced that, while they are on the right track, their approaches fail. I shall briefly summarize what I consider to be the problems with their approaches before presenting my own version of a justice-based defense of the use of age as a criterion for allocating health resources.

Daniel Callahan's Setting of Limits.[3]   His claim is that there is a natural end to the life-span. Medical resources should be used to get people up to that natural completion and then only to use resources for the elderly to provide comfort and inexpensive treatments of acute illness.

The result is that medical care needed to complete the major phases of the life cycle generates a higher moral claim than care to sustain life after the life cycle is completed. According to Callahan, "The old should step aside in an active way."[4]

To be fair, Callahan has sometimes been terribly misunderstood. He was not suggesting that we be cruel.[5] Rather his position was that all of us ought to have a realistic conception of what counts as a full life. There comes a time when life is complete. While Callahan does not directly make his argument in terms of justice, it seems to be an appeal to fairness considerations rather than aggregate utility.

The problem with Callahan's approach is that it rests on a controversial stance regarding the value of life after what he takes to be the end of the natural life-span. Moreover, it rests on an even more controversial claim about life having a natural span. His use of age as a criterion for limiting certain life-sustaining resources for the elderly rests on a conviction that life after some purported natural end point is not very valuable in any case. For him, it is, thus, all too easy to argue that it deserves low priority.

There is a more practical problem as well. The notion that life after its natural end point calls for a lower priority in health resource allocation seems to call for a precipitous cessation of claims for a certain group of life-sustaining services at some age—the age at which the life cycle has been completed. As one is "over the hill," there is a precipitous fall "over the cliff." Yet, even if we are willing to accept the notion of a natural life-span, many of us would be acutely uncomfortable with the idea that there is some identifiable end point at which, for public policy purposes, some health-care resources would no longer be funded.

Yet, we would need some easily administered, if arbitrary, age cut-off. We could not tell insurance companies and hospital administrators to cut people off whenever it appears they have completed their life span without giving them some specific age. Callahan, at one point early in the discussion, suggested that a life span of 75 years was as good as any.[6] In *Setting Limits,* he was slightly more conservative, identifying the range of the late 70s to early 80s.

Whether we pick 75 or 85, administrators and clinicians would have to have some specific, cut-off age. It is the precipitous cut-off that seems both necessary and implausible in a theory grounded in the notion of completing a life-span. Consider, for example, two patients medically similar in need of some high-tech, life-extending technology such as a transplant. If one were 74 and the other 76 (or 84 and 86), the former would get the full treatment (because he has not yet completed his life-span) while the latter would get no life-extending interventions. I doubt that such a cut-off would be tolerable, yet it seems appropriate based on a theory that differentiates people into two groups, one which has completed the life-span and one that has not.

There is one final problem with Callahan's theory. He readily acknowledges the continuing need for relief of suffering, basic nursing care for cleanliness and dignity, and so forth. What the "life-span completion" theory cannot explain is why we should spend resources on these when others will never reach their full life-span. If these lives are over, why do they have claims for even these services? Would not those whose life span is not over have claims for these resources as well?

Here Callahan's instincts are stronger than his theory. It is intuitively obvious that we should continue to provide comfort care. I do not think Callahan's theory can explain why.

Norman Daniels' Prudential Life-Span Account. The account of Norman Daniels attempts to rectify some of these problems.[7]

There are problems, however, with Daniels' account as well. It is not obvious that it is only a matter of prudence how the resources get allocated to different stages of one's life-cycle. Even if it is prudent for people to save for their old age, it may not be just or fair.

The problem is especially acute when one takes into account the fact that not all people will reach old age. Daniels implies at one point that a prudent allocation would be one in which an equal portion of each age-specific need was met.[8] That seems reasonable, provided we are dealing with a group who will live through all stages of the life-cycle. The Rawls-Daniels scheme is based on a model in which rational, self-interested heads of households (blinded as to their specific interests and needs) are viewed as the ones making the allocation choices. That model, however, has built into it the implication that all will at least reach adulthood. They therefore have a very high probability of reaching old age, and it would be rational to include a prudent amount (if only a prudent amount) for their period of old age.

In the real world, however, some are treated more harshly by the natural lottery. They are born with congenital and genetic problems such that they will suffer from critical, fatal, or permanently handicapping conditions. If a majority of rational adults would spend equally on conditions of infancy, middle age, and old age, it does not follow that it is fair to those who will never reach adulthood. The real ethical issue is what is fair or just. In the same way that I would say to Callahan that completion of the life-span is not the relevant criterion, so I would say to Daniels that prudence is not. The real question is whether justice either permits or requires limits on care to the elderly.

A JUSTICE-BASED LIMIT ON CARE TO THE ELDERLY

I think there is another nonconsequentialist argument that supports limits on some care to the elderly, one based more directly on appeals to justice. I agree with Daniels, and with the work of Ronald Dworkin that precedes Daniels,[9] that an ethical health insurance is one that is based on intrapersonal allocational decisions made by those behind a veil of ignorance about their own personal desires, needs, and interests. I would, however, see them further constrained to choose what is fair rather than simply what seems prudent.[10] In particular, I would see them as obliged by the principle of fairness to deal with the just claims of those who have critical or fatal conditions in infancy. It is not just a matter of being prudent. It is not a matter of efficiently serving the common good. Rather, it is a question of which allocation is fair. Justice requires identifying the worst-off individuals and allocating resources so as to give those persons an opportunity to be as well off as others. I shall argue for certain kinds of health care that give priority to the young.

Age in Deciding Who Is Worse Off

Consider two dialysis patients, medically similar, both of whom have a five-year life expectancy if dialyzed and both of whom will die soon if not dialyzed. One is age 40; the other age 60. Can we identify one of them as worse off or do we say that they are equally poorly off? In a hypothetical situation in which there was only one dialysis machine, can we identify who should get it?

If we add the further assumption that we can expect the two to lead equally useful lives during their remaining five years, it should be clear that a utilitarian should be indifferent. For the nonconsequentialist considering egalitarian justice, the problem is more complex.

The Slice-of-Time and Over-a-Lifetime Perspectives

We should consider two different ways of calculating who is worse off. The first, call it the slice-of-time perspective, asks who is worse off at a given moment, say, when the two patients are near death. The second, call it the over-a-lifetime perspective, views well-being cumulated over the lifetimes of the individuals involved. From the slice-of-time perspective these two patients seem equally poorly off. They are both about to die if they do not get the machine and will live for five years with it. From the over-a-lifetime perspective, however, they seem to be in significantly different positions. The 60-year-old has had twenty more years of life. From the slice-of-time perspective they are equal. On a per–lifetime basis, the 40-year-old has had much less opportunity for well-being. He would seem to have a much greater claim of egalitarian justice.

Justifying Acute Care and Basic Care Needed for Dignity and Pain Relief

This brings us back to the problem faced by Callahan of why the elderly have a claim for basic medical care, for treatment of acute illness and relief of suffering, and for nursing care for cleanliness and dignity. It seems that the relevant consideration has nothing to do with whether a lifespan is deemed to have been completed. Rather, it seems related to whether it is legitimate to cumulate one's well-being.

I see the problem as related to contemporary debates over the theory of personal identity. A person is one who has continuity of personal identity over a period of time. That continuity of identity requires continuity of awareness of oneself such that one can say, "I am the same person who existed at some previous time."

For some conditions, well-being (or lack thereof) is easily seen as cumulating over time. It makes good sense for people to say that, since they have lived a long time, they have had many opportunities for well-being. In fact, the longer one has lived, the more such opportunities one has had.

By contrast some needs present themselves anew at each moment in time. They cannot be cumulated over a lifetime. There is noncontinuity of personal identity that prohibits the summing up of acute, severe pain over a lifetime. We cannot plausibly say that because one's first eighty years have been relatively pain-free, the acute, severe pain one experiences at age eighty-one gets low priority morally. Acute pain forces radical discontinuity with one's previous life. Life in acute pain is detached from experiences accumulated over the years. Past life experiences seem irrelevant in deciding whether one in acute pain is among the worst off. A similar conclusion seems right regarding significant assaults on personal dignity such as those that come from absence of basic nursing care.

The slice-of-time perspective is appropriate in these cases because people in acute, severe pain or in a state in which they experience significant assault on dignity are entities separate from their life-histories. They are comparable to the child trapped in a well who cries out for assistance. Deciding whether it is ethical to respond is independent of any cool calculation of utility *or* of who is worst off over a lifetime. For those conditions that separate oneself from one's personal identity over a lifetime, the slice-of-time perspective is the correct one in deciding who is worst off. For those conditions such as chronic threat to continued existence, which still leave one recognizing personal identity over a lifetime, the cumulative time perspective is the correct one. That seems to me to explain how we should differentiate kinds of care for the elderly much better than either the "natural lifespan" view of Callahan or the "prudential lifespan" account of Daniels. My conclusion is that for these conditions that permit accumulating over-a-lifetime, age is one relevant factor in deciding who is worse off and therefore a *prima facie,* justice-based reason for allocating scarce resources.

NOTES

1. See Robert M. Veatch, *The Foundations of Justice: Why the Retarded and the Rest of Us Have Claims to Equality.* New York: Oxford University Press, 1986, for my development of the case for this interpretation.
2. Jerry Avorn. "Benefit and Cost Analysis in Geriatric Care: Turning Age Discrimination into Health Policy," *New England Journal of Medicine* 310 (May 17, 1984):1294–1300; Nancy S. Jecker, "Disenfranchising the Elderly from Life-Extending Medical Care," *Public Affairs Quarterly* 2 (July 1988):51–68; John F. Kilner, "Age Criteria in Medicine: Are the Medical Justifications Ethical?" *Archives of Internal Medicine* 149 (Oct., 1989):2343–2346; Eric Munoz, Fred Rosner, Don Chalfin, et al., "Age, Resource Consumption, and Outcome of Medical Patients at an Academic Medical Center," *Archives of Internal Medicine* 149 (Sept. 1989): 1946–1950; Margaret P. Battin, "Age Rationing and the Just Distribution of Health Care: Is There a Duty to Die?" *Ethics* 97 (January 1987):317–340; Larry R. Churchill, "Should We Ration Health Care by Age?" *Journal of the American Geriatrics Society* 36 (July, 1988):644–647.
3. Daniel Callahan. *Setting Limits: Medical Goals in an Aging Society.* New York: Simon & Schuster, 1987.
4. Ibid., p. 43.
5. In his sequel, Daniel Callahan, *What Kind of Life: The Limits of Medical Progress.* New York: Simon and Schuster, 1990, Callahan is much more bold about appealing to "the common good" as a criterion for health resource allocation.
6. Daniel Callahan, "Natural Death and Public Policy," *Life Span: Values and Life-Extending Technologies,* edited by Robert M. Veatch. San Francisco: Harper and Row, Publishers, 1979, p. 174.
7. See Norman Daniels, *Am I My Parents' Keeper?: An Essay on Justice Between the Young and the Old.* New York: Oxford University Press, 1988.
8. Ibid., pp. 58–59.
9. See Ronald Dworkin, "What is Equality? Part 1: Equality of Welfare," *Philosophy and Public Affairs* 10 (Summer 1981):185–246; and "What Is Equality? Part 2: Equality of Resources," *Philosophy and Public Affairs* 10 (Fall 1981):283–345.
10. It should be clear that this commits me to a different version of the hypothetical contract than that supported by Rawls and Daniels. I view contractors as discovering a preexisting moral structure, not simply choosing what is prudent.

SUGGESTED READINGS FOR CHAPTER 9

A. CASE STUDIES

VEATCH, ROBERT M. Commentary on "The Costs of Addiction: The Case of Rita Anderson." *Casebook on the Termination of Life-Sustaining Treatment and the Care of the Dying.* Cynthia B. Cohen (ed.). Bloomington, IN, and Briarcliff Manor, NY: Indiana University Press and The Hastings Center, 1988, pp. 130–133.

B. THE ECONOMICS OF TERMINAL CARE

GILLICK, MURIEL. "The High Costs of Dying: A Way Out." *Archives of Internal Medicine* 154 (October 10, 1994):2134–2137.

MAKSOUD, ALFRED, DENNIS W. JAHNIGEN, AND CHRISTINE I. SKIBINSKI. "Do Not Resuscitate Orders and the Cost of Death." *Archives of Internal Medicine* 153 (May 24, 1993):1249–1253.

PIRO, P.A., AND T. LUTINS. *Utilization and Reimbursement Under Medicare for Persons who Died in 1967 and 1968.* Washington, DC: Social Security Administration, 1973.

RILEY, GERALD, JAMES LUBITZ, RONALD PRIHODA, AND MARY ANN STEVENSON. "Changes in Distribution of Medicare Expenditures Among Aged Enrollees, 1969–82." *Health Care Financing Review* 7(3, 1986):53–63.

SCITOVSKY, ANNE A. "The High Cost of Dying: What Do the Data Show?" *Milbank Memorial Fund Quarterly* 62(4, 1984):591–608.

WEEKS, WILLIAM B., LIAL L. KOFOED, AMY E. WALLACE, H. GILBERT WELCH. "Advance Directives and the Cost of Terminal Hospitalization." *Archives of Internal Medicine* 154 (1994):2077–2083.

C. MORAL REFLECTION ON THE ECONOMICS OF TERMINAL CARE

BAYER, RONALD, DANIEL CALLAHAN, JOHN FLETCHER, THOMAS HODGSON, BRUCE JENNINGS, DAVID MONSEES, STEVEN SIEVERTS, and ROBERT VEATCH. "The Care of the Terminally Ill: Morality and Economics." *New England Journal of Medicine* 309 (December 15, 1983):1490–1494.

BROOME, JOHN. "Good, Fairness and QALYs." *Philosophy and Medical Welfare.* J.M. Bell and Susan Mendus (eds.). Cambridge: Cambridge University Press, 1988, pp. 57–73.

CALLAHAN, DANIEL. "Vital Distinctions, Mortal Questions: Debating Euthanasia and Health Care Costs." *Commonweal* 115(3, July 15, 1988):399–402.

FLETCHER, JOHN. "Ethics and the Costs of Dying." *Genetics and the Law II.* Aubrey Milunsky and George J. Annas (eds.). New York: Plenum, 1980, pp. 187–209.

TOMS, STEVEN A. "Outcome Predictors in the Early Withdrawal of Life Support: Issues of Justice and Allocation for the Severely Brain Injured." *Journal of Clinical Ethics* 4(3, Fall 1993):206–211.

VEATCH, ROBERT M. "Justice and the Economics of Terminal Illness." *Hastings Center Report* 18 (August/September 1988):34–40.

WILLIAMS, ALAN. "Ethics and Efficiency in the Provision of Health Care." *Philosophy and Medical Welfare.* J.M. Bell and Susan Mendus (eds.). Cambridge: Cambridge University Press, 1988, pp. 111–126.

D. AGE AND THE ALLOCATION OF RESOURCES

AVORN, JERRY. "Benefit and Cost Analysis in Geriatric Care: Turning Age Discrimination into Health Policy." *New England Journal of Medicine* 310 (May 17, 1984): 1294–1300.

BATTIN, MARGARET P. "Age Rationing and the Just Distribution of Health Care: Is There a Duty to Die?" *Ethics* 97 (January 1987):317–340.

BROCK, DAN W. "Justice, Health Care and the Elderly." *Philosophy and Public Affairs* 18(3, Summer 1989):297–312.

BROCK, DAN W. "Justice and the Severely Demented Elderly." *Journal of Medicine and Philosophy* 13(1, February 1988):73–100.

CALLAHAN, DANIEL. *Setting Limits: Medical Goals in an Aging Society.* New York: Simon and Schuster, 1987.

CHILDRESS, JAMES. "Ensuring Care, Respect, and Fairness for the Elderly." *Hastings Center Report* 14(5, 1984):27–31.

CHURCHILL, LARRY R. "Should We Ration Health Care by Age?" *Journal of the American Geriatrics Society* 36 (1988):644–647.

DANIELS, NORMAN. *Am I My Parents' Keeper?: An Essay on Justice Between the Young and the Old.* New York: Oxford University Press, 1988.

JECKER, NANCY S. "Toward a Theory of Age-Group Justice." *Journal of Medicine and Philosophy* 14 (1989):655–676.

KILNER, JOHN F. "Age Criteria in Medicine: Are the Medical Justifications Ethical?" *Archives of Internal Medicine* 149 (1989):2343–2346.

KUHSE, HELGA, and PETER SINGER. "Age and the Allocation of Medical Resources." *Journal of Medicine and Philosophy* 13(1, February 1988):101–116.

MCKERLIE, DENNIS. "Equality and Time." *Ethics* 99 (April 1989):474–491.

MOODY, HARRY R. *Ethics in an Aging Society.* Baltimore: Johns Hopkins University Press, 1992.

SIEGLER, MARK. "Should Age Be a Criterion in Health Care?" *Hastings Center Report* 14(5, 1984):24–27.

U.S. Congress, Office of Technology Assessment. *Life-Sustaining Technologies and the Elderly,* OTA-BA-306. Washington, DC: U.S. Government Printing Office, 1987.

WIKLER, DANIEL. "Ought the Young Make Health Care Decisions for Their Aged Selves?" *Journal of Medicine and Philosophy* 13(1, February 1988):57–72.

BIBLIOGRAPHICAL SOURCES AND REFERENCE WORKS

REICH, WARREN (ed.). *Encyclopedia of Bioethics.* New York: Macmillan, 1995, articles on:

AIDS
Aging and the Aged: Theories of Aging and Life Extension
Aging and the Aged: Life Expectancy and Life Span
Health Care Resources, Allocation of
Life, Quality of
Triage

General Bibliography

American Medical Association. Council on Ethical and Judicial Affairs. "Decisions Near the End of Life." *Report B.* Adopted by the House of Delegates (1991), 11–15; and "Decisions Near the End of Life." *Journal of the American Medical Association* 267 (April 22/29, 1992):2229–2233.

BEAUCHAMP, TOM L., AND JAMES F. CHILDRESS. *Principles of Biomedical Ethics.* 4th ed. New York: Oxford University Press, 1994. Chapter 4.

BROCK, DAN W. "Death and Dying." In Veatch, Robert M. (ed.). *Medical Ethics.* Boston: Jones and Bartlett Publishers, 1989.

BROCK, DAN W. *Life and Death: Philosophical Essays in Biomedical Ethics.* New York: Cambridge University Press, 1993.

BRODY, BARUCH A. *Suicide and Euthanasia: Historical and Contemporary Themes.* Boston: Kluwer Academic, 1989.

CALLAHAN, DANIEL. *The Troubled Dream of Life: Living with Morality.* New York: Simon and Schuster, 1993.

CANTOR, NORMAN. *Legal Frontiers of Death and Dying.* Bloomington, IN: Indiana University Press, 1987.

COHEN, CYNTHIA (ed.). *Casebook on the Termination of Life-Sustaining Treatment and the Care of the Dying.* Bloomington, IN: Indiana University Press, 1988.

Hastings Center. *Guidelines on the Termination of Life-Sustaining Treatment and the Care of the Dying.* Briarcliff Manor, NY: The Hastings Center, 1987.

HORAN, DENNIS J., AND DAVID MALL (eds.). *Death, Dying, and Euthanasia.* Washington, DC: University Publications of America, 1977.

LYNN, JOANNE (ed.). *By No Extraordinary Means.* Bloomington, IN: Indiana University Press, 1986.

MEISEL, ALAN. "The Legal Consensus About Forgoing Life-Sustaining Treatment: Its Status and Its Prospects." *Kennedy Institute of Ethics Journal* 2(4, Dec. 1992): 309–345.

MEISEL, ALAN. *The Right to Die.* New York: John Wiley and Sons, 1989, with Cumulative Supplements published in 1992 and 1993. New York: Wiley.

Momeyer, Richard W. *Confronting Death.* Bloomington, IN: Indiana University Press, 1988.

Pence, Gregory. *Classic Cases in Medical Ethics.* 2nd ed. New York: McGraw-Hill Publishing, 1995.

President's Commission for the Study of Ethical Problems in Medicine and Biomedical and Behavioral Research. *Deciding to Forego Life-Sustaining Treatment.* Washington, DC: U.S. Government Printing Office, 1983.

Ramsey, Paul. *Ethics at the Edges of Life.* New Haven, CT: Yale University Press, 1978.

Ramsey, Paul. *The Patient as Person.* New Haven, CT: Yale University Press, 1970.

Regan, Tom (ed.). *Matters of Life and Death.* 3d ed. New York: Random House, 1992.

Society for the Right to Die. *The Physician and the Hopelessly Ill Patient.* New York: Society for the Right to Die, 1985, pp. 39–80; and *1988 Supplement,* pp. 17–34.

Veatch, Robert M. "Forgoing Life-Sustaining Treatment: Limits to the Consensus." *Kennedy Institute of Ethics Journal* 3(1, March 1993):1–19.

Veatch, Robert M. *Death, Dying, and the Biological Revolution: Our Last Quest for Responsibility.* Revised Edition. New Haven, CT: Yale University Press, 1989.

Weir, Robert F. (ed.). *Ethical Issues in Death and Dying,* 2d ed. New York: Columbia University Press, 1986.

BIBLIOGRAPHICAL SOURCES AND REFERENCE WORKS

Becker, Lawrence, and Charlotte Becker (eds.). *Encyclopedia of Ethics.* New York: Garland Publishing, 1992.

Johnson, Gretchen L. *Voluntary Euthanasia: A Comprehensive Bibliography.* Los Angeles: Hemlock Society, 1987.

Lineback, Richard H. (ed.). *Philosopher's Index.* Vols. 1-. Bowling Green, OH: Philosophy Documentation Center, Bowling Green State University. Issued Quarterly. See under "Active Euthanasia," "Death," "Dignity," "Dying," "Euthanasia," "Killing," "Letting Die," "Life," "Sanctity of Life," and "Suicide."

Walters, LeRoy, and Joy Kahn. *Bibliography of Bioethics.*

Reich, Warren (ed.). *Encyclopedia of Bioethics.* New York: Macmillan, 1995, articles on:

Death: Anthropological Perspectives
Death: Eastern Thought
Death: Western Philosophical Thought
Death: Western Religious Thought
Death in the Western World
Death: Art of Dying
Death, Attitudes Toward
Death Education
Hospice and End of Life Care